Shakespeare and the Allegory of Evil

Shakespeare and the Allegory of Evil

THE HISTORY OF
A METAPHOR
IN RELATION TO HIS
MAJOR VILLAINS

BY BERNARD SPIVACK

NEW YORK 1958
COLUMBIA UNIVERSITY PRESS

Copyright © 1958 Columbia University Press
Published in Great Britain, Canada, India, and Pakistan
by the Oxford University Press
London, Toronto, Bombay, and Karachi
Library of Congress Catalog Card Number: 57-12758
Manufactured in the United States of America

TO CHARLOTTE

Where the heart lies, let the brain lie also

This study, prepared under the Graduate Faculties of Columbia University, was selected by a committee of those Faculties to receive one of the Clarke F. Ansley awards given annually by Columbia University Press.

PREFACE

In Shakespeare's characters scholarship finds, or creates, ten thousand problems, but in a few, among them his major villains, it finds something more—a mystery. The issue at stake is their elementary meaning, for the dramatic image expressing each is obscure at its very heart. They have the effect upon Shakespearian criticism of making it, in its own way, as myriad-minded as their creator. Obvious examples of this mystery among villains of the first magnitude are Aaron the Moor, Richard of Gloucester, and Iago. Others of lesser stature will appear in the course of this study, which rests on the opinion that all these figures are related on the side of their profound difficulty, and that examination of any one of them will suggest the nature of the trouble common to all.

The pages ahead are involved, therefore, in a double commitment. They try, in the first place, to dig out of late medieval dramatic tradition the explanation for Iago, as well as for several other figures in Shakespeare and elsewhere in the Elizabethan drama who, by virtue of unmistakable kinship, belong to the Family of Iago. At the same time they cultivate a thesis with wider application than to the present subject alone: namely, that the popular stage for which Shakespeare wrote was in transition from one dramatic convention to another one radically different—a revolution in subject matter with its corresponding revolution in organic method and purpose—and that, in consequence, his plays often enfold a profound heterogeneity which escapes us while its effects baffle us. Sooner or later we must suspect that our long trouble with several major problems in Shakespeare lies in the way we construct them. We look at his plays with eyes adjusted to what the drama has become, since, like so much of their vocabulary

viii   *PREFACE*

which seems modern but isn't, they give the *surface appearance* of having arrived. Especially we are trained to be naturalistic, neglectful that tradition, particularly the highly traditionary art of the stage, hath its reasons of which naturalism knows nothing. Our naturalism is complicated, moreover, by a stubborn romantic mystique concerning the nature of art, especially the art of Shakespeare, which still turns away from its historical conditions and from what may be called its theatrical archaeology. Facing Shakespearian issues of the widest compass, a great deal of modern criticism, however sensitive, is hopelessly subverted by its aesthetic preconceptions. It has the wrong image of its quarry and repeatedly chases a psychological scent to a dead fault.

Although the present study is, therefore, unabashedly archaeological, it probably is not able to exhibit the kind of confident efficiency which ought to belong to such a method. I arrived at the method, and its accompanying thesis, only after long dissatisfaction with the evasions or irrelevancies of naturalistic criticism as applied to Shakespeare's villains, and only after long groping toward a better way of dealing with them; and the book undoubtedly shows the marks of such origins. The first two chapters, in fact, are a debate with my own preconceptions in an effort to break through them to clarity about the real nature of the problem and its proper solution. And it is fair to say that only when the last page was finished did I feel I had grasped the subject with sufficient control to begin the first. At any rate, I understand at last how profoundly the Shakespearian drama is divided between two different worlds of perception and technique, how inadequate must be any system of interpretation which tries to lock the plays within a portal they have only half entered, and how much their better elucidation depends on greater familiarity with the earlier theater—on deeper penetration than any yet achieved into what poor J. P. Collier once called "the impenetrable stores of our ancient dramatic compositions."

On its road toward such conclusions this book has been a wayfarer through several libraries, receiving comfort and sustenance from each of them; and to the Huntington Library, the Folger Shakespeare Library, the library of Vanderbilt University, and the library of the Englisches Seminar at the University of Munich I owe a debt of gratitude which, these words notwithstanding, remains unpaid. To a Cut-

PREFACE

ting Fellowship awarded me long ago by Columbia University I owe the opportunity for research which began the book, and to a Ford Foundation grant the opportunity for writing it into its present form. To several persons my obligation is profound. The uncompromising scholarship of Professors Alfred Harbage of Harvard and William Nelson of Columbia rescued the text from serious errors of fact, and the literary eye of Mr. Stanton Kreider did as much for its prose. The rowdy manuscript which came to the Columbia University Press was refined by the editorial energy of Mr. Raymond J. Dixon into the decent demeanor of a book, and the transformation, which seemed impossible, remains astonishing. My gratitude in another direction goes where words stumble, and are better unsaid, for it would be easier to write another book than to express what this one owes to Professor Oscar James Campbell of Columbia University.

About another kind of obligation I am content to remain cryptic. During a year or more of daily travel on the New York subways I stared at an advertisement which proclaimed the analgesic effect of a certain unguent, and vivified its point through the pictorialized triumphs and frustrations of a little green devil named "Peter Pain." To Peter, from whom I learned a great deal about allegory and Iago, I dedicate a new trident, very sharp.

BERNARD SPIVACK

Fisk University
November, 1957

CONTENTS

I.	*IAGO*	3
II.	*THE FAMILY OF IAGO*	28
III.	*THE PSYCHOMACHIA*	60
IV.	*THE MORALITY PLAY*	96
V.	*EMERGENCE OF THE VICE*	130
VI.	*MORAL METAPHOR AND DRAMATIC IMAGE*	151
VII.	*CHANGE AND DECLINE IN THE MORALITY CONVENTION*	206
VIII.	*THE HYBRID PLAY*	251
IX.	*THE HYBRID IMAGE IN FARCE*	304
X.	*THE HYBRID IMAGE IN SERIOUS DRAMA*	337
XI.	*THE HYBRID IMAGE IN SHAKESPEARE*	379
XII.	*IAGO REVISITED*	415
	NOTES	455
	BIBLIOGRAPHY OF MORALITY PLAYS	483
	INDEX	495

Shakespeare and the Allegory of Evil

Bei euch, ihr Herrn, kann man das Wesen
Gewöhnlich aus dem Namen lesen,
Wo es sich allzu deutlich weist,
Wenn man euch Fliegengott, Verderber, Lügner heiszt.

FAUST, PART I

Shakespeare and other Masters of Mind

CHAPTER ONE

IAGO

"Fie, there is no such manl It is impossible."
IAGO

I

Long before *Othello* St. Paul addressed the Thessalonians on the *mystery of iniquity*. Applied to the play, the apostle's phrase is a haven of comprehensive explanation compared to all the others that have been advanced to account for Shakespeare's tragedy and for the nature of its agent. Having pursued the meaning of Iago by ingenious and labyrinthine ways, critics and scholars are left, like his greatest victim, "perplex'd in the extreme." It would be ungenerous to the literature on *Othello* not to acknowledge that it affords deep and sensitive insight into the meaning of the play. And in this literature Iago has been rationalized to the last inch of his human similitude. But the hard and literal enigma of Othello's fatal ancient remains intractable. There is still no successful mediation between his terrible vividness, as we *feel* it on the one hand, and the blank he presents to our scrutiny on the other. To his bad eminence above all other figures of evil in the Elizabethan drama he is elevated not only by the shock of his turpitude, the pathos of his victims, and the poetry of his role, but also, and in no small measure, by his mystery. "Qu'est-ce qu'Iago?" asked the Duc de Broglie in a penetrating critique on *Othello* in 1830.[1] The question came after half a century of criticism had already tried to answer it, and the attempts have been legion ever since. But the question abides, and in 1945 Granville-Barker hopelessly threw up his hands at it: "Behind all the mutability there *is,* perhaps, no Iago, only a poisoned and poisonous ganglion of cravings after evil." [2]

What indeed is Iago? In Shakespeare's most compact and painful tragedy he is the artisan of an intrigue that first alienates and then destroys a pair of wedded lovers, in an action fraught with the pathos

IAGO

that attends the loss of noble love and noble life. He is also the divisive agent of another kind of separation, probably a more tragic theme for the Elizabethans than for us—the divorce of friendship between two generous men. His victims are a beautiful and pure-hearted Venetian woman, a noble and heroic Moorish prince, a loyal and ingenuous fellow soldier, his own honest wife, and a foolish gentleman whose wealth he has drained into his own pocket. He is a soldier, a liar, an adept at dissimulation and intrigue, a cynic, an egotist, a criminal. His crimes, he explains, are motivated by his resentment over the denial of an office to which he aspires and by his desire to recover it, by his suspicion that he is a deceived husband and by his desire for revenge, and by his need ultimately to cover up his previous malefactions. He inflicts unendurable suffering, destroys love and friendship and four lives, and at the end moves off in defiant silence to torture and his own death.

From the foregoing epitome one is not likely to be impressed with any serious problem in the interpretation of the agent of the tragic intrigue. He appears open to unperplexing definition as a malevolent creature, moved to an action of revenge by his real or fancied wrongs. In numerous monologues and asides he is voluble in explanation of his causes and intentions. Of late he has even received the sympathy of several critics, who have tried to create what has come to be known as *The Romantic Iago*—a tragic figure whose suffering merits a place in our compassion alongside the agony of his victims.[3] But we need not go so far. There is a complacent point of rest, attracting a good deal of critical allegiance, in the untroubled characterization by the late Professor Kittredge, who described Iago as "a passionate and revengeful Italian" whose initial motive is defined with "perfect clearness" and expressed with "passionate vigour." He is "actuated by resentment for injustice," namely, the rejection of his suit for an office to which "he seems to have the better claim." Added to this initial motive, said Kittredge, is Iago's "raging torment" of suspicion that his wife is Othello's mistress:

There is no difficulty, then, in finding a motive for Iago, and (what is vital in every tragic action) this motive is not only human but has a kind of foundation in reason and justice. In Iago's cankered nature, resentment for real or fancied injury brought with it boundless possibilities of crime.[4]

IAGO

Common sense and scholarship combine here apparently to compel such an interpretation. Let us but assume, as Kittredge assumed, what seems to be obvious—that tragedy, since it contemplates human life, necessarily portrays human beings in the grip of human passions—and does it not follow unerringly that the motives which drive the aggressor against his victims in the tragedy of *Othello* must be both human and passionate? And what other motives are there for Iago than those explicit in his own words? Does he not expatiate very directly upon them in soliloquy? And is it not an undeviating practice of the Elizabethan dramaturgy that the soliloquy is an instrument of direct revelation, providing information that the audience need to have and would not otherwise get clearly, or at all? Furthermore, the fact that he really entertains the motives he expresses—does it not receive unmistakable corroboration from other characters in the play? His suspicion of an adulterous relationship between his wife Emilia and Othello—is it not glanced at by Emilia herself in unequivocal language?

> Some such squire he was
> That turn'd your wit the seamy side without
> And made you to suspect me with the Moor.
> [IV.ii.145–47]

And another of his motives, his aspiration to the lieutenancy given to Cassio—is it not confirmed when he is elevated to that office after Cassio becomes disgraced and suspected, and additionally confirmed by the presentiment of Emilia?

> I will be hang'd if some eternal villain,
> Some busy and insinuating rogue,
> Some cogging, cozening slave, to get some office,
> Hath not devis'd this slander; I'll be hang'd else.
> [IV.ii.130–33]

And when late in the play he plots the destruction of both Cassio and Roderigo, do not his reasons for it, as he expresses them, grow out of the inescapable logic of his position? [5] These things are all in the play *literatim,* and by every canon of Elizabethan dramaturgy they are intended as unequivocal revelation. Surely, to ignore them is to fly in the face of the play and to resign ourselves to the unhappy conclusion that Shakespeare didn't know his own mind when he wrote *Othello*.

Moreover, why should anyone be troubled merely by the fact that

6   *IAGO*

Iago is provoked against Othello for at least two reasons and against Cassio for three or four? There is nothing in experience that prevents us from believing that a man may be stirred to crime or vengeance as readily by several causes as by one, and for illustration we need go no further than other plays of Shakespeare. Practically no one quarrels with the several motives Shylock has for his enmity toward Antonio; or with the confession of Claudius that he has been moved to crime by multiple temptations ("My crown, mine own ambition, and my queen"); or with Hamlet's awareness that he has more provocations than one for avenging himself upon his uncle—

> He that hath kill'd my king, and whor'd my mother;
> Popp'd in between th'election and my hopes;
> Thrown out his angle for my proper life . . .
> > [*Hamlet* V.ii.64–66]

And if some, or all, of Iago's expressed motives are groundless, mere vaporings of self-delusion, do they not all the more confirm thereby his membership in the human community, his kinship with Othello himself, and his resemblance to other men and women in Shakespeare —Leontes of *The Winter's Tale,* for instance, who is moved to passionate tyranny by his fantastic suspicion of Hermione? Merely the fact that Iago has more motives than one, or that some of them are chimerical, is thin justification for all the pother about them. Malevolence and hallucination, with perhaps a modicum of just resentment, create him an agent of destruction whose energies are devoted to the ruin of others; and of this species of men he is neither the first nor the last, in literature or in life.

Why is it then that so obvious a portrait, supported so patently by the text of the play, requires the repeated affirmations of the successive generations of critics and scholars who uphold it? It is scarcely necessary to rediscover and reaffirm the triple instigation for Claudius, or the strength of the hallucination within Leontes, or the destructive force that can be generated in anyone by frustrated ambition and sexual jealousy. And is it mere obtuseness in Coleridge, Hazlitt, Swinburne, Bradley, Stoll, Granville-Barker, and Wilson Knight—not to exhaust the list—that they reject an explanation so unperplexing and comprehensive? And is there any reader of *Othello* who can rise from

IAGO

the play untroubled by the question: What is Iago, and why does he do the things he does?

For the fact is, the literal interpretation of Iago and his motives will serve only until we read the play and find ourselves entangled in the mystery to which an enormous literature of conjecture pays tribute. The problem that confronts lay reader and scholar-critic alike—and renders uneasy even the most ardent defenders of literalism—arises from the inescapable impression that a profound ambiguity vitiates each of Iago's motives individually, and divorces all of them together from his dramatic personality and his actions. Adequate enough in the abstract as motives theoretically sufficient—and this is what the literalist seizes upon—they are invalidated by the way they are expressed and by their failure to conform with the dominant impression Iago makes as a character in a play. Lifted from the play and paraphrased, they point the ancient human way of sensible injury and passionate retaliation; but in the play itself Iago goes a very different way, dragging his motives backward, as it were, in spite of themselves. The result has been more than one hundred and fifty years of perplexed speculation over a problem that can be illustrated as threefold.

2

We need to notice, first of all, the remarkable equivocation which, in his monologues, infects his private utterance of his injuries and aims. The force of his provocations is dissipated by the very texture of the language in which he expresses them, by a literal and formal frivolity that resides in the vocabulary and syntax of his statements. Although we cannot avoid their nominal meaning, which is that Iago is moved to his deadly intrigue by desire for vengeance and for office, his explanations lack the emotional sincerity and dignity of such motives. Not only do his suspicions, for instance, lack objective support in the play, they do not even possess the quality of hallucination, but are studiously voiced by him as the flimsiest hearsay and conjecture. And once so voiced early in the play, they are forgotten, as we shall see, for all the rest of it. It is because of such a context that the very number of his motives augments their ambiguity. They come crowding in frivolous profusion and jostle each other off into oblivion. They sound

IAGO

like parenthetical remarks, postscripts, marginalia—like a clutter of opportunisms for an action that was inevitable before they were ever thought of.

For an example we need not go beyond the very beginning of his first soliloquy. The passion of sexual jealousy, sufficient apparently in Iago's case to drive him to the most rigorous retaliation, has probably never expressed itself in language so flippant as in his significant first statement of it:

> I hate the Moor;
> And it is thought abroad that 'twixt my sheets
> 'Has done my office, I know not if't be true;
> Yet I, for mere suspicion in that kind,
> Will do as if for surety.
>
> [I.iii.392–96]

We can, for the moment, neglect the anterior hatred except to note in passing that it has clear priority over the fantastically worded suspicion (with due allowance for the Elizabethan sense of "mere") to which it is so curiously linked. He is aware of a rumor which he has no reason to believe, but will use it as sufficient pretext for bringing about what his hatred of Othello, antecedent to all suspicion, provokes him to desire. This is the whole statement of his provocation as a hypothetical cuckold in the first of his two references to it. The other occurs soon after in his second soliloquy, and thereafter he forgets the subject completely.

His second soliloquy introduces a second suspicion in language even more bizarre, for the levity of the conjecture in the first two verses is accentuated by the frivolous chant of parisonic clauses and approximate rhyme:

> That Cassio loves her, I do well believe it;
> That she loves him, 'tis apt and of great credit.
> The Moor (howbeit that I endure him not)
> Is of a constant, loving, noble nature,
> And I dare think he'll prove to Desdemona
> A most dear husband.
>
> [II.i.295–300]

Here is once more the thematic hatred of Othello, joined this time to suspicion of an affection beyond friendship between Cassio and

IAGO

9

Desdemona, a suspicion that is never mentioned again. There turns out to be additional justice, then, in his already well-established plot to accuse Cassio and Desdemona of adultery, since one may very well believe that they are really in love with each other. Othello loves Desdemona, she loves Cassio, Cassio loves her; and immediately thereupon he announces his own novitiate in this family of love: "Now I do love her too . . ."—but only in part out of genuine desire, he hastens to explain. For the other part he is motivated by the compulsive artistry of a revenge that would even the score with Othello, "wife for wife"—but this love, or lust, of his for Desdemona never receives mention again. And then suddenly, and parenthetically—this is still his second soliloquy—he has another excuse for his plot, this time in respect to Cassio alone. Cassio deserves to be accused of adultery, not only because of the likelihood that he is guilty of unlawful love for Desdemona in the first place, but also because it is likely that he has committed, or is capable of committing, adultery with Emilia in the second place:

> For I fear Cassio with my nightcap too.
> [II.i.316] [6]

But this parenthetical fear never gets mentioned again. In fact, to none of these specific provocations, or vindications, of his intrigue does he ever again allude in the three quarters of the play remaining after this second soliloquy, and this remarkable amnesia includes every motive that can be attributed to him, except the pertinent reasons he meditates in the fifth act for a late necessity of his plot, the deaths of Cassio and Roderigo. In the end, when he stands uncovered, he has not a word to offer by way of justification, or even explanation, although he is directly asked for both or either. He is anything but reticent in the last three and a half acts, but in them his loquacity is engrossed by a very different subject matter, to which the insouciant temper of his utterance throughout the play, so out of square with passionate motivation, is perfectly suited. As we shall see eventually, his motives and his life in the play are at variance, and his words equivocate his motives because they express his life.

But where are we left, then, in respect to this group of sexual provocations? That they are suspicions that lack even the slightest

IAGO

justification is, of course, beside the point. Merely as hallucinations they would sufficiently explain Iago and supply the emotional energy for his intrigue; and we need so to accept them, but how can we? They are vitiated in their utterance by a frivolity in conjecture that is grotesque when measured against the compulsive force they seem to exert in action. They are fantasies stabbed to death in the very moment of their birth by equivocation as deliberate as a jest, and as invariable as a formula:

> 'Tis thought abroad
> I know not if't be true
> I do well believe it
> 'Tis apt and of great credit
> I fear Cassio with my nightcap too
> I do suspect the lusty Moor

After receiving in this giddy language their single exposition (except for his suspicion of Othello, which is mentioned twice) they sink into oblivion, as far as Iago is concerned, for all the remainder of the play after the first scene of the second act. And to this immediate effect of levity and ambiguity in each of his motives—including others which still remain to be examined—their very multitude necessarily contributes. There is an inverse ratio between Iago's loquacity and his clarity. The more he explains the less we understand. His explanations, growing to a pleurisy, die in their own too much. They twinkle on and off like the will-o'-the-wisp, now here now there, flickering all around for the instant before they extinguish forever to leave us mired in perplexity and groping in total night.

3

But there is another kind of equivocation that invests Iago's motives generally and is even more disturbing than their literal and formal frivolity. The point concerns two very different levels of motivation, one of which we have already examined in part. On that level there exist Iago's resentment of Cassio's promotion and his desire to gain the lieutenancy for himself; his jealousy of Othello and Emilia; his suspicion of Cassio and Desdemona; his suspicion of Cassio and Emilia;

IAGO

his love, which is part revenge, for Desdemona. In one sense, as it has already appeared for all of them except the first, these motives are unreal. They are not convincing as an explanation of Iago's intrigue because they exhale flippancy instead of a passion equivalent to their gravity, because their multitude dilutes their seriousness, and because we cannot feel that they really govern Iago's life and action in the play. But in another sense they are incontrovertibly real: they have a literal existence in Iago's monologues, and in several instances they receive corroboration, as motives, outside his monologues, particularly in some remarks of Emilia which we have already noticed. Their simultaneous reality and unreality is exactly the problem that afflicts us and nourishes the endless controversy over them.

When compared, however, with several additional reasons that Iago gives for his actions, the motives already canvassed possess an important kind of reality, or verisimilitude, in another sense: for all their failure to convince, they are theoretically intelligible. They adhere abstractly to the conventional possibilities in human behavior. No matter how much they fall short of imparting emotional integrity to Iago's conduct, they are at least the unfulfilled outlines of recognizable provocations. They have the shape, if not the life, of familiar resentments, suspicions, and desires. They are like fragmentary sketches of humanity on a page of Leonardo's notebooks: an oddly disposed assortment of heads, limbs, and torsos, lacking vital color and unified composition; yet to what species of animal they belong is not doubtful. So it is with these motives of Iago already examined. To believe in them it is only necessary to do what those literal scholars who accept them for true currency have done. Single out each of them from the medley in which they inflict on each other a mutual contamination, rephrase it free from the wanton idiom that dissolves its sincerity, disregard the oblivion that annihilates it as an influence and even as a memory for every moment of the play except the one in which it is uttered—and it stands up as a conventional force in human behavior, and particularly in that imitation of human behavior which occurs in the play before us.

But these are not the only motives of Iago. Attached to them by the closest syntax, in a pairing so habitual as to constitute a formal characteristic of his utterance, there appear in his soliloquies several ex-

IAGO

planations that do not have intelligible reference to the human situation inside the play, or, for that matter, to the conventions of human behavior outside it. We have already noticed this trick of combination in the very beginning of his first soliloquy—the close mating of a specific provocation with a generalized and vague, but impelling, animosity:

> I hate the Moor;
> And it is thought abroad that 'twixt my sheets
> 'Has done my office.

And in the first lines of his second soliloquy there has also appeared this union of precise suspicion and nebular enmity: it is credible that Cassio and Desdemona love each other; as for Othello, "howbeit that I endure him not," his nature is full of constancy, love, and nobility. This habit of coupling in such close syntax and almost in the same breath a brace of motives so different in their breed gives to Iago's speech an unmistakable style, which repeats itself exactly in respect to Cassio—the marriage of the concrete and intelligible purpose to an intention so comprehensive as to render superfluous all other motives for his intrigue, if it were not at the same time so cryptic as to leave us groping forever for its meaning:

> To get his place, and to plume up my will
> In double knavery.
>
> [I.iii.399–400]

And once more, toward the end of the play, such a discordant pair of reasons keep strange company in his words as he formulates his own advantages for fulfilling Othello's assignment in the death of Cassio— the second of them explicit in its criminal cogency, the first a shrouded visitor from worlds unrealized:

> If Cassio do remain,
> He hath a daily beauty in his life
> That makes me ugly; and besides, the Moor
> May unfold me to him; there stand I in much peril.
>
> [V.i.18–21]

Following in part the romantic formula for the role supplied by Coleridge, A. C. Bradley interprets this last passage, although hesitantly, as "another symptom of the obscure working of conscience or humanity" in Iago.[7] But its real meaning escapes Bradley, as we shall see eventually.

IAGO

Our present concern is with the additional confusion Iago heaps on his already confusing portrait by offering a second set of explanations for his intrigue that are even more bewildering than those previously discussed, although for a different reason. These are not simply additional motives of the kind to which we are already accustomed; they belong, if we examine them carefully, to a different world of causation; and their close merger with Iago's jealousy and ambition suggests something very much like crossbreeding between widely different species. Their existence in the play is a second element of the confusion inhabiting his motivation in general, creating, in effect, a double equivoque.

What can be made out of the instigation that exists for Iago in Cassio's daily beauty, in the attractions of double knavery, and in his frequently voiced hatred of Othello? As motives they have always been a puzzle in a way that his pragmatic resentments and suspicions are not. The language of the first two is so cryptic that they cannot even be paraphrased with any certainty; and the third, his thematic hatred, receives commonly a facile explanation that is in no way satisfying. The two that are usually acknowledged as enigmas can properly remain so for the present. It is the third, Iago's hatred for Othello, which needs to be restored to mystery by separating it from the explanation it frequently receives.

Hatred has often been regarded as Iago's ruling passion, a hatred that feeds on events and creates its own multiple provocations. So the great actor Edwin Booth interpreted the role, and such an interpretation receives the approval of George Woodberry:

Inside, Booth has no doubt, Iago was a spirit of hate. . . . And perhaps in that most difficult moment of the *rôle,* the climax of Iago's fate, the elder Booth was right in making the expression of this intense enmity dominant in the Parthian look which Iago, as he was borne off, wounded and in bonds, gave Othello,—a Gorgon stare, in which hate seemed both petrified and petrifying.[8]

And Professor Edgar Stoll, having wavered over Iago from essay to essay, came in a late opinion to much the same conclusion: "At bottom Iago is moved by simple 'hatred' . . . which he flatly avows at the outset and reiterates again and again." [9] There is in such a view a great deal of apparent justice. Iago's hate, as Professor Stoll says, is a significant iteration in the early part of the play, receiving expression in soliloquy and outside it no less than five times,[10] although after the first scene of the second act it endures the fate of all his other motives— it is forgotten. Another thing about it, already noticed, is that it is anterior to his professed suspicion of cuckoldry, and indeed he seems open-eyed to the fact that his suspicion ("I know not if't be true") is only a convenient excuse for the action to which his hatred moves him in the first place. Finally, it is the only one of his multiple provocations that he shares with his gull Roderigo—shares it with him, in fact, even before the play begins, as appears from their conversation at the beginning of the opening scene:

> *Rod.* Thou told'st me thou did'st hold him in thy hate.
> *Iago.* Despise me if I do not.

And he proceeds thereupon with an exposition of grievance that passes current, in every literal interpretation of Iago, as the explanation for his hatred, since it contains, as Kittredge has called it, Iago's "initial impulse" and "prime incentive."

But in this explanation and what follows it there is a curious and disturbing obliquity. He is resentful because Othello has denied him the vacant lieutenancy, to which, he says, merit and seniority entitle him, and instead has allowed favoritism to dictate the appointment of Cassio, a textbook soldier merely. Having so far edified Roderigo, he concludes with a declaration of the state of his feelings toward Othello which is just about right when measured against his provocation, but falls notably short of the inveterate enmity he later invokes to justify his fatal intrigue:

> Now, sir, be judge yourself
> Whether I in any just term am affin'd
> To love the Moor.
> [I.i.38–40]

And what directly follows in their conversation is no less notable when it is considered in the light of his subsequent expressions of hatred and of the terrible results for which his hatred seemingly is responsible. For out of Iago's professional frustration Roderigo derives a very natural consequence in respect to Othello: "I would not follow him then." It is at this point that Iago's explanation for his continuance in service expresses an intention the mildness of which has the effect of converting all that he says and does thereafter into a *non sequitur*. He remains

IAGO

with Othello "to serve my turn upon him," a threat whose e[x]
easily be exaggerated through an unwary reading of the text. [I]
further reach than that he will continue in Othello's service [...]
his own advantage and profit, without regard to love and duty. In his
revenge, in short, he expresses no higher ambition than to play the
fallax servus, imitating those retainers of great men

> Who, trimm'd in forms and visages of duty,
> Keep yet their hearts attending on themselves;
> And, throwing but shows of service on their lords,
> Do well thrive by them, and when they have lin'd their coats,
> Do themselves homage.   [I.i.50–54]

Here, then, is his initial provocation and its moderate, even normal,
consequence in knavery. It will serve very well to explain a dishonest
servant or disloyal follower; but it cannot explain, because it is inadequate to inspire, the antiphony of hate that responds to it and becomes apparently the first cause of his enormous aggression:

> Though I do hate him as I do hell pains . . .
>   [I.i.155]

> I have told thee often, and I retell thee
> again and again, I hate the Moor.
>   [I.iii.372–73]

Furthermore, if Iago's feelings can be measured by their consequence
in action, it is scarcely to be allowed that his hatred for Othello is any
degree greater than it is for Cassio or Desdemona. His "revenge" does
not discriminate among them, nor does his expressed purpose either,
which is to "make the net that shall enmesh them all." [11]

There remains, however, one consideration which asks to be laid to
rest. Is there, perhaps, for this hatred, so often expressed and apparently so widely operative, a better meaning elsewhere in the play
than anything the opening scene discloses? Although the expository
technique of first scenes in the Elizabethan dramaturgy must be respected, it is a temptation, knowing what we do of Iago and of the
relationship between the two men, to discount anything he tells
Roderigo. The latter is Iago's dupe, not his confidant. Why should the
serpentine ancient be uniquely candid in this place with the silly gentleman he hoaxes everywhere else in the play? Such a hope, alas, seeks to

16 **IAGO**

open a door that does not, in fact, exist. Elsewhere and in other matters
we know exactly how, why, and to what extent he beguiles Roderigo,
for he himself tells us. In this matter he tells us nothing, and we learn
nothing further. The explanation Roderigo gets is the only one there
is. It is too frail a vessel for the cargo of animosity with which it is
laden, but where do we find a better?

For Iago's hate is subject to the same comment that T. S. Eliot makes
about Hamlet's grief—it lacks an "objective correlative." [12] It has no
particular connection with the opportunities of the human situation displayed within the tragedy, but reflects, instead, a vague, pervasive, and,
in a sense, static condition of Iago's being. It is more like the enduring
biological characteristic of a species than an aspect of the personality
of a single man in reaction to particular events. For the present it must
remain cryptic and superfluous, as though Iago were invoking motives
out of another world to buttress and vitalize the provocations available
to him in this one. Actually, as it will turn out, the exact reverse is
true. A figure out of another, older, world is being naturalized into
the drama of the Renaissance, and part of the process is to array him
in new garments of the prevailing cut. Iago's resentments and his
jealousies are, in fact, just such motives as a dramatist might employ to
refashion into tragic naturalism a stock figure out of an archaic dramatic convention that had no use for the conventional incitements of
human life.

4

So far we have been concerned with only one large aspect of the riddle
of Iago—the ambiguity resident within the language of the motives
themselves, as he expresses them in his monologues and during his
converse with Roderigo in the fundamental exposition of the opening
scene. But this first difficulty is compounded by a second which is no
less disturbing. The trouble with Iago's "hate" and with all his other
revengeful "passions," as well as with the causes that seem to provoke
them, spreads out beyond their inherent difficulties. Between the emotions Iago says he feels and Iago himself throughout the play there
exists a profound disjunction in mood; between his provocations, as he
describes them, and the actual premises of his behavior there is a profound discrepancy in logic.

Who can read the play without becoming aware that his motives

IAGO

inhabit his words but not his emotions? As Bradley h⟨as⟩
he displays none of the passion that belongs with resent⟨ment⟩,
jealousy, or outraged honor.[13] His injuries, he says, excite ⟨his⟩
retaliation, but they do not excite *in him* anything like a feeling
equivalent to their character and consequence. The "hate" that seems
so dominant a theme has only a nominal existence. It is naked of any
feeling that carries the impression of hatred. Who can doubt Shylock's
hate or believe in Iago's? The disappointed ambition, the sexual
jealousy, the affronted honor never find expression, with one minute
exception, in that rhetoric of passion which was the elementary equipment and resource of every Elizabethan playwright, not to speak of
Shakespeare. Iago's aggression far outsoars his causes, but his emotions
lie infinitely beneath them. The "wrongs" he has endured are merely
so many words, displayed and withdrawn with slick rapidity, like a
frivolous performance of sleight of hand, forever giving way to glee,
to mordant irony, to contemptuous triumph over the innocent fools
who are his victims. There is indeed a unique moment when something like an outburst emotionally consistent with sexual jealousy
crosses his lips. His "love" for Desdemona, he says, is not so much real
desire as it is a means to achieve evenhanded vengeance for the intimacy he suspects between Othello and Emilia:

> the thought whereof
> Doth, like a poisonous mineral, gnaw my inwards;
> And nothing can or shall content my soul
> Till I am even'd with him, wife for wife.
>
> [II.i.305–308]

If this is "stagey," as one critic described it,[14] it is so because it is
singularly at odds with the whole impression of Iago throughout the
play. Everywhere else his emotions are simply variations on the
monolithic passion of laughter. He is a creature of leaping jubilation
and sardonic mirth, most subdued when he is merely brisk and
ebullient:

> If consequence do but approve my dream,
> My boat sails freely, both with wind and stream.
>
> [II.iii.64–65]

> By th' mass, 'tis morning!
> Pleasure and action make the hours seem short.
>
> [II.iii.384–85]

IAGO

Myself the while to draw the Moor apart
And bring him jump when he may Cassio find
Soliciting his wife. Ay, that's the way!
Dull not device by coldness and delay.

[II.iii.391–94]

What reader does not make the astonishing discovery that jocularity is the true passion of the tragic agent throughout this play, and that against this jocularity his professed motives are verbal and marginal, when they are not actually contaminated by it? By the end of the first scene of the second act he is completely done with them, and nothing competes with his intense pleasure and single-minded concentration upon the felicity of his intrigue. There are moments later on when the passion of his cause or the passion of his revenge begs in vain for expression. One such moment occurs in the fourth act, just after he has left Desdemona, already deep in her agony, and stands over Othello, now prostrate under his. Now if ever he has his opportunity to utter the passion of his provocation, or simply the gratified feeling of his vengeance. But something so very different comes from his lips—he has divulged it before but never so completely as now—that at the laughter-laden sound of it the whole elaborate fabric of passionate cause and conventional revenge fades into air, into thin air:

Work on,
My medicine, work! Thus credulous fools are caught,
And many worthy and chaste dames even thus,
All guiltless, meet reproach.

[IV.i.45–48]

And with these words Iago confronts us with another aspect of his multiplex enigma. His opinion of his several victims is a chaos of contradictions. Whenever he is engaged in the exposition of his injuries he presents them uniformly in one light. Whenever he regards them as his victims, which is most of the time, he pronounces upon them a moral commentary different in the extreme. For it is not merely that *we* cannot for a moment believe his accusations; he himself does not believe them, and plainly says so. He declaims at one instant his suspicion that the "lusty Moor" is guilty of adultery with Emilia. Yet in the very same soliloquy—only four lines earlier in fact— adulterous Othello "Is of a constant, loving, noble nature" and will

IAGO

make Desdemona "A most dear husband." The Othello who carries on a stealthy intrigue with the wife of one of his soldiers, who, when the "three great ones of the city" solicit the lieutenancy for Iago,

> Evades them with a bombast circumstance,
> Horribly stuff'd with epithets of war;
>
> [I.i.13–14]

is also of "a free and open nature"; the libertine Moor who is making love to Emilia behind Iago's back is also Desdemona's devoted, doting husband:

> His soul is so enfetter'd to her love
> That she may make, unmake, do what she list,
> Even as her appetite shall play the god
> With his weak function.
>
> [II.iii.351–54]

And if we require a paradigm of the endless bewilderment with which honest Iago afflicts us, we have only to try to see Othello through his ancient's bifocal vision—both as the "lusty Moor" and as the middle-aged man of "weak function."

But his opinion of his other victims is no less baffling. Cassio, whom he also suspects of a liaison with Emilia, who in addition, he believes, is making illicit love to the wife of Othello—Cassio, who is a precocious amorist and faithless friend, is also an "honest fool" who "hath a daily beauty in his life. . . ." Of Desdemona he believes it likely that she loves Cassio in adulterous violation of her marriage vows; yet she is also a woman who inclines to "any honest suit," whose "virtue" he intends to turn into pitch, out of whose "goodness" he will weave a net to enmesh them all. And when her suffering becomes testimony to the success of his intrigue, he offers her to the audience as an example of how

> many worthy and chaste dames even thus,
> All guiltless, meet reproach.

At one moment all his victims are guilty of moral turpitude and devious faithlessness; at another they are all exemplars of virtue, all honest fools whose simple-minded rectitude and credulity render them his natural prey. This remarkable cleavage in his attitude toward them— which must be accepted at face value since, except for his remark about Othello's "bombast circumstance," it is all in his monologues—

corresponds exactly to the schism between the tenor and the tone of his soliloquized motives, between his words and his behavior, between the passional implications of his grievances and his joyous, exuberant life throughout the play.

Nor does his *schizoid* attitude toward Othello, Cassio, and Desdemona exhaust the range of his ambivalence. Is it not extraordinary that the only person of any significance of whom he expresses no resentment, against whom he weaves no plots, is his wife Emilia?—a singular complacency in an Elizabethan husband who believes himself twice a cuckold. Where can we find that he is conscious of that aspect of the adultery he fears which touches his emotions and his honor most nearly? Nowhere in his soliloquies does he accuse her, or blame her, or in any way vent upon her the feelings of an outraged husband. The astonishing fact is that he never so much as mentions her in any connection with the adultery for which he professes to take revenge, his expression of his suspicion forever taking the form of a metaphor at once coarse and, in respect to her, nimbly evasive:

> And it is thought abroad that 'twixt my sheets
> 'Has done my office.

> For that I do suspect the lusty Moor
> Hath leap'd into my seat.

> For I fear Cassio with my nightcap too.

It is true that in the end he stabs her, calling her "villainous whore," but the provocation then has nothing to do with adultery, and the epithet belongs to the indiscriminate vocabulary of abuse. In an earlier scene he addresses to her a cynical jest upon her "common thing," but when she challenges him to explain, he retreats quickly behind an evasion, and the total effect is that of a characteristic animadversion upon women in general.[15] Elsewhere, without exception, he treats her with amiable contempt, reflecting the easy familiarity of a settled marriage and his inveterate cynicism toward the feminine sex. As far as the adultery he suspects is concerned, she simply does not exist. Nothing about Iago is more bewildering than his utter neglect of Emilia's crucial role in his dishonor and her inescapable primacy in his revenge—nothing discloses so nakedly the fissure cleaving through the whole extent of his life in the play. The entire Elizabethan and

IAGO

Jacobean drama—in which no theme is more prominent than adultery, actual or suspected—offers no parallel to this oblivion of a husband to his wife's part in the adultery for which he seeks vengeance.

When we consider that none of the great tragedies gives the over-all impression of being more carefully wrought than *Othello*, we are bound to put aside any suggestion that such dislocations are due merely to Shakespeare's oversight. Besides, they are not simply discrepancies in detail, like Hamlet's age or Lady Macbeth's children. They achieve in their effect the total disruption of the emotional and logical premises that create, albeit superficially, the human image of Iago in the first part of the play. Nor can they be taken as a lapse in Shakespeare's creative power. Few of his characterizations are more consistently vivid from first to last than is Iago. If anything, he grows more vivid as he discards the human garments to which literal criticism clings in its baffled effort to apprehend him.

5

And if it appears so far that Iago bewilders us because he defies analysis in any terms that are consistent with the dramatic representation of human behavior, especially in tragedy, we have only to go a step further to discover a third side of him which exposes the folly of attempting such an analysis in the first place. For in close association with his scornful proclamation of the virtue and credulity of his victims there appears in his monologues the iterated avowal of a purpose that has nothing to do with vengeance. By itself it shatters into failure every effort to achieve a consistent interpretation of him as a passionate avenger of his real or illusory wrongs. Concentrating, as we naturally do, on his resentment and jealousy, we neglect an entirely different order of motivation that is more real for him than any impulse of conventional life could be. We neglect it because we are not accustomed to view it for what it actually is; or if we do not neglect it altogether, since it is there to disturb us, we find it inexplicable by itself and regard it as, somehow, attached to his vengeful purpose. But it has a source and nature altogether different and apart. In respect to Othello, to confine it to a pair of illustrations only, it appears thus:

> The Moor is of a free and open nature
> That thinks men honest that but seem to be so;

IAGO

And will as tenderly be led by th' nose
As asses are.

[I.iii.405–408]

Make the Moor thank me, love me, and reward me
For making him egregiously an ass
And practising upon his peace and quiet
Even to madness.

[II.i.317–20]

Let us notice in passing that to make Othello "egregiously an ass" by filling him with suspicion that Desdemona and Cassio are in love with each other has no cogent relation to his own belief, expressed a few lines earlier in the same monologue, that they really are in love. In respect to Desdemona, as well as to Cassio and Othello, this same purpose appears in words already familiar:

So will I turn her virtue into pitch,
And out of her own goodness make the net
That shall enmesh them all.

[II.iii.365–68]

Behind such aims there is a cause that has no connection at all with resentment or jealousy, or with any other motive that we can think of in conventional humanity. It has its a priori meaning in the obscured, but basic, nature of its agent. Nor is he reticent about revealing, at least in part, what he really is, beneath his appearances, except that our eyes are distracted by these very same appearances, and our ears are not attuned to listen. Nothing that he utters in the privacy of his monologues is as dominant or persistent a theme, or as effectively divorces his conventional motives from verisimilitude, as his portrait of himself, garlanded in laughter. How can there be any doubt concerning the veil when he himself lifts it?

I have't! It is engend'red! Hell and night
Must bring this monstrous birth to the world's light.

[I.iii.409–10]

O, you are well tun'd now!
But I'll set down the pegs that make this music,
As honest as I am.

[II.i.201–203]

IAGO

> 'Tis here, but yet confus'd.
> Knavery's plain face is never seen till us'd.
>
> [II.i.320–21]

> How am I then a villain
> To counsel Cassio to this parallel course,
> Directly to his good? Divinity of hell!
> When devils will the blackest sins put on,
> They do suggest at first with heavenly shows,
> As I do now.
>
> [II.iii.354–59]

If we are looking for an explanation of the mirth that is Iago's only real emotion, it is now amply supplied. The thwarted aspirant and tormented husband is not only completely missing from these sentiments, there is no room for him in them. The place is occupied. The veil once withdrawn, the figure who glimmered through it at all times, distorting the surface image, now grins at us in the full light; and it appears at once that he has nothing whatever to do with the grave passion of frustrated ambition or the graver passion of sexual jealousy. Although the nature of the substitution and of the thing substituted so far escapes us, we discover at once that we can discard these conventional motives without creating the slightest vacuum in the play.

The result, in fact, is surprisingly otherwise. The conventional incentives are not convincing because, among other reasons, they are superfluous. Beneath them and showing through them, like a dark ground lightly painted over, is the dominant Iago, and he is there with all the impulsion his archaic nature needs for his multiple aggression. The connection between the credulous virtue of his victims and his own self-proclaimed, ebullient villainy; his voluntary association with hell and his zest for "double knavery"; the vague dynamic of the "hate" that seems to propel him; his provocation in Cassio's "daily beauty"— these are all an archaeological stratum beneath the familiar motives of human life that time and changing dramatic convention sifted upon the primary configuration of Iago. And it is because our only habituation for three centuries has been to a stage and a literature that imitate these familiar motives of human life that we confront in Iago, and not only in him alone on the Elizabethan stage, a partially concealed order of motivation we no longer recognize, the logic and energy of which elude us.

IAGO

6

Up to this point we have canvassed the threefold objection to a literal interpretation of Iago and his motives, such as that represented by the opinion of Professor Kittredge, which draws the picture of a man passionately moved to revenge by frustrated ambition and sexual jealousy. Perhaps it is clear by now how evasive in respect to the play as a whole such an interpretation must necessarily be. It would keep the balance even to enter at this time a demurrer against an inviting alternative. It might seem that if we cannot accept at face value the explanations Iago offers for his intrigue, nothing remains for us except to agree with Coleridge and Bradley that these explanations portray, with infinite psychological finesse, the "motive-hunting" of Iago's flickering moral sense and rudimentary conscience, that they "clearly betray his uneasiness and his unconscious desire to persuade himself that he has some excuse for the villainy he contemplates." [16] This is a point of view at the opposite pole to literalism, and it represents that kind of subjective interpretation that the sensitive student consistently prefers to literalism when confronted by a problem like that of Iago, or by the similar problem of Hamlet.

But is not such an alternative simply a short flight from one horn of the dilemma to the other? Shakespeare, this theory says in effect, in the high noon of his dramatic power and popular artistry, creates a character whose self-deception is so complete that he is never able to distinguish for himself, or able to help the audience to distinguish, between his true and his forged motivations. Such a description fits more nearly the hieratic mysteries of ancient Egypt than a consummate dramatist in the popular Elizabethan tradition, whose plays were interpreted by actors who had to understand their parts, to an audience that had to understand the play. To exalt Shakespeare's subtlety at the expense of his clarity is to have desperate recourse to a solution that is valid neither for Shakespeare's dramatic practice nor for the consistent practice of the entire Elizabethan and Jacobean drama. It is an explanation contradicted by all that scholarship has learned about the invariable—and, from our modern viewpoint, frequently undramatic—technique of clarity of every Elizabethan playwright in respect to the motives and intentions of his dramatis personae, particularly as that

IAGO 25

clarity is realized through the organ precisely contrived to achieve it—the direct exposition of the dramatic soliloquy. Professor Schücking is on unassailable ground when he says,

It must be made a principle to deny that Shakespeare makes any character in a monologue state reasons for his actions that are not meant to be substantially correct and sufficient.[17]

And Professor Stoll's opinion on Iago's monologues is likewise unassailable:

The Elizabethan soliloquy is the truth itself, and though in real life a liar may lie to everybody, even to himself in a way, Iago cannot be lying when he expresses his ambitious jealousy of Cassio, his sexual jealousy of Othello, and his lust for Desdemona. . . . The soliloquy or aside, and the confidence of friend to friend, are for information, like prologue and chorus, and in treating them psychologically Shakespearian criticism has ignored dramatic convention. . . . Most of his motives Iago touches on but once, and he demeans himself, as Professor Bradley says, not at all like one stung with resentment, fired by ambition, or consumed with hatred . . . sexual jealousy or lust. . . . Having motives, then, he acts as if he had them not. Shall we, therefore, discard them, and, like the critics, get him new ones of our own? In doing so we discard Shakespeare, and, unawares, cease from criticism.[18]

To argue for Iago's motive-hunting is to argue, in effect, that Shakespeare is perverting the soliloquy in its most central function. It is to argue for the existence of something in Iago that is simply not expressed anywhere in a play that offers its loquacious villain a hundred opportunities to reveal himself—as in fact he does, but not as a hunter after motives to appease a conscience he does not possess. And it is, finally, to argue for an equal—and equally untenable—subtlety whenever we are similarly baffled by an equivalent problem of motivation elsewhere in Shakespeare and elsewhere in the drama of his age—in *Titus Andronicus,* for instance, for which play "subtle" is scarcely the proper adjective, in *Richard III,* in *Much Ado,* in Marlowe's *Jew of Malta,* and in at least a dozen other plays of the time through which the scions of the family of Iago spread themselves.

"A play," observes an acute analyst of the corpus of *Hamlet* criticism, "is not a mine of secret motives. We persist in digging for them; what happens usually is that our spade goes through to the other side of the drama." [19] This is exactly what happens to Bradley's

26   IAGO

sensitive ingenuity. After demonstrating how impossible it is to accept Iago's motives literally, he breaks out into the emptiness on the other side of the play and builds his own interpretation in the void. His criticism weaves for Iago a psychological wardrobe out of invisible thread, and then says: Behold now, how suitably he is clothed. But stare as much as we can, with the greatest good will in the world, we still look on the naked problem. Bradley's supersubtle probing of the nonexistent proceeds out of very much the same fallacy that creates the bad auspices for Shakespearian criticism generally, including the literalism that he himself rejects. The nature of that fallacy, and how it keeps criticism in a treadmill in respect to more Shakespearian characters than Iago alone, remains for later consideration.

The timeless effort of all drama everywhere, as of all art and thought that contemplate man, is to elucidate human life, not to obscure it; and no stage was ever more overt than Shakespeare's. The exposition of reliable motives is so much an imperative of an Elizabethan dramatic plot that it consistently takes place before the earliest duplicity, aggression, or intrigue appears. The audience must know, and Shakespeare very often goes out of his way to let the audience know, the springs of malice and the springs of intrigue. If a case arises wherein the aggressor is doubtful as to his motives, that very doubt is made clear. Consider Oliver of *As You Like It* the very first chance he has to express himself in monologue:

Now will I stir this gamester. I hope I shall see an end of him; for my soul (yet I know not why) hates nothing more than he. Yet he's gentle; never school'd and yet learned; full of noble device; of all sorts enchantingly beloved, and indeed so much in the heart of the world, and especially of my own people, who best know him, that I am altogether misprised. But it shall not be so long.

[I.i.170–78]

And if, as sometimes happens, a character has appeared to act upon motives he does not really entertain, that too is made clear. An example of such integrity in explanation occurs in that scene of *Henry V* in which the conspiracy against the King's life is exposed and the conspirators charged with selling their love and allegiance for French gold. One of the traitors, the Earl of Cambridge, not content to rest his

IAGO

treason on so adequate a temptation, fetches a superfluous revelation out of Holinshed:

> For me, the gold of France did not seduce,
> Although I did admit it as a motive
> The sooner to effect what I intended.
>
> [II.ii.155–57]

The players cannot keep counsel; they'll tell all. Shakespeare belonged to a dramatic tradition that cultivated the rhetorical art of introspection to a degree that is remarkable to us today. The soliloquy was an instrument, not simply for motives perfunctorily uttered, but for motives lavishly canvassed, for the conflict of motive with motive, for the effect of conscience upon iniquitous incentive. It is precisely from Shakespeare's concern with motivation that the problem of Iago arises. If he had intended Iago's expressed motives to be the searching for justification by an uneasy conscience, or "the motive-hunting of a motiveless malignity," he would have revealed such a fact with perfect clarity very soon in the play. What he could not reveal was a different kind of motive-hunting, in which, not Iago, but he and some of his fellow playwrights were engaged.

CHAPTER TWO

THE FAMILY OF IAGO

I

To proceed on its course the present enterprise must cut through a paradox that stands in the way. The examination so far takes on a viewpoint that rejects each of the two substantial and directly conflicting halves of the body of criticism dealing with Iago—whose representatives for our purpose are Kittredge and Bradley—but agrees, in a sense, with both of them. Actually it is a viewpoint that employs literalism to put down the supersubtlety of romantic criticism, and invokes the superior sensibility of the romantic school to expose the evasions of the literalists. For both are right in what they deny and wrong in what they affirm. Romantic criticism, for the sufficient reasons already noted, cannot accept Iago's conventional motives as an explanation of what he is and does; but it is unreasonably prone to forget that these motives exist ineluctably. Literalism, supported by scholarship, rightly argues that these motives cannot be overlooked, or volatilized into an inexplicable motive-hunting provoked by Iago's invisible conscience; but in its turn it concentrates on some of Iago's motives to the neglect of others, and to the more serious neglect of everything in the play that invalidates all of them. As a result of a fallacious assumption within Shakespearian criticism generally, the criticism of Iago consists of two hemispheres, each endlessly estranged from the reality of its complement, each successful only in destroying the other. This paradox can be resolved, but only by substituting a new one. Iago's conventional motives are at once unmistakably valid and unmistakably invalid. As we observed earlier, the long controversy over them is maintained precisely by their simultaneous reality and unreality.

But we can try to unchain ourselves at once from this wheel of

THE FAMILY OF IAGO

paradox lest we revolve with it through endless cycles. Can it be that an idea is both right and wrong because it contemplates two things which through force of habit it persists in regarding as one? Can it be that seemingly opposite views do not clash because in fact they do not meet, being directed toward different objects? Is it possible that we are dazzled by the simultaneous reality and unreality of these motives only because we are the victims of an illusion which merges into one figure the person to whom they do belong and another person to whom they do not belong? Is it possible that Kittredge's scholarly literalism quarrels with Bradley's sensitive insight simply because each sees only one of the two faces of Janus? Are not two such irreconcilable views both right in the respect that together they affirm a fundamental duality, but each alone wrong because unable to take this duality into account? Is there a chance that it is only the metaphysical habit of unity which prevents us from seeing that the whole criticism of the subject is futile because the basic tenet of its faith is false—because, in fact, the Lord its God is *Two?*

Perhaps it no longer comes as a surprise that the course of this inquiry is directed toward more than one Iago—that his "character," impenetrable to coherent analysis, can be unwoven into two very dissimilar roles governed by two very different motive principles. On the one hand there is the cankered Iago of the thwarted ambition—except that he is never really cankered or ambitious; the passionately moved husband of a wife he believes unfaithful—except that, apart from one flicker of emotion, he is never passionately moved or in any way aware that the adultery he suspects involves his wife; the aspirant who seeks to gain an office by disgracing its incumbent—except that he does not show the slightest interest in the office before or after he achieves it; the hot-blooded Italian whose latent depravity is fired into action by a sense of injury—except that he does not display a sense of injury; the irascible soldier who finds himself deviously and shamefully wronged by Othello and Cassio—except that he proclaims that Othello and Cassio are honest fools, openhearted, generous-minded, noble, ingenuous men, whose artless virtue makes them the easy and natural victims of his duplicity.

On the other hand there appears a figure strange to us, but familiar and fascinating to the Elizabethan playgoer. The Iago who craves

THE FAMILY OF IAGO

revenge for a slight or for dishonor, or seeks advancement to a post held by a rival, dissolves; and in his place appear the features, wrinkled in mocking laughter, of another Iago, concerned with a purpose that has nothing to do with either revenge or ambition. This second Iago is an artist eager to demonstrate his skill by achieving a masterpiece of his craft. He is working upon exactly the right material—ingenuous virtue, or (as in the case of Roderigo) ingenuous folly. His motivation is implicit in his self-proclaimed nature, in the proclaimed nature of his victims, and in the traditional dynamic of his role. His action, he announces, is to be an illustration of his natural talent through a display of virtuosity in aggression against the high spiritual values of love and friendship, and the susceptible naïveté of virtuous, but frail, humanity.

Nor is the foregoing the whole of the difference between the two Iagos. Only the first, the literal Iago of the conventional motives, is actually inside the play, in the sense that he has a biography as an individual person within the particulars of the story of *Othello,* in the sense that he is involved in the formal tensions of the literal plot and in immediate personal relationship with the other dramatis personae. It is only this conventional figure who is sufficiently individualized by a local habitation and a name—as Iago of Venice, ancient to Othello, husband of Emilia—to be aware of other individuals in the play: of an Othello who has denied him an office and has, as he believes, cornuted him; of a Cassio whose place he covets, and who has also, he fears, cornuted him, or is about to do so; of a Desdemona he can properly accuse of adultery because it is likely she loves Cassio anyway. It is only such a character—circumstantially related to the other characters of the play, individualized as a person in time and space, and impelled by the conventional motives of human nature—that the Elizabethan playgoers of 1604 were prepared to accept in tragedy. That was why he was draped on top of a primordial figure of the stage who still titillated them powerfully, but in himself was no longer either fashionable or completely intelligible.

But this earlier figure, Iago's *Doppelgänger* as it were and still sufficiently, albeit obscurely, alive on the stage of 1604 to be for this play the more vital agent of tragedy, is not individualized within the plot of *Othello.* His relationship to his victims is as abstract as a moral

THE FAMILY OF IAGO

proposition, for it exists only in so far as they exemplify values he is bent on destroying—virtue, love, friendship. He has no emotion other than the pleasure of his work because he has no personal affinity to anyone or anything that could provoke him to any other emotion. He is aware of human beings who are his natural prey because they are exalted by values that are spiritual and romantic, but in no further particular of their individual lives is he aware of them. And if a woman called Emilia is the wife of the conventional Iago who is Othello's ancient and Cassio's fellow soldier, for this other figure, since she is not a relevant subject for his talent to operate upon, she does not exist at all. He is not aware of her or of the others as individuals because he is not indigenous to the play and not a member of the human world it displays. He existed before *Othello* was conceived, and is merely brought into it to do a job that is his traditional specialty, just as many times before and a few times after he does the same job in other plays of the period. And he is no more personally concerned with an Othello, a Desdemona, a Cassio than he was personally concerned in earlier plays with a Lavinia, a Lady Anne, or a Hero.

He is outside the play in another sense. He is the showman who produces it and the chorus that interprets it, and his essential relationship is with the audience. His monologues are intended to be unqualified public addresses, and when properly delivered that is what they are, without any pretense at self-communion overheard by an eavesdropping auditory.[1] Words of his, to some of which we have already listened, begin to suggest their proper import when restored to their right, their unnaturalistic, perspective. He announces to the audience his nature and quality, the question he asks them needing no answer:

> And what's he then that says I play the villain? . . .
> [II.iii.342]

and the ductile nature of the material on which he works—

> The Moor is of a free and open nature
> That thinks men honest that but seem to be so;
> And will as tenderly be led by th' nose
> As asses are.
> [I.iii.405-408]

THE FAMILY OF IAGO

He proclaims the artistic effect he strives for:

> So will I turn her virtue into pitch,
> And out of her own goodness make the net
> That shall enmesh them all.
>
> [II.iii.366–68]

carefully elaborates on each step of the process—

> For whiles this honest fool
> Plies Desdemona to repair his fortunes,
> And she for him pleads strongly to the Moor,
> I'll pour this pestilence into his ear—
> That she repeals him for her body's lust.
>
> [II.iii.359–63]

and reveals the secrets of his technique—

> When devils will the blackest sins put on,
> They do suggest at first with heavenly shows,
> As I do now.
>
> [II.iii.357–59]

He points, in passing, to a felicitous stroke here and there:

> The Moor already changes with my poison.
> Dangerous conceits are in their natures poisons
> Which at the first are scarce found to distaste,
> But with a little act upon the blood
> Burn like the mines of sulphur. I did say so.
> Look where he comes!
>
> [III.iii.325–30]

And finally unveils with a flourish the completed work of art—

> Thus credulous fools are caught,
> And many worthy and chaste dames even thus,
> All guiltless, meet reproach.
>
> [IV.i.46–48]

It is a triumphant exhibition of virtuosity, and if actually the conventional matrix of the play prevents the artist from taking up a collection or delivering a formal public lecture at the end, some of his ancestors did even that, as we shall see. It is also, let us note, a moral sermon, with the preacher, satirical though he be rather than solemn, homiletically on the side of God and the angels.

This is the earlier of the two Iagos. The process of conventionalizing

THE FAMILY OF IAGO

him, when the theater could no longer take him straight, produced for a time a hybrid. The origin of this hybrid and his history on the stage until he is bred out of the drama altogether is the task of this study and will occupy the chapters to follow. It is a history that will unfold itself through a survey of the transition from one dramatic convention to another that took place from the middle of the sixteenth century onward. The problem with which we are dealing arises because a stock dramatic figure persisted on the stage during a period of rapid change away from the theatrical convention that gave him birth and supplied his existence with meaning. He himself is gradually transformed, but because of his powerful hold on the popular stage in his original form and nature, it is a compelled and reluctant transformation, lagging behind the rapidly evolving naturalism of the English drama after 1550. He links the old dramatic auspices to the new and owes allegiance to both. In 1603–4, while still in transition, he is domesticated in *Othello* and vitalized by Shakespeare's mature genius, so that he is suffused by the glow of his own transcendent utterance and by the contagious magic of the poetry round about him in the play. But he is nonetheless a transitional figure, hovering between profoundly different modes of drama, upon whom a conventional human nature has been superimposed; and the double image is opaque to every effort to view it as a coherent personality or to give it psychological formulation. In the older drama his name sufficiently explained his nature and his actions. Moving into the new drama, he continues to exhibit in his behavior the archaic compulsion of his name and nature, his whole action being an illustration of what he is. But also he is gradually draped in the decent clothing of motivations habitually human, to accommodate him to a stage no longer willing, or able, to receive him naked. Such was the process, and we need to observe it.

2

Such an undertaking will proceed more freely, however, if it is delayed until the existence of the hybrid strain in which Iago participates can be more fully established and its nature more fully described. Although it is still an incorrigible habit to attempt to define him by a coherent psychological formula that is doomed to be evasive or super-

THE FAMILY OF IAGO

subtle, modern Elizabethan scholarship, foraging through the entire drama before, after, and round about Shakespeare, has gradually become aware that the mystery of Othello's ancient is not unique. The unreality of his conventional motives considered by themselves, and the incongruity between all of them taken together and his life in the play, are found to be duplicated in other Shakespearian roles and, what is even more suggestive, in an astonishing number of roles belonging to the non-Shakespearian drama of the period. Poetic richness and theatrical skill measure the main differences between them and Iago, and since they are transient phenomena in a rapid dramatic evolution, the time of their creation qualifies them in important ways; but the problem for all of them is the same. They are all of one hybrid stock, and they are all involved in explanations that do not explain.

That they exist outside Shakespeare has been more or less recognized by a good deal of recent scholarship which detects the resemblance without quite analyzing it. The Barabas of the last three acts of *The Jew of Malta* exhibits an obvious kinship, and the problem of a dual Barabas is exactly the same as the problem of the two Iagos, except that in Marlowe's play the double role is sharply compartmented between the first two acts and the last three, whereas in *Othello* it is more closely woven together, though not so closely that we cannot detect the change in Iago between the first four scenes and the remainder of the play. The resemblance between Iago and Clois Hoffman, the revenger-protagonist in Henry Chettle's *Tragedy of Hoffman* (c. 1602), was remarked by Thorndike, who found a broad discrepancy between Hoffman's ostensible project of revenge and his actual behavior throughout the play.[2] Joseph Quincy Adams observed the "Iago-like" quality of the Duke of Epire in *The Dumb Knight* (1607-8), by Gervase Markham and Lewis Machin.[3] Professor Farnham found "a sort of morality Iago" in the figure of Politick Persuasion in the morality play of *Patient and Meek Grissill* (1561-65)—how much he understates the resemblance remains to be seen.[4] Patent similarities have been noted, but not always wisely interpreted, between Iago and Lorenzo of *The Spanish Tragedy* (1587-89), Eleazar of *Lust's Dominion* (1599?), Francisco of *The Duke of Milan* (c. 1616), in all of whom there exists the puzzling dislocation between a sharply defined intrigue and motives which are obscure, inapplicable, belated, or nonexistent. There is,

THE FAMILY OF IAGO

in short, sufficient indication that the problem of Iago, rather than being private to Shakespeare or peculiar to the world of *Othello,* is only a single vivid instance out of a tradition that produced many such baffling stage criminals. A score of major figures in as many plays between 1585 and 1616 reveal so plainly the common features of this dramatic lineage that it is astonishing it can be overlooked. It is a useful coincidence that Thorndike, dealing with one of these plays although for a different end, expresses the same view that these pages seek to apply to Shakespeare's relationship with the tradition in question:

Inferences in regard to Shakespeare's subjective moods and personal experiences may be less likely to furnish clues for the reasons of his choice and treatment of subjects than a study of contemporary plays and dramatic fashions.[5]

And if the problem of Iago is not private to Shakespeare, neither in Shakespeare is it confined to *Othello.* Who can fail to become aware of an unmistakable kinship in ambiguity between Iago on the one hand and such characters of earlier plays as Aaron the Moor of *Titus Andronicus,* Richard III in the play of the same name, and the bastard Don John of *Much Ado?* In all four there is the familiar discrepancy, which we feel more easily than we can formulate, between their behavior and their explanations, or at least that part of their explanations which finds penetrable ground in our comprehension. Their reasons have neither a logical correspondence with their actions, nor—what is more important—an emotional correspondence with their dramatic personalities. They express themselves as moved by resentment, ambition, hatred, professional and sexual jealousy, but they do not behave as if they were so moved. In the case of all of them we are aware of an inexplicable disjunction between the passional implications of their expressed incentives and their inextinguishable vivacity and hilarity. Their one real emotion is an effervescent zest in the possibilities of mischief and a jubilant savoring of success therein. There is simply no logical or psychological filament that will unite, for instance, the irrepressible gaiety of Aaron with his own words:

> What signifies my deadly-standing eye,
> My silence, and my cloudy melancholy,
> My fleece of woolly hair that now uncurls

THE FAMILY OF IAGO

Even as an adder when she doth unroll
To do some fatal execution?

. . . .

Vengeance is in my heart, death in my hand,
Blood and revenge are hammering in my head.
[II.iii.32–39]

or his words, for that matter, with each other:

O, how this villany
Doth fat me with the very thoughts of it!
Let fools do good, and fair men call for grace,
Aaron will have his soul black like his face.
[III.i.203–206]

The discrepancy is so complete both ways that it becomes idle to seek
an answer to what would be otherwise a very pertinent question: Just
what is it exactly that provokes him to "blood and revenge" in the first
place?

On the same ambiguity in Richard, every sensitive reader of the
play finds his own trouble expressed by Richard Moulton, who describes an effect which bewilders him because he does not understand
its cause:

It is to be observed that there is no suggestion of impelling motive or
other explanation for the villainy of Richard. He does not labour under
any sense of personal injury. . . . Nor can we point to ambition as a sufficient motive . . . in all his long soliloquies he is never found dwelling
upon the prize in view. There appears, then, no sufficient explanation for
the villainy of Richard: the general impression conveyed is that to Richard
villainy has become an end in itself needing no special motive. [my italics] [6]

And everyone must sympathize with the complaint of Quiller-Couch
upon the behavior of Don John in *Much Ado:*

Don John has no quarrel with Claudio or with Hero, nor any hope of
advancement through the success of his villainy. . . . Shakespeare, who
afterward created Iago, could easily, by taking a little more trouble, have
given Don John an intelligible motive, and thereby made him a more intelligible villain. [7]

The comparison with Iago is either brilliant or absurd, depending on
how it is understood, since we know already how intelligible Iago's
motives make *him.* As for Don John's motivelessness, a close reading
of the play will reveal that "Q" was wrong in the way he made his

THE FAMILY OF IAGO

point. Don John is equipped with an explanation for his intrigue against Claudio and Hero, but, like Iago's whole arsenal of motives, it is once more a conventional explanation which does not explain an aggression that takes place for reasons that are not conventional. In his case the dislocation is even clearer because he is drawn so slightly and fades out of the play so quickly that he does not blind us with that vitality we discover in the other three. But the real meaning of even his role escapes us because it is expressed in a way no longer patent and because it is obscured by the distracting language of a conventional provocation. Actually all four reveal clearly enough why they act the way they do and why their victims qualify as such, if only we can free ourselves from preoccupation with their psychological coherence. They belong to the same hybrid family and show themselves simultaneously on two levels of meaning. We do not understand them because we do not realize that we are looking at photographs in which double exposure has merged two sets of features and two sets of dimensions. Unable to make this distinction, the eye wavers endlessly over the bewildering fusion of passion with hilarity, of motives that do not apply with others that do if only we might understand them, of an intelligible outline with an unintelligible content.

3

How distinctly these four qualify as members of a special genre becomes even more evident when they are compared with Shakespeare's other criminals. Against them a Claudius, an Angelo, a Goneril, a Macbeth, a Iachimo, even Shylock and Cymbeline's Queen, are cogent portraits of humanity. They are verbally and emotionally consistent, and their behavior is morally perspicuous. Their motives exist incontestably and are pertinent, specific, continuous, and logically directed to fulfillment. They respond to temptations and provocations that are valid results of the interplay between their natures and the circumstances of their lives. Their desires or their enmities are plainly reflected by the language of passion and clearly oriented toward unmistakable purposes—lust, aggrandizement, kingship, revenge, or the destruction that envy or rivalry inspires. No matter how vicious their natures, how monstrous their actions, they are bad for ends which explain their

THE FAMILY OF IAGO

badness and define them morally. Whether they are inwardly at war with themselves, savoring in monologue the bitterness of their frailty and confessing in the end their guilt and remorse, or whether they are indurated criminals and die bad deaths, they all exist within the moral world of cause and consequence, and exist therefore entirely within the illimitable convention of human nature. Although they and their transgressions are as individual and various as the plots in which they have their lives, they bear to each other the patent resemblance of their common humanity. Conceived in poetry, they are rich in the imaginative overtones that inundate formula and classification; they reverberate in regions of meaning where paraphrase cannot follow them. But from first to last they remain morally consistent with themselves and with all mankind, for they live and die according to the clear interplay of character and circumstance. They are concrete images in dramatic poetry of those logical relationships that can be found abstractly expressed in any system of morals, whether it be the Code of Hammurabi, the theological *Summa* of St. Thomas, or the *Ethics* of Spinoza.

The majority of Shakespeare's criminals, in brief, are intelligible because they are individually conceived dramatic portraits in imitation of the universal convention of human life, without which history itself would be unintelligible. In spite of a thousand details which separate them from the modern world and stamp them as sixteenth-century Elizabethan, they and their actions exist wholly within the ambit of those timeless and ubiquitous forces that shape the behavior of men on any street, or in the plot of any play. Elizabethan rhetoric and dramatic technique, the physiological and essentially mechanistic psychology of Shakespeare's time, the ethical vision of an age that regarded ambition and innovation as great evils—these are only styles and modes of the high poetic expression of our substantive humanity which renders Shakespeare a rich heritage even for those who are not Elizabethan scholars. And it is because most of the criminal figures in his plays participate in this universal bond that they are lucid in spite of all the problematical details which absorb the energy of scholarship. They are intelligible because they are bound by the moral convention of human life and exist in moral relationship to their crimes.

It is just here—in their relationship to crime—that the great point of

THE FAMILY OF IAGO

difference appears between the majority of Shakespeare's malefactors and those four who are obviously related to each other and belong to a class apart—Aaron, Richard, Don John, and Iago. Perhaps the best way to make this difference clear is to state it negatively in respect to Shakespeare's intelligible criminals—that is, to show what they are not in contrast to what the other four are. The generalities that follow are, in the nature of the case, extremely broad, and they ask at least temporary indulgence from the reader who is aware of specific distinctions, qualifying details, and even exceptions which they deliberately avoid.

1. In the behavior of the intelligible criminals there is never any real ambiguity to obscure the moral distinction between cause and effect, between ends and means. Just as the ends are always practical, in the large sense of the word, and always clear, even when they are pursued by an Angelo or a Macbeth with a soul divided between desire and conscience, so are the means clearly distinguished as means and their existence explained by purposes beyond themselves to which they are auxiliary. Beyond the crime itself there is always the comprehensive motive which, so to speak, compels it. In all of them there is an element of resistance to the evils they commit or attempt, in the sense that their appetite is not toward the criminal act as such, but toward its consequence. It is not incorrect to say that they all *succumb* to evil because they cannot resist the temptation of the ends toward which evil is the only effective means. This formula applies as well to those who are hard of heart as to those who are merely frail—to Goneril as well as to Claudius. For it is precisely this distinction between ends and means, defining a moral relationship between the criminal and his crime, which preserves even the doghearted daughters of Lear as intelligible portraits of humanity.

2. It is a further condition of their moral verisimilitude that Shakespeare's intelligible criminals are never isolated from the tension and strain which announce the impact of resistance upon human desires in a moral world. The technical differences between comedy and tragedy are unimportant in this respect. Both forms are seriously concerned with human values, and both are separated fundamentally thereby from the painless world of farce. To extend the point to its largest dimension in Shakespeare, every role he created, provided it is not anesthetized by the amoral artistry of farce, expresses, with more or less inten-

THE FAMILY OF IAGO

sity, the elementary suffering inherent in human limitation. This *humanity*—if the word can escape its sentimental and psychological associations—is, in varying degree, the condition of all literature, and probably of all the arts. Shakespeare's eminence is so great because, the whole body of his plays considered, his humanity in this sense—the sense of the Virgilian *mortalia*—is enormous. In this common theme of pain and pleasure attendant on human limitation he occupies more ground more deeply and—by virtue of the expressive felicity that belongs to poetry and drama beyond all other arts—more intensively than any other artist. Within the unrivaled immediacy of dramatic utterance his experimental width and poetic depth are so huge he seems to encompass the whole of the great theme—

> All pains the immortal spirit must endure
> All weakness that impairs, all griefs that bow . . .

In this theme his fools participate alongside his tragic heroes, and Feste's song at the end of *Twelfth Night* is as much a part of it, although in a lower key, as are Hamlet's soliloquies. Berowne as well as Macbeth endures the passion of experience, Rosalind as well as Ophelia.

His intelligible malefactors are no exceptions to this sense of human limitation. In both comedy and tragedy they endure the tension of desire, stretched to augmented pain by defeat or relaxed to transient pleasure by temporary victory. They all reflect the suffering that appetite experiences in an environment that resists it. Revenge, ambition, lust are in all of them a fever, albeit a cold fever in those who, like Goneril and Regan, are hard of heart. They have, as it were, a career of illness inside the dramatic action that contains their lives, and all their words and deeds are consistent symptoms of its course toward crisis. They begin with intelligible motives they really feel and end in frustrations to which they are really sensitive. Most instructive is the fact that they endure ends in a sense that is deeper than death or punishment simply. They suffer a defeat, the pain of which lives in their souls, although it is not always a matter of conscience. It is a pain as evident in Shylock's departing words—

> I pray you give me leave to go from hence.
> I am not well.
>> [*Merchant of Venice* IV.ii.395–96]

THE FAMILY OF IAGO

as in the desperation that compels Goneril's suicide and Macbeth's search for death. It is as clear in the remorse and repentance of Angelo or Iachimo as in the Christian agony of dying, prognostic of the throes to come, that expresses the iniquity of Cardinal Beaufort, Lady Macbeth, and Cymbeline's Queen: "So bad a death argues a monstrous life." [8]

In one way or another the life of each of them has passion and pain in its retinue, and in each of them there is a continuous and consistent movement of soul through five acts. Apply the same standard to Richard III and the difference becomes evident in a moment. Richard also dies miserably, a retribution dictated by popular history and conventional morality. But what filament of character or experience can unite the doomed tyrant tormented by bad conscience on the night before Bosworth with the merry, and motiveless, genius of seduction and dissension earlier in the play? There are no premises in Richard's dramatic life that can explain his transformation, for it is not simply the intelligible change from the triumphant alacrity of initial success to the irresolution and despair brought on by a sense of sin and of ultimate defeat, although this too is in the play. Under the single name of Richard there exist two roles in different dimensions, with no continuous life between.

3. It is testimony to their complete moral involvement in the human relationships of their respective plots that in their soliloquies the intelligible criminals are never, so to speak, outside the play. Lacking the astonishing showmanship of Iago and his kindred, they do not appear to address their monologues directly to the audience. Nor do their monologues give the impression that the speakers exist on the stage primarily to impress the audience with a demonstration of their criminal skill and versatility. In varying degree all Elizabethan stage soliloquies offend the dubious modern canon of verisimilitude. And from our modern viewpoint it is equally a violation of verisimilitude that nearly every criminal in Shakespeare is compelled by his didactic heritage in the Elizabethan drama to self-conscious awareness of his iniquity, with the soliloquy his opportunity to express it. But between Shakespeare's intelligible criminals and those who, because of their dramatic kinship, can properly be called *The Family of Iago,* it is an awareness with a conspicuous difference, and the technical effect of

THE FAMILY OF IAGO

this difference upon their soliloquies is important. The former really soliloquize: their monologues are kept within the bounds of private rumination by the fact that they themselves are bound within the cordon of moral relationships between person and person, or person and circumstance, which defines the naturalistic verisimilitude of the play. Conferring with themselves, they communicate by indirection the purposes at which their actions aim, their awareness that they are criminals, their emotional and mental sympathy with their wickedness, or the division in their souls between temptation and conscience. Even the most confirmed and hardened of them—the adjectives themselves are a moral definition—display the strain, the tension, the seriousness of their moral involvement. Their open-eyed assessment of their own iniquity and their almost bravura dedication to it at times are didactic and rhetorical commonplaces of the Elibabethan drama which stylize the soliloquy without impairing its integrity as private rumination. In spite of both these qualities in the highly colored language with which Lady Macbeth expresses her reaction to the news of Duncan's approach to Inverness, her words are still a soliloquy:

> Come, you spirits
> That tend on mortal thoughts, unsex me here,
> And fill me, from the crown to the toe, top-full
> Of direst cruelty! Make thick my blood;
> Stop up th'access and passage to remorse,
> That no compunctious visitings of nature
> Shake my fell purpose nor keep peace between
> Th' effect and it!
>
> [*Macbeth* I.v.41–48]

It is not too much to say that the monologues of Shakespeare's conventional and intelligible transgressors are forced out of them by moral pressure. Although their words are not always rhetorically passionate, there is always in them the unmistakable tone of moral tension. The audience are only the technical reason for their existence; the speaker's inner necessity supplies them their moral integrity, so that, in fact,

> They are close dilations, working from the heart
> That passion cannot rule.

4. Shakespeare's intelligible criminals never proclaim that they are types rather than individuals, as Iago and his kindred invariably do,

THE FAMILY OF IAGO

or that their purpose on the stage is to illustrate a generic name and nature. Nor do they compromise their individuality and freedom of action by labeling themselves with a beforehand definition of what they are dramaturgically—a definition that would make their dramatic careers implicit, and independent of the circumstances of the plot. And by comparison with Iago and his kindred they assert their individuality still another way. They are never given over to that monolithic and duplicate display of a single form of intrigue, to mere multiple exhibition of a single talent, which shapes Aaron, Richard, Don John, and Iago, beneath their surface differences, into variant expressions merely of the same dramaturgic formula. For the important discrimination here is that these four display their distinctive homogeneity in a word—in a self-imposed title, a verbal fixture which rigidly defines their behavior before it ever begins. It is a title that meant to the Eizabethan audience that they were about to witness another display of competitive brilliance in a very special sort of aggression, whose form and method had been made thoroughly familiar to them by its repetition on the stage through several generations—an aggression, moreover, that ran its traditional and independent course and paid no more than lip service to the particulars of the plot in which it happened to appear.

4

The majority of Shakespeare's criminals, to repeat, are intelligible because they are dramatic portraits in conformity with the universal convention of human life under the impress of the culture of Renaissance England. Their actions and their feelings are consistent with their motives, and their motives are perspicuous either absolutely or in the terms of that culture. Desire satisfied and desire unsatisfied express their share in the elementary tragedy of human limitation. About them there is the individuality of free response to the circumstances in which they find themselves. Their criminality, in spite of problems of detail, is fundamentally lucid because it is conventionally human, because their relationship to crime is invariably moral.

Aaron, Richard, Don John, and Iago are not lucid because, beneath the drapery of conventional humanity which never fits them, they have

THE FAMILY OF IAGO

nothing to do with the moral imperatives of human life. Their essential relationship to their crimes and to their victims is not moral but *artistic,* or at least we may call it so before we reach a more accurate appraisal of that relationship.[9] They are, then, first of all great artists, and if, incidentally, they are also great criminals, that is because the traditional expression of their talent moved from its origin in one dramatic convention, where they were full of meaning in their artistic amorality, into another, where they were no longer viable without a surface accommodation, at least, to moral values. The source of our trouble with them is that by Shakespeare's time they had lost their original import without losing their dramatic popularity, so that they had to undergo a gradual reprocessing to meet the demand of his age for what in our own is called "realism."

It is a datum of considerable importance in aesthetics that art differs from other forms of human activity in the fact that its end is patent in itself. A statue or a symphony is its own excuse for being, in need of nothing beyond itself to express the reason for its existence. To put the same thing another way, art, as art, has no ulterior purpose in the practical, or moral, world. The same is true of the artist. Although a painter may—and, as the world goes, invariably does—create his picture for the sake of his living, that is, strictly speaking, the inartistic side of his life. As artist, he paints only for the sake of the picture.

It is unnecessary to extend this point beyond its relevance to Iago and his fellow artist-criminals in Shakespeare's plays. All of them unmistakably announce themselves as possessors of a talent which they are about to display, and they make it perfectly clear in the course of their intrigues that what they are doing is being done for art's sake. And if they also express ulterior purposes, that is because they could not remain stationary as mere artists but had to submit to the evolutionary sway of the drama toward the realistic imitation of the practical conventions of human morality. It is exactly their superficial involvement in this conventional morality that makes them hybrid, and creates the problem that defies the ingenuity of conventional criticism.

In the first years of the seventeenth century their moral verisimilitude is still only a veneer, for in the very traditional art of the drama such a process is bound to be gradual and partial. The archaic part of them

THE FAMILY OF IAGO

is still dominant in their behavior, cropping out in their words and controlling the emotional tone of their roles. That is why, whatever practical motives they express, they display in respect to them a nearly complete emotional indifference; for their whole action remains essentially an artistic demonstration that is not concerned with practical ends. Nor is there anything personal about their choice of victims. Not only are their motives extrinsic and verbal—grudging concessions to the convention of moral realism at work upon them—but their victims qualify as such by species, and it is only another concession to the same convention that these victims are detailed as particular persons who provoke revenge or stand in the way of ambition. If from the monologues of Iago and his kindred we subtract those formal expressions of cause which are mere draperies on the essential figure, we discover that their aggressions are directed against virtue and honor and that mixture of religious and secular values that defined the eminence of human life in Shakespeare's time. Ultimately their assault is upon unity and order and the piety of love in all its forms. But we need to avoid the easy fallacy of assuming that they *hate* these high moral values of the Elizabethan culture. Hate, we shall see, is a constant verbal fixture of the moral apparatus that was screwed upon them, but like all the rest of that apparatus it is only a superficies. These values are the natural materials on which they do their work; they do not hate or envy them any more than the sculptor hates or envies the clay which is the material condition of his art.

Furthermore, the evil in the plays in which they appear is never really committed; it is only suffered. For the agents of evil are not moral; only their victims are. *Evil* is a word that describes the human and moral view of what they do. But since at bottom they are neither human nor moral, evil is for them solely an organic function and an artistic pleasure. They are aware of iniquity in the same way that a self-dedicated crusader is aware of the banner under which he gladly serves—as a standard to be advanced and planted on the highest ramparts of virtue. Their devotion is single and complete, their enormous energy and its direction constitutional. A total euphoria leaves in them no room for the slightest shred of conscience. Their monologues, as it has already appeared in the case of Iago, are not simply overheard ruminations, but are, in fact, buoyant announcements of intention and triumphant declarations of achievement addressed directly to the audience. And if they maintain their original character to the end, as Richard III does not, the last scene finds them defiant, triumphant, and utterly careless of the "cunning cruelty" of the punishment in store. They are rigid, undeviating, monolithic, pursuing endlessly their single action and indulging endlessly their single emotion until they are stopped by superior physical force and thrown off the rails with their wheels still spinning in the air.

Finally, not only are they artists essentially; all of them are essentially one and the same artist, and their works all one work. For what are the actions of Aaron, Richard, Don John, and Iago except the fourfold repetition of a single stratagem whose meaning is immeasurably wider and deeper than the local details of four separate plots? It is not simply coincidence that Aaron, by contriving the rape of Lavinia, destroys virginity and defeats the consummation of chaste love in marriage; that Richard seduces Lady Anne out of the bonds of matrimonial piety that tied her to the memory of her dead husband; that the slander manipulated by Don John is an aggression against the values of chastity and matrimony; that Iago destroys the bond of love and marriage which, in the persons of Desdemona and Othello, unites transcendent virtues—love and purity with valor and magnanimity. Neither is it chance that all four gleefully demonstrate their skill in divorcing lover from lover, husband from wife, child from father, brother from brother, ruler from subject, friend from friend. Nor is it chance that they concentrate their wit and energy upon the art of making fools and victims out of human beings who express those values and relationships which defined for the Elizabethans the highest possibilities in human life—virtue, heroism, loyalty, love. Beneath the superficial differences of four separate plots there appears the strong outline of a single role four times repeated. We are witnessing four performances by the same craftsman. He may call himself Aaron, Richard, Don John, or Iago, and he may be more brilliant at one time than another; but his métier is undeviating, his style and theme unmistakable, his signature clear on all his works. He is an artist in dissimulation, seduction, and intrigue; and his purpose on the stage is to display his

THE FAMILY OF IAGO

talent triumphantly at work against the affections, duties, and pieties which create the order and harmony of humane society. His specialty is the destruction of unity and love. His genius receives its affirmation from the existence of hate and disorder. Shakespeare, who put him through four performances and no doubt saw him on exhibition in the plays of others, has not neglected, in several lines that belong, it is true, to a different context, to describe him and his enterprise:

> Such smiling rogues as these,
> Like rats, oft bite the holy cords atwain
> Which are too intrinse t'unloose.
> [*King Lear* II.ii.79–81]

Perhaps it is now clear to us, at least as a working hypothesis while awaiting the detailed evidence to come, that this figure who appears at least four times in Shakespeare is confusing because he is the hybrid product of two conventions that met and merged in him. It should also be clear that we apprehend him in the most superficial and evasive way if we view him only in the literal terms of his conventionally human motives. His partially concealed but organic role is that of an artist whose actions are implicit in his nature, a laughing aggressor and intriguer so traditional and popular that he had to be disguised, because he could not be abandoned, as the stage shifted, in the space of one generation, from one dramatic method to another. In his archaic role over almost two centuries he performed his stock function, which was to confound his human victims by playing upon their gullible honesty and human frailty, and particularly to confound them in respect to those values that governed any play in which he appeared. Over the long span of his career on the stage these values changed, but he was flexible enough to adjust his aggression accordingly. In the early period of his vogue they were ascetic and transcendent. Later they became political and social and reflected the ideological conflict of the Reformation. By Shakespeare's time they had become fairly secular, although not without deep religious implications in the immediate background. But especially they had become concentrated, at least in the popular drama, in the high value of romantic love; hence the four times repeated aggression against love and marriage by the four figures who concern us in Shakespeare.

THE FAMILY OF IAGO

5

We turn now from the family resemblances of these four destructive artists and confine our attention to Iago for the remainder of this chapter. In addition to his dual role and twofold meaning, result of the merger in him of widely different conventions, he exists on a third level of significance which is so vivid in Shakespeare's great tragedies that it must be treated as personal to his unique poetic power and the reach of his ethical imagination even though it is everywhere part of the spiritual atmosphere of the Age of Elizabeth.

Although Iago is essentially an amoral figure, we fail to grasp the deepest moral *consequence* of his action upon his victims unless we can appreciate the full meaning of his assault upon the "holy cords" that express Shakespeare's vision of the Good that suffers destruction in all his great tragedies. They are the bonds that knit nature, human society, and the cosmos into hierarchic order and unity and create the divinely ordained harmony of the universe. In the little world of men they are those ties of duty, piety, and humane affection which give a religious meaning to all domestic and social relationships, for in Shakespeare "religion" frequently has this wider sense.[10] Our typical modern view, by comparison, is fragmentary and limited. Having lost the vision of a spiritual destiny, we read into love and morality no higher purpose than private happiness inside the pitiful span of mortal life, create an exclusive secular absolute to define the meaning of society and the state, and display the desperate tendency to equate salvation with romantic love. Shakespeare's vision, by contrast, has a profound metaphysical reach. Everywhere in his plays, but particularly in his great tragedies, human behavior on every level of life and in every kind of relationship receives its moral definition from its adherence or lack of adherence to the spiritual harmony and order of the universe. It is all religion. Filial piety, matrimonial love, fraternal loyalty, and the immutable social degrees under God's royal regent are spiritual alliances that express man's conformity with the divinely established order of the cosmos and create the health and happiness—the very possibility in fact—of human society:

> Piety and fear,
> Religion to the gods, peace, justice, truth,

THE FAMILY OF IAGO

> Domestic awe, night-rest and neighbourhood,
> Instruction, manners, mysteries and trades,
> Degrees, observances, customs and laws . . .
> [*Timon of Athens* IV.i.15–19]

It is probably correct to say that in Shakespeare's system of values there are no secular absolutes. They were brought into the modern world by the revolution taking place just in his time, and his plays are full of the anguish of anticipation. Recent Shakespearian scholarship has dwelt upon this point,[11] but its full significance still remains to be exploited, especially its implication for the poet's choice of themes in his so-called tragic period. The metaphysical range of his moral vision is the main literal and imaginative cargo of the great tragedies, controlling their origin and direction to a degree that still escapes us. The evil in each of them is much broader than simply the violation of private love and natural fealty between person and person. In each a great bond of piety, electric with cosmic meaning, is ruptured; the religious foundations of society are shaken and the universe is racked with disorder. A brother's murder, the unfaithfulness of a wife to the memory of her dead husband, filial ingratitude, the assassination of a king by his subject, the presumed adultery of a wife with her husband's friend—these are acts with infinite repercussion in the poet's ethical imagination. They violate the nature of man, the nature of society, the nature of the universe. It is in this deep sense that they all receive their great condemnation as *unnatural* acts. They are, in fact, all one crime. Their distinguishing details as separate malefactions dissolve and merge into a single large affront to the unity and harmony of the world. The bias of Shakespeare's choice for his great tragic themes and the depth of treatment he brings to them are a double consequence of his vision that evil in its greatest magnitude expresses division and disorder. This single burden of all the great tragedies, a meaning deeper than the actual deed of fraud or bloody violence, unites all their separate and literal crimes into a vision of metaphysical evil, single and undifferentiated. Superstitiously interpreting the "late eclipses in the sun and moon," the Earl of Gloucester details this evil of division into its individual parts and effects:

Though the wisdom of nature can reason it thus and thus, yet nature finds itself scourg'd by the sequent effects. Love cools, friendship falls off, broth-

THE FAMILY OF IAGO

ers divide. In cities, mutinies; in countries, discord; in palaces, treason; and the bond crack'd 'twixt son and father. This villain of mine comes under the prediction; there's son against father: the King falls from bias of nature; there's father against child. We have seen the best of our time. Machinations, hollowness, treachery, and all ruinous disorders follow us disquietly to our graves.

[King Lear I.ii.113–25]

The Duke of Albany expresses its social meaning:

> If that the heavens do not their visible spirits
> Send quickly down to tame these vile offences,
> It will come,
> Humanity must perforce prey on itself
> Like monsters of the deep.

[King Lear IV.ii.46–50]

And the cosmic implication in these fractures of the human bond stretches into tremendous significance the death of love and fidelity, so that Queen Gertrude's remarriage is more, much more, than the faithlessness of a wife and the private agony of her son:

> O, such a deed
> As from the body of contraction plucks
> The very soul, and sweet religion makes
> A rhapsody of words! Heaven's face doth glow;
> Yea, this solidity and compound mass,
> With tristful visage, as against the doom,
> Is thought-sick at the act.

[Hamlet III.iv.45–51]

This tragic dilation into religious and metaphysical significance of crimes which in our secular modern view have only a personal or social meaning is undoubtedly part of the explanation of Shakespeare's magnitude. His language, subdued to his dramatic purpose, is rarely theological, as Dante's is, and his religious emphasis is upon human society rather than upon eternity. But in the great tragedies Evil receives a treatment that is uniformly metaphysical: it severs the "holy cords" of love and loyalty, cancels and tears to pieces the great bond that holds the universe in order. And in each of them, with one exception, it achieves its cosmic meaning through the language of a moral astronomy and is dyed into high relief by the iterated imagery and visionary atmosphere of the play.

THE FAMILY OF IAGO

51

The apparent exception, in spite of the giant evil in it, is *Othello*. From it seems to be absent that quality of transcendental vision that creates in *Hamlet,* in *Lear,* in *Macbeth,* in *Antony and Cleopatra* even, a level of meaning above the merely dramatic level of action, conflict, and passion. Also absent from it is that characteristic thematic imagery which in the other great tragedies elucidates the evil into symbol and metaphor and weaves out of them the imaginative texture of the play. The pervasive motif of disease and death in *Hamlet;* the elemental, weather-beaten, bestial world of *Lear;* the blood and darkness, the fear and sleeplessness of *Macbeth*—these great unitary atmospheres do not appear to have a counterpart in *Othello*. Bradley speaks of "the comparative confinement of the imaginative atmosphere," and continues:

Othello has not equally with the other three [*Hamlet, Lear, Macbeth*] the power of dilating the imagination by vague suggestions of huge universal powers working in the world of individual fate and passion. It is, in a sense, less 'symbolic.' We seem to be aware in it of a certain limitation, a partial suppression of that element in Shakespeare's mind which unites him with the mystical poets and with the great musicians and philosophers.[12]

And Wilson Knight, discriminating *Othello* from the other great tragedies in the same respect, calls it "a story of an intrigue rather than a visionary statement." [13]

This is not to say that *Othello* is without its cosmic reference, or devoid of thematic iterations both imagistic and verbal. But these are somehow irrelevant to the enormous evil in the play or lack the clairvoyant power to interpret it into a statement or an atmosphere that could be perspicuous to the imagination of the reader. The cosmic range is there in Othello's words to Desdemona, words reminiscent of Hamlet's to his mother, but they apply in this case to a purely fictitious evil, not to the wicked reality:

> Heaven stops the nose at it, and the moon winks;
> The bawdy wind, that kisses all it meets,
> Is hush'd within the hollow mine of earth
> And will not hear it.
>
> [IV.ii.77–80]

There is also an abundance of verbal and metaphorical iteration, but it is no less inapplicable. Equally incident in the speech of Othello and

THE FAMILY OF IAGO

Iago there is the language of the sea, distilling apparently the maritime setting of the play and the salt-water careers of two soldiers in the employ of sea-fostered Venice. And there is, of course, in the word "honest," which adheres to Iago like a constant epithet, the thematic irony that highlights his success in dissimulation and the fatal misapprehension of him entertained by his noble-natured gulls. Furthermore, by himself on several occasions and by others in the last scene, he is equated with the devil; and he wears his satanism with pleasure—first in the vanity of self-comparison:

> When devils will the blackest sins put on,
> They do suggest at first with heavenly shows,
> As I do now.
> [II.iii.357–59]

and later in the polite derision with which he interprets the wound Othello inflicts upon him in wonder-stricken experiment:

> *Oth.* I look down towards his feet—but that's a fable.
> If that thou be'st a devil, I cannot kill thee.
> [*Wounds Iago*]
> *Iago.* I bleed, sir, but not kill'd.
> [V.ii.286–88]

The importance of such words is not particularly in the diabolism itself, which is an incidental metaphor leading nowhere. For Othello in his passion Desdemona is also a "fair devil," and he applies the epithet to her three times more in the scene in which he strikes her. In the last scene Emilia applies it twice to him. Far back in Iago's ancestry there were devils and the cronies of devils, but his descent is collateral rather than direct, and his association with the diabolic, frequent as it is, is too much a moral cliché to be enlightening. Intrigue, dissimulation, and the seduction of virtue define the enterprise of the Common Enemy throughout the Christian mythos; and the diabolism in the language of this play is a figure for the similar behavior of Iago. But it does not explain him. The Devil is what Iago, considered in human terms, is *like*. What he *is,* is another matter.

But if the diabolism is not in itself enlightening, his joyous self-assertion in respect to it is. The distinction is important, for in Iago's case it makes all the difference between morality and art. The point needs to be examined in the company of another verbal repetition that

THE FAMILY OF IAGO

rings through every scene of the play, reaching in the last one a pitch of clamorous iteration that amounts almost to frenzy. Nothing about Iago's career is more murky than its end. In the last scene he is uncovered and at bay. It is a moment in which the human instinct for self-justification would provoke a declaration of cause out of anyone who had even one of the motives that flourish in Iago's early monologues. The situation fairly pleads for his avowal of his provocations. What has happened to the professional resentment, the jealousy, the hatred? If they all conceal a deeper mystery, here at least in the denouement is the time for revelation; and the express demand for it burns on the lips of the great victim:

> Will you, I pray, demand that demi-devil
> Why he hath thus ensnar'd my soul and body?

But Iago is an alien to the moral conventions of the world of the play, and his real answer would be no more intelligible to Othello than to us. In his reply, therefore, there is no answer:

> Demand me nothing. What you know, you know.
> From this time forth I never will speak word.

These are his last words. Round about him rings a clamor of imprecation. He is called an inhuman dog, a Spartan dog, a viper, a pernicious caitiff, a damned slave, a cursed slave, and a variety of epithets beside—a frantic rhapsody that constricts the imagination, leaving us, in respect to the meaning of the evil, depressed because unenlightened. We look for an explanation that has moral significance either literally or through some liberating symbolism, but find none. And in the words of all the other characters there is none either. Like the reader or playgoer, they belong to the moral world, so they too are unenlightened. They call Iago names.

One name in particular, expressing the sternest kind of moral condemnation, reaches out for Iago in almost every scene of the play. From the exclusively moral viewpoint of the other characters it tells us what Iago appears to them to be in the terms of humanity. In the last scene, where there is almost no end to its iteration, it beats upon him almost beyond, not his endurance, but ours:

> O mistress, villany hath made mocks with love!
> I know thou didst not; thou'rt not such a villain.

THE FAMILY OF IAGO

Villany, villany, villany!
I think upon't, I think! I smell't! O villany!
Precious villain!
'Tis a notorious villain.
I'll after that same villain . . .
Bring the villain forth.
O villain!
This damned villain . . .
To you, Lord Governor,
Remains the censure of this hellish villain.
This wretch hath part confess'd his villany.
O villany, villany!

Now perhaps no word in the lexicon of moral condemnation—especially in the theater, where it is a stock epithet—is more common or hackneyed than this one which designates Iago in the frantic rhapsody that ends the tragedy. Sooner or later every malefactor in every play, particularly an Elizabethan play, is a villain, and we are scarcely edified by so universal a stereotype. What is a villain? If that is the extent of what Iago is, how are we helped toward understanding him? No wonder the critics have felt—Bradley and Wilson Knight have already been quoted—that in *Othello* the liberating symbolism of the other great tragedies does not appear, that in this play of intrigue the imagination of Shakespeare is confined within an uninterpretable evil.

6

But we need to review these verbal associations and epithets from a different perspective. Although they come off with a moral meaning from the lips of the other characters, they have a further existence in a dimension that is not moral. The endless references by Iago's victims to his honesty is an elaborate piece of tragic irony that is not by itself especially enlightening as to the real meaning of his role. But his own sardonic awareness of the position is most enlightening. He is the very spirit of dishonesty; he is Dishonesty personified, and how joyously and derisively he proclaims it:

Whip me such honest knaves! . . .

[I.i.49]

THE FAMILY OF IAGO

The Moor is of a free and open nature
That thinks men honest that but seem to be so . . .

[I.iii.405–406]

I protest, in the sincerity of love and honest kindness.

[II.iii.333–34]

O, you are well tun'd now!
But I'll set down the pegs that make this music,
As honest as I am.

[II.i.201–202]

And although the diabolism, as it is expressed by the others, is a moral metaphor not especially useful, his own happy assumption of the satanic is his absolute definition of his behavior, rendering all moral causation superfluous. And beyond anything else in the play, what is enlightening about his villainy is that he himself proclaims it as his proper name and nature and proceeds thereupon to act accordingly. Villainy is the badge Iago thumbs to announce his dramatic profession. It is an identification card which he himself several times flashes gleefully at the audience, and an Elizabethan audience knew him unmistakably thereby beneath his "motives," for they had seen him many times before in many plays. His role had a stage history that made his villainy self-explanatory in an absolute sense, for villainy such as his defined a stock dramatic figure, and defined, moreover, his purpose on the stage regardless of the plot of the play in which he happened to appear. His essential role, behind the moral façade, exists in a professional and artistic dimension that is perpendicular to the morally conventional plot of the plays in which he survived after the dramatic method that created him disappeared from the English stage.

"Thou art a villain," cries out Brabantio upon the dim figure in the darkness below who, with enormous relish, hurls up at the father the gross images that make intolerably vivid to him the elopement of his daughter. And the villain replies in kind, and just as accurately, "You are a senator." [14] Both designations are professionally exact, and the former is the thread that leads us to the fundamental Iago. For he is not essentially a man who is provoked to act villainously, but *Villainy* disguised by late convention to act like a man. The play concerns the oppression of Virtue by Villainy, and if the clamorous iteration of the latter word beats on our brains without enlightening us, that is because

THE FAMILY OF IAGO

we are habituated to look for moral significance in it. But as it is used by Iago to label himself it defines an action that is artistic rather than moral, and it draws its meaning out of an earlier dramatic convention whose characteristic protagonist was at once an abstraction and a professional artist, a laughing *farceur* who had no further purpose than to confound his human victims by a series of intrigues that illustrated the meaning of his abstract name. The First Folio has made a strenuous effort to help us out. There, in the dramatis personae attached to *Othello,* we find professional explanations for most of the roles. Cassio is "an Honourable Lieutenant," Montano "Gouernour of Cyprus," Brabantio "Father to Desdemona," Lodovico and Gratiano "two Noble Venetians," Bianca "a Curtezan." And Iago—what of him?

Iago, a Villaine.

The full stop at the end of the designation proffers a world of meaning. Iago is a villain, and that's all there is to it. He is a villain in a sense so special it has nothing to do with moral condemnation and is not receptive to the moral symbolism through which evil is interpreted in the other great tragedies. Villainy, to paraphrase a kindred artist in another play, is Iago's vocation, and it is no sin for a man to labor in his vocation. He is the villain as artist, who, deeply considered, has nothing to do with evil. Into the word "Villain," as it defines his role, is compressed a formula, not moral but profoundly dramaturgic, which determined the nature of the English stage between 1400 and 1570–80, and maintained itself in disguise for several decades thereafter until it was eventually digested by the radically different convention of the *literal* drama that took its place. The formula is that of allegory, and especially that central type of Christian allegory known as the Psychomachia, in which personified forces of good and evil contend for possession of the human soul. Out of medieval allegory came the morality play, which for two centuries provided a type of drama whose purpose and method were homiletic, whose structure was schematic and rigid, whose characters for the most part were personified abstractions with names that expressed the motive and predetermined the nature of their actions.

The morality play not only created allegorical drama out of Christian homiletics but produced also a homilist of amazing popularity. In the

THE FAMILY OF IAGO

early part of Elizabeth's reign he was the *sine qua non* of the stage—so popular and indispensable in fact that his name is the prominent feature of the titles of several plays that have survived in print. In his role as sardonic intriguer in every play in which he appeared he inflicted upon his gullible victims a variety of deceits and seductions—tragedy for them but laughter for him—which illustrated the meaning his abstract name of the moment expressed—Envy, Avarice, Sensual Suggestion, Ill Report, Ambidexter, Iniquity, and numerous designations besides of qualities abstract and pejorative. But all his separate performances, under whatever name, in play after play are merely variations on a single theme—his dexterity in effecting, through artful dissimulation and intrigue, the spiritual and physical ruin of frail humanity; and all his particular names are enveloped within his generic title of *The Vice*. The details of his evolution after 1550 supply the answers to most of the questions that surround Iago. For as the morality play surrendered to the literal drama, its medley of tragic farce giving way to the separate types of comedy and tragedy, the Vice with equal facility moved into both, so entrenched on the popular stage that he outlived by many years the dramatic convention that had created him. His survival in Elizabethan comedy has been to some extent traced and acknowledged.[15] But his significant career in tragedy still goes begging for recognition.

And yet in tragedy he is not so far removed from his origins in homiletic allegory that he does not reveal his breeding through his new title, equally homiletic and almost as abstract, which he proclaims and exemplifies in action. Iniquity has had to be rechristened Iago, but the dominant Vice in him, tenaciously clinging to his old role as artistic intriguer and destroyer, merely acquires a new label—concession to changed surroundings—for his old nature, and an appreciative audience knows him now as the self-proclaimed Villain. And as a further, unavoidable, step in the process of adaptation he acquires something which as an undisguised abstraction in the earlier drama he didn't need—passionate motivation. The energy for his aggressions supplied him previously by allegory is crossbred with the conventional motives of human morality. But since the vital part of him on the stage is still the old Vice, still the laughing, amoral, and self-explanatory artificer of ruin, the motivation is always superfluous, never really fits

THE FAMILY OF IAGO

him, invariably fails to fuse with his archaic nature and function. So criticism writhes.

"What's he then that says I play the villain?" Iago asks his audience, and the question, of course, is a sneer. He is playing the villain in a way so self-conscious and deliberate that, separated as we are today from allegory and conditioned as we are by a very different literary convention of passionate cause and moral consequence, we are unable to see beneath the surface of his performance to grasp its deeper meaning. And so too are Aaron, Don John, and Richard playing the villain; and they tell us so unmistakably, but we don't understand them either. For it escapes us that in all four we confront the lingering tradition of the morality play. We are blinded by a flimsy coverture of motivation that our own literary habits compel us to accept. We postulate a psychological unity in the name of which we squeeze together in Procrustean distortion the unassimilable elements of profoundly different conventions.

We have now to see how, by a series of accommodations, the central figure of the late morality plays was able to survive the decay of his own dramatic world and for a time to flourish in disguise within the alien auspices of the secular drama. The Christian allegory of the Psychomachia produced for two centuries a type of play that was half a tragedy, half a farce. At stake was the soul of man, and contending for it were the forces of good and evil. The nature of the subject created a dramatic form of which intrigue was the invariable dynamic —the intrigue of the agents of damnation against the human soul. By a characteristic medievalism, reflecting the moral baseness they personified as well as their essential impotence in being ultimately subject to the will of God, these destructive forces were always dramatized as grotesque or ludicrous figures, rich and vivid in their coarseness and obscenity, their blasphemous mockery, their horseplay and raucous quarrels among themselves. They provided a rough-and-tumble high jinks that delighted the popular audience and reconciled them to the dull dignity of the homiletic theme. But these risible imps of hell were also grimly efficient seducers, employing moral and physical deceit with deadly success against human frailty. The agony and eternal peril of the sin-invested soul wrought in the play its serious issue and fundamental pathos; the prescribed plot shaped it as a drama of intrigue; personification staffed it with characters whose actions grew out of

THE FAMILY OF IAGO

their names; and the buffoonery of its evil personae bred a harlequinade in the heart of tragedy.

By the end of the fifteenth century the purely eschatological theme was worn out, a victim of the secular revolution of the Renaissance. Nevertheless the morality play survived vigorously through the first two decades of Elizabeth's reign and beyond, for at least two reasons. Its organizing principle, the Psychomachia, was energetic enough to shift the ground of its serious issue from heaven and hell to reward and punishment in the life of this world, and supple enough to enfold for a time the secular interests of the new age—ethics, politics, and history at first, and then love and romance. In the second place, the motor of the Psychomachia, the Vice, continued to function with undiminished vitality in plays that in all other respects were no longer in the allegorical tradition—a fact that touches the heart of our problem. For while allegory, by the very process of its adjustment to secular themes, suffered a constant decay, until by 1590 it had practically disappeared from the professional stage, its most significant and vital personage did not. The abstractions all about him gave way to the concrete and individualized men and women of the literal drama. The play gradually freed itself from its homiletic purpose, whereby it was essentially the dramatized exemplum of a sermon, and acquired autonomous life and justification as dramatic spectacle. The stage ceased to be a pulpit or the audience a congregation, the action and the actors retreating into a discrete and independent world that no longer acknowledged the presence of the audience or sought their moral improvement through formal homily. The growth of literary sophistication, plus the influence of the classical and Italian drama, distilled the morality's medley of tragical mirth into the separate genres of comedy and tragedy. Plot and characterization became diversified and organic, deriving their shape and energy from the moral conventions manifested by human life in history true or fabulous. But the Vice stubbornly resisted the process and only succumbed in the end to a much slower transformation. Reluctantly draping his allegorical nakedness, he persisted in his allegorical function. Having refurbished himself with the name, the clothing, the motives of a "formal man," he conducted in Elizabethan tragedy a Psychomachia without benefit of allegory.

CHAPTER THREE

THE PSYCHOMACHIA

Two such opposed kings encamp them still
In man . . . grace and rude will.
ROMEO AND JULIET

I

Toward the end of the fourteenth century the profound allegorical and homiletic tradition of the Middle Ages began to receive dramatic expression in the form we know as the morality play. A single example of allegorical drama does indeed survive out of an earlier period—the twelfth-century Latin play *Antichristus,* in which appear such figures as Heresis and Ypocrisis, Iustitia and Misericordia, Ecclesia and Synagoga, and Gentilitas;[1] but there is no further evidence that allegory made anything more than sporadic appearance on the stage before the middle of Chaucer's lifetime. The earliest records of the performance of moralities in Europe are English, and they refer to *Paternoster* plays in which apparently the separate clauses of the Lord's Prayer were related to the Seven Deadly Sins and the Seven Christian Virtues, and dramatized in cyclical pageants that displayed these two sets of moral personifications in allegorical competition for the human soul. The existence of such a play at York is mentioned by Wyclif about 1378;[2] and in it, according to a later document (1389), "all manner of vices and sins were held up to scorn, and the virtues were held up to praise"; while a later notice still (1399) refers to one division of that play as a "ludus Accidie." A *Paternoster* play at Lincoln is mentioned in various records as having been performed, perhaps annually, between 1397 and 1521. And a third, at Beverley, receives an illuminating account in the *Minute Book* of that town under the date May 29, 1469.[3] The Beverley play consisted of eight pageants (*ludi*), one for each of the Seven Deadly Sins, and the eighth for a performance whose theme and mean-

THE PSYCHOMACHIA

ing are uncertain, the "pageant of Viciose." [4] It is clear from the records available that in all three towns the moral play of the *Paternoster,* though probably making a later appearance than the great mystery cycle of Corpus Christi, rivaled the latter in popularity, was produced no less lavishly, and owned equal powers of endurance from one generation to another. At York it was performed at least as late as 1572, when Archbishop Grindal asked for the playbooks and received "a trewe copie of all the said books even as they were played this yere." [5]

These *Paternoster* plays have not survived, the oldest of the extant moralities being *The Castle of Perseverance* and the fragmentary *Pride of Life,* which belong to the period 1400–1425. Thereafter for almost a hundred and fifty years the morality play had continuous and lively existence on the English stage as the most popular form of the professional drama. More than any other type of dramatic entertainment it incorporated the native tradition of the theater, especially the professional and popular theater, just preliminary to the great development of the Elizabethan stage. In the eighth and ninth decades of the sixteenth century moral plays were still presented in London and in the provinces, according to the evidence of contemporary documents; still performed at court, according to the evidence of the Revels Accounts; still published to supply a reading public, according to the evidence of the Stationers' Register. The testimony is copious for their traditional status and impress at the very time the great age of the drama was stirring into life.[6] It is inconceivable that during Shakespeare's pupilage the plays performed at Stratford by touring companies of actors did not include a solid number of moralities alongside the histories and romances just then becoming popular, or that those very histories and romances were not deeply qualified—the subject will concern us later—by features of the morality tradition. Just such a performance in the city of Gloucester is remembered in a little volume of autobiography and confession by one R. Willis, published in 1639. Willis, seventy-five years old when his book appeared, was born the same year graced by the birth of Shakespeare. He describes that customary event, the arrival of a troupe of "Players of Enterludes," and the play he attended when he was so small his father "made mee stand betweene his leggs, as he sate upon one of the benches where wee saw and heard very well." What he saw and heard was *The Cradle of*

THE PSYCHOMACHIA

Security, a morality whose theme can be gathered from its roles: "This Prince did personate in the morall, the wicked of the world; the three Ladies, Pride, Covetousnesse, and Luxury, the two old men, the end of the world, and the last judgement." [7]

No copy of *The Cradle of Security* remains, and it is a fair guess, amounting almost to certainty, that most of the moralities have likewise perished. Those that have survived whole or in part, including transitional plays with obvious morality features, number close to sixty. They compose a substantial body of dramatic literature with prominent common traits and with a significant development from the time of its origin until it is supplanted, in the period between 1570 and 1585, by the literal drama of the Elizabethan stage. No more than six or seven of these plays can be placed with any certainty inside the fifteenth century. About twenty-five others belong to the first half of the sixteenth, and another twenty-five come in the three or four decades between 1550 and the end of the morality convention. As the occasion arises, these three groups of plays will be designated, according to their chronology, as *early, intermediate,* and *late* moralities.

Such a classification, besides its convenience, has intrinsic utility, for it agrees substantially with phases of evolution in the morality plays themselves. They exhibit a threefold development that reflects the whole secular revolution of the Renaissance. From the early to the intermediate moralities the change is essentially a shift of emphasis from spiritual to secular values—that is, from Christian eschatology, with its contempt for the world and its concentration upon the post-mortem destiny of the soul, to consideration of human life in its own terms of success or failure. Transition from the intermediate to the late moralities is largely characterized by progressive reduction in scope as compared with the original subject matter of these plays—that is, by increasing specialization of the moral theme into topics of limited significance and by gradual *thickening* of intention and method, converting the abstract toward the concrete, the general toward the specific. The third and final step in this secular process, occurring mainly in the late moralities, is the gradual substitution of history for allegory— that is, of a literal plot, real or imaginary, for a metaphorical one; and of literal personages, real or imaginary, for type figures and personified abstractions.[8] But this last stage, properly considered, is not a development within the nature of the morality plays themselves; rather it is the intrusion of an alien element that expands until it puts an end to the formal existence of the allegorical drama.

To follow this threefold process in detail is to receive insight into the decline and fall of a literary convention of considerable magnitude, and later on there will be occasion to do so. But these changes, while they modify, do not obliterate the radical characteristics that define the nature of the allegorical play so long as it is recognizable as such, or so long as allegorical remnants survive in the plots and personae of plays that *seem* to belong entirely to a different convention. It is precisely for the sake of exposing one of these vestiges in troublesome amalgamation with the later drama of concrete life and literal humanity that we need to examine the principles that generate the nature of the whole morality convention. And these principles are contained within the fact that, with almost no exception, the moralities dramatize the central type of medieval allegory—the homiletic allegory of the Psychomachia. Transcending change, the same subject, method, and purpose that appear in the *Paternoster* plays, at the very origin of the morality drama, uniformly govern all the plays that have survived. They all dramatize the war between vice and virtue for possession of the human soul; their method is personification; their purpose moral instruction. The only plays that appear to be exceptions to any part of this generalization are *Pride of Life* and *Everyman,* but they are not really so. An examination of the morality drama in the three aspects of its substantive nature—as Psychomachia, as personification, and as homiletics—is a necessary preface to the curious history of its chief figure, the Vice.

2

Four themes of medieval allegory supply the content for the entire body of English moralities. Three of them—the Summons of Death, the Debate of the Soul and the Body, and the Parliament in Heaven—are of secondary importance in the whole development of the morality drama. Not only are they infrequent, but when they do appear they are subsidiary to a greater theme. Furthermore, with a single exception,[9] they do not survive beyond the early plays. They embodied in allegory the hopes and fears of Christian eschatology, and by the end

THE PSYCHOMACHIA

of the fifteenth century they lose their place on the stage for causes that are both doctrinal and dramaturgic. The spiritual considerations they allegorized—that is, death and judgment—do, in fact, survive as important influences upon thought and action in the Elizabethan and Jacobean drama; but the three allegories themselves, as actually presented on the stage, belong to the earlier history of the moralities.

The theme of the Summons of Death expresses what is almost the most striking feature of the religious faith of the late medieval centuries. The stupendous system of otherworldliness that had developed throughout the Christian era produced at its climax, just before it bowed beneath the secular onslaught of the Renaissance, a frenzied concentration on "Death and its bitterness." The art of the period teems with death, and so does its literature. Church walls and windows gleamed with the menace of the *Danse Macabre;* in household and tavern the *memento mori* thrust its inescapable comment on business or pleasure; the skull on the ring pressed its sermon into the jeweled finger.[10] What is particularly notable about this late medieval concern with death is its terrible effort at realism—its fascination not simply with the idea of mortality, but with death in its most horrible shapes and attitudes: the disembowled and rotting corpse, the decapitated head and dismembered limbs, the grim physical details of dying, and, more than anything else, the personification of hollow-eyed Death the skeleton:

> With synnews wyderyd,
> With bonys shyderyd,
> With hys worme-eten maw,
> And his gastly jaw
> Gaspyng asyde,
> Nakyd of hyde
> Neyther flesh nor fell.[11]

Timor mortis conturbat me—Dunbar's cry rings everywhere in late medieval literature. Today we are prone to exaggerate its morbidity unless we restore to horror its counterpoise of hope and read Dunbar's poem for what it says elsewhere:

> Sen for the deid remeid is none,
> Best is that we for dede dispone,
> Eftir our deid that lif may we.
> [*Lament for the Makaris*, ll. 97–99] [12]

THE PSYCHOMACHIA

Decay and death got their ugly emphasis as reminder to the medieval Christian that his real destiny lay elsewhere. The divided universe held on one side the eternal joy of heaven, or the pain, no less eternal, of hell; on the other, the corrupt and mutable world of nature in which mortal flesh ached with immortal longings, craving and fearing. And at the juncture of these two worlds stood Death the invincible foeman, the fell sergeant strict in his arrest, summoning mankind, not to anni- hilation, but to the throbbing crisis of the Last Things: the pangs of dying, the fearful rendering of account before the Seat of Judgment "even to the teeth and forehead of our faults," the convulsive pause before the irrevocable sentence of heaven or hell. We do not understand Hamlet's most famous soliloquy unless we derive it from such terms— from the terms of the Prayer of Villon's Mother to the Virgin:

> Femme je suis povrette et ancienne,
> Ne riens ne sçay; oncques lettre ne leuz,
> Au monstier voy dont suis parroissienne
> Paradis painct, où sont harpes et luz
> Et ung infer où damnez sont boulluz:
> L'ung me faict paour, l'autre joye et liesse.
> La joye avoir fais-moy, haulte Deesse,
> A qui pecheurs doivent tous recourir,
> Comblez de foy, sans faincte ne paresse.
> En ceste foy je vueil vivre et mourir.[13]

With such an inspiration building up over the Christian centuries, it is scarcely a wonder that the late medieval imagination gave it full play by "painting death to the life." The personification of Death, as ani- mated cadaver or grinning skeleton, strode through literature and art and developed into the somber mockery of the *Danse Macabre,* which, originating in France in the end of the fourteenth century, spread throughout Europe in the fifteenth. Disqualified either by the nature of the dramatic story or by a more native tradition, the Dance does not actually appear in the English moralities, where the allegorical image of Death is martial or legal, an assault or a summons.[14] In *The Castle of Perseverance* the earthly career of Humanum Genus comes to an end when "drery Dethe" enters with his dart and strikes him down, after reciting his power over the "lordys & ladys in euery londe." [15] In the *Ludus Coventriae* (c. 1475), a cyclical mystery permeated by alle- gorical elements, Herod, exulting in the slaughter of the innocents and

THE PSYCHOMACHIA

reveling with his two knights in wine and song, is suddenly and spectacularly visited by Mors, "goddys massangere," and stricken at the very moment he bids the music strike up: "Hinc dum buccinant mors interficiat herodem et duos milites subito et diabolus recipiat eos." [16] The coming of Death is the focal point of the plots of two other moralities, *Pride of Life* and *Everyman,* creating in the latter the whole moral crisis of the play. The lesson attached to all these visitations is threefold: the universal and impartial power of Death over all life and all social classes; the folly of concentration upon the transient pleasures and goods of this world; the need for chastening all one's life by the mortifying thought of its end and of the judgment to come. Sooner or later in each of these plays comes the insistent, melancholy warning:

> Thinke, þou haddist beginninge
> Qwhen þou were i-bore;
> & bot þou mak god endinge
> þi sowle is fforlore.
>
> . . . .
>
> þis world is bot ffantasye
> & fful of trechurye;
> Gode sire for ȝoure curteysye
> Take þis for no ffolye.
>
> . . . .
>
> & eke þat þou art lenust man,
> & haddist begyning,
> & euirmore hau þout opon
> þi dredful ending.
>
> [*Pride of Life,* ll. 183–398]

> To saue you fro synnynge,
> Evyr at the begynnynge
> Thynke on youre last endynge!
>
> [*Perseverance,* ll. 3647–49]

> The story sayth:—Man, in the begynnynge
> Loke well, and take good heed to the endynge,
> Be you neuer so gay!
> Ye thynke synne in the begynnynge full swete,
> Whiche in the ende causeth the soule to wepe
> Whan the body lyeth in claye.
>
> [*Everyman,* ll. 10–15]

This somber advice *de arte moriendi* received its dramatic emphasis from the entrance of Death, dreadful in his visible form—God's all-

THE PSYCHOMACHIA

powerful, unbribable, inexorable messenger, who summoned the trembling soul to its accounting in the spiritual world:

> I am Dethe, that no man dredeth;
> For euery man I rest, and no man spareth;
> For it is Goddes commaundement
> That all to me sholde be obedyent.

> . . . .

> I set not by golde, syluer, nor rychesse,
> Ne by pope, emperour, kynge, duke, ne prynces;
> For, and I wolde receyue gyftes grete,
> All the worlde I myght gete;
> But my custome is clene contrary.
>
> [*Everyman*, ll. 115 ff.]

The personification of Death on the English stage is confined, in plays that survive, to his role in the *Ludus Coventriae* and in the three early moralities already mentioned. It is an important sign of the loss of eschatological values that he does not continue as a dramatic figure beyond 1500. Instead of altogether disappearing, however, his role undergoes a transformation that points up the profound shift toward secular and prudential values signaling the Renaissance. It is taken over by a series of allegorical figures who signify judgment and punishment in this life. In Skelton's *Magnificence* it is Adversity who enters suddenly at the climactic moment of the hero's pride and folly to humble him. He is also God's messenger; and so are Divine Correction in Lindsay's *Three Estates,* Nemesis in *Respublica,* God's Visitation in *The Trial of Treasure,* Correction in *The Tide Tarrieth No Man,* Horror in *The Conflict of Conscience,* and similar figures besides in other late moralities—all of whom come in at the end to inflict on the sinner his sublunar suffering,[17] and are in the mind of Edmund, in *King Lear,* when he makes his comment on the entrance of his brother: "Edgar—and pat! he comes, like the catastrophe of the old comedy." [18]

The Summons of Death, with its dreadful figure of the Summoner, is the first of a series of allegorical themes that develop the full meaning of the great crisis of death in the Christian history of the spirit. Next in order and closely related to it is the Debate between the Soul and the Body, a motif prolific in the homiletic literature of the whole of medieval Europe.[19] In its standard version it consists of two parts: the complaint of the jeopardized Soul addressed to the Body after

THE PSYCHOMACHIA

death, blaming it for its addiction to sin; the reply of the Body lamenting its past loveliness and present decay, and shifting responsibility for its errors to the negligent Soul. This theme appears only twice in the surviving moralities, and is confined to the two oldest of them. The prologue to *Pride of Life* informs us that in the missing second half of the manuscript,

> Qwhen þe body is doun i-broȝt
> þe soule sorow awakith;
> þe bodyis pride is dere a-boȝt:
> þe soule þe ffendis takith.

> & throgh priere of Oure Lady mylde
> Al godenisse scho wol qwyte;
> Scho wol prey her son so mylde
> þe soule & body schul dispyte.
> [ll. 93–100]

In *The Castle of Perseverance* the Debate is compressed within a single stanza, in which the Anima of the dead Humanum Genus stands over the corpse and laments:

> body! þou dedyst brew a byttyr bale,
> to þi lustys whanne gannyst loute;
> þi sely sowle schal ben a-kale;
> I beye þi dedys with rewly rowte;
> & al it is for gyle.
> euere þou hast be coueytows,
> falsly to getyn londe & hows;
> to me þou hast brokyn a byttyr jows;
> so welaway þe whyle!
> [ll. 3013–21]

It is another sign of the loss of eschatological values that this popular medieval theme should have so small a place in the moralities. Only one of them after *Perseverance* carries the spiritual history of man beyond the moment of death itself,[20] although many of them continue to train on the events of life a moral focus sharply adjusted to view them chiefly in relation to their consequences beyond the grave. As for the Debate itself and its two Debaters, they are to be heard all over again in the most Christian of Shakespeare's sonnets:

> Poor soul, the centre of my sinful earth,
> . . . these rebel pow'rs that thee array,

THE PSYCHOMACHIA

Why dost thou pine within and suffer dearth,
Painting thy outward walls so costly gay?
Why so large cost, having so short a lease,
Dost thou upon thy fading mansion spend?
Shall worms, inheritors of this excess,
Eat up thy charge? Is this thy body's end?
Then, soul, live thou upon thy servant's loss,
And let that pine to aggravate thy store;
Buy terms divine in selling hours of dross;
Within be fed, without be rich no more.
  So shalt thou feed on Death, that feeds on men,
  And Death once dead, there's no more dying then.
                          [Sonnet CXLVI]

The last episode in this allegorical trilogy is also a debate—in this case a Parliament in Heaven before the throne of God—and it has its Biblical source in the 85th Psalm:

> Mercy and truth are met together;
> Righteousness and peace have kissed each other.

The personifications in these Old Testament verses fell in fruitfully with the allegorical disposition of medieval Christianity, and became a familiar text and story in homiletic literature as early as the twelfth century, a development stimulated no doubt by the great names of Bernard of Clairvaux and Hugo of St. Victor. Both churchmen cultivated the allegory, which is, in its oldest form, an explanation of the redemption of mankind through the sacrifice of Christ. Mercy, Truth, Justice, and Peace appear as the Four Heavenly Sisters, personifications of major qualities in the Divine Nature. Their original harmony in a perfect world has been disturbed by a world that has become imperfect, and they argue the fate of depraved humanity after the Fall. It is only because Mercy's plea triumphs over the legal argument presented by Justice for mankind's condemnation that the Son goes to earth as the Redeemer. The disputation thus resolved, all Four Sisters are reconciled to each other by Peace. In feudal dress the incident occurs in the *Chasteau d'Amour* of Robert Grosseteste (1175–1253) and in its fourteenth century English version, *The Castel of Love*.[21] It also has substantial place in such homiletic favorites as the *Cursor Mundi*,[22] the *Meditationes Vitae Christi*,[23] and the Anglo-Latin versions of the *Gesta Romanorum*.[24] In the fourteenth century it

THE PSYCHOMACHIA

is introduced into Langland's *Vision*,[25] and in the fifteenth it is used by Lydgate in his *Court of Sapience*.[26] Also in the fifteenth century the same theme gets lavish dramatization in two French plays, the *Mystère de la Passion* by Eustache Mercadé and the enormous work of the same name by Arnould Greban.[27]

In the English drama the debate and reconciliation of the Four Sisters is one of the large allegorical intrusions into the *Ludus Coventriae,* where they appear just before the episode of the Annunciation in order to give it its heavenly motivation.[28] Otherwise they exist in only two of the English moralities, and in only one of these, *Perseverance,* do they serve their original eschatological function, even here modified, by debating the fate of the errant soul that appears before God for judgment.[29] In *Respublica* (1553) they appear on earth to save the Lady Respublica from the enemies that assail her. Their terrestrial role in this play, as a sort of *posse comitatus* on the trail of social evils, is another illustration of the loss of eschatological emphasis in the moralities after 1500; and they deserve the comment put upon them by one of the malefactors they confront:

> Dwell ye in heaven and so madde to come hither.
>
> . . . .
>
> Why, what folke are ye that cannot heaven endure?
> [ll. 1676 and 1686]

Elsewhere in the moralities they survive only by a clear allusion in *Mankind* and a doubtful one in *Hickscorner*.[30] But although they have no more than a thin role on the English stage and, except for their secular activity in *Respublica,* disappear early from the drama, the profound medieval hope they symbolize does not. When in *Respublica* Mercy exclaims, "If offendours were not, wherefore might mercye serve?"[31] the sound of her voice reaches into *The Merchant of Venice* and *Measure for Measure,* and her very words re-echo through the despairing cry in *Hamlet:*

> What if this cursed hand
> Were thicker than itself with brother's blood,
> Is there not rain enough in the sweet heavens
> To wash it white as snow? Whereto serves mercy
> But to confront the visage of offence?
> [III.iii.43–47]

THE PSYCHOMACHIA

3

Before attending to the fourth, and last, of the allegories which supply the plots of the morality plays, we need to return briefly to a point already made: namely, that the three so far discussed are really three parts of a single theme, the fate of the soul upon the death of the body, and that their early disappearance from the stage corresponds with the growth of secular ideals in the Renaissance. But it is also noteworthy that in the early plays in which they do appear these three allegories have only a contributory function and exist in dependency on a larger subject. The Summons or Assault of Death appears an exception, for it seems to engross the main action of two plays: the fragmentary *Pride of Life* and *Everyman*. It is, however, worth a moment's consideration whether at the dramatic and moral center of both these plays the main issue is actually Death's advent or another. In *Pride* the chief figure is the King of Life (Rex Vivus), epitome of blindly confident mankind. Sustained in his arrogance by Strength and Health, his knights, and diverted from spiritual issues by Mirth, his courtier-jester, he scorns the holy admonitions that come to him from his queen and the Church. He is not summoned by Death, but presumes so far that he sends Death a challenge; and in the lost second part, as the prologue relates, Death and the King of Life meet in fierce encounter, with Death the victor:

> Sone affter hit befel þat Deth & Life
>   Beth togeder i-take;
> & ginnith & striuith a sterne strife
>   King of Life to wrake.
>
> [Deth] him driuith adoun to grounde,
>   He dredit nothing his kniʒtis;
> & delith him depe deþis wounde
>   & kith on him his miʒtis.
>
> [ll. 85–92]

But this event is not the climax of the play, only corridor to the region where in so early a morality the climax can take place: to wit, the everlasting world beyond. There justice gives way to mercy, and the sinful soul "þat þe ffendes haue i-kaʒte" is redeemed through the intercession of "Oure Lady mylde."

THE PSYCHOMACHIA

Pride of Life, in short, is essentially concerned to present the issue between vice and virtue in the human soul, with hell or heaven the outcome. And so, in a real sense, is *Everyman* in spite of the prominence of the Summons of Death in the first part of it. For the burden of the play is much less in the Summons itself than in its sequel. Arrested by Death because of his sinful life, and summoned to his reckoning before God, Everyman confronts eternal damnation. Good Fellowship, Kindred, Worldly Goods are actually his soul's enemies since they represent his concentration upon things that are spiritually destructive; and Worldly Goods is explicit: "My condycyon is mannes soul to kyll."[32] As they turn from him in his need, so he turns from them to their opposites, his true spiritual friends—to Good Deeds, Confession, and the sacramental ministrations of the Church. Our modern view of human destiny, since it goes no further than the grave, is prone to miss the point that in *Everyman* the real issue lies beyond it. The death of the body attracts only the incidental pathos of the play, and we ought not to read it as if it were *The Great Lover* by Rupert Brooke. Its deeper feeling, as well as its dramatic center, resides in the fact that its hero hovers between contending forces of spiritual death and spiritual life, each side arrayed against the other through its cogent personifications. He saves his soul in the end because he becomes a convert from sin to virtue. The real meaning of the play is perfectly clear in its epilogue:

> This morall men may haue in mynde.
> Ye herers, take it of worth, olde and yonge!
> And forsake Pryde, for he deceyueth you in the ende.
>
>   . . . .
>
> For, after dethe, amendes may no man make;
> For than mercy and pyte doth hym forsake.
> If his rekenynge be not clere whan he doth come
> God wyll saye:*"Ite, maledicti, in ignem eternum!"*
>
>   [ll. 902 ff.]

If then, as it appears, both plays are largely concerned with presenting the conflict of spiritual opposites, they are not exceptions to the one motif that governs the content and shape of every other surviving morality—the war of moral personifications that goes under the name of the Psychomachia. Nothing about the English moralities is more

THE PSYCHOMACHIA

central to them than the fact that they are, from first to last, dramatizations of the homiletic allegory of the Psychomachia. At the heart of each of them, dictating the action it presents and the lesson it imparts, is the struggle between Good and Evil for possession of the human soul. When other allegories also appear, as in the oldest moralities, they are merely extensions of this dominant theme. The dramatic and homiletic energy of this whole dramatic corpus flows from the concept, basic to Christianity, of endless and universal conflict between God and the Devil, or between their auxiliaries, virtue and vice—a concept that defines the earthly life of man as the arena of a Holy War between the contending forces of his own nature. As well as dramatizing the Psychomachia, the moralities verbalize it exactly:

> The temtacyon of the flesch ȝe must resyst lyke a man
> For ther ys euer a batell betwyx the soull & the body;
> *Vita hominis est milicia super terram.*

> Oppresse yower gostly enmy & be Crystes own knyght;
> Be neuer a cowarde ageyn yower aduersary.
> If ȝe wyll be crownyde ȝe must nedes fyght.
> [Mankind, ll. 219–24]

More vividly, in Medwall's *Nature* Reason instructs Man on the meaning of human life by expressing the metaphor of the Psychomachia in one of its most common medieval forms—the siege of the allegorical castle:

> I assemble the lyfe of mortall creature
> To the assyege agayn a strong town or castell
> In whyche there ys myche besy endeuure
> Myche warly polycy wyth dylygent trauayll
> On euery syde whyche parte shall preuayll
> By sleyght of ingyns or by strong power
> That other to subdue and bryng into daunger.
>   In suche case and maner of condycyon
> Is wreched man here in thys lyfe erthly
> Whyle he abydeth wythin the garyson
> Of the frayll carcas and carynouse body
> Whom to impugn laboreth incessantly
> The world, the fleshe, the enemy, these thre
> Hym to subdue and bryng into captyuyte.
> [part II, ll. 1–14] [33]

THE PSYCHOMACHIA

This war between Good and Evil, the common subject of all the morality plays, is a theme older than Christianity, older than human speculation itself, for its source is probably coeval with the earliest response of human consciousness to the tension of existence. In its ultimate formulation, as in Zoroastrianism, it contemplates a dualistic universe divided between contending principles of Light and Darkness engaged in endless conflict, with human life a microcosmic battleground of the same struggle. A similar metaphysical dualism is fundamental doctrine in Manichaeism, which received the allegiance of St. Augustine during nine years of his youth. Cosmological dualism defines the speculation of Anaxagoras, who assigned the creation of the world to the operation of an ordering principle, *Nous,* upon the undifferentiated chaos of matter.[34] Dualism, both metaphysical and moral, is profoundly involved in the thought of Plato. In its former aspect it appears in his radical separation of the world of Ideas from the world of Sense, and in his distinction, prominent in the *Timaeus,* between God as the source of the soul and the Demiurge as the source of the body in which the soul is imprisoned. His moral dualism is everywhere in the dialogues, getting spectacular expression in his famous equine metaphor, and myth, of the soul in the *Phaedrus.*[35] Practically all ethical thought in Western culture during the sixteen centuries between Philo Judaeus and Spinoza—that is, the vital epoch of Christianity—is profoundly oriented to a dualistic conception of human life as oscillating between antithetic poles of Good and Evil. This same dualism, although temporarily obscured today by the "scientific" consideration of human behavior, nonetheless remains deeply imbedded in our more imaginative reflection on the human situation; and we can scarcely speak about ethical issues without employing the language of antinomies—spirit and matter, soul and body, heaven and hell. The medieval Faust would have no difficulty understanding his namesake, the modern man of Goethe:

> One impulse art thou conscious of, at best;
> O, never seek to know the other!
> Two souls, alas! reside within my breast,
> And each withdraws from, and repels, its brother.
> One with tenacious organs holds, in love
> And clinging lust, the world in its embraces;

THE PSYCHOMACHIA

The other strongly sweeps, this dust above,
Into the high ancestral spaces.[36]

Among the early and medieval heresies that distracted Christianity
none was more stubbornly rooted and recrudescent than the belief in a
universe ultimately dualistic, with Evil a second, and competing, god-
head. Against the sects that held it, or seemed to hold it, the Church
fought bitterly, employing anathema and exclusion against the Manichees and Gnostics in the fourth and fifth centuries, and extermination
against the Albigenses in the thirteenth. But at the same time the
reality of moral evil in a positive and absolute sense was basic to
Christianity from its origin. The source of all evil, the Devil, was at
first one of the brightest of the angelic retinue of God; but, corrupted
by pride and envy, he rebelled against the Deity, was defeated and
thrust into hell, and became the tireless enemy of God and man,
assailing the impervious Creator through His pervious creature. His
endless and subtle assaults upon the human heart created the invisible
war between Good and Evil which was for Christianity, primitive and
medieval, the profoundest reality of life, since upon the issue hung the
eternal destiny of the soul. The salvation of the hard-pressed soul was
the supreme prize of existence, and mortal life became subject to a
single evaluation—the soul's progress toward God or its defection away
from Him. The adventure of life was inward and spiritual, and the attention of mankind became riveted upon an invisible drama, in comparison with which the external actions and relations of the world were
vanities and shadows. History lost its ordinary secular meaning, gaining a new one about which the whole literature of early Christianity
is explicit, and for which a single quotation from Eusebius (260?–340?),
the historian of the victory of Christianity in the Roman world, must
suffice:

Other writers of historical works have confined themselves to the written
tradition of victories in wars, of triumphs over enemies, of the exploits
of generals and the valour of soldiers, men stained with blood and with
countless murders for the sake of children and country and other posses-
sions; but it is wars most peaceful, waged for the very peace of the soul,
and men who therein have been valiant for truth rather than for country,
and for piety rather than for their dear ones, that our record of those
who order their lives according to God will inscribe on everlasting monu-
ments: it is the struggles of the athletes of piety and their valour which

THE PSYCHOMACHIA

braved so much, trophies won from demons, and victories against unseen adversaries, and the crowns at the end of all, that it will proclaim for everlasting remembrance.[37]

For Eusebius—and before him Tertullian, Cyprian, Lactantius, and other fathers of the early Church are equally expressive on the same theme—every affliction of the faithful was a trial imposed on their souls by the Enemy, who sought their spiritual destruction by every means. Every distress of the Church, in its struggle against the Empire without and discord and defection within, had its origin in the envy and jealousy of "the devil who hates what is good, as the enemy of truth, ever hostile to man's salvation."[38] Martyrdom, heresy, the surviving superstitions of the old religions, the distractions of the world, and the sins of the flesh were as so many legions of the demonic commander who "marshalling his death-dealing forces . . . stripped for action" against the citadel of the soul.[39] This fateful contest in the immaterial world of the spirit expressed for Christianity the real meaning and effort of mortal life, and defined, consequently, the real nature of history. The affairs of men and nations, of war and empire; actions associated with honor, patriotism, ambition, familial piety, personal affection; every hope and fear brought on by the vicissitudes of this world—all these, from the uncompromising viewpoint of militant Christianity, were products of the vanity and blindness of paganism. History was still a record of war, of defeat or victory, of valor or cowardice and their consequences—but it was a different history and a different war: "wars most peaceful, waged for the very peace of the soul" in which "the struggles of the athletes of piety" gained "trophies won from demons, and victories against unseen adversaries, and the crowns at the end of all."

Having thus acquired for Christianity a new meaning and a new subject matter, history needed also a new language and literary method. It is the insistent tendency, if not the essence, of the human imagination to express itself in concrete images and to receive its most vivid impressions in the same way. Entities that are not material, or qualities without independent life apart from the thing they qualify, create a problem in communication which is solved by dressing them in the metaphor of a sensible image. The immaterial realities of the spiritual world, and the Holy War between unseen forces inside the human

THE PSYCHOMACHIA

soul, needed to be expressed thus concretely to the senses if the homiletic and proselytizing efforts of militant Christianity were to be served. We have not far to look therefore to discover, at the very fountainhead of Christian faith, a statement of the real history of man and his significant warfare couched in the language of personification. St. Paul, writing to the Ephesians, provided for later Christianity a model of the literary method that the great theme demanded:

Put on the whole armour of God, that ye may be able to stand against the wiles of the devil. For we wrestle not against flesh and blood, but against powers, against the rulers of the darkness of this world, against spiritual wickedness in high places. . . . Stand therefore, having your loins girt about with truth, and having on the breastplate of righteousness; and your feet shod with the preparation of the gospel of peace; above all, taking the shield of faith, wherewith ye shall be able to quench all the fiery darts of the wicked. And take the helmet of salvation, and the sword of the spirit, which is the word of God.[40]

From its very beginning Christianity formulated the moral issues of this life in terms of the soul's destiny in the life beyond. Almost as early, the result perhaps of the influence of Oriental dualism, which had already been absorbed by Judaic culture, these moral issues assumed the shape of a conflict between opposites of vice and virtue: "For the flesh lusteth against the Spirit, and the Spirit against the flesh: and these are contrary the one to the other." [41] By what must be regarded as a natural accommodation of method to subject, the language of personification became the means to render this invisible struggle explicit and its unseen soldiery vivid. Even the philosophical subtlety and conceptual power of St. Augustine do not exempt him from the martial imagery of this dualism when he contrasts our embattled earthly life with the bliss of the Heavenly City, where the breach in our mortal nature is healed and the will no longer divided:

There the virtues shall no longer be struggling against any vice or evil, but shall enjoy the reward of victory, the eternal peace which no adversary shall disturb.[42]

In the imaginations of other Christian moralists, earlier and later than Augustine, this metaphorical warfare of the spirit is gradually enriched by its inherent possibilities. The metaphor grows from one generation to the next, and burgeons shortly with the whole panoply

THE PSYCHOMACHIA

and arsenal of war, as well as with war's violence and variety. "Would you have also fightings and wrestlings?" asks the ardent Tertullian (160?–230?), in one of his attacks upon the amusements of the Roman theater and arena—"Well, of these there is no lacking, and they are not of slight account":

Behold unchastity overcome by chastity, perfidy slain by faithfulness, cruelty stricken by compassion, impudence thrown into the shade by modesty; these are the contests we have among us, and in these *we* win our crowns.[43]

For Tertullian the personifications are still an incidental device of expression, but under the pen of Cyprian, a generation later, they acquire the details and autonomy of an episode:

What else in the world than a battle against the devil is daily carried on, than a struggle against his darts and weapons in constant conflicts? Our warfare is with avarice, with immodesty, with anger, with ambition; our diligent and toilsome wrestle with carnal vices, with enticements of the world. The mind of man, besieged, and in every quarter invested with the onsets of the devil, scarcely in each point meets the attack, scarcely resists it. If avarice is prostrated, lust springs up. If lust is overcome, ambition takes its place. If ambition is despised, anger exasperates, pride puffs up, wine-bibing entices, envy breaks concord, jealousy cuts friendship.[44]

The Devil is not a personification but a concretely historical figure in the Christian mythos. His agents, however, who carry out his assault upon man, are personifications of the destructive feelings and inclinations that invade the human heart. These the Christian moralists invariably objectified as the shock troops of Satan and developed the military figure in its most natural ways—as a siege laid to the fortress of the soul, or as field warfare waged for possession of the battleground, also the soul. This marriage of the rhetorical device of personification with the profound spiritual and subjective impulse of Christianity is the first stage in the development of the vast homiletic allegory of the Middle Ages. And this stage is concluded when Prudentius (*flor.* 400), a Christian poet with the epic tradition in his veins, unfolds the latent resources of the military image and spreads them into the continuous and diversified action of Virgilian battle. Personification, or prosopopoeia, which was, to begin with, an occasional device of classic rhetoric and poetry—Quintilian calls it an "embellishment"—becomes in the hands of Prudentius an independent literary

THE PSYCHOMACHIA

genre; and his poem, the *Psychomachia,* supplies the generic name for the most common form of medieval allegory.

In an earlier poem, the *Hamartigenia,* Prudentius at one point develops the conflict of vice and virtue into the metaphor of the besieged fortress:

Alas, with what armed forces does the ruthless enemy press upon the race of men, with what attendant trains under his command does he wage his iron wars, with what dominion triumph over the conquered. . . . With his stealthy forces he infiltrates into men's hearts and they draw him in. He sows all manner of wickedness into their inmost parts, and scatters his agents through their frames.[45]

Like any poet writing in the tradition of the classic epic, he is bound to enumerate the forces of the enemy, the "plagues of sin" with which "the powerful robber besets our sickened souls," and to describe the nature of the action:

For there a large force serves under this wicked commander and invests men's souls with dreadful weapons—Anger, Superstition, Sickness-of-Heart, Strife, Affliction, foul Thirst-for-Blood, Thirst-for-Wine, Thirst-for-Gold, Malice, Adultery, Craft, Slander, Theft. Hideous and frightful are their shapes, threatening their carriage. Vaunting Ambition is puffed up, Learning is proud, Eloquence thunders, Deceit contrives snares in secret. Here Abusive Speech snarls throughout the courts, there paltry Philosophy wields the club of Hercules . . . while Idolatry coats smoke-grimed stones with wax and in pale fear falls prostrate before altars that cannot hear.[46]

This siege of the soul by the personified soldiery of the Devil is only a single passage—a brief flare-up of imagination—in the more discursive content of the *Hamartigenia.* The poem as a whole fulfills its title by explaining the origin of sin, in refutation of the heresy, which it imputes to Marcion the Gnostic, that there is a god of evil as well as of good and that dualism is ultimate in the universe. But in the *Psychomachia* Prudentius puts epic prosopopoeia into play from beginning to end and fills 915 verses with the swaying fortune and confused alarums of allegorical battle, signifying "the vicissitudes of our soul's struggle." Christ is the muse whose aid the poet invokes in cataloging the combatants on either side. The opposing leaders—all personifications and all feminine—meet and engage with boast and challenge. Retreat, pursuit, and flying weapons fill the air with motion and with clamor. The ears of the dying are insulted by the taunts of the victors.

THE PSYCHOMACHIA

First Fides takes the field against Veterum Cultura Deorum and soon strikes her foe to death while the host of the virtues rejoices. Next Pudicitia sends her sword through the throat of Sodomita Libido and then washes her weapon clean of gore in the waters of Jordan. In the third encounter Ira, "showing her teeth with rage and foaming at the mouth," having vainly exhausted her missiles against the impenetrable armor of unflinching Patientia, finally is driven by sheer exasperation to suicide. Then Superbia on horseback gallops toward Mens Humilis, standing in the midst of her poor little band of Righteousness, Honesty, Soberness, Fasting, Purity, and Simplicity; but in mid-career the vice tumbles into a pit dug by Deceit, and while she lies thus prostrate her throat is piously cut by Mens Humilis, urged on by Hope. But now a more dangerous foe appears—Luxuria, in a golden chariot, her only weapons violets and rose petals, which she scatters, as if in sport, over the ranks of the faltering virtues; and they yearn to surrender and are about to do so when staunch Sobrietas exhorts them. She herself moves against Luxuria, thrusting the Christian cross upon the chariot steeds so that they bolt and throw their mistress into the dust, whereupon Sobrietas puts her to the sword. In the sixth action Avaritia, with her crooked hand, seeing her sister vices defeated in open battle, employs a more sinister form of aggression. She disguises her grim nature by putting on the affable countenance and modest clothing of Thrift. By such dissimulation she is able to seduce and demoralize the ranks of virtue, until Operatio (Good Works) seizes her in an iron grip, chokes and stabs her to death, and distributes to the poor the trinkets and money she strips from the corpse. One more action remains, but it takes place after the triumphant virtues have returned to their camp for the night and are about to celebrate their victory. Then Discordia, whose other name is Heresy, having ambushed herself in their midst, rises suddenly and wounds Concordia, who reacts promptly by sending her javelin down the throat of the vice that afflicted the early Church with doctrinal strife. Finally, with peace, purity, and unity established, the virtues erect on the battleground of victory (the body cleansed of its sins) the temple of the soul, with wide entrances to receive God and His Son.

It is unnecessary to exaggerate the literary merit of the *Psychomachia*

THE PSYCHOMACHIA

in order to acknowledge the achievement of Prudentius. His modest performance as a poet does not diminish his importance as an innovator. In his hands the whole epic machinery is put to work to generate Christian allegory. For all his epic afflatus, he never forgets the end for which he is writing. He is first of all a moralist, but a moralist with a literary sense strong enough to recognize the homiletic value of concrete image and continuous story. By collecting the dispersed elements of what was still only a tendency in Christian literature, and by articulating them into a running narrative enriched by imaginative detail, he created a new literary type—the allegorical poem. And he is sufficiently aware of his innovation to join to it a manifesto of purpose and achievement, for in a single important sentence he formulates the whole utility of personification for Christian homiletics:

The way of victory is before our eyes *if we may mark at close quarters the very features* of the Virtues and the monsters that close with them in deadly struggle. [my italics] [47]

We need to combine this statement with another, for together they are womb and cradle for the great pageant of moral abstractions in medieval art and letters. To the end of his poem Prudentius appends a *significatio* which not only expresses the meaning of his own allegory but proclaims the subject of almost the whole body of allegorical literature to come. The violent, bloody warfare on the spacious plain is dissolved into its spiritual meaning and restored to its invisible arena inside the human breast:

Savage war rages hotly, rages within our bones, and man's two-sided nature is in an uproar of rebellion; for the flesh that was formed of clay bears down upon the spirit, but again the spirit that issued from the pure breath of God is hot within the dark prison-house of the heart, and even in its close bondage rejects the body's filth.[48]

More than three hundred surviving manuscripts attest the popularity and influence of Prudentius throughout the Middle Ages.[49] It is probably a mistake, however, to ascribe to him the single, or even the major, role in the vast proliferation of the theme of the Holy War in allegorical literature and art. As it has already been remarked, the concept is implicit in every part of the Christian view of life, and Mr. C. S. Lewis is no doubt correct in his broader observation that "the *bellum intestinum* is at the root of all allegory." [50] In any case, in one form or another—as battle, siege, tournament, disputation, or perilous journey—the theme of the Psychomachia flourished in the millennium separating Prudentius from the morality plays. In its several forms it provided a moral definition of life, a psychological method, and an artistic motif; and in the art and literature of the Middle Ages it is usually all three at once. The conflict of the vices and virtues became the familiar subject of the pulpit sermon; and the figures of the various combatants in this struggle—the vices usually as ugly and deformed imps, the virtues as dignified and beautiful women—heavily populate all the forms of religious art: paintings, cathedral sculpture, mosaic pavements, tapestries, miniatures, and manuscript illumination.[51] By the time of the Renaissance, in fact, the method of allegory and its chief subject, the Psychomachia, became so assimilated to each other as to be indistinguishable, and Puttenham in 1589 can write of allegory as if in its very nature it is a Holy War: speaking of various figures of speech as properly forms of allegory, he concludes: "all these be souldiers to the figure *allegoria* and fight vnder the banner of dissimulation." [52]

The literature of the Psychomachia, outside the drama, is too extensive and various for methodical treatment in this place, but a few important examples will at least suggest the tradition. In the eighth and ninth books of the *Anticlaudianus,* a Latin poem of the twelfth century by Alanus de Insulis, there occurs the warfare between the vices that attack and the virtues that defend "divinus homo," whose creation by God and Natura and whose spiritual and intellectual development occupy the previous books.[53] The thirteenth-century poem by Huon de Meri, *Li Tornoiemenz Antecrit,* develops at great length a battle in which vices and mythological figures mingle in the forces led by Antichrist against the virtues whose leader is Christ.[54] The same mixture of allegory and mythology occurs in the warfare between vice and virtue in Lydgate's *Assembly of the Gods,* the battleground being, as the poet tells us, the human soul.[55] That version of the Psychomachia which appears in the *Hamartigenia* as a siege laid by the forces of evil to the fortress of the soul repeats itself in the twelfth-century *Chasteau d'Amour* of Bishop Grosseteste.[56] Likewise in the *Vision of Piers Plowman* the Castle of Unity, defended by Conscience, is beleaguered by the Seven Deadly Sins led by Antichrist:

THE PSYCHOMACHIA

And there was Conscience constable   Cristene to saue,
And biseged sothly   with seuene grete gyauntz
That with Antecrist helden   hard aʒein Conscience.[57]

Nor is the erotic allegory of the *Roman de la Rose* an exception to allegorical siege warfare, for one of its extensive episodes consists of the attack of Love's army, aided by Venus, upon the Castle of the Rose, defended by Daunger, Fear, and Shame.[58] In the Renaissance two major English poems apply the same image to their own specialized themes. Besides diversifying the *bellum intestinum* into a hundred chivalric episodes, illustrating "how many perils doe enfold / The righteous man to make him daily fall," *The Faerie Queene* exactly recreates in one of them the figurative siege. The enemies of Temperance (Alma) invest her castle, whose architecture and economy compose a metaphor of the human body and its functions. Five of their twelve troops assault the bulwarks of the five senses; the other seven, who concentrate upon the castle gate, are doubtlessly the Seven Deadly Sins.[59] In *The Purple Island* Phineas Fletcher, imitating Spenser in this respect as well as in others, expends the second half of his anatomical allegory upon similar warfare. Both poems sophisticate the original theme, their concern with the body being somewhat more modern than medieval. But also in the Renaissance the spiritual metaphor reasserts itself once more, and powerfully, in John Bunyan's *Holy War,* describing the history of the siege laid to the fortress of Mansoul by Diabolus, "a mighty Gyant," and his personified cohorts.[60]

A variation on the theme of the Psychomachia, more flexible and subtle than open battle or siege assault, is the spiritual journey, with its reflection of time and vicissitude, its changes of allegorical scenery and topography, its variety of spiritual encounters along the way, and its chance of the wrong fork of the road. And once more medieval homiletic allegory stretches into the modern world as far as Bunyan, this time through *The Pilgrim's Progress.* But before Bunyan there are the falsely attributed *Parables of Bernard* (of Clairvaux), the first of which takes the Prodigal Man through the Mountains of Pride, the Vale of Curiosity, the Meads of License, the Groves of Desire, the Marshes of Carnality, and binds him in the Castle of Despair.[61] There is also the massive *Pèlerinage de la Vie Humaine* (1330–35) by Guillaume de Guilleville, at least twice Englished, once by Lydgate, in the

THE PSYCHOMACHIA

fifteenth century. The metaphor lived naturally in the Christian imagination, and it is an effort as unnecessary as it is futile to relate the *Pèlerinage* as an influence upon the uneducated Bedford preacher. The sermons of the medieval pulpit, as Dr. Owst shows, were filled with the allegorical imagery of the Road to Salvation, along which the sins lurk to intercept the soul by force or guile.[62] An example worth adding consists of the description of the *via recta* in *John the Evangelist* (c. 1517–18), a moral and saint play combined. In it the preaching of St. John is supplemented by the exhortation of Irisdision addressed to the reprobate Eugenio, urging him to seek the "holy Syone," to which castle, guarded by the two porters Hope and Faith, "full strayte is the waye":

> Ouer the mede of mekenesse marke thou the waye
> Than to the pathe of pacyence shalte thou passe
> In to the lande of largenes holde for the laye
> And in the lane of besynesse loke thou not basshe
> Than measure in a marsshe a fayre maner hasse
> Reste ther hardely and abyde all nyght.
>
> [ll. 95–100]

This spiritual scenery is familiar to everyone acquainted with the wayfaring of Bunyan's Pilgrim; and the "marsshe" and the "fayre maner hasse"—what else are they except the prototypes of the Slough of Despond and the Palace Beautiful? As for the other way, *via obliqua et via circularis,* it also receives its descriptive due in imagery that spells out the Seven Deadly Sins:

> It brynges men to the feete of rufull araye
> The lady of confusion lyeth therin
> That Babylone is called; she is the ende of all synne.
>
> . . . .
>
> With bowes and trees it is meruaylously paled
> There groweth the elders of enuye
> Staked with pryde full hye
> And the breres of bakbytyng with wrath wrethed aboute
> Full of slouthy busshes and lecherous thornes drye
> With glotonous postes and couetyse rayled throughoute
> And at myscheues gate many dothe in roone.
>
> . . . .
>
> Downe to the dongyon where the deuyll dwelleth.
>
> [ll. 146 ff.]

THE PSYCHOMACHIA

4

Having carried the Psychomachia as far as Bunyan, we need to return to the poem of Prudentius for one further variation on its theme, and examine briefly in this instance a type of spiritual aggression that governs almost the whole use of the Psychomachia by the morality plays. Let us recall how Avarice, seeing her sister vices defeated and slain in open fight, decides to achieve her ends through guile—*nil refert armis contingat palma dolisve*.[63] Assuming the countenance and dress of Thrift, so often greed's respectable exterior, she brings about by dissimulation what violence was unable to achieve. Her deceived victims follow her and become her spoil, until Good Works (Operatio) comes to their rescue and puts Avarice, alias Thrift, to death. Almost the exact duplicate of this motif appears in one of the two oldest morality plays, *The Castle of Perseverance*. The vices assault the Castle which encloses the now aged Humanum Genus, but are beaten back by the defending virtues and retire in grotesque dismay from this open warfare. Their leader Avarice, however, achieves success another way —through seduction.[64] He advances with polite, solicitous address, proclaims himself Mankind's "best frende," and invites him with alluring words out of "øat castel colde" into the world where wealth and pleasure await him. His enticement is skillful and his success complete. Humanum Genus forsakes his virtuous resolutions and gives himself over to covetousness, the vice peculiar to old age, and to all the evils that accompany it, dying a sinner whose soul is saved in the end only by Mercy's plea on his behalf. Something very much the same occurs in the allegorical part of the hybrid Digby play of *Mary Magdalene* (1480–90). The Seven Deadly Sins, equipped no less for fraud than force,

> With wrath or wyhylles we xal hyrre wynne
> Or with sum sotyllte set hur in synne.
>
> [ll. 377–78]

first besiege the castle of "Maudleyn" until Mary, although she has successfully resisted their onslaught, decides to go to Jerusalem. Thereupon Lady Lechery attaches herself to Mary in the guise of maidservant and traveling companion, and with fair words of flattery and encouragement on the way soon brings about her fall. In both plays

THE PSYCHOMACHIA

the battle and its preliminaries, wherein, in patterned contrast, vice and virtue declaim to the audience their contrary natures, are homiletic pageantry rather than dramatic action, elocution and spectacle rather than plot. This form of the Psychomachia soon gives way, in plays that follow, to another, to which the stage is more tractable than it is to epic warfare.

Only two other moral plays preserve the military Psychomachia in anything like its original form, but in them it is even more vestigial. They need to be discussed together because of their obvious kinship and because they lead us up an irresistible bypath, along which we can take only a few steps before returning to the main theme. In Henry Medwall's *Nature* (1490–1501) a pitched battle impends between the Seven Deadly Sins, led by Man already seduced and depraved, and the forces of virtue whose leader is Reason.[65] The battle itself is never actually fought—Man suddenly feels his old age, loses his stomach for fighting, and finds it the better part of valor to reconcile himself to Reason—but there is an elaborate scene in which the vices mobilize for it. The other play is John Rastell's humanistic morality *The Nature of the Four Elements* (c. 1517), which imitates Medwall's earlier play in many respects. Both men belonged to the intellectual and literary circle that seems to have had its center in the household of Cardinal Morton and contained as well the young Thomas More. Medwall was Morton's chaplain and Rastell became More's brother-in-law, and there can be little doubt of their personal acquaintance, or of Rastell's knowledge of Medwall's plays. One of them, *Fulgens and Lucres*, Rastell himself printed, and his son William later did the same for *Nature*.[66] *Nature* and *The Four Elements* are the earliest of a line of humanistic moralities, all of which are oriented to the new values of the Renaissance—to Reason and Science and the classic virtue of moderation, against which are arrayed, as natural enemies of the intellectual discipline, Sensual Indulgence, Idleness, and Ignorance. Both plays are full of topical reference, social satire, and the rowdy energy of London street life. In both the delinquent hero (Man in *Nature,* Humanity in *The Four Elements*) gives himself over to the pleasures of the Cheapside taverns and the Bankside brothels, and the dialogue celebrates epicurean banquets and frolics with "lytell Nell," "Jane with the blacke lace," and "Bounsynge Besse"—all three "Ryght feyr and smotter of

THE PSYCHOMACHIA

87

face." In *The Four Elements* there is a merry taverner a little too fond of his own wine:

> Now if ye put it to my lyberte,
> Of all metes in the worlde that be,
> By this lyght, I love best drynke.
> [p. 34]

In Medwall's play the roistering companions of Man are the Seven Deadly Sins after he has been induced to their fellowship by the blandishments of Sensuality. In *The Four Elements* the seducer and bad companion of Humanity is Sensual Appetite himself.

If we turn now to the unfought military Psychomachia in *Nature,* for which the vices assemble after the summons comes to them in the midst of their tavern junkets, we confront several of a set of images that survived on the stage until Shakespeare put them together in one figure who marched to a Psychomachia of his own—at Shrewsbury. The image of Gluttony (whose pseudonym is "Good Felyshyp"), as fat no doubt as bombast could make it, claims our attention first. As the direction has it, to the other vices gathering for the fray "then cometh in Glotony wyth a chese and a botell" and protests that these are sufficient harness since he does not intend to fight anyway:

> What the deuyll harnes shuld I mys
> Wythout yt be a botell
> A nother botell I wyll go puruey
> Lest that drynk be scarce in the way
> Or happely none to sell.
> [part II, ll. 778–82]

Falstaff, of course, doesn't do his own purveying "in the way"—he sends Bardolph ahead to Coventry for "A nother botell"—but that is the only difference. His military equipment is identical. As for his military sentiment ("Give me life") and his catechism on the theme of honor, they are so much an improvement upon their original that we can forgive the borrowing. But borrowed they are. Bodily Lust (Lechery), summoned to Medwall's Psychomachia, has the same opinion on the same subject, and his is earlier:

> I wyll not com where strokys be
> I am not so mad a man
> And I wys yt ys not for any fere
> But yt ys a thyng that I can well forbere

THE PSYCHOMACHIA

And wyll as long as I can
Of lust and pleasure ys all my mynde
It longeth to me of properte and kynde
And yf I shuld to the warre
And ly in myne harnes as other men do
It shuld me vtterly marre.

[part II, ll. 672–82]

When we turn from *Nature* to the closely related morality of *The Four Elements,* we uncover another branch of Sir John's lineage on the military side. Eight leaves are lost from the middle of the one surviving copy of the play, and with them has disappeared what is undoubtedly another version of the martial Psychomachia—but not altogether disappeared; for just following the lacuna Sensual Appetite, leader of the evil personifications in the play, comes breathless onto the stage to describe to Ignorance ("Yngnoraunce"), his fellow vice, "a shrewd fray" in which he has just been fighting after his own fashion. The dialogue deserves quoting in full:

Sen. Gogges nayles, I have payed som of them, I tro.
Yng. Why, man, what eylyth the so to blow?
Sen. For I was at a shrewd fray.
Yng. Hast thou any of them slayn, than?
Sen. Ye, I have slayn them every man,
Save them that ran away.
Yng. Why, is any of them skapyd and gone?
Sen. Ye, by gogges body, everychone,
All that ever were there.
Yng. Why than, they be not all slayne.
Sen. No, but I have put some to payne,
For one horeson there was that torned again,
And streyght I cut of his ere.
Yng. Than thou hast made a cut hym purs. [sic]
Sen. Ye, but I servyd another wors!
I smot of his legge by the hard ars,
As sone as I met hym there.
Yng. By my trouth, that was a mad dede!
Thou sholdest have smyt of his hed,
Than he shold never have troublid the more.
Sen. Tushe! than I had ben but mad,
For there was another man that had
Smyt of his hed before!
Yng. Than thou hast quyt the lyke a tal knyght!

[pp. 42–43]

THE PSYCHOMACHIA

Is it possible to miss in these lines a later knight just as "tal" in prowess, the composite image of Gluttony, Lechery, and all the rest of the fleshly sins, who behaves in the same way at Gadshill and Shrewsbury and tells much the same story in a tavern in Eastcheap?

Nor is it only the warlike parts of Falstaff that Shakespeare collected from the vices of these two moralities. It would be strange if, having more flesh than another man and therefore more frailty, Sir John did not buckle within his belt the sin of pride. For the Tudor period pride had several related meanings, not the least of them referring to the vanity of extravagant apparel. There is everlasting solemn and satirical to-do on the subject in the Tudor drama. " 'Tis pride that pulls the country down" warns the old song, urging the good example of worthy King Stephen, "whose breeches cost him but a crown." [67] Falstaff's pride gets prominent exposition on his first appearance in the second part of *Henry IV,* "with his *Page* bearing his sword and buckler." The spectacle of the enormous knight floating forward, with his diminutive attendant, his "agate," in the lee and foundering under the outside cargo of iron, must have stirred recollection as well as laughter, especially when the talk, having brilliantly exploited the physical contrast between the knight and the "whoreson mandrake" behind him, turned to the satin sought on credit from reluctant Master Dommelton—two-and-twenty yards of satin for a short cloak and slops! The dramatic and the moral image was not new. In Medwall's *Nature* Pride, on his first entrance, displays himself sartorially to the audience:

> How say ye syrs by myne aray.
>
> .   .   .   .
>
> My doublet ys on laced byfore
> A stomacher of saten and no more
> Rayn yt snow yt neuer so sore
> Me thynketh I am to hote
> Than haue I suche a short gown
> Wyth wyde sleues that hang a down
> They wold make some lad in thys town
> A doublet and a cote.
>
> [part I. ll. 740 ff.] [68]

Pride has more to display—his weapons and the little boy, his "garcius," who attends him as page:

> Than haue I a sworde or twayn
> To bere theym my selfe yt were a payne

THE PSYCHOMACHIA

They ar so heuy that I am fayne
To puruey suche a lad
Though I say yt a praty boy
It ys halfe my lyues ioy
The vrchyn ys so mad

. . . .

Somtyme he serueth me at borde
Somtyme he bereth my two hand sword
Com forth thou lytell lyk tord.

. . . .

Se thys brat
Thys boy ys passyng taunte
Com behynd and folow me
Set out the better leg I warne the.

[part I, ll. 780 ff.]

The dismemberment of Falstaff into allegorical fragments might be
continued in other moralities, reversing the synthesis that put him
together. The homiletic allegory of youthful delinquency and personified vice in a dozen morality plays, perennial on the stage, supplied
Shakespeare with the moral and dramatic structure of the Falstaffian
epos, and also with the images of the personae who fit into it.[69] That
provenance has been indicated, but it has not yet been sufficiently exposed, nor its implications sufficiently canvassed.[70] The delinquent
prince, his precocious first soliloquy, and his rejection in the end of
"that reverend vice, that grey iniquity," who has been such "Good
felyshyp" to him for so long, create problems of interpretation mainly
because the play has become isolated from its source in homiletic allegory. The robbery at Gadshill, the tavern frolics, Doll Tearsheet meretrix, the endless jests about hanging, the antinomy of Falstaff and the
Lord Chief Justice, are all stock motifs of action, dialogue, and "character" in the moralities. The brilliance is Shakespeare's of course, but
the elementary stage images belong to the allegorical drama. The
problems arise because two worlds, one metaphorical the other literal,
have been fused. Allegory has been overlaid by history—by historical
places, literal events, and the moral drapery of concrete humanity—
without altogether losing its traditional features or the moral sentiment
appropriate to them. Falstaff himself, at Gadshill, Eastcheap, Shrewsbury, and marching before his page, oscillates between an historico-
moral figure and a personification. The "aged Councellor to youthfull

THE PSYCHOMACHIA

sinne" is also the jolly good fellow and harmless boon companion. The liar and coward, who exploits himself in these characteristics as if he were a pageant, is also somehow Sir John Falstaff with a reputation for honor and bravery. At least since the time of Maurice Morgann he has been a baffling figure because all interpretation insists on taking him for the coherent image of a human being, morally unified and self-consistent. But Falstaff is neither morally unified nor self-consistent. He was originally a personification, or a set of cognate personifications, to whom, because he was too theatrically attractive to die with the dramatic convention to which he originally belonged, Shakespeare gave a local habitation and a name. Although he walks like a man his innards are allegorical, and this fact will appear more clearly later on when the subject is riper for analysis.

5

No one less than Falstaff could have distracted us from the severe pursuit of the military Psychomachia in the moralities, and we need to return to it if only to mark its end. As outright warfare, either pitched battle or siege, it survives only in the four plays so far discussed.[71] Three of them are early moralities, and the fourth, Rastell's *The Four Elements,* is one of the oldest of the intermediate group. In all four the theme of physical combat between the vices and virtues has already shriveled into an episode of homiletic pageantry on the margin of a plot of intrigue. The old conflict has been caught up in a new way, more suitable to the stage; and the consistent method of the Psychomachia, as the shaping principle for the morality drama, becomes malevolent intrigue—the skillful employment of moral deception and verbal cajolery to pervert unsuspecting innocence or unfortified virtue.

The motif of open warfare does not, however, disappear entirely from the moralities. In one of its degenerate forms it becomes a verbal quarrel—a logomachy stiffened with insults—between vice and virtue, examples of which appear in Bale's *Three Laws* (1530–36) and in the allegorical part of *King Darius* (1559–65), the vices in both plays effectively losing the argument when they are driven off the stage by fire from heaven. In another it maintains its feature of physical violence,

THE PSYCHOMACHIA

as in *Mankind* (1461–85), where the three vices, Nought, New-guise, and Now-a-days, trouble Mankind, a farmer, at his labors until he beats them off with his spade. They retire to nurse their injuries and to invoke the help of their chief, Titivillus, who succeeds by craft where they failed by open aggression, exactly as in *Perseverance* and the Digby *Mary Magdalene*. A diminished fight of this sort also takes place in *Mundus et Infans* (1500–1520), where Manhood exchanges blows with Folly, with the human hero victorious in the physical contest but an easy victim of the verbal blandishments that follow. Thereafter the military Psychomachia, along with its large doctrinal meaning, dwindles into a functionless but characteristic piece of farcical stage business that persists throughout the morality convention—the familiar episode of rowdy quarrel and rough-and-tumble fighting among the vices themselves; or, where a single vice survives in later plays that are mainly outside that convention—*Horestes* and *Cambises* for example—a quarrel and brawl between him and several rustics. In all these stock imbroglios the vices flourish all that is left them from their formidable armament in the original Psychomachia—their wooden daggers.

For this degeneration of the epic hostilities that supplied the earliest version of the Psychomachia, and for the ascendancy of intrigue, the causes are not far to seek. One of them consists simply of the introduction of a new figure into the metaphor. In its original form, as in the poems of Prudentius, the allegorical conflict occurs directly between two antithetic groups of personifications, who objectify the opposition of good and evil in man's nature. Man himself cannot appear as a figure in the action because, in the logic of the metaphor, he is the battleground on and for which the battle is fought, or the castle besieged and defended. Similarly in Lydgate's *Assembly of the Gods* the *significatio* at the end clarifies the allegorical relationship of man to the Holy War that has just been waged between personified opposites of vice and virtue:

> So ys man the felde to whyche all were sent
> On both partyes.[72]

None of the surviving moralities maintains this allegorical purity, which dictates that a substance and its personified accidents cannot appear together as if they were parallel entities. A few of the plays, superficially examined, seem to abide by such logic, but not really. In

THE PSYCHOMACHIA

the early morality of *Wisdom* (1461–85), for example, man does not seem to be present; but in fact he is, distilled into his spiritual essence which is personified as Anima or the Soul, and she is accompanied by her accidents, her Five Inward Wits and her Three Powers. In a few other moralities, which clearly do not include man among the personae, he is also not the subject of the metaphorical action. In Bale's *Three Laws* the violent debate between virtue and vice has reference to the social and geographical entity which is the whole of England, not to man. The same is true of such plays as *King Darius, New Custom,* and several others that deal with the Reformation controversy. Man does not appear either in the two late moralities attributed to Robert Wilson, *The Three Ladies of London* (1581) and *The Three Lords and Three Ladies of London* (1589), for the very good reason that the virtues and vices belong not to him but to the city, and the city is the scene of the action.

Otherwise, into the morality drama from its beginning there intruded, under his various names and aspects, the figure of mankind, who, strictly speaking, does not belong in the allegory at all. He is not a personification but a universalized type; and he is placed in the position, absurd from the viewpoint of allegory, of fraternizing with his personified attributes. In Medwall's *Nature,* for instance, Man stands by a mute listener while his Sensuality and his Reason argue their separate claims to dominion over him, until finally he bursts out like a wonder-stricken and utterly forlorn third party:

> O blessyd lord what maner of stryf ys thys
> Atwyxt my reason and sensualyte.
> [part I, ll. 371–72]

The popular stage easily tolerated the paradox for at least two reasons. By the fourteenth century moral allegory had become so conventional that its personifications assumed independent life as artistic motifs and existed without reference to their ultimate moral or metaphorical logic. Mankind could appear in the company of his vices and virtues because they had become autonomous figures in the medieval imagination.[73] In the second place, the omission of man from *his own drama,* while tolerable in the diffuse and discursive method of other forms of art, violated every instinct of the homiletic theater, which, by its traditional commitment to popular entertainment and moral instruction, culti-

THE PSYCHOMACHIA

vated the obvious rather than the subtle. The morality stage was compelled by its own necessities to present mankind along with his vices and virtues; and he remains, in his various forms, a standard figure in the dramatized Psychomachia, making a third element in a tripartite grouping of personae. Since he is not a personification, his appearance in the allegory is actually the first of a series of literal intrusions that ultimately bring the metaphorical convention to an end. And it is worth noting now, although the point will get more attention later, that he is the first of the three groups of "characters" to be replaced by a concretely individualized person.

With man in the allegory, the massive military Psychomachia between the vices and virtues gives way to an action of another nature directed toward him. No longer imagined as battleground or fortress to be fought over, he now appears *in propria persona* as a sentient and responsive being to be *won over*. The old warfare dwindles from what it was in *The Castle of Perseverance*—

> Pride a-saylyth Meknesse with all his myth;
> Ire, a-geyns Paciensse, ful fast ganne he fyth;
> Envye, a-geyn Charyte strywyth full ryth;
> But Coveytyse a-geyns Largyte fytyth over longe.
>
> Coveytyse, Mankynd euere coveytyth for to qwell:
> He gaderith to hym Glotony, a-ȝeyns Sobyrnesse;
> Leccherye, with Chastyte ffytith ful fell,
> & Slawthe in Goddis seruyse, a-geyns Besynesse.
> Þus vycys, a-geyns vertues fytyn ful snelle;
> Euery buskith to brynge man to dystresse.
>
> [ll. 62–71]

—and moves aside for the richer possibilities of a dramatic method the essence of which is expressed in the epilogue to *Jack Juggler* (1553–58), a blend, typical for its time, of moral play and Plautine farce:

> Such is the fashyon of the worlde now a dayes
> That the symple innosaintes ar deluded
> And an hundred thousand diuers wayes
> By suttle and craftye meanes shamefullie abused.
>
> [ll. 1150–53]

Both poles of the transition and its direction are obvious in Skelton's *Magnificence,* an intermediate morality. The martial strife between moral opposites has here become verbal, a formal debate in the begin-

THE PSYCHOMACHIA

ning of the play between Felicity and Liberty (unrestrained will), each pressing his claim for dominion over the hero. From this moral argument Magnificence emerges safely, for Liberty loses his case and is put under the close supervision of Measure. But the respite is brief, for onto the scene comes Fancy, who doesn't argue. By deceit and flattery he soon installs himself in the bosom of his victim, and his followers, waiting their turns on the road now open to them, can gloat:

> Fansy hath cachyd in a flye net
> This noble man Magnyfycence,
> Of Largesse vnder the pretence.
> [ll. 403–405]

A second, equally cogent, reason for this transformation of the Psychomachia, once it is dramatized, exists in the nature of the stage itself—in its limitations and possibilities, already tested by the mystery plays. A battle may be richly described in an epic poem; in the theater it is never impressive. The pageantry of vices and virtues, which is what the allegorical battle became on the stage, was bound to give way to an articulated and sinuous plot; the hurly-burly of warfare to the dramatic interplay of individual action and dialogue; mere spectacle and declamation to the richer values resident in wit and word play, irony, insinuation, and deft persuasion; the blatancy of physical violence to the psychological and histrionic opportunities in temptation and seduction. A consideration of a different order, but no less compelling, is economy. Warfare, even when it is presented as a succession of small engagements, requires an army for its enactment; and an army is not only a cumbersome thing on the stage, it is also in every way uneconomical. Intrigue is another matter: it requires only an intriguer.

The marriage of the Psychomachia to the stage had for its issue just such an intriguer, a figure as constant to the moralities as the Psychomachia itself, and in the end more durable than the dramatic convention that gave him birth. His protean nature and devious history are the main objects of this study. But he will be seen more clearly if, before turning to him directly, we continue with the general examination of the morality drama.

CHAPTER FOUR

THE MORALITY PLAY

Vice is a monster of so frightful mien
As to be hated needs but to be seen.
POPE: ESSAY ON MAN

I

Allegory is a troublesome subject because its general nature is habitually confused with its specialized employment by Christianity.[1] It is an understandable mistake, growing out of its proliferation in medieval art and letters, to regard allegory as a mode of thought and expression invented by the Christian spirit, or by the pre-Christian spiritual impulse of the late Graeco-Roman world, and to treat it as such. As a result, it commonly receives an interpretation that limits its function to its characteristic use by Christianity, and identifies it almost exclusively with personification and abstraction. In its essential nature, however, allegory is not restricted to the unseen entities of the moral or spiritual world, nor is it essentially related to personification. If it seems to be fundamentally involved with both, that is only because Christianity, striving to express the immaterial, frequently so employed it.

In its widest literary sense, allegory is simply an allusive use of language, usually in the form of imagery and narrative, whereby one thing, which may be either concrete or abstract, is suggested through the appearance, the behavior, or the nature of another. As such it was known to the rhetoricians of the classic world—Quintilian for example:

Allegoria, quam inversionem interpretantur, aut aliud verbis aliud sensu ostendit aut etiam interim contrarium.[2]

And Quintilian, by way of illustration, can cite a passage from the *Bucolics* for the only reason that Virgil refers to himself when he speaks of the shepherd Menalcas. In the same broad and basic sense of allegory,

THE MORALITY PLAY

the various animals that appear in the first canto of *The Divine Comedy* are taken, on their political side, to signify Florence, the royal house of France, and the Papal See. Similarly the political allegory of *The Faerie Queene* alludes to nothing more abstract than the persons of Elizabeth, Leicester, Grey, and other prominent contemporaries of Spenser. More modern examples of allegorical allusion no less concrete come to mind in Poe's poem of "The Haunted Palace," which creates an architectural metaphor for the human head and countenance; and in Whitman's "O Captain! My Captain!" with its figurative elaboration of the death of Lincoln. "If we should call," says the Elizabethan Puttenham, following the Roman Quintilian, "the common wealth a shippe, the Prince a Pilot, the Counsellours mariners, the stormes warres, the calme and [hauen] peace, this is spoken all in allegorie." [3]

This demurrer against abstraction can also be inverted. Just as one side of the allusive equation does not necessarily involve an insensible, so the other side is not dependent on personification, and of this fact we sometimes need to be reminded. Otherwise we may wonder, as we move through Dante's concretely crowded worlds of punishment, purgation, and bliss, what the poet means by describing his poem as an allegory in his letter to Can Grande, when, in fact, its personifications, if indeed it contains any at all, are, by count, negligible.[4] We face the same consideration in the "continued Allegory" of *The Faerie Queene,* with its mixed population of personifications and of other figures who obviously are not personifications, neither the several knights who are the "patrones" of single virtues, nor Prince Arthur, whose "magnificence" embraces all of them. Una indeed is Truth personified, but the Redcross Knight is simply the Christian man dedicated, not without occasional default, to her service. This distinction, always present in Spenser's poem, is also sometimes explicit. In the second book, Sir Guyon, paying court to one of the damsels in the House of Alma, is disconcerted by her downcast eyes and preternatural blushing, until the explanation comes to him from Alma herself:

> Why wonder yee
> Faire Sir at that, which ye so much embrace?
> She is the fountaine of your modestee;
> You shamefast are, but *Shamefastnesse* it selfe is shee.
> [II.ix.43]

THE MORALITY PLAY

When we disengage allegory from the characteristic error which identifies it intrinsically with personification, we are also able to get rid of another misapprehension, in this case the fallacious distinction, sometimes attempted, between allegory and symbolism. Such a distinction is invalid for the reason that symbolism, properly considered, is simply one form of allegory; and the real discrimination concerns the difference between symbolism and another tool of the allegorical method, namely, personification. Symbolism and personification are both modes of thought, since otherwise, without such prior station in the mind, they could never have become modes of expression; but they are modes of thought moving in opposite directions between the material and immaterial worlds, those two great poles of human apprehension. A symbol is both an object and an emblem; that is to say, it is a concrete and literal thing so seen or employed as to suggest a meaning, or several meanings, beyond itself. The important point is that it always remains itself, always retains its character as an object or action in the sensible world, no matter what insensibles it suggests. The rose so often engraven on the tombs in the catacombs is emblematic of the paradisal life whose hope comforted the dying Christian, but it is nonetheless a carved imitation of the living, natural flower. The panther or unicorn of the medieval Bestiary, whatever sacramental meaning it also signifies, remains a panther or a unicorn. The punishments in Dante's Hell, while they are symbolic of the moral obliquities in the sins for which they are retribution, are not deprived thereby of their literal reality; and *The Divine Comedy* is an allegorical poem because its persons and actions in all three worlds, while retaining their literal existence, signify also, as symbols, several other levels of meaning. Successive moral states in the life of Halvard Solness are expressed through an architectural allegory whose symbols are the structures actually erected by the Master Builder. In Camus's *La Peste* the description of a North African city stricken by the plague is also, through its extended meaning, a general statement on the condition of human life in the world. A symbol, in other words, is a simile creating an equivalence between a sensible and an insensible, or between a particular and a generalization, moving from the former to the latter. Its medieval development reflects a habit of mind that does not invent symbolism

THE MORALITY PLAY

but exploits it, because to a remarkable degree that mind took a sacramental view of the physical world—its objects and events.

The same habit of mind, reversing its direction on the same path, is responsible for the efflorescence of personification in medieval literature and art. Personification, however, is not a simile involving an equivalence but a metaphor involving a transformation. It is always a sensible human image created by the imagination for the sake of materializing what is immaterial or vivifying what is inanimate, and may be the quality of Patience expressed through the figure of a woman sitting "on a monument, smiling at Grief," or the force of the north wind represented through the inflated cheeks and streaming breath of Boreas. But here a caveat is necessary. Personification, strictly understood, is only one mode of the metaphorical activity involved in allegory, for that activity is not necessarily anthropomorphic—witness Spenser's House of Temperance or Bunyan's Slough of Despond. *The Pilgrim's Progress,* in fact, is very little dependent on personification, since most of its human figures are not abstractions but types. The chief function of metaphor in Bunyan's allegory is topographical and scenic, expressing the vicissitudes in the inner life of the dedicated Christian through the variable landscape of his figurative journey. It is of some use to understand that the allusive use of metaphor creates a type of allegory which frequently employs personification without being limited to it. Medieval allegory is full of metaphorical castles, weapons, animals, landscape, and vegetation as well as metaphorical persons; and Bunyan, the last of the medievals in this respect, illustrates the mixture. In the House of the Interpreter, Christian watches the sweeping of a dusty room and receives the following interpretation:

This Parlor is the Heart of a Man that was never sanctified by the sweet Grace of the Gospel: the Dust is his Original Sin, and inward Corruptions that have defiled the whole Man. He that began to sweep at first is the Law; but She that brought Water, and did sprinkle it, is the Gospel.[5]

In short, Bunyan, employing personification without being restricted to it, creates a metaphorical journey, whereas Dante, moving with literal precision through three worlds, creates a symbolic one; and both journeys together exhibit the two hemispheres of the allegorical method.[6]

THE MORALITY PLAY

The morality plays are allegories because they are dramatized metaphors, and they are *moral* allegories because their metaphors allude to the moral and spiritual conditions of human life. But they do not have the metaphorical latitude enjoyed by other forms of allegorical literature. The representation of an abstract meaning through inanimate objects or through forms of life other than human, while congenial to narrative poetry and prose, is obviously not well suited to the physical limitations and uniquely human processes of the stage. Except for a metaphorical castle called Perseverance in the play of that name, a sword called Comfort in Redford's *Wit and Science,* and a few figurative objects besides that a diligent search might disclose,[7] it is almost altogether through its personae that the allegorical drama expresses its meaning—that is, through its personifications. If Man, who is a typical rather than an abstract figure, is subtracted from the characteristic tripartite grouping of the roles, there remain in the morality play two sets of personifications, aligned in opposition to each other according to the scheme of the Psychomachia. The virtues abet and exhort Man in the direction of his salvation; the vices are committed to tireless efforts aiming at his damnation. Among the games played by his Utopians, Sir Thomas More describes one in terms that reproduce the Psychomachia in what is probably the form originally enacted by the *Paternoster* plays:

The other [game] is wherein vices fight with virtues, as it were in battle array, or a set field. In the which game is very properly shewed both the strife and discord that vices have among themselves, and again their unity and concord against virtues: and also what vices be repugnant to what virtues; with what power and strength they assail them openly; by what wiles and subtlety they assault them secretly; with what help and aid the virtues resist and overcome the puissance of the vices; by what craft they frustrate their purposes; and finally by what sleight or means the one getteth the victory.[8]

Although this is the primitive military version of the struggle, its later replacement by a plot of intrigue does not change the nature of the issue or the opposed forces on each side of it. Whether expressed through combat or through persuasion, the activities of these two groups of antithetical figures, signifying the invisible conflict between Good and Evil in the human soul, compose the basic metaphor of the morality drama.

THE MORALITY PLAY

But the metaphor is actually twofold, or, if one wishes, the image of the moral *conflict* is supplemented by another in which Christianity was intensely interested, namely, the image of the moral *sequence*. Imitating Christian thought, Christian allegory always conceives human life as inescapably committed to movement, whether upward or downward, and the direction of that movement as determined by the outcome of the war between virtuous and vicious impulses. As a matter of proper moral edification, therefore, the Christian allegorist was concerned with charting the progressive stages of ascent or decline. Virtue leads upward toward virtue in the soul striving for beatitude, and, by a corresponding dynamic, in the soul headed downward vice follows vice in a descending scale of turpitude. In medieval allegory outside the drama the natural image for such a sequence is the allegorical journey, hindered or helped, kept to the true path or diverted from it, by figurative encounters along the way. And these encounters do not occur by caprice or accident, but represent, in their nature and sequence, a deliberated moral or spiritual formula, as perspicuous in its details to the initiated as it is perspicuous in its large outline even to the uninitiated when Dante describes his progressive liberation from a state of sin, first through the guidance of Reason, then of Theology, and finally of Revelation. Bunyan's Pilgrim, Spenser's Knights, and Dante himself travel a road on which, by rigid doctrinal logic, one thing leads to another.

Such an allegorical journey governs the structure of only three plays, the relatively late "wit" moralities. Otherwise it is absent from the morality drama. But the metaphor of the moral sequence, in more or less detail, is always present, and its intention always open to interpretation in the terms of traditional doctrine. For instance, in several of the moralities before 1525, notably *Perseverance, Mundus et Infans,* and *Nature,* the plot has a double movement. The human hero, born relatively innocent, sins and is recovered, but lapses once more into viciousness, until in his old age, or even after his death as in *Perseverance,* he is finally saved for good. A double action of this kind is provoked solely by the aim of communicating the theological meaning of Perseverance, without which virtue has only a precarious hold on the human heart. But not only the plot in general, the very entrances and exits of the separate personae take place in a sequence that obeys a

THE MORALITY PLAY

moral formula. At the climax of Skelton's *Magnificence,* for example, when the hero is at the very nadir of his well-earned wretchedness, the spiritual moments of his soul in their doctrinal succession are demonstrated by the entrance to him of a set of characters in a sequence about which there is nothing arbitrary. Despair comes in first advising suicide, and is followed by Mischief who brings a knife and a halter. Magnificence is just about to kill himself when Despair and Mischief flee before the entrance of Good Hope, who snatches the lethal instruments out of the hero's hands. Good Hope now recovers the sinner from his *desperatio* and turns his mind toward the opportunity afforded by penitence, whereupon Redress comes in patly and clothes Magnificence in new garments, signifying his moral conversion. Next enters Sad Circumspection to review for the hero his unhappy past and the lessons to be learned from it. Finally Perseverance comes in to perfect the penitent in moral fortitude.

It would be wrong to assume, because it has been illustrated, for brevity's sake, out of the end of the play alone, that such a method in the hands of the playwright is capricious or sporadic. The whole action of *Magnificence* up to its climax charts the hero's progressive decline in a sequence equally cogent. And every other morality play imitates the same method. For it is a structural principle of this kind of drama that whatever happens in it should be determined by a sequential thesis in fulfillment of an instructive purpose, and such a thesis maintains itself throughout the whole reach of the plot and in every part of it. When Sin, one of the evil personifications in *All for Money,* addresses the audience at the end of the play in explication of its meaning, his summary of mankind's career of vice defines the serial movement of the play as a whole:

> His money brings him to pleasure, and pleasure sendes him to me,
> And I sende him to Damnation, and he sendes him to hell quickly.
> [ll. 1417–18]

Medwall's *Nature* conveniently illustrates the same principle through some of its details. Sensuality describes to Worldly Affection the tavern revels of Man in the company of the Deadly Sins, who are now his cronies, but is interrupted by a doctrinal question:

> But yet I haue great maruayll
> That couetyse shuld dwell in hys company.

THE MORALITY PLAY

His reply is equally doctrinal:

> By my trouth lo and so haue I
> But one thyng I ensure you faythfully
> And that I haue espyed well
> That hyderto our mayster setteth no store
> By hys councell nor hys lore.
> Mary whan hys hed waxeth hore
> Than shalbe good season
> To folow couetyse and hys way.
>
> [part I, ll. 1236–45]

Avarice is properly the vice of old age, and since Man has not yet reached that point in his progressive moral decline, but will eventually, the idea is rendered explicit by the image of Avarice already in his vicinity but not yet admitted to his close company. In the same play Pride is about to depart alone, but Sensuality insists on going with him for no other except the good doctrinal reason that

> It ys accordyng for Sensualyte
> Wyth Pryde for to go.
>
> [part I, ll. 1271–72]

For on the stage the figurative journey of narrative allegory is, in a sense, reversed: the hero does not travel in order to encounter his moral adventures; they come to him in the shape of persons who seek to be admitted to his company and counsel, or depart as former friends and advisers now disgraced and banished. And the order of their appearance or disappearance is pregnant with meaning.

It is within this metaphorical framework of moral conflict and moral sequence that the plot of the morality play presents through visible forms and actions the invisible history of the human soul according to the Christian formulation. Such a play is a *sermo corporeus,* and the actors who move about in it are "the motives and impulses of man's own heart . . . taken from him, clothed in flesh and blood, and given him again for companions." [9] Nothing about their roles is arbitrary or idiosyncratic. Each part of the action (even the comic passages, as we shall see) has its homiletic compulsion as part of a schematic exposition of vice and virtue, their operation and effect. Each moment of the performance was a transparent allusion and solemn exhortation to every member of its audience. The dramatized story before him was not about men, but *Man.* It did not concern itself with diverse careers

THE MORALITY PLAY

among the miscellaneous and variable incidents of the external world, but with the universal experience of the soul among the central moral forces of human life, operating endlessly and uniformly on every member of the species. Vividly objectified to his eyes and ears were his own vices, the jeopardy of his own soul, and the way he too must take through repentance and perseverance to his own salvation. More effectively than any sermon could, the animated lesson brought home to his senses and reflection the moral implications of Christianity. And at no moment of the play did he feel himself more the object of its intention than during that standard piece of consolation which occurred at its end:

> For, thoughe a man had do alone
> The deedly synnes euerychone,
> And he with contrycyon make his mone
> To Cryst our heuyn kynge,
> God is also gladde of hym
> As of the creature that neuer dyde syn.
> [*Mundus et Infans*, ll. 862–67]

The theme was solemn and inspirational. To deny it dignity and power in its own time and place, on the score that its effort was reformatory or its meaning abstruse, is a modern prejudice. It was consecrated to an end for which the dramatic vesture was only a means— an end that remained for the morality drama exactly what it had been for Prudentius a thousand years before:

The way to victory is before our eyes if we may mark at close quarters the very features of the Virtues and the monsters that close with them in deadly struggle.

Nor did such a purpose die with the morality plays themselves. Like any great convention, it succumbed slowly and maintained a lingering authority as an idea even while it was being undermined in practice. In the epilogue to *Impatient Poverty,* by way of excuse for the "symple interlude" just performed, the audience received the justification traditional for all the morality plays: "It is but a myrrour vice to exclude." The same apology is made by the prologue of *Like Will to Like:*

> Herein, as it were in a glass, see you may
> The advancement of virtue, of vice the decay.

A generation later, although the drama has changed greatly in the interval, Hamlet has the very same idea about "the purpose of playing,"

THE MORALITY PLAY

whose end, both at the first and now, was and is, to hold, as 'twere, the mirror up to nature; to show virtue her own feature, scorn her own image, and the very age and body of the time his form and pressure.

[III.ii.23–28]

His words, carefully examined within the context of Elizabethan dramatic tradition, derive their meaning from the older drama of allegory and *personification*. To "catch the conscience" of the audience is the professed aim, just as it is implicit in the very nature, of every morality play. If, in the process, some concessions had to be made to that audience's craving for entertainment merely, they became accepted as adjuncts to the success of the godly objective. The whole relationship of dramaturgic means to pious ends, at least in theory, is effectively expressed in the epilogue of Skelton's *Magnificence,* the greatest of the English moralities for its literary power and dramatic skill:

> This mater we haue mouyd, you myrthys to make,
> Precely purposyd vnder pretence of play,
> Shewyth Wysdome to them that Wysdome can take:
> How sodenly worldly Welth dothe dekay;
> How Wysdom thorowe Wantonesse vanysshyth away;
> How none estate lyuynge of hymselfe can be sure,
> For the Welthe of this worlde can not indure.

[ll. 2547–53]

2

But the metaphors of the morality drama, while they define its allegorical substance, do not exhaust its reformatory zeal. In addition to them it is equipped with an apparatus of interpretation and appeal that characterizes not moral allegory in general but the didactic intention of a special type of moral allegory, and reflects the condition of its origin. Apart from the distinction between metaphor and symbol, another difference separates Bunyan from Dante, and divides as well the whole body of allegorical literature produced by the Middle Ages and the Renaissance. In part it is the difference between the patently instructive purpose within the explication previously quoted from *The Pilgrim's Progress* ("This Parlor is the heart of a Man . . . the Dust is his Original Sin," etc.) and the impossibility of such naked didacticism in *The Divine Comedy.* More largely, however, it distinguishes two schools of moral allegory, separated from each other by temper and technique—the one popular, homiletic, and conservative; the other aristocratic, literary, and experimental. The former, with a continuous history from Prudentius to Bunyan, addressed itself to common men and women, iterated the traditional themes and insights of Christian morality, presented them through images and actions equally traditional, and brought to moral allegory the homiletic clarity of the popular sermon. The other school, extending at least from the *Anticlaudianus* of Alanus de Insulis in the twelfth century to *The Purple Island* of Phineas Fletcher in the seventeenth, is marked by its literary, particularly its classic, affinities, by its complex and sophisticated meanings, and especially by its effort to be allusive rather than obvious, challenging the educated reader's powers of interpretation even at the risk of remaining obscure. Out of the popular tradition came the homespun hero, the overt metaphors, the Biblical and patristic dependence, the crude power of *Piers Plowman*. Out of the aristocratic tradition came the knights and ladies, the covert meanings and ingenious complexity, the indebtedness to classical and Italian literature, and the poetic elegance of *The Faerie Queene*. Defined by content and purpose, both poems are moral allegories. But the former, inheriting the spirit and method of the medieval sermon, is properly *homiletic*. The latter, by virtue of its heritage in poetry and rhetoric, is properly *literary*.

Such a discrimination opens a way into the special temper of the morality drama by affording some insight into its origin. For in homiletic allegory, whether narrative or dramatic, we hear the corrective energy and didactic candor of the medieval preacher. It is never characterized by that kind of allusive finesse which creates an Archimago or a Duessa to be interpreted as personifications of hypocrisy or deceit. Instead the homiletic metaphor nakedly presents Hypocrisy and Deceit and they preach their own exposure. Toward the end of the *Psychomachia* of Prudentius, for example, the virtues, having returned to camp after their victorious battle against the vices, confront a figure who suddenly rises up in their midst and wounds Concordia. They ask the assailant her name and get the following reply:

I am called Discord, and my other name is Heresy. The God I have is variable, now lesser, now greater, now double, now single; when I please, he is unsubstantial, a mere apparition, or again the soul within us, when

THE MORALITY PLAY

I choose to make a mock of his divinity. My teacher is Belial, my home and country the world.[10]

Such a speech is a sermon, and to see it called as much we have only to turn to that part of the *Roman de la Rose* composed by the moralist Jean de Meun. His long continuation, so opposite in spirit to the delicately allusive metaphor created initially by Guillaume de Lorris, effectively illustrates, by its proximity to the original poem, the contrast between the homiletic and the literary temper in allegory. One of the large digressions in Jean's part of the *Roman* deals with the council of war summoned by the God of Love as preliminary to an assault upon the Castle of the Rose. Among the captains present is Fals-Semblant, who is invited by Love to explain his quality and talent. Fals-Semblant explains at first that he is the child of Guile and Hypocrisy, and then continues at enormous length to describe his way of life, his habitations in the world among laity and religious, as well as among all stations and trades:

> Withouten wordis mo, right than,
> Fals-Semblant his sermon bigan,
> And seide hem thus in audience:
> "Barouns, take heede of my sentence!
> That wight that list to have knowing
> Of Fals-Semblant, full of flatering,
> He must in worldly folk hym seke,
> And, certes, in the cloistres eke." [11]

And so on for several hundred verses more he "sermoneth," warning his hearers against himself. This sort of translucent self-revelation is a standard feature of medieval homiletic allegory, and explains a good deal, incidentally, about the otherwise astounding confession, also in the context of a sermon, of Chaucer's Pardoner, whose words often derive verbatim from Fals-Semblant's predication. In *Piers Plowman* the same method is obvious when Reason preaches so compellingly to "þe felde ful of folke" that the Seven Deadly Sins, though in fact they are generalized types of vicious humanity rather than personifications, come up one at a time and make confession of their turpitude.[12] Although the poem is narrative, its homiletic pageant of the Sins is as dramatic as the living human voice, the give and take of dialogue, profane humor, vivid emotion, and implicit gesture can make it. And the pageant reveals its derivation through its auspices, for the preacher creates the event, his place of preaching the stage, and his congregation the audience. The verbal style of such a pageant also belongs to the church, being the style of the confessional or the pulpit.

The century that bore Langland's allegorical pageantry, the English translation of the *Roman de la Rose,* and Chaucer's Pardoner (his Parson as well) was also pregnant with the origins of the morality drama. That these origins took the form of pageants of the Deadly Sins and Christian Virtues has already appeared from surviving documents at York, Lincoln, and Beverley. From these accounts, as well as from Sir Thomas More's later testimony,[13] such pageants were military, with each vice matched in combat against its contrasting virtue. Unquestionably they were also pageants of verbal self-exposure, with each personification declaiming its nature and operation. For centuries priest, parson, and preaching friar had fashioned and conventionalized the Christian formula of vice and virtue until that formula took on visible shape and spoke in its own voice in the medieval marketplace. Dr. Owst has shown how heavily medieval preaching leaned for its effects upon the rhetorical and psychological opportunities afforded by allegory, and how easy was the transition from the allegorized sermon of the pulpit, naturally vivid and dramatic and often in dialogue, to actual pageantry and rudimentary stage action.[14] Wyclif's reference to the York *Paternoster* play is a testimonial to such a transition:

herfore freris han tauȝt in englond þe paternoster in engliȝsch tunge, as men seyen in þe pley of ȝork.[15]

In the early plays, moreover, there is frequent admonition to "Loue God & Holy Chirche" and even more frequent warning that the only way out of sin is through the sacramental offices of the Church. *Everyman* contains a long celebration of priesthood which has the sound of self-advertisement:

> There is no emperour, kinge, duke, ne baron,
> That of God hath commycyon
> As hath the leest preest in the worlde beynge.
>
> . . . .
>
> For preesthode excedeth all other thynge:
> To vs holy scrypture they do teche,

THE MORALITY PLAY

And conuerteth man fro synne heuen to reche;
God hath to them more power gyuen
Than to ony aungell that is in heuen.

[ll. 713 ff.] [16]

In short, just as the mystery cycles grew out of rudimentary dramatizations of the ritual of the mass in the early Middle Ages, it is possible to detect a similar development in the later Middle Ages whereby the morality drama evolved from allegorical pageantry that theatricalized the pulpit sermon. The earliest moralities, according to the oldest records, staged what Chaucer's Parson preached: the schematic exposition, by contrasting pairs, of the Deadly Sins and Christian Virtues.

For such a derivation the moralities themselves, from first to last, supply abundant internal evidence, since the method of the drama retains the method of the homily. The fact that they are moral allegories does not by itself account for the homiletic technique at work within them. In addition to their metaphorical action they invariably are equipped with a complex apparatus of exposition, and carry onto the stage the method of direct discourse and exhortation employed by a preacher toward his congregation. Prologue and epilogue, for instance, are undisguised sermons based on the text provided by the play between. This feature of the whole genre gets early exemplification in *Mankind,* in the long opening speech addressed by Mercy to the spectators of all conditions, the poor who stand as well as those rich enough to sit:

O souerence, I be-seche you yower condycyons to rectyfye
Ande with humylite & reuerence to haue a remocyon
    To this blyssyde prynce that ower nature doth gloryfye,
That ye may be partycypable of hys retribucyon.

. . . .

In goode werkys I a-wyse yow, souerence, to be perseuerante,
    To puryfye yower sowlys that thei be not corupte;
For yower gostly enmy wyll make hys a-vaunte,
    Yower goode condycions yf he may interupte.
    O ye souerens that sytt, & ye brothern that stonde ryghte wppe,
Pryke not yower felycytes in thynges transytorye!
    Be-holde not the erthe, but lyfte yower ey wppe!

[ll. 13 ff.]

THE MORALITY PLAY

And after the action itself has illustrated his exhortation, he industriously hammers the point once more in the admonition of his epilogue, closing with a theological flourish of Latin and a prayer:

> Wyrschepfyll sofereyns, I haue do my propirte;
>   Mankynd ys deliueryd by my sunerall patrocynye.
> God preserue hym fro all wyckyd captiuite
>   And send hym grace hys sensuall condicion to mortifye!
>
> Now for hys lowe that for vs receyuyd hys humanite,
>   Serche your condicyons with dew examinacion!
> Thynke & remembyr the world ys but a wanite,
>   As yt ys prowyd daly by diuerse mutacyon.
>
> Mankynd ys wrechyd, he hath sufficyent prowe;
>   There-fore God kepe ʒow all, *per suam misericordiam,*
> That ye may be pleseres with the angelles abowe,
>   And hawe to ʒour porcyon *vitam eternam. Amen!*
>
> [ll. 896–907]

How completely the action itself is a demonstration within the context of a sermon and how direct the homiletic relationship between stage and audience appear in some other words from the same play. Having rescued Mankind from the wickedness into which he had fallen, Mercy preaches to him on the subject of his spiritual enemies, the World, the Flesh, and the Devil, and concludes thus:

> These be your iij gostly enmys in whom ʒe haue put your confidens;
> Thei browt yow to Myscheffe to conclude ʒour temperull glory,
> As yt hath be schewyd this worschypfyll audiens.
>
> [ll. 881–83]

In one of the oldest of the surviving moralities, *Pride of Life,* the sermon appears in all its clerical trappings, delivered by Episcopus to the peccant Rex Vivus; and, in one form or another, the sermon remains a feature of the morality plays through the period of their decay. In addition to prologue and epilogue, moreover, any moment of the plot can provide an opportunity for one or several of the good personae to exhort the audience to take note of what is happening on the stage and to profit from it. In *Mundus et Infans,* after Manhood has repulsed him and gone off to revel with Folly, his new friend, in the taverns and stews, Conscience makes the audience the outlet for his heaviness:

> Lo, syrs, a grete ensample you may se:
> The freylnes of Mankynde,

THE MORALITY PLAY

How oft he falleth in folye
Throughe temptacyon of the fende.
[ll. 721-24]

And he continues for many lines more to bring home to their hearts the meaning of the sad example before their eyes, expostulating with them not to imitate it. In the *Interlude of Youth,* Charity, having been put into the stocks by Riot, Pride, and the young reprobate hero, preaches to the audience from that spectacular, though uncomfortable, position:

Lo maisters here you maye see beforne
That the weede ouergroweth the corne
Nowe maie ye see all in this tide
How vice is taken, and vertue set aside.
[ll. 541-44]

The audience that attended *Nice Wanton,* having observed the dramatic spectacle of youthful delinquency and its bad end, received in the epilogue the sermon proper to such an exhibition:

Right gentle audience, by thys interlude ye may se
  How daungerous it is for the frailtye of youth,
Without good gouernaunce, to lyue at libertye.

.   .   .   .

Therfore exhort I al parentes to be diligent
  In bringing up their children, yea, to be circumspect;
Least they fall to euill, be not negligent,
  But chastice them before they be sore infect.
[ll. 524 ff.]

Nor does the pulpiteering energy of this whole dramatic genre expend itself upon the audience alone. Sooner or later, and often more than once, the frail and erring human hero finds himself exposed to formidable moral lectures by his good counselors, who seek thereby to prevent his fall or to lift him being fallen.

But the technique of the pulpit and its reformatory effort in these plays go even further, repeating in all of them what we have already seen as a characteristic of homiletic allegory outside the drama: every personification of evil is converted into a preacher of straight exhortation. Vice, not content with disclosing itself for what it is and vaunting its power and ubiquity, must also deliver serious remonstrances against itself. The homiletic pageantry of the Deadly Sins in

112   *THE MORALITY PLAY*

The Castle of Perseverance is notable in this respect, each of the vices, as well as the World, the Flesh, and the Devil, declaiming to the audience the quality of the evil he personifies, and its pernicious opera-tion on the human race. Nothing in Skelton's *Magnificence* is more brilliant, satirically and metrically, than the separate expositions by the several vices of their natures and effects, of which the following by Courtly Abusion is only a slight example:

> Abusyon
>   Forsothe I hyght;
> Confusyon
>   Shall on hym lyght
>   By day or by night
>   That vseth me,—
>   He can not thee.
>   [ll. 829–35]

In *The Trial of Treasure,* Sturdiness, one of the vices, can step out of his role so far as to sermonize the audience against Lust, his personified companion in evil:

> This Lust is the image of all wicked men,
> Which in seeking the world have all delectation;
> They regard not God, nor his commandments ten,
> But are wholly led by their own inclination.
>
>   .   .   .   .
>
> Thus you see how men, that are led by their lust,
> Dissent from the virtuous, goodly and just.
>   [Dodsley, III, 275]

And in Lupton's *All for Money* the personification of Sin delays his last exit until he can digest the whole meaning of the play into a solemn warning to the audience:

> Doo you not see howe all is for money, masters?
> He helpes to make good all wrong and crooked matters:
> He cares not though at length he go to the deuill,
> So that with money he may his bagges fill.
>
>   .   .   .   .
>
> Therefore if any wilbe maried to my faire sonne Damnation
> Let them not blame me for I haue tolde his behauiour:
> Before you proceede therefore in this mariage
> Wey well with your selfe the daunger and charge.
>   [ll. 1413 ff.]

THE MORALITY PLAY

Could any moralist be more fervent on the side of right, or more uncompromising in the condemnation of evil?

Such examples of the sermonical apparatus within the moralities could be multiplied indefinitely. Each of the plays furnishes abundant internal evidence for the clerical origin of this whole dramatic genre and, what is still more important, illustrates the unique dramatic method specialized to fulfill on the stage the purposes of homiletic allegory. The metaphorical action remains a text with universal application, the stage remains a pulpit, and the audience, as they are frequently denominated by the plays themselves, remain a "congregation"—always within the homiletic consciousness of the play and the players, and subject at any moment to direct admonitory address. At the very beginning of *The Trial of Treasure* the actors are plainly instructed in their purpose: "Do all things to edify the congregation." This didactic intimacy between such a play and its spectators creates drama in a special dimension—a dimension which is, so to speak, perpendicular to the recessed and secluded plot which the audience merely overlooks and overhears in the modern theater. If we look for the origin of that most intimate—and perpendicular—feature of the sixteenth-century playhouse, the apron stage, we find it in this traditional intercourse. It is difficult to see how the close liaison between the morality drama and its spectators could have been achieved without just such a homiletic platform.[17] And the shrinking of that stage through the sixteenth and seventeenth centuries until it became the modern proscenium—to what better cause can it be assigned than to the corresponding withdrawal by the action it supported, that is, to the gradual divorce between play and audience resulting from the decline of the didactic convention in the English drama?

3

There is, however, another side to the morality play, its leavening element. Against so much moral seriousness in its plot and homiletic fervor in its preachments, both prescriptive, the unregenerate instincts of playwright and audience maintained a running quarrel. "A cuckowe for Conscyence," cries Folly in *Mundus et Infans*, "he is but a dawe! He can not elles but preche." And in the same play, Manhood, the

114 THE MORALITY PLAY

depraved hero, hurls his own feelings, as well as those of the popular theater, after the solemn figure who has just departed, having lectured him, and the audience, to distraction:

> Ye, come wynde and rayne,
> God let hym neuer come here agayne!
> [ll. 491–92]

The grave theme was accepted and respected, but in order to hold the allegiance of mere flesh and blood it required its countertheme, and the whole morality drama is marked by its large concession to farcical stage business and verbal humor.

One of the notable features of this mixture of high seriousness and mirth is the stress it receives in the "advertisements of levity" appearing in title and prologue.[18] The prologue of *Pride of Life* announces almost at once that "Here ye schullin here spelle Of mirth & eke of Kare." The title of *The Four Elements* describes it as "a new Interlude and a mery," and continues with advice to the actors that, for the sake of a shorter performance, "yf ye lyst ye may leue out muche of the sad mater." *Magnificence* is also "A goodly interlude and a mery" as well as a play whose high moral seriousness appears in the lines of the epilogue quoted previously. The title of Bale's *Three Laws* describes the play as a "Comedy" whereas within the text it is referred to as "thys tragedye." *Respublica* is "A merye enterlude," and *New Custom* maintains that it is "no lesse wittie then pleasant" although in fact it is neither. Lewis Wager's morality of *The Life and Repentance of Mary Magdalene* commends itself as "learned and fruiteful, but also well furnished with pleasaunt myrth and pastime." *The Longer Thou Livest* ends in tragedy, but is not prevented thereby from declaring itself "A very mery and Pythie Commedie." In *Enough Is as Good as a Feast* the human hero dies in sin and goes to hell, but the play is nonetheless "A Comedy . . . ful of pleasant mirth." Similarly the ending is unmitigated catastrophe for the erring hero of the "New and Mery Enterlude called the Triall of Treasure." *The Tide Tarrieth No Man* presents a variety of frail social types who meet a variety of bad ends, but the play insists that it is "A moste pleasant and merry commody, right pythie, and full of delight." Beggary, disease, and hanging are the fates of the sinners in *Like Will to Like,* "very godly and ful of pleasant mirth," and a self-conscious prologue provides an explanation:

THE MORALITY PLAY

And because divers men of divers minds be,
Some do matters of mirth and pastime require:
Other some are delighted with matters of gravity,
To please all men is our author's chief desire.
Wherefore mirth with measure to sadness is annexed:
Desiring that none here at our matter will be perplexed.
[Dodsley, III, 308]

Some of the late moralities and transitional plays announce even
sharper contrasts of mood. *All for Money,* the end of which shows Judas
and Dives making "a pitiefull noyse" as they are driven to hell by
Damnation, is entitled "A Moral and Pitifvl Comedie" while the
prologue inverts the paradox by describing the play as "a pleasant
tragedie." The title page of *The Conflict of Conscience* proclaims "An
excellent new Commedie. . . . Contayninge A most lamentable example of the dolefull desperation of a miserable worldlinge," with the
prologue invoking the principle of *dulce et utile:*

And though the Historie of itselfe, be too too dolorus,
And would constraine a man with teares of blood, his cheekes to wett,
Yet to refresh the myndes of them that be the Auditors,
Our Author intermixed hath, in places fitt and meete,
Some honest mirth, yet alwaies ware, DECORVM, to exceede.

The last examples are furnished by plays which are inspired by Seneca
and stand at the beginning of popular Elizabethan tragedy, without,
however, forsaking entirely the allegorical convention. The title page
of *Appius and Virginia* announces "A new Tragicall Comedie," a
description which does not refer to the later genre of tragicomedy
but to the very same medley of sadness and mirth that has already
appeared. Finally, and ultimately as well, there is the "Comedie" of
Cambises, enormously popular in its time, which wraps up its "Many
wicked Deeds and Tyrannous Murders" within the enticing formula:
"A Lamentable Tragedie Mixed full of Pleasant Mirth." These are the
plays, along with the early dramatic romances which also drew their
comic passages out of the morality tradition, that Sidney contemned as
"neither right Tragedies, nor right Comedies" but as deserving to be
called "mungrell Tragy-comedie." [19]

Such invitations to merriment and morality together, characterizing
the whole allegorical convention and surviving into the period of the
literal drama, express a popular taste that was never content with

116   THE MORALITY PLAY

sententious loftiness alone. Occasionally, as in the prologue to Rastell's *The Four Elements,* this appetite for comedy gets acknowledgment in words that betray diffidence, as if the playwright were hoping against hope that his serious theme would somehow slip into minds that were being held open for mirth alone:

> But because some folke be lytyll disposyd
> To sadnes, but more to myrth and sport,
> This phylosophycall work is myxed
> With mery conseytis to gyve men comfort,
> And occasyon to cause them to resort
> To here this matter, wherto yf they take hede
> Some lernynge to them therof may procede.
>
> [p. 7]

But more often the author simply accepted the character of his audience and the conditions of his stage and catered to both generously. That the mirth was not always "honest" and that vice was sometimes made more attractive than reprehensible appear from the frequent condemnations of the "lascivious toys" of "unchaste interludes" in criticisms of the stage, as well as from the contents of some of the plays and the protestations of others:

> And though perchaunce some wanton worde, doe passe which may not
>   seeme
> Or gestures light not meete for this, your wisdomes may it deeme,
> Accoumpt that nought delightes the hart of men on earth,
> So much as matters graue and sad, if they be mixt with myrth,
> Of both which here I trust you shall, as in a myrrour see,
> And that in such a decent sort as hurtfull shall not be.
>
> [*Virtuous and Godly Susanna,* ll. 16–21]

It is too easy, however, to look with modern eyes upon this pungent, earthy merriment and to misunderstand it. Whatever it sometimes became, at least in its origin and traditional aim it served a sober homiletic purpose, and was not a perversion of the reformatory intention of the morality drama. Although elements of farce are everywhere in these plays (and grossness in some of them), there is no such thing as a morality that is essentially a farce, unless it be the late and degenerate play of *The Marriage between Wit and Wisdom.* Nor, with the same exception, is there one whose humor is factitious in the sense that it is not a natural extension of its serious theme, according

THE MORALITY PLAY

117

to a relationship that will soon be evident. However far the risible urge of the playwright might carry him, he could protest, with theoretical justification at any rate, that his comic passages were aimed, as the prologue to *The Longer Thou Livest* puts it, "Not to thaduauncement, but to the shame of vice." A brief inspection of the comedy in these plays will lend meaning to such a protest.

Their mirth is versatile and complex, inhabiting all gradations between coarse and subtle, between rude foolery and deft satire. On its coarse, physical side it consists of such antics as sudden and grotesque entrances, shoving aside of the audience on and off stage with a traditional "make room, sirs," outlandish attire, brawls and beatings, obscene gestures, and numerous bits of improvised stage business inviting laughter. As broad verbal comedy its ingredients are insults, scabrous language, profanity, long speeches of pure fustian, puns, malapropisms, garbled proclamations, *doubles-entendres,* elegant foreignisms, and endless jests about anatomy, virginity, marriage, and the gallows. A standard item in this comic bill of fare is music, and sooner or later in every morality there are songs, sometimes accompanied by dance or jig, sometimes by musical instruments. *The Four Elements* contains a discussion on the difference between plain song and prick song, and a musical score is attached to the end of the play.[20] In *The Longer Thou Livest* the depraved hero Moros comes on stage "Synging the foote of many Songes, as fooles were wont," one of them worth quoting because it held the fancy of a later fool:

> Com ouer the Boorne, besse,
> My little pretie Besse,
> Com ouer the Boorne, besse, to me.
> [ll. 94–96]

Frequently these humorous elements combine into a substantial comic sequence. In *Mankind,* for instance, there is the mock court of Mischief, to which the hero, having surrendered to vice, is brought to be sworn "in forma iurys" as a member of the evil fellowship, while his warm old-fashioned coat is taken from him to be cut down into a gay jacket of the latest mode.[21] Bale's *King John* achieves an effective piece of doctrinal comedy when Sedition insists on being carried to the stage on the backs of the other three vices so that the audience may have ocular demonstration of the fact that he is their leader and they his underlings.[22] In the intermediate and late moralities this same contest for leadership usually precipitates a quarrel and brawl among the vices, with one of them finally acknowledged by the others as supreme in the hierarchy of evil, and the significance of this rivalry will receive attention later. Among the "lascivious toys" for which these plays were criticized is the stock sequence of amorous byplay between the strayed human hero and the meretrix, to a chorus of profane witticisms by the vices who have introduced him to her. More innocent but more durable is the laughter provided by that scene of Redford's *Wit and Science* in which Idleness exhausts her pedagogic patience upon Ignorance, a reluctant scholar, in the effort to teach him to spell his own name.[23]

In addition to such broad comedy, the moralities were capable of a more sophisticated type of humor equally useful to their corrective purpose. Satire is the weapon of the moralist, its laughter, mild or ferocious, draping its sermon; and the satire of the moralities is probably their most signal literary achievement. The range of their satirical energy is wide, reaching every form of private vice and public abuse that engaged the attention of contemporary social criticism. Four subjects, however, are satirized with such frequency and vehemence that they have a prominence in the plays beyond all others. These are the corruption of the law, sartorial excess, papacy in all its aspects (in plays dating from the Reformation), and the frailties of the feminine sex. In addition to these large themes, or in combination with them, the moralities abound in ironic reference to topics as familiar to the audience as their daily bread—to legal chicanery at Westminster, highway robbery on Blackheath, the amusements of the Bankside and the opportunities for dicing, drinking, and drabbing at taverns or inns specified by name, the momentary outrage in fashionable dress, the treatment of poor tenants by rich landowners, the domestic comforts afforded by the Counter, Marshallsea, and Newgate, usury and the tricks of the London moneylender, and a multitude besides of allusions equally pregnant and provocative. A satirical comedy of manners and morals twists in and out of the serious, often tragic, temper of these plays, leavening them with laughter that ranges from grave to gay.

The humor of the moralities has also a third side, structural and dramatic, which encloses a good deal of their verbal comedy and satire, and is especially relevant to the purpose of this study. It has

THE MORALITY PLAY

already been suggested that, according to the available evidence about the *Paternoster* plays, the allegorical drama grew out of homiletic pageantry, in which the virtues and vices defined themselves and their moral effects in human life by speeches they addressed to the spectators —the virtues solemn and hortatory, the vices sardonic, boastful, and indecent. The method of this pageantry is strong in all the surviving moralities, particularly on the side of evil. In *Perseverance,* for instance, the World, the Flesh, and the Devil, each on his separate stage, disclose their qualities and purposes in declamations filled with vaunt and seriocomic malice; and the Deadly Sins, when they are summoned by their three overlords, do the same, parading themselves before the spectators and expatiating on their names and natures. This familiarity between actors and audience maintains itself throughout the play, and when the Bad Angel makes his last exit with the soul of Mankind on his back, he bids everybody within earshot a polite but instructive goodbye: "Haue good day! I goo to helle." Such direct intercourse between play and audience is bred, as already shown, by the very nature of homiletic allegory, and remains a native characteristic of the whole allegorical drama after formal pageantry itself has disappeared. The spectators are always within the purview of the play, and at every opportunity their presence is acknowledged and exploited, but not only for the purpose, previously described, of treating them to solemn preachment. This homiletic intimacy gave rise, as its by-product, to a dramaturgic feature that supplied the morality with its liveliest humor and its greatest theatrical appeal. It consists of the continuous rapport throughout the play between its most important evil personage and the audience, whom he enlightens and amuses by conversing with them in a series of dramatic monologues (not to be confused with the soliloquies of the later drama) and sardonic asides. The range of this one-way conversation is large, but essentially it is an exposition of the speaker's allegorical nature and of his activity as contriver and manipulator of a play of intrigue. And although the tone is nearly always jocular, it is jocularity that can shift with ease from sheer badinage to the grimmest sort of homiletic mordancy. As broad comedy it can regale the audience with outright fustian:

> At Black heath field where great Golias was slain,
> The Moon lying in childbed of her last son:

THE MORALITY PLAY

> The Tiborne at Warwick was then King of Spain,
> By whom the land of Canaan then was won.
>   It happend between Peterborough and Pentecost,
> About such time as Ivy was made of Wormwood:
> That Childs work in Basil Wood with fire was lost,
> And all through the treason of false Robin Hood.
>   [*Enough Is as Good as a Feast*, Sig. B2 *recto*]

In almost as light a vein it can be a warning to the audience against "cousin cutpurse" lurking in their midst, or a bit of satirical byplay with the masculine spectators:

> Now must I to the stewes as fast as I may
> To fetch thys gentylman, but syrs I say
> Can any man here tell me the way
> For I cam neuer there
> Ye know the way parde of old
> I pray the tell me whyche way shall I hold.
>   [*Nature*, part II, ll. 405–410]

Or it can achieve a parting fillip of raillery directed at a startled female in the audience:

> Fare ye well no remedie I must depart,
> Fare well God be with you my Pigges nie with all my hart,
> If you had Grissils pacyence and condiscyons excelent,
> You and I would make a match to marye incontinent.
>   [*Patient and Meek Grissill*, ll. 1231–34]

Or it can, with a laugh of triumph, invite the audience to admire the achievement of the speaker:

> Hath not Corage contagious now shewd his kind
> By encouraging Greedinesse unto euil:
> Which late was drawing to a better mind,
> And now againe doth follow the deuil.
>   [*The Tide Tarrieth No Man*, ll. 424–27]

Although such monologues will come in for fuller discussion later, in connection with the allegorical personage to whom they invariably belong, it is useful to notice now that their service to laughter does not interfere with their service to homiletics. They are an integral part of the didactic intention of the allegorical stage, and achieve unique utility by charging moral instruction with humor and theatrical excitement.

THE MORALITY PLAY

In fact, all the humor of the moralities serves the same dual purpose, but in a more fundamental, more subtle way, and reveals its true nature, as well as its original significance, less through its actual content than through its auspices. It is from first to last and in all its forms the monopoly of the vices, eked out now and then by the depraved contribution of the human hero while he is under their influence. Otherwise he is as solemn as his guardian virtues always are. This whole body of mirth is purveyed by vice in a context where there is no such thing as innocent merriment, where levity, even in a form so apparently harmless as music, is the positive sign of virtue's absence. The comedy of the morality drama, in short, is entirely the *comedy of evil*. The farce, the satire, the direct titillation of the audience, the whole range of mirth from gross indecency to edged wit, proceeded from a traditional conception of vice and its characteristic behavior that marks not only the morality plays but has its roots deep in the theology and psychology of the Middle Ages. The façade of any Gothic cathedral displays the contrast between the stiff beatitude of the saint and the grinning, supple beastliness of the gargoyle. The devil of the mystery plays appears in a risible form, undignified and indecent, strutting and roaring his malice and then cringing and roaring his bafflement under the foot of God's omnipotence. Dante's demons in Malebolge (*Inferno* XXI–XXII) are dangerous but constrained by divine will, savage but also grotesque, indecent, and stupid. The Seven Deadly Sins of *Piers Plowman* compose a comedy of moral weakness and physical degradation. It is easier to observe than to explain this comic portrayal of evil everywhere visible in medieval art and letters. Probably it obeyed the same impulse evident today in the political cartoon—the degradation by caricature of a dangerous enemy, and an anodyne, therefore, applied to fear and pain. And the method of this degradation is at least twofold: as an image of frustration it expressed the essential impotence and vulnerability of evil, comforting the Christian with the pleasing vision of its defeat by God's will and its subjection to His purpose; as an image of baseness it allowed him contempt and laughter for the nature of evil by depicting it as rudely physical and bestial, a mirror of what is lowest, because least spiritual, in human nature and in the universe.

What distinguishes the mirth of the moralities from the medieval comedy of evil in general is its precise homiletic intention. The passages of farce in the plays have, at bottom, the purpose of making particular revelations about the nature of moral turpitude—its frivolity, its irreverence, its animalism, its destructive appetites, and its brainsick folly. About the homiletic aim, for instance, within that standard piece of morality fun, the quarrel and brawl of the vices, Sir Thomas More, in the passage from his *Utopia* already quoted, tells us something (not everything) when he says that it "shewed both the strife and discord that vices have among themselves." The aim is always to "show" something. If, as in *Mankind,* the foolery tastes greasy on the modern tongue, that must be regarded as the excess of the same intention. To say, as one scholar does, that *"Mankind* has as nearly as possible no plot," [24] or, as another does, that "this is a very degraded type of morality, aiming at entertainment rather than edification," [25] evinces a failure to read the play in terms of its proper substance, which is the complex homiletic meaning enclosing its humor—a failure, in other words, to read the play as a metaphor. A similar caution signals at us from the opposite direction. It is too easy today to exculpate merriment which the moralistic rigor of the allegorical playwright found guilty. The world of virtue in these plays is solemn and ardent, and levity of any sort is its enemy. In *Pride of Life,* for example, the figure of Mirth, jovial, musical, and the favorite of Rex Vivus as well as his jester and messenger, seems honest enough to a cursory view; but in fact he is not. He sits on the knee of the human hero, fondles and flatters him, and offers him the profane diversions that deflect the human heart from its proper striving upward. He is, according to the eschatological view of the play, a vice, along with Strength and Health—all three signifying the loss of spiritual concentration through distractions belonging to the World and to the Flesh.

The mirth of the moralities, in short, consistently pursued a homiletic purpose even if it pursued as well the favor of the playgoers. It is only toward the end of the allegorical convention, as the plays gradually lost their metaphorical transparency, that their "lascivious toys" also lost their allusive significance and took on the character of comedy or titillation for its own sake. But the significant development from the viewpoint of dramatic history does not concern the fact that vice on the stage became, according to contemporary criticism, morally seduc-

THE MORALITY PLAY

tive. It concerns the fact that the personified vices, because of their comic and dramatic vitality, became theatrically fascinating. For it is the paradox of the allegorical plays, anticipating the similar paradox of *Paradise Lost,* that their theatrical achievement was at the opposite pole to their ethical intention. Proclaiming the moral superiority of virtue, they uniformly demonstrated the dramatic superiority of vice. The personified virtues were verbose and wooden preachers, the personified vices trenchant and versatile actors. The former sought to dominate the conscience, but the latter actually dominated the stage. Shaped by the method of homiletic allegory, both sides of the Psychomachia undertook, as their common purpose, to persuade the audience that it is better being good than bad. As promulgated by the vices, this lesson became effective theater through the flexible energy of their enactment; and while their purpose was deadly serious, it was seriousness subtilized into satire, into derision, into comedy. Furthermore, by its very nature, the morality plot was put into motion by their aggression and sustained by their intrigue, leaving very little to the other side except to unpack its heart with words. While the virtues talked the vices acted, and by their physical exuberance and verbal pungency transmuted the pious monotony of the homily into the profane excitement of the play.

4

This dramatic verve on the part of evil, as well as its typical method, gets a primitive illustration in the early play of Mankind, where it contrasts vividly with the inert polysyllabic tedium of Mercy, the human hero's guardian personification. As always, the method is cast as a demonstration, conducted in this instance by Titivillus, an allegorized figure whose motive for contriving the ruin of Mankind is impersonal, professional, and implicit in his name and nature, for "propyrlly Titiuilly syngnyfieth the fend of helle."[26] His concern is with his audience, for whom he provides both a display of his evil artistry and a moral lesson, serving at once their pleasure and edification. He has already proclaimed his name and talent:

> *Ego sum dominantium dominus,* & my name ys Titivillus!
> ȝe that haue goode hors, to yow I sey *caueatis.*
>
> [ll. 468–69]

THE MORALITY PLAY

Now he announces his special intention in regard to the pious, seemingly impervious, hero:

> To speke with Mankynde I wyll tary here this tyde,
> Ande assay hys goode purpose for to sett a-syde.
> The goode man, Mercy, xall no lenger be be hys syde;
> I xall make hym to dawnce a-nother trace!
>
> [ll. 518–21]

He invites the audience to observe carefully each step of his device for driving Mankind, a poor farmer, from patience to impatience, from piety to impiety:

> To yrke hym of hys labur I xall make a frame.
> Thys borde xall be hyde wnder the erth preuely;
> Hys spade xall enter, I hope, on-redyly;
> . . . he xall be uery angry
> And lose hys pacyens, peyn of schame.
>
> [ll. 525–29]

And in the name of their entertainment and instruction he invokes their cooperative silence:

> Ande euer ȝe dyde, for me kepe now yower sylence!
> Not a werde, I charge yow, peyn of xl pens!
> A praty game xall be schowde yow or ȝe go hens.
>
> [ll. 582–84]

Mankind enters, tries to delve the intractable earth, gives it up as a bad job and falls to his prayers. Titivillus, having stolen his spade, returns now "invysybull," whispers in his ear that "a schorte preyere thyrlyth hewyn," and finally distracts him utterly from his devotions by the profane insinuation of a physical need. With Mankind off the stage, Titivillus pockets the prayer beads and invites the admiration of the audience for his skill and success so far:

> Mankynde was besy in hys prayere, ȝet I dyde hym aryse;
> He is conveyde, by Cryst! from hys devyn seruyce.
> Whether ys he, trow ȝe? I-wysse, I am wonder wyse.
>
> . . . .
>
> Titivillus kan lerne you many praty thynges!
>
> [ll. 558 ff.]

He discusses with them the remainder of his intrigue, promises them more fun if they will be patient, and heralds the reappearance of his victim:

THE MORALITY PLAY

3e xall se a goode sport yf 3e wyll a-byde.
Mankynde cummyth a-geyn, well fare he!

. . . .

I hope of hys purpose to sett hym a-syde.
[ll. 569 ff.]

Back on the stage, Mankind reveals his spiritual decay by going to sleep although he should be at church for evening services. The last enterprise of Titivillus is to bring about his victim's complete fall from grace by alienating him from his good counselor Mercy, and for this end his device is to whisper slanders about Mercy into the ear of the sleeping hero. Once more he invites the attention and silence of his audience:

3e may here hym snore, he ys sade on slepe.
I-wyst, pesse! The deull ys dede! I xall go ronde in hys ere.
[ll. 585–86]

His purpose achieved, his virtuosity fully demonstrated, Titivillus takes his leave of the spectators, not, however, without a homiletic valedictory that keeps the moral record straight:

For-well, euerychon, for I haue don my game,
For I haue brought Mankynde to myscheff & to schame.
[ll. 598–99]

The pivotal action of the allegorical drama, repeated as many times almost as there are plays, is a more sophisticated version of just such a demonstration and such a lecture. Although Titivillus is a figure in transition from devil to vice and his guile still largely physical, the Psychomachia in *Mankind* has already evolved into a deft spiritual intrigue—a curious merger of solemn meaning and comical method—manipulated by a laughing artist who presents himself to the audience like a sleight-of-hand performer in vaudeville, with the important addition that he is also a moralist whose running comment exposes the tricks of his trade and the serious consequence of his success. The play governed by such a theatrical method can never forget, or pretend to forget, that it has an audience to edify and reform. Its function is always expository and each role a self-conscious moral exhibition. The figures of evil are no exception to this didactic principle. They, no less than the virtues, preach on the side of the angels and contribute their efforts to "the scorn of vice." But here a distinction intervenes. The

THE MORALITY PLAY

virtues, no longer warriors in a military Psychomachia, are reduced to solemn, pontifical, lifeless homilists; whereas the vices monopolize the theatrical life of the play—its diversified intrigue and its humor. All the elements of comedy and satire are concentrated in their hands and the whole energy of the plot springs from their activities. They are the playmakers, the chorus, the comedians, the satirical moralists, and the agents of destruction of every play in which they appear. As personifications in homiletic allegory it belongs intrinsically to their nature that they should put themselves, their intrigues, and their human victim on moral display, conducting themselves as masters of dramatic ceremonies whose first duties are to the spectators. They always say in effect: "This is what I am, and now I'll show you what I can do with frail and foolish humanity. Watch the demonstration and be amused and edified at once." Such a role, in short, is characterized by an expository relationship with the audience that has already been defined as its *homiletic dimension,* by a unique fusion of serious purpose with comical method that creates a *comedy of evil,* and by a metaphorical aggression through *deceit* that represents the evolved form of the Psychomachia.

Something else is intrinsic in the nature of such a role and characterizes it uniformly. Although the moral personifications appear on the stage in the shape of human beings, the similarity does not go much deeper. They are elemental parts of the moral life of humanity, but as elements they have no moral life of their own. No feature about them is more basic, or obvious, than their *allegorical motivation.* Mankind, as the representative human creature, is subject to all the moral impulses belonging to human nature. He moves backward and forward between avarice and generosity, pride and humility, envy and love, and so on, through all the phases of the inward life as they are codified by Christian ethics. If he does not finally succumb to the evil tendencies that flock within him and define his human frailty, that is because he has the strength, or grace, to overcome them, and because he is helped by the contrary tendencies toward good residing within his soul. In any case, his life is a moral conflict and a moral choice among a multitude of contending impulses. But each of these impulses, as it is personified on the morality stage, expresses in its behavior a very different dynamic. A personification, no matter how persuasive its human

THE MORALITY PLAY

similitude and vital energy in play or story, is subject to none of the multiplicity which defines the moral condition of human life. It is an elemental force, constrained to its single activity by what C. S. Lewis calls its "esse." What it does is what it has to do by virtue of what it explicitly and indivisibly is. Personifying one of the irreducible modes of life's complex substance, its behavior and motivation are inherent in its name.

The morality plays themselves are sufficiently explicit on this point. In *Pride of Life,* the nuntius, whose name is Mirth (or Solas), departs with alacrity and with a song on a mission from the Queen to the Bishop, explaining to his mistress:

> Madam, i make no tariyng
> With softe wordis mo;
> Ffor I am solas, i most singe
> Ouer al qwher i go. *et cantat.*
> [ll. 319–22]

In a bit of byplay in Medwall's *Nature,* Pride, who is Man's favorite among the Deadly Sins, is the victim of a deceitful stratagem by Envy, who informs him that he has fallen into disgrace and that his safest course is to go into retirement, out of the reach of Man's wrath. When Pride runs off to hide, Envy offers for his trick an explanation that makes an effective distinction between the motives of practical life and those which are allegorical:

> Mary cause had I none
> But only yt ys my guyse
> Whan I se an other man aryse
> Or fare better than I
> Than must I chafe and fret for yre
> And ymagyn wyth all my desyre
> To dystroy hym vtterly.
> [part II, ll. 931–37]

In the same way, in *New Custom,* Perverse Doctrine can be motivated to renewed effort by an appeal to the meaning of his name:

> Remember also, that it were a great shame
> For thee to have forgotten thy own name.
> Perverse Doctrine, of right, must the truth so pervert
> That he never let it sink into any man's heart.
> [Dodsley, III, 28]

THE MORALITY PLAY

When the young hero of Redford's *Wit and Science,* an educational allegory, lingers in indecision between Idleness and Honest Recreation, confused by their contrary claims to his allegiance and asking both to declare themselves, he receives from the latter the pertinent reply:

> What woolde ye more for my declaracion
> Then evyn my name, Honest Recreacion?
> And what wold ye more her to expres
> Then evyn her name, to, Idlenes?
>
> [ll. 351–54]

And in *The Conflict of Conscience* one of the evil personifications undisguises himself in words that explain his homiletic function as well as his monolithic commitment to action:

> Zeal nay, no Zeale, my name is Tyranny,
> Neither am I ashamed who doth my name knowe
> For in my dealings the same I will showe.
>
> [ll. 838–40]

This kind of motivation is properly allegorical in the sense that it is constrained by the unitary principle resident in personification; and, since it has nothing to do with choice or passion, it is amoral. The personification is timeless and so is his behavior. His appearance in the play is simply another illustration of what he has always done and always will be doing. Once he makes clear his signification in speeches addressed to the audience, his action has all the motivation it needs. Sometimes in the later moralities his role consists of a series of actions, providing by accumulation an impressive exposition of his name and nature. And sometimes, in plays which retain only a partial allegiance to allegory, his allegorical motive is complicated by the addition of other causes belonging to the practical issues of human life. In the play of *Sir Clyomon and Sir Clamydes,* an amalgam of chivalric romance with allegorical vestiges, Subtle Shift piles one dishonest stratagem on top of another, offering all sorts of reasons. Beneath them all, however, remains his abstract name, with its uncomplicated basic explanation for everything he does:

> Although vnder the tytle of Knowledge my name I do faine,
> Subtill Shift I am called, that is most plaine.
> And as it is my name, so it is my nature also,
> To play the shifting knaue wheresoeuer I go.
>
> [ll. 211–14]

THE MORALITY PLAY

But he is a later development and belongs to a later chapter. What needs to be reckoned with now is that, as an almost invariable feature of the morality plays, a stage figure, in all the habiliments of humanity, promotes an intrigue, or a series of intrigues, for the sake of illustrating to the audience his allegorical meaning. He is the creator of the action and its interpreter, as well as being the central display in a moral pageant of his own designing. His motivation is implicit in his name and nature, and does not need to grow out of any relationship with the other characters, except insofar as his victims present to him the instigation of their virtue. It is only necessary that during his first appearance he should announce his name and declare his strategy, supplementing both by a running moral commentary throughout the play. The audience that attended Lewis Wager's *The Life and Repentance of Mary Magdalene,* for instance, found themselves addressed as follows by the grinning figure on the stage:

> Infidelitie is my name, you know in dede;
> Proprely I am called the Serpent's sede.
> Loke, in whose heart my father Sathan doth me sow,
> There must all iniquitie and vice nedes growe.
> The conscience where I dwell is a receptacle
> For all the diuels in hell to haue their habitacle.
> You shall see that Marie's heart within short space
> For the diuell hym self shall be a dwellyng place.
> I will so dresse her that there shall not be a worse.
> To her the diuell at pleasure shall haue his recourse.
> I will go and prepare for her such a company,
> As shall poison her with all kyndes of villanie.
>   [ll. 235–46]

Such a figure, laughing instigator of mirth and damnation, presents himself for consideration another way. Hitherto in this study the theme of evil in the moralities has enveloped the vices in general. But from the crowd of his personified fellows one of them gradually emerged to unique prominence. Dominating the stage right up to the Shakespearian drama, he impressed upon successive generations of playwrights and playgoers the traditional image of an intriguer who moved against his victims for a reason that had nothing to do with the passionate impulses of human life.

CHAPTER FIVE

EMERGENCE OF THE VICE

Now sylence I desire you therefore,
For the Vyce is entering at the door.
KING DARIUS, *Prologue*

I

The Devil, who in the Christian mythos is the father of evil, has only a negligible place in the morality drama. In the cyclical mysteries and in the miracles he is a familiar personage—indispensable to such dramatized episodes of the Christian story as the Revolt of the Angels, the Temptation of Christ, and the Harrowing of Hell. But for several reasons he does not properly belong in homiletic allegory, and the morality plays reflect that fact. As Belial, Lucifer, or Satan he exists in only nine of the almost sixty surviving plays that adhere, altogether or in part, to the morality convention; and even in these nine his roles, with one exception, are insignificant. The exception is *Wisdom* (1461–85), where Lucifer in the disguise of "a goodly galont" appears to the central figure of Anima and argues her out of her ascetic purity. But even here his action is brief and confined to the first part of the play, its homiletic burden depending not on him but on the dances and pageantry of the numerous vices that afflict the depraved Anima in the latter half. Elsewhere in the morality drama, when he does appear at all, he is on the fringe of the play, part of its evil scenery rather than an active participant in its plot.

By their distribution as well as by their dearth, the Devil's few roles in the moralities reveal how alien a figure he is in that type of drama. His appearances on the allegorical stage are almost entirely confined to the formative period of its infancy or to its last few decades, the period of its dotage. In the early moralities, in addition to his role in *Wisdom,* he is Belial in *Perseverance,* one of the homiletic trio whose other two

EMERGENCE OF THE VICE

members are Mundus and Caro. He is also a member of the same group in the hybrid miracle-morality of *Mary Magdalene* (Digby). The Devil who thus appears in schematic association with the World and the Flesh is no longer the compact "historical" figure of Christian theology and folklore, but half a moral personification in close company with two other personified abstractions, the chief significance of all three lying in the triple classification they provide for the Seven Deadly Sins. His half abstracted meaning in these early plays is prologue to his almost total disappearance from the moralities that follow. After 1500 and up to 1560, the central period of the allegorical drama, when at least forty of the surviving plays were composed, the Devil makes a trivial appearance in only one of them, *Lusty Juventus,* where in a single scene he implores the help of the Vice Hypocrisy against the religious truth and purity of the Reformation.[1]

It is only in the late period of the moralities, when the allegorical convention is rapidly losing its hold on the stage, that he once more appears with any frequency, and then he has very minor roles in five plays, all of which are also adulterated by other nonallegorical features. In none of these latter plays is he anything more than the functionless and undifferentiated source of all evil, whose deputies in the real action of the plot are the vices. In *The Conflict of Conscience* he exists only as a prologue. In *Enough Is as Good as a Feast* he comes in once, at the end, to clear the stage by lugging off the corpse of Worldly Man to hell. In *Like Will to Like, Virtuous and Godly Susanna,* and *All for Money* he associates exclusively and briefly with the Vice, commissioning him to his work, while the Vice belabors him with insults and treats him generally with mocking contempt. In all these plays he is for the most part a grotesque and lugubrious figure, without verve or alacrity —a lumbering, helpless target at whom the Vice shoots his scurrilous jests. He never has any part in the intrigue itself and never associates with its human victims. His sole, easily dispensable, business is to commission the Vice, without whose aid he is helpless. It is only in the later Elizabethan drama of literal plot and compact human characters that the Devil reasserts himself as a dramatic figure of some consequence, as in *Doctor Faustus, Grim the Collier of Croydon, A Knack to Know a Knave,* and *Histriomastix,* to confine ourselves to plays of the sixteenth century.

EMERGENCE OF THE VICE

For this estrangement between the morality drama and the Devil the reasons are not far to seek. He is not a personification but an historical figure out of Christian theology and folklore, and an illogical intrusion, therefore, into the drama of abstraction. He is too much the composite of undifferentiated evil to be homiletically useful, his few appearances serving only to demonstrate the source of all vice, whereas the moralities were mainly concerned to analyze and illustrate the operation of the separate vices upon the human soul.[2] And, as in the mystery plays, he is traditionally a humorless figure who provoked laughter chiefly by his fantastic appearance, his obscenities, and his grotesque exclamations of dismay.[3] The moralities wanted a homiletic showman and satirist—a nimble trickster, dissembler, and humorist—on the side of evil; and the traditional stage Devil, besides suffering the disqualification of his nonallegorical nature, had none of these talents. As far as the allegorical drama is concerned, therefore, the Devil is dead.

In his place, as energetic and witty exponents of the evil side of the Psychomachia, are the numerous vices, who fulfilled the homiletic purpose of the moralities by illustrating in detail the moral evils in human life. Although the vices of the later moralities occasionally refer to the Devil as their father or godfather, their relationship to him is doctrinal and hierarchic rather than genetic. He is their father only in the loose sense that he is the universal source of evil; and they are, figuratively, his children because by their domination over man they serve the Devil's purpose, which is to bring the human soul to hell. In the early moralities the metaphorical relationship is not filial but feudal, the Seven Deadly Sins adhering to the World, the Flesh, and the Devil as their knights and retainers.[4] This generic distinction between the Devil and his agent vices is well expressed by Charles M. Gayley:

The Vice is neither an ethical nor dramatic derivative of the Devil; nor is he a pendant to that personage, as foil or ironical decoy, or even antagonist. The Devil of the early drama is a mythical character, a fallen archangel, the anthropomorphic Adversary. The Vice, on the other hand, is allegorical,—typical of the moral frailty of mankind. Proceeding from the concept of the Deadly Sins, ultimately focussing them, he dramatizes the evil that springs from within.[5]

EMERGENCE OF THE VICE 133

Nothing illustrates more clearly the difference between the genus vice and the genus Devil than the contrasting ways they are motivated. The latter in all his stage appearances is invariably anthropomorphic and passionate, for his assault upon mankind has its cause in emotions that make him a moral personage. He is moved by hatred of God and by envy of man, and his purpose is to achieve revenge upon the Creator by destroying the creature. The Lucifer of *Wisdom,* the only one of his diabolic kind in the moralities who is an active aggressor, expresses himself like the aggrieved villain in any melodrama of passionate human life:

> Owt harow, I rore
> For envy I lore,
> My place to restore,
>   God hath mad a man;
> All cum they not thore
> Woode & they wore,
> I xall tempte hem so sorre,
>   For I am he that syn be-gane.
>
> I was a angell of lyghte;
> Lucyfeer, I hyght,
> Presumynge in Godis syght,
>   Werfor I am lowest in hell;
> In reformynge of my place, ys dyght
> Man, whan I haue in most dyspyght,
> Euer castynge me with hem to fyght;
>   In that hewynly place he xulde not dwell.
>   [ll. 325–40] [6]

This is the violent stage Devil of the mysteries, whence he was borrowed for the nonce at a time when the moralities were still searching for their proper style and method. A century later, in the decline of the moralities, the same figure reappears occasionally, full of the same sound and fury, except that he is now completely impotent and reduced to imploring the help of the whimsical Vice. In the late morality of *All for Money* he is brought on stage by the following direction: "Here commeth in Satan the great deuill as deformedly dressed as may be." A moment later, having treated "Sinne" the Vice with insufficient deference, he is inundated by a shower of abuse and threats of

EMERGENCE OF THE VICE

bodily harm. The Vice calls him "bottell nosed Knaue" and worse epithets besides, threatens to forsake him, and keeps the dismayed demon at a distance by offers of violence: "Stande backe in the mischief, or I will hit you on the snout." Satan has no recourse except to cajole and implore ("Ohe my friend Sinne, doe not leaue me thus"), while a stage direction has him hysterical with grief and impotence: "Here Satan shall crie and roare." [7]

But for all his grotesquerie, his elongated nose, and his fantastic array, the Devil's motives are passionate and clear. In *Virtuous and Godly Susanna* Satan succeeds in gaining the cooperation of Ill Report against the reputation of that Biblical heroine—not, however, without meekly absorbing the Vice's insolent jests—and departs confident:

> And let vs see if God with all his myght,
> Can defende this soule from oure auncient spyght.
> [ll. 115–16]

Left alone on the stage, Ill Report lectures the audience on the motivation of the Devil:

> The pollicy of the Deuill, the enuie he doth beare,
> The man he seekes to ouerthrow, all such as God doth feare.
> [ll. 147–48]

and, incidentally, makes obvious the very different order of motivation which sends him into action:

> My selfe will blow the leaden Trumpe of cruell slaunderous fame,
> Lo thus my Dad I please I trowe, *and thus my nature showe.*
> [my italics; ll. 180–81] [8]

Here, in juxtaposed contrast, is the distinction between moral evil and that kind of homiletic exposition to which the moral plays were committed. The purposes of the Devil are those of a complex moral being. The whole purpose of the Vice is to illustrate his name and nature and to reflect upon the audience the single moral idea he personifies. The former acts to achieve his desires, the latter only to show what he is. Between the two no ethical continuity is possible because in the nature of a personification there is nothing that is subject to ethical definition.

2

One discrimination invites another. Since the Devil is not significant in the integral content of the moralities, there remain on the side of

EMERGENCE OF THE VICE

evil the significant vices, and among them, in play after play, there appears a distinction, hitherto unfathomed, between *the vices* and *the Vice*. So far in these pages both words have been used indiscriminately, but the difference between them is of signal importance in the development of the Tudor drama and challenges clarification. In spite of considerable dispute on the subject, there can be no real question about the origin of the dramatic figure of the Vice, or about the derivation of his name.[9] He is not, as some scholars have supposed, the "summation" of the Seven Deadly Sins; but he springs, by a century-long process of doctrinal emphasis and dramatic specialization, from the numerous vices, including the Deadly Sins, who came upon the morality stage out of the diffuse homiletic allegory of medieval Christianity.

We have already seen that the limitations of the stage and the needs of the dramatic plot, with its human hero, gradually transformed the Psychomachia from warfare to intrigue. The same needs and limitations, plus a homiletic principle within the moralities which has not yet come forward, magnified one of the vices in almost every play into a figure of special prominence, the intriguer par excellence. By dint of his doctrinal eminence and leading role in play after play he acquired distinctive theatrical personality and status beyond the allegorical features he shared originally with his many brethren on the evil side of the Psychomachia. And as he became the most persistent and popular character stereotype on the early Tudor stage, the word *vice,* which originally had simply a moral meaning, acquired in his case a special dramaturgic significance. It became the familiar theatrical label for the stock role of the homiletic artist who, as protagonist of the forces of evil, created and sustained the intrigue of almost every morality play. The Vice is at once the allegorical aggressor, the homiletic preacher, and the humorist of the moralities—and of plays which, except for his part in them, belong to the later convention of the literal drama. He is designated "the Vice" in the players' lists and stage directions of no less than twenty plays surviving out of the sixteenth century, and in a score of others his functions reveal him clearly although his title does not actually appear.[10] His remarkable impress on the imagination of his own time and on the memory of the generation that outlived his active career on the stage is affirmed by so many notices and recollections of him in sixteenth and seventeenth century documents that in

EMERGENCE OF THE VICE

this respect at least no other feature of the morality drama can compete, even remotely, with the Vice.

Confusion as to his origin arises largely from the comic side of his role, frequently overstressed by scholarship to the neglect of his serious homiletic meaning and of the tragedy he always tries to, and often does, inflict. It also arises from the opinion that the theatrical label of "the Vice" appears for the first time in two plays mainly outside the allegorical convention. These are the *Play of the Weather* and the *Play of Love,* both by John Heywood, and printed, for the first time apparently, by William Rastell in 1533 and 1534 respectively. Both plays, neither of them characterized in any obvious way by the distinguishing features of the morality drama, contain what seem to be the earliest notices of the dramaturgic role of the Vice. In *Weather* the comic manipulator of the action appears in the list of players' names as "Mery reporte the vyce"; and in *Love* the four roles are presented as follows:

> A man a louer not beloued.
> A woman beloued not louyng.
> A man a louer and beloued.
> The vyse nother louer nor beloued.[11]

Both roles, superficially examined, seem to present nonallegorical comedians, provoking at least one scholar to argue that the Vice is essentially a dramatic outgrowth of the medieval clown or jester, extraneous to the morality drama and brought into it merely to create its comedy.[12] Another, the editor of Skelton's *Magnificence,* was similarly misled, and in his otherwise valuable introduction to that play makes superfinical distinctions between its evil personifications, conferring vicehood only on those roles that seem sufficiently comic to deserve it.[13] What such students of the subject fail to notice is that by Heywood's time one of the vices in each morality play had become distinguished doctrinally and dramatically from his allegorical cohorts (all of them more or less comic), and had developed, in consequence, a theatrical personality and an apparatus of stage business substantial enough so that he could be lifted out of his allegorical and homiletic context and cultivated in comedy of the type Heywood was writing. What they also fail to notice (although Ramsay indeed is struck by the fact that the only abstract name in *Weather* belongs to "Mery reporte the vyce") is that Heywood's two Vices retain a variety of allegorical features out

EMERGENCE OF THE VICE 137

of their morality origins. Nor do they notice that other plays in the decade of the thirties, and they indisputable moralities, also provide the word "vice" as a theatrical label for their evil personifications.

At the end of *Three Laws,* a morality written by John Bale as early, it is probable, as 1531,[14] the following direction appears:

The aparellynge of the six vyces, or frutes of Infydelyte.

Lete Idolatry be decked lyke an olde wytche, Sodomy lyke a monke of all sectes, Ambycyon lyke a byshop, Couetousnesse lyke a pharyse or spyrituall lawer, false doctryne, lyke a popysh doctour, and hypocresy lyke a graye fryre. The rest of the partes are easye ynough to coniecture.

[after l. 2081]

Such sartorial advice respecting "the six vyces" in Bale's morality severely challenges Heywood's priority in this type of nomenclature. Nor is Bale's play the only such challenge. Sir David Lindsay's *Satire of the Three Estates,* the great Scottish anti-Catholic morality, is of doubtful date; but a record of its performance is contained in a letter, dated January 26, 1540, sent by Sir William Eure to Thomas Cromwell; and the play presents internal evidence that it was written and produced as early as 1535.[15] In Lindsay's *Satire,* as it is preserved in the Bannatyne manuscript of 1568, occur the following stage directions:

Heir sall the thre vycis cum and mak thair salutatioun to the king . . .
Heir sall the thre vycis pass to ane counsale.
Heir the vycis gais to the sprituall estait . . .

[after ll. 1925, 2057, 2101 respectively]

In short, contrary to the usual assumption that the earliest theatrical reference to the role of the Vice exists in Heywood's *Weather* and *Love,* two plays largely outside the morality convention, it appears that similar reference occurs in unimpeachable moralities belonging, according to the best evidence, to the same decade as Heywood's two comedies. Even if we could assume a priority of two or three years for Heywood's plays, it remains very unlikely that his type of secular farce could supply a provenance for the allegorical drama of the English zealot or the Scottish reformer. Their plays belong to an older and wider convention—one, moreover, that supplies its own natural resolution of the issue before us, as we are about to see. Should it be objected that the several vices designated in the stage directions of the plays of Bale and Lindsay are not altogether the equivalent of Heywood's single special-

EMERGENCE OF THE VICE

ized figure of the Vice, it will appear before long that the difference is more specious than real.

We can, in fact, remove every difficulty about the origin of the figure with whom we are concerned as soon as we realize that he is the product of a very natural process of homiletic emphasis and theatrical exploitation. Before it acquired its distinctive theatrical meaning, the word *vice,* in its obvious moral sense, was the ordinary appellative in the texts of the moralities for every personification of evil.[16] The inimical members of the Psychomachia are regularly described in the singular or plural as a *vice* or as *vices,* by themselves and by the other characters. The double point of distinction, separating its prior common usage from its consequent development into a proper name and distinctive title, is that the word originally has only a moral meaning precisely because it does exist inside the text, and it refers to any or all of the evil personae precisely because it does have its original moral meaning, not a dramaturgic one. In the following examples, ranging from the earliest to the latest plays, we see the word as it appears in the text, not in the players' lists or stage directions, and we see it, therefore, in its ordinary, uncapitalized, moral sense. The prologue to *Perseverance* anticipates part of the military action of the play in the following language:

> Þus vycys, a-geyns vertues fytyn ful snelle;
> Euery buskith to brynge man to dystresse;
> But Penaunce & Confescion, with Mankynd wyl melle;
> Þe vycys arn ful lyckely, þe vertues to opresse:
> Sann dowte;
>
> [ll. 70–74]

In *Wisdom* the numerous vices who attend on Mind, Will, and Understanding, the three corrupted Powers of the now depraved Soul, fall into a quarrel and then into a brawl in the midst of their pageantry and dancing, whereupon Mind comments: "Wer vycis be gederyde, euer ys sum myschance." [17] In Skelton's *Magnificence* Liberty addresses the audience in homiletic exposition of what he stands for as a quality in human life:

> For I am a vertue yf I be well vsed,
> And I am a vyce where I am abused.
>
> [ll. 2101–102]

EMERGENCE OF THE VICE

The "six vyces" of Bale's *Three Laws* are agents of Infidelity, under whose leadership they serve. As he summons them in pairs to assign them their specialized assaults upon true religion in England, they come forward, according to the invariable method of the moralities, to address the audience in homiletic exposition of their qualities. When it comes the turn of Sodomismus, he says in part:

> I am soche a vyce trulye
> As God in hys great furye,
> Ded ponnysh most terryblye,
> In Sodome and in Gomorre.
> [ll. 556–59]

The text of *Respublica* is filled with the word *vice* as the moral appellation of its four malefactors, who are Avarice, Insolence, Flattery, and Oppression. Of all four the prologue observes:

> But thoughe these vices by cloked collusyon
> And by counterfaicte Names, hidden their abusion,
> Do Reigne for a while to comon weales preiudice,
> Pervertinge all right and all ordre of true Iustice,
> Yet tyme trieth all and tyme bringeth truth to lyght,
> That wronge may not ever still reigne in place of right.
> [ll. 23–28]

When the Four Daughters of God come down from heaven to help Respublica out of her great distress, they reveal to her the truth about the personifications in whom she has mistakenly placed her trust:

> Ah, good Respublica, thow haste been abused,
> Whom thowe chosest are vices to be refused.
> [ll. 1369–70]

And of Avarice, leader of the four, Verity says:

> He first enveigled thee, and his purpose to frame
> Cloked eche of these vices with a vertuous Name.
> [ll. 1377–78]

When the four vices are cornered and exposed, Respublica denounces them thus: "Well, the best of youe is a detestable vice."[18] At the end of the play she invokes the help of Justice and her sisters in putting them down:

> Nowe will I to Iustice & thother ladies three,
> And praie that these vices maie all suppressed bee.
> [ll. 1573–74]

EMERGENCE OF THE VICE

One more illustration, in this case from *The Longer Thou Livest,* makes the same point with versatile felicity, because at the same time it also makes another, which is no less than the key to the development with which we are concerned:

> *Incontinence.* What, Idlenes, the parent of all vice?
> Who thought to haue found the heare.
> *Idleness.* Then art thou neyther mannerly nor wise,
> As by thy salutation doth appeare;
> For if I of vice be the parent,
> Then thy parent I must needes be.
> Thou art a vice by all mens consent,
> Therfore it is like that I begat thee.
>
> [ll. 595–602]

This last quotation does double duty. Not only does it contribute to the evidence that the word *vice,* as a moral designation for *all* personifications of evil, is prevalent in the texts of the moralities and is as old as the oldest of them, but it also explains in large part the emergence of the single figure who ruled the morality stage and stood out with special theatrical prominence, in allegorical and literal plays alike from 1530 onward, as *the Vice.* It reveals the homiletic principle at work in almost every morality to distinguish one vice from his fellows and to make him, as it were, the arch-vice of the play.

3

Every morality before the time of Elizabeth—with the single exception of *Mundus et Infans,* freakishly compressed for only two actors—has more evil personifications than one, and they are all vices in the moral sense. The numerous vices, including the Seven Deadly Sins, of the early moralities are condensed to three or four in almost all the plays that come after 1500, the reasons for such contraction being several. For one, it is brought about by the need for dramatic economy and clarity as the allegorical drama came to depend less on pageantry and more on a plot of intrigue. For another, the need arose to fit the morality to the limitations of a small professional troupe, usually consisting of three, four, or five men, and a boy.[19] A third reason lies in the shift of doctrine and values which loosened the plays from the hold of the rigid penitential system of Deadly Sins versus Christian Virtues, the

EMERGENCE OF THE VICE

moralities after 1500 turning their attention to the issues of the Reformation, to political problems, to humanistic ethics, to social and religious abuses, and to a variety of special prudential texts—all reflecting the secular trend and all providing lessons that could be expressed by relatively few vices and virtues. But as long as the allegorical play is clearly recognizable as such, it almost invariably has several figures of evil in homiletic association with each other, and all of them are vices.[20] Their relationship, however, is not egalitarian. The crux in the development we are discussing exists in the fact that one of the vices is almost always distinguished from the others as their *immoral* superior and dramatic leader. He is captain of the forces of evil and they are his privates. When they contest his supremacy or show him insufficient deference, he puts them down with threats and blows, producing the inveterate quarrel of the vices along with its homiletic purpose, the exposition of who is top dog in the hierarchy of evil. For there is nearly always a homiletic intention within the comedy of the moralities. A recollection of this piece of morality stage business and also of its significance occurs in George Chapman's play *The Widow's Tears:*

Nay, the Vice must snap his authority at all he meets; how shall't else be known what part he plays.

[V.iii.275–76] [21]

Between the doctrinal and dramatic explanations for the existence of this *führer prinzip* among the vices, it is hard, and perhaps unnecessary, to decide which has priority. Both operate together in the moralities to distinguish a vice-in-chief from his allegorical henchmen, making him the brains of the intrigue, the seducer par excellence, and making his the heavy role of the play. The dramatic cause for his pre-eminence exists in the important fact, already elaborated in a previous chapter, that the pageantry of the military Psychomachia became transformed on the stage into a plot of intrigue. Such a plot, the persistent structural feature of the whole morality drama, required the services of a single intriguer, a voluble and cunning schemer, an artist in duplicity, a deft manipulator of human emotions. His operation upon his human victim is closet work, close and private. After he succeeds in breaking down the pales and forts of virtue and insinuating himself into the bosom of mankind as servant, counselor, or crony, he brings his subordinates through the breach; and all of them exist in close fellowship

EMERGENCE OF THE VICE

with the human soul, to its great jeopardy. He is the dramatic star of the play on the side of evil, and the other vices are, by contrast, diminished figures who troop in his train.

But now the question arises—by what form or logic of election is he elevated to such dramatic prominence above his fellow vices? Here we are brought, or rather returned, to the presence of that pervasive formula in medieval homiletics which explains his emergence. Let Chaucer's Parson, as he introduces his schematic exposition of the Seven Deadly Sins, preach us into perception:

Now is it bihovely thyng to telle whiche been the sevene deedly synnes, this is to seyn, chieftaynes of synnes. Alle they renne in o lees [leash], but in diverse manneres. Now been they cleped chieftaynes, for as muche as they been chief and spryng of alle othere synnes. Of the roote of thise sevene synnes, thanne, is Pride the general roote of alle harmes. For of this roote spryngen certein braunches, as Ire, Envye, Accidie or Slewthe, Avarice or Coveitise (to commune understondynge), Glotonye, and Lecherye. And everich of thise chief synnes hath his braunches and his twigges, as shal be declared in hire chapitres folwynge.[22]

The sins that grow in our lives are not coeval, but spring from each other contingently: one is the root and trunk (not always Pride, but variable according to a variable moral text) of which others are branches and still others twigs. This commonplace of the medieval moralist is also the prescriptive schema, although often simplified, of the moralities. Transmuted into its proper dramatic form, it appears in them as the metaphor of the moral sequence, already discussed. By their didactic purpose and analytical method they are committed to the exposition of the sequence by which one moral evil, having established itself in the human heart, makes a path for the next; and especially they are committed to the exposition of that vice which is first of all, the *radix malorum*. He is acknowledged by the other vices as their leader and governor, and he is offered homiletically to the audience as the vice preceding all others in the destructive assault of evil upon the heart of man, the true religion, or the structure of society, depending on the didactic focus of the play. If we now turn back to the quotation from *The Longer Thou Livest,* we grasp the large meaning of the exchange between Incontinence and Idleness in a morality whose subject is juvenile delinquency. It points up the lesson that the sins of the young have their origin in idleness, the vice which first invades and weakens the

EMERGENCE OF THE VICE 143

moral constitution of youth. The insidious proliferation of a radical vice into an *arbor mala* was not only a dominant theme for the medieval pulpit and for pious iconography; it also supplied the stage with a homiletic idea that was subject, as it turned out, to sensational dramatic exploitation.[23]

Examples of this doctrinal and dramatic superiority of one of the vices over his fellows are almost as many as there are morality plays, so that a few perforce must serve, with the early moralities showing its incipience, obviously, rather than its fulfillment. The prominent role among the many vices of *Perseverance* is that of Covetousness. He is the sole and special representative of Mundus, whereas the other six of the Deadly Sins, to whom he introduces Humanum Genus, are grouped by threes under Caro and Belial. It is he who initiates the attack on the Castle, and when the other vices fail in open warfare it is he who finally succeeds by seduction, drawing Humanum Genus by silken words out of his haven. His position of leadership is affirmed by his unrivaled prominence in the dramatic action and by the fact that he alone of the Deadly Sins has a scaffold to himself in the diagram of the "platea" that survives with the play. And his corresponding doctrinal priority is uttered by Largitas as she stands by, a helpless witness of his successful wooing of Mankind:

> Þer is no dysese nor debate
> Þorwe þis wyde werld so rounde,
> Tyde nor tyme, erly nor late,
> But þat Coueytyse is þe grounde.
> Þou norchyst pride, Envye & hate,
> Þou Coueytyse, þou cursyd hounde!
> . . . .
> Swete Jhesu, jentyl justyce,
> Kepe Mankynde fro coueytyse!
> For I-wys he is, in al wyse,
> Rote of sorwe & synne.
> [ll. 2454–66]

Radix malorum est cupiditas—the text reminds us that Chaucer's Pardoner, reaching middle age, might have attended a performance of the morality of *Perseverance*. And because the play advances such a text, the large figure occupying the foreground in the moral and dramatic landscape of *Perseverance* is that of Covetousness.

EMERGENCE OF THE VICE

In *Mankind* it is Titivillus who is prominent as the successful intriguer, who is acknowledged by the other vices as their leader, who is pointed out by Mercy as Mankind's chief enemy since he is supreme over all the evil forces in the play—"he ys master of them all."[24] In *Nature* Man is seduced by Pride, the other vices following on the trail he blazes; and it is Pride's role which is magnified to the neglect of theirs. The homiletic point behind his dramatic eminence is explicit in the verbal jest addressed to him by Sensuality: "Ye be radix viciorum. Rote of all vertew."[25] Bale's *Three Laws* presents Infidelity as the dominant, because initial, vice of the play. He is rarely off the stage, whereas the other vices come and go as his agents. Doctrinally they are the "frutes of Infydelyte" and he is their head and source in the scheme of evils that afflict Christianity; and Vindicta Dei, before she finally drives him off the scene, makes the relationship clear: "Of whom spronge they first? but of Infydelyte?"[26] In *King John* Bale inverts the sequence, presenting Sedition not as the source but as the culmination of the evils that subvert a kingdom after the other vices have done their work and paved the way for him. On this point the play achieves an effective piece of homiletic comedy when Sedition insists on being carried onto the stage on the backs of the other three vices so that the audience may have ocular demonstration of the fact that when Dissimulation, Private Wealth, and Usurped Power are permitted to flourish in England they finally bring into the country the crowning evil of Sedition. Instruction on this theme extends through more than 150 verses, coming to an end only when Sedition formally introduces all the vices to the audience in the order of their doctrinal rank and sequence:

> Here ys, fyrst of all, good father Dyssymulacion,
> The fyrst begynner of this same congregacion;
> Here is Private Welthe, which hath the Chyrch infecte
> With all abusyons, and brought yt to a synfull secte;
> Here ys Usurpid Power that all kyngs doth subdwe
> With such autoryte as is neyther good nor trewe;
> And I last of all am evyn, sance pere, Sedycyon.
>
> [ll. 810–16] [27]

It is Sedition, therefore, who is dramatically the most prominent of the vices. He is the first to appear, making a lavish entrance, whereas the other three come on stage almost in a group; he marshalls them to their

EMERGENCE OF THE VICE
145

knavery; and he stays on for the climax of the play after they have vanished. The same distinction separates Infidelity from the other three vices who attend him in Lewis Wager's *Life and Repentance of Mary Magdalene*. They are his "impes" and his "ofspryng," his auxiliaries obeying his directions; and one of them, Pride of Life, makes clear the homiletic sequence and dramatic relationship:

> If thou be once rooted within the hart,
> Then maist thou make an entrance by thy craft and art,
> So that we may come into hir at pleasure,
> Fillyng hir with wickednesse beyond all measure.
>
> [ll. 287–90]

Earlier in the play Infidelity himself, in a fifty-six verse lecture to the audience, leaves no doubt that he is the foundation of the structure of evil, the *radix* of the *arbor mala:*

> Beware of me, Infidelitie!
> Like as Faith is the roote of all goodnesse,
> So am I the head of all iniquitie,
> The well and spryng of all wickednesse.
>
> [ll. 33–36]

This differentiation, both doctrinal and dramatic, between leader and followers in the forces of evil could be pursued through all the later moralities, where it is even more fully confirmed and accentuated. In each of them one of the vices is homiletically supreme in the hierarchy of evils that appear, and his role gradually expands in individuality and dramatic prominence while the roles of the other vices diminish and fuse in the same ratio. It was inevitable that sooner or later the distinction should receive formal theatrical recognition in the players' lists, in the stage directions, and even on the title pages of the printed plays. The first of them to grant such recognition is *Respublica* (1553). In that play there are four unmistakable "moral" vices, but in "The partes and Names of the Plaiers" they appear as follows:

> Avarice. allias policie, The vice of the plaie.
> Insolence. " Authoritie, the chief galaunt.
> Oppression. " Reformation, an other gallaunt.
> Adulation. " Honestie, The third gallaunt.

Avarice's title proclaims his dramatic elevation over the other three vices and his special theatrical rank. It also proclaims the gradual ascendancy of theatrical over homiletic values in the moralities after

1550. The role he fills has expanded beyond its original moral meaning to take on, in addition, the status of *protagonist* and *dramatic lead* in the stereotyped intrigue of the morality plot. If we ask why he, beyond the other vices, is "The vice of the plaie," the answer repeats the story that has already unfolded. Doctrinally he is the root and source of the evil in *Respublica*. The other vices, in their various ways, are all moved by the acquisitive energy he personifies, and they all acknowledge him as their "founder." When he appears to them they salute him as such enthusiastically: "All Haille our Fownder & Chiefe, Mr. Avarice."[28] He is, as it were, the spiritual leader of the other vices, and when they are all brought to judgment Nemesis singles him out as the special "plague of Comonweales," punishing him with unique severity; while Respublica learns in the denouement that he is the vice "who first enveigled thee." Dramatically the distinction is equally clear, his homiletic eminence receiving its theatrical due. His is the largest and richest role of the four, and it is highlighted and individualized while the other three are merged into a background cluster. He is the leader and strategist of the vices, initiating the conspiracy against Respublica and carrying it through unaided, introducing his followers to her only after he has ensnared her by his own efforts. The other vices simply obey him—sometimes badly, gaining his reproof; and they are glad to acknowledge their dependence on his cunning and their obedience to his control:

> But we maie herein, nothing attempte in no wyse,
> Withowte the Counsaile of our fownder Avaryce.
> [ll. 149–50]

Other distinctive features, dramatic and rhetorical, belong to him, but they can be neglected for the present. After *Respublica,* "The vice of the plaie," or an equivalent phrase, became the familiar honorific that acknowledged the expanding theatrical prominence of this metaphorical archconspirator and his stock intrigue in moralities, in hybrid plays, and in plays whose only allegorical element is his portentous role. To illustrate him once more, this time out of one of the late moralities, *Enough Is as Good as a Feast* has four figures of evil, Temerity, Inconsideration, Precipitation, and Covetousness—all four working together to achieve the damnation of Worldly Man. But whereas

EMERGENCE OF THE VICE 147

in the list of players three of the vices appear simply by their moral names, each role slight enough to be combined with two or three others played by the same actor, the fourth has his telltale histrionic title, and his role is immediately distinguished from theirs by its substance, by the fact that it is large enough to require the undivided attention of one of the players: "Couetousnes the Vice for another." In the text itself the distinction is even sharper in two stage directions, the second only twelve lines after the first:

Enter Temeritie, Inconsideration, and Precipitation singing this Song.
Enter Couetouse the Vice alone.

[sig. B2 *recto*]

If we seek to know why Covetousness must be the Vice, must enter alone, and why his role must dominate the play, crowding the other three vices into insignificance, the answer is the same as it is for the same situation in all the moralities. The metaphorical plot of intrigue required a significant single intriguer, and its homiletic aim required that he should be conspicuous as the *root* of all the evils represented. The play in question wastes no time establishing Covetousness in this double eminence. He demands and gets, after fuming and foining through a comic quarrel, the allegiance and homage of the other three vices:

> For you knowe wel inough that of you all three:
> I am worthy the gouernour and Ruler to be.
> Couetouse (saith the wise man) is the root of all euil:
> Therfore Couetouse is the cheefest that cometh from the deuil.
>
> [sig. B4 *recto*] [29]

A little later, after he browbeats them out of their reluctance, they acknowledge him "The king, Emperour, yea the God of all vice." [30] Thereafter he rules the play.

4

Whatever has become clear so far in this history of the emergence of the Vice, one point at least remains obscure. It is the still unexplained existence of his theatrical label in the two plays of Heywood, *Weather* and *Love,* some twenty years before it appears in the morality of *Respublica.* The explanation comes from careful inspection of Hey-

EMERGENCE OF THE VICE

wood's two Vices. They are morality Vices transplanted into Heywoodian didactic comedy. They display almost all the stock dramaturgic and comic features of their lineage, with the serious homiletic side omitted—as it very well could be, and as, we shall find, it is omitted, not only in Heywood's plays, but in several others as well that stand at the beginning of Elizabethan comedy. For the morality Vice, like the morality play itself of which he is the essence, is a composite of homiletic "sadness" and dramaturgic "mirth." This ambivalence in his nature, which will be examined later, made him plastic and adjustable to almost any dramatic mood. Heywood borrowed and emphasized that half of the morality Vice which makes him the *farceur* of the play and its intriguer—the comic artist who displays his cunning operation upon his human dupes, who is in intimate relationship with the audience and addresses his asides and monologues—witty, ironic, satiric, and choric—directly to them, who regales them with a dozen typical tricks of language and stage business, who sings and jests, who reveals through his behavior his allegorical origin and motivation, and who is still sufficiently a homiletic figure so that his actions are intended to demonstrate his name and nature, to show what he is. Consider the allegorical *significatio* of Merry Report in the *Play of the Weather*:

> And for my name: reportyng alwaye trewly,
> What hurte to reporte a sad mater merely [merrily]?
> As, by occasyon, for the same entent,
> To a serteyne wedow thys daye was I sent,
> Whose husbande departyd wythout her wyttynge,—
> A specyall good lover, and she hys owne swettynge!
> To whome, at my commyng, I caste suche a fygure,
> *Mynglynge the mater accordynge to my nature,*
> That when we departyd, above al other thynges
> She thanked me hartely for my mery tydynges!
> And yf I had not handled yt meryly,
> Perchaunce she myght have taken yt hevely;
> But in suche facyon I coniured and bounde her,
> That I left her meryer then I founde her!
> What man may compare to shew the lyke comforte
> That dayly is shewed by me, Mery-reporte?
>
> [my italics; ll. 137–52]

This is not the place for a thorough examination of all the traits that Heywood's two Vices bring with them out of the morality drama, but

EMERGENCE OF THE VICE

one substantial point can be made quickly: both of them are playing directly to the audience in homiletic exposition of their abstract natures. The Vice in the *Play of Love,* after a long dramatic monologue, both text and exemplum, to show that he is the very personification of "lovelessness," even enrolls the audience upon his side of the *débat* to follow:

> And syns my parte now doth thus well appere
> Be ye my partyners now all of good chere
> But sylence euery man vpon a payne
> For mayster woodcock is nowe come agayne.
>
> [ll. 685–88]

And nowhere in the moralities themselves do we find a better illustration of the intimacy, originating in homiletic allegory, between Vice and audience than in the stage direction from the same play: "Here the vyse cometh in ronnynge sodenly aboute the place among the audiens. . . ." [31]

It was because the subtle intriguer of the allegorical drama was so borrowed and so specialized in the unusual context of Heywood's two comedies that he received in them his theatrical title of "the Vice" a score of years before it appeared in the moralities themselves. The designation occurred sooner, because its need and usefulness were greater, in plays that were not otherwise allegorical. The point is simple. In any moral play the indispensable roles of the vices, and of the Vice, were traditional and taken for granted, and they revealed themselves at once by their names in the list of players. In the morality of *Youth,* for example, there could be no question as to who the vices were in a cast that contained Youth, Charity, Humility, Riot, Pride, and Lechery. And in the morality plot itself, as we have already observed, one of the important homiletic aims is exactly to demonstrate who, among several cognate figures of evil, is the Vice-in-chief by virtue of his primacy as *radix malorum,* so that his designation as "the Vice" in the cast or stage directions is actually a piece of supererogation. These homiletic conditions, however, did not hold for Heywood's two plays, or for other secular plays that likewise borrowed the Vice; and it was precisely because they did not hold that he was in special need of his generic title. In such plays he was not a traditional figure but a theatrically attractive importation. Nor did his homiletic eminence appear in them from his association with other vices, because he was borrowed

EMERGENCE OF THE VICE

without the company of his allegorical cohorts, and exploited theatrically for his dramatic verve, not homiletically for his immoral primacy or metaphorical significance. In such plays, therefore, he soon received the title that made his dramaturgic function patent. If it was of some use to have the Vice in a play to which he was not native, it was also useful to indicate his presence. In the cast of *Love,* for instance, the Vice without his title would not be recognizable:

> A man a louer not beloued.
> A woman beloued not louyng.
> A man a louer and beloued.
> The vyse nother louer nor beloued.

In *Jack Juggler* (1553–58), the next nonallegorical play after Heywood's pair of comedies to designate the Vice, the same conditions apply, and "The Players names" tell the same story:

> Maysters. Boungrace.   A galant
> Dame coye.   A Gentelwoman
> Iacke Iugler.   the vyce.
> Ienken careaway   A Lackey.
> Ales trype and go   A mayd.

Not only do all the names in the cast occupy the same level of abstraction, but there is nothing in the name of "Iacke Iugler" that specializes his role on the side of moral evil. His distinction, which is theatrical rather than moral, is expressed through his histrionic title. He is not just another personage in the dramatic story, not just one character among several in a play. He is *the* dramaturgic darling of the popular stage in another version of his traditional role, and the definite article in his title is the badge of his special status.

By his evolution, moreover, the Vice illustrates a principle that we cannot afford to neglect: for he is simply the most vivid example of the fact that the tangible character of the morality stage and its theatrical characteristics—its monolithic plot, its personages and their personalities, its paraphernalia of technique and device, even its seriocomic medley—drew their substantive life and motive force from a complex of intangible homiletic conceptions.

CHAPTER SIX

MORAL METAPHOR AND DRAMATIC IMAGE

What man so wise, what earthly wit so ware,
As to descry the crafty cunning traine,
By which deceipt doth maske in visour faire,
And cast her colours dyed deepe in graine,
To seeme like Truth . . .

THE FAERIE QUEENE

I

Having produced the figure of the Vice, the Tudor stage submitted to his spell. As homiletic showman, intriguer extraordinary, and master of dramatic ceremonies, he emerged, before the middle of the century, into acknowledged theatrical prominence—both in the moralities proper and in plays that do not participate, except for his presence in them, in the allegorical convention. His role, much older than his histrionic title, came into its key position as soon as the martial allegory of the Psychomachia was transformed by the stage into a plot of intrigue. From the first he is elevated above his companion vices by his homiletic distinction as *radix malorum,* and exploited into special dramatic magnitude to illustrate his primacy in a sequence of moral evils—a sequence the schematic exposition of which is an important part of the homiletic purpose of nearly every moral interlude. His development over a century (roughly 1425–1525), until he earns the title which expresses his popularity and unique theatrical status, consists largely of his growing individuality and in the expansion of his role through its accumulation of standard pieces of stage business. Into his stock performance the Psychomachia distills its essence, its theme the source of his aggressive energy, its method as homiletic allegory the source of his dramatic style. In the moralities proper he invariably functions

152 MORAL METAPHOR AND DRAMATIC IMAGE

in homiletic association with several subsidiary vices, who follow him through the breach he makes in the moral defenses of humanity. This association disappears only when he is transferred into plays which, save that they exploit his role for its great theatrical value, are but partially within the allegorical convention or not at all, and are not, therefore, concerned with the exposition of a sequence of moral evils. Such plays will receive attention later. For the present we need to examine, in his typical character and performance, the Vice of the moralities.

It cannot be stressed too much that his whole action as intriguer and seducer is a dramatized metaphor with a meaning beyond its literal enactment on the stage. The principles governing his role are inevitably homiletic in their origin, and his typical stage behavior is inevitably abstract in its ultimate significance. Just as his very existence resulted from the homiletic concept of a *root* evil, so are the whole scope and the parts of his behavior concrete images of similar generalizations. His aim is the moral and spiritual ruin of his victim in order that he may demonstrate thereby the destructive force and characteristic effect of the evil he personifies. His separate actions and stock characteristics are likewise allusive, metaphorical, and expository—at least in plays that are thoroughgoing moralities. His performance, in its whole range and in its details, is a stereotype because as often as he appears on the stage he is a metaphor for the homiletic stereotype that medieval Christianity formulated in respect to the origin of moral evil and the method of its operation on the human heart. To illustrate this fact is to reproduce, at the same time, the typical dramatic image of the Vice—an image that remained alive on the stage for a considerable time after its original significance and the morality drama itself had passed away.

The heart of his role is an act of seduction, and the characteristic stratagem whereby the Vice achieves his purpose is a vivid stage metaphor for the sly insinuation of moral evil into the human breast. For its consummation he displays himself as an artist in persuasion who deftly manipulates his victim out of his virtuous inclination and turns him about in the direction of his ruin. Translated into dramatic terms, his stratagem is twofold. In one part it is to create a divorce between the human hero and the personifications of virtue who support and

MORAL METAPHOR AND DRAMATIC IMAGE 153

counsel him. In *Mankind,* as we have seen, Titivillus, by his insinuations and slanders, is able to alienate the hero from Mercy, his guardian personification. Folly, in *Mundus et Infans,* having created a similar breach between Manhood and Conscience, assures the audience "That Conscyence he shall awaye cast." [1] In *Nature,* Pride achieves his initial success in depraving Man by prevailing on him to get rid of Reason, and is soon able to announce:

> Reason nay nay hardely
> He ys forsaken vtterly
> Syth I cam to hys [Man's] company
> He wold not onys appere.
>
> [ll. 1090–93]

Likewise in *The Four Elements,* Sensuous Appetite persuades Humanity to free himself from the solicitous tutelage of Studious Desire. In *Magnificence* the success of the plot of the vices against the well-being of the hero is signalized when Measure, who has been his counselor, is thrown out of favor and driven from court. In the Protestant morality of *Lusty Juventus* the young hero of that name, having been set on the right path of life and religion by Good Counsel and Knowledge, is induced by Hypocrisy, in a long scene of clever seduction, to forsake his guardian personifications and to devote his attention to Abominable Living. In each of these actions, and in others too numerous to mention, the homiletic purpose creates the dramatic image of the Vice as the artful breeder of strife and alienation between his victim and his victim's true spiritual friends, the attendant personifications of virtue. He is the cunning instigator of discord and debate, and his success in this part of his stratagem appears when the frail hero attaches himself to the company and guidance of the Vice, rebuffing and insulting Virtue, who is left on the stage to vent his grief and admonition upon the audience.

According to the same homiletic logic, expressing the human decline from moral good to moral evil, the Vice accomplishes the remaining part of his enterprise in seduction when he is able to unite himself to his victim in the bond of friendship, in the relationship of servant to master, or in that of preceptor to pupil.[2] "Your seruaunt wyll I be," says Folly to Manhood in *Mundus et Infans,* as the hero abandons his

154 MORAL METAPHOR AND DRAMATIC IMAGE

allegiance to Conscience and goes off, Folly guiding him, to dine in Eastcheap and to sample sweet wine at the Pope's Head Tavern.[3] "Putte yourselfe nowe wholye into my handes," is the ruinous advice that Avarice, alias Policy, urges upon Respublica.[4] In *Impatient Poverty* the Vice attaches himself to the hero as his "cosin," and, since doctrinally he is the pioneer beating a way for other moral evils to follow, he advises his victim to expect more company:

> I come hyther wyth you to dwell
> Ye muste haue moo seruauntes I do you tell
> Soche as were necessarye for youre person.
>> [ll. 584–86]

And Mary Magdalene, in Lewis Wager's play of that name, is so taken by Infidelity's blandishments that she fairly leaps at his sly bid to be her servant and counselor:

> I perceiue right well that you owe me good will,
>> Tendryng my worshipfull state and dignitie:
> You see that I am yong and can little skill
>> To prouide for myne owne honor and vtilitie.
>
> Wherfore I pray you in all thyngs counsell to haue,
>> After what sort I may leade a pleasant life here;
> And looke what it pleaseth you of me to craue,
>> I will geue it you gladly, as it shall appere.
>> [ll. 138–45]

The Vice is only too willing:

> Say you so, mistresse Mary? Wil you put me in trust?
>> In faith I will tell you, you can not trust a wiser.
> You shall liue pleasantly, euen at your heart's lust,
>> If you make me your counseller and deuiser.
>> [ll. 146–49]

So much then for the intention of the Vice's stratagem, which, while he remains in the moralities proper, is always one and the same: to manipulate the human hero out of the virtue which is the Vice's homiletic opposite and to insinuate himself instead (that is, the evil he personifies) into his victim's bosom, dominating him and enticing him headlong down the road to damnation. The constant and compact stage image created by the metaphor of the Psychomachia is that of an artless and credulous dupe who is tempted, fooled, and ensnared by a master craftsman in the fine art of seduction.

MORAL METAPHOR AND DRAMATIC IMAGE 155

2

As for the Vice's method in his stratagem, it is first, last, and always deceit. Deceit, in a dozen forms, is his most indelible dramatic characteristic and the greatest source of his professional pride as often as he invites the audience to admire his talent, or invokes the applause of the Devil himself:

> The time were too long now to declare,
> How many and great the number are,
> Which have deceived bee;
> And brought cleane from God's law
> Unto thy yoke and awe,
> Through the enticement of me.
>> [*Lusty Juventus,* Dodsley, II, 64]

It will help us in dealing with him, however, if we keep in mind that his alacrity in deception defines the method of his operation, but has no essential relation to the particular evil he personifies. No Vice is actually named Deceit in the moralities; but whether he is Pride, Avarice, Infidelity, or any other pejorative quality in human life, his infinite guile expresses metaphorically, as a universal principle, the devious beginning and insidious growth of every evil in our mortal nature. His endless behavior that way simply translates into dramatic terms the evolved formula of the Psychomachia—formerly warfare, now intrigue —out of which he derives his origin and prescriptive performance. "The first vices," says Gregory the Great, "force themselves into the deluded mind as if under a kind of reason."[5]

In the arsenal of his deceit the chief weapon is dissimulation in the form of moral, abetted often by physical, disguise. Like nearly everything else in the moralities, the art of his dissimulation obeys a homiletic tenet, which is especially evident in the commonest of his devices, the virtuous alias under which he conceals his name and dissembles his nature. "All *Vices* maske themselues with the vizards of *Vertue,*" observed Thomas Dekker, continuing, "they borrowe their names, the better and more currantly to passe without suspition: for murder will be called *Manhood, Dronkennesse* is now held to be *Phisick, Impudence* is *Audacitie, Ryot,* good fellowship &c."[6] The whole literature of homiletics and moral allegory, both medieval and Tudor, supports

156 MORAL METAPHOR AND DRAMATIC IMAGE

such a commentary; and we may recall in this connection the success of Avarice in the *Psychomachia* of Prudentius when she disguises herself as Thrift. In several places of his *Moralia* Gregory stresses and interpets the same point:

And there are some vices which present an appearance of rectitude, but which proceed from the weakness of sin. For the malice of our enemy clokes itself with such art, as frequently to make faults appear as virtues before the eyes of the deluded mind. . . . For cruelty is frequently exercised with punishing sins, and it is counted justice; and immoderate anger is believed to be the meritoriousness of righteous zeal. . . . Frequently negligent remissness is regarded as gentleness and forbearance. . . . Lavishness is sometimes believed to be compassion. . . . When a fault then appears like virtue, we must needs consider that the mind abandons its fault the more slowly, in proportion as it does not blush at what it is doing.[7]

The homiletic logic behind the moral dissimulation of the Vice is consistent with the fact that he is at bottom a personification of a fault in human nature. He dissembles his name and quality because it is an obvious trait of frail humanity to disguise under a fair semblance the moral evil to which life is prone; and the plays themselves are not chary about providing this psychological explanation for his typical behavior. In a part of the *Ludus Coventriae* clearly influenced by the method of moral allegory, the prologue to the Second Passion Play, Lucifer reads the audience a satirical lecture on their euphemistic proclivities in respect to the Seven Deadly Sins:

> I haue browth ȝow newe namys, and wyl ȝe se why
> Ffor synne is so pleasaunt, to ech Mannys intent
> Ȝe xal kalle pride oneste and naterall kend lechory
> And covetyse wysdam there tresure is present.
> Wreth manhood and envy callyd chastement . . .[8]

This characteristic effort of human nature to miscall by a palatable name the evils to which it is addicted is a constant theme of the moralities themselves. The virtuous figure of New Custom, in the Protestant morality of the same name, laments long and loud over such a tendency:

> Sin now no sin, faults no faults a whit:
> O God seest thou this, and yet wilt suffer it?
>
> . . . .

MORAL METAPHOR AND DRAMATIC IMAGE 157

Adultery no vice, it is a thing so rife,
A stale jest now to lie with another man's wife!
For what is that but dalliance? Covetousness they call
Good husbandry, when one man would fain have all.

. . . .

For pride, that is now a grace; for round about
The humble-spirited is termed a fool or a lout.
Whoso will be drunken, that he scarcely knoweth his way,
O, he is a good fellow, so now-a-days they say.
Gluttony is hospitality, while they meat and drink spill,
Which would relieve diverse whom famine doth kill.

. . . .

Theft is but policy, perjury but a face,
Such is now the world, so far men be from grace.
[*New Custom*, Dodsley, III, 16]

In *Hickscorner* the same lament comes from Pity, as he preaches from the stocks:

Alas! now is lechery called love, indede,
And murdure named manhode in every nede;
Extorsyon is called lawe, so God me spede:
Worse was hyt never!
[ll. 557–60]

It is in consequence of this important homiletic principle, valid for human life universally, we may suppose, and common to all the moralities, that no facet of the typical performance of the Vice is more prominent than his skill in moral dissimulation, nor is there any other part of his talent in which he takes more pride. Such deceit is the central characteristic of his role, translating into vivid dramatic image the habitual self-deception or blindness of mankind to the real nature of the temptations to which it succumbs—a subject which receives nowhere a more searching treatment than in the plays of Shakespeare, with their continual emphasis on appearance and reality:

There is no vice so simple but assumes
Some mark of virtue on his outward parts.

. . . .

The seeming truth which cunning times put on
To entrap the wisest.
[*The Merchant of Venice* III.ii.81–92]

158 MORAL METAPHOR AND DRAMATIC IMAGE

We can listen to the Vice himself in his matter, for he is never slow to utter the homiletic explanation for his behavior. For one example out of many there is the speech of Avarice as he takes the audience into his confidence in the very beginning of *Respublica:*

> But nowe, what my name is and what is my purpose,
> Takinge youe all for frendes, I feare not to disclose:
> My veray trewe vnchristen Name ys Avarice,
> Which I may not have openlye knowen in no wise;
> For though to moste men I am founde Commodius,
> Yet to those that vse me my namme ys Odius.
> For who is so foolishe, that the evell he hath wrought
> For his owen behouff he wolde to light sholde be brought?
> Or who had not rather his ill doinges to hide,
> Thenne to have the same bruted on everye syde?
> Therefore to worke my feate I will my namme disguise
> And call my Name polycie in stede of Covetise.
> The Name of policie ys praised of eche one
>
> .   .   .   .
>
> The Name of policie ys of none suspected;
> Polycye is ner of any cryme Detected:
> So that vnder the Name and cloke of policie
> Avaryce maie weorke factes and scape all Jelousie.
>
> [ll. 69–86]

Derived from such a concept, the metaphorical dissimulation of the Vice takes several noteworthy forms. Its most compact expression is his almost invariable device of the virtuous, or at least equivocal, pseudonym, as it has already appeared in the foregoing monologue of Avarice. In the few moralities after 1500 in which the device of the pseudonym does not appear, its absence is due to several obvious reasons, chief among them being that in such plays Man does not figure as the victim of a seductive stratagem. In *Three Laws* and *King Darius,* for example, the action consists mainly of violent debate between opposing personifications, and the Vice has no use for a deceptive alias. In a few other plays, notably *The Four Elements* and *The Tide Tarrieth No Man,* the name of the Vice (Sensual Appetite in the first and Courage in the second) is sufficiently equivocal to begin with, so that he can urge his name in its best sense while intending to produce upon his victim an effect corresponding to its worst. In such plays as *Youth* and *John the Evangelist* the human hero is already depraved upon his first

MORAL METAPHOR AND DRAMATIC IMAGE 159

appearance, his affinity for vice so strong at the start that he does not need to be further deceived. This point is made explicit in the text of another play with the same kind of hero, *The Longer Thou Livest*. Its human figure is Moros, incorrigibly delinquent from the first, the sad product of parental indulgence. Idleness, who has been his companion from childhood under the name of Pastime, has ripened Moros for graver evils, and is now prepared, in the usual homiletic way, to introduce him to the consequent vices of Incontinence and Wrath. For that purpose he advises them to take on their appropriate pseudonyms:

> With me he is very well aqueinted,
> For all his bringing vp hath been with me,
> So that any vertue he coulde neuer se:
> Therefore pastime he calleth me alway,
> In plaies and games he hath no measure.
> Incontinencie, to him thou must say,
> That thy name is called pleasure.
>
> [ll. 669–75]

Incontinence accepts the proffered alias, although dubious about its necessity in the present instance, and in turn suggests the usual one for wrath: "Wrath is wonte to be called manhode." But Wrath rejects the whole device, seeing no need for any sort of deceit when their intended victim is so outright a fool:

> In good faith, litle needeth this deuise,
> To be called by our names is as good:
> Doth he know what Idlenesse doth meane,
> Knoweth he incontinencie to be leacherie?
> He discerneth not cleane from vncleane,
> His minde is all set on foolerie.
>
> . . . .
>
> For he discerneth not cheese from chalke . . .
>
> [ll. 676–729]

Apart from such exceptions to the standard intrigue of the Psychomachia, and they are not many, the moral obfuscation of the pseudonym is an inevitable part of the strategy of the Vice. To cite the plays in which it exists would be tantamount to a roll call of almost the entire morality drama. As one of the minor vices of Lewis Wager's *Mary Magdalene* says:

160   *MORAL METAPHOR AND DRAMATIC IMAGE*

> In our tragedie we may not vse our owne names,
> For that would turne to al our rebukes and shames.
> > [ll. 365–66]

And Infidelity, the Vice of the same play, lectures the audience on his whole system of deceptive nomenclature for the Seven Deadly Sins, whose leader he is according to the play's moral perspective:

> Mary, syr, yet I conuey my matters cleane!
> > Like as I haue a visour of vertue,
> So my impes, which vnto my person do leane,
> > The visour of honestie doth endue;
>
> As these: Pride I vse to call cleanlynesse;
> > Enuie I colour with the face of prudence;
> Wrathe putteth on the coate of manlynesse;
> > Couetise is profite in euery man's sentence;
>
> Slouth or idlenesse I paint out with quiete;
> > Gluttonie or excesse I name honest chere;
> Leachery, vsed for many men's diete,
> > I set on with the face of loue, both farre and nere.
> > [ll. 37–48]

Afterwards, as the brains of the intrigue, he confers on his dependent vices the aliases designed to penetrate the moral guard of Mary—such a scene of homiletic conspiracy and name-shifting, wherein the Vice proper assumes the leadership to which his bad eminence as *radix malorum* entitles him, being a fixture of the moralities. As for himself, he explains, he has a large stock of pseudonyms at his beck, each specialized to the occasion and the nature of his victim:

> With publicans and sinners of a carnall pretence
> I am sometime called counsel, and sometime Prudence.
> I cause them the wisedom of God to despise,
> And for the fleshe and the world wittily to deuise.
> Prudence before Marie my name will I call,
> Which to my suggestions will cause hir to fall.
> > [ll. 393–98]

Infidelity's manipulation of the moral pseudonym illustrates the common practice of the moral plays, where the Vice habitually disarms his victim by presenting himself under the assumed name of virtue, beguiling him thereby with heavenly shows. But Infidelity's resourcefulness in dissimulation goes further. Like many another Vice, his apparatus of deceit includes physical disguise, a grosser form of duplicity,

MORAL METAPHOR AND DRAMATIC IMAGE 161

and he parades himself before his accomplices in new clothing congruent with his new name:

> I haue a garment correspondent to that name.
>
> . . . .
>
> A vesture I haue here to this garment correspondent:
> Lo, here it is; a gowne, I trowe, conuenient.
>
> [ll. 391–400]

In *Respublica,* likewise, Avarice turns his coat inside out to conceal the money bags hanging from it, and throughout the play he is frantic lest it come open and reveal them. And Flattery, alias Devotion, in *The Three Estates,* invokes the audience to help out with garments suitable to his plot against Rex Humanitas: "Hes na man Clarkis cleathing to len vs?"[9]

Another part of the Vice's talent in deceit is his virtuosity in the art of false faces. "Two faces in a hode couertly I bere," says Cloaked Collusion in *Magnificence,*[10] and his comment on himself applies to the Vice generally. He has one countenance for his dupe and another for his audience, and the rapid transformation of his features, depending on which way his business lies, is a standard and sensational part of his repertory. His quality as a personification of evil gets its typical anthropomorphic expression through his vulgarity, insolence, cynicism, scorn, and triumphant hilarity—every trait, in short, that is the opposite of moral and social refinement; and the native cast of his visage reflects a nature so addicted. But when he appears to his victim it is with a "grave countenance," full of pious solicitude. In *Respublica* Avarice urges his accomplices to "counterfaite gravitee"; the Vice of *Patient and Meek Grissill* advises the audience that "My countenaunce shalbe graue, sad and demure";[11] and the Infidelity of *Mary Magdalene* composes his features, not without some difficulty, to create upon Mary the same impression:

> Lyke obstinate Friers I temper my looke,
> Which had one eie on a wench, and an other on a boke.
>
> [ll. 413–14]

An even more vivid characteristic of his role, condensing his duplicity into its most acute dramatic form, is the Vice's trick of tears and laughter. His weeping feigns his affection and concern for his victim; his laughter, for the benefit of his audience, declares the triumph of his subtle fraud and his scorn for the puny virtue of humanity; and his

162 MORAL METAPHOR AND DRAMATIC IMAGE

rapid transition between convulsions of simulated grief and genuine hilarity is one of his most startling effects. "I can dyssemble, I can bothe laughe and grone," says Cloaked Collusion in *Magnificence*.[12] The love and compassion which Covetousness pretends for Mankind in *Perseverance,* as he seeks to draw him out of "þat castel colde," is accentuated in the moralities that follow until it becomes a standard motif—the weeping of the Vice. "Then he wepyth" is the stage direction for Sensuality in Medwall's *Nature,* as he endeavors to separate Man from the companionship of Reason and to draw him once more to the good old times in the taverns and stews.[13] "Et plora" is the gloss for the behavior of Envy, alias Charity, as he bids Conscience a sorrowful farewell after deceiving him into running for his life out of England:

> Thys is an heauy departynge
> I can in no wyse forbeare wepynge
> Yet kysse me or ye go
> For sorowe my harte wyll breke in two.
> Is he gone, then haue at laughynge
> A syr is not thys a ioly game
> That conscience doeth not knowe my name.
> > [*Impatient Poverty,* ll. 508–14]

His laughter, of course, is addressed to the audience, with whom he shares his triumph. "Enter Corage weeping" is the stage direction for the Vice of *The Tide Tarrieth No Man*.[14] The long and cunning seduction scene of *Enough Is as Good as a Feast* is inundated by the tears of the Vice, three successive directions making him as lachrymose as possible: "Weep," and again "weep," and finally "Let the Vice weep & houle and make great Lamentation":

> Oh Sir, oh good Sir, oh, oh, oh my hart wil breke
> Oh, oh, for sorow God wot I cannot speak.
> > [sig. D *recto*]

Indeed, so expert is the Vice in dissembled weeping and his faculty that way so copious that he is able to supply his tears at a need for the service of anyone. In the surviving fragment of *The Cruel Debtor* Ophiletis pleads to King Basileus for remission of his debts, but too coldly, so that the Vice, standing by, first urges him on to a more pathetic effort, and then steps into the breach himself:

> Weepe, body of god can you not weepe for a neede?
> You must loke pyteously if you intende to speede,

MORAL METAPHOR AND DRAMATIC IMAGE 163

If you can not weepe, I wyll weepe for you:
Ho, ho, ho, I pray you be good to vs now.
[ll. 186–89]

To look piteous, to shed tears plentifully, and to howl dismally are the inveterate method of the Vice with his victim—his grappling irons whereby he boards the human soul. They show his affection, his compassion, his moral refinement; and compose the "flag and sign of love" behind which evil moves into position for its destructive assault. "Wepe" urges the stage direction in *Horestes,* and "O oo oo, you care not for me," moans the Vice until he brings the hero around to the unnatural destruction of his mother.[15] We shall have cause to remember the Vice's tears and his grief in later plays that, at first glance, do not appear to have the slightest resemblance to the morality drama.

And we shall have cause also to remember his mirth. For clamorous as the moralities are with the dissembled sorrow of the Vice, they are even noisier with the crepitation of his triumphant laughter. His rapid alternation between one mood and the other, and the no less rapid conversion of face and body to suit, as he oscillates between his victim and his audience, express in compact theatrical metaphor the homiletic duplicity that is at the heart of his role. No stage direction of the moralities is more common than that one which documents his hilarity: "Here cometh in Crafty conueyaunce [and] Cloked colusyon with a lusty laughter" or "Enter Inclination, laughing" or "Here cometh enuye runnynge in Laughyng" or "Here entereth Nichol Newfangle the Vice laughing."[16] And if one monosyllable can be said to be more frequent than any other in the moralities, it is the interminable "ha, ha, ha" of the Vice's laughter, as he brays out to the audience the triumph of his guile. His vaulting dissimulation makes him a creature of grotesque contrasts—no small part of his popularity—and his mirth is sharply outlined, not only against his own feigned weeping, but just as sharply against the very genuine sorrow of his dupes. In *Three Laws,* to offer one instance only, Naturae Lex and Moseh Lex come on stage to lament the corruption that Infidelity, through the subtlety of his lieutenants, has been able to inflict upon their respective laws; and hard upon their misery the Vice himself comes forward with his laughter:

Ha, ha, ha, ha, ha, ha, ha, ha, ha, ha, ha
A pastyme quoth A, I knowe not the tyme nor whan,
I ded laugh so moch, sens I was an honest man.

164   *MORAL METAPHOR AND DRAMATIC IMAGE*

> Beleue me and ye wyll, I neuer saw soch a sport
> I wolde ye [the audience] had bene there . . .
>
> [ll. 793–97]

Allowing for the refinements of characterization in the later drama, are we not, nonetheless, reminded of the "sport" of another "honest man" who announces that "pleasure and action make the hours seem short" a few moments after the high artistry of his fraudulent "love" and "grief" gain the highest sort of compliment from his chief dupe:

> Honest Iago, that looks dead with grieving,
> Speak. Who began this? On thy love, I charge thee.
>
> [*Othello* II.iii.177–78]

Although this looks ahead too soon to the end of our history, it also tells us what to look for now—the Vice's "honesty," for instance; for that is a facet of his moral imposture in which he takes especial delight. He forever dissembles himself as an honest man, is forever taken as such by his dupes, and forever shares the jest with his audience. "Beleue me as I am an honest gentleman here is my hand," says the Vice of *Common Conditions* to one of his victims, and to the audience a few minutes earlier: "By my honesty it doth me good that I so crafty should bee." [17] The Vice of *Virtuous and Godly Susanna* is equally fond of such ironies:

> In fayth I was an honest man,
> Yet I cannot tell whan.
>
> [ll. 914–15]

It will save us another whirlwind tour of the moralities if we concentrate on the "honesty" of the Vice in one of them, *The Three Ladies of London*. He makes his entrance in the array of a farmer and falls into his homiletic exposition thus:

> Nay, no less than a farmer, a right honest man,
> But my tongue cannot stay me to tell what I am:
> Nay, who is it that knows me not by my party-colour'd head?
> They may well think, that see me, my honesty is fled.
>
> [*Dodsley*, VI, 251–52]

He concludes with the announcement of his purpose, which is to go to London and "To get entertainment of one of the three ladies like [in the guise of] an honest man." To him enters Simplicity, who wishes to go along with him to London because "I love honest company"; and he tells the Vice his name "Cause thou art an honest man." A little

MORAL METAPHOR AND DRAMATIC IMAGE   165

later, when the Vice turns away from him to join the company of Fraud, Simplicity invokes him to stay but immediately thereupon penetrates his disguise:

> Nay, come and go with me, good, honest man;
> For if thou go with him, he will teach thee all his knavery.
> There is none will go with him that hath any honesty.
> A bots on thy motley beard! I know thee; thou art Dissimulation:
> And hast thou got an honest man's coat to 'semble this fashion?
>
> [*Dodsley*, VI, 257]

All these samples of the Vice's "honesty" come within little more than one hundred lines of the play, with a good deal more of the same in the rest of it. Nothing, in fact, is more thematic for his role throughout the entire homiletic drama, especially in the later plays, where human particulars crowd upon him.[18]

Another verbal formula expressive of the Vice's deceit consists of his "hate" and "love," although neither word is attached to any correlative emotion within him. His "hate" is only a word for the natural war between vice and virtue, and his "love" is the imposture that conceals his aggression. By definition he is the enemy of the virtues or values that prevail in any play in which he finds himself, and for this antinomy his "hate" is another anthropomorphism. In the same way the intersection of two lines at right angles to each other might be described in a personified geometry as enmity between the vertical and the horizontal. Actually the point of this hatred can be turned the other way, as in the comprehensive statement of this moral conflict that appears in *Like Will to Like:*

> So vice and virtue cannot together be united;
> But the one the other hath always spited.
> For as water quencheth fire, and the flame doth suppress,
> So virtue hateth vice, and seeketh a redress.
>
> [*Dodsley*, III, 338–39]

However, since the action of the moral play belongs to the Vice, the stress is on his "hate" for the virtues, the values, and the victims he attempts to destroy. In *King John,* for instance, as uttered by the Vice to the King, the word defines the conflict between papal authority and national sovereignty:

> I am Sedycyon playne:
> In euery relygyon and munkish secte I rayne,

166 MORAL METAPHOR AND DRAMATIC IMAGE

Havyng yow prynces in scorne, hate and dysdayne.

[ll. 186–88]

Moseh Lex in *Three Laws* describes in similar language the antagonism between himself and the minor vices matched against him:

One was Ambycyon, whych euer ought me hate,
And Couetousnesse the other enemye hyght.

[ll. 1301–302]

In *The Trial of Treasure* Elation advises Lust to join the war of vice against virtue and "unto the just bear hate and malignity." [19] Likewise the Vice of *Impatient Poverty* merrily informs the audience that "I hate conscience, peace loue and reste." [20] For by inevitable extension of the antinomy of the Psychomachia into the language of human feeling, the Vice commonly expresses enmity for his victim or for virtue in general, although the emotion connoted by such a word is not, in fact, part of his dramatic equipment. When he is described by those who virtuously oppose him, the same extension appears a fortiori, especially in late plays, where his original transparency as an abstraction has been clouded by the acquired traits of human personality. In *Patient and Meek Grissill* the elemental conflict which sets him against the welfare of the heroine gets its description in the following words addressed to him:

The Scorpion forth will flinge, his poyson to anoye,
And passingers that passe him bye, with Vennome to distroye,
So thou whose mallice doth abound, thy stinge doste now prepare,
To vex and harme those wightes, whose liues most vertuous are.

[ll. 932–35]

That they are addressed to a broadly comic trickster apparently, with whose farcical composition their gravity seems strangely at odds, remains a problem to be dealt with, although we have already traced in a previous chapter the broad lines of its resolution.

Against this background, at any rate, of the Vice's "hate" for virtue, the art of his deceit shows itself through his pretensions of love and sympathy, as in the following information he imparts to the audience in the play last mentioned:

I will not cease priuely her confusion to worke,
For vnder Honnie the prouerbe saith poyson maye lurke:

MORAL METAPHOR AND DRAMATIC IMAGE 167

So though I simulate externally Loue to pretend,
My loue shall turne to mischife, I warrant you in the end.

[ll. 897–900]

While the Vice's weeping renders him inarticulate in *Enough Is as Good as a Feast,* his crony assures their victim that "Pure loue causeth him, Sir I wus./ I am sure that he loues you at the hart." [21] Hypocrisy gives the young hero of *Lusty Juventus* the same assurance of affection: "By the mass I love you so heartily,/ That there is none so welcome to my company." [22] And the Vice of *Love Feigned and Unfeigned* announces his talent in the following words:

I can speake fare to a man and Imbrace hime as my brother
Whome Inwardlie I disdayne and hate above all other.

[ll. 85–86]

His "hate," explained by the Psychomachia, explains his "love," the reality, by doctrinal compulsion, generating the matched pretense of its opposite. Committed to enmity, he is bound to feign affection because his role, moved by its interior homiletic logic, proliferates into as many forms of deceit as possible, each exhibited by him as a supporting detail within the comprehensive design of his duplicity.

The same design fulfills itself in details precisely verbal. One of them is his sneering, witty aside—either a *sotto voce* interpolation into his colloquy with his dupe, or a moral comment frankly and swiftly directed to the audience. His mental and vocal agility in this respect never forsake him. "Ye, Folye, wyll thou be my trew seruaunt?" asks the deceived and ensnared hero of *Mundus et Infans,* proposing a drink to seal the bargain, "For that is curtesy." The Vice is gravely compliant, "Ye, syr Manhode; here my hande!" but his voice is immediately elsewhere:

A ha! syrs, let the catte wynke!
For all ye wote not what I thinke,
I shall drawe hym such a draught of drynke
That Conscyence he shall awaye cast.

[ll. 649–52]

Around their talk, as they prepare to leave for the promised entertainment in the taverns and stews, he runs his quick circles of mordant commentary:

168 MORAL METAPHOR AND DRAMATIC IMAGE

> *Manh.* Now, gramercy, Folye, my felowe in-fere!
> Go we hens; tary no lenger here;
> Tyll we be gone me thynke it seuen yere,—
> I haue golde and good to spende.
>
> *Folye.* A ha! mayster, that is good chere.
> [aside] And or it be passed halfe a yere,
> I shall the shere ryght a lewde frere,
> And hyther agayne the sende.
>
> [ll. 684–91]

And at the end of the same scene Folly glides out of his conversation with his victim just long enough for the ironic gloss that fulfills his homiletic duty to the audience:

> Lo, syrs, this Folye techeth aye,
> For where Conscyence cometh with his cunnynge,
> Yet Folye full fetely shall make hym blynde:
> Folye before and Shame behynde,—
> Lo, syrs, thus fareth the worlde alwaye!
>
> [ll. 695–99]

The verbal deceit of the Vice takes another form—a unique piece of oral legerdemain, delighting the audience, which appears scores of times in the moralities, and is, in fact, a prominent signature of his role in plays after 1550. It consists of a short exchange wherein he flashes a gleam of truth in the face of his dupe, but quickly withdraws it, pretending a slip of the tongue or other words to another effect. To treat this truth-revealing jest of his as an aside, as some modern editions of the moralities do, is an editorial mistake. He is talking directly to his victim, playing with him, confounding him, and parading his own talent for deceit. Also, like everything else in his role, it has its homiletic logic: his dupe must always be deceived, but the audience must always hear the moral truth. A rudimentary, because early, example of this verbal duplicity occurs in *The Four Elements,* in the following dialogue between Sensual Appetite and Humanity:

> *Sen.* And yf that I ever forsake you,
> I pray God the devyl take you!
> *Hum.* Mary, I thanke you for that othe!
> *Sen.* A myschyfe on it! my tonge, loo,
> Wyll tryp somtyme, whatsoever I do,
> But ye wot that I mene well.
>
> [p. 21]

MORAL METAPHOR AND DRAMATIC IMAGE 169

Another early version of the same trick of equivocation, moving toward its final form, appears in Bale's *Three Laws,* in Infidelity's first words, as he enters, to Naturae Lex:

> *Infid.* I thought I shuld mete a knaue,
> And now that fortune I haue
> Amonge thys cumpany.
> *Nat. Lex.* Why dost thu call me knaue?
> *Infid.* I sayd. I wolde be your slaue
> Yf your grace wolde me haue.
>> [ll. 200–205]

By the middle of the century this jest had become a staple of conversation between Vice and victim, its language always consistent with the following example in *Impatient Poverty,* where Prosperity (the prosperous man), enticed by Envy, is impatient for the wine and wenches in the tavern called the Fleur-de-Lis:

> *Pros.* Then let vs go our waye
> I syt on thornes tyll I come ther.
> *Envy.* That shall make your thryfte full bare.
> *Pros.* What wyll it do?
> *Envy.* I say we shall haue good chere
> When we come there.
>> [ll. 787–92]

Almost none of the late moralities omits this display of his verbal guile, and in several he is so addicted that it becomes a fixture of his conversation each time he encounters his victim. Here, for instance, are three excerpts from separate colloquies between the Vice Inclination and Lust (lusty humanity, filled with the pride of life) in *The Trial of Treasure:*

> *Lust.* Ye have heard of the combat between me and Just?
> *Inc.* Yea, marry, I heard say that you lay in the dust.
> *Lust.* What say ye?
> *Inc.* Neither one word nor other, ye may me trust.

> *Lust.* [looking forward to the arrival of Pleasure]
> Truly of him I would fain have a sight,
> For because that in pleasure I have marvellous delight.
> *Inc.* Then honesty and profit you may bid good night.
> *Lust.* What say'st thou?
> *Inc.* I say he will shortly appear in sight.

170 MORAL METAPHOR AND DRAMATIC IMAGE

Lust. My lady is amorous, and full of favour.
Inc. I may say to you she hath an ill-favoured savour.
Lust. What sayest thou?
Inc. I say she is loving and of gentle behaviour.
[Dodsley, III, 270, 289, 292, successively]

A late instance of the same trick is furnished by *Common Conditions* (S.R. 1576), where the Vice of the same name (the only personification in the play) has his joke with the knight Lamphedon:

Condi. Gentleman whatsoeuer lyes in my hand is to your ease.
Commaund me euen what you list and Ile do what I please.
Lamphe. What sayst thou?
Condi. I say commaund me what you lyst, and Ile do what you please.
[ll. 592–95] [23]

An even later example awaits us in Shakespeare's *Richard III,* where the Vice, now a duke and later a king, employs it in display of his own repertory of deceit. Richard will receive his due later, but for the sake of dealing with the guile of the Vice in its most comprehensive aspect it is useful to recall, in passing, the scene between Richard and Lady Anne, its quality and method matched by only one other in Shakespeare, the great seduction scene in *Othello.* Both are amplifications of the style and method of the typical seduction effected by the Vice in the pivotal scene of the moralities. At such a moment the Vice displays the full extent of his virtuosity. Step by step, with every device at his command, he dissolves his victim's allegiance to virtue and binds him to the evil which he, the Vice, personifies. No other scene of the morality plot is more a stereotype than this one, in which, with swift efficiency, he pulls the wool over the eyes of his human dupe. It is just at this crisis of the play that he puts to work all those tricks of deceit which, as they appear in him, are characteristic parts of the extended metaphor by which the morality stage vivified the Christian idea of evil. And to them he adds one more, in its effect equal to all the others—his deadly talent for moral sophistry, for masking evil under "glist'ring semblances of piety." "Gode lowyt a clene sowll & a mery," says Lucifer to Anima in *Wisdom,* as he persuades her to abandon spiritual strenuousness and to give herself over to the pleasures of the world.[24] "Can you deny, but it is your duty / Unto your elders to be obedient," urges Hypocrisy in beguiling Lusty Juventus, in the play of

MORAL METAPHOR AND DRAMATIC IMAGE 171

that name, out of his adherence to the reformed religion and the life of virtue that goes with it.[25]

We need to examine a scene of this sort for the sake of gaining an impression of the stage image perpetuated by the Vice as the result of his characteristic behavior in his characteristic function; and *Enough Is as Good as a Feast,* a late morality, will serve our purpose. In this play Worldly Man has converted his energies to spiritual effort and put aside the acquisitive desires of the life temporal. His companion and counselor in this effort is Enough, who stands for contentment with the bare necessities of life. Against them are arrayed the Vice Covetousness and his three homiletic followers: Precipitation, Temerity, and Inconsideration; all four plotting to regain their old authority over Worldly Man. He and Enough appear on stage, where the Vice and Precipitation lie in wait for them. The Vice approaches them with polite address:

> God speed you Sir, I pray you might I be so bolde,
> As to haue a worde or two with you in your eare?
> > [sig. C4 *verso*]

At once he cuts Enough out of the conversation with "I would fain speak with him a word or twain alone." Worldly Man asks the polite stranger, "What say you to me?" But the only response he gets is a grief-stricken face, groans, and a deluge of tears. Curiosity and compassion provoke the prey to ask, "What is the matter? wherefore weep you thus?" Whereupon Precipitation, standing by, puts in his stroke:

> Pure loue causeth him, Sir I wus.
> I am sure that he loues you at the hart.
> > [sig. D *recto*]

Meanwhile the lament of the Vice climbs to crescendo, just intelligible enough to whet his victim's curiosity further:

> I cannot chuse, oh, oh, I cannot chuse:
> Whow! I cannot chuse if my life I shuld lose.
> To hear that I hear, oh wel it is no matter:
> Oh, oh, oh, I am not he that any man wil flatter.
> > [sig. D *recto*]

Worldly Man is drawn in neatly: "To hear what you heer, why what hear you of me?" And now the Vice flings upon him the first light strands of the web, beginning with an accusation brilliant in its irony:

172   *MORAL METAPHOR AND DRAMATIC IMAGE*

Couetouse, couetouse, euery man saith you be:
A shame take them all pratling knaues for me.
I am of such a nature as no man is but I:
To hear my freend il spoken of I had rather dye.
Yea wisse man, you are called euen so:
All the cuntrey of you speak bothe shame and wo.
He was wunt (saith one) to keep a good house:
But now (saith an other) there is no liuing for a mouse.

* * * *

Yea God wot, it is none other, it is none other:
I loue you as wel as mine owne borne brother.
Thinke you that it greeueth me not to hear eche boy and Girle:
To say that the worldly man is become a Churle?

[sig. D *verso*]

Worldly Man decides that he cannot please everybody and turns to rejoin Enough, but the stage direction has the Vice "pluck him back," saying:

Nay hear you, this greeueth me worst so God me saue:
They say you keep company with euery beggerly knaue.

* * * *

Hark you, hark you, in faith knowe you not me?

[sig. D *verso*]

The Vice now achieves his characteristic and decisive stroke by introducing himself as Policy, and Precipitation as Ready Wit: "I dare say your father knew vs bothe very wel." His dupe is sufficiently taken in by now to want them both for his friends. But Enough does not like the new company and says so, whereupon the inevitable rift develops between him and his protégé, the latter saying peevishly:

Your parables truely I do not wel vnderstand:
Except you mene I shuld haue no freend but you by me to stand.

[sig. D2 *verso*]

And the Vice is not slow to drive a wedge of moral sophistry into the breach:

I perceiue that against vs two you do grutch:
Can a man of policy and redy wit haue to much?
The noble king Salomon was rich & had wisdome great store
Yet he seassed not dayly to pray to God for more.

[sig. D2 *verso*]

MORAL METAPHOR AND DRAMATIC IMAGE   *173*

Step by step he turns his victim's mind against Enough, growing bolder as he feels the human clay temper to his touch. The theme of riches, from having had no part in the beginning of his discourse, and after creeping, almost as by inadvertence, into the middle of it, now swells into his main subject, as he replies with infinite courtesy to the brusque objections of Enough:

> He sayes wel by[re] Lady, yea and like an honest man,
> But yet Sir, riches to be good, wel prooue I can.
> For euery man is not called after one sorte:
> But some are called to prophecy, some to preach & exhorte.
> And he by that meanes Heauen ioyes to win:
> But euery man knoweth not that way to walke in.
> Therfore euery man (as his vocation is) must walke:
> I am sure that against this you wil not talke.
>
> [sig. D3 recto]

But Enough does continue to talk against the sweet reasonableness of the Vice, until Worldly Man, now thoroughly enmeshed, throws him off in exasperation:

> Mary fare wel! adieu to the deuil:
> Body of me, he would make me his driuil.
>
> . . . .
>
> Oh Sirs me thinks if I had money and treasure again:
> In faith I would be a liuely lad I tel you plain.
>
> . . . .
>
> The best heauen is me thinks is [sic] rich for to be.
>
> [sig. D3 verso]

He embraces the Vice, who assures him ("if you wil be ruled by me") of "a thousand, thousand, thousand waies" of making money; and Precipitation, in the prescribed homiletic sequence of the *arbor mala,* makes sure that he will be receptive to all the vices that follow hard upon Covetousness:

> Sith worthy Policy you haue intertained:
> Now none of his instruments must be disdained.
>
> [sig. E recto]

Worldly Man's reply reveals that his feet are now set squarely on the road to damnation:

174 MORAL METAPHOR AND DRAMATIC IMAGE

> Disdained? no faith let him teache me what he wil:
> And I wil do it, if it were mine owne father to kil.
>
> [sig. E *recto*]

The Vice and his victim go out hand in hand, not however before Covetousness, true to his homiletic function, edifies the audience through a long, triumphant monologue:

> Whow, of this world I rule the whole state,
> Yea faith I gouern all lawes, rites and orders:
> I, at my pleasure raise war, strife and debate,
> And again I make peace in all Costes and borders.
>   Nay, yet a much more maruail then that,
> Beholde, see you this little pretty hand?
> This is an Arme of steele for it ouerthroweth flat,
> The strongest walles and towers in a whole land.
>
> . . . .
>
> Moreouer I haue in this little hand,
> The harts of all men & women upon Earth:
> I rule them bothe by Sea and by land,
> Plenty I make and I make also derth.
>   Whow, it is wunderful that is don by policy,
> While you liue take heed striue not aginst policy:
> The best of them all are glad of Policy,
> Yea in Westminster hall they vse much policy.
>
> [sig. D4 *verso*]

The play is a tragedy. Having given his avaricious race the rein, Worldly Man plunges headlong into usury, bribery, and a host of related evils. He is especially wicked as an extortionate landlord—the Vice is now his steward—who oppresses his poor tenants. Greed leads him on to other sins, and he becomes

> An abhominable drunkard, a stinking Lecherer,
> A filthy Sodomite, a corupt conscience within:
> A priuy slanderer, and a suttle murtherer,
> To be short, a very dunghil and sink of sin.
>
> [sig. G *verso*]

At the height of his depravity and insolence he is visited by God's Plague and stricken into his last illness. To the end his mind is so filled with concern for his goods that he has no thought for repentance, and his last effort is to dictate a testament that will cheat his creditors after his demise. But he does not get any further than "In the name

MORAL METAPHOR AND DRAMATIC IMAGE 175

of—of—of—of—" before he collapses and expires while struggling in vain to utter the name of the deity. The play ends when Satan appears to carry body and soul to hell; but before that the Vice stands over the corpse and expounds to the audience the meaning of the tragedy, his homiletic candor prescriptive for his role:

> This is the end alwaies wher I begin:
> For I am the root of all wickednes and sin.
> I neuer rest to teach and instruct men to euil:
> Til I bring them bothe body and soule to the Deuil.
> As we haue doon this worldly man heer as you see.
>
> . . . .
>
> Come, let vs go hence, heer is no more to be said:
> Farewel my masters our partes we haue playd.
>
> [sig. G *recto*]

A synopsis such as the foregoing presents, broadly outlined, the typical action of the Vice in its large significance as homiletic metaphor. In more or less detail, and with marginal variations, the same action and the same characteristics of Vice and victim repeat themselves in almost all the plays that compose the allegorical drama. The originality available to the playwright lay in his didactic aim, not in his dramatic form. Between play and play the difference exists almost entirely in the special homiletic pointing that the author imposed on the standard dramaturgic formula of the Psychomachia. The metaphorical action is a stereotype although its moral scenery changes. The evils dramatized, as well as the corresponding virtues, shift with all the winds of re-ligious, moral, social, and political doctrine that blew between the beginning of the fifteenth century and the end of the sixteenth. But through the whole range of homiletic applications for which it was employed, the dramaturgy of the Psychomachia remained constant— and not merely constant, for, with repeated use, it etched itself ever more sharply upon the stage, until it finally stood bare with a dramatic life and status of its own after the matrix of moral allegory which had shaped it dropped away. In a purely theatrical evaluation, it and its chief personage are the one solid wedge of dramatic gold within the didactic dross of the moral play, and able to maintain themselves, there-fore, on a stage rapidly dominated by naturalistic values in the second half of the sixteenth century.

176 MORAL METAPHOR AND DRAMATIC IMAGE

We have only to separate the radical allegory and homiletic method of such a plot from the dramatic image it created to discern in the latter the theatrical stereotype that perpetuated itself into the later drama. The action presents an unsuspecting dupe, an *innocent*—guileless and gullible because he is the epitome of frail humanity—flattered and fooled to the top of his bent, turned inside out and made a plaything by a consummate artist in the craft of deceit. The degree of trouble into which, in consequence, he is plunged, and his recovery or destruction, depend on the degree of comic or tragic bias governing the play. As for the artist himself, his characteristic achievement is to ensnare and mislead his victim, to demonstrate his power over him, and to create dissension and debate where formerly there were unity and affection. His invariable method in that achievement consists of all the forms of deceit and moral sophistry, pretending love when he intends destruction, assuming the "visour of vertue" and the "visour of honestie" when actually he is the very embodiment of their opposites. So much for his role in its dramatic dimension. In its homiletic dimension it is turned directly to the audience, interpreting to them the action of the play, its moral significance, and his own meaning and motivation. It is to his relationship with the audience that we need now to give our attention.

3

We saw earlier (Chapter Four) that the audience attending the morality drama witnessed a type of play that was, by its explicit avowal no less than by its nature, a demonstration. Originating in moral allegory and homiletic pageantry, the morality stage created drama in two dimensions—one more than we are accustomed to in the modern theater. The metaphorical plot itself, or what today we should distinguish as the plot, did not exist by any theatrical right of its own, but was actually a moral exposition—a dramatized homily inserted between the outright sermons of prologue and epilogue which it illustrated, and subject at any moment of its action to additional moral commentary by any of its personages. The constant verbal formula of the didacticism that frames and pervades this homily is: *you shall see, thus you see,* and *thus you have seen.* Such a stage was fundamentally a pulpit

MORAL METAPHOR AND DRAMATIC IMAGE 177

and its audience fundamentally a congregation. Addressed as *lordings, sirs, masters,* or *sovereigns,* they received a running lecture which anticipated, accompanied, and followed the allusive action they overlooked and overheard; and the lecture was delivered by the very same personages who illustrated it by their enactment.

The moral play, in short, divides itself into the dramatic dimension of its allegory and the homiletic dimension of its *significatio,* although the two are always closely interwoven. The latter was frankly and naturally addressed to the audience, and this intimacy between play and playgoer is an organic principle of the allegorical drama. By homiletic compulsion its roles are so inveterately "out of character" that to apply such a criterion at all to their behavior is only a modern naïveté, wrought by our addiction to our own theatrical standards. We need to accept this homiletic transparency of the moralities without reservation in order to avoid being startled by some of its manifestations—by the human hero of *Perseverance,* for example, who, although gaily addicted to all seven of the Deadly Sins in the full flower and felicity of his wicked life, is nonetheless able at the very same time to point himself out to the audience for the horrible example he is of turpitude and impending damnation:

> 'Mankynde' I am callyd be kynde,
>   with curssydnesse, in costis knet,
> In sowre swettenesse my syth I sende,
>   with seuene synnys sadde be-set.
> Mekyl myrþe I moue in mynde,
>   with melody at my mowþis met:
> My prowd pouer schal I not pende,
>   tyl I be putte in peynys pyt,
>   to hellë hent fro hens.
>   [ll. 1241–49]

Such moral precocity and prescience from the lips of the hero is an extreme instance and belongs mainly to the early moralities, where the element of pageantry is still strong. With some slight expansion of the naturalistic instinct in later plays he becomes less transparent and therefore more thoroughly a dupe, edifying the audience on his bad life only after he himself has gained moral enlightenment out of his own sufferings and out of the mouths of the personifications of virtue who helped to restore him. It is because he has recovered from his own

178   MORAL METAPHOR AND DRAMATIC IMAGE

earlier folly that the hero of *Lusty Juventus* is in position to urge upon the audience the lesson of all they have seen:

> All Christian people which be here present,
> May learn by me hypocrisy to know,
> With which the devil, as with a poison most pestilent,
> Daily seeketh all men to overthrow.
>
> [Dodsley, II, 40]

As for the opposing personifications of good and evil, they are, as we have already noted, incorrigible homilists. The virtues never ceased preaching so long as the stage tolerated their presence, and their didactic quality is always the same—somber, elevated, interminable, and dull. Mere talkers and theatrically inert, they and their function dwindle from the stage with every advance of the dramatic instinct in the second half of the sixteenth century. It remained for the evil personae to develop homiletics into a theatrical art by inverting it into irony, satire, and innuendo, by charging it with scornful laughter, and especially by translating it into dramatic action. And in particular it remained for that unique protagonist of evil, the Vice himself, to exploit the dramatic possibilities in his homiletic function. His talent for converting moral instruction into exciting theater explains his great popularity and long life on the stage. He creates a play to demonstrate a moral text, and he interprets every stage of the demonstration with a homiletic zeal matched only by his derision. His relationship with the audience, originating in the homiletic principle organic in his role, is one of the remarkable features of the moralities and the cause of remarkable confusion when he survives in plays that are not otherwise moralities. That relationship, although it has already been intimated, is complex, inviting our deeper inspection.

Of the several standard elements that compose his obligatory program of moral elucidation none is more prescriptive than his exposition of himself: his formal proclamation of his name and its moral significance. Such a revelation, obeying a rhetorical tradition as old as homiletic allegory itself, is no less than a formal sermon.[26] It is also the necessary preface to his action in the play, since it provides the large formula for that kind of motivation which we have already defined as allegorical. Actually it would be misleading to treat such an exposition as exclusive to the Vice, for it belongs to all personifications of good and evil, and in early plays to the human figures as well. In *Mundus et*

MORAL METAPHOR AND DRAMATIC IMAGE 179

Infans, for example, every role, upon its first appearance, introduces itself to the audience with the standard expository formula:

> For all the Worlde wyde, I wote well, is my name;
>   All rychesse, redely, it renneth in me,
> All pleasure worldely, both myrthe and game.
>   My-selfe semely in sale I sende with you to be,
> For I am the Worlde, I warne you all
>   Prynce of powere and of plente.
>
> [ll. 9–14]

>   Cryst, as he is crowned kynge,
>   Saue all this comely company.
>
> . . . .

>   Me thynke it is a nessarye thynge
>   For yonge and olde, both ryche and pore,
>   Poore Conscyence for to knowe;
>   For Conscyence clere it is my name.
>
> [ll. 283–301]

>   Syrs, Perseueraunce is my name;
>   Conscyence [my] borne broder is;
>   He sente me hyder mankynde to endoctryne,
>   That they sholde to no vyces enclyne . . .
>
> [ll. 757–60]

The human hero does the same each time he comes forward to present himself in a separate stage of the pageantry of his life.

>   A ha! Wanton is my name!
>   I can many a quaynte game:
>
> [ll. 76–77]

>   A ha! now Lust and Lykyng is my name!
>   I am as fresshe as flourys in Maye;
>   I am semely shapen in same
>   And proudely apperelde in garmentes gaye.
>
> [ll. 131–34]

And so on. As for the Vice of the same play, he is not likely to prove an exception to the method, and to it he imparts that brusque familiarity with the audience which is the stamp of his race:

>   What, hey how, care awaye!
>   My name is Folye! Am I not gaye?
>   Is here ony man that wyll saye naye!
>   That renneth in this route!
>
> [ll. 522–25]

180 MORAL METAPHOR AND DRAMATIC IMAGE

To Juliet's question, "What's in a name?" the answer, as it concerns moral allegory, is *everything*—particularly in respect to the evil personae of the moralities. For the dramatic energy that moves the plot is, in fact, the allegorical energy latent in their names, defining and prescribing their monolithic natures. No literary feature is more constant for the whole body of moralities than just such an exposition of his name by the Vice as the logical preliminary to his aggression. It enables us to recognize him even when he intrudes into places where we would least expect him. A variety of personifications in the *Ludus Coventriae* reveal the influence of moral allegory upon that mystery cycle: the prologues and epilogues spoken by "Contemplacio" beginning with the New Testament sequence, the heavenly debate of the Four Daughters of God, the figure of "Mors" in The Death of Herod, and the several personified virtues referred to in the episode of Mary in the Temple. But the most striking intrusion of this kind occurs in The Trial of Joseph and Mary. The figure who comes forward at the start of this episode belongs neither to the New Testament nor the Old, and his style is not the style of the mysteries:

> A serys god saue yow all
> Here is a fayr pepl in good ffay
> Good serys telle me what men me calle
> I trowe ye kan not be this day
> Yitt I walke wyde and many way
> But yet ther I come I do no good
> To reyse slawdyr [sic] is al my lay
> Bakbytere is my brother of blood.[27]

Here is the Vice once more with the prescriptive exposition of his name and his rallying familiarity with the audience. A few lines later Raise-Slander is joined by his fellow personification, upon whom he urges a similar revelation:

> But yitt good brother I yow pray
> Telle all these pepyl what is your name.
> Ffor yf thei knew it my lyf I lay
> They wole yow wurchep and speke gret fame.[28]

To which the other is immediately compliant:

> I am bakbytere that spylleth all game
> Bothe kyd and knowyn in many a place.[29]

MORAL METAPHOR AND DRAMATIC IMAGE 181

Having announced their moral quality, they proceed to demonstrate it in action by stirring up "hate" and "debate" as the two "detractors" who accuse the obviously pregnant Mary of unchaste relations with Joseph, her betrothed. Speaking in quatrain sequence in the trial scene, after she denies any misconduct, they subject her to a barrage of ironic scurrility, exactly the style of the Vice:

> In Ffeyth I suppose that this woman slepte
> With-owtyn all coverte whyll that it dede snowe
> And a flake ther of in to hyre mowthe crepte
> And ther of the chylde in hyre wombe doth growe.
>
> Than be-ware dame for this is wel i-knowe
> Whan it is born yf that the sunne shyne
> It wyl turne to watyr ageyn as I trowe
> Ffor snow on to watyr doth evyr more reclyne.[30]

Returning to the moralities proper, we discover that the introductive formula of the Vice appears in them as often as he himself does, and a few examples from different plays must suffice:

> Now here begynneth a game ywys
> For Manhode they wene my name is
> But trust mee syrs if I shuld not lye
> My name is called Iniury.
> > [*Albion Knight,* ll. 126–29]
>
> For I am a chylde that is pas[t] grace
> Ilwyll I am called that in euery place
> Doth much mischiefe this is a playne case
> Vertue I doo vtterly dispise.
> > [*Wealth and Health,* ll. 337–40]
>
> How say you, woman? you that stand in the angle,
> Were you never acquainted with Nichol Newfangle?
> Then I see Nichol Newfangle is quite forgot,
> Yet you will knowe me anone, I dare jeopard a groat.
> Nichol Newfangle is my name, do you not me know?
> > [*Like Will to Like,* Dodsley, III, 309]

An additional element of vivacity enters his exposition when, as in several of the later plays, he becomes coy about his name, or pretends to forget it, as he does in *Cambises:*

> Ha! my name? My name would ye so faine knowe?
> Yea, iwis, shall ye, and that with al speed!—

MORAL METAPHOR AND DRAMATIC IMAGE

I have forgot it, therefore I cannot show.
A! a! now I have it! I have it, in-deed!
My name is Ambidexter: I signifie one
That with both hands finely can play.

[ll. 144–51] [31]

His declaration of his name is only one part of the Vice's expository commitment, and Ambidexter's last statement introduces another: namely, a bill of particulars elucidating the meaning of the name and providing illustrative details for the moral quality it signifies. In this part of his sermon the Vice tells the audience what he can do, or has done, as preliminary to what he is going to do in the play of the moment. Any one of the evil personae of *Three Laws* illustrates this homiletic device—Avarice, for example:

I Covetyse am
The deuyll or hys dam
For I am insacyate.
I rauysh and plucke
I drawe and I sucke
After a woluysh rate.

Father nor mother
Syster nor brother,
I spare not in my moode.
I feare neyther God,
Nor hys ryghtfull rod,
In gatherynge of goode.

Both howse and medowe
From the poor wydowe,
I spare not for to take.
Ryght heyres I rob
And as bare as Job
The fatherles I make.

[ll. 1068–85]

For another example there is the more relaxed satirical monologue of "Sinne," the Vice of *All for Money,* as he demands the reverence of the spectators for his proficiency in his craft:

What, of with your cappes sirs, it becomes you to stande bare,
None can foreswear them selues in trading for ware,
No picking of purses can be at market or fayer,
No thefte or robberie, no murther or killing

MORAL METAPHOR AND DRAMATIC IMAGE   183

Can be without me, ne yet whordome or swearing,
No pride, no slothe, no gluttonie can be vsed,
No periurie without me, neither enuie nor hatred,
As my qualities be good, so my personage is proper.

. . . .

Therefore to beholde my persone, you cannot chuse but ioye.

[ll. 432–45]

As self-glorification and as sardonic invitation to the members of the audience to reverence the evil forces ruling them, such set pieces of moral rhetoric create the personality of the Vice, but at bottom they are transparently didactic. They provide the amplifying details that enlighten the audience about the typical activities of the speaker, and enlighten them, therefore, in respect to the concrete manifestations of moral evil in the affairs of their lives. He is particularly fond of emphasizing his universal power and his habitation in all men at all times. "A lorde I am of gretter pusans / Than the Kynge of yngland or fraunce," is the vaunt of Ignorance in *The Four Elements*.[32] "All states of men me cherishe and falshode Imbrace," boasts Falsehood in *Love Feigned and Unfeigned*.[33] The Vice of *Like Will to Like,* who has learned from Lucifer "All kinds of sciences . . . that unto the maintenances of pride might best agree," cajoles his audience to admit that they are very well acquainted with him:

Know you me now? I thought at the last!
All acquaintance with Nichol Newfangle is not pass'd.
Nichol Newfangle was and is, and ever shall be:
And there are but few that are not acquainted with me.

[Dodsley, III, 310]

Similarly in *The Trial of Treasure* Inclination boasts of his "daily increase" and invites the audience to acknowledge an old familiarity:

I perceive by your looks my name ye would know;
Why, you are not ignorant of that, I dare say;
It is I that do guide the bent of your bow
And ruleth your actions also day by day.

[Dodsley, III, 268]

Sometimes the Vice's preachment of his name and quality takes the more concrete form of a vita or *moral pedigree,* as in *Mundus et Infans* and *John the Evangelist,* wherein he relates his antiquity throughout England and throughout the world.[34] He is a great traveler,

184 MORAL METAPHOR AND DRAMATIC IMAGE

so popular with all classes, trades, and professions that he is welcome and influential everywhere. But his chief aim in this kind of discourse is to describe the various manifestations of his special faculty and his competence in them. He has learned his trade well, has applied it universally, and has now come forward to display it once more for the enlightenment of the present audience. But before he displays it he must describe it, as Envy does in *Impatient Poverty*. He has just sent Conscience into hiding by the same sort of deception that his namesake puts upon Pride in the earlier morality of *Nature*, and he is now ready to brief the spectators on the business just finished as well as on the main stratagem to come:

> A syr is not thys a ioly game
> That conscience doeth not knowe my name
> Enuy in fayth I am the same
> What nedeth me for to lye
> I hate conscience, peace loue and reste
> Debate and stryfe that loue I beste
> Accordynge to my properte
> When a man louethe well hys wyfe
> I brynge theym at debate and stryfe
> This is sene daylye
> Also betwene syster and brother
> There shall no neyghboure loue an other
> Where I dwell bye.
>
> [ll. 513–25]

What need to lie indeed! Between the Vice and his audience understanding is perfect, and he is about to unfold to them his device for achieving his major enterprise in the play. But before we follow him into that let us note once more that his exposition of his name, his nature, and his characteristic activity is a constant rhetorical formula for every Vice of the morality drama. It is the necessary sermon prefacing the dramatic action of the play, for that action is, in fact, arranged by him as one more demonstration of his timeless and universal quality. There will be occasion later to observe that just such a formula survives, along with the Vice, in plays that in other respects are not within the allegorical convention.

Another aspect of his communication with the audience grows naturally out of his homiletic mission and is, in fact, indistinguishable

MORAL METAPHOR AND DRAMATIC IMAGE 185

from it. Creating for them as he does the moral lesson of the play, he continues his didactic assignment by interpreting that lesson for them at every opportunity, interlacing the action with a running commentary. Occasionally serious and somber, but more often scornful or cynical, he is always ready with a moral gloss on the blindness or weakness of his victim, forever elucidating the human frailty which he is busily exploiting. In a late scene of *The Trial of Treasure* the Vice Inclination is just such a chorus to a part of the action which he himself has brought to pass. Incited by him, the human hero Lust is about to marry Lady Treasure, and she comes forward accompanied by her brother Pleasure, the latter invoking all human experience on the question whether "all men us two do not love." Whereupon the Vice is prompt with his aside:

> Love? yes, they love you indeed, without a doubt,
> Which shutteth some of them God's kingdom without.
> They love you so well, that their God they do hate,
> As time hath declared to us even of late.
>
> [Dodsley, III, 291]

And his commentary continues until it deviates into his typical trick of verbal legerdemain at the expense of his dupe:

> *Inc.* But he that on such things his study doth cast
> Shall be sure to be deceived at the last.
> *Lust.* What dost thou say?
> *Inc.* Of Treasure, forsooth, ye must ever hold fast.
>
> [Dodsley, III, 291]

Or once more, when Pleasure promises the hero that if he marries Lady Treasure, "then will I Pleasure remain with you still," the aside of the Vice holds up that pledge for close moral inspection:

> You are both as constant as snow in the sun,
> Which from snow to water through melting doth run.
>
> [Dodsley, III, 292]

In Lewis Wager's morality of *The Life and Repentance of Mary Magdalene*, Infidelity, as befits the Vice of a playwright who is also a "learned clarke," falls into Latin for his moralizations during his ironic conversation with Mary. When she offers him courtesy and affection because he was a friend of her parents, he turns from her to the audience to recite: "Verba puellarum foliis leuiora caducis." [35]

186 MORAL METAPHOR AND DRAMATIC IMAGE

And when she describes her free and easy life as a result of parental indulgence, he is ready once more in the same style: "Puellae pestis, indulgentia parentum." [36] A less learned, more rowdy Vice, Ambidexter of *Cambises,* is no less diligent in moralizing the death inflicted by the tyrant on his brother Smirdis—an act of violence, incidentally, which Ambidexter has brought about in demonstration of his ability "with both hands to play":

> The king through his cruelty hath made him away,—
> But hath not he wrought a most wicked deed,
> Because king after him he should not proceed,
> His owne naturall brother, and having no more,
> To procure his death by violence sore?
>
> . . . .
>
> If the king use this geere still, he cannot long thrive.
>
> [ll. 745–53]

But the choric diligence of the Vice has a reach beyond his constant moral commentary. He is also, by natural extension of his homiletic energy, the liaison between the audience and the dramatic business of the play. The source and center of the action, especially in the later moralities, he is also its spokesman; and his primary subject that way is his outline of his enterprise against the hero. Having introduced and anatomized himself in an exposition of which the serious basic meaning is frequently spiced with comic business—some fustian, a flash of raillery directed upon Joan, Meg, or the woman standing "in the angle," and a claim for the respect due his universal power and handsome person—he proceeds to make the audience the confidants of his intrigue. For the sake of viewing the Vice in this part of his typical function as master of dramatic, as well as of moral, ceremonies, we can take up once more with Envy, of *Impatient Poverty,* a short distance beyond the point we left him earlier. To him in the meantime has come the human hero, formerly poor and bitter about it, now wealthy and arrogant, and named, for the nonce, Prosperity. The Vice is quick to board his victim and is soon in his bosom as his "cosin" and counselor under the name of Charity. When Prosperity departs "to solace me wyth some recreacyon" before they meet again, the Vice speeds him on his way with a pious couplet before sharing his laughter and his stratagem with the audience:

MORAL METAPHOR AND DRAMATIC IMAGE 187

He that sytteth aboue the mone
Euermore be in youre protection
A ha here is sporte for a Lorde
That prosperite and I be well at accorde
I shall brynge hys thryfte vnder the borde
I truste wythin shorte space.

   .   .   .   .

I muste fynde some proper shyfte
That from hys good he maye be lyfte
To brynge hym to mysrule I holde it beste
For he [Misrule] can soone brynge it to passe.
        [ll. 595–607]

This sort of conspiratorial monologue, as the Vice ponders his purposes
in a score of plays, announces its own future development. In the
literal drama it will become simply literal, the method remaining
identical. Let us listen to the familiar style and cadence as they appear in
the similar speech of another moralist—in this case Hypocrisy, the
Vice of *Lusty Juventus,* standing forward among the audience on his
pulpiteering platform of a stage, reaching for the device that will
ensnare the play's hero:

I will be with Juventus anon,
And that, ere he be ware;
And, i-wis, if he walk not straight,
I will use such a sleight,
That shall trap him in a snare.
How shall I bring this gear to pass?
I can tell now, by the mass,
Without any more advisement:
I will infect him with wicked company,
Whose conversation shall be so fleshly,
Yea, able to overcome an innocent.
This wicked Fellowship
Shall him company keep
For a while:
And then I will bring in
Abhominable Living,
Him to beguile.

   .   .   .   .

Thus will I convey
My matter handsomely;

188   MORAL METAPHOR AND DRAMATIC IMAGE

> Trudge, Hypocrisy, trudge!
> Thou art a good drudge
> To serve the devil.
>
> [Dodsley, II, 19–20]

Nor is the Vice content with sketching the scheme of his intrigue before he puts it into action. So completely subdued is he to his didactic mission that he commonly re-edifies his audience at every stage of the business, as Pride does at one moment of Medwall's *Nature:*

> Syrs remember ye that thys other day
> Man promysed me euen in thys stede
> That I shuld wyth hym dwell and now I here say
> The wylde worm ys com into hys hed
> So that by reason only he ys led
> It may well be so but I am sure
> That Reason shall not alway wyth hym endure.
>
> [part II, ll. 304–10]

Indeed, his rapport with them extends to the point where it is pregnant with irony: he treats them as his fellow conspirators in the "game" or "sport" unfolding to their eyes and ears. "Ande euer ȝe dyde, for me kepe now yower sylence," urges Titivillus as he begins his work upon Mankind, promising, "ȝe xall se a goode sport yf ȝe wyll a-byde." [37] And the Vice of Heywood's *Play of Love,* having impressed upon the spectators a sample of his ability and experience, invites their confidence in his skill:

> And syns my parte now doth thus well appere
> Be ye my partyners now all of good chere.
>
> [ll. 685–86]

Let us also remember the deft irony in the expository monologue of Avarice in *Respublica:*

> But nowe, what my name is and what is my purpose,
> Takinge youe all for frendes, I feare not to disclose:
> My veray trewe vnchristen Name ys Avarice . . .
>
> [ll. 69–71]

"Takinge youe all for frendes"—from now on the audience are his accomplices, and he has the right to whisper to them as he approaches the unsuspecting Lady Respublica:

> Remember nowe: my name ys Maister Policie.
> All thing, I tell yowe, muste nowe goe by policie.
>
> [ll. 478–79]

MORAL METAPHOR AND DRAMATIC IMAGE 189

It is not easy, without employing for the purpose an amount of space disproportionate to the scope of this study, to do justice to this unique intimacy between Vice and audience. But even our brief examination must reveal how consistent it is throughout the Vice's career on the stage and how integral and pervasive a part of his role. It has its origin in the profoundly expository nature of the allegorical drama, its reformatory energy unhampered by naturalistic canons. And like that drama, whose creature he is, he exists on the stage in two dimensions: the primary and enveloping homiletic dimension that links him directly to the audience, and the properly dramatic dimension of his stereotyped intrigue. He is a lecturer in moral philosophy who first of all stages himself and puts on a practical, and public, illustration to confirm the moral idea he personifies. In the later moralities and hybrid plays, the whole design of which consists of a succession of his stratagems illustrating his ability to deceive and dominate, and extending from him upon the other characters like spokes from a hub, he occupies the stage almost constantly, prefacing and concluding each part of his activity with his explanatory and triumphant monologues. He not only tells the audience what he is about to do, but also predicts the consequences of his various stratagems, describes off-stage developments, heralds the entrances of his separate victims, and when they leave he usually remains behind to supply the commentary, dramatic and moral, which is always a fundamental part of his office. The whole effect of his role is that of a demonstration, or, as in the later moralities, a series of demonstrations; and his monologues and asides are inevitably couched in the language of demonstration. "A praty game xall be schowde yow or ʒe go hens" promises *Titivillus* in the early morality of *Mankind;* [38] and in a late one, *The Conflict of Conscience,* the demonstrative principle basic to his role has lost none of its force:

> What shall become of foolish Goose, I meane Philologus:
> In actuall maner to your eyes, shall represented bee:
> For though as now, he seemes to be, in state most glorious,
> He shall not long continue so, eche one of you shall see.
>
> [ll. 1926–29]

So committed is he by the inner logic of his performance to this type of discourse that he is bound to fall into it at one time or another dur-

190 *MORAL METAPHOR AND DRAMATIC IMAGE*

ing his exhibition, coloring it with the triumph and derision which are the conventional mood of his stage personality. Essentially he is demonstrating himself, and he rarely concludes his performance without a reflexive Q.E.D. In such terminal lectures his characteristic word is *thus,* and almost as characteristic are words that pertain to showing and seeing, as in the following examples from different plays:

> Lo, syrs, this Folye techeth aye,
> For where Conscyence cometh with his cunnynge,
> Yet Folye full fetely shall make hym blynde:
> Folye before and Shame behynde,—
> Lo, syrs, thus fareth the worlde alwaye!
>
>   [*Mundus et Infans,* ll. 695–99]

> Now may you see how Corage can worke,
> And how he can encorage both to good and bad:
> The Marchaunt is incouraged, in greedinesse to lurke,
> And the Courtyer to win worship, by Corage is glad.
>
>   . . . .
>
> Thus may you see Corage contagious,
> And eake contrarious, both in me do rest.
>
>   [*The Tide Tarrieth No Man,* ll. 698–707]

> How like ye now, my maisters? Dooth not this geere cotten?
> The proverbe olde is verified: soone ripe, and soone rotten!
> He wil not be quiet til his brother be kild,
> His delight is wholly to have his blood spild.
> Mary, sir, I tolde him a notable lye;
> If it were to doo againe, I durst not doo it, I!
> Mary, when I had doon, to it I durst not stand;
> Thereby ye may perceive I use to play with eche hand.
>
>   [*Cambises,* ll. 694–701]

The first line spoken above by Ambidexter in *Cambises* supplies another locution remarkably typical of the Vice in his role as playmaker, and, in fact, another verbal trade-mark of his performance. "Dooth not this geere cotten?" means simply: Does not this stratagem prosper? With minor variations around the inevitable word *gear,* the phrase and its sentiment are a fixture in his utterance. It is nearly always addressed to the audience, inviting their attention to the skill of his device and the success of his aggression. "By the messe I laugh, to se how thys gere doth wurke"—Infidelity in *Three Laws.*[39] "Surs, marke well this gere, for now yt begynnyth to worke"—Sedition in *King*

MORAL METAPHOR AND DRAMATIC IMAGE   191

John.[40] "How shall I bring this gear to pass?"—Hypocrisy in *Lusty Juventus.*[41] "This gere will worke after my fantasye"—Injury in *Albion Knight.*[42] "But marke well this game, I see this gear frame"—Nichol Newfangle in *Like Will to Like.*[43] "Is not this good geare"—Ill Report in *Virtuous and Godly Susanna.*[44] "Ah syr this geare doth trimly fall out"—Courage in *The Tide Tarrieth No Man.*[45] In late plays the commonest form of the phrase is substantially like that uttered by Ambidexter, as the following examples from plays after 1560 testify:

> Nowe this gere to cotten doth begin
> > [*Patient and Meek Grissill,* l. 956] [46]

> A, sirra, in faith this geer cottons
> > [*Wit and Wisdom,* p. 29]

> Ah ah ah this geare cottens I may say to you
> > [*Common Conditions,* l. 894] [47]

> Masse, this geare will not coten; I must another way
> > [*Misogonus* IV.iii.76]

The "gear" of the Vice is noteworthy because it is sometimes a touchstone for detecting him when he survives obscurely in plays that have nothing otherwise to do with allegory. In *Gammer Gurton's Needle,* for instance, Diccon, who creates the "sporte" of the play by a series of deceits that victimize several country people, is just such a survivor. And he gives his lineage away not only by his intimacy with the audience but also by the fact that such intimacy takes the following form: "Now this gere must forward goe, for here my gammer commeth." [48] Actually the phrase merely confirms what will be obvious in every moment of his role when we come to examine it. For the Vice, by natural extension of the theatrical side of his allegorical nature and homiletic enterprise, becomes in later comedy exactly what Diccon is— the playmaker whose histrionic deceits and beguilements create the action of the play as *game* or *sport* for the playgoer. The environment of the stage, especially the popular stage, inevitably stimulated the dramatic aspect of his moral demonstration and provoked in him, accordingly, that kind of theatrical transparency which is constantly a mark of his role on its dramatic side, just as his moral transparency is a mark of his role on its homiletic side. "Now wyll I contryue the dryft of an other playe" announces Infidelity in *Three Laws,* as he summons

192 MORAL METAPHOR AND DRAMATIC IMAGE

his aids "to begynne thys tragedye." [49] "In our tragedie we may not vse our owne names" is the opinion of Pride in *Mary Magdalene*, expressing as well his proprietary attitude toward the play in question.[50] "Farewel my masters our partes we haue playd" is the valedictory of the Vice to the audience attending *Enough Is as Good as a Feast*.[51] "Ah, my masters, how like you this play?" asks Nichol Newfangle toward the end of *Like Will to Like*.[52] And the first words of the Vice in *A Marriage between Wit and Wisdom* are equally thespian:

> A! sirra, my masters,
>   How fare you at this blessed day?
> What, I wen, all this company
>   Are come to se a play!
>
> [p. 12]

And he proceeds, accordingly, to give them a play, after announcing his name, his nature, and his stratagem. We need not wonder that in one of the Martin-Marprelate tracts the Vice is referred to as though he were, not simply a metaphorical fiction of the stage, but another struggling playwright or actor of the times:

Roscius pleades in the Senate house; Asses play vpon harpes; the Stage is brought into the Church; and vices make plaies of Churche matters. . . .[53]

This histrionic intimacy of the Vice with his audience, extending from the homiletic principle organic in his role, explains, at least in part, his survival. He outlives the decay of the allegorical drama because he has developed into a stage personality remarkably attractive to the popular audience, and no small reason for that attraction exists exactly in his unique intimacy with them. His performance, in consequence, is double, both choric and dramatic, and as such it survives in both comedy and tragedy.

How it could survive in both remains the next consideration. Strange as it may seem at first, he is able to become both Diccon and Iago. The difference between them is mainly the difference between farce and tragedy—between country yokels and the noble Moor, between the commonplace needle and the romantic handkerchief. If that difference seems offhand too wide to sustain a bridge between the two intriguers, that is because we are thinking of comedy and tragedy in their classic, or academic, purity of distinction, not of the realities of the Elizabethan stage. The tragedy of *Othello* exists in Iago's victims, not

MORAL METAPHOR AND DRAMATIC IMAGE 193

in Iago. The serious motives which accommodate him to tragedy only obscure, for they are too thin to conceal, the allegorical nature, the amoral enterprise, and the histrionic performance of the traditional *farceur*. As for Diccon, his role, carefully examined, will reveal the same features, as well as a degree of demonic asperity that is not altogether comic. The Vice was able to evolve into both figures because his role is double in more senses than we have so far discussed.

4

We have already noted how sedulously the English moral plays catered to the popular taste for humor, and with what diligence they advertised their ware as a mixture of "sadness" and "mirth." Even when they are most somber in theme and treatment they almost never fail to relieve their serious reflection on mortal life and human weakness by an infusion of comic business. Sometimes indeed the humorous bias of the playwright—the author of *Mankind* for instance—is responsible for so lavish a seasoning of buffoonery that it comes perilously close to obscuring, for modern eyes at least, his serious primary meaning. But that serious meaning is always present as the governing purpose of every morality, and the elements of comedy or farce that are also present either contribute to that purpose by inverting it into humor or simply provide it with comic relief without in any way dissolving its gravity. For the comedy of the moralities, to repeat, is entirely the comedy of evil—a revelation of viciousness by those figures who personify it. There is no better sign of the secondary status of these comic motifs, no matter how generously they are exploited, than that they have their origin in the same personage who is also the source of the moral evil in the play and the jeopardy of its human hero. It is only in the manner of his execution that the Vice is comic; his effect is serious. He laughs as he bites, but his bite rankles and is often fatal. "My speche is all Pleasure," says Cloaked Collusion in *Magnificence,* "but I stynge lyke a waspe." [54]

This double nature of the Vice, which makes him, to use the happy phrase of Brandl, *ein spitzbübischer Verführer,*[55] can be illustrated in its most elementary form by the morality of *Everyman.* Perhaps no evidence is more conclusive against a native English inspiration for the

194 MORAL METAPHOR AND DRAMATIC IMAGE

play, and for its derivation from the Dutch *Elckerlijk,* than the fact that it maintains its somber tone throughout, never deviating into humor—an omission not duplicated by any of the English moralities. Yet even in *Everyman* the Vice, with his deceit and laughter, is incipient in the figure of Worldly Goods. He is the climactic personage among the several representations of Everyman's earthly attachments who abandon him to his fate in the spiritual world. But whereas the others forsake him with some polite expression of concern or regret, Worldly Goods is immune to such courtesy. In the expository rhetoric of homiletic allegory he describes his destructive operation upon the human soul, and, having edified his victim, concludes his sermon with words that stress what is most characteristic of the role of Evil in the moralities:

> Therfore to thy soule Good is a thefe;
> For whan thou arte deed, this is my gyse—
> Another to deceyue in this same wyse
> As I haue done the, and all to his soules represe.
> [ll. 447–50]

In the passionate reply of Everyman the dominant feature in the stereotyped image of the Vice, his deceit, is caught up and expanded:

> O false Good! cursed may thou be,
> Thou traytour to God, that hast deceyued me
> And caught me in thy snare!
> [ll. 451–53]

But the image of the Vice would be imperfect without his merriment, and the very next words of Worldly Goods supply it. The sorrow of his victim is the occasion of his laughter, and we may imagine that he gives vent to it generously:

> Mary! thou brought thy selfe in care!
> Wherof I am right gladde.
> I must nedes laugh; I can not be sadde.
> [ll. 454–56] [56]

If such an illustration is limited it is also compact, and suggests in miniature the contrapuntal tone of the moralities generally as well as the ambivalent role of the Vice. It explains why such plays are, by their own advertisement, both *pleasant tragedies* and *pitiful comedies,* with their implicated extremes of high seriousness and broad hilarity.

MORAL METAPHOR AND DRAMATIC IMAGE 195

The secret of this double mood lies in the radical difference between the nature of the Vice and the nature of his victim. The latter is a moral being in a moral universe, a prey to his own frailty and to the punishment and pain that follow hard upon his dereliction. Desperately human, he is subject to death and damnation as well as to the sorrows that afflict humanity this side of the grave. His own folly and consequent suffering in this world or the next create the pathos of the moral play, his sad example and the surrounding moral commentary create its purpose—the lesson directing the audience how to avoid both the folly and the suffering. Mankind, in short, is consistently a pathetic, if not quite a tragic, figure. His final redemption in the early and intermediate moralities prevents them from being tragedies in the technical sense of the word. In late plays, however, as we shall see, even that technical disability drops away, and human folly sinks beneath the full tragic weight of irredeemable disaster.

But the Vice, the source of the hero's tragic suffering, is, as we have already seen, a figure of very different substance and texture. His humor, which he shares with his evil associates, springs not only from those causes which were our subject in an earlier chapter, but it is sustained in a special way by his essential nature as an abstraction. In his typical role in the moralities proper he is fundamentally, beneath his human features and habiliments, a moral personification. That is to say, he is neither moral nor a person, only a homiletic formula designed to express, through his standard intrigue, the insinuation of evil into the human heart. To deceive all men is his professional enterprise, his "guise," as Worldly Goods says in *Everyman,* to which he is committed by his allegorical meaning; and the didactic commitment of the play makes his success certain, at least initially. Free from human limitation, he is equally free from human passion and responsibility, and his residual emotion is a limitless, amoral merriment, heightened by his jubilation over the success of his intrigue. Professional and impersonal, he is immune to the gravity of his aggression—a gravity that exists everywhere in the play except in him. Nor, by the same token, is his pleasure actually malignant, for such a feeling would render him personal and passionate; and although the anthropomorphic tendency at work upon him frequently invests his speech with the language of such emotions, it is a language without real content, without genuine

196 MORAL METAPHOR AND DRAMATIC IMAGE

relevance to the color and tone of his life in the play. The words of Worldly Goods are true of the Vice in all his performances: "I must nedes laugh; I can not be sadde" (that is, grave, solemn). Insulated by his allegorical status, as well as by the demonstrative nature of his role, against the passions and provocations of human life, yet bound in some degree to parody them by virtue of the human semblance the stage conferred upon him, he inevitably becomes the only thing possible—a figure of farce.

This connection in his role between allegory and farce is subject to fairly pat illustration. In the early moralities the Vice, having done his work, simply disappears from the play, and the remainder of it is given over to its proper concern, the fate of the hero. However, as his role gains stature and popularity in the moralities that come after 1530 and gradually moves into the dramatic center of the play, the Vice begins to assert his right to survive to the very end of the story and to make his final exit a notable dramatic event. Sometimes he is the last personage on the stage, concluding the play by pointing up its moral before he bids the audience goodbye and goes off to hell or to further exploits in this world. Almost as often he is caught by the forces of virtue and receives a punishment proper to the evil he personifies. Thus in *Respublica* Avarice is sentenced to be pressed like a sponge until he disgorges his pelf to the last mite. Inclination at the end of *The Trial of Treasure* is bridled and shackled, penalties fitting his nature, and led off to prison. Occasionally the Vice is banished, as Flattery is in *The Three Estates,* or as Gluttony and Riot are in the surviving fragment of *Good Order*. But the penalty he suffers most often is no less than hanging, and at least once (Ill Report in *Virtuous and Godly Susanna*) he is actually executed on the stage. Now although such punishments, especially the last, are administered seriously because they are administered by those in the play who are capable of seriousness, they are received and endured in a very different mood by the figure at whom they aim. The allegorical immunity of the Vice to any real curtailment of his universal and timeless existence inevitably subdues the effect of his capture and condemnation into a kind of dark-grained farce. His behavior in this situation is no more than a parody of the alarm and resistance of the human criminal confronting the same fate. Either he tries to slip away with a jest, pretending urgent business elsewhere, or he brandishes his wooden dagger and

MORAL METAPHOR AND DRAMATIC IMAGE 197

struggles to escape (Iago re-creates this stage image with a dagger no longer wooden), filling the air with oaths or seriocomic threats, as "Corage" does in *The Tide Tarrieth No Man:* "They striue, he draweth his dagger and fyghteth"; [57] or as Iniquity does in *Nice Wanton:* "They take him in a halter; he fighteth with them." [58] And Iniquity's defiance of his fate, with its sense of allegorical immunity, is typical:

> He that layeth handes on me in this place,
> Iche lay my brawlynge-yron on his face!
> By Gogs bloud, I defye thy worst!
> If thou shouldest hange me, I were a-curst.
> I haue bene at as low an ebbe as this,
> And quyckely a-loft again, by Gisse!
> I haue mo frendes then ye thynke I haue;
> I am entertained of all men lyke no slaue.
> Yea, within this moneth, I may say to you,
> I wyl be your seruaunt, and your maister, to,—
> Ye, crepe into your brest!
>
> > [ll. 416–26]

Filled with the same sense of immunity, the last words of Haphazard in *Appius and Virginia* are merely frivolous:

> Must I needes hange, by the gods it doth spight me,
> To thinke how crabbedly this silke lase will bite me:
> Then come cosin cutpurs, come runne haste and folow me,
> Haphazard must hange, come folow the lyuerie.
>
> > [ll. 1174–77]

Another example, equally compact, of the way the farcical side of the moralities grows out of the status of the Vice as a personification—a status which renders him impervious to the serious temper of the play—is furnished by Bale's *King John.* Toward the end of the play Dissimulation, who is also Simon of Swinstead, comes in with the poisoned potion he has prepared for John and informs Sedition that he will induce the King to drink by swallowing half the poison himself. Sedition feels bound to advise his comrade of the consequences:

> If thu drynke the halfe, thu shalt fynde it no scoff:
> Of terryble deathe thu wylt stacker in the plashes.
>
> > [ll. 1996–97]

But Dissimulation is too much a personification to be anything but cavalier about his own demise: "Tush, though I dye, man, there wyll ryse more of my ashes." Having drunk off his share of the poison, he

198   MORAL METAPHOR AND DRAMATIC IMAGE

staggers back to Sedition and makes his imminent "death" serve for an anti-Catholic sneer:

> I do not doubte it but I shall be a saynt;
> Provyde a gyldar myne image for to paynt.
>
> . . . .
>
> No doubt but I shall do myracles in a whyle,
> And therfore lete me be shryned in the north yle.
>
> [ll. 2095–2100]

Impervious to his own destruction, the Vice is equally impervious to any emotion corresponding to the moral seriousness of the play or the very real jeopardy of his human victim. The gradual contamination of his allegorical nature by traits and appetites belonging to humanity, a process that was inevitable over the long years of his vogue on the stage, will concern us later. By degrees his original status as a personification becomes compromised by the inevitable tendency to dramatize him—that is, to invest him with human traits and to subject him to human experiences and emotions. His eventual subjection to punishment—imprisonment, exile, hanging—is merely one aspect of the humanizing effort at work upon him. But at the same time the whole process is resisted by the allegorical law of his nature, and he is always more or less hybrid—an amoral, elemental force overlaid with the traits of humanity. In the moralities proper he is always essentially a personification, not a person, a fact which renders unreal whatever serious emotion he may verbalize or whatever serious experience may happen to him. His "death" is a parody of death, and his "hate," expressing his elementary opposition to virtue, is, as we have already seen, a parody of that emotion. His action is serious only as it is felt by his victims, who are both moral and mortal creatures, and as it is interpreted, in the terms of human life, by the ethical message of the play. But since he himself is neither moral nor mortal he is free to supply the craving of the popular audience for something besides high seriousness. His role, in consequence, opens itself up to an expanding variety of comic motifs. He appears as a practical joker and clever fool, delighting the audience by his satirical wit, his frequent grossness, his antics (both physical and verbal), and above all by his consummate artistry in deceit.

It is not surprising that such a role should appear to most of the

MORAL METAPHOR AND DRAMATIC IMAGE   199

scholars who have examined it to have no option for survival beyond
the moralities except in the baldest kind of farce, maintaining as they
do that it undergoes steady comic degeneration.[59] In this opinion they
seem to be supported by a variety of sixteenth- and seventeenth-century
comments. In his own time and after, the Vice is often identified explicitly as the fool of the play, or his behavior is described in such a way
that the association is unmistakable.[60] Thus Phillip Stubbes in his
Anatomy of Abuses (1583) asks, "For who wil call him a wiseman,
that plaieth the part of a foole and a vice?"[61] In his *Art of English
Poesie* (1589) Puttenham refers to "Carols and rounds and such light
or lascivious poems, which are commonly more commodiously uttered
by those buffons or Vices in playes then by any other person."[62] Cotgrave in his *Dictionary* of 1611 defines the French *Mime* as "A vice,
foole, jeaster, scoffer, dauncer, in a Play."[63] A passage in *Alphonsus,
Emperor of Germany,* of doubtful date and doubtfully ascribed to
Chapman, is to the same effect:

> *Mentz.* I am the Jester.
> *Edward.* O excellent! Is your Holiness the Vice?
> Fortune hath fitted you, i' faith, my Lord;
> You'll play the Ambidexter cunningly.
> [II.ii.47–50] [64]

It is unnecessary to pursue all such notices, including those prominent
ones in Jonson's two plays, *The Devil Is an Ass* (1616) and *The Staple
of News* (1626), to realize that the comedy of the Vice made an extraordinary impression on the theatrical audience or that his role was
vividly recollected well into the seventeenth century. His popularity and
the mirth his antics provided for Londoners who sought relief from
solemnity are effectively condensed in the following lines from Nashe's
play of *Summer's Last Will and Testament* (1592). After listening to
a long moral discourse by Summer (the season) that put him half
asleep ("I thought I had bene at a Sermon"), Will Summer (the
jester) falls into Welsh English to describe his preference as between
a solemn preacher and a merry one:

Hur come to Powl (as the Welshman sayes) and hur pay an halfepenny
for hur seat, and hur hear the Preacher talge, and a talge very well, by
gis; but yet a cannot make hur laugh: goe ae Theater, and heare a Queenes
Fice, and he make hur laugh, and laugh hur belly-full.

> [ll. 341–46] [65]

200 MORAL METAPHOR AND DRAMATIC IMAGE

To form an opinion of the Vice exclusively from such evidence, however, is to neglect the direct testimony of the plays themselves, as well as available evidence outside the plays that bears in a different direction. It is not necessary to minimize his farcical aspect to realize that farce alone is only the dramatic glitter of his role, not its homiletic substance. His double nature and the double nature of the moral play make it impossible to resolve him into a buffoon merely, as much as we may be tempted to get rid of the problem by so resolving him. For whatever consolation there is in it, the Elizabethans, who knew him intimately, could not resolve him either. The same Phillip Stubbes who was quoted earlier as objecting that it does not suit a wise man to play "the part of a foole and a vice," presents a very much darker picture of the Vice in a passage of the same work that inveighs against the bad examples to be learned from plays and interludes:

If you will learne falshood; if you will learn cosenage; if you will learn to deceiue; if you will learn to play the Hipocrit, to cogge, lye, and falsifie; if you will learn to iest, laugh, and fleer, to grin, to nodd, and mow; if you will learn to playe the vice, to swear, teare, and blaspheme both Heauen and Earth . . . [etc., etc.] [66]

And this darker picture is endlessly confirmed by the moralities themselves, where he is painted in colors that match the seriousness of his aggression. In *Three Laws* the Vice is a "vengeable wretch" and a "cruell enemye"; in *King John* he is a "detestable thiefe"; in *Lusty Juventus* he is "wicked hypocrisy"; in *King Darius* he is execrated as a "wycked feend and full of ill," as a "cruell enymy," as "more wicked then the Deuill," and condemned for his "cruell hatred," his "malice and enuie," with the virtue Equity determined

> To speake agaynst your euell vsage,
> Your flaterynge, your hordome and wycked actes,
> Your malycyousnes and euell factes.
> [ll. 298–300]

In *Impatient Poverty* the "ioly game" the Vice provides the audience is almost cut off at its start by Peace, who sees through him early in the play and threatens him with condign punishment:

> Go hence wretche, thou make bate
> It were almes to set the in newgate.
> [ll. 83–84]

MORAL METAPHOR AND DRAMATIC IMAGE 201

In *New Custom* he is denounced in language conformable to the evil he stands for:

> O imp of antichrist, and seed of the devil!
> Born to all wickedness, and nusled in all evil.
> [Dodsley, III, 43–44]

And in *The Tide Tarrieth No Man* he is apprehended in the end as a "crafty caytife" whose punishment serves as a warning to other "malifactors."

Cursing the Vice is a favorite pastime of the moralities, and it would be tedious to continue with the execrations and epithets to which he is subjected by the virtues who oppose him and by the human figures he has ensnared. One additional example, however, is too useful to be omitted. There is no more mirthful Vice in the moralities than Nichol Newfangle of *Like Will to Like,* with his laughter, his songs, his jests, his fustian gabble, his uninhibited vulgarity, and his rallying familiarity with the women ("kind worms") in the audience, with "little Meg," and with the "good gentle boy" whose critical opinion of the play he invokes at its end. To put him down, however, as a witty fool merely is to be blind to the overwhelming seriousness of his aggressions against his several victims. Two of them are driven to beggary, two others become permanent inmates of the spital-house, and a final pair are hanged for highway robbery. They have all been thoroughly duped and broken by him in his successive demonstrations to the audience of the evils brought on by the loose living and spendthrift addiction to sartorial finery for which he stands. In the end they go out to their separate fates, their ears ringing with his scornful and triumphant laughter. But before they go they curse him with a vehemence that is a long remove from the merely jovial side of his role:

> O cursed caitiff, born in an evil hour,
> Woe unto me, that ever I did thee know.
> For of all iniquity thou art the bow'r;
> The seed of Satan thou dost always sow.
> Thou only hast given me the overthrow.
> Woe worth the hour, wherein I was born!
> Woe worth the time that ever I knew thee!
> [Dodsley, III, 353–54]

And one of them treats him to an epithet which is applied to the Vice with sufficient frequency in the later moralities to indicate how his role, as it strained against its allegorical leash in the decline of the morality convention, came to be conceived on its serious side: "Thou, villain, art only the causer of this woe."[67]

It should be obvious that, like the moralities themselves, the figure of the Vice is a composite of farce and high moral seriousness, and that the combination is deeply rooted in the convention of the allegorical drama. Nor is it possible to discover any comic degeneration in his role so long as he performs in a context of allegory, where his characteristic intrigue is never without its sharp edge of homiletic significance and his effect never without grave moral consequences. In addition to his serious meaning he is more or less comic, in one morality or another, depending as the disposition of the playwright led him to cultivate the mirth as well as the conscience of the audience. But so long as the convention of homiletic allegory prevails over his performance it inevitably shapes the Vice as a purveyor of mirth only within his primary function as a purveyor of damnation. The comments already quoted which stress his humor need to be qualified by others which show that even in the final period of the moralities he was not regarded only as a jester. There is, for instance, the following couplet from one of the poems of the eighties directed against Martin Marprelate:

> Now Tarleton's dead, the Consort lackes a vice:
> For knaue and foole thou maist beare pricke and price.[68]

Equally revealing of the same division in his role is the marginal comment spoken by Hypocrisy in *The Conflict of Conscience* (Pr. 1581) while Tyranny holds forth in the center of the stage: "He can play too parts, the foole and the K[nave]."[69]

Perhaps nowhere do we find richer confirmation of the double nature of the morality Vice than in the recollections of him that occur in Shakespeare's plays. One feature of his clownish side, his addiction to word play, is recalled in an exchange between the pair of fun-makers in *The Two Gentlemen of Verona*:

Speed. How now, Signior Launce? What news with your mastership?
Launce. With my master's ship? Why, it is at sea.
Speed. Well, your old vice still—mistake the word.

[III.i.279–84]

In *Twelfth Night* the song of the clown, as he tantalizes the imprisoned Malvolio, recaptures the typical features of the comic passages

MORAL METAPHOR AND DRAMATIC IMAGE   203

between the Vice and the Devil, whenever in the moralities the former
comes to the aid of the frustrated demon ("your need to sustain") and
badgers him unmercifully:

> I am gone, sir;
>   And anon, sir,
> I'll be with you again,
>   In a trice,
>   Like to the old Vice,
> Your need to sustain;
>
> Who, with dagger of lath,
> In his rage and his wrath,
>   Cries 'aha!' to the devil.
> Like a mad lad,
> 'Pare thy nails, dad.'
>   Adieu, goodman devil.
>   [IV.ii.130–41]

So much for the comedy of the Vice as it is evoked in Shakespeare by
stage fools who identify themselves with him. But elsewhere in Shakespeare the Vice is recalled in a different fashion by persons who are
not comedians and do not identify themselves with him, but view him
as the personifications of virtue do in the moralities when they advise
Mankind against him. There are the words of Hamlet, for instance, as
he tries to make his mother see Claudius in a truer light than her
infatuation permits:

> A murtherer and a villain!
> A slave that is not twentieth part the tithe
> Of your precedent lord; a vice of kings;
> A cutpurse of the empire and the rule . . .
>   [*Hamlet* III.iv.96–99]

Or there is Falstaff once more, as he is described in words representing
the counsel of the King to his son, although they are actually spoken
by the son as he impersonates his father in the tavern play of the first
part of *Henry IV*:

Why dost thou converse with . . . that reverend vice, that grey iniquity,
that father ruffian, that vanity in years? . . . wherein cunning, but in
craft? wherein crafty, but in villany? wherein villanous, but in all things?
        [II.iv.494–504]

204 MORAL METAPHOR AND DRAMATIC IMAGE

It is hard for us, if not impossible, to regard Falstaff as a villain in any sense, Shakespeare having marvelously exploited his affinity with the comic aspects of the Vice. But Falstaff's high comedy is still sufficiently close to its origins in the double nature of his allegorical forbear to prevent him from being a comic figure merely. In him the direct accent of the Vice's wit is not quite free from the faint echo of the Vice's evil. The comic hyperbole describing him as "That villanous abominable misleader of youth" is his vestigial appendix: it does not actually function in his dramatic life, but it creates the illness of which he dies. The shadow of a serious moral judgment hovers about him, disturbing us as it disturbed Maurice Morgann, and when it finally closes in on him Falstaff succumbs to the moral severity which is always present in the traditional stage image of the Vice, no matter how comic his performance. His banishment and imprisonment are regular punishments for the Vice, who, we must remember, is at bottom a personification and incorrigible; and we are in debt to Shakespeare's clemency that the fat knight escapes the even more common punishment of the gallows. If Falstaff's end distresses Bradley and us, that is because our modern sentiment, innocent of the old moral and dramatic convention that survives in him and controls his fate, craves a unified impression consistent with that side of him into which Shakespeare's genius mainly poured—his gorgeous wit and innocuous good fellowship. The Elizabethans, however, habituated by their transitional stage to hybrids of this sort, were completely at home with the double image and the double sentiment.

At any rate, Shakespeare's recollections of the morality Vice confirm his double nature and point the cleavage his role underwent when the dying stage convention of homiletic allegory bequeathed him to the secular drama and to its instinct for artistic discrimination between comedy and tragedy. So long as he remained in the moralities, which lack that instinct because their effort is mainly didactic rather than dramatic, he is an inextricable mixture of farce and high moral seriousness, the source of both the gaiety and gravity of the play. It is only when he is taken over by the secular drama, with its at least partially specialized genres of comedy and tragedy, that he becomes correspondingly specialized, and his intrigue takes on a coloration that conforms to the tragic or comic spirit. But the process is gradual, and in the early

MORAL METAPHOR AND DRAMATIC IMAGE 205

years of the seventeenth century the Vice still trails his double nature into both comedy and tragedy, something of a villainous *farceur* in the former and a deadly villain with a farcical style in the latter. His abstract name necessarily disappears, but the allegorical and homiletic method of his performance linger, and so do his traditional intrigue and his characteristic devices of deceit. In comedy his performance is a demonstration of his wit, in tragedy of his villainy. The Elizabethan poets of the secular drama took him as they found him and reworked him gradually, his traditional status and rooted popularity more authoritative for them than the sort of psychological analysis that troubles us today.

CHAPTER SEVEN

CHANGE AND DECLINE IN
THE MORALITY CONVENTION

A local habitation and a name.
MIDSUMMER NIGHT'S DREAM

I

So far we have dealt with the moral play and the Vice more or less in cross section, canvassing their typical features without taking into account, except incidentally, the changes wrought in both over the long period of their vogue. The process of change in the plays themselves, although rich in details, obeys a single law: like the epoch they mirror, they gradually submit to the secular revolution that separates the Renaissance from the late Middle Ages. The first as well as the most thorough effect of this revolution upon the moralities consists of the shift that takes place in the nature of the issues they present. Their initial absorption with the spiritual crisis of death and the consequent destiny of the soul gradually becomes distracted by a variety of less ultimate crises and less metaphysical forms of salvation. Alongside this change in focus there occurs a corresponding shift in the values governing their moral outlook and the tenor of the lessons they impart. The rigorous ascetic principle that marks them in the beginning and inspires their solemn warnings against the world, the flesh, and the Devil slowly relaxes into a growing tolerance of the first two and a growing neglect of the third. The moral drama, in brief, becomes diverted in the course of its history from heaven to earth, from the One to the Many, with all that such a change implies in moral emphasis and in heterogeneity.

The so-called "full scope" of the earliest moralities is the result of their powerful eschatological emphasis, as we have already seen it. They survey the whole of man's life on earth in order to contrast its mean-

CHANGE AND DECLINE

ness and brevity against the life to come, their analysis extending over the soul's eternity both in this world and the next. Although so large a reach actually appears only in *Perseverance* and *Pride of Life* (if we may trust the prologue of the latter for the contents of its lost second part), it is also present by vivid implication in *Everyman*. Other moralities by comparison, even early ones, are reduced to a smaller, because less spiritual, canvas. Plays like *Mankind, Nature,* and *Mundus et Infans* are relatively curtailed because the transcendental part of their theme has already begun to fade into background, their main concern being with man as the creature of the phenomenal world. When the hero of the last of these three plays appears old, ill, impoverished, and desperate after his career of folly, his punishment already afflicts him in the flesh, and the lesson of the play is, at least in part, prudential. Such plays, although early, mark the beginning of the recession by the moralities from their infinite stage and story, and the start of their more restricted examination of issues within the context of this life.

After 1500 this tendency toward contracted scope and specialized examination becomes sharply accelerated. In only two plays after that date does the human hero bear his generalized name—Humanity in *The Four Elements* and Rex Humanitas in *The Three Estates*—but in neither case does he stand any longer for the universalized concept of mankind. Rather, he is limited in the former to that side of man which engages in intellectual pursuits, and in the latter he is man as a king. Elsewhere in the intermediate and late moralities the human situation, as the name of the hero reveals, is treated from some partial point of view, and restricted to the vices characteristic of some special mode or station of life. Thus in *Magnificence* Skelton confines his analysis to the weaknesses and follies to which the man of royal or noble estate is peculiarly subject. In *Impatient Poverty* the hero of the same name exemplifies a limited moral thesis—the defects revealed in human nature when it is strained by either indigence or wealth. *The Trial of Treasure* demonstrates the ultimate futility of a life given over to unrestrained indulgence of the animal appetites. The ruin to which Worldly Man is brought by his acquisitive impulse is the theme of *Enough Is as Good as a Feast*. In these plays, as well as in all the others of the new century, the trancendental view of the first moralities has declined too close to earth to take in more than a part of the mi-

CHANGE AND DECLINE

crocosm and its moral landscape. This fragmentation of Humanum Genus applies equally to his vices and virtues. After 1500 the medieval penitential system no longer appears in its full array of the Seven Deadly Sins and the Seven Christian Virtues. They survive singly within the limited aim of one play or another and compete with new moral abstractions expressing the miscellaneous issues—sectarian, political, social, and humanistic—that come into being with the sixteenth century.

These new issues are a decisive force in diverting the morality drama from the universal theme and transcendental emphasis with which it began. They create a variety of homiletic topics that are mainly secular, and result in several groups of plays, each group cultivating its own limited theme and special set of values, and each a minor convention within the larger one of the moralities generally. One such group is concerned with the moral delinquency of youth and with the lessons for parents provided by the dramatized spectacle of youthful folly. This topic produced the moralities of *Hickscorner, Youth, Lusty Juventus, Nice Wanton,* and *The Longer Thou Livest,* and relates them to such literal plays as *The Disobedient Child, Misogonus,* and Gascoigne's *Glass of Government.* In greater or less degree most of these plays reveal the influence of the continental humanists and educators who adapted Terence to Christian purposes and used him as model for the construction of prodigal son dramas. Another group is composed of plays related to these "youth" moralities, except that they are even more specialized in subject and humanistic in temper. They are concerned not so much with the moral as with the educational delinquency of youth, and present him as a scholar striving for knowledge but impeded by sensuous temptations and by a lack of patience and discipline. The earliest of these plays is Rastell's *The Four Elements,* after which appear successively *The Play of Wit and Science* by John Redford, a close imitation of Redford's play called *The Marriage of Wit and Science,* and finally *A Marriage between Wit and Wisdom* written perhaps by one Francis Merbury. In almost all these delinquency plays no more of the life of man is involved than that part of it which belongs to youth and young manhood, and the moral issue extends very little beyond his success or failure in the world as the result of his upbringing and education.

CHANGE AND DECLINE

No theme engaged the allegorical drama more thoroughly or distracted it more effectively from its original scope and subject than the Reformation controversy with its political and social implications. It is the whole burden of half a dozen plays and a prominent secondary topic in at least a dozen others—*Lusty Juventus,* for instance, which is a "youth" morality with a sharp Protestant bias, or the much later hybrid play of *Mary Magdalene* by Lewis Wager, which suffers the dramatic energy with which it begins to stray into a waste of doctrinal polemic. Although about religion, the Reformation moralities are not actually religious but sectarian. The "pitiful conditions of humanity" and the redemptive effort of Christianity are lost sight of in the heat of the vehement debate. Ritual and doctrine, the corruption of the clergy, and the secular power of the pope are the prominent issues in these plays, stimulating the most effective satire of the whole morality convention, especially in the moralities of John Bale and in Lindsay's *The Three Estates.* Furthermore, since the viewpoint of the Reformation plays is not private and eschatological but social and political, their concern being with the effect of organized religion upon the national welfare and upon public vice and virtue, they are able to dispense altogether with a representation of mankind. In his stead they substitute a variety of figures who stand for society as a whole or for its various classes. Thus in *King John* the victims of the papistical vices are representations of the several estates—Clergy, Nobility, and Commonalty, and in addition there are the figures of Civil Order and the Widow England. In the pro-Catholic play of *Respublica* the deluded central figure is the lady bearing the titular name, faithfully attended by her rustic servant People, "representing the povre Commontie."

Even more directly concerned with the public issues of Tudor England are several plays which are properly socio-political moralities, their concern being the safety and health not of the individual but of the whole state. Their dramatis personae have civic or national significance and so do their values. Thus in *Albion Knight,* with a hero of the same name, the vices are Injury and Division, the virtues Justice and Peace, and the issue is civil harmony and prosperity versus disorder and ruin. The theme of *Wealth and Health* is likewise social and patriotic, its virtues and vices standing for the preservative and destruc-

CHANGE AND DECLINE

tive forces "of this realme." The same subject, this time more or less confined to urban scope, occupies the late morality of *The Three Ladies of London* and its continuation, *The Three Lords and Three Ladies of London*. The social and political theme, in fact, maintains a continuous tradition from the allegorical plays, through their decline, into the literal drama of the Elizabethan and Jacobean theaters. Robert Wilson, who is conjecturally the author of the two London plays mentioned above, is beyond conjecture the author of *The Cobbler's Prophecy,* a medley of allegory and mythology, but mainly a conspectus of the vices of English society and the decline of public virtue in time of peace. Its Vice is named Contempt, and he stands for the envy and dissension among the several estates and for the resultant turmoil and injustice in the realm. Later plays, which preserve or at least reflect the tradition of the moral drama, cultivate the same broad subject, notably *A Knack to Know a Knave, The Peddler's Prophecy, A Looking Glass for London* by Lodge and Greene, and the revised version of *Histriomastix* which is almost certainly by John Marston. In almost all these plays the supreme value is social unity, brought about through the harmonious submission of the several estates to their established place and function within the hierarchic order. The supreme evil correspondingly is represented by vices that instigate social division, bending their efforts to destroy the bond of mutual trust and loyalty which holds the commonwealth together and guarantees peace and justice.

Within this large theme, or alongside it, all these plays richly preserve for the social historian of Tudor England the specific issues toward which that age was sensitive. In their pages rack rents, enclosures, and grasping landlords create the distress of the poor rural tenant; usury, excessive residential rents, and dishonest tradesmen do as much for the city dweller; ignorant and profligate clergy neglect their parishioners and degrade religion; bribable magistrates pervert justice while unscrupulous lawyers impoverish their clients; international trade, exchanging English necessities for foreign luxuries, drains and enervates the commonwealth; the influx of alien craftsmen, particularly the Flemings, deprives the native English of their dwellings and livelihoods; the poor scholar out of the university, lacking patronage, looks in vain for employment; and pampered or neglected children provoke the times by the timeless spectacle of juvenile delinquency.[1] Although

CHANGE AND DECLINE

social evils such as these are not absent from the earliest moralities, there they are merely glanced at as incidental manifestations of the spiritual wickedness that threatens the soul's eternity. But in these later plays they are no longer incidental, and the jeopardy of the soul gives way to the jeopardy of the state.

2

At the same time that the large and uniform subject of the earliest moralities, the issue of heaven or hell for the soul with all its maladies, is diverted in the sixteenth century by a variety of special topics and partial viewpoints, the issue itself slowly withdraws from its ultimate meaning even in those plays that, unlike the Reformation and socio-political moralities, continue to examine the private war between vice and virtue in the heart of man. Although the eschatological vision is not wholly lost, its moral authority and emotional force deteriorate. The transformation of values that is at work in the Renaissance to make the earth less vile also makes the afterlife less vivid; and we have already seen that the purely eschatological themes—the Summons of Death, the Debate of Soul and Body, and the Parliament in Heaven— do not survive beyond the fifteenth century. Furthermore, the sharp ascetic dualism between the life of the spirit and the pleasures available to the life temporal is gradually compromised. The distinction between heaven and earth, like the opposition between soul and body, becomes less acute; and the virtues that give the human soul entry to the one tend to become identified with the virtues that permit comfort and prosperity in the other. The plays continue to urge the vanity of the world and the fragility of human life, their *contemptus mundi* heritage persisting in them as an habitual overtone. But actually they are diverted more and more into a secular morality. Thus although Skelton can apply the epilogue of *Magnificence* to the traditional lesson that "the Welthe of this worlde can not indure," his play, in its actual effect, is a prudential text advising a prince in the right way of living and governing so that his worldly wealth and felicity may endure. The discrepancy is even more marked in *Impatient Poverty*, where the playwright's ascetic left hand is largely ignorant of what his very worldly right hand is doing. The main intent of the play is to demonstrate the

CHANGE AND DECLINE

virtues that support and the vices that hinder the achievement of riches, as its prologue succinctly announces:

> I speake for this cause, dayly ye may se
> Howe that by enuy and malyce, many be destroyed
> Which yf they had lyued in peace with pacyent humilite
> Ryches and prosperite with them had ben employed
> For there as is peace, no man is annoyed
> For by peace men growe to greate rychesse
> And by peace men lyue in greate quyetnesse.
>
> [ll. 9–15]

But after devoting itself to just such a thesis, with the final redemption of its hero signified by the change of his name from Poverty to Prosperity, the play permits itself the naïve inconsistence of an epilogue that echoes the medieval formula:

> Soueraynes here may ye se proued before you al
> Of thys wanton worlde the great fragilyte
> Euer mutable of the turnyng as a bal
> Nowe flode of ryches nowe ebbe of pouerte
> What shulde men set by this worldes vanyte
> Thynke on this lesson and do it not forget
> The gayest of vs al is but wormes meate.
>
> [ll. 1070–76]

Elsewhere in the intermediate and late moralities such a dissonance is more or less resolved by modulation of its extremes, by a tendency to bridge the gap between heaven and earth. Not only do they display a growing respect for the affairs of men and for events beneath the moon, they also dignify both by a characteristic stress, not found in the earliest plays, on God's providence. His action, hitherto reserved for the single great stroke of judgment upon the soul after it sheds the body, becomes increasingly detected in the currents of the world, distributing benefits and penalties that are felt in the flesh. Virtue, in consequence, qualifies for double reward—both here and in the life to come. In *The Trial of Treasure,* for instance, there is assurance to the virtuous that not only will they attain "double felicity at the last" but also that "in all earthly doings God shall give you success." *Like Will to Like* offers the similar assurance that "virtue and fortune be not at strife," for "Where virtue is, fortune must needs grow." [2] If they do not always offer the gross prizes of wealth and good fortune,

CHANGE AND DECLINE

they make an increasingly large point of honor and fame, considerations that the earliest plays treated with as much contempt as they did all other mundane appetites and aspirations. Both Honor and Good Fame are personages in *Like Will to Like*—the leading figures among those who personify the forces opposite to vice—and the former speaks for both in promising a double remuneration to the virtuous:

> For in this world I Honour with you shall remain,
> And Good Fame from you cannot refrain:
> And after this life a greater crown you shall attain.
> [Dodsley, III, 342]

In the late moralities and transitional plays Honor and Fame become increasingly prominent as the main rewards for virtue just as the world becomes increasingly prominent as the place of reward. Fame (in the older neutral sense of the word) is a personification in *The History of Horestes,* in Redford's *Wit and Science,* and in *The Three Ladies of London.* In *Appius and Virginia* practically nothing is said of a heavenly recompense for the virtue of the martyred heroine, but a great deal of her renown, and Fame and Memory are both at hand at the end of the play to memorialize her to succeeding generations. And it is characteristic of the forces at work in the Renaissance to undermine the Christian ideal of the previous epoch by creating substitute types of beatitude that *The Tide Tarrieth No Man* should quote with approval a saying of Periander's: "Honor (sayeth he) Immortalis est." As both symptom and result of the decline of the eschatological vision, virtue's credit with heaven for heavenly redemption is no longer enough. In the moralities after 1500 it has also become a negotiable instrument in the currency of this world. By the same token vice becomes subject to earthly punishment, but this is a topic for later consideration.

Such changes inevitably bring with them another—a new concept of the nature of virtue itself. The oldest moralities, since they are actually dramatized versions of the *ars moriendi* theme so emphatic in the fifteenth century, present the whole moral effort of life as a preparation for death, and stress an ideal of virtue appropriate to that effort. Their formula for salvation is mortification, life everlasting being the soul's reward for dying to the world while still in it. Since all men are sinners the Church supplied its necessary aid through its exhortation, its sacraments, and especially through its ministrations in the fivefold

CHANGE AND DECLINE

formula of repentance, confession, contrition, satisfaction, and absolution. Above all there is God's mercy to temper His justice, and that mercy is free to any Christian, whatever his sins, whose heart is humble enough to ask for it. But their ideal of virtue, no matter how far beyond man's power to realize it, is an uncompromising asceticism, a strenuous rejection of this world, which is, as the preacher urges in *Pride of Life,* "bot ffantasye & fful trechurye." The secular sway of the sixteenth century, however, aiming virtue in a new direction and orienting it to a new ideal, by the same process enlivens its complexion. As earthly life becomes a value to be cultivated for its own sake and a challenge to be met on its own terms, virtue exchanges its ascetic pallor for a more vital hue, and turns from its former alliance with mortification to a new one with mediation and restraint. Held back by their religious and medieval auspices, the moralities keep in the rear of this transformation, but they participate in it nevertheless. In them also the old Christian enmity between spirit and flesh is at least partially compromised, and by degrees they hold up an image of virtue whose features are borrowed from the classic ideal of moderation.

This new ideal of virtue is best discussed in connection with its source, which, no less than the ideal itself, represents a signal change in the moralities that come after 1500. The citation of moral authority in plays before that date is exclusively Christian—the Bible and the Fathers. It is impossible to find in them a single classic reference, unless Medwall's *Nature,* the date of which is somewhere between 1490 and 1501, is regarded as a play of the earlier century. *Nature,* however, is a transitional play and a milestone in the new dispensation. Although it adheres to the older tradition in its dramatic style and scope, surveying as it does the whole life of man on earth within the schematic array of all the Deadly Sins and Christian Virtues, its eschatology is a faded echo and its moral emphasis mainly humanistic. The representative of God in the phenomenal world is Lady Nature, a pagan deity. The virtue of virtues, and Man's guardian angel therefore, is Reason personified. And the doctrine of the play is not mortification, but moderation under the tutelage of Reason:

> Lo here Reason to gouerne the in thy way
> And sensualyte vpon thy other syde
> But reason I depute to be thy chyef gyde.
>
> · · · ·

CHANGE AND DECLINE

> I wot well sensualyte ys to the naturall
> And graunted to the in thy furst creacyon
> But not wythstandyng yt ought to be ouerall
> Subdued to reason and vnder hys tuycyon.
>
> [part I, ll. 101–65]

This sort of moral program appears in its time as altogether a new thing in the moralities, and so are its auspices, which are not far to seek. Lady Nature advises Man, if he wishes to know the truth about the natural world, to take "Counsell with Arystotell my phylosopher electe," and if he wishes a sufficient authority for God's creation of the world, there is none better than "Ouyde in hys boke cleped the transformacyon." [3] Rastell's play of *The Four Elements,* closely imitative of *Nature* as we have already seen, is so thoroughly committed to "phylosophy naturall" rather than to Christian doctrine that the author's acknowledgement of his authorities is almost superfluous:

> The greks the romayns with many other mo
> In their moder tonge wrot warkes excellent.
>
> [p. 3]

And the moral lesson of the play is consistent with its intellectual loyalties. In the last speech of the mutilated text Natura Naturata counsels Humanity against excess but not against a decent affirmation of the world and the flesh:

> Though it be for the full necessary
> For thy comfort somtyme to satysfy
> Thy sensuall appetyte
> Yet it is not conuenyent for the
> To put therin thy felycyte
> And all thy hole delyte.
>
> [p. 52]

Let us notice that the word "conuenyent," although it had for Rastell a sense several degrees stronger than its modern meaning, is nonetheless a humanistic rather than a religious comment on the sins of desire.

This shift in emphasis from mortification to moderation, creating an image of virtue fit to cope with the world rather than to reject it, is nowhere more conclusive than in *Magnificence.* In this, the most literary and artistic of the allegorical plays, the secular revolution and the classic spirit enjoy a success that is no less than precocious when we

CHANGE AND DECLINE

consider the proximity of Skelton's play, certainly written no later than 1518, to the eschatological moralities of the previous century. Although the structure of *Magnificence* and several of its personifications—Mischief, Despair, Perseverance—belong to the older tradition, the older ascetic piety is relegated to a few lines of conventional rhetoric in its epilogue. Otherwise the moral fabric of the play is thoroughly prudential, an allegorization of the *Nichomachean Ethics* for the benefit of Henry VIII or for princes generally, depending how the allusion is understood. The name of the hero combines the sense of several Aristotelian virtues signifying large-scale liberality and spiritual greatness. The grand prize to be won or lost by him is expressed by the figure of Felicity; and Felicity is no other than the personification of Aristotle's *eudaimonia,* the earthly happiness, crowning moral success, in respect to which all other human aims are partial and subordinate. As for the moral endeavor itself, its entire meaning is concentrated in the key figure of Measure, who steps into Skelton's pages out of the very center of the Aristotelian system of virtue. It is Measure whose moral authority over the hero in the beginning of the play creates the latter's initial well-being. It is the usurpation of this authority by Fancy (that is, wayward, unchecked inclination) that starts him down the road of misfortune. And his restoration in the end is marked by his determination to live under the rule of Measure. If any passage of the play is able to express the moral lesson of the whole, it is the following speech by Measure himself as he puts in his claim for moral "domynyon" over Magnificence:

> With euery condycyon measure must be sought:
> Welthe without measure wolde bere hymselfe to bolde,
> Lyberte without measure proue a thynge of nought.
>
> . . . .
>
> Where measure is mayster, plenty dothe none offence;
> Where measure lackyth, all thynge dysorderyd is;
> Where measure is absent, ryot kepeth resydence;
> Where measure is ruler, there is nothynge amysse;
> Measure is treasure: howe say ye, is it not this?
>
> [ll. 115–25]

Although Skelton's dependence on Aristotle for the homiletic substance of his play makes it unique among moralities for its large use

CHANGE AND DECLINE

of a single pagan author, the employment of classic authority in the plays that follow is impressive another way—for its variety. By the middle of the century the moral drama has become a conventional reservoir for the ethical wisdom of antiquity—its original waters, which slaked the Christian thirst for the life everlasting, subtly qualified by the earthy flavor of pagan tributaries. *The Tide Tarrieth No Man* is not exceptional among the latter plays for documenting its moral lesson by reference to Sallust, Socrates, Plautus, Periander, Juvenal, Antisthenes, Plato, Aristotle, Pythagoras, and Seneca. Nor is *All for Money* exceptional for summoning the moral authority of Diogenes, Cicero, "the learned Seneca," Terence, Themistocles, Cato the Elder, Sallust, Pliny, Juvenal, and Horatius. And the host of classic authors is accompanied by no less a crowd of instances and evocations out of classic history and myth—the heroes, real or imaginary, and the divinities of the ancient world becoming familiar names in the pages of the later moral drama. The resulting effect is the characteristic Renaissance medley of Christian and classic, with a significance for the present examination that is at least twofold. The expanding moral authority of the classic writers in the allegorical drama is prologue to the renovation of the English stage, including the disappearance of homiletic allegory altogether, under the influence of their artistic authority. However, their more immediate influence shows itself through a gradual reformulation of the ideal of virtue which divests it largely of its ascetic nature and transcendent aspiration, and recreates it into a formula for avoiding the pitfalls and gaining the prizes of human existence "upon this bank and shoal of time." And the formula consists mainly in subjugating passion and desire to the authority of reason, while identifying the rule of the latter with prudence and moderation. When the very Christian figure of God's Visitation rebukes the human sinner of *The Trial of Treasure* he does so in terms that come out of a tradition far apart from his own:

> Thou never rememb'red'st Thales his sentence,
> Who willeth men in all things to keep a measure,
> Especially in love to uncertainty of treasure.
>
> [Dodsley, III, 293]

3

An influence from a very different direction, but no less a sign of the secular sway toward the Elizabethan theater to come, consists of motifs drawn into the moralities out of the romantic tradition of western Europe—in particular the motifs of knight errantry and romantic love. In such early plays as *Perseverance,* the Digby *Mary Magdalene,* and *Mundus et Infans* the relationship of the vices, presented as knights or potentates, to their overlords, the World, the Flesh, and the Devil, reflects the social structure of feudalism, but never its romantic patina. As for the relationship between the sexes in the earlier plays, it invariably serves to illustrate the sin of lust specifically, or moral evil generally. Its exponents are such discouraging (according to the pious intention, at any rate) females as Lady Lechery, the meretrix Abominable Living in *Lusty Juventus,* and the numerous off-stage population of the stews and taverns who entertain and speed the erring hero along his primrose way. The ditty of love-longing sung by the young hero of *Lusty Juventus,* although its caroling birds in an "herber green" and its dream-vision of a ladylove grace the English stage with the first trills of the coming music, does not alter the point. The charm that suffuses it is inadvertent, and at odds with its purpose, which is to reveal the depraved state of the singer. Nor does honest love in marriage fare any better, since, apart from the starkly formal relationship between the Rex and Regina of *Pride of Life,* it is altogether absent from the purview of life in the early plays. In them Mankind is either addicted to lechery or he exists in a womanless world. The eschatological moralities, in short, employ the sexual principle in human life as a symbol of evil, or they are indifferent to it altogether.[4]

The change, which is prepared for by the moral changes already noticed, is brought about through the elevation of the image of the earthly feminine to represent the Good toward which the hero is striving, her beauty his inspiration, and his eventual union with her in marriage the new symbol of moral achievement. It is not surprising, since their doctrine is essentially profane, that the combination of chivalric romance and moral allegory should first appear in the education, or "wit," moralities; moreover they have behind them the example of Hawes' *Pastime of Pleasure* with its similar theme and method in

CHANGE AND DECLINE

narrative poetry. In Redford's *Wit and Science* (1538–46) the pursuit of the educational ideal is expressed through the courtship addressed by the youthful hero Wit to Science, the beautiful daughter of Reason and Experience. Perhaps no passage in any of the plays more perfectly reveals the change in moral vision that marks the later history of the allegorical drama than the following one in which the devoted lover despairs of winning his lady:

> Alas! that lady I have now lost
> Whome all the world lovth and honoryth most!
> Alas! from Reson had I not varyd,
> Ladye Science or this I had maryd;
> And those fower gyftes which the World gave her
> I had woon, to, had I kept her favor;
> Where now, in-stede of that lady bryght
> Wyth all those gallantes seene in my syght,—
> Favor, Ryches, ye, Worshyp and Fame,—
> I have woone Hatred, Beggry and Open Shame.
>
> [ll. 779–88]

The course of this intellectual love, with one eye prudently open to the dowry of Renaissance beatitudes—favor, riches, worship, and fame—is presented through the metaphor of the typical chivalric journey of the adventurous knight to the castle where his lady abides. Wit has been "stryken in love" and sets out "For my dere hartes sake to wynne my spurres." No less typically it is a journey beset by enemies whom he must overcome before he can gain her—the tyrant Tediousness, who is a Saracen knight, like Chaucer's Sir Olifaunt, and swears by Mahound; the siren Idleness, who is the foe of the intellectual discipline and has in addition an intense puritanical dislike for honest pleasures. Young Wit, ardent but rash, encounters Tediousness without the necessary aid of his squires Confidence and Instruction, and without waiting for the sword Comfort, which Science, like a proper damosel of romance, sends forward to him as token of her love. He is overthrown but revived momentarily through the diversion tendered him by Honest Recreation. Daunted however by his hard experience, he insists in remaining in that lady's company beyond all measure, until at last Idleness enters to take over. He is soon fast asleep in her lap, creating a moral image like that of Spenser's Bower of Bliss with Verdant asleep in the lap of Acrasia, or a dramatic one like that of Bottom and Titania.

And like Bottom he is "translated." He rises from his debilitating sleep with blackened face, the coat of Ignorance on his back, a cockscomb on his head, having been "Cunjurd from Wyt into a starke foole!" Unaware of his changed condition, he maintains his suit to Lady Science, who has come forward to meet him, charmed by the portrait she has seen of him in his pristine state. Now she turns from him in disgust, giving him a mirror in which he may see himself for what he has become. From this desperate ebb of his fortunes Wit recovers by humbly accepting the counsel of Reason; and before long he is once more on his journey perilous, but now fully provided with the sinews of intellectual war. The audience is assured that this time "A maryage betweene them ye shall see shortlye," and so it turns out. Wit comes to the "pyth" of his journey, which is Mount Parnassus guarded by his old enemy Tediousness. He slays his foe in a brisk encounter and "cumth in and bryngth in the hed upon his swoorde." For his reward—guerdon no doubt is the better word—he is united in love and marriage with his lady. She has thrilled to his exploit from her place "upon yonder mowntayne" and is now won to him "bodye and all." She comes down to greet him, her parents with her, and the two parties join in an antiphonal love song, expressing the joy of the lovers, their "love so sweete," and their mutual devotion "till deth us depart!"— the afterlife no longer even a blur on the moral landscape.

The metaphors of love and chivalry that animate the play are not deflected from their significance by the fact that ultimately they express an educational allegory. Through them Eros becomes dignified into the symbol of the moral Good, the love between man and woman spiritualized into a type of salvation. The theme almost sums up the last four centuries of our literature, and how fruitful it has been on the stage all the world knows. There is a further consideration, just as important for the main purpose of this study as for the present branch of it: metaphor, originally transparent, tends to become opaque, ceases to be metaphorical. Both the history of religion and the history of language testify to this phenomenon, and the theater is no exception. The dramatic metaphors developed by the allegorical plays as artistic means to homiletic ends eventually occupy the stage in their own right when allegory withers and the literal drama gains the ascendant. In Redford's play allegory already shows signs of being distracted by the

CHANGE AND DECLINE

artistic and sensuous possibilities in its metaphors. The figurative meaning suffers not thinking on when, as in the second song of the play, it is invaded by a very unallegorical *Compleint d'Amour:*

> Exceedyng mesure, wyth paynes continewall,
>   Langueshyng in absens, alas! what shall I doe,
> Infortunate wretch, devoyde of joyes all,
>   Syghes upon syghes redoublyng my woe,
>   And teares downe fallyng fro myne eyes toe?
> Bewty wyth truth so doth me constrayne
> Ever to serve where I may not attayne!
>
> [ll. 575–81]

The amatory and chivalric complexion of the play is further heightened by the fact that it is full of women—four in all—and three of them are nobly planned as desirable types of the earthly feminine. The heroine herself is as enticing an object as any lady of them all in courtly romance, and in the kisses the hero seeks from her metaphor plays a poor second to his "amorous love." The play, in brief, reserves a shock for anyone who, without warning, wanders into it subdued by the steep and thorny way to heaven in the older moralities. Here heaven is no higher than Parnassus Hill, its felicity no more ethereal than the outstretched arms of two terrestrial lovers, its unexpressive nuptial song the very clear language of romantic passion and requital.

The anonymous *Marriage of Wit and Science,* licensed 1569, is not an original play, but Redford's earlier morality rewritten in septenary couplets, in classic act and scene division, and with a pair of scenes omitted. The plot is the same and so are most of the roles. And it is no less charged than its predecessor with the values of romantic love and chivalry. The approach of his lady sends Wit into a rhapsody of oxymorons:

> I see her come, her [face my] sorrow and my joy,
> My salve and yet my sore, my comfort and my care,
> The causer of my wound, and yet the well of my welfare;
> O happy wight, that have the saint of your request,
> O hopeless hope, that holdest me from that which likes me best!
>
> [Dodsley, II, 358]

Tediousness damns the young hero and all other such knights-errant who "promise, for their woman's love, to vanquish me in fight"; and like any true cavalier the lover drinks valor out of his mistress's beauty:

CHANGE AND DECLINE

Here in my sight, good madam, sit and view:
That, when I list, I may look upon you.
This face, this noble face, this lively hue,
Shall harden me, shall make our enemy rue.
                                    [Dodsley, II, 388–89]

His victory earns him the applause of his squires, "O valiant knight, O conquest full of praise!" and with due chivalric courtesy he returns the compliment, "You, you, my faithful squires, deserve no less." His words at the end sum up the universal romantic formula: "My foe subdued, my lady's love possessed." Of the old somber moralizing there is not a word. Instead the audience is promised that the two lovers will live according to the new religion—"one soul in bodies twain." We have come a long way from the insistent warning of the old moralities: *Memento, homo, quod cinis es et in cinerem reverteris.*

In the last play of this series of "wit" moralities, *A Marriage between Wit and Wisdom,* which belongs to the decade of the seventies and survives in manuscript only, the same plot is distracted by homely comedy. The homiletic purpose and the allegory itself are pushed aside by an inordinate concentration on the deceitful antics of the Vice Idleness—an indication of the way the wind is blowing in the late period of the moralities. Romantic values, however, dominate as much serious meaning as the play possesses. After tumbling into a variety of pitfalls set for him by Idleness, young Wit finally arrives at the house of Wisdom, the fair object of his affections. She welcomes him in a style that does justice to Montaigne's remark that the surest sign of wisdom is a constant cheerfulness: "Tantara tara tantara, My husband is at hand!" He is allowed to embrace her "comly corpes," and the play ends with their nuptials, which Idleness attends disguised as a priest, for Catholicism is always fair game in any of the moralities that come after the Reformation, no matter what their subject.

The influence of the romantic theme can be traced in the method of other plays that have nothing to do with education. The social meaning of *Albion Knight* is organized into a projected marriage between the titular hero and Dame Plenty, who is the daughter of Peace and the niece of Justice—a marriage which the vices of the play plot to prevent. *The Trial of Treasure* presents the moral success of the virtuous hero Just as a marriage between him and the lady named Trust, signifying

CHANGE AND DECLINE

his earthly happiness in consequence of his "trust" in God. His opposite number, the erring hero Lust, is married more gorgeously to Lady Treasure, "a woman finely appareled," the symbol of his blind addiction to pelf and pleasure. The two late moralities attributed to Robert Wilson, *The Three Ladies of London* and *The Three Lords and Three Ladies of London,* are full of the motifs of gallantry and courtly love. After a series of misadventures, the result of giving their hearts to the wrong personifications, the three ladies, who are Lucre, Conscience, and Love, are lavishly wooed and wed by the right ones, the noble cavaliers Pomp, Pleasure, and Policy. By the time of both these plays, however, John Lyly is already composing his amatory comedies, and the romantic theme has become a commonplace of the English stage. But what one scholar finely says of Lyly must be qualified by what has appeared in the foregoing pages, and understood as marking the crest of a tendency rather than its beginning:

Lyly's love-apprehension is new and striking. His faith in the naked impulse of sexual attraction is exceptionally pure and independent of all moralizings. . . . *Love has become, for the first time, dramatic,* challenging the religious consciousness which, through the centuries preceding, held a monopoly over drama.[5]

It is impossible to leave the subject of romantic love, with its accompanying manifestation of a secular ethic, without a word about its existence in the hybrid plays, in which the personifications of the moralities mingle with concrete men and women inside literal plots out of history or legend. Whatever resistance the religious heritage of the "pure" moralities offers to the love theme is dissolved immediately we encounter these transitional plays, about which the reader may expect to hear more in the next chapter. Their writers understand how to dramatize love by presenting its careless rapture in sharp contrast to misfortune before or after, and they apply the method to almost any material that comes to hand. It is instructive to see how the romantic impulse, together with its dramatic usefulness as peripeteia, moves them to work transformations on starkly unromantic stories by steeping them in this erotic chemistry, often with strange results. In *The History of Horestes,* Clytemnestra and Aegisthus, just before they are captured and executed by the hero, engage in a long and light-hearted duet of love with the refrain of "My deare Lady," one stanza of

224   *CHANGE AND DECLINE*

which is enough to show what an Elizabethan romanticist is capable
of doing to classic story:

> And was it not a worthy sight
> Of Venus childe, kinge Priames sonne:
> To steale from Grece a Ladye bryght,
> For whom the wares of Troye begon?
> Naught fearinge daunger that might faull,
> > Lady, ladie:
> > From Grece to Troye he went with all,
> > My deare Lady.
> > > [ll. 538–45]

The same play ends with the celebration of love and marriage between
the hero and Hermione, their vows of love and loyalty giving a new
glow to the old denouement. *Virtuous and Godly Susanna* presents
the heroine and her husband in a setting of domestic bliss just before
their troubles come upon them—he a generous and indulgent husband,
she a devoted and solicitous wife, worrying over his health and his
lateness to dinner. In the end, of course, they are restored to their
previous happiness. In *Patient and Meek Grissill* the old virtue story is
transformed by its new romantic aura. The very moment before the
Vice begins his work of alienation the two married lovers join in a
ditty expressive of their felicity, the first stanza of which, sung by the
Marquis, is interesting for its early reference (the play was licensed in
1565) to another tale of love:

> Syth Fate and Fortune thus agree,
> My onlie ioye and Ladie deare:
> A *Romeo* I will rest to thee,
> In whome the fruites of Faith appeare:
> > Heigh hoaw, my true loue,
> > I ioye in thee my Turtell Doue.
> > > [ll. 840–45]

Cambises is not so engrossed by the theme of tyranny and its punishment as to forgo a scene of the amatory-idyllic. The lady whom the
tyrant forces to become his wife although their kinship forbids it,
enjoys, a moment before this violence comes upon her, the *pleasaunce*
of nature and love in the company of the young lord who woos her:

> Lady deer, to king a-kin, forthwith let us proceed
> To trace abroad the beauty feelds, as erst we had decreed.

CHANGE AND DECLINE

The blowing buds, whose savery sents our sence wil much delight;
The sweet smel of musk white-rose to please the appetite;
The chirping birds, whose pleasant tunes therein hear record,
That our great joy we shall it finde in feeld to walk abroad;
On lute and cittern there to play, a heaven'y harmony:
Our eares shall heare, hart to content, our sports to beautify.

[ll. 861–68]

In such a passage we see some of the gathering forces that eventually overthrew completely the drama of homiletic allegory. The stage is invaded by the colors of earth—by the excitement and glamor of sexual love; by courtesy, that earthly substitute for the heavenly virtues; by the pleasures of the natural world. One is tempted to say that in *Cambises* the ascetic and abstract tradition is already wholly overthrown. The story is historical, and so are most of the characters. A Persian king stands in the old place of Humanum Genus, and the virtuous personifications have disappeared without being replaced by anyone. But a dozen abstractions remain in the cast, although some of them are abstract in name only; and the Vice Ambidexter, as vigorous as any of his forebears although in a different way, reminds us that the old tradition lingers inside the new.

A step further takes us into a dramatic world completely dominated by romantic values, whose unpath'd waters and undream'd shores provide endless room for knightly adventure and amorous distress. Such plays are *Sir Clyomon and Sir Clamydes* and *Common Conditions,* the former probably and the latter certainly composed in the seventies. Both are rife with the motifs of honor, fame, chivalry, and love. With the same exception in both plays, the homiletic method no longer exists for either, having given way to sheer spectacle and titillation; and they exactly fit Stephen Gosson's wrathful description of plays that are no longer morally edifying:

Sometime you shall see nothing but the aduentures of an amorous knight, passing from countrie to countrie for the loue of his lady, encountering many a terible monster made of broune paper, & at his retorne, is so wonderfully changed, that he can not be knowne but by some posie in his tablet, or by a broken ring, or a handkircher, or a piece of a cockle shell. What learne you by that? [6]

As for personification, in one respect it comes to no more in both plays than the brief appearance of Rumor and Providence in *Sir Clyomon,*

226 *CHANGE AND DECLINE*

the former merely choric exactly as in *2 Henry IV,* the latter repeating the old morality role of the virtue who appears in the nick to save the despairing sinner from suicide, except that in this case the despair afflicts a pretty heroine, and not for sins but for the loss of her lover. But in another respect personification and the homiletic method in both these plays come to a great deal. The enemy of all the romantic values in *Sir Clyomon,* and therefore of all the figures who embody them, is Subtle Shift the Vice. And in *Common Conditions* the Vice so thoroughly dominates the play as the tireless foe of love and knighthood that his name supplies its title. He is the old Vice still, performing in the same homiletic and histrionic dimension as of yore, but with certain differences that can best be examined after we trace the decline of the method of homiletic allegory from the stage and the rise of the literal convention that replaced it.

4

The shift in view and values, which reveals itself in the foregoing pages as the primary aspect of the secular revolution within the moralities, partly anticipates but mainly accompanies another feature of that revolution, which is no less than the decay of the morality drama and its disappearance—at least in its overt form and obvious character— from the English stage. The two processes are, in fact, interwoven strands of a single development, and we have already detected the nature of the second while tracing the first. Together they mark the disintegration of that original vision which embraced the universal drama of mankind and viewed it *sub specie aeternitatis,* comprehending the entire human race within a single spiritual formula and a typical destiny. Such a vision, directly trained upon abstraction and generality, found its natural literary method in personification, which vivified the abstract by creating the figures of vice and virtue in medieval homiletic art and by dramatizing them in the moralities. The same vision, dealing with the race of men, who are not abstractions, assimilated the human variety into a type figure as generalized as possible: namely, Mankind, Humanum Genus, or Everyman. The spread of the secular spirit constricted the vision and subverted its method. From the arena of Christian metaphysics the action moves, as we have

CHANGE AND DECLINE

seen, into the arena of the world, and finds habitation even more local in England or London. The single transcendental subject is replaced by a world of particulars—by detailed issues respecting the Reformation, youthful delinquency, education, political unity, social justice, national prosperity, domestic happiness, and other topics equally specialized and secular. Simultaneously the ascetic ideal withdraws before the advance of moral standards in and of the world. These changes in vision inevitably have their effect upon theatrical methods and values, and they are the large cause for the eventual birth of an artistic standard independent of homiletic purpose and, therefore, for the new dramaturgy that eventually flowers into the Elizabethan and Jacobean theater. At the same time they alter the morality drama itself to the limit that it can absorb alteration while still retaining its identity, and when that limit is reached they bring its formal existence to an end. In the sixteenth century these two dramatic conventions—the one crescent, the other waning—merge frequently to produce plays variously designated as hybrid, polytypic, or transitional. Such plays concern us greatly but not immediately. They will have their day after we carry the moralities somewhat closer to the end of their tether.

Any definition of death is likely to be more practical than profound, since life is not actually gone from cells and members the moment the heart stops beating. The same problem is intensified for an institution like the morality drama, whose homiletic method remains vigorous as an influence and whose dramatic fragments survive in disguise and in dispersal after it itself no longer exists in a visible form. As a matter of practical definition, however, we may say that the moral play disappears when the two sets of figures who define its formal existence, its personifications and its types, succumb to the secular tendency pressing the drama toward the concrete, the particular, the literal. But these two sets of figures, being of different natures, succumb in different ways. As we have already seen in part, the generic figure of Mankind becomes divided and specialized into narrower types to suit the limited viewpoints of later plays. As Youth, Magnificence, Wit, or Impatient Poverty, he appears in exemplification of what is typical not of mankind generally but of some selected aspect of human nature and human existence; and his career in the play does not extend to ultimate Christian issues but achieves its denouement within the con-

CHANGE AND DECLINE

fines of a particular moral problem. It is instructive in this regard to compare the very early morality *Pride of Life* with one written more than a century later, Lindsay's *Satire of the Three Estates*—a comparison invited by the fact that in each play the central figure bears the title of king. The Rex Vivus of *Pride* is attended by a wife with the title Regina, by the knights Fortitudo and Sanitas, and by a *nuntius* named Mirth or Solas. He is displayed as a monarch of great prowess and unlimited dominion. But he is Everyman nonetheless, and the entire regal setting is essentially a metaphor with the broadest possible meaning for humanity in general. It expresses that imperial arrogance that afflicts human nature when it is in the full flush of material success, physical strength, and sensuous vigor—when decay, death, and the soul's eternity are annihilated from the mind by that *Superbia,* or Pride of Life, which is the Christian equivalent of the classic *Hubris.* Lindsay's play, on the other hand, has no eschatological message, and its Rex Humanitas is literally intended to represent the state of kingship. His humanity is not presented at large but only in those restricted terms relating to the duties and moral requirements of his royal station. Even more narrowly, he is displayed as the type figure of a *Scottish* king, for the play is directly and frankly concerned with the welfare of Scotland. His attraction to pleasure and his negligence of his high office expose his realm to a host of evils richly topical for the situation in that country in the second quarter of the sixteenth century. After he is aroused from his sloth and sensuality by Correction, God's messenger, the remainder of the play is largely devoted to an exposure of Scottish abuses and to their reformation. *The Three Estates* is actually an amalgam of two types of the morality play, the private and the public. Its first part, which resembles *Magnificence,* is devoted to the personal life of Rex Humanitas, detailing those vices to which royalty is prone. In its second part, however, it is another example of those socio-political moralities already described which examine the evils in the national life according to their appearance in the several estates, these latter being victimized by the same vices who previously misled the king. In either case the generalized figure and condition of Humanity has fractured into human types and situations of limited significance.

In *The Three Estates,* however, we are only at the beginning of

CHANGE AND DECLINE

this process of limitation which in the moralities of the sixteenth century curtails the original figure who encompassed the whole human race. Having been specialized in the manner recounted, he now undergoes a further reduction, of considerable dramatic import, for which there is no better name, perhaps, than *fission*. Instead of a single human personage to exemplify the lesson of the play, several of the moralities after 1550 present us with two, one on each side of the moral ledger. An early instance appears in *Wealth and Health,* whose two titular figures engage in a long debate before Wealth acknowledges the superior worth of Health in the economy of private and national life. Later both are deceived and led astray by the vices, and both are eventually recovered from their distress by the efforts of Remedy, who is the play's single personification of the Good. More significant in this development, *The Trial of Treasure* organizes its homily around the contrasting pair of Lust and Just, the former addicted to a life of heedless pleasure and aggrandizement, the latter religiously aware of God and of the need for virtuous restraint. Lust, in consequence, ends wretchedly, betrayed by his devotion to the wrong objects; while Just enjoys happiness in this life and the certainty of bliss in the next. In the same way *Enough Is as Good as a Feast* presents contrasting types of humanity in the Heavenly Man and the Worldly Man, their careers corresponding to their names, their ends corresponding to their careers. Worldly Man, as we saw earlier in the synopsis of the play, persists in his turpitude, dies suddenly and miserably, and is carried off to hell. Heavenly Man, on the other hand, lives to enjoy a double satisfaction: his own obvious moral success and the chance of edifying the audience in the epilogue with pious contrasts between himself and his now hapless opposite number. It is not merely fortuitous that the catastrophes with which these two plays end, together with the no less unhappy termination to the career of Moros, the very specialized type of humanity in *The Longer Thou Livest,* provide the earliest examples, save one, of unmitigated tragedy in the moralities. The prior example of *Nice Wanton* will demonstrate very much the same point. As we shall see before long, the development of a tragic conclusion in the later morality drama is closely involved with the movement toward the concrete and the particular which we are at present examining.

To carry this movement to its limit we need to inspect a group of

230   *CHANGE AND DECLINE*

three plays that belong to the seventh and eighth decades of the century and represent almost the farthest extension of the morality drama as an autonomous form still confined within the lists of its own governing principles. Perhaps the earliest of the three is *Like Will to Like* by Ulpian Fulwell, published in 1568 and probably revived as late as 1600 by the Earl of Pembroke's Players.[7] The division of humanity into specialized figures of virtuous and evil inclination maintains itself in this play; and Virtuous Living, vehemently rejecting the solicitations of the Vice, enjoys a happy life and happy prospects in eternity. Erring humanity, on the other hand, is presented not through one role alone but through no less than half a dozen; and the range of typical significance in each is reduced in a ratio corresponding to this sixfold multiplication. Each is the type of a particular form of excess or knavery, reminding us of the humour characters to come in the later drama. They are all wastrels, but more or less specialized, as their names indicate, in dissipation and roguery, with a racial classification thrown in for good measure. Ralph Roister and Tom Tosspot are types of the profane young bloods about town who waste their patrimony on finery and tavern frolics, and in the end they are reduced to beggary. Hance and Philip Fleming, like their earlier compatriots in *Wealth and Health,* represent the drunken, gluttonous Lowlander living and working in England, the moral purpose here being crossbred with xenophobia, and they end their days as diseased inmates of the spital. The final pair are Cuthbert Cutpurse and Pierce Pickpurse, obvious professional types, who leave the world by way of the gallows. The members of each duo are brought together by the Vice, on the principle of like will to like, and bound together in the common fate he metes out to them. All six, as well as Virtuous Living, their moral opposite, descend as specialized heirs of the broadly generalized figure of Mankind, who in himself contained all seven of the Deadly Sins, whose soul was finally saved by mercy in heaven or by pious counsel on earth, and who occupied the center of the stage in a comedy of redemption. His six reprobate descendants in this play sin without redemption in narrow categories of evil that reflect the concern of the playwright over the topical vices of his time and place. The disasters which end their careers of folly do not wait for the flight of their souls to judgment but visit their mortal lives as sharp reminders of what this world can

CHANGE AND DECLINE

do to those who offend against its canons. And they do not occupy the center of the stage but come and go as so many moral exhibits; for the same revolution that has dispersed Mankind into plurality, with the consequent loss of dramatic concentration, has cut away the numerous secondary vices of the original moralities from the single large figure who introduces the play, brings it to its close, and stands throughout at dead dramatic center, engrossing the action.

The Tide Tarrieth No Man by George Wapull, licensed and published in 1576, continues this development within the moralities toward the concrete and particular, and confirms its influence upon the structural change by which the Vice dispossesses his victims from the central role. Like Fulwell's play above, *Tide*'s limited purview and restricted homily are indicated by the special-text admonition within its proverbial title. The theme of the play neatly paces the secular revolution we are discussing, for it is a Christian comment on the loss of eschatological aim in the life of the sixteenth century and the consequent misdirection of human energy toward acquisition, ambition, and sensual fulfillment. The title, constantly repeated in the text, has double significance. As employed by the Vice in its bad sense, it drives humanity to make the most of life while it lasts by feverish pursuit of wealth, position, and animal satisfactions. In its pious meaning, as the play's virtuous figures intend it, it urges the shortness of life as compelling reason for preparing one's soul for eternity. The representative of the human minority who live according to the better sense of the proverb goes under the name of Faithful Few, and he is abetted by personifications of Authority (civil), Correction (judiciary and police), and Christianity. The other side of human life is partitioned among half a dozen persons who move in and out of the play and reveal themselves in passing as separate examples of human folly. The first is Greediness, the type of the grasping, dishonest businessman, who comes to a bad end by dying "in a great madnesse" brought on by theological *desperatio*. Another, with a name made to order for John Bunyan, is No-Good-Neighborhood, typifying the selfish landowner who deprives his poor neighbors of their livelihoods by buying out the property they hold in lease. Next is the Courtier, his characteristic passion expressed by his name of Willing-to-Win-Worship, who succumbs to the usurious rate and multiple cheats of the moneylender so that he may have the

CHANGE AND DECLINE

wherewithal to maintain himself in the style demanded by the society "of Courtyers, so iolly a rout, and eke of Ladies a company so trim." The conclusion of his history may be guessed from a later scene presenting that London commonplace—the wretched Debtor (whether the same Courtier or another person is not clear) in the grip of the sergeant who is haling him to the Counter. The last two representatives of mankind's lower nature are Wantonness and Wastefulness— she a "pretty peate" of fourteen in haste to get married against her mother's wish to have her first reach years of discretion; he a young man of slender will who, as her husband, squanders his means and neglects his occupation to give her the finery and entertainment she craves. They are in good time reduced to beggary, going their separate ways to grovel and scrounge for sustenance; and he is driven by despair to the edge of suicide, from which he is saved by the timely intervention of the forces of virtue.

In this clinical display of human error each of the subjects, at the crux of his moral history, encounters the Vice and succumbs to his blandishments. The latter is practically never off the stage or away from its center, and his victims enter to him by turn in their moment of hesitation, when they are poised in suspense between conscience and desire. His energetic sophistry overcomes their scruples and shoves them headlong to perdition on the highway of their baser impulses. His name, which is "Corage," gives trouble to the modern reader who neglects its older meaning. It stands for the blind will and appetitive energy governing the lives of animals, Chaucer's "smale fowles" for instance; but as the animal *élan* in our human nature it is potent for ill unless subject to a more spiritual authority. In *The Pastime of Pleasure* it is "vylayne courage," and, like Liberty in Skelton's *Magnificence,* whose "corage must be croppyd," it must be checked and guided to an end purer than its own by the light of reason or the light of eternity. Otherwise, in its free-ranging effect, the equivalent of limitless self-indulgence, it is sinful and destructive, reducing human life to blind desire and brutish passion. It is within the frame of this moral thesis that the play arranges its multiple, and contracted, types of humanity—each an example of the effect of "corage contagious" in a common walk of life, each hastening to make hay while the sun shines, except that it is the wrong kind of hay.

CHANGE AND DECLINE

The last of this trio of late plays illustrating the sway within the moralities from the general to the particular, from the typical to the individual, is *All for Money* by Thomas Lupton, licensed in 1577 and published the year following. Here again the special-text title limits the moral thesis, which is even further limited by the fact that its sense is mainly applied to the corruption of the law through bribery. A prologue indeed makes the point that cupidity is the root of all evil, and thereafter the three figures of Theology, Science, and Art come in to complain that the virtues of their separate faculties are in the present age perverted by this craving. Linked to the general theme but with no dramatic coherence to the action of the play, a later scene contains an isolated debate, exactly in the style of Heywood, involving four types of humanity: Learning-with-Money, Learning-without-Money, Money-without-Learning, and Neither-Money-nor-Learning. And the same moral lesson is made as trenchant as possible in another isolated scene at the end, in which appear Judas "like a damned soule, in blacke painted with flames of fire" and Dives "with such like apparell," both complaining bitterly of the pangs they now suffer for their former sin of avarice. The play, in short, with each of its thirty-two roles making, with the exception of the Vice, a single appearance in discontinuous scenes, is held together by the sense of its homily, with no sense at all of dramatic unity. But woven through these fragments a continuous action of a sort does exist, involving the genealogy of "Sinne" the Vice and displaying his seductive force upon the type figures of a realistic *comédie humaine*. The Vice and his grandfather Money organize a thriving business for their most fervent human adherent, who is All-for-Money "apparelled like a ruler or magistrate." Setting him up in the authority of his office, with the Vice himself as usher to his presence, they drum up for him a stream of petitioners who plead in the coin of the realm. The first to come is Gregory Graceless "like a ruffian," who seeks relief from imminent hanging and gains it at the expense of half the booty from the highway action for which his neighbors have condemned him—a piece of business that gets its eloquent summary in Shakespeare: "And oft 'tis seen the wicked prize itself buys out the law." Another, who cannot come in person but sends a hundred pounds to speak for her, is a young woman accused of murdering her illegitimate child. In return she is sent assurance that

234 *CHANGE AND DECLINE*

> They that should giue euidence shalbe all tongue tyde,
> And the twelue men shall finde her gyltles, let her not be afrayde.
>
> [ll. 1070–71]

By way of contrast, the next applicant, who has taken "a fewe ragges and clothes" from a hedge, is treated to the rigor of the law because he is, as his name explains, Moneyless-and-Friendless. After him comes William-with-the-Two-Wives, with "fourtie olde angels" to help him out of his unpleasant first, and legal, marriage, together with his promise of a yearly Christmas capon—a traditional perquisite that kept the English justice of the peace "in fair round belly with good capon lin'd." He is followed by Sir Laurence Livingless, a hedge priest seeking redress because he has been deposed from his multiple livings only for being illiterate, lascivious, and exceptionally proficient at cards and dice. He is presented as the typical cleric of the old religion, one large side of the Reformation declaring itself in his reply to the Vice's question concerning the number of epistles written by Paul:

> By the masse he writ to manie, I would they were all burned,
> For had not they bene and the newe Testament in English,
> I had not lacked liuing at this time I wisse.
>
> [ll. 1286–88]

All-for-Money is sufficiently taken by his spiritual quality and his hundred groats of "good siluer and olde" to make him his own chaplain and steward. The last petitioner is almost completely realized as an individual portrait—a rustic edition of the Wife of Bath in her old age. She is Mother Croote, "an hundreth yeres olde" and blind for the last thirty, her request complicated by the "cham," "cha," and "chill" of country speech and by outright malapropisms which the Vice politely corrects. Her money, which speaks plainly enough however, is also the cause of her coming. For it, she readily admits, a "holsome yong man" of twenty-three has made advances to her, and now she insists on having him for husband:

> My loue in my youth was neuer so feruent
> As it is on my sweete heart, nowe at this present.
>
> [ll. 1361–62]

The Vice himself is somewhat dismayed and raises obvious considerations, but she is adamant: "Yea, but he is good in my bedde to keepe my backe warme." Unfortunately the young man is now in love with

CHANGE AND DECLINE 235

a girl of his own age, so that Mother Croote is forced to apply her gold to the ingenuity of the court. The remedy is simple, consisting of two purchased witnesses who will testify to a formal act of betrothal between her and her young man:

> And then will he, nyll he, he must be compelled
> To forsake the other and to you to be maried.
> [ll. 1389–90]

In each case the human portrait is contracted and thickened to the point where its typical features verge on the idiosyncratic. The separate petitioners are at least as individualized as those that appear in the similar action, also with its Vice as usher, of Heywood's *Play of the Weather,* and that such a comparison is possible marks a considerable advance toward diversified human portraiture in the moral drama. Both plays alike are satirical comedies of manners, for the purpose of *All for Money,* as its title page announces, is that of "Plainly representing the maners of men, and fashion of the world noweadayes." Such a purpose comes close to the limit beyond which the moral plays were not able to go while retaining their determinative features, especially their radical didacticism. *The Three Ladies of London,* which advertises itself as "A Perfect Patterne for All Estates to looke into," and its sequel, *The Three Lords and Ladies of London,* printed respectively in 1584 and 1590, with their various type figures of humanity in the trades and stations of life, pause at the same line of demarcation. *The Cobbler's Prophecy,* licensed and printed in 1594, is also an "estates" morality in that part of its medley which belongs to the allegorical convention, presenting its social thesis through the operation of the Vice Contempt (alias Content) on types of sixteenth century society: Courtier, Soldier, Country Gentleman, and Scholar. Such type figures, as well as the others already seen, are the farthermost development in a continuous line from their parent type of Humanum Genus, and they stand at the barrier dividing the morality from the play of literal plot and personae which grew up alongside it during the first three quarters of the century and replaced it entirely in the final quarter.

In this respect it is enlightening to see how and for what reasons a playwright with the morality convention in his veins resists the secular trend toward dramatic literalness and attempts to turn it backward.

CHANGE AND DECLINE

The Conflict of Conscience, printed in 1581, is unique among moral plays because it is derived from the history of an individual life. Composed by Nathaniel Woodes, a minister of Norwich, it is based on the real story of Francesco Spira, an Italian lawyer who abandoned under pressure the Protestant for the Catholic faith, and then in remorse over his apostasy tried to commit suicide and finally died in despair in 1548, some thirty-three years before Woodes' play came to press.[8] We may imagine what such a story would have been if fashioned a decade later for the popular stage by the author of *The Tragical History of Doctor Faustus,* who wrote under very different auspices from those governing the Norwich minister.[9] The influences of the morality convention would have been obvious in it, just as indeed they are in Marlowe's tragedy. But such a play's first impulse would have been dramatic, its method concrete, and it would have presented, no matter how qualified by selection and embellishment, the literal career and literal figure of Francesco Spira. In Woodes' play, however, the method of homiletic allegory is not simply influential, it is regnant, and his prologue in this respect is revealing. He speaks of reading "Frauncis Speraes History, to most men fully knowen," which he undertakes to present in a play in order to "Styrre vp their myndes to godlynes, which shoulde it see or heare." But how present it so that its lesson may be most relevant, and therefore most fruitful, to the audience or reader? The minister's homiletic instinct and the method of the allegorical drama dictate the answer, which is to dissolve the career and features of the historical individual into a type figure representing a characteristic weakness, as Woodes sees it, in Protestant Christianity: the religious faith that is only verbal and skin deep, unable to withstand the temptation or coercion that assails it. For avoiding all mention of Spira in the text of the play its author provides two interesting reasons in his prologue. The fact that the play is a "Comedy" prevents him, he says, from taxing the vices of an individual man:

> Burt Speraes name for causes iust, our Author doth omit,
> And at this tyme imagine him Philologvs to be,
> First, for because a Comedy will hardly him permit,
> The vices of one priuate man, to touch particulerly.
>
> [prologue, ll. 36–39]

We can disregard, since it is alien to the immediate purpose, the meaning or meaninglessness of "Comedy" as designation for a play which

CHANGE AND DECLINE

in its first version at least ends in stark disaster, or the playwright's tenderness about attaching the faults he presents to an Italian more than thirty years dead. But Woodes' second reason has a cogency which, in the light of his homiletic purpose, we cannot disregard:

> Againe, nowe shall it styrre him more, who shall it heare or see,
> *For if that Spera had ben one, we would strayght deeme in mynde,*
> *That all by Spera spoken were, our selues we would not finde.*
>
> But syth Philologvs is nought else, but one that loues to talke,
> And common of the worde of God, but hath no further care,
> According as it teacheth them, in Gods feare for to walke,
> *If that we practise this in deede, Philologi we are,*
> *And so by his deserued fault, we may in tyme beware.*
>
> [my italics; prologue, ll. 40–47]

Francesco Spira, in consequence, is got rid of altogether, and in his place stands Philologus, the type of the Christian of many words but little faith, whose bad actions and wretched end are a mirror for all Christians of the same tepid piety. He is, moreover, attended by the customary personifications of good and evil in a play determined to achieve its didactic aim by converting to generalization and abstraction the concrete events from which it is derived.

As a self-conscious explanation for his resort to a dramatic tradition that is rapidly being supplanted, Woodes' prologue is providential. It illuminates the organic relation between purpose and method in the whole morality genre. Nothing is more characteristic of the allegorical play than that it intends to be obviously typical in order to be obviously instructive and reformatory. Such didacticism is not incidental but a definitive standard deliberately cultivated, and it relies upon the patent generalization in its human figure, or figures. Beyond its type figures the morality, qua morality, could not go in the direction of concreteness, although the spirit of the age provokes the late morality to make them as concrete as possible. It is not, therefore, the absence of personification that first marks the breakdown of the morality convention, for the personifications of good and evil remain in plays of the sixteenth century that are clearly hybrid plays rather than moralities. Historically considered, the significant departure from that convention occurred when plays appeared in which the typical human hero, or heroes, was replaced by a literal person and the literal events of his life. The same secular pressure toward the historical and topical that, as we have

238 CHANGE AND DECLINE

already seen, dismantles the generic figure of Humanity into multiple types of limited compass, carrying the morality thereby to the furthest degree of concreteness permitted by its own organic form and purpose, also leaps outside the convention to dramatize the history of individual men. The result is a new species of play and, eventually, a new artistic standard which invites the drama to be theater rather than homiletics. The hybrid plays, which we shall examine before long, illustrate this development and its effect on the fortunes of the Vice.

5

The Conflict of Conscience brings up another topic in the evolution of the moralities which is germane to the history of the Vice: namely, the development within them of a tragic resolution. Woodes' play has claim to unusual interest in this respect. It survives in two issues of a single edition, the difference between them confined to the title page, the prologue, and the speech of the *nuntius* which in both comprises the whole of the sixth and final act. Both issues, for the reasons already presented, get rid of the historical person by generalizing him into Philologus, but it is only the earlier of them that mentions him at all. Besides naming Spira in its prologue, it offers itself in its title as "the most lamentable Hystorie, of the desperation of Frauncis Spera." The second issue blots out the historical name from its title by substituting "A most lamentable example of the doleful desperation of a miserable world-linge, termed, by the name Philologvs," and also from its prologue by a similar substitution, freeing its homiletic aim thereby from all contamination by historicity (even to the point of replacing the word "Hystorie" by "example"). Otherwise, except for the sixth act, the two issues are identical. In both Philologus submits to pressures epitomized by the papistical Vice Hypocrisy and his three companions, Tyranny, Avarice, and Sensual Suggestion. He renounces his Protestant faith, resists the appeals of Conscience and Spirit, and lives pleasantly for a time as a Catholic. Before long, however, Horror arrives to torment him, and soon thereafter he is writhing in the grip of *desperatio,* longing to die. His friends urge him to repent, but he cannot, nor even pray—his heart is too reprobate. The fifth act leaves him thus in his suffering, and it is at this point that the two issues part

CHANGE AND DECLINE

company. In the earlier the speech of the *nuntius* turns the end of the play into unrelieved tragedy, informing the audience that after thirty weeks of agony, during which he refused all food, Philologus moved from despair in this world to damnation in the next by committing suicide:

Oh doleful newes, which I report, and bring into your eares,
Philologvs by deepe dispaire hath hanged himselfe with coard.

. . . .

And his owne hand, now at the last, hath wrought his endles paine,

[ll. 2411–24]

The second issue, however, alters a few words of this speech to enormous effect. The despairing sinner is saved at the end, makes his peace with God, and dies happily. Rarely in the history of the drama has the issue between tragedy and comedy been decided so economically:

Oh ioyfull newes, which I report, and bring into your eares,
Philologvs, that would haue hangde himselfe with coard,
Is nowe conuerted vnto God, with manie bitter teares,
By godly councell he was won, all prayse be to the Lorde,
His errours all, he did renounce, his blasphemies he abhorde:
And being conuerted, left his lyfe, exhorting foe and friend,
That do professe the fayth of Christ, to be constant to the end.

. . .

And nowe the Lord, in mercy great hath easde him of his payne.

To fathom the cause for so radical a change while the book was still in press is perhaps impossible. It may have come to Woodes' notice at the last minute that the numerous sixteenth-century accounts of Spira's career offer conflicting versions of the manner of his death, ranging, in fact, between the alternatives the playwright himself employs.[10] It is even more suggestive, since the happy ending belongs to that version which cuts itself off most completely from the concrete individual and the historical source, that the playwright, retreating more deeply into the morality convention, should also retreat from tragedy, for a reason that will presently appear. In any case, the two versions, taken together, encompass a wide arc of change in the moral drama.

Despite their happy endings the early moralities are described by Owst, with a good deal of justice, as "the earliest group of stage

CHANGE AND DECLINE

Tragedies in our language." [11] Their common theme is uniformly serious at its center and never far from seriousness anywhere, even in their comic passages. The issue by which they are all engrossed, the relation of the human soul to God and, *per consequens,* its destiny beyond the grave, is more crucial and poignant than any other in the metaphysics of true belief. Even if we no longer know it in our own time, *The Tragical History of Doctor Faustus* instructs us that the prospect of "incessant pain" in hell once qualified eminently as the stuff of tragedy. [12] The same tragic temper inhabits the suffering, none the less real for being vicarious and anticipatory, of the human hero in any of these early moralities. His sorrow has a darker theme than any belonging to worldly misfortune, physical pain, or even death itself, for death in his case is only the gateway to catastrophe. Nor is it limited to his anguish over the eternity of hell-fire that confronts him. For all their fumbling execution, the early plays manage to communicate that sense of moral or spiritual loss which is at the heart of all great tragedy: the sense of human life cut off from its deepest purposes and most essential sustenance, making existence an unendurable burden. Such high tragedy, in a deeply Christian context, afflicts Dante's people in hell. They are most wretched, not because of the pain their senses endure, but because they have lost the good of the intellect ("le genti dolorose ch' hanno perduto il ben dello intelletto"), which is the knowledge of God. [13] The deepest suffering of the sinner in the early moralities is very little different though it is scarcely so well expressed. He too is cut off by his sins from the divine source of his being and the vision that gives meaning to life.

But he is not allowed to remain in despair or to endure the damnation which in justice he deserves. A profound doctrinal stress on repentance and mercy contributes to the benevolent resolutions of the early plays and helps turn them all into comedies of redemption. Without ever being shallow, their criticism of life is, to use a pair of modern adjectives, optimistic and constructive. They offer hope to the most desperate sinner with their constant message that while he is still alive it is never too late to repent. Indeed they carry such comfort even further, as in the following very typical lines from the concluding speech in *Nature,* addressed to the aged Mankind when he has finally made his peace with heaven at the end of a lifetime of iniquity:

CHANGE AND DECLINE

Haue good perseueraunce and be not in fere
Thy gostly enemy can put the in no daunger
And greter reward thou shalt therfore wyn
Than he that neuer in hys lyfe dyd syn.
[part II, ll. 1411–14]

At the moment Death summons him, Everyman, in the play of the same name, is guilty of all "the seuen deedly synnes dampnable." But he is allowed time to redeem himself, inspired by the memory of his meritorious deeds and aided indispensably by the formal penitential system of the Church Catholic. When he finally descends into the grave he is received in heaven as an exceptional candidate for beatitude, the angel in the wings hailing him as "excellente electe spouse to Iesu," whose "synguler vertue" has made his "rekenynge . . . crystall clere." Formal repentance has made all the difference in the next world to this paradigm of sinful humanity at large, and the epilogue, inverting his escape into an admonition, grinds the great alternative to a sharp edge:

For, after dethe, amendes may no man make;
For than mercy and pyte doth hym forsake.
If his rekenynge be not clere whan he doth come
God wyll saye: *"Ite, maledicti, in ignem eternum!"*
[ll. 912–15]

Although nothing in the early moralities is more common than such a warning, none of them actually dramatizes its fulfillment. Alongside their Catholic emphasis on formal penitence through the offices of the church, the great medieval theme of mercy—so powerful later in Shakespeare—invests their denouements and averts catastrophe. The same divine mercy that granted the sacrifice of Christ for mankind's redemption in the first place, although mankind did not deserve it, remains abundant to all who ask for it among the guilty generations since, although in their own right they are equally undeserving. Repentance itself draws its inspiration and logic from this plenitude of mercy, as in the prayer of the sin-spotted Anima of *Wisdom:*

What ys yt xall make me clene?
Put yt, Lorde, in-to my thowte!
Thi olde mercy, let me remene [remember].
[ll. 958–60]

242   CHANGE AND DECLINE

"Ewyr to offend & euer to aske mercy, that ys a puerilite" protests the despairing reprobate of *Mankind,* "I am not worthy to haue mercy, be no possibilite." But Mercy himself assures him that it is not so, as long as the heart is able to ask for mercy while the flesh is still alive:

In this presente lyfe mercy ys plente tyll deth makyth hys dywysion.

. . . .

Aske mercy & haue, whyll the body with the sowle hath hys annexion.
[ll. 854–56]

And in *Perseverance* even Humanum Genus, a backslider who dies imperfectly repentant, is allowed with his very last breath to cry for mercy and to get it. The debate between Misericordia and her heavenly sisters is warm, with Justicia opposing a formidable argument:

Ouyr late he callyd confescion;
Ouer lyt was his contricion;
He made neuere satisfaccion;
    Dampne hym to helle be-lyve!
    [ll. 3428–31]

But Misericordia wins in the end by the judgment of "Pater Sedens in trono" because she personifies the major bias in the divine nature of her Father:

To make my blysse perfyth,
I menge with my most myth,
Alle pes, sum treuthe, and sum ryth,
    And most of my mercy.
    [ll. 3571–74]

This mercy, however, although it flows to all men no matter how sinful or tardy, is not open to abuse by premeditated reliance. It responds to men's weakness and humility, not to their calculation, as the hero of *Mankind* is warned:

Synne not in hope of Mercy; that ys a cryme notorie!
To truste ouermoche in a prince yt ys not expedient,
In hope when ʒe syn to haue mercy; be-ware of that awenture.
    [ll. 838–40]

Such warnings, which are frequent,[14] and the severe admonitory character of all the early plays lead to a question which is not fully satisfied by the repentance-mercy formula of their endings. Why, since

CHANGE AND DECLINE 243

they are not chary of threatening damnation, do they not actually present it? Their human hero supplies the most comprehensive answer. Although, like Dante's epic, they pay their respects to hell, finally they are also comedies of redemption for almost the same reason. They could not be otherwise since their subject is the whole of humanity, just as Dante could not do otherwise because his subject is himself. Their very universality compels them to a happy ending if they are not to shut the gates of mercy on all mankind and renounce thereby the whole gospel of Christianity. Humanum Genus, Everyman, Mankind, and the other heroes of the early plays who typify the entire human race, require to be saved in the end if their histories are to be edifying to a Christian audience. In such a play, with its medieval and Catholic auspices, the frailty of all men is taken for granted; and even if the salvation of all men is not, it could not in the end confer anything except salvation on the figure who stood for everybody. His wickedness, like his name, is typical rather than exceptional, and the extent of the warning his universality allows is that he should be saved precariously. In *Pride of Life* and *The Castle of Perseverance* the issue is indeed carried to the very edge of the pit, since the hero of each dies in sin, and it is only by the intercession of the Virgin in the first case and of Misericordia in the second that the soul is saved from the fiends who snatch at it. But saved it is, for it is the composite soul of all mankind. The early moralities, in brief, while they could and zealously did address the threat of hell to individual men, could not enact such a consummation on their universal stage without becoming unintelligible to the Christian spectator. Of necessity they turn away from tragedy although it is latent in their theme and temper.

The moralities of the sixteenth century present a different story. Although they commonly fall short of the tragic atmosphere of the early plays, they go through a number of developments, several of them already described, which put within their reach that technical requisite of tragedy, the tragic denouement. The loss of eschatological concentration and the equivalent growth of emphasis on mortal life and prudential ethics qualify virtue, as we have seen, for reward in this world's goods—honor, fame, prosperity. By the same token and even more emphatically they expose transgression to penalties no longer confined to the hereafter. Adversity, while it remains generally an

CHANGE AND DECLINE

omen of the wrath to come, first of all afflicts the living man. *Mundus et Infans,* early in the century, offers useful coincidence between its language and its action in this kind of secularization. The great eschatological warning of the early plays—ever at your beginning, remember your ending—degenerates in this one into advice worthy of *Poor Richard's Almanack:*

> In what occupacyon that euer ye be,
> Alwaye, or ye begyn, thynke on the endynge,
> For blame.
>
> [ll. 484–86]

Corresponding to this success morality, the distress of the hero proceeds from the fact that a lifetime of self-indulgence has brought him in the end to decrepitude, illness, and beggary—afflictions which do not appear at all in the early plays. Likewise the hero of *Magnificence,* his folly ripe for pricking, "is beten downe and spoylyd from all his goodys and rayment" and lies prostrate while Adversity lectures him (and the audience) on such consequences as "hunger & colde," "botches and carbuckyls" and "the bone ake," hanging and suicide.[15] The sinner in *Impatient Poverty,* having lived under the guidance of Misrule, also suffers extreme want and is made to do public penance "with a candell in his hande." In almost every moral play of the sixteenth century the punishment for the transgressor, whatever else it may involve in the next world, rigorously afflicts his flesh and fortune in this one. With increasing frequency after the middle of the century, moreover, it becomes a punishment imposed by society rather than by God and administered by its agents rather than His. Pathos, in consequence, ceases to be exclusively eschatological—that is, it becomes diverted from its concentration upon spiritual jeopardy and receives a new stimulation in the disasters of mortal life.

Such punishments, however, are not necessarily irreparable and do not of themselves constitute tragedy. In each of the three cases above suffering is followed by recovery and moral improvement. The sinner has had his lesson and is a better man thereafter. Although their context is secular, these plays are also comedies of redemption, with mercy manifesting itself in them through a penalty that is also a moral medicine. And, in fact, a benevolent ending is a constant feature of all the moralities in which the human hero is allowed to remain the representative of humanity at large, or of one of its universal aspects

CHANGE AND DECLINE

such as Youth or Wit, or of one of its universal estates such as Magnificence or Albion Knight—so long, in other words, as he remains, by the logic of his significance, the single hero of the play. The appearance of the tragic denouement accompanies the appearance of morally specialized, and frequently contrasted, types of humanity in a single play, many of them with names that pronounce them badly destined from the beginning. The comminatory side of Christianity fulfills itself in the moralities as soon as it can do so without involving all mankind, or all kings, or all youths in a blanket condemnation.

Although we have already traced this process of division and specialization, its connection with tragedy needs a more particular comment. In addition to being the product of the secular spirit at work upon the moralities, it has an important doctrinal aspect in Protestantism, which is or is not, depending on the viewpoint, also a form of secularism. The Catholic plays of the fifteenth century stressed free will, God's bountiful mercy toward a world which is more or less an ecumenical democracy of sinners, and remission of spiritual guilt for all men through repentance and the cleansing sacraments of the Church. By contrast, the Protestant plays of the next century move within a context of predestination, justification by faith alone, God's promises to the elect, and an emphasis on divine grace that makes the divine mercy somewhat harder to come by. Especially must predestination and grace be allowed their divisive force in the moralities that distinguish the sheep from the goats among mankind, as in Cassio's drunken Calvinism: "Well, God's above all; and there be souls must be saved, and there be souls must not be saved." Whereas the Catholic plays chart the course from sin to salvation available to every mortal, the Protestant allegiance of the later moralities moves them to put their human figures through a display of behavior rigidly consistent from first to last as indication that they are unalterably saved or damned from the beginning. However, it is impossible to attribute the development we are discussing to Protestantism alone. As it manifests itself in the dramaturgic evolution of the moralities, Protestantism is only a part of the larger tendency of the age. We have also to reckon with the forces of change and ramification inherent in a continuous dramatic tradition, as well as with influences from the classics and from the continent. And perhaps as much as anything else, we must allow for the natural tendency of the theater toward concreteness and personality, at work from the begin-

246   *CHANGE AND DECLINE*

ning, although slowly, to make abstraction and generalization a losing business on the popular stage.

Nice Wanton, which belongs to the reign of Edward VI, is the earliest morality of private life to depart from the single hero and to create its lesson through the contrasted behavior of several types of humanity. It is not merely coincidence, therefore, that it is also the first with an ending unmistakably tragic. A play about youthful delinquency with a general resemblance to the *Rebelles* (which has a happy ending, however) of the Dutch playwright Macropedius, it is one of several that transfer this theme to the English stage from the humanistic drama of the Continent. Its derivation somewhat modifies its morality characteristics, and at first glance it seems to belong among hybrid plays rather than with the moralities proper, for its human figures bear the names not of types but of discrete individuals. But such an impression is deceptive. The names are plainly borrowed from Biblical and classical story for their typical meaning, each a definition of character and behavior. Xantippe, the bad mother who spoils her children by indulgence, is a "curst shrew" and bears the name that the famous domestic character of the wife of Socrates had made a label for such a woman. She insultingly resists good counsel, spares the rod herself, and protests its use upon her wild son and daughter at school. In the end she suffers bitterly from personal loss and public shame when they move through crime to wretched deaths. Her two ill-fated children, Ishmael and Delilah, also display in their lives the moral traits implicit in their names. Their youth under their mother's care gets a compact summation:

> Al was good that these tidlynges do might,—
> Sweare, lye, steale, scolde, or fight,
> Carde, dyce, kysse, clippe, and so furth:
> All this our Mammy would take in good worth.
>   [ll. 449–52]

From such elementary skills Ishmael advances into "felony, burglary and murdre," his progress reaching its end when he is "hanged in chaynes and waueth his locks." Delilah graduates into the profession of her famous namesake and dies "of the pockes, taken at the stewes."

The third child, Barnabas, accords no less with the literal meaning of his name, borrowed along with its etymology from chapter four of the books of Acts, for he is, as the prologue makes clear, "by interpretacyon,

CHANGE AND DECLINE

the sonne of comfort." He is also, as he himself makes clear to his mother, distinguished from his brother and sister and saved from their fate by the special grace of God:

> In that God preserued me, small thanke to you!
> If God had not geuen me speciall grace
> To auoyd euil and do good,—this is true—
> I had liued and dyed in as wretched case
> As they did, for I had both suffraunce and space.
>
> [ll. 503–507]

Taking on himself in part the role of the virtuous personifications of other moralities, he saves her from suicide ("She wold stick herselfe with a knife") and subdues her despair with the news that both sinners cleansed their souls by repentance before they died. Such eschatological comfort, however, is only a trifle against the tragic pathos that flows from dishonor, domestic pain, and death itself—from the sorrows of temporal life, in short, rather than from the soul's jeopardy in eternity. Against the background of benevolence in earlier moralities, the tragic conclusion here discloses its origin in the play's secular temper, its Protestantism, but especially its bifurcation of the universal figure of Youth into contrasting types of youth good and bad.

The Longer Thou Livest, the More Fool Thou Art by W. Wager, a play of the sixties most likely, is also concerned with juvenile delinquency, its title advertising it as "A Myrrour very necessarie for youth, and specially for such as are like to come to dignitie and promotion." But it is also more than that, for it spreads the display of folly and its fruits over the whole lifetime of its hero Moros, presenting him in three stages. As a youth, the child of rude parents, he is incorrigible to all efforts to give him schooling, discipline, and piety. His mind is apt enough, but his nature's bent is expressed through his boon companions, the personifications Idleness, Incontinence, and Wrath. From his juvenile absorption in love songs and spinning tops he matures into gambling, drinking, brawling, and wenching. So much for his youth. He next appears as a man "gaily disguised and with a foolish beard," whom capricious fortune has advanced to wealth and power. His rooted viciousness now mainly shows itself through his ignorance, atheism, and cruelty; and the figure of People comes on to lament the oppression suffered by Moros' tenants and neighbors. The last scene of his history finds him a brainsick old man who enters "Furiousely with a

248 *CHANGE AND DECLINE*

gray beard," thrusting with his sword at an imaginary enemy. God's Judgment "with a terrible visure" now arrives to strike him to the ground with his last illness and to admonish him at the same time:

> If thou hast grace, for mercy now call,
> Yet thy soule perchaunce thou maist saue:
> For his mercy is aboue his workes all,
> On penitent sinners he is wont mercy to haue.
>
> [ll. 1788–91]

But Moros, who has no grace, diagnoses his seizure as a "qualme" and calls instead for "a cuppe of good wine," earning thereby the doctrinal prediction of his doom:

> Indurate wretches can not conuert,
> But die in their filthines like swine.
>
> [ll. 1794–95]

Finally Confusion comes in to carry him off—eventually to hell, but this consummation, which was all that counted in the moralities of the previous age, is delayed by inference until Moros can have his fill of earthly punishment. He is stripped of his fine clothes and borne out to his proper "hyre," which is

> Confusion, pouertye, sicknes, and punishment,
> And after this life eternall fyre,
> Due for fooles that be impenitent.
>
> [ll. 1837–39]

The tragedy in this instance, parceled out between irredeemable suffering in both worlds, is clearly shaped by the Protestant emphasis on grace. And the discrimination between man and man in such an emphasis, as well as the tragedy itself, is made possible by the fact that Moros is neither Mankind nor Youth, but a special example of the depravity that afflicts only a fraction of the human race. His name, at the same time that it condemns him from the start, separates him from humanity at large. His career and destiny illustrate only such "wicked fooles" as he is, as the prologue makes clear:

> Do we not see at these daies so many past cure,
> That nothing can their crokednes rectefie,
> Till they haue destroied them vtterly?
> The Image of such persons we shall introduce,
> Represented by one whom *Moros* we do call.
>
> [ll. 47–51]

CHANGE AND DECLINE

Other moralities whose unhappy endings earn for them the right to be called tragedies have already come to our attention. Beneath their homiletic variations they all obey the same pattern of specialization. In *The Trial of Treasure* mankind is discriminated between the contrasted types of Just and Lust, the former happy in a disciplined life and in his assurance of salvation, the latter an example of those who "Are subjects and slaves to their lusts and affection." Having concentrated his life upon pleasure and treasure, Lust eventually is disabused by God's Visitation, who afflicts him with "pain in thy members continually," so that his pleasure departs. His treasure soon follows when Time's operation turns it "to rust and slime." He suffers the "anguish and grief" of his ailments and poverty before he too is taken off by Time to "Vulcan's fire." What remains of him and his treasure is shown to the audience when Time reappears at the end "with a similitude of dust and rust," pressing home to them the moral difference between one kind of man and another:

> Behold here, how Lust is converted into dust;
> This is his image, his wealth and prosperity;
> And Treasure in like case is turned into rust,
> Whereof this example showeth the verity.
>
> . . . .
>
> But whereas Lust and Treasure in time is come to nought,
> Just, possessing Trust, remaineth constantly.
>
> [Dodsley, III, 299–300]

Enough Is as Good as a Feast makes a similar distinction between Heavenly Man and Worldly Man. The latter in the end is visited by God's Plague, afflicted by pains in head and heart, but so utterly without grace that try as he will he cannot pronounce the name of God. He suffers through a long and detailed death scene, attended by a physician and a popish priest, before he expires on the stage and is carried off to hell. The success of the former while alive is preliminary to the success of his soul after death. In *Like Will to Like* Virtuous Living stands in contrast to the six figures who typify rascality and lawlessness. He sternly resists vice and enjoys felicity in the world below together with the promise of it in the world above. They, for their part, endure an assortment of punishments—beggary, disease, hanging—and the ministers of retribution are not the agents of God but of society: Severity the judge and Hankin Hangman. *The Tide*

CHANGE AND DECLINE

Tarrieth No Man also stresses a social viewpoint, and Faithful Few, the happy representative of those who live according to the law of God and man, is supported by the police power of society, represented by Authority and Correction. Opposite him are arrayed half a dozen types of erring humanity who meet a variety of bad fates, including penury, imprisonment, and suicide. Finally *All for Money,* which has no continuous plot, only a series of actions illustrating the theme of avarice, concludes with a spectacle of unrelieved tragedy: Judas and Dives wrapt in the flames of hell and with barely enough time to moralize their woe before they are prodded off the stage by Damnation:

> But had I had grace to haue asked mercie therefore
> And repented my faulte as Peter did before,
> I should haue bene pardoned as other sinners be,
> And accounted no sinner, God will haue mercy,
> So that they aske mercie so long as they do liue,
> All which time he is readie their sinnes to forgiue.
>
> [ll. 1454–59]

The theme of mercy lasts, we see, to the end of the morality convention, although qualified by the Protestant emphasis on grace. What does not last is Mankind. The universal figure succumbs to the sway of the particular which marks the later history of the moralities and is strained into divergent types of limited application. These, in turn, become even further compressed by individuality and idiosyncrasy, or finally give way entirely to the discrete historical person of a Judas or a Dives. Tragedy, inhibited by the universality of the early moralities, in which it is nonetheless thematic and potential, steps onto the stage as soon as it is allowed to do so by this gradual displacement of the general by the particular, of the One by the Many, which is perhaps the most conspicuous feature in the evolution of the morality drama, as well as the main clue to its disintegration. As for the connection between this development of tragedy, or indeed between the whole process reviewed in this chapter, and the history of the Vice, that must be delayed and the reader's patience begged for. Before we can come to it, the morality play, having lost its typical hero, must, in the next chapter, surrender the stage to the secular drama, except for a few stragglers and a single bastion.

CHAPTER EIGHT

THE HYBRID PLAY

I

This seems a good moment to perform a service to clarity by disclaiming for the previous chapter and this one any ambition to inspect all the beginnings of the secular drama in their complex manifestations throughout the sixteenth century. The narrower interest of both is in the changes the morality convention undergoes before it comes to its end, and in its interpenetration with early plays that plainly herald the drama we know today as Elizabethan. Along these roads, as it will appear, the Vice is shaped and exercised to fit him for his later role. Up to now we have followed the morality through alterations which, without being exhaustive, are typical of its history in what may be called its essential form, while it still retains, however modified, its constitutional features. These have already been seen as mainly three. For one, there is the unbroken allegiance to the stereotyped moral plot of the Psychomachia. Again, there is the transparent didacticism that creates the morality's demonstrative and expository method, openly affiliates the play with the audience, and allows it to be only incidentally *dramatic,* as we understand the word today. Finally, there is the engrossment of its dramatis personae, making such a didactic method possible, by moral personifications and type figures, and their tripartite organization into vices, virtues, and the representative—or, as later, representatives—of humanity.

That the convention survives without any real abridgement of its essential features into the seventh, eighth, and even ninth decades of the century is indicated by many of the plays noticed in the previous chapter. They belong to those decades and retain all the necessary characteristics. There is, furthermore, the very useful information to the same general effect in Professor Harbage's *Annals of English*

252   *THE HYBRID PLAY*

Drama, which is able to apply the designation "moral" or "interlude" to more than sixty of the almost three hundred pieces of all sorts (nearly two thirds of them have perished) appearing in its columns between and including the years 1560 and 1589.[1] Also, Professor Chambers can reckon that of forty-two plays printed between 1565 and 1585 seventeen were moralities, and that of sixty-five plays distinguishable in the Revels Accounts as performances at court during the same period fourteen were likewise moralities.[2] These modern calculations, exposing the radical mélange and transition in that period of drama which was threshold to Shakespeare, get ample Elizabethan confirmation, especially in the theatrical criticism of the same decades. Energetically condemning or defending what the popular stage was currently presenting, the critics of the drama, notably in the decade of the eighties, advert upon it in terms of its histories, comedies, tragedies, and its "morrals."[3] Not only did the metaphorical play live side by side with the literal play on the same stage, but in at least one instance, suggesting others, both came from the same indiscriminate hand. When Stephen Gosson, a playwright himself before his vehement reformation, attacked the stage, his theatrical past arose to grin at him, as he acknowledges in *Plays Confuted in Five Actions* (1582): "Since my publishing the *Schole of Abuse* [1579], two Playes of my making were brought to the Stage: the one was a cast of Italian deuises, called, The Comedie of Captaine Mario: the other a Moral, Praise at parting."[4] Later in the same book he again elucidates the drama of the eighties in a way that serves our present purpose. Against attacks such as his the stage resorted to the stage, and he himself describes at length "the Playe of plays showen at the Theater, the three and twentieth of Februarie last," produced as a defense of the drama.[5] Its personae were Life, Delight, Zeal, Recreation, and related personifications, enough to tell us what kind of play it was. Intending to abolish the London stage, Gosson, in such passages, contributes materially to its history during that time when it was filled with the complex pregnancy of the drama we now call Elizabethan.

The same period, however, marks the dead end and dissolution of the allegorical drama, at least on the popular stage. After 1590 its whole method is rather imitated than repeated in a few ingenious pieces which make a strange appearance among the plays of their own time.

THE HYBRID PLAY

The Contention between Liberality and Prodigality, although performed before Elizabeth in 1601, is in all likelihood a refurbished play of the sixties. At the Rose in 1600 the Earl of Pembroke's company, according to Henslowe, presented "the [devell] licke vnto licke," but that is almost certainly Ulpian Fulwell's morality of the same name which survives in an edition dated 1568. But the old convention explains the *modus* of Thomas Nashe's *Summer's Last Will and Testament* (1592), in which the seasons of the year appear as personifications of distinct moral qualities as well as of the weather. And the Psychomachia glints in the title and is fulfilled in the text of another archaic play, fostered characteristically by the academic stage: *Lingua, Or the Combat of the Tongue and the Five Senses* (licensed and printed in 1607) by Thomas Tomkis of Trinity College, Cambridge. Tomkis may also be the author of another academic play filled with metaphorical warfare: *Pathomachia, Or the Battle of Affections,* written probably around 1616. The elaborate "moral maske" of *Microcosmus* (1634–35) by Thomas Nabbes also has roots in the old tradition. But the sporadic and sumptuous staging of allegories at court or in the universities during the first part of the seventeenth century does not much concern us. They were composed for genteel or educated audiences and show a degree of sophistication that removes them far from the homely spirit of the popular morality.

The way the formal convention dies is much less our subject, however, than the ways its influence and some of its elements continue to live. To this end we turn now to a group of more than a dozen plays out of the middle half of the sixteenth century which deserve to be called *hybrid,* or *transitional,* because in them exists the *open* fusion of two radically different dramatic methods, the abstract and the concrete. They are products of interaction between the old convention and the new, and they are a sufficient number to indicate that they represent a substantial body of dramatic literature most of which has not survived. It is an interesting, even if unanswerable, question to ask of the numerous lost plays which in the *Annals of English Drama* are classified as Biblical stories, histories, or romances—frequently on the strength of the only available evidence, their titles—whether many of them were not also in fact hybrid amalgamations of both dramatic conventions in the extensive period when both were alive on the stage together. For who

254 **THE HYBRID PLAY**

could conjecture the significant elements of the allegorical drama that exist in the following plays if they too had come down to us only as titles: *John the Evangelist, Godly Queen Hester, King Darius, King John, The Life and Repentance of Mary Magdalene, Virtuous and Godly Susanna, Patient and Meek Grissill, The Cruel Debtor, Appius and Virginia, The History of Horestes, Cambises King of Persia, Sir Clyomon and Sir Clamydes, Common Conditions, The Cobbler's Prophecy, Tom Tyler and His Wife?* Luckily they survive through texts as well as titles, and combine with a mass of other evidence to support the following proposition: that the formative decades of the Elizabethan drama compose a period of gradual change from a metaphorical to a literal, from an unnaturalistic to a naturalistic, stage; and that the mingled elements of both conventions in play after play became the customary method of the playwright and the unremarkable experience of his audience.

About all these plays together several observations can be made immediately. With only one exception (Bale's *King John,* whose unique characteristics present a problem outside the scope of this study) they all dramatize stories out of history or legend and present individual men and women in the place of that touchstone of the unadulterated morality—the type figure representing mankind or a portion of mankind. But they also retain the personifications of the morality convention and combine them, strangely to our modern eyes, with the original story, which, because of their presence in it, is commonly reshaped into a Psychomachia. Also, the history of these plays does not begin in time where the moralities leave off but occupies the period from 1520 to 1585 and runs parallel to the development of the intermediate and late moralities. Finally, although a third line of plays will appear later in which the allegorical method also survives, they are omitted from the present consideration because in them it is submerged or disguised, whereas in the plays now before us it is overt and earns for them the name of *hybrid*.

Three of these plays show a structural resemblance to each other of a sort that exhibits this hybridization in its most rudimentary form. In *John the Evangelist, Godly Queen Hester,* and *King Darius*—the first probably and the last two certainly printed in the sixties, but two of them full of indications that they were composed a good deal earlier

THE HYBRID PLAY

—a narrative theme out of the Bible alternates with scenes that are pure morality, with no dramatic nexus between. Like the discontinuous acts of vaudeville, the parts derived from Biblical story and those devoted to the personifications seem to take no cognizance of each other. It is clear that in each case the morality business is wedged into the play to meet a popular demand for the Vice and his humorous diversion within the serious story and also for the sake of dealing topically—and satirically—with matters of English import. But a more comprehensive explanation remains. To charge these plays with an absolute lack of coherence is to measure them by modern theatrical standards which recognize unity only when it is dramatic. But in the three plays before us the governing purpose is didactic, and the unity is homiletic. In each the single lesson is fortified through a double presentation— through the moral meaning *suggested* by the dramatized story and through the direct exposition of the allegorical method. Both actions are harnessed, tandem fashion, to the same homiletic carriage.

John the Evangelist, which may be as early as 1520,[6] is a confusing play, partly because of the corrupt text in which it survives. Its direct dependence on the Bible exists mainly in the figure of John, and perhaps in the role of Irisdision, whose name presents difficulties and who is not always clearly distinguished from the Evangelist himself, if they are in fact separate personages.[7] However the lesson of the play is clear enough as it is presented in three sermons, the pillars of its structure and frankly addressed to the audience ("this congregacyon"). It contrasts spiritual love (with a strong emphasis on chastity) and its heavenly hope against the misdirected love toward pelf and pleasure which takes one "downe to the dongyon where the deuyll dwelleth." During these sermons, as well as in between, the stage is held by two roisterers who first listen only to mock, but in the end succumb to eschatological hopes and fears and are converted. Eugenio, as his name suggests, is the well-born and rich young man too fond of his worldly goods and the pleasures they buy. His friend Actio, although his energy and credo seem confined to "sporte and playe," stands more largely for the acquisitive and passionate activity of the profane world as opposed to the life devout and contemplative which St. John and Irisdision preach. Both youths are wenchers and tavern haunters until they are won over by the exhortations of the Evangelist to the "trowe loue" and

THE HYBRID PLAY

to "that holy nacyon" in the life beyond "Where loue dothe dwell with virgynyte."

So much for the story line, such as it is, of the play. But into its middle is thrust a single scene of the kind long known and enjoyed. Pushing his way through the audience, the Vice leaps onto the stage and immediately addresses them in the familiar style:

> By your leaue let me come rere
> What dothe all this company here
> Where after is your gapynge
> [ll. 367–69]

He proceeds thereupon to the exposition of his name, his moral quality, and launches into a satirical preachment of his previous activities throughout England. He is Evil Counsel, who has "sought Englande thorowe and thorowe," and he is now looking to serve a new master with his skill in purveying women and money. His current victim soon appears, bearing the name of Idleness, although he is in fact not intended as a personification but as the type of shiftless humanity, disposed to just such temptations as the Vice is master of. After several venereal gags and anecdotes, neither better nor worse than what is usual between the modern comedian and his straight man, they fall into a quarrel which leads to blows—this last a piece of business that the Vice's performance is rarely without, since it is, in fact, a vestige of the military Psychomachia. Soon reconciled, they go out to the pleasures the Vice can provide, escaping at the same time what they suspect is coming on—a sermon by him "That layde fyrst In principio togyther." The scene is a diversion, but its comedy should not blind us to its homiletic intention. In the method of the morality it enforces the same point that the rest of the play is about: namely, that the love of money and of pleasure is at the opposite pole to that love of God which is mankind's salvation.

Godly Queen Hester, licensed and printed as a "newe enterlude" in 1560–61, dramatizes the triumph of that Biblical heroine over her enemy Haman. But the familiar story seems in this instance so strongly flavored with allusion to Cardinal Wolsey's last years of power that in all likelihood the play belongs to 1525–29. It is less interesting for its reasonably faithful rendition of the scriptural event than for several additions which reflect the temper and practice of the early Tudor

THE HYBRID PLAY

stage. Imitating the theme and method of *Fulgens and Lucres* and *Gentleness and Nobility,* as well as the large body of nondramatic literature on the same subject, it opens with a debate in which King Ahasuerus and the members of his counsel, among them Haman, discuss whether riches, noble birth, or virtue is most deserving of honor. Agreeing on virtue, they agree further that justice is the preeminent virtue in a king. On this thesis the play moves, for Haman is later condemned by the very same royal justice which at this point he so strongly advocates. For another addition to the original story the play offers in the role of Hardy-Dardy what seems the earliest surviving dramatization (with the doubtful exception of Mirth in *Pride of Life*) of the professional court fool. The jests with which he entertains his master Haman are edged and pregnant, and he suggests his great descendant in *Lear* by his ironic comparisons between the wise man and the fool, his sharp allusions to his lord's folly, and his covert prophecies of the latter's fate. One more characteristic of the play as a whole, distinguishing it from the conventional enactment of sacred story in the miracles and mysteries, is its precise homiletic intention. It is a virtue play, offering the example "of the vertuous and godly Queene Hester" for other women to follow, and the invitation is specific on the title page:

> Com nere vertuous matrons & women kind
> Here may ye learne of Hesters duty,
> In all comlines of vertue you shal finde
> How to behaue your selues in humilitie.

Other Tudor accretions appear when we turn to the moral personifications who invade this play of concrete story and personage, and to the method of their performance. They are three, all vices, their names Pride, Adulation, and Ambition; and they enter in that order in the course of a single scene which divides the first third of the play from its remainder. Their performance, purely choric and covertly topical, takes an unusual form in imitation of the satiric, often scabrous, Testament Literature of the late Middle Ages. Their discourse, among themselves and to the audience, is altogether a moral indictment of Haman on counts, some of them irrelevant to the play, that keenly suggest the career and reputation of Cardinal Wolsey, just as the whole play shadows, more vaguely, the Cardinal's relations with Henry and

258 THE HYBRID PLAY

Catharine, and offers in Haman's persecution of the Jews a parallel to Wolsey's first actions against the monasteries.[8] Pride enters "poorely arrayed," complaining to the audience that he has no pride left, for it has all been engrossed by Haman, who "hath as many gowns, as would serue ten townes." And he goes on to paint Haman as the image of hypocrisy in terms that seem to apply more cogently to the English prelate on his mule and to the Lord Chancellor's part in the continental wars

Outward honestie, inward infidelitie,
Bothe rydes on a mule:
In peace he is bolde, but in war he is colde,
That soonest wyll recoyle.

. . . .

But such men by battail, may get corne and cattell
Bullyon and plate:
And yf they once get it, let vs no moore craue it,
By GOD we comme to late.

[ll. 350–65]

Adulation enters next to complain likewise that he "must chaunge his occupation" because Haman-Wolsey has cornered the market in that quality, especially in his behavior as a judge:

For al law est & west, & adulation in his chest
Aman hathe locked faste:
And by his crafti pattering, hath turned law into flattering.

. . . .

For yf Aman wynkes, the lawyers shrynckes,
And not dare saye yea nor naye.
And yf he speake the lawe, the other calles hym daw
No more then dare he say.
So that was law yisterday, is no lawe thys daye,
But flatterynge lasteth alway, ye may me beleue.

[ll. 402–16]

Moreover he has corrupted religion by advancing his minions into pluralities, by taking all the larger benefices for himself, by mulcting and engrossing right and left. The third vice's lament has the same burden. The ambition of Haman-Wolsey is so insatiable that by comparison Ambition himself is fit for nothing except "To dwell amonge fooles." The king's arrogant first minister despises "all rewlers & lawes,"

THE HYBRID PLAY

overturns all "Ordynances & foundation[s]," funnels every "office and fee" into his own pocket. There is neither bread nor meat, and the poor are without relief,

> Wherefore yf warre should chaunce, eyther wyth Scotland or Fraunce,
> Thys geare woulde not goe ryght.

[ll. 479–80]

All three vices agree that there is nothing left for them except to "make merye, euen tyll we dye" and to prepare their testaments against that eventuality. Pride therefore bequeaths to the king's minister "Al my presumptuous pryde" and also the certainty that pride must have a fall. Adulation leaves him "All my subteltie, & forged fydelite, To hym and hys espyes" with the hope that such qualities may lead them all to the gallows. Ambition's testament is in the same vein, and the three of them go out with a song, their destination being "the tauerne dore." That is the extent of their performance, and we hear no more of them except for a single recollection of their legacy by Hardy-Dardy (who does not associate with them) during his all-licensed foolery with Haman. They are here elaborately specialized in one feature of their many-sided roles in the moralities—their choric function, which is to bring the play's meaning, both topical and moral, home to the bosoms of the audience. If their relationship to the play as a whole is not dramatic, it is very distinctly homiletic.

King Darius, licensed and printed in 1565, ends with a prayer for Elizabeth, nor is there anything in the play to contradict the evidence that it belongs to her reign. Structurally, however, it looks back to the time of the two previous plays, for it shows the same dramatic rift, the same patchwork of morality and Biblical story. The latter is developed out of the apocryphal book of Esdras and concerns the debate by three members of the king's bodyguard on the subject of the strongest thing in the world. The first two urge respectively the strength of wine and the strength of the king. The third, who is Zorobabel, leader of the Jews captive in Babylon, wins the contest by arguing first for the superior strength of woman and love among all earthly things, and then, raising the polemic to a higher level, by celebrating the indefeasible strength of God's truth over all things whatsoever. Darius rewards him with permission to rebuild Jerusalem and the Temple. The other two debaters, anonymous and forgotten in the original story, are condemned by the moral indignation of the play as types of flattering and lying counselors and named Stipator Primus and Stipator Secundus. Zorobabel, on the other hand, is held up as an exemplar of religious constancy: "He remayned in Constancye and was still wyse." It is through such moralizing additions that the play unfolds its topical meaning. For the whole of *King Darius* is a reaction to Elizabeth's obscure course in religion during the first years of her reign, and it is filled with Protestant anxiety over the chance of a Catholic restoration. It prays in its epilogue that God may send the queen "his cleare syght" and "his worde" and that she may give "true precepts" to her subjects. Especially it prays that God may direct her counselors to imitate Zorobabel's constancy "in the true fayth."

This sense of urgency over the true faith, which creates the covert meaning of the Darius episode, also creates the open conflict over religion in those other parts of the play that are outright morality. When we turn to them we find ourselves squarely in the old arena of the Psychomachia. The Darius-Zorobabel story exists in two scenes, the second and fourth, composing much the smaller half of the play. Alternating with them, but completely without dramatic relation to them, are two long scenes of doctrinal quarrel and abuse between three Protestant virtues and three papistical vices. Charity, Equity, and Constancy are matched against Iniquity, Importunity, and Partiality, the first named of the evil trio being the *radix malorum* and, therefore, "the Vyce" of the play. Each side attempts to drive the other off the stage—that is, out of England. To that end the virtues employ solemn lectures and fervent denunciations while the vices retort with an endless flow of billingsgate punctuated by sporadic shows of violence. Iniquity flourishes his dagger, and at one point he "casteth at Constancye" what he describes as "A pece of a brasse pan" as well as similar missiles at the other virtues. However Constancy—the same virtue celebrated in Zorobabel—wins the day for Protestantism in England by resorting to his own brand of pious violence. The Vice is driven from the stage by heavenly fire ("Here sombody must cast fyre to Iniquytie"), crying on the way out, "Nay, I go to the deuil, I fere." [9] At the end of the play the three virtues appear once more as the epilogue to knit both parts of the presentation into their single meaning. We can give the morality scenes their due allowance as a sop to the audience's craving for the

THE HYBRID PLAY

comedy of the Vice and still find that they have a weightier explanation in their homiletic alignment with the meaning of the play as a whole.

Before we turn away from *King Darius* it is useful to notice how the influence of the morality convention exerts itself to subdue even the historical elements in the play to its own method. Darius' two servants are named Agreeable and Preparatus and his two advisers are Perplexity and Curiosity. There is not, of course, any warrant for such names in the Biblical episode, nor do they have any real significance in the play, for the roles they fit are perfunctory in the extreme. Such moral nomenclature illustrates the tenacious habit of homiletic allegory and of the old dramatic order when it stiffens its feet against the tug of the new. Elsewhere in the hybrid plays we shall find the same reactionary effort to dissolve the individual into a moral abstraction by providing him with a moral label for a name.

A few general observations on the foregoing plays will help us to move beyond them. All three have their source in sacred literature, but in purpose and method they differ widely from the mysteries and miracles. The latter sought to stimulate Christian faith by the vivid enactment of its historical events, whereas the plays in question aim not at faith but at conduct, either the conduct of private life or of national affairs, or both together. Their purpose throughout is moral edification, their method either openly didactic or covertly so. Two of them are virtue plays, offering a moral hero (Zorobabel) or a heroine (Esther) as an example for imitation by the generation contemporary with the play. In all three the historical material is shaped to suggest a moral lesson, and that lesson is made as explicit and topical as possible by the addition of scenes filled with the homiletic voices of moral personifications. Although from a dramatic view alone there is no relation between the historical and allegorical scenes in these plays, the latter appearing mainly as chaotic excursions away from the main purpose for the sake of the comedy of the vices, such a view is the wrong one for a drama whose conscious standards are overwhelmingly homiletic. As for the personifications themselves, it is worth noting that although all three plays have their vices, only *King Darius,* because it is some thirty years later than the other two, is able to advance the evolved figure of "the Vice." The virtues are less numerous, existing in only one of the plays

262   THE HYBRID PLAY

(also *King Darius*). The two sides of the Psychomachia are not equally popular or durable.

2

From the panel of hybrid plays remaining it is possible to carve out a group of four which, while they have important features in common with the three plays already considered, show others that belong to a more advanced dramatic method. They are also virtue plays with an overriding homiletic intention, each presenting a moral heroine for the audience to admire and imitate. Only the first two, however, have their source in the Bible and show a clear Christian orientation. In the latter pair, which take their stories out of profane literature, Christian sentiment is sharply qualified by classical or romantic influence. In all four we can trace the progressive effect of the secular evolution already seen in the "pure" moralities, as it leavens, *pari passu,* the hybrid plays. It shows itself especially through the dramatic instinct working darkly within them, obscurely militant against their homiletic auspices. Unlike the plays previously considered, they merge history and allegory into a single action, with the result that the latter is exposed to a theatrical atmosphere ultimately fatal to its existence. The personifications of virtue are cast off from the main current of the plot by its new ebullience and survive for a time as homiletic froth around its margin until they are skimmed off altogether. As for the secondary personifications of evil, like their fellows in the late moralities they droop from the stage, leaving it to the expanding figure of the Vice. To him who hath shall be given, and the Vice, always theatrically effective, thrives on the very climate that decays the other members of the Psychomachia. Not only does his role swell in size and importance, but for the first time in our survey he directs his energy against individual men and women, and his aggression gains new zest from its new quarry.

The earliest of these plays, *The Life and Repentance of Mary Magdalene* by Lewis Wager, although licensed in 1566 and printed the same year as "A new Enterlude," refers in its prologue to "true obedience to the kyng" and belongs very probably to the reign of Edward VI. Not only is the play motivated by its author's vigorous Protestantism, but, more particularly, it is shaped from first to last into an

THE HYBRID PLAY

263

exposition of that cardinal tenet of the reformed religion—justification by faith. It is exactly to such a homiletic end that Wager dramatizes the story of the Magdalene. His purpose is to show that the start of all evil in Mary came from her lack of faith. Accordingly the Vice, as in Bale's *Three Laws,* is named Infidelity. The moment of her conversion is marked by the arrival on the stage of "the holy vertue of Faith"; and the last part of the play stretches into a long homily, innocent of the slightest dramatic artifice, on the supreme position of faith in the Christian scheme of salvation. For "by Faith onely Marie was iustified," and her life, therefore, is dramatized as a fruitful example which both prologue and epilogue offer to the audience:

> Here an example of penance the heart to grieue
> May be lerned, a loue which from Faith doth spring;
> > [prologue, ll. 56–57]

> Praying God that all we example may take
> Of Mary, our synfull lyues to forsake;
> > [ll. 2077–78]

The seventh and eighth chapters of Luke supply the Biblical part of the play as well as the three literal figures in its cast—Christ, Simon the Pharisee, and Mary. The author accepts the traditional identification of the Magdalene with the unnamed "woman in the city, which was a sinner" who in Luke comes to Jesus during his repast with Simon, washes his feet with her tears, dries them with her hair, and annoints them with precious ointment out of an alabaster box. For her humility and her faith in him Christ frees her from her sins: "And he said to the woman, Thy faith hath saved thee; go in peace." But the scriptural story furnishes Wager with less than a quarter of his play and its cast. The larger part of both are constructed according to the abstract and analytical method of the moralities. More than eight hundred lines at the beginning are devoted to the seduction of Mary by Infidelity and the three vices in his retinue: Pride of Life, Cupidity, and Carnal Concupiscence. Her wanton life under the tutelage of Infidelity and the appearance to her of The Law and Knowledge of Sin fill up almost three hundred more. Christ appears at this point to cast the seven evil spirits out of her, but her actual redemption awaits the entrance to her of Faith and Repentance, who lecture her (and the audience) for a hundred lines before they bring her around to the true

264   THE HYBRID PLAY

belief and a proper remorse. It is only now that Wager inserts the Biblical episode in the house of Simon, a matter of some four hundred lines which also include the extra-Biblical plotting against Christ of two allegorical guests at the banquet, Infidelity and Malicious Judgment. In the end Mary enters with Justification, with Love arriving on the scene a moment later to complete, in their exact doctrinal sequence, the stages of Mary's progress toward salvation. Love comes in at the last because it is important to Wager's doctrine that love is only a consequence of redemption, not its cause, which is faith:

> But loue foloweth forgiueness of synnes euermore,
> As a fruict of faith, and goth not before.
>
> [ll. 1987–88]

The standards and status of the popular drama at the midpoint of the century (as distinguished from the stage of the universities, the inns of court, and the royal court) receive a fair illustration in this play. Its purpose, its methods, its very entrances and exits are doctrinal and homiletic, but it also shows a diffident instinct in a new direction. The virtuous personifications, six in all, have not the least dramatic quality. They are simply walking voices, uninflected and abstruse, who come on the stage only to lecture. Each makes a single appearance in a sequence that expresses, according to the author's doctrine, the spiritual moments that follow one another in Mary's soul:

> Such persons we introduce into her presence,
> To declare the conuersion of hir offence.
> Fyrst, the lawe made a playne declaration,
> That she was a chylde of eternall damnation:
> By hearyng of the law came knowledge of synne . . .
>
> [ll. 2031–35]

As for Mary herself, her fall, bad life, and conversion furnish the audience with an example very little different from the example supplied them by the typical figure of Humanity in the moralities proper. And as in the moralities, the fitful moments of this play that have even rudimentary dramatic quality occur during Mary's association with the vices led by Infidelity. To some extent she is her own woman then and not the play's puppet. Her status as an individual rather than as a type teases the author into touches that are personal and idiosyncratic—her yellow hair, her musical ability, her pride in her noble lineage, her

THE HYBRID PLAY

blushes when the vices shame her. Falling and fallen, she has about her the charm, affection, and even modesty of a girl who is willful and spoiled rather than vicious. She is vexed by the bad cut of her clothes and the poor attendance of her servants, but it is the petulance of a child. Her nature expands to the possibilities of pleasure, but the bold insinuations of the vices startle her into shamefast laughter or even leave her uncomprehending. She is, in fact, an example of how the appearance of a literal person within the moral drama stirs a sleeping nerve within the moral dramatist.

Also stirred, we may suppose, by her individuality and her sex, the vices surpass their usual verve and present an instructive theatrical contrast to the moribund virtues. The efforts of Infidelity and his "impes" toward her perversion fill up the first two fifths of the play, turning it into an oasis of stage business, topical satire, and the arts of deceit and insinuation. He has promised the audience:

> You shall see that Marie's heart within short space
> For the diuell hym self shall be a dwellyng place.
> I will so dresse her that there shall not be a worse.
> To her the diuell at pleasure shall haue his recourse.
> I will go and prepare for her such a company,
> As shall poison her with all kyndes of villanie.
> [ll. 241–46]

Enticing her, therefore, by flattery and sympathy into his governance, he introduces her to his three followers, and all four, under disguised names, subtly infect her with the evils they personify—atheism, avarice, sensuality, and proficiency in all the alluring tricks of posture, clothes, and cosmetics. Her downfall at their hands gets an unusual sexual coloring, and there is even the suggestion that the initial triumph over her chastity belongs to the Vice himself, an enlightening point in his anthropomorphic development.[10] Later on, after they reach Jerusalem, he is her pander, jesting with her over the merits of this "mynion felowe" or that one with "the flaxen beard." And he remains in the play beyond her conversion to become the motivating force in the conspiracy of the Jews against Christ. Long before that the minor vices have faded from his side. They are only branches of the moral evil of which he is the root, and therefore expendable, once their sequential meaning has been exposed, in a play that declares that "Foure may

266 THE HYBRID PLAY

easely play this Enterlude." His survival to the end, as well as his dramatic vigor throughout, results directly from his primacy as the *radix malorum*. Indeed, for the homiletic burden of the play his role is more important than that of the titular heroine: she is simply one exemplification of the fideistic tenet he embodies, and illustrates another way by his action against Jesus.

Thomas Garter's *Comedy of the Most Virtuous and Godly Susanna*, licensed in 1568–69 and published as "neuer before this tyme Printed" in 1578, celebrates, as its title indicates, the piety and moral excellence of its heroine. In its main lines the play is faithful to its source in the apocryphal book of Susanna and reproduces the story of wifely virtue, the lust of the two elders, their attempt upon Susanna during her bath in the garden, the hard choice they present her, her steadfastness and trust in God, the accusation and the trial, her exoneration through the divinely inspired wit of Daniel, and the death of the two accusers at the hands of the people. Its roles also reproduce all the Biblical figures —Susanna herself, her husband Joachim, her father Helchias and his wife, the prophet Daniel, and the two elders. However the play's own time and place invade its temper in several characteristic ways. Susanna's two maids compare the pleasures of court with the more wholesome method of their previous life in the country in language that reads like *Colin Clout's Come Home Again*. Joachim discourses on the duties and defects of rulers like a Tudor moralist. One of the elders celebrates the beauty of Susanna in a methodical *blazon* that belongs to the Renaissance rather than to the Bible:

The fewter of her formed face, the glistering of her eyne,
Her shoulders that are quadrant to, her nose that is so fyne.
Her cheekes that are so chery red, her lippes so red and thin,
Her smyling cheare which often showes the pittes vpon her chin.
Her brestes that are so round and fayre, her armes that are so long,
Her fyngers straight with vaynes beset, of blew and white among.
Her middle small, her body long, her buttockes broade and round,
Her legges so straight, her foote so small, the like treades not on ground.
[ll. 411–18]

Several other features that give the play its Tudor countenance concern us more directly because they come to it out of the moral drama. At the beginning a frustrated Satan laments that though he has "the

THE HYBRID PLAY

world at will" Susanna's virtue resists all his craft; at the end he comes in once more to belabor with insults the "hanged" Vice for failing in his appointed task. The two elders, by the same kind of atavism that has already appeared in *King Darius*, surrender their historical individuality to the homiletic intention of the play and step forth as moral types under the names of Voluptas and Sensualitas. And the drama of homiletic allegory also supplies the play with its two moral personifications, one on each side of the Psychomachia. But although each is the homiletic counterweight to the other, in the dramatic scales their roles weigh very unevenly. The slight figure of True Report appears twice, each time briefly, and his role is trivial. He is one of the two male servants of Susanna who respond to her cries for help in the garden, and at the end he helps the Servus and the Jailer to arrest the Vice, to unmask his true nature, and to "hang" him on the stage. Ill Report the Vice, on the other hand, has easily the most substantial role of the play. He has shed his traditional retinue of secondary vices, and the whole field of allegorical evil and of comic relief is his alone to revel in. His commission from the Devil is not specific—simply the overthrow of Susanna's virtue by whatever device his wit can contrive. His name and significance are an obvious accommodation to the slander which is the crux of the original story, and his aggression against her consists in spreading about the countryside, in fulfillment of his nature, the libel that the lustful elders have invented against her. But his intrigue is double, with the elders themselves also grist for his mill, as he informs the audience after the pair have hired his aid in their lust's behalf:

> Iudge what I will doe for this ten pounde,
> Teach them a way themselues to confounde.
> [ll. 271–72]

They are, in fact, his real victims. When they are condemned he jeers at them, and when they are stoned he is the most vigorous of their executioners. Having done his worst in all directions, he is captured and subjected to an equivocal hanging "in signe of releefe," which means apparently that in the present instance at least the evil he personifies is at an end. He himself assures everybody that his execution is not as serious as it looks:

> Must Ill Reporte dye:
> No no, I trow,

THE HYBRID PLAY

> The world goes not so,
> Then all were awry.
> For neyther of Prince ncr King,
> Nor of any other thing,
> But my tongue shall walke,
> The prowdest of them all,
> Shall not giue me such a fall
> Or shall let me to talke.
>
> [ll. 1270–73]

Despite his leading role and enormous energy, however, he is clearly superfluous to the action when it is considered from a dramatic view alone. The play needs him no more in the dynamic of its plot than did the original story. Why then is he thrust into it with a part so large and active that it eclipses every other? We must reckon of course with his comedy and his great popularity. But that alone does not fully explain his presence just as it does not explain at all the other elements of the morality convention that also appear in the play as additions to the Biblical narrative. The larger answer lies in the fact that *Susanna* is still primarily a homiletic play, and its chief mission is to instruct the audience in morality, with the dramatized story itself still only a means to that end. Not only is it a virtue play which offers its steadfast heroine as an "ensample good . . . meete in these our dayes," but it is also a more general "myrrour" reflecting upon its own time every possible moral lesson it can extract from her story—especially the evils resulting from malicious slander and corrupt magistrates. For such a purpose the morality drama supplied the traditional apparatus, especially the Vice, with his mordant intrigue in exposition of the evil he personifies and with his satiric communion with the audience. He is the comic relief of the play, but he is also its destructive protagonist and its instructive voice. The spectators are very soon assured by him that slander was not confined to the time of Susanna:

> Euill Reporte mary he is a jolly man, and had in such a pryce,
> That no man liueth now adayes, but will him excercyse.
>
> [ll. 143–44]

Touching on Susanna's wifely patience and submissiveness, ironically he invites the women in the audience not to imitate her:

> But here you wiues, I would not wish that you should take her part,
> But if your husbandes anger you, beshrew their crooked hart.
>
> [ll. 161–62]

THE HYBRID PLAY

He also advises them not to imitate her chastity. And the moment after he incites the two elders to their aggression against Susanna he moralizes the large Elizabethan implication of their turpitude:

> Must now a common welth,
> Be needes in good health,
> That haue such Rulers . . .
>> [ll. 581–82]

The same didactic compulsion and a corresponding homiletic apparatus invest *The Tragical Comedy of Appius and Virginia,* licensed in 1567 and printed in 1575. The popular medieval story derived from Livy becomes in this instance another virtue play. "Wherein," as its title page announces, "is liuely expressed a rare example of the vertue of Chastitie." [11] The prologue not only offers Virginia's example to all Elizabethan virgins but also, by an extension of the idea to include marital constancy, urges the "Lordings all that present be" and all wedded ladies "to imitate the life you see, whose fame will perish neuer." Nor does the epilogue neglect a last reminder:

> And by this Poets faining here example do you take,
> Of Virginias life, of chastetie, of duty to thy make.
> Of loue to wife, of loue to spouse, of loue to husband deare,
> Of bringing vp of tender youth, all these are noted heare:
>> [ll. 1209–12]

For the play's range of exemplification extends beyond its heroine's chastity. It includes also her filial piety, and in Virginius it shows the model of a father and husband. Judge Appius is an examplar of another kind, for in his desperate suicide "the finall ende of fleshly lust wee see."

But although the literary method of the play is moralistic in the conventional way, it is so with a difference. Here, for the first time in these hybrid plays, we are taken outside the Bible. We are taken even further, for "this tragidie," as it is called in its prologue, is very clearly influenced by the Senecan drama, and its atmosphere is Renaissance-classical rather than Christian. There are occasional lapses into Christian eschatology, as when Appius fears "that fier eternall, my soule shall destroy," or when Virginius is glad that his dead daughter, "a virgine pure and chast, in heauen leades hir life." But they are not many, for the deliberate theology of the play is pagan. The piety of the Virginiae

THE HYBRID PLAY

consists in their reverence for the Roman "Gods that rule the Skies." Virginia's chastity is "Dianas gifte" and under the protection of that goddess. Appius invokes the whole classical pantheon to pity his lovesick suffering. Every scene is rife with the mythology of the ancient gods and heroes. Furthermore the morality of the play is oriented to the distinctly secular motifs of fame, honor, and fortune. "Immortal fame" is Virginia's reward for her martyrdom, and Appius is much more worried about his honor and reputation than about his immortal soul. As for the theme of fortune, it plays so large a part that, as we shall see shortly, it is responsible for the whole moral significance of the Vice.

The secular morality of the play and its marked transitional character are also reflected in its allegorical machinery. Less than a third of the cast of sixteen is made up from figures belonging to the old story—Virginia, her father, her mother, Judge Appius, and Claudius his instrument. A substantial addition, which is also a structural development of considerable moment in the evolution of the Vice, consists of the three servants of Appius: the married pair Mansipulus and Mansipula, and Subservus. The other eight roles belong to personifications, seven of whom are virtues. But in these seven moral allegory has gone to seed, surviving only as so much homiletic bric-a-brac retained by piety or habit in a play where it is no longer part of a functional design. Conscience and Justice have their brief moment when they enter to embody the short seizure of remorse and fear that divides the soul of Appius from his lust, and the stage direction at this point is interesting:

Here let him [Appius] make as rhogh [sic] he went out and let Consince and Iustice come out of him, and let Consience hold in his hande a Lamp burning and let Iustice haue a sworde and hold it before Apius brest.

[opposite ll. 499–512]

They remain, however, no longer than the very short time it takes the Vice to rally his victim out of his hesitation. Later in the play Rumor comes on for a single speech which informs Virginius of the judge's real intention toward Virginia. The moment after Virginius kills her, Comfort appears to save him from despair and to advise him to proceed resolutely against Appius. In the denouement Justice enters once more, alongside Reward, to condemn Appius to death and also to take care of the by now conventional business of "hanging"

THE HYBRID PLAY

the Vice. Finally Fame, Doctrina, and Memory arrive to eulogize the martyred heroine and to guarantee her enduring renown. In all these shrunken and scattered survivors out of moral allegory we witness the decay of the beneficent half of the Psychomachia. The largest role among them has no more than a score of lines, and some of the others have fewer than half a dozen. Clinging to the play out of the abstract and expository world from which it emerges, they are being pushed off its stage by their own dramatic ineptness as well as by the men and women who make up its actual story and herald the concrete dramatic world toward which it is groping. The two moral virtues who "come out of" Appius in the unusual stage direction above are a sign that such moral symbolism is becoming self-conscious and inhibited. It is also a sign of the same development that they are reduced to dumb show while Appius himself interprets the passionate division of will *within him*:

> But out I am wounded, how am I deuided?
> Two states of my life, from me are now glided,
> For Consience he pricketh me contempned,
> And Iustice saith, Iudgement wold haue me condemned:
> Consience saith crueltye sure will detest me:
> And Iustice saith, death in thende will molest me,
> And both in one sodden me thinkes they do crie,
> That fier eternall, my soule shall destroy.

> [ll. 501–508]

This, in a cruder style, might be Angelo or Macbeth speaking, or Richard III debating with his conscience on the night before Bosworth. We have arrived, in short, at the Elizabethan soliloquy. The "Holy War" externalized by the morality convention is now being restored to subjectivity as the divided voice within the heart of individual men.

But what is true of one side of the Psychomachia is far from true of the other. Consolidated into the single large figure of Haphazard the Vice, abstract evil pulsates with theatrical life. His name defines a code of behavior accommodated to the belief that all things are governed by chance, and that, accordingly, reward and punishment have no essential relation to virtue and vice but proceed indiscriminately from the caprice of blind fortune. Since there is neither justice nor moral law, but the world is all "hap," one ought boldly to "hazard." It is with this doctrine that he incites the lust-stricken but hesitant judge to his crime and supplies him with a stratagem:

272   *THE HYBRID PLAY*

> There is no more wayes, but hap or hap not,
> Either hap, or els haplesse, to knit vp the knot:
> And if you will hazard, to venter what falles,
> Perhaps, that Haphazard, will end al your thralles.
>
>   .   .   .   .
>
> Of this kinde of conspirasie now let vs common,
> Some man, Virginius, before you must summon,
> And say that Virginia is none of his Daughter.
>
>   [ll. 474 ff.]

Appius, however, is not his only victim. The structural development that in the late moralities split the figure of Mankind into multiple types, each the dupe of the Vice, is repeated in the hybrid plays, where his aggression shows a corresponding proliferation. The comic passages between Haphazard and the three servants are not merely humorous relief. They are an important part of the Vice's demonstration that the evil he personifies invades all classes high and low, and the servants are just as much his victims as their master. They come on as faithful retainers, zealous about the performance of their duties and fearful of the punishment for slackness. But he soon turns them into reckless pleasure seekers, as conscienceless about their dereliction as Appius is about his lust, and hoping likewise to escape punishment because the world is "haphazard." The two actions, otherwise dissociated, are homiletically one, two examples of a common affliction. What the Vice cannot actually demonstrate to the audience he tells them about—his universal influence over all classes and occupations: courtiers, plowmen, merchants, scholars, schoolmasters, wives, and maids. All subscribe to the doctrine of haphazard fortune:

> Most of all these my nature doth injoy,
> Somtime I aduaunce them, somtime I destroy . . .
>
>   [ll. 222–23]

For a last demonstration he victimizes himself. Unable to get a recompense for his "service" from the doomed Appius, he seeks it recklessly from Justice and Reward ("hap that hap may, I wyll put it in hazard, I geue it assay") and gets it in the shape of the gallows.

The Griselda legend, made to order for the homiletic method of the virtue play, is so exploited in John Phillip's *Comedy of Patient and Meek Grissill,* in an undated quarto but licensed in 1565. The intention

THE HYBRID PLAY 273

explicit in the title is confirmed by the words that directly follow: "Whearin is declared, the good example, of her pacience towardes her husband: and lykewise, the due obedience of Children, toward their Parentes." The prologue makes the point once more ("Let Grissills Pacience swaye in you, wee do you all require"), the epilogue repeats it, and the play itself is full of the same emphasis, with the Vice never tired of inverting it into satirical comparisons between the heroine and the generality of wives "at this daye." The play is faithful to the established lines of the story and reproduces, under their original names, all the characters who belong to it—Grissill, her father Jannickle and his wife, the Marquis Gautier, the Countess of Pango, and Grissill's two children. Several minor characters are added—a nurse, a pair of pages, a midwife, and a maid. The didactic intention, as the title shows, is actually twofold, exemplifying in the heroine the wifely virtues of obedience and meekness in the face of outrageous provocation, and also in her as well as in her children the proper behavior of offspring to their parents.

In addition to this self-contained scheme of events and persons, the hybrid convention to which the play belongs asserts itself in the abstract and homiletic ways with which we are already familiar. The old habit and allegiance fill in the crevices of the literal story with allegorical supernumeraries. The messenger of the marquis is allegorized, if only in name, into the chief virtue of his office and called Diligence. Rumor has a single speech of sixteen lines filled with what his name describes, addressed to Vulgus through whom the common people speak a total of twenty-two. Grissill's parents have a neighbor called Indigence whose perfunctory role exists simply to make the point that they have lived very close to poverty all their lives. When the heroine is sent back to them their grief is vanquished by their moral resources, signified by the appearance to them of Patience and Constancy. And since the play has a point to make about the relations between courtiers and their lord, the marquis is attended by Fidence, Reason, and Sobriety, who are simply a group of three honest counselors, indistinguishable from each other and personifications in name only. All these figures are at once marginal in their significance and trivial in their action—metaphorical fragments ill at ease in a play that is no longer a metaphor. The compact interplay of human relationships in-

274   *THE HYBRID PLAY*

side a literal story robs them of their previous force and function, and they survive merely as homiletic embroidery around its edges.

But alongside these fading vestiges of the moral play we encounter once more the startling exception of the Vice, and so theatricalized that he is one of the most interesting members of his line. He has no cohorts, for that homiletic detail, so important in the analytical method of moral allegory, has been rubbed out by the dramatic economy of the hybrid plays. In his name, Politick Persuasion, and in his actions he partly signifies what seemed to the Renaissance the most typical as well as the most insidious danger to which a ruler is subject—the evil influence of the parasite whose flattering tongue holds his ear and sways his mind and heart. For the sake of this topical point, as well as for the reason that his presence on the popular stage at this time is indispensable apparently, the play is filled, dominated, and motored by the multiple stratagems of the Vice. He has his first chance when the courtiers petition the marquis to take a wife:

> Now Polliticke perswasion shoe forth thy skyll,
> I will make him obstinate stoberne and frowarde,
> If that I may atchiue my purpose and will.
>   [ll. 138–40]

He has another, this time as a demonstration of his influence over the court, when Gautier reserves the choice of a wife to himself and keeps her identity a secret:

> But to none of his court the gentilwoman is knowne,
> And therfore to wonder there mindes I incence,
> So that euery man longeth to vew the Ladyes presence.
>   [ll. 357–59]

The election of the lowborn Grissill provides him with his next opportunity, as he explains to the audience:

> I tell you I haue found out such an inuension,
> As among the common sort, shall kindle discencion:
> A Marquis maried to a beggerlye Grissill,
> Her father an olde foole, and an impotent criple,
> His store and substaunce in value not worth twentie pence,
> This geare cannot chuse but breed inconuenience,
> I will not cease priuely her confusion to worke,

THE HYBRID PLAY

For vnder Honnie the prouerbe saith poyson maye lurke:
So though I simulate externally Loue to pretend,
My loue shall turne to mischife, I warrant you in the end:

[ll. 891–900]

It is only after his failure with both the court and the people that he really gets under way as he invades the main business of the old story and instigates the marquis to each of the three trials the latter imposes on Grissill's wifely virtue:

Sith my former deuice, is thrust to exemption,
And that I cannot preuayle with rancor and contencion:
I will frequent through pollicie, another meane,
Wherwith I will molest and distroye her cleane,
I will trye her pacience, another kynde of waye:
Let mee see euen so, it shallbe I swere by this daye,
Peace conceale thy purpose as yet Polliticke perswacion:
Till such time as thou see farther occasion,
Not a word more my Lorde Marques entreth the place,
Nowe maist thou contriue thy drift within short space.

[ll. 958–67]

Here is the fascinating crux of the play for its intimation of *Othello*. The marquis enters lyrical with love's excitement and devotion, the song on his lips expressing his "ioyfull iollytie" and celebrating the peerless virtues of "my true loue and Ladye deare." The standard peripeteia of the morality drama, whereby the Vice, as special testimony of his skill, begins his work of perversion when his victim is at the height of his virtue, is here transformed into its romantic equivalent:

God ge goddeauen my Lorde wyth all my hart,
If your wyfe be so vertuous as nowe ye import,
Surelie, surely shee is worthy commendacion,
Shee may be made a saynte for her good conuersacion:
But harke my Lorde nay nowe harken in your eare,
Try hir that waye and *by myne honestie* I sweare . . .

[my italics; ll. 992–97]

His dupe is in his hands, and from this point the trials of Grissill begin, each one separately insinuated by the Vice. Having demonstrated his "property" and ability in every way possible, he moves out of the play to make room in the end for the restoration of the heroine and the celebration of her excellence:

THE HYBRID PLAY

Ah syra this geare is trimly handled by St. tan,
Howe saye you hath not Pollicie nowe playd the man,
Shee shall home to her father shee, this is trim:
But her sudden fall will trouble the harte of him,
Fare ye well all, I will bee packing,
Tush ther wants a man, where Pollicie is lackyng.

[ll. 1665–70]

His various aggressions, no joke to his victims, sparkle at his end with all the comical and rhetorical features inveterate in his role. Wrapt into that continuous intimacy with the audience which is the special expository dimension of his performance are the bawdy jests, the endless word play, the fustian speeches, the choric information, the long monologues of allegorical exposition and topical satire, the boasting and self-gratulation over each sharp device, the scorn and laughter—all of which they delighted in and demanded. Most remarkable is his tireless satire on marriage and the female sex. He never misses a chance to catalogue the tribulations of matrimony and the sins of wives—their pride and vanity, their self-indulgence and wastefulness, their faithlessness and deceit, their craving for "mastership," their idleness and chatter, their spite, meanness, willfulness, shrewishness, and hypocrisy:

I speake plainlye I can not flatter,
Thinke not that enuy doth giue me occasion,
No there natures be knowen to Pollyticke perswasion,
Trie them who will shall my words true fynde,
Sume of them I tell you will be stoberne and vnkynde,
Denye them of ther willes and then ye mar all,
Ye shall see what there after is like for to fall,
Ether brauling, iaulynge, sknappinge, or snarringe,
Ther tounges shall not cease but alwaies be iarringe,
Or els they will counterfait a kind of hipocrisye;
And symper lyke a fyrmentie pot, the finger shalbe in there eye.

.   .   .   .

Tush, tush, I know full well theire meaninge and intent
They be the craftiest cattell in Cristendome or kent.

[ll. 419–33]

The conditions of the play make his resemblance to Iago inescapable, but it need not be exaggerated into a direct influence. It is one expression simply of the more massive influence exerted by the conventionalized role he enacts. If the kinship in his case seems especially

THE HYBRID PLAY

prominent, that is because his aggression, like that of every Vice, is polarized by the values governing the play in which he finds himself; and in this instance they are romantic—married love, feminine virtue, and masculine devotion. Let us remember also that he has no motives as we commonly understand the word. He is merely putting on a demonstration of the fact that he is Politick Persuasion, and he is carrying on the Vice's hereditary work, which is, as he explains, "To vex and harme those wightes, whose liues most vertuous are."

The four plays just behind us illustrate the fusion of homiletic allegory and concrete story. Each dramatizes a heroine out of history or legend, but she, no less than the generic figure of Mankind in the moralities, is presented as an edifying moral example, and about her are the subsidiary examples of the persons who belong to her story. Each, moreover, is invested with the apparatus and method of the Psychomachia—with opposed personifications who externalize the moral forces working in the plot and extend their significance into lessons profitable to the play's contemporaries. All four, in short, cling to a tradition that uses the stage primarily for moral exposition and only incidentally for literal representation, and in all of them the unifying principle is homiletic rather than dramatic. Such a standard and such a sense of unity make it easy for them to tolerate the intimate association between the abstract and the concrete, the figurative and the literal, so that Virginius, for instance, can hold converse with his own embodied Comfort, and invite his company on the way to Judge Appius: "Come on good Comfort, wend we then, there is no other shifte." The fact that each of these plays inhabits two disparate worlds at one and the same time, and is from beginning to end a mixed metaphor, is an insight available to us today who look at them with literary eyes through the perspective glass of four centuries. In their own time the paradox was much less apparent, if at all. Wavering between very different conventions, their conscious standards were still fixed upon the old one while they were being invaded imperceptibly by the spirit of the new.

Almost in spite of themselves, however, they testify that this mixture of persons and personifications, of a literal story and a dramatic method rooted in homiletic allegory, could only be a temporary ferment of uncongenial elements. One or the other was bound to be consumed or

THE HYBRID PLAY

thrown off, and the direction of the stage, no less than of the age, is clear in all four plays. They begin to cultivate the new opportunities afforded them by a story in time and place, whose movement is created by the interplay of human individuals. Narrative variety and personal idiosyncrasy compete in the same plot with the rigid formula of the metaphorical Psychomachia to the disadvantage of the latter. A Mary Magdalene, an Appius, a Gautier show the stirrings of personality. The personifications of virtue lose their functional integrity and become one-speech supernumeraries, with many of them—Fame, Memory, Rumor—no longer clearly Christian. The minor personifications of vice fade and disappear as the homiletic sequence they embody ceases to be part of the play's design. Both sets of figures are crowded off the stage by its new population and its unfolding sense of a new kind of stage business. The role with which we are chiefly concerned, needless to say, enjoys a more prosperous history. It survives vigorously but, as we shall see, it does not survive unchanged.

3

As we trace his career through the hybrid plays we discover in the latest of them the inevitable effect of his new environment upon the Vice. He was originally conceived and subsequently developed as a native of a metaphorical world which supported in all its parts the subjective logic of his role. But as he moves onto a new stage filled with human individuals and the diverse events of history or fable—a stage, moreover, rapidly transferring its allegiance from a homiletic to an aesthetic purpose—his original significance is compromised by his new surroundings, and his activity, though his energy is unimpaired, undergoes an important transformation. His traditional behavior is bent and twisted to accommodate him to events and persons too confirmed in history or fable to be accommodated to him, and too self-sufficient in their own concreteness to have any real use for his metaphorical presence among them. In the four plays we are about to consider the Vice is so clearly an imposition that his presence would be inexplicable without our awareness of the homiletic tradition still within these plays and of his peculiar hold on the stage as the most durable feature of that tradition. But his presence remains possible for **another reason: in a**

THE HYBRID PLAY

dramatic world that is no longer a metaphor he himself ceases to be metaphorical.

John Pikering's *Horestes,* printed in 1567, presents the revenge taken by the hero upon Clytemnestra and Aegisthus for their murder of his father.[12] Despite the nature of the plot, the play derives it from nothing more classical than Caxton's *Recuyell of the Historyes of Troye* (c. 1475),[13] and fashions it according to the dramatic method and moral interests of its own time. The full title is a useful index to the state of the popular drama in the decade of the sixties: *A Newe Enterlude of Vice, Conteyninge the Historye of Horestes, with the cruell revengment of his Fathers death, vpon his one naturtll* [sic] *Mother.* Here at once and compactly are the characteristic mixture of history and morality, the homiletic intention of the play, and the extraordinary theatrical prominence of the Vice. The cast of twenty-six ("deuided for VI to playe") confirms the title. It contains seven Greek figures more or less connected with the legend—the three already mentioned plus Idumeus [Idomeneus?], Nestor, Menelaus, and Hermione. The morality convention equips it with such personifications as Nature, Fame, Truth, Duty, not to speak of the Vice himself. And the native spirit fulfills itself additionally by supplying mirth and didacticism together in a brawl, instigated by the Vice, between the farmers Hodge and Rusticus (a pair of names that speak volumes for the mixed auspices of the play), and in another brawl between a pair of homely soldiers, Haltersick and Hempstring.

The events of the play, as well as its moral theme, concern revenge, making it the first of the long Elizabethan line in this genre. The action of Horestes against his mother places him squarely between the teeth of his provocation and his filial piety. His inward division and irresolution are the single burden of his first soliloquy:

> To caull to minde the crabyd rage of mothers yll attempt
> Prouokes me now all pyttie quight from me to be exempt.
> Yet lo, dame nature teles me, that I must with willing mind
> Forgiue the faute and to pytie some what to be inclynd.
>
> . . . .
>
> O paterne loue, why douste thou so of pytey me request,
> Syth thou to me wast quight denyed, my mother being prest!
> [ll. 171–80]

280 THE HYBRID PLAY

Later on, when he advances with his army against the stronghold of the guilty pair, Nature confronts him with an appeal to refrain from so "unnatural" a deed as matricide. But his determination to revenge his father is now unshakable:

> No, nought at all, oh nature, can my purpose now withstand.
> Shall I forgiue my fathers death? my hart can not agre
> My father slayne in such a sorte, and vnreuengyd to be.
>
> [ll. 409–11]

He has a second moment of hesitation, however, when his mother pleads for her life. But the Vice soon stiffens him to his vengeance, and she goes to her death. Thereafter Fame appears to deplore the act and to lament that she has to spread Horestes' reputation throughout the world as a second Nero(!). From having been the agent of revenge Horestes now becomes its object, for Menelaus, objecting to his nephew's cruelty, is himself stirred by the spirit of retribution. This feud is resolved, however, by the judgment of Idumeus and Nestor that Horestes acted out of sufficient cause; and his marriage to Hermione at the end establishes amity between himself and her father.

Although the moral question of Horestes' revenge is left unresolved, it is at least discriminated. The revenge of a prince, especially if it is commanded by the gods, is a necessary punishment for the guilty and a deterrent to others viciously inclined. The nicer question of a revenge that takes the form of matricide the playwright, although he deplores it, is content to leave essentially unanswered after developing the argument on both sides. On the negative there is the unnatural aspect of the deed as it is proclaimed by Nature and Fame; on the affirmative its justification by Idumeus and Nestor as "a ryghtuous facte" because "the gods commaundyd him there to." But in reality Pikering is occupied by a larger thesis than revenge itself, and that is social unity and order, of which crime is one form of disruption, and revenge, crime's consequence, another. That is what the two virtues, Truth and Duty, intend when in the epilogue, just after the marriage of the hero and heroine has brought a new harmony in place of the old violence and family strife, they draw for the audience the play's most topical lesson. Truth proclaims that "A kyngdome kept in Amyte, and voyde of dissention," which is not "deuyded in him selfe" and whose members are not provoked against each other by "wordes of reprehen-

THE HYBRID PLAY

tion," avoids ruin and lasts a long time. Duty says the same thing negatively:

> Where I, Dewtey, am neclected of aney estate,
> Their stryfe and dyssention my place do supplye:
> Cankred mallyse, pryde, and debate,
> Therefore to rest, all meanes do trye.
> Then ruin comes after of their state, whereby
> They are vtterly extynguyshed, leuinge nought behynde,
> Whereof so much as their name we maye fynde.

[ll. 1171–77]

It is within a moral context so specifically Tudor that we can best understand the Vice of the play. His theatrical and homiletic importance is clear, not only from his prominence in the title, but no less from the fact that he is first on the stage, his long speech of exposition to the audience having become by now the conventional opening for almost every play in which he performs. His name is Revenge, the force that animates every part of the action, even its comic passages. It is he who, as "messenger of godes," appears to Horestes in his perplexity, abolishes his moral scruples, and sends him forward "to reueng thy fathers death." His moral pseudonym for the purpose is Courage, a word whose equivocal meaning we have already encountered. He becomes a kind of aide-de-camp to the hero in his wars, close at hand to rally him out of a momentary fit of conscience, to make him obdurate against Clytemnestra's plea for mercy, and, in fact, to be her executioner himself. After her death the Vice informs the audience in a song that, having done his worst by Horestes (who "now doth rew" his matricide), he has no further use for him, and seeks new employment:

> A new master, a new!
> And was it not yll
> His mother to kyll?
> I pray you, how saye you?

[ll. 853–56]

His new master is soon forthcoming. Menelaus, whom "Reuenge hath set on fyare," arrives to punish Horestes, and strife impends between uncle and nephew. But the judgment of the Greek princes erases the enmity between them, the marriage cements their friendship, and the Vice is once more masterless. He bids the audience good-by for the

282 THE HYBRID PLAY

nonce in an uninterrupted monologue of eighty-four lines filled with satirical exposition of his quality and force in human affairs. Entering "with a staffe and a bottell or dyshe and wallet," he explains how it happens that he has come down in the world:

> This one thinge, you knowe, that on caulyd amyte,
> Is vnto me, reuenge, most contrarey;
> And we twayne to geather could not abyde,
> Whych causyd me so sone from hye state to slyde.
> Horestes and his ounckell, Kynge Menalaus,
> Is made such sure frendas, without paraduenture.
>
> . . . .
>
> I was dryuen with out comfort awaye from their gate;
> I was glad to be packinge, for feare of my pate.
>
> [ll. 1062–72]

His last effort to create division between them took place, as he explains, at the marriage ceremony, symbol of concord:

> Yet, befor I went, my fancey to please,
> The maryage selebratyd at the church I dyd se.
> Wyllinge I was, them all to dysease;
> But I durst not be so bold, for master Amyte
> Sot by Menalaus, and bore him companye,
> On the other syde Dewtey with Horestes boure swaye,
> So that I could not enter, by no kynde of waye.
>
> [ll. 1073–79]

He lets his hearers know, however, that he is of good comfort for he is sure to have employment: "the most parte of wemen to me be full kynde" and "knowe Reuengys operation":

> Yf they haue not all thinges, when they do desiare,
> They wyll be reuengyd, or elles lye in the myare.
>
> . . . .
>
> Ye, faull to it, good wyues, and do them not spare!
> Nay, Ille helpe you forward, yf you lacke but perswacion.
>
> [ll. 1085–90]

And after celebrating the well known discomfort of Socrates at the hands of Xantippe, he concludes with a reminder than an Elizabethan audience could appreciate:

THE HYBRID PLAY

Farwell, cosen cutpursse, and be ruled by me,
Or elles you may chaunce to end on a tre.

[ll. 1120–21]

Revenge, in brief, as the Vice personifies it, is a significant aspect of the great Elizabethan theme of order. He is represented as the force that disrupts what duty and degree promote—harmony and peace in the state, in and between social classes, in kinship, in marriage. His operation in the present story is responsible for the violence of son against mother (unfilial whatever her guilt), of uncle against nephew, and he seeks to do as much for husband and wife. He is responsible, furthermore, for the internecine war that ravages Mycenae. Nor are these disorders the limits of his demonstration. He extends his quality and its effects upon members of all estates, and what seem at first to be merely comic diversions in the play are, in fact, important contributions to its homiletic aim. The country pair, Hodge and Rusticus, come on as friends, but each is soon stirred by the Vice's whispered incitements (his pseudonym for the purpose is Patience!) to seek revenge of the other ("Naye, I wyll be reuenged, by his oundes, and I maye"), and before they are through they have not only exchanged bitter words but broken each other's head with their staves. Having paid his respects to the rural estate, the Vice does as much for the military. Although he is not actually present, his quality soon displays itself at work upon Haltersick and Hempstring as their friendship degenerates into quarrel and blows: "I wyll be reuengyd, or eles I shall bourste." His multiple aggressions weave the classic legend into a topical lesson, and his presence does for *Horestes* what it does for nearly all the hybrid plays: it creates a plot with a double orbit and a double center, the result of the merger of two disparate conventions. As dramatic story *Horestes* moves around its hero; as homily (*A Newe Enterlude of Vice*) it moves around the Vice (the other personifications are trivial). One other feature needs to be observed about him since he is the last of his race in our survey in whom it remains unequivocal. His name and his role retain their subjective meaning as personification of a property in the nature of human beings who are his victims. He instills the spirit of revenge into them, and it is they, not he, who act out what he personifies. He attaches himself to them as servant or companion, sig-

THE HYBRID PLAY

284

nifying that they have embraced the moral quality he stands for. In other words, the Vice of this play is still a metaphor, as his words to Horestes make clear when he comes forward to his victim for the first time, posing as the messenger of the gods:

> And I as gyde with you shall go, to gyde you on the way.
> By me, thy mind, ther wrathful dome shalbe performed in dede.
>
> [ll. 192–93]

Or again, when he shames him out of his hesitation:

> Why waylst thou, man? leaue of, I say; plucke corrage vnto the;
> This lamentation sone shall fade, if thou imbrasydest me.
>
> [ll. 203–204]

Cambises by Thomas Preston, licensed in 1569, offers a spectacle of tyranny in the "many wicked deedes and tyrannous murders" of that Persian monarch.[14] And in the tyrant's "odious death by Gods Iustice appointed" the playwright is able to point up an admonitory example of the penalty to which evil rulers and magistrates are subject at the hands of divine providence. In one respect at least *Cambises* is closer to the original moralities than any other of the hybrid plays with the exception of Wager's *Mary Magdalene:* it encompasses the whole moral career of its hero, presenting a life rather than an episode. Like the moralities also, it offers the contrast of Cambises good with Cambises bad, tracing his moral degeneration from the "one good deede of execution" with which he begins his reign. Leaving Persia to make war on the Egyptians, he appoints Sisamnes to govern in his place. When he discovers upon his return from his victorious campaign that Sisamnes has been a dishonest and oppressive magistrate, perverting justice for his own profit, Cambises has him put to death. Moreover, having appointed Sisamnes' son to his father's place and duties, he compels him to witness the execution in order to bring home to him the punishment awaiting malfeasance in high office. But after this meritorious act the evil in Cambises' nature asserts itself. He becomes addicted to drink and for the rest of his life he is berserk. Because his faithful counselor Praxaspes dares exhort him against drunkenness, he demonstrates that his aim at least is sober by shooting an arrow through the heart of Praxaspes' little son. When his virtuous younger brother Smirdis is maligned to him he has him murdered incontinent. His next

THE HYBRID PLAY

outrage is to marry against her will a lady related to him within the prohibited bounds of kinship. And when she weeps in recollection over the cruel death of Smirdis she quickly suffers the same fate. Finally the providential justice of God steps in. The tyrant is pierced by his own sword in a fall from his horse and, since no one is willing to help him, dies wretchedly.

Despite its admonitory theme, however, and the auspices from which it derives, *Cambises,* as compared with the hybrid plays so far examined, shows a marked falling away from the temper of the homiletic stage. Its ethical formula is undermined by a melodramatic impulse toward sensationalism for its own sake, and it is easy to do the play some injustice by reading it as an unprincipled farrago of violence and rant. The many deaths, for instance, which fill up the plot are exploited with a tabloid appreciation for bloody detail. Sisamnes, his son a looker-on, is flayed as well as slain on the stage, the direction urging, "Flea him with a false skin." Praxaspes' son is transfixed in full view, and his heart is cut out and presented to the father to show the arrow piercing its center. When Smirdis is stabbed "a little bladder of vinegar prickt" colors the deed with verisimilitude. The tyrant's own death is made as scenic as possible: "Enter the King, without a gowne, a swoord thrust up into his side, bleeding." A piece of mythological business and its theme do violence of another sort to the moralistic tradition. Cambises' passion for his "cosiniarmin nigh of birth" is explained by the entrance of Venus "leading out her sonne, Cupid, blinde" and guiding his shot to hit the king with the arrow of love. The play itself aims ostentatiously in one direction but shoots in another. Pointing at the ethical nerve of the audience, it actually hits their melodramatic sense. It was a great success in its own time because it was, for its popular audience, a novel advance toward spectacle and theater.

The melodramatic bias of the play also reveals itself in the subtler ways of omission. The bad career of its chief figure is a warning for anyone in a position to profit from it, but, unlike the forthright didacticism of the other hybrid plays, he is never offered to the audience in so many words as an "example." On the other hand he is pungently theatricalized as a roaring, strutting tyrant whose "vein" became a byword for the bombastic style that tears a passion to tatters. The epilogue especially is interesting for what it does not say. Instead

286   *THE HYBRID PLAY*

of expounding the meaning of the play in the traditional manner and generalizing it into topical relevance, it presents a moral synopsis as brief as the posy of a ring:

> Right gentle audience, heere have you perused
> The tragicall history of this wicked king.
>
> [ll. 1199–1200]

Further evidence of the play's defection from the homiletic convention exists in its allegorical machinery. Abstract roles are numerous, the playwright having sprinkled personification with a free hand upon the historical ground of his plot. But they are also, apart from the Vice, both perfunctory and empty of real ethical significance. Literary habit and enervated traditionalism rather than genuine purpose are responsible for such scattered and nondescript figures as Commons Complaint, Commons Cry, Proof, Diligence, Preparation, Attendance, Murder, Cruelty, Execution, Shame, Trial, and Small Ability. They have neither the collective force nor the ethical meaning that marks the personifications in the moral plays, and all of them enter just once for some trivial action that earns them their abstract names. Thus Murder and Cruelty are simply first and second murderers, Execution an executioner, Preparation a servant, and so on. As a result the Psychomachia exists only to the extent that it is upheld by the Vice, and even he, in as large a role as ever, displays noteworthy aberrations.

Ambidexter, the Vice of the play, is one of the most versatile members of his line. He is also, for a reason that will soon appear, one of the most complicated. Without companions and without opposition, since all other members of the Psychomachia have fallen by the wayside, he cuts a triumphant swathe through half a dozen actions and as many victims. *Cambises* is as much his play as it is the titular hero's, and all its otherwise disparate parts, comical and serious, are tied into one homiletic package labeled with his moral signification. His name, as he never tires of informing the audience, signifies one "That with both hands finely can play," or, as the *New English Dictionary* has it, "a double-dealer, a two-faced actor." The earliest English sense of the word restricts it to actions at law and describes the judge, lawyer, or juryman who takes bribes from either litigant, or from both together.[15] We may suspect, therefore, that he was originally conceived in the present play as a homiletic comment on Sisamnes, who is a more or

THE HYBRID PLAY

less honest magistrate, although painfully aware of his opportunities, until the Vice encounters him:

> Jesu, Maister Sisamnes, with me you are wel acquainted!
> By me rulers may be trimly painted.
> Ye are unwise if ye take not time while ye may:
> If ye wil not now, when ye would ye shall have nay.
> What is he that of you dare make exclamation,
> Of your wrong-dealing to make explication?
> Can you not play with both hands, and turn with the winde?
>
> [ll. 315–21]

To which Sisamnes replies, "Beleeve me, your words draw deepe in my mind" and gives himself over wholly to the malfeasance that brings upon him the punishment already described.

But the demonstration of his moral quality through his first victim ("How like you Sisamnes for using me? / He plaid with both hands, but he sped ilfavourdly!") exhausts neither the ambition nor the energy of Ambidexter. He is a Vice for all estates, as he announces in his first address to the audience, his purpose being "To see if I can all men beguile":

> Now with King Cambises, and by-and-by gone,—
> Thus doo I run this way and that way.
> For [a] while I meane with a souldier to be,
> Then give I a leape to Sisamnes the judge,—
> I dare avouch you shall his destruction see!
> To all kinde of estates I meane for to trudge.
> Ambidexter? Nay, he is a fellow, if ye knew all!
> Cease for awhile; heereafter heare more ye shall!
>
> [ll. 152–59]

His aggressions consequently range wide as he exerts himself upon men of all sorts in order to demonstrate the broader meaning of his name through a variety of applications. Since the play begins with Cambises' war against the Egyptians, he first appears as the image of that kind of ambidexterity which characterizes the cowardly soldier. The influence of Latin comedy shows itself at once when he comes forward in the attire of a *miles gloriosus* ("Enter the Vice, with an old capcase on his head, an olde paile about his hips for harnes, a scummer and a potlid by his side, and a rake on his shoulder") shouting his prowess and announcing that he is "appointed to fight against a snaile." In this guise

THE HYBRID PLAY

he encounters the three "ruffins" Huff, Ruff, and Snuff, who are on their way to the wars; and after a good deal of comic byplay which includes a meretrix, they exchange friendship with him as token that his moral quality governs their soldiering:

> Gogs hart, to have thy company needs we must prove!
> We must play with both hands, with our hostes and host,
> Play with both hands, and score on the poste;
> Now and then, with our captain, for many a delay,
> We wil not sticke with both hands to play.
>
> [ll. 214–19]

The same moral quality creates the homiletic relationship between the Vice of *Cambises* and the whole career of its peccant hero. It exhibits itself through the ambidextrous swerving of the king from virtue to wickedness—from his one good deed to his numerous tyrannies, from justice to wanton cruelty, from brotherly love to fratricide, from his passion for the lady he marries to his vicious order for her execution. Since in addition to personifying the evil in the play he is also its moral voice, Ambidexter clarifies the point many times over in his choric pronouncements which preface and conclude almost every episode:

> The king himselfe was godly uptrained;
> He professed vertue, but I think it was fained.
> He plaies with both hands, good deeds and ill;
> But it was no good deed Praxaspes sonne for to kill.
> As he for the good deed on the iudge was commended,
> For all his deeds els he is reprehended.
>
> . . . .
>
> And yet ye shall see in the rest of his race
> What infamy he will work against his owne grace.
>
> [ll. 607–20]

The Vice, in brief, supplies the homiletic unity of the play, parts of which have little to do with the career of King Cambises, but all of which, including its comic passages, demonstrates the evil that Ambidexter personifies. Sometimes that unity seems forced and the Vice himself an imposition, but this is a later topic. As it is, he never misses a chance to translate everything and almost everyone into an example of moral ambidexterity, diversifying his homily with news about off-stage

THE HYBRID PLAY

developments, with quips about "My cosin Cutpurse" among the spectators, or with a satirical thrust upon a theme that is never out of season for the Vice in any of his roles—the badness of womankind.

But Ambidexter presents another side neglected so far—a complication in the stage image of the Vice as he hovers in transition between his subjective status as a moral personification and the growing tendency to dramatize and objectify him. It is not absent from his brothers who have already appeared in these hybrid plays, notably Ill Report and Politick Persuasion, but in him it is especially prominent and makes him at once a confusing figure and a turning point in this history. He is no longer wholly conceived as an evil *accident* residing in the moral *substance* of humanity, although he remains that in part. In respect to Cambises, Sisamnes, and the three soldiers he is still a dramatized metaphor for the evil which invades their natures and governs their behavior. Cambises plays with both hands, so does Sisamnes, and the three soldiers commit themselves likewise. As far as they are concerned the Vice is faithful to his original meaning in the morality drama, where his action allegorized the insidious entrance of the evil he personified into the heart of his victim, where his deceits and aggressions were transparent stage metaphors, and where he himself was simply the dramatized embodiment of a moral fault within the human soul.

Like all metaphors after long use, this one thickens and loses its transparency. In another part of his performance and in relation to other victims the Vice no longer has an inward meaning. His behavior remains a demonstration, for his performance retains its homiletic dimension, but now it is a demonstration which has nothing to do with the moral nature of his dupes. Without perverting them, he simply deceives them and breeds dissension between them as a demonstration of *his own nature*. Not only does he appear in the guise of a *miles gloriosus* in order to infect others with that kind of ambidexterity in warfare, but he plays the boaster and coward himself, running out of several quarrels when they turn into physical violence ("The Vice must run his way for feare"), explaining to the audience afterward:

> I may say to you I was in such a fright,
> Body of me, I see the heare of my head stand upright!
> [ll. 295–96]

THE HYBRID PLAY

Even more illuminating in this respect is the program of activity he announces on his first appearance: "To see if I can all men beguile," for his beguilements have a subjective meaning only in those instances already recounted. At court he displays himself as a two-faced sycophant at the expense of the virtuous Smirdis. At one moment he counsels the latter as a friend and in the next incites the king against "His owne naturall brother"—for whom Cambises has just shown deep affection—by whispering in his ear that Smirdis seeks his throne and prays for his death. Having by this double game turned brotherly love into hatred and provoked the crime of fratricide, his boast to the audience reveals the true focus of the demonstration:

> Mary, sir, I tolde him a notable lye;
> If it were to doo againe, I durst not doo it, I!
> Mary, when I had doon, to it I durst not stand;
> Thereby ye may perceive that *I use to play with eche hand.*
>   [my italics; ll. 698–701]

For his final action of this sort he illustrates himself as a *promoter* in the Elizabethan sense of the word—that is, an *agent provocateur.* When the two rustics Hob and Lob come on with guarded comments on the king's cruelty, he too plays the aggrieved subject until by his own frank language he draws them into statements amounting to treason. Whereupon, with an aside to the audience: "Now with both hands will you see me play my parte," he turns upon them:

> A, ye fooles, ye have made wrong matches!
> Ye have spoken treason against the kings Grace,—
> For it I will accuse ye before his face;
> Then for the same ye shalbe martered,—
> At the least ye shalbe hang, drawne and quartered.
>   [ll. 789–93]

The two simpletons, beside themselves with fright, offer him pear pies and a fat goose for his silence. But he is not finished with them before he puts them through a piece of stage business which the Vice rarely neglects, no matter what his name, because apparently the popular audience could not do without it. He transforms their friendship into a quarrel and then into a brawl, the stage direction urging that "the Vice set them on as hard as he can." Nothing in the whole action has subjective meaning in respect to Hob and Lob. They are simply comic

THE HYBRID PLAY

victims upon whom the Vice demonstrates his traditional guile, and his traditional skill in creating dissension, just as Cambises and his brother Smirdis are victims of the same arts on a tragic level.

In short, like the play to which he belongs, Ambidexter is the Vice theatricalized and in transition—a metaphor so common that it has partially lost its dependent meaning and become self-sufficient. In part of his demonstration he retains his subjective force as the personification of a condition in the moral life of man. In another part, however, he demonstrates himself alone—or rather, he demonstrates, independent of its figurative sense and exploited simply for its theatrical effect, the stage behavior that is always characteristic of the Vice. His very name proclaims the change in his status. It is no longer a moral designation simply, like Pride, Envy, or Avarice. It describes the role rather than the evil, and it is, in fact, an accommodation to the chief histrionic feature of the composite Vice—*his dexterity in deceit*. For instance, one of the commonest tricks of the Vice, no matter what his name, is, as we have seen, his rapid transition from tears to laughter. But in Ambidexter's case the name is made to fit the trick. After the assassination of Smirdis he informs the audience of the sorrow at court, and continues:

> Ah good Lord! to think on him, how it dooth me greeve!
> I cannot forbeare weeping, ye may me beleeve.
> O my hart! how my pulses doo beate,
> With sorrowfull lamentations I am in such a heate!
> Ah, my hart, how for him it doth sorrow!
> Nay, I have done, in faith, now, and God give ye good morrow!
> Ha, ha! Weep? Nay laugh, with both hands to play!
> [ll. 738–44]

On the allegorical stage the name of the Vice applied to the moral meaning behind the metaphorical performance, a performance which, in its effect, made every Vice an ambidexter. In *Cambises*, on a literal stage, the performance has half escaped from metaphor, has sent forth roots of its own, has itself become halfway literal, and has, in consequence, acquired a name in its own right.

Two plays remaining for consideration are so naked of homiletic intention and the apparatus of moral allegory that they barely retain the right to be called hybrid. Almost the only vestiges of the morality convention surviving in *Common Conditions,* licensed in 1576, are the title and the Vice, and they are one and the same: "An excellent and pleasant Comedie, termed after the name of the Vice, Common Condicions, drawne out of the most famous historie of Galiarbus Duke of Arabia." The "famous historie" is unknown, but clearly it was either one of the many chivalric romances that since the Middle Ages fed the popular appetite for *love-drury* and knightly adventure, or one of the Greek romances that in the sixteenth century catered to the same taste. The play transfers this vogue to the stage, not as the metaphorical vesture for a moral theme in the manner of the "wit" plays, but in a deluge of literalness that completely overwhelms the homiletic tradition. The plot is a wholesale extravaganza of romantic love and exotic adventure. Although Schelling's arithmetic is excessive when he says that "the turbulent stream of true love runs through three continents," it certainly spreads itself over two. Arabia and Phrygia, adjacent localities on the same stage, supply the *Lebensraum* for the separations, wanderings, knightly encounters, and reunions that spin the story through its interminable vicissitudes. Parasites, tyrants, jealous dames, dishonorable knights, robbers, pirates, mistaken identities, and capricous fortune put masculine courage, feminine devotion, and filial affection to the test on sea and shore, in strange forests and on stranger islands. The sudden onset of love is blissfully reciprocated or agonizingly rejected, and passion finds its vent in septenary couplets stuffed with alliteration and classic mythology. Nature decorates adventure with the song of birds and the flowers of woodland or meadow. A foreign physician (Spanish) who makes fritters of English is one of the first examples of a role that appears in many Elizabethan plays,[16] and a female "naturall foole" called Lomia makes her contribution to the play's "delectable mirth." Three tinkers turned robbers give high romance a fillip of vulgarity, and a group of sailors turned pirates salt it with the brine of the sea. On the other side chivalry distills its essence into the figure of the knight Cardolus, who guards a castle full of captive maidens on "Marosus Ile," a spot beyond geography. The play, in short, offered God's plenty to its popular audience and survives as the earliest of a line of dramatized romances that, in spite of the derision of sophisticates like Sidney and the fulminations of moralists like Gosson, persisted well into the seventeenth century, exerting no slight influence on the major dramatists.

THE HYBRID PLAY

A summary of the plot aids our business with it. First Duke Galiarbus and then his two children, Sedmond and Clarisia, are the victims of machinations that force them to flee Arabia. Each comes to Phrygia unknown of the other two. Clarisia is seen and loved by Lamphedon, son of that region's duke, and returns the feeling. But the duchess's jealousy of Clarisia creates a danger that puts the two lovers to flight, in the course of which they are captured by pirates and separated. Clarisia escapes the pirates and disguised as Metrea becomes a servant in the household of the Phrygian knight Leostines, who soon adopts her as his daughter on condition that she gain his consent before disposing of her heart and hand. Her brother Sedmond meanwhile has become a "wandryng knight," having also disguised himself by the inversion of his name into Nomides, and as such provokes the love of Sabia, daughter of the Spanish physician Montagos. He scorns her but develops a passion for Metrea, his disguised sister, when he wanders into her neighborhood. She, without recognizing him, is faithful to her absent Lamphedon, who all this while is having his own adventures. Also escaping the pirates, he is brought by his search for her to the castle of Cardolus, overthrows him and frees the captive maidens. He finally comes to the dwelling of Leostines, discovers his Clarisia, but their joy is shortlived. Fearing the displeasure of Leostines, she hides Lamphedon in her chamber; but the two lovers are betrayed, falsely accused of unchastity and of plotting the old knight's death by poison. He dooms them to the same kind of death, and abruptly the play ends, or rather stops, at the moment they swallow the potion. Nothing better is offered by way of explanation than the following lines of the epilogue, which read as though the author had the same feeling about his play—his justification is no less—that Chaucer's host has about *Sir Thopas:*

> As wee are now by Time cut of from farther time to spende.
> So time saith to vs seace now here, your audience mutch ye wrong
> If farther now to weary them the time ye do prolonge.
>
> [ll. 1892–94]

Unquestionably the story demands a happy ending, and it is possible, with fair assurance, to extend the plot somewhat further toward the resolution that existed in the playwright's source or in his mind. The potion the two lovers drink is not actually poison, for the physician

THE HYBRID PLAY

who prepares it is surely no other than Montagos, father of the love-lorn Sabia. And to get rid of the obstacle of her seeming low birth, he is probably the disguised "Mountaynio kinge of Thrace" referred to twice in the play. As for Leostines, it is not very hazardous to guess that he turns out to be Galiarbus, father of Sedmond and Clarisia, living in disguise according to his previously announced intention. In the end, Lamphedon has his Clarisia and Sabia her Sedmond, although it is impossible to say through how many more perilous adventures and impenetrable disguises they need to struggle before reaching permanent happiness and prosperity.

What can the Vice have to do with such a plot and in such an atmosphere, where he is not lent the support of any discernible homiletic aim or the company of a single moral personification besides? To carry the question even further, what can he do in such a play, where he is essentially an interloper, that earns him the titular role? The answer, in a word, is that he does everything. He is responsible for the banishment of Galiarbus out of Arabia, for the flight of Sedmond and Clarisia, for the jealousy of the duchess of Phrygia that sends the two lovers fleeing, for their capture by pirates, for their jeopardy at the hands of Leostines; and in the end, although they are his master and mistress, he goes with alacrity to fetch and administer the poison they are condemned to drink. In the complicated action of the play he overlooks no chance to display his virtuosity and to take credit, in his monologues of exposition which frame every phase of the plot, for all the bedevilment to which the knights and their ladies are subjected. A dozen times he rubs his hands in pleasure over his successful guile and over the fact that "this geare cottens." He is the enemy of the play's romantic values, especially in his disparagement of women. Given license to settle a minor dispute between Sedmond and Clarisia, he strikes instead the Vice's everlasting note:

> It is geuen to weemen to be obscure & ful of simpriety by the way
> Proffer them the thing they most desier they wold it denay.
> They are so full of sleights and fetches that scarce the Fox hee,
> In euery poinct with weemen may scarce compared bee,
> For when men pray they will denay, or when men most desire:
> Then marke me a woman she is sonest stirred vnto ire.

THE HYBRID PLAY

Their heds are fantasticall and full of variety strange,
Like to the Moone whose operation it is often times to change.
And by your leaue howsoeuer it goes the mastery they must haue,
In euery respect or in ought that they seeme for to craue.
But Madam, I hope you will inpute no blame vnto mee,
Considering you are a mayden, and full of imbycillity.

[ll. 346–57]

His name need not be taken too seriously nor its meaning too closely scanned, for it is mainly an accommodation to his prescriptive role. In its subjective Elizabethan sense *conditions,* or its more usual singular form, signifies the moral constitution of a man, what today we should call his disposition or character; and *common conditions* expresses a mixed disposition, inclined both to good and ill. His real name, he explains in his long initial monologue, is Mediocrity, which amounts to the same thing. Woven into the story as the agent of its vicissitudes, he also equates himself with the caprice of fortune and offers a sample of his past achievement to guarantee his present skill:

And Mediocritie is my name though condicions they mee call,
Nere kinde to dame fortune to raise and to let fall.
As for experience, it was my chance to blesse one the other day,
And within two dayes after hee was hanged out of the way.

[ll. 165–68]

For special occasions, as deception requires, he adopts the pseudonyms of Affection (that is, amorous passion) and Gravity, both names directly opposite to his nature. But none of all these titles possesses any longer the subjective force belonging to the genuine moral personification. Empty survivals of the old homiletic habit, they exploit the traditional behavior of the Vice without defining in any way the moral effect of his operation in any of his victims. What was only partial in Ambidexter is complete in Common Conditions. From this play of concrete life and literal story the metaphorical significance of the morality Vice has evaporated. What remains is simply its dramatic by-product, the stage image perpetuated by a century of repetition. In *Common Conditions* the Vice has lost his subjective meaning and become simply the unprincipled exponent of the art of deceit and wily subterfuge, illustrating only himself and delighting the audience by his stratagems and jubilant explanations:

THE HYBRID PLAY

> Ha ha ha, this geare fauls out excellent well in deede.
> Welfare a craftie knaue at a time of neede.
> Affection quoth you, why? what a counterfeit knaue am I,
> Thus vnder the title of affection, my condicions to apply?
>
> . . . .
>
> For at length it will redowne to my profit I do not doubt.
> Roome for a turne coate, that will turne as the wynde,
> Whom when a man thinkes surest he knowes not where to finde.
>
> [ll. 610–23]

If he appears inconsistent by seeming to help at one time the same persons whom he victimizes at others, that is because his impartial deceit turns in a new direction: he now deceives their enemies; and his name, to a large extent, is a rationalization of this weather-vane quality in him. Having enabled the pirates to capture his mistress Clarisia, he shortly after helps her to escape to apparent safety, weeps with her at parting, and then invites the audience to admire his serpentine artistry in respect to her as well as to them (he has been their captain):

> Ha my good mistres leaue you of your wayling so sore for mee
> For I know you to well, kinde harted for to bee.
> What is she gone? haue I bin howling all this while & know not wherfore
> Nay and she be gone so soone, by her leaue ile lament no more.
> Ah sira, to see the dissimulation of a craftie counterfit knaue,
> That by flatterie can brynge to pas the thinge he would haue.
> Wept quoth you? I haue wept in deed to put you out of doubt,
> Euen as mutch as will driue halfe a dousen milles aboute.
> But I must laugh to thinke on my Pirats filching knaues,
> Their captayne hath boarde them through their noses like slaues.
>
> [ll. 1251–60]

But as the incarnation of deceit, with everyone grist for his mill, he occupies uneasy ground in a play concerned with people rather than with types or abstractions; and this fact exposes the large problem of the Vice's history from this point on. Having lost its old environment, where it rested on its metaphorical meaning in a metaphorical play, the dramatic image has now to be assimilated to the concrete terms of its new scene. In the two speeches above we see the process at work. What is the "profit" at which Common Conditions aims by one trick of deceit after another directed against anybody and everybody, and what

THE HYBRID PLAY

is "the thinge he would haue"? Time and again the vague suggestion of a practical motive creeps into his explanations:

> And therfore for my owne aduantage beleeue me you may,
> As nere as I can ile vse a mediocratie by the way.
>
> [ll. 163–64]

> Now this geare cottons law, now shall you plainly see,
> Which waies so euer the winde blowes it is for my commoditie.
>
> [ll. 576–77]

> I will bring them together sure how so euer it fauls out,
> For at length it will redowne to my profit I do not doubt.
>
> [ll. 620–21]

> But howsoeuer the world goes parasites part I must play,
> For to get my lyuing I can finde no other kinde of way.
> Well I must after to the Dukes place, euen as fast as I may,
> But in the end marke how the crafty knaues part I will play.
>
> [ll. 728–31]

> Are they gone? Conditions? Nay double condicions is my name
> That for my owne aduantage suche dealynges can frame.
>
> [ll. 977–78]

We shall never learn anything more about his motives, for there is nothing more to learn. They have neither clarity nor depth nor continuity, but begin and end in the words already quoted. They are the apparatus of accommodation, parts of a new vesture that gives his old performance entry into a new world of men and women. Unlike the old Vice, who came into a metaphorical play out of hell or from his ubiquitous activities in the whole world round about, Common Conditions is fitfully realized as a person at the Arabian court, a servant to various masters, a captain of pirates, and a parasite—this last bespeaking the influence of Latin comedy. To adjust his role to a play unable to tolerate a naked moral personification as the leading figure among its literal dramatis personae, he is clothed with the traits of human life and given a local habitation and a biography. And since the traditional aggression is thus bereft of its metaphorical, or subjective, *raison,* the practical motives of human life flow in to fill up the vacuum. Assimilation is the keynote of the Vice's history from this time forth. Unfortunately, the role, in its essential nature, is not amenable to such exterior transformation. At its heart, giving it the shape and dynamic

THE HYBRID PLAY

that made it so popular and long-lived, are characteristics that belong to its origin in metaphor—its amoral temper, its homiletic dimension, and its self-sufficiency as a demonstration. To such a role human motives are superfluous, and they do not adhere no matter how energetically they are daubed on. They do not adhere to Common Conditions; and his successors, depending on how much of the old Vice remains in them, suffer in varying degree from the same cleavage and the same lack of verisimilitude.

As for the line of succession itself, any doubts that remain concerning it can perhaps be satisfied by allowing Common Conditions to project himself homiletically in the new language which is part of his transformation. Many times in the course of his demonstrations he invites the audience to admire the duplicity of a crafty knave hiding behind the vizor of honesty. Like the Vice of earlier plays—morality and hybrid—he delights to parade himself ironically as an honest man: "Beleue me as I am an honest gentleman here is my hand." But Common Conditions also strikes a new note and descants on it tirelessly:

> But I am the arrants villaine that you shall finde or see,
> For the banishment of Galiarbus was all longe of mee.
> $\qquad$ [ll. 179–80]
>
> What a mad man are you? take mee with a lye,
> And whip mee that all villaynes may take example thereby.
> $\qquad$ [ll. 943–44]
>
> Ha, was there euer villaine in such kinde of takyng as I,
> I am so beset that tis vnpossible to deuise a lie.
> $\qquad$ [ll. 1536–37]

The evolution of the Vice toward literalness has carried him to the point where he emerges as that familiar figure on the Elizabethan stage who joyfully proclaims his own villainy and baffles our modern scrutiny. The details of this villainy obey the circumstances of the plot in which it appears, but its governing features are clear and consistent with its origin. At its heart it is a demonstration of deceit which takes the form of feigned honesty and affectionate good will. The aim of this deceit, perpetuating the original aim of the Vice without its metaphorical meaning, is invariably twofold. It seeks, in the first play, to transform the feelings and intentions of the victim into something quite opposite from what they are; in the second, it seeks to turn people

THE HYBRID PLAY

against each other, to break up the human bond which expresses the
values governing the play—to set them by the ears, as Common Conditions puts it to his audience:

> Ah ah ah this geare cottens I may say to you.
> I haue wrought a fetch to set them by the eares hap what shall ensue
> By my honesty it doth me good that I so crafty should bee
> For the Dutches is fallen out with clarisia long of mee.
>
> . . . .
>
> Thus haue I set them together by the eares hap what hap shall.
>
> . . . .
>
> I must away [!] rome for a cutter that is euery ynche a man,
> A villain that will set a thousand by the eares if hee can.
>
> [ll. 894–909]

Printed in 1591 as a play that "hath bene sundry times Acted by her
Maiesties Players," *Sir Clyomon and Sir Clamydes* almost certainly
belongs to the seventies and may even come from the same hand that
wrote *Common Conditions*. Not only does it deal in the same kind
of dramatic merchandise, knight errantry and love, but between the
two plays there are narrative and verbal affinities so close they amount
nearly to iteration.[17] However, *Sir Clyomon* shows the greater metrical
dexterity and a romantic imagination even less inhibited. The action
whirls from Denmark to Suavia to Macedonia to Norway and back
again. Excursions en route lead to a Forest of Marvels which holds a
flying serpent and a castle full of imprisoned knights, victims of the
magician Brian Sans Foy, and to the Isle of Strange Marshes, whose
princess Neronis is one of the pair of love-smitten heroines. The way is
eventful with knightly combats, alarums and rescues, a storm at sea, a
crew of mariners, disguises, impersonations, and perhaps the earliest
dramatic exploitation of the pastoral-idyllic. Ladies and their cavaliers
take an outing along the seashore to enjoy "of fragrant fields, the dulcet
fumes," and Neronis, an earlier Rosalind, escapes to the forest in the
guise of a boy and tends sheep for the shepherd Corin, who, like his
Shakespearian namesake, compares the manners of the court with
those of the country. The classic world supplies Alexander the Great,
who holds a tournament to determine the rightful ruler of the Isle of
Strange Marshes, and allegory supplies the perfunctory figures of
Rumor and Providence, as well as the Vice. The prologue epitomizes

THE HYBRID PLAY

the values and temper of the plot, and even pays lip service to the homiletic convention that the play, in fact, flouts:

> Wherein their liues are to be seene, which honour did delight.
>
> . . . .
>
> Wherein the froward chances oft, of Fortune you shall see,
> Wherein the chearefull countenance of good successes bee:
> Wherein true Louers findeth ioy, with hugie heapes of care,
> Wherein as well as famous facts, ignomius placed are:
> Wherein the iust reward of both, is manifestly showne,
> *That virtue from the roote of vice, might openly be knowne.*
>
> [my italics]

True love, honor, and gallantry are the virtues that sustain the heroes and heroines through fortune's trials and mischances. On the "ignomius" side, Brian Sans Foy is a coward who overcomes gallant knights by sorcery and tries to cheat love by impersonation; the King of Norway violates both love and chivalry by resorting to abduction; and Subtle Shift the Vice is the cynical negation of everything good in the play—love, valor, and honor.

Needless to say, his name is but another rationalization of the Vice's established performance. It describes a role which is no longer a moral metaphor and defines a relationship between him and his dupes which is no longer subjective. His pseudonym is Knowledge, an alias intended to enhance his value as servant and counselor to a wandering knight in strange places. His chief business consists of betraying and forsaking one master after another, and he is, among other things, the negation of the chivalric virtue of loyalty. He forsakes Sir Clyomon for Sir Clamydes, promising the latter, "Ah Noble Clamydes, heres my hand, ile deceiue you neuer." It does not take him long to betray Sir Clamydes to Brian Sans Foy and to seal his service to the latter with a similar promise: "Then here is my hand, ile be your seruant euer." Consequently he betrays him in turn and frees Sir Clamydes from the sorcerer's clutches, deceiving the knight a second time in the very act of liberating him:

Well, seeing I haue played the craftie knaue with the one, ile play it with the other:

Subtill Shift for aduantage, will deceiue his owne brother.

[ll. 714-15]

THE HYBRID PLAY

So shall they both deceiued be
And yet vpon neither part mistrust towards me.

[ll. 868–69]

His essential business in the play is to illustrate himself endlessly and indiscriminately. All circumstances suit him and all persons qualify as his dupes. It is no special clairvoyance in him, therefore, that he should predict to the audience the outcome of each new employment and each new pledge of loyalty—in respect to Sir Clyomon for one: "I promise you, I entend not very long to be his man"; or in respect to Brian Sans Foy for another:

Well after Bryan I will, and close with him awhile,
But as well as Clamydes, in the end ile him begile.

[ll. 635–36]

He has no genuine alignment with the plot—he is still too much the old Vice to have an organic role in a concrete story—but comes into it as to a fertile ground on which he can sow his stratagems broadcast. When, in consequence, he reverses his field, hurting where he has helped and helping where he has hurt, it is neither help nor hurt but only deceit for its own sake. He is an inexplicable weather vane only when we neglect his roots and try to assess him morally. The moral standards of human life—its loyalties, enmities, appetites, and practical aims—are as inapplicable to him as to any other Vice:

Although vnder the tytle of knowledge my name I do faine,
Subtill Shift I am called, that is most plaine.
And as it is my name, so it is my nature also,
To play the shifting knaue wheresoeuer I go.

[ll. 211–14]

It is easy, of course, to be misled by his moral façade, for he is the Vice in transition, his performance overlaid with a patchwork of explanations referring to his "advantage" or his "commodity." No longer sustained by its figurative meaning, the role, as we have already noticed in the case of Common Conditions, re-equips itself with an arsenal of "motives." He is a coward who is disloyal out of fear, he explains; or he goes over to Brian Sans Foy to escape his enchantments, not to speak of the tug of kinship: "For he and I am both one consanguinitie"; or, having betrayed Sir Clamydes for several reasons, he now saves him for several others—remorse, contempt for the sorcerer, and

THE HYBRID PLAY

again his own advantage. But through these shallow anthropomorphisms, nullifying them, there invariably shows the deeper stratum of his performance—the amoral temper and homiletic demonstration of the essential Vice: "Shift shall not be voide of a shift." In his endless confabulation with the audience his original dynamic and the thin veneer of a practical aim roll out together huggermugger from the very same couplet:

Well, such shifting knaues as I am, the ambodexter must play,
And for commoditie serue euery man, whatsoeuer the world say.

[ll. 633–34]

Ah sirra, here was a shift according to my nature and condition,
And a thousand shifts more I haue, to put my selfe out of suspition.

[ll. 934–35]

The gradual contraction of the Vice is apparent in him another way—in that verbal turn, already seen in Common Conditions, which translates the metaphorical aggression into its human equivalent. When he is not describing himself as a "deceitfull knaue," a "craftie knaue," a "subtill shifting knaue," he concentrates upon an even more comprehensive word, running it through a scale of moods—ironic, frank, and even half-regretful—but always the homiletic definition of his performance:

Vse me that all other villains may take ensample by me, if I digresse.
   (to Sir Clamydes)

[l. 345]

The veryest cowardly villaine that euer was borne, thats of a certaintie.

[l. 537]

Euen the cowardlyest villaine ant shall please you that liues vnder the sun.

[l. 591]

Gogs bloud what a villaine am I my maister to betray.

. . . .

Am I not worthie to be hangd, was euer seene such a deceitfull knaue?
What villany was in me, when vnto Bryan vnderstanding I gaue
Of my maisters being in this forrest.

. . . .

Well, seeing it is through my villany, my maister is at this drift
Yet when he is in prison, Shift shall not be voide of a shift.

[ll. 682–90]

THE HYBRID PLAY

The traditional role, we see, has outlived its traditional environment and is now clothing itself in a vesture that will acclimate it to a new kind of play. The aggression that was formerly explicit in its metaphorical context is now no longer so in a literal one. Its agent is no longer intelligible as a personification of an interior moral quality, and his victims are no longer types of humanity. They are men and women, and he himself is in an uneasy stage of transition to a similar status. Of necessity, therefore, his stock performance gropes toward a new rationale in the conventional motives of human life, and through its homiletic dimension it showers the audience with explanations that belong to the irascible or concupiscible causes, to use an Elizabethan classification, of human behavior. At the same time, however, these new motives are robbed of vitality by the fact that the essential role remains very much the same, its amoral temper and homiletic showmanship resisting change. It goes its ancient bravura way, obeying the metaphorical compulsion in which it originated, and remains a demonstration of deceit, or, rather, of a series of deceits imposed upon as many dupes as the literal story with its plurality of men and women can be stretched to contain. Its homiletic transparency also resists the naturalistic transformation and keeps the moral record straight through a formula of self-exposure of which the key word, since it is no longer able to be Avarice, Hypocrisy, or any other personified quality, is now literalized into *villainy*.

CHAPTER NINE

THE HYBRID IMAGE
IN FARCE

I

The stages of transformation that bring the Vice to the point at which we now find him are, it ought to be clear, inseparable from the history of change and decline in the homiletic drama. That history, in its turn, is chiefly conditioned by the moral play's *tertium quid:* the human prize between the opposed forces of abstract Good and Evil. The figure of Mankind, under his various generic names, actually created the morality theater, for his appearance in the Psychomachia transformed the blatant warfare of the vices against the virtues, essentially a pageant, into an intrigue directed against himself, essentially a play. The largest view of the subject suggests that he is the contribution of the stage to the Psychomachia once the latter was introduced upon it. Although his presence among his own vices and virtues violates the logic of the allegory, it is a theatrical necessity. What narrative literature, such as the poem of Prudentius, can describe or interpret to the imagination, the stage must *present* to the senses. Its very nature and limitations demand a plot rather than a battle, and demand, moreover, the visible presence of that figure upon whom the whole meaning of the plot converges. The role of Mankind, therefore, must be regarded as the creation of the stage in response to its own needs. He illustrates, in fact, the intensely human character of the theater: its dependence on persons to a degree beyond that of any other major art; and his history, which means also the history of the morality drama, indicates that the popular stage was a soil in which abstraction and generalization could take root only to be transformed.

For at least a century and a half the morality stage presented this tripartite version of the Psychomachia, and presented, accordingly, a

THE HYBRID IMAGE IN FARCE

plot that was invariable, although its implication could be turned toward whatever moral lesson the dramatist had in mind. Any homily for any way or station of life could be dramatized as the figurative attempt of vice, any vice, to insinuate itself into the bosom of its human victim, to divorce him from the counsel and protection of virtue, to gain ascendancy over him, and to bring him thereby to his ruin. Throughout the whole period of these plays, however, their human hero was subject to a constant process of limitation which shortened their homiletic scope and in the end invalidated the metaphor. He became divided and specialized into man religious, man political, man juvenile, man intellectual, and so on, remaining, however, the proper subject of such an intrigue so long as he remained a generalization sufficiently broad. But this process of curtailment went further, producing contrasted types of good and bad humanity in respect to a limited moral thesis, and eventually a multitude of sinners, the representative nature and homiletic relevance of each proportionately confined. At the same time, largely as a corollary of such multiplication, the tragic ending, always implicit in the moralities, became a feature of the late plays, sharpening the moral lesson by discriminating the wages of sin from the rewards of virtue. When the convention reaches its end in the last quarter of the sixteenth century its human figures have contracted to the point where they appear as personalities rather than as modes of human life. They come on the stage with their moral natures already inside them, with souls committed to good or ill from the start—as individualized, although elementary, human portraits, equipped with the rudiments of character and personal history. The effect of this trend toward concreteness is to disorganize the original metaphor and to dispossess the personifications of vice and virtue from their original function. As the human object of their concern ceases to be a moral void, they themselves, in corresponding measure, lose the right to be externalized on the same stage with him. The metaphor of the Psychomachia, clouded by the introduction of Man in the first place, becomes cloudier as he becomes more inward and opaque. Strictly considered, however, the moral plays, although they press steadily toward a literal world of men and women, cannot, by definition, be said to reach so far. The convention maintains itself unequivocally only so long as its human figures remain in some degree ob-

THE HYBRID IMAGE IN FARCE

viously typical. When it is invaded by persons out of history or legend the result is the mixed dramatic metaphor of the abstract and the concrete; and the plays so characterized are more accurately described as *transitional* or *hybrid* than as moralities.

This evolution toward concreteness within the moralities themselves, however, has notable effect upon the fortunes of the Vice. As Mankind undergoes division and becomes plural, the Vice moves in a direction precisely opposite. Having begun his career as one of many abstractions, he is first distinguished from his evil associates by his dramatic and homiletic pre-eminence, and then by his tendency to absorb them and to stand alone as the aggressive force of the play. In *Mundus et Infans* Folly comprehends in himself all seven of the Deadly Sins, but the play, which is early, is exceptionally contracted for only two actors. A more normal development is shown by the later moralities. Although there are roles for three inferior vices in *The Tide Tarrieth No Man,* they are no more than emaciated survivors of the old homiletic concern with the evil branches growing from the *radix malorum.* The Vice not only subdues them to his authority, but his monopoly of the stage allows them only the most trifling roles. The same is true of *All for Money,* where a variety of evil personifications, presented at the beginning in complex homiletic relationship, are soon swept out of the play, leaving the whole field of action in exclusive possession of Sin the Vice. What we witness in these late moralities is the tendency to shear off the fringes of the homily in favor of dramatic compactness, with the Vice the natural beneficiary of this trend. His own theatrical vitality drains the force out of his henchmen and comes near to abolishing them altogether as theatrical values gain the ascendant. In *Like Will to Like,* where the stage rather than the sermon has the upper hand, he actually does so. But, as a rule, so long as his performance remains inside the morality plays it is governed by their homiletic determination to document a complex of moral evils according to their origin and sequence, and his associates at least have entry into the play even if they have no more.

But not only does the Vice of the later morals monopolize his own half of the Psychomachia, he also engrosses the play as a whole. It is no exaggeration to say that whereas the older moralities were about man, the later ones are about the Vice. Early in his career he was an incident,

THE HYBRID IMAGE IN FARCE 307

albeit a decisive one, in the moral history of his human victim. The latter possessed the play before the Vice entered to do his work, and held it after the Vice made his last exit. The dispersion of Mankind into plurality, however, and the theatrical magnetism of the Vice produce a reversal in dramatic focus and structure that is as obvious in the later history of the moralities as its significance is inescapable. It is now the Vice whose role bounds the scope of the play, as Mankind degenerates, in a dramatic sense, into a series of incidental figures upon whom he repeats his performance and multiplies the display of his cunning. They come and go on a stage dominated by him, their roles reduced to no more than support for his. The moral drama, moreover, accommodates its structure to its new protagonist. From having been a chronicle of human life, it becomes a succession of his activities. Typically the late morality begins with his entrance and expository monologue, and it ends when he is captured and punished, attended by a clamor of execration, or when he bids the audience good-by, pressing home the lesson of his performance before he departs to exercise his talent elsewhere. In between it has its substance in his multiple stratagems, each an application to some segment of the human race of the special moral text he embodies, and each, on its dramatic side, one more demonstration of his ability to inveigle his dupes into a ruinous course of action or way of life.

His initial eminence on the side of evil, his theatrical force, and his enormous vogue fulfill themselves thus logically as the repressed dramatic sense of the morality drama responds, in its period of decline, to the theatrical leaven at work upon the homiletic stage. But in the moral plays proper, since their context is able to sustain him metaphorically, he remains the embodiment of a moral aspect of human life, and his action in its final significance is subjective. The words applied by Fortune to Incontinence in *The Longer Thou Livest* define the usual nature of the Vice in the moralities:

> I trow your name is incontinencie,
> One of the properties of Moros.
> [ll. 1087–88]

In *The Trial of Treasure* the defiance of the Vice Inclination has the same subjective meaning when, bridled and shackled, he is led off to prison:

THE HYBRID IMAGE IN FARCE

Well, yet I will rebel, yea, and rebel again,
And though a thousand times you shouldest me restrain.
[Dodsley, III, 299]

The same self-assurance laughs at the same punishment when Ill-Will defies his captors in *Wealth and Health:*

Lock us up and kepe us as fast as ye can,
Yet yll-will and Shrewdwit shalbe with many a man.
[ll. 894–95]

And Rigor's hold upon his victim in *The Cruel Debtor* is no different: "Yea, from hys harte I am neuer absent." [1]

Having exploited him to the limit of their resources, the moralities take the Vice to this point without being able to take him further. The hybrid plays, however, use him even more richly and carry him through a partial transformation that ripens him for the later drama. In them, as we saw, personification withers away in an atmosphere fatal to its existence. That it endures at all is tribute to the grip of moral allegory upon the stage and to the persistence of a homiletic standard for the drama, the latter a fact sometimes neglected. For almost the entire sixteenth century a didactic purpose, however undermined it was in practice, remained the only respectable standard for the popular stage; and only at the end of the century does the great transition to a naturalistic standard get under way, not without fearful controversy. "What learne you by that?"—Stephen Gosson's angry and formidable challenge to the dramatic romances demands simply what right they have, since they offer no obvious moral lesson, to exist at all. His voice, echoed by every vocal moralist of the age, affirms the traditional view of the stage against a clear and present danger. And throughout the century the popular drama professes allegiance to its traditional purpose even when in the play itself there is no such matter. *Sir Clyomon and Sir Clamydes,* although its subject is love and chivalry and its code of morals certainly not that intended by Gosson, proclaims nonetheless as its aim "That virtue from the roote of vice, might openly be knowne." More cogently, George Whetstone, in his epistle prefixed to *Promos and Cassandra* (1578), assures the reader that "what actions so ever passeth in this History, either merry, or morneful: grave or lascivious; the conclusion showes the confusion of Vice, and cherishing of Vertue." Earlier, Lewis Wager defends from attack the "comely and

THE HYBRID IMAGE IN FARCE

good facultie" of acting by the argument that its purpose is, from first to last, morality:

> Doth not our facultie learnedly extoll vertue?
> Doth it not teache, God to be praised aboue al thing?
> What facultie doth vice more earnestly subdue?
> Doth it not teache true obedience to the kynge?
> What godly sentences to the mynde doth it brynge!
> [*The Life and Repentance of Mary Magdalene*, prologue, ll. 31–35]

Such an aim, prescribed by the critics and professed by the dramatists, is continuous throughout the century; and it is the background without which we do not understand, since it no longer thoroughly applies to its own context, Hamlet's explanation of "the purpose of playing." [2] The art of Shakespeare and the other great Elizabethans of the theater sublimed the homiletic formula of vice and virtue into a more penetrating image of men and the world, into a profounder, because more immediate, sensation of good and evil; but their intense moral energy has its roots in this soil, while the later Jacobean drama becomes enervated as it becomes merely theatrical.

Inside this homiletic standard, however, the latent art of the theater tunneled like a mole until it could come out into the open—through Sidney, Lodge, and the other apologists—and assert its own right, justifying itself eventually through a *dulce et utile* which in art is one and the same, instead of two as in a medicine show or a morality play. The hybrid plays show very clearly this blind stirring of a new spirit within the body of the old convention. All of them are more or less under the aegis of a homiletic purpose, addressed to the audience through the mouths of those stage figures traditionally designed to express it—the personifications of Good and Evil. But their men and women out of the literal world offer a rival subject matter, a rival set of images and values. Once brought into the homiletic citadel, they gradually subvert it and eventually drive out its garrison, except for the one figure tenacious and resourceful enough to survive among them. The other moral personifications first shrink into supernumeraries, then retreat entirely out of the plot to survive for a time on its outskirts in the static functions of chorus, or prologue and epilogue. That is where we find them when they continue as homiletic vestiges in the later drama. For the habit of prosopopoeia out of the moralities explains the scattered abstractions in Elizabethan plays. Honesty is such a vestige in *A Knack to Know a Knave,* and he still has an active part in the homiletic underplot. *The Spanish Tragedy* may derive its theme of revenge from Seneca, but its choric figure of Revenge belongs to the native morality tradition. Death, Fortune, and Love are the choric voices in the prologue and epilogue of *Soliman and Perseda.* The same place and function are filled by Envy and Comedy in *Mucedorus. A Warning for Fair Women,* strongly homiletic in its temper and intention, offers History, Tragedy, and Comedy in its induction, and Tragedy alone in its epilogue. The action between is wedged with dumb shows presenting Murder, Lust, Chastity, Justice, and Mercy in pantomime. Vice, Virtue, and Fortune are more active in the plot of *Old Fortunatus,* but they are, in fact, the machinery of a moral masque which Dekker added to an older version of the play when he revised it for court performance. *Histriomastix,* which is doubtlessly an old moral play made over into a satire on the theater and the times, is rife with the choric comment of moral personifications.

Other abstractions in other Elizabethan and Jacobean plays testify to the same decayed convention and also to its surviving influence, with Shakespeare contributing to the evidence. Such a detail in *Titus Andronicus* as Tamora's disguise as Revenge and her two sons as Rape and Murder came to him (with an assist perhaps by Kyd) from the morality stage. From the same source he drew the method of such choric figures as Time in *The Winter's Tale* and Rumour in the second part of *Henry IV.* The latter's speech to the audience is exactly in the expository style of his allegorical forebears—his name, his property, a satirical reference to his dominion over his hearers, and his business in the play before them:

> Open your ears, for which of you will stop
> The vent of hearing when loud Rumour speaks?
> I from the Orient to the drooping West,
> Making the wind my posthorse, still unfold
> The acts commenced on this ball of earth.
> Upon my tongues continual slanders ride,
> The which in every language I pronounce
> Stuffing the ears of men with false reports.

. . . .

THE HYBRID IMAGE IN FARCE

> But what need I thus
> My well-known body to anatomize
> Among my household? Why is Rumour here?
>
>   . . . .
>
>   My office is
> To noise abroad that Harry Monmouth fell
> Under the wrath of noble Hotspur's sword,
> And that the King before the Douglas' rage
> Stoop'd his anointed head as low as death.
>
>   . . . .
>
>   The posts come tiring on,
> And not a man of them brings other news
> Than they have learnt of me. From Rumour's tongues
> They bring smooth comforts false, worse than true wrongs.
>
>   [induction, ll. 1–40]

Such surviving personifications can remain as obviously abstract as they ever were, because they are no longer inside the play and do not need to conform their behavior and appearance to the world of literal humanity. On the contrary, they and their special function need to be as clearly distinguished from the essential plot and its normal inhabitants as a frame is from its picture. Shakespeare's Rumour, therefore, enters "painted full of tongues," and his Time, as the text suggests, is decorated with a pair of wings.

But the survival of the Vice, who remains very much inside the plot, requires his transfiguration, and in the hybrid plays it is, as we saw, under way. In their literal world he himself becomes half literalized as a person in time and space. He acquires a degree of biographical reality, achieves a personal or professional relation to his victims, who treat him as their fellow member of the human species, and even decks himself vaguely with conventional human motives for his traditional aggression. He is also, on occasion assimilated to type figures out of Latin comedy, the parasite and the *miles gloriosus*. At the same time his performance becomes opaque. It loses its figurative and inward meaning and gets its explanation instead from what it appears to be—the cunning beguilements of a witty villain exerted upon everyone within reach. Furthermore it becomes flexible in respect to its objects, bending itself against a world of values and loyalties—social, political, sectarian,

THE HYBRID IMAGE IN FARCE

domestic, and romantic—that replace the original value of the Christian virtues and the original loyalty of the soul to God. The whole effort, in short, of the world in which he now finds himself is to naturalize him to its human laws and conventions, to change him into a moral creature, in order to preserve his role on a stage very different from the one which brought it into being. That effort, as we can see from our vantage point, is caught within an inescapable paradox. To the extent that he remains himself, he does not admit of such a moral transformation.

In the hybrid plays, however, this effort to assimilate him to the literal world is only slight in comparison with what it is destined to be in the later drama, or in the secular comedy growing up alongside them. In each of them he is clearly an imposition on the plot—an intrusion upon an established legend that moves according to its own perspicuous logic; and his presence would be bewildering if we did not know the theatrical and homiletic compulsion behind it. The elders are inflamed by lust for Susanna and scheme to force her to their will or to punish her for not submitting. Appius is similarly moved by Virginia and fashions his plot to gain her. The tale of Griselda in Boccaccio, Petrarch, or Chaucer grows out of its own premises as a virtue story:

> This markys in his herte longeth so
> To tempte his wyf, hir sadnesse for to knowe,
> That he ne myghte out of his herte throwe
> This merveillous desir his wyf t'assaye;
> Nedelees, God woot, he thoghte hire for t'affraye.[3]

The revenge sought by Orestes, the tyranny of Cambises, the jealousy of the Phrygian Duchess belong to their souls by traditional right and do not require the activity of a personification or of a villain. His gratuitous addition to all these plays testifies to the force of the homiletic habit and the popular craving for his role.

Furthermore, he is not really fused with the story but moves through it rather on an orbit of his own and in a set performance that obeys a stage tradition, not the nature of the plot. He is still "the Vice," married to many plays but never really at bed and board with any. So mechanical a relationship, tolerable in an incidental stage clown or between the stock roles of farce, does violence to plays which, however crude their execution, rest on serious values to which he must somehow be

THE HYBRID IMAGE IN FARCE 313

accommodated. Once his performance loses the integrity of its subjective meaning it remains a piece of unregulated theatricalism, needing a new integration.

Finally, in the hybrid plays he is still sufficiently out of another world to retain a name whose style is still abstract. As Ill Report, Revenge, or Common Conditions, he still wears the badge of homiletic allegory, however he may be grafted otherwise to the traits of humanity. Such a name and our knowledge of its origin save us, of course, the trouble of puzzling over the nature of his performance or of attempting to define him in psychological terms. It is when his transmutation reaches the point where he qualifies for the name of Barabas or Iago and where he is no longer labeled "the Vice of the play" that such trouble comes upon us. In the hybrid plays he himself is already a hybrid, but largely the "old vice still" and still so designated. His state there is uneasy and his weather-vane behavior bewildering, for he has lost his old alignment with metaphor without quite achieving a new one with the literal world of the secular drama.

Some foresight into that new alignment comes to us from the confused temper of his aggressions in both the moralities and hybrid plays. Having traced the growth of a tragic conclusion in the former and examined several tragic plots among the latter, we are aware that the element of tragedy in both groups of plays is governed by their human personnel, not by him. His influence and direction get his dupes into trouble, but it is trouble only as it is suffered by them, not as it is committed by him. As they become increasingly individualized in moralities that become increasingly concrete, or when they are committed to disaster by the established lines of the story in the hybrid plays, the seed he now sows in such a ground converts to a harvest in tragedy. But it is tragedy brought forth by the nature of the ground rather than of the seed or the sower. So long as he remains largely outside the moral world, his performance is indifferent to its consequence in the human sphere. It has its cause in homiletic demonstration and its temper in farce, and this mixture is constant whether he is inveigling Judge Appius to destruction or provoking a brawl between a pair of rustics. Either way he scores his homiletic point and at the same time diverts his audience with the "sport" his "wit" provides them. When Clarisia (alias Metrea), in *Common Conditions,* hides Lamphedon in

THE HYBRID IMAGE IN FARCE

her chamber, the Vice is elated over the chance of a new piece of business which will get them into the deepest trouble, not because he is their enemy—he has, in fact, just brought them together—but because their situation invites his impartial guile and offers him another opportunity to demonstrate himself as the agent of fortune's vicissitudes:

> Ha ha this geare cottons, now if her master Leostines hee,
> Knew that Lamphedon in lady Metreas chamber should bee,
> There were all the sport and pastime that should excell.
> [ll. 1728–30]

And this sport, the Vice never tires of reminding the audience, is the product of his wit, which deserves their admiration:

> Though the Deuill himselfe, could not tempt Susans grace
> The wit of Mayster Ill Report hath her and it defaste,
> Oh goodly wit, oh noble brayne, whence commeth this deuyce.
> [*Virtuous and Godly Susanna,* ll. 183–85]

Now the only thing that sustains this relationship between the Vice and such victims is its figurative meaning. It not only supplies the "cause" for his aggressions, it also lends dignity to their otherwise farcical temper, and makes possible what would otherwise be a gross indecorum from a dramatic standpoint—the very real jeopardy to which persons of rank and moral seriousness are subjected by a broadly comical *farceur.* How, to beg the question, could a role so tempered survive in the secular drama, where it is no longer sustained by metaphor? The answer, clearly, is that, without an increment of moral dignity and serious motivation, it qualifies naturally for farce alone, and that is where we find it. As farcical protagonist he inhabits a series of plays that stand at the beginning of English secular comedy, with the line of his descent from the homiletic stage clear in his behavior, in his intimacy with the audience, and in the motifs of language and action he brings along with him. His victims in this genre are, for the most part, proper to it: rustics, servants, and common folk, who naturally qualify for farce on the Renaissance stage, where the distinction between the inhabitants of serious drama and those of broad comedy is mainly social.[4] They are, in fact, the same victims as those swept within the compass of his aggression against all estates in the hybrid plays—the servants in *Appius and Virginia,* the rustics and common soldiers in *Horestes* and *Cambises,* the tinkers in *Common Conditions.* Against

THE HYBRID IMAGE IN FARCE

them the Vice is able to display his wit in the traditional way and provide his audience with their traditional "sport," and he no longer requires the support of a serious figurative meaning. The context of farce sustains him instead as he continues, more or less in the guise of a man among men, to bedevil his dupes to the top of their bent. Also tradition sustains him when his aggressive energy sometimes goes beyond farce; and his audience, of course, understood the familiar figure who turned his laughter their way and sought their admiration for his cunning.

2

Latin comedy is thoroughly reclothed in English garments in *Jack Juggler,* licensed in 1562–63 although it may be a decade older. It is a simple farce of one act, an "Enterlued for Chyldren to playe." This fact and his classic source strengthen the unknown author to an announcement which has almost the force of a manifesto. The audience is invoked not to expect "mattiers substancyall Nor mattiers of any grauitee," for such serious business does not become "litle boyes handelings." The whole prologue, in fact, is a claim for dramatic entertainment independent of homiletic purpose, clearly disclosing the background of convention and expectation from which the playwright is departing. It begins with a quotation from Cato on the need for "honest mirthe" as refreshment for mind and body, and builds up support for this theme out of Ovid, Plutarch, Socrates, Plato, and Cicero, until it gets around to the main point, which is that the present play has its purpose in entertainment alone: "you shall heare a thing that onlie shal make you merie & glad." Since the author is a Tudor playwright, however, he is a moralist after all—not in the plot itself, which classic authority instructs him to keep free from sententiousness, but in the epilogue. There he succumbs to his own time and place and explicates "this trifling interlud" into an "example playne" of how "symple innosaintes ar deluded" by craft, or compelled by force to affirm the contrary of what they believe. He also explicates, inadvertently, a detail of dramatic history: when morality is forced out of the plot, it finds a refuge in prologue and epilogue, where it survives in many later Elizabethan plays, imitating thereby the declining career of the moral personifications themselves.

316   *THE HYBRID IMAGE IN FARCE*

The plot is based squarely, and candidly, on "Plautus first commedie," the *Amphitruo,* or rather on the first part of it, wherein Mercury masquerades as Sosia, Amphitryon's slave, and keeps the actual
Sosia away from the house of his master while Jupiter is inside with
Alcmene. Although often an exact translation of its original, the play
manages to breathe English at every pore, its characters within their
tight domestic relationship as native to London as St. Paul's. Sosia has
become Jenkin Careaway, as harassed and fearful a page as ever pil-
fered a shilling and diced it away again in neglect of his indentured
time and duties. Amphitryon has been made over into Master Bongrace, an Elizabethan man about town with an acrid wife to appease.
Mistress Bongrace, although she stands in the place of Alcmene, savors
much less of Latin Plautus than of English Chaucer:

> For she is an angrie pece of fleshe and sone displeasyd
> Quickely moued but not lyghtlye appesed
> We vse to call hir at home dame Coye
> A Cresie [queasy?] gingerlie pice god saue hir and saint Loy
> As denty and nice as an halpeny worthe of syluer spoons
> But vengable melancolie in the aftir noons.
>
>   [ll. 217–22]

Alison Trip-and-go, who is Jenkin's fellow servant and his natural
enemy therefore, replaces Alcmene's Bromia, but also shows the Chau-
cerian burnish:

> She simperith, she prankith and getteth with out faille
> As a pecocke that hath spred and sheweth hir gaye taylle
> She mynceth, she bridelethe, she swimmith to and fro
> She tredith not one here a wrye, she tryppeth like a do
> A brod in the stret going or cumming homward
> She quauerith and warbelith like one in a galiard.
>
>   [ll. 229–34]

Jupiter disappears entirely, the English play purging the erotic theme by
purging the god.

As for Jack Juggler in the title role, his stratagem is the stratagem of
Mercury, but his voice and performance belong to what he is called,
"the vyce." He supplies the whole plot by the deception he imposes on
Jenkin and by the several troubles, including a trio of beatings, into
which he beguiles him. But this action, which in the *Amphitruo* draws
its meaning from the effort of Mercury to safeguard the adulterous

THE HYBRID IMAGE IN FARCE

317

privacy of Jupiter and Alcmene, transfers itself here to a divided premise whose alien halves illustrate the paradox of a role that has outlived the metaphor which begot it. The confusion at its heart, model of the greater confusion to come when it moves into more serious drama, is trimly contained within the expository monologue of 108 uninterrupted lines with which the Vice begins the play. His first words are a lavish salutation to the audience, very similar to the greeting of Avarice in *Respublica,* also a children's play. He proceeds to the exposition of his name and purpose, both of which, since, unlike Avarice, he is the Vice only in a histrionic sense, define simply the chief dramatic feature of the traditional performance, its deceit:

> I am called Iake Iugler of many an oon
> And in fayth I woll playe a iugling cast a non
> I woll cungere the moull and god before
> Or elles leat me lese my name for euer more
> I haue it deuised and compacced hou
> And what wayes I woll tell and shew to you.
> [ll. 108–13]

Added to this familiar promise of a demonstration is another promise equally familiar:

> And now if all things happin ryght
> You shall see as mad a pastime this night
> As you saw this seuen yers!
>
> . . .
>
> But and if Ienkyne wold hither resort
> I trust he and I should make sum sport.
> [ll. 104–91]

Here, in a play that has renounced didactic morality, is the naked performance without its metaphor and the homiletic dimension without its homily; and the process of transition from a metaphorical to a literal meaning spreads itself plain when, in the same monologue, the role reaches out for new clothing from the literal world:

> This Ienkine and I been fallen at great debate
> For a mattier that fell betwine vs a late
> And hitherto of him I could neuer reuengid bee
> For his maister mentainyth him and louethe not mee.
> [ll. 120–23]

THE HYBRID IMAGE IN FARCE

What better motive than revenge for explaining a stock aggression that has lost its older explanation, even if we never know what this revenge is for, even if the chemistry of the performance will not unite with such a motive, even if the very next lines dissolve it to nothing:

> Albeit the very truth to tell
> Nother of them both knoweth me werie well.
> [ll. 124–25]

Here in little is the large problem of the later plays, as well as the manner of its origin. Although the play is a farce, its landscape is literal, its performers persons, its action concrete; and the Vice is drawn of necessity to become a part of such a scene, although, in fact, he cannot while remaining the Vice. His motive is genuine so far as he himself offers it, and he refers to it again in the monologue which ends his performance ("But now I haue partelye reuenged my quarell"), although it is once more canceled out by four lines of the same speech:

> Hou saye you maisters I pray you tell
> Haue not I requited my marchent well
> Haue not I handelyd hym after a good sort
> Had it not byne pytie to haue lost this sporte.
> [ll. 870–73]

But so far as it is offered by a transitional drama it is motive-hunting for the sake of verisimilitude. The playwright, of course, was not concerned that the familiar stage image so pat to his purpose was of a nature to which the motives of the moral world do not adhere. He simply took the role available to him, and illustrates, by the adjustment he makes, the process of adaptation by which the metaphorical aggression within its homiletic dimension was preserved on a literal stage.

Roister Doister by Nicholas Udall was licensed in 1566 and published shortly after, but it was certainly written before 1553, and probably for performance by his students between 1534 and 1541, when Udall held a mastership at Eton.[5] The work of a teacher and humanist, it goes beyond *Jack Juggler* as an open-eyed departure from the homiletic stage, proclaiming the step in a prologue remarkably similar. Urging the salubrious effect upon young and old of "mirth which is vsed in an honest fashion," it dedicates itself to "mans recreation"; and it is sensitive enough to moralistic cavil to make the plea that no

THE HYBRID IMAGE IN FARCE

one of "good nature can gainsay . . . [the] mirth we intende to vse, auoidyng all blame." Like *Jack Juggler* also, it justifies itself by classic precedent:

> The wyse poets long time heretofore
> Vnder merrie comedies secretes did declare,
> Wherein was contained very vertuous lore,
> With mysteries and forewarnings very rare.
> Suche to write neither Plautus nor Terence dyd spare . . .
> [prologue, ll. 15–19] [6]

Both the epilogue to *Jack Juggler* and these words of Udall's prologue declare the gradual nature of the escape from the radical didacticism of the homiletic convention. Both invoke the Renaissance habit of allegorizing the classics in order to justify plays which do not preach within their plots, but through their specific representations suggest a general meaning, and are, in other words, true moral allegories, allusive rather than obvious. For *Roister Doister,* while it asserts the right to be a play rather than a generalized homily, conforms so far to the native tradition as to declare that by implication it "against the vayneglorious doth inuey." [7]

The formal influence of Latin comedy is everywhere apparent in Udall's play, and everywhere transfigured by its vernacular spirit. It is faithful to the classic unities and to regular division into "actus" and "scena." Its action and characters derive from the comic plot and personae of the Roman drama, especially the *Miles Gloriosus* and the *Eunuchus;* but the indebtedness is diffuse, unlike the precise relation of *Jack Juggler* to the *Amphitruo.* All the braggart soldiers in Plautus and Terence, rather than any one of them, are digested into Ralph Roister Doister, the play's comic hero. Dame Christian Custance is mainly a purified version of Terence's Thais (*Eunuchus*), but other ladies of Latin comedy have their part in her. And a dozen clever slaves and parasites in both Roman playwrights, although Gnatho is chiefly conspicuous, supply the raw material for Matthew Merrygreek, who concerns us most directly because he is sharply modified by the very English quality of the Vice. All the main roles are at once borrowed and original, having undergone a sea change into the idiom, manners, humor, and moral atmosphere of sixteenth-century England. Most remarkable is the absolute moral transfiguration. The comedy and intrigue that courtesans, pimps, and slave girls promoted on the

320 THE HYBRID IMAGE IN FARCE

Roman stage in an environment of lupanars and marketable love is here sustained within a chaster ethic. The Thais for whose professional favors Thraso and Phaedria are rivals in the *Eunuchus* has become an honorable English widow whose hand is sought in marriage; the slave girls and the rest of the venereal staff have been transformed into her trim and dutiful maids; and the brothel itself has been remade into her industrious and efficient household.

The role of Matthew Merrygreek and the theme of his relationship to Roister Doister are roughly supplied to Udall by Terence's pair of Gnatho and Thraso, the parasite and the cowardly braggart of the *Eunuchus*. But the resemblance is only on the surface. Although Gnatho is the wittiest of parasites, he is still too typical of his breed to be a sufficient model for Merrygreek's wit and gratuitous energy in deception and intrigue. The parasite of the Roman stage is mainly a coarse and worried feeder, whose conversation, no less than his existence, centers about his stomach—an outrageous sycophant in the name of an outrageous appetite, whose humor is usually as heavy as his diet. The long and short of an Artotrogos or a Gnatho is that he lives to eat, and to that end hooks on to some wealthy idiot, soothing his folly while battening on his table. Although there is a strain of such a character in Merrygreek, it is certainly not his essence. He does indeed show the parasitical side of his lineage by the occasional respect he pays to food and maintenance:

> Yet wisdome would that I did my-selfe bethinke
> Where to be prouided this day of meate and drinke.
>
> [I.i.11–12]

And his attachment to Roister Doister unquestionably has its predatory aspect:

> For truely of all men he is my chiefe banker
> Both for meate and money, and my chiefe shootanker.
> For, sooth Roister Doister in that he doth say,
> And, require what ye will, ye shall haue no nay.
>
> [I.i.27–30]

But as we always discover when the role with which we are concerned is merged with another, the spirit of Merrygreek's behavior belies such a purpose, and other words of his also belie it. Unlike the Roman parasite who cravenly flatters his patron, Merrygreek dominates and manipulates his, putting him on display as a creature of wax in his

THE HYBRID IMAGE IN FARCE

hands. His program in the play is utterly a demonstration of what he announces to the audience in the long monologue which occupies the opening scene—a program in defiance of food and drink:

> But such sporte haue I with him as I would not leese
> Though I should be bounde to lyue with bread and cheese.
> For exalt hym, and haue hym as ye lust, in-deede,—
> Yea, to hold his finger in a hole for a neede.
> I can with a worde make him fayne or loth,
> I can with as much make him pleased or wroth,
> I can, when I will, make him mery and glad,
> I can, when me lust, make him sory and sad,
> I can set him in hope and eke in dispaire,
> I can make him speake rough, and make him speake faire.
>
> [I.i.53–62]

His whole behavior, accordingly, is a merry aggression against his dupe for the sake of the "sporte" and the demonstration, a far remove from the behavior and aim of the parasite. He turns Roister Doister inside out, inflating or deflating him at will, subjecting him to endless physical abuse; and his familiar phrase adheres to the traditional temper and dimension within his performance: "He is in by the weke, we shall haue sport anon," and again, "We shall haue sport anone; I like this very well!" He has no purpose beyond this purely manipulatory one, which contradicts, when it does not actually dissolve, his partial affinity with the gastric logic of the parasite's role. He is the Vice transferred to farce, merged, for the sake of a reasonable exterior in a play of literal circumstances, with a type figure out of Latin comedy. Unlike a Gnatho, he is a transient visitor to the scene for a day, for he lives among many people in many places, as he instructs the audience in his opening monologue, which is essentially the traditional exposition of the Vice. And at least one episode in his serial manipulation of his dupe is worth noting for its striking similarity to the Vice's treatment of another victim in another play, not farce but tragedy. He brings Roister Doister the news that Dame Custance has flatly rejected his suit:

> *R. Royster.* Well, what should I now doe?
> *M. Mery.* In faith, I can not tell.
> *R. Royster.* I will go home and die.
> *M. Mery.* Then shall I bidde toll the bell?
>
> [III.iii.47–48]

THE HYBRID IMAGE IN FARCE

He recites a mock requiem over the prostrate Ralph—*placebo, dilexi, dirige,* plus a jumble out of the rest of the ritual—and having had his jest one way, continues it another by reversing the mood of his gull:

> Now folow my counsell. . . . If I were you,
> Custance should eft seeke to me ere I would bowe.
>
> . . . .
>
> Ye must now take vnto you a lustie courage.
> Ye may not speake with a faint heart to Custance,
> But with a lusty breast and countenance,
> That she may knowe she hath to answere to a man.
>
> . . . .
>
> Let vs see how to behaue your-selfe ye can doe.
> Ye must haue a portely bragge, after your estate.
>
> . . . .
>
> Well done! so loe! vp, man, with your head and chin!
> Vp with that snoute, man! so loe! nowe ye begin!
>
> . . . .
>
> That is somewhat like for a man of your degree!
> Then must ye stately goe, ietting vp and downe.
> Tut! can ye no better shake the taile of your gowne?
> There, loe! suche a lustie bragge it is ye must make!
> [III.iii.97–123]

Although language and action here are more primitive, the essence of this stage image survives when Roderigo is shaken out of his own love-prostration and persuaded to "make money" and to defeat his favor with an usurped beard.

The only known early edition of *Gammer Gurton's Needle,* "Played on Stage, not longe ago in Christes Colledge in Cambridge" and "Made by Mr. S. Mr. of Art," belongs to 1575, but the play itself is undoubtedly a good deal earlier. It is probably the same as the "Dyccon of Bedlam, &c." licensed in 1563, and it may go back to the last years of Edward VI if its author, as seems reasonably certain now, is William Stevenson, a fellow of Christ's in 1551–54 and again in 1559–61. The college records for 1559–60 contain an item of five shillings "Spent at Mr. Stevenson's plaie," but this performance may be no more than a revival from the earlier period of Stevenson's fellowship, when he was also credited with a play.[8] At any rate, *Gammer Gurton's Needle* is one of the few surviving examples of vernacular comedy at the uni-

THE HYBRID IMAGE IN FARCE

versities in the sixteenth century. No doubt this distinction explains in part another: unlike the popular drama of the same period, it is completely free from the homiletic tradition, which it does not even acknowledge by way of apology or valediction. The scholarship of its author appears in its obedience to the formal structure of classic comedy: five act division, change of scene for each entrance and departure, a single locale abutted by several houses, an action contained within one day. Unlike *Roister Doister,* however, its plot and characters have not even a derived affinity with Latin comedy but originate in the life and manners of rural England. For all its classic technique the play is native to its core. Hodge, Tib, Dame Chat, and Gammer Gurton herself are the primitive human scenery of the English countryside. They speak its dialect with lusty vulgarity and spend their lives upon its major issues—cats, poultry, livestock, middens, clouted breeches, and jolly good ale and old. Dr. Rat, the curate in this genre piece, is a cut above them in language but in little else. Master Bailiff, who restores them all to peace after their war of the needle, is a cut above them in sophistication, but no less native to their rustic society on the manorial estate.

Diccon the Bedlam, whose name supplies the title by which the play was licensed and whose devices supply its plot, belongs to a different fellowship. He is in the country but not quite of it, a visitor upon the scene after having, as he explains to the audience, covered "Many a myle . . . diuers and sundry waies" and tasted hospitality at "many a good mans house." His unprovoked aggressions against practically everyone in the play are subject to a kind of explanation in the fact that by his name he belongs to the race of crackbrained vagrants out of St. Mary of Bethlehem, with a reputation for thievery and mischief. But the play itself never urges such an explanation, and he shows, in fact, none of the fantasticality associated with this type of madman-beggar elsewhere in the literature of the times, of which Edgar's speech in *Lear* is a summary:

> My face I'll grime with filth,
> Blanket my loins, elf all my hair in knots,
> And with presented nakedness outface
> The winds and persecutions of the sky.
> The country gives me proof and precedent

THE HYBRID IMAGE IN FARCE

Of Bedlam beggars, who, with roaring voices,
Strike in their numb'd and mortified bare arms
Pins, wooden pricks, nails, sprigs of rosemary;
And with this horrible object, from low farms,
Poor pelting villages, sheepcotes, and mills,
Sometime with lunatic bans, sometime with prayers,
Enforce their charity.

[II.iii.9–19]

Such a description has nothing to do with Diccon. His clothing is sober, his language trim and sophisticated, his behavior sane and efficient. Nor is he treated by the others like a tolerable lunatic, but as a welcome visitor and counselor at first. In the end, when he stands uncovered, they are content to know no more than that they have been victimized by a "villain knaue" and "false varlet." To a deeper curiosity he is none of all these things essentially, but the Vice once more adjusted to farce and once more assimilated to a formal image of humanity. He moves against his dupes by an impetus that has lost sight of its origin, but retains the unmistakable features of his heredity.

Although the loss of the needle is none of his doing, all its consequences are. On the strength of it he weaves a net of bedevilment around everyone within reach, inciting them by his lies to reciprocal mayhem; and his whole program unrolls in a speech whose style and content are familiar:

Here is a matter worthy glosynge,
Of Gammer Gurtons nedle losynge,
    And a foule peece of warke!
A man, I thyncke, myght make a playe,
And nede no worde to this they saye,
    Being but halfe a clarke.

Softe, let me alone! I will take the charge
This matter further to enlarge
    Within a tyme shorte.
If ye will marke my toyes, and note,
I will geue ye leaue to cut my throte
    If I make not good sporte.

[II.ii.7–18] [9]

The "sporte" he provides is rough, but his devices are subtle. Extracting a promise of secrecy in respect to himself, he arouses Dame Chat with the finespun lie ("Because I knew you are my friend, hide it I

THE HYBRID IMAGE IN FARCE

cold not") that Gammer Gurton accuses her of the theft of a favorite rooster. Leaving that redoubtable female to nurse her wrath, he stokes up a contrary fury in Gammer Gurton and her man Hodge, desperate for the recovery of the needle because of his torn breeches. His instigation is wonderfully astute. To Hodge, who ran away previously in great fright from Diccon's conjuration of the Devil, he now imparts (at Hodge's request) what that demon is supposed to have told him:

> The horson talked to mee I know not well of what:
> One whyle his tonge it ran and paltered of a cat;
> Another whyle he stamered styll vppon a rat;
> Last of all, there was nothing but euery word chat! chat!
> But this I well perceyued, before I wolde him rid,
> Betweene chat and the rat and the cat, the nedle is hyd.
> Now, wether Gyb, our cat, haue eate it in her mawe,
> Or Doctor Rat, our curat, haue found it in the straw,
> Or this Dame Chat, your neighbour, haue stollen it, God he knoweth!
> [II.iii.19–27]

To Gammer Gurton he recites a circumstantial tale of how he saw Dame Chat stoop down before the Gurton gate and pick up "a nedle or a pyn." He remonstrated with her, he continues, but the "crafty drab" outfaced him: "Ech other worde I was a knaue, and you a hore of hores." Having fired passions all around to the boiling point, he delivers his typical communique to the audience on the sport about to begin. Thereafter he gets out of the way of the impending carnage, leaving Gammer Gurton and Hodge to advance upon Dame Chat and clash with that amazon in a long scene of primitive violence, both verbal and physical.

With three of his puppets thus manipulated into mutual discomfiture, Diccon turns his skill upon a new victim. To Dr. Rat, who has been summoned by Gammer Gurton to help recover her property, he gives the advice that he has only to creep into Dame Chat's house in the night to catch her red-handed with the needle. To Dame Chat he imparts that Hodge, in revenge for his beating, will break in upon her to steal her poultry. The curate, in consequence, is received in the darkness by a cudgel that sends him out again with a broken head and fury in his heart. He summons the bailiff to redress his injuries, and the latter patiently unweaves the enormous confusion, while every-

THE HYBRID IMAGE IN FARCE

one talks at cross-purposes, until he penetrates to the agent of all their troubles:

> I weene the ende wil proue this brawle did first arise
> Upon no other ground but only Diccons lyes.
>
> . . . .
>
> My Gammer here he made a foole, and drest hir as she was;
> And goodwife Chat he set to scole, till both parties cried alas;
> And D[octor] Rat was not behind, whiles Chat his crown did pare;
> I wold the knaue had ben starke blind, if Hodg had not his share!
> [V.ii.166–203]

Diccon, summoned, readily admits his guilt but is sorry for nothing. In reply to the bailiff's question: "Hast thou not made a lie or two, to set these two by the eares?" he asserts—and it is the Vice speaking— his prescriptive right to his habitual activity:

> What if I haue? fiue hundred such haue I seene within these seuen yeares.
> I am sory for nothing else but that I see not the sport
> Which was betwene them when they met, as they them-selues report.
> [V.ii.223–25]

He is roundly cursed by all his victims, and the curate strikes him. Under pressure from the bailiff, however, who can appreciate a jest of which he is not the butt, they ultimately let him off with a mock penance, during which, by taking his oath with a vigorous hand on Hodge's breeches, he makes the latter feelingly aware of the precious needle sticking in them. The end is a celebration in the tavern with ale provided by Gammer Gurton's halfpenny.

The nature of his victims converts to farce the deceit and injury he inflicts on them, and in farce he is under no great pressure to acquire moral plausibility. As Diccon the Bedlam he conforms sufficiently to the world he enters to deflect a deeper scrutiny. But the temper of his performance, no less than the familiar character of his actions, reveals to our acquired perspective what he really is and where he comes from. The demonstration, no longer homiletic, is still a demonstration:

> Ye see, masters, that one end tapt of this my short deuise!
> Now must we broche tother, to, before the smoke arise.
> [II.iii.1–2]

The Vice survives in him even more minutely—in the "gear" he promotes, in his conspiratorial intimacy with the audience, and in his urging that they make room for the action on the stage:

THE HYBRID IMAGE IN FARCE

> Now this gere must forward goe, for here my gammer commeth.
> Be still a-while and say nothing, make here a litle romth!
>
> [II.iv.1–2]

> Now, sirs, do you no more, but kepe my counsaile iuste,
> And Doctor Rat shall thus catch some good, I trust.
>
> [IV.iii.1–2]

And if farce is where we find him specialized at present, out of the medley of dramatic moods in which he originated, one scholar at least, in dealing with the play before us, was able to divine what Diccon could become:

> In the central figure of the piece, Diccon the Bedlam, a merry-spirited village Iago, laying plot upon plot with no other purpose than the gratification of his own super-subtle imagination, English drama received the very finest comic creation which it had yet to show.[10]

There is little reason to suppose that the play of *Misogonus* is much earlier than 1577, the date on the title page of the imperfect manuscript which preserves it. The name of Laurentius Bariona, also on the title page, is generally taken for that of the author, although immediately after the prologue there is the rival name of Thomas Richardes. Although *Misogonus* has a considerable element of farce, which accounts for its position in this study, it is by its theme a prodigal son play with clear affinities to the education drama of the continental humanists.[11] The type names of all the main characters are a moral scaffold for the structure of the plot, and an occasional speech that is nakedly homiletic carries us back somewhat, though not much, into the native morality convention:

> All yow that loue your children take example by me:
> Lett them haue good doctrine and discipline in youth;
> Correct them be tyme, least afterwarde they be
> Frowarde and contempteous and so bringe yow to great ruth.
>
> [II.v.97–100]

These words to the audience are from the sorrowing father, Philogonus, whose son, Misogonus, has grown up into a defiant wastrel, the bad product of pampered upbringing. Unable to redeem him from his evil courses and companions, Philogonus gives himself over to despair, until he discovers that he actually has a second son, Eugonus, hidden away from him since birth, who turns out to be as good as the other is bad. The manuscript ends before the play does, but not before the happy

THE HYBRID IMAGE IN FARCE

conclusion is established with Eugonus brought home, and Misogonus, now displaced and disinherited, repentant and on the verge of reconciliation with his forgiving parent.

The classic influence upon the play is slight and probably indirect, coming to it out of Christian Terence. The playwright obeys, with some latitude, the formal act and scene division of the Roman drama. But the action spreads over several weeks and is loosely conceived in several places, although they may all be intended as abutments on a central locale. The scene is Italy—Laurentum, to be exact—but only in the vaguest way. In every vital detail—allusions, local color, and characterization—the play is entirely and intensely English. A quartet of secondary characters are even more natively rustic than the bucolic population of *Gammer Gurton's Needle*. A sharp Protestant bias gets dramatic expression in the notable role of the licentious priest Sir John, whose deck of cards is his breviary. The language is virile and racy and the episodes of low life filled with depraved vigor, especially the tavern scene (II.iv), which adds the meretrix Melissa to the other profligates, both lay and clerical, and spins them all through a frenzy of dicing, drinking, dancing, and drabbing. Despite its moralistic aim and the exotic derivation of its theme, *Misogonus* is at once richly dramatic in execution and thoroughly English in spirit, its scenes of knavery the most vivid of their kind before the great age of the drama sets in.

At the center of this knavery stands Cacurgus, a figure perplexing in every way unless we see him for what he really is—the Vice assimilated to concrete dramatic story. Although he himself is no longer a personification, his behavior is still charged with the old metaphorical energy and logic, and his role, in consequence, is charged with contradiction. As his name suggests, he is the evil genius of the play. On the title page, however, he is defined as "morio," a fool. Not only do both labels together add their confirmation to the double nature of the Vice, they also show how refractory his performance has become to any label in a play where the original one is no longer viable. To Philogonus, in whose household he is literalized as a servant, he appears "a simple thinge," whose moronic fancies and clownish babble give the old man great amusement. He has had him clothed in fool's coat and cockscomb, calls him Will Summer, and delights to humor him. Furthermore, he regards his "poore fole" as a useful spy upon the behavior of

THE HYBRID IMAGE IN FARCE   329

his wayward son, finding in his reports the primitive honesty of the simpleton. How completely the situation is reversed and he himself the fool, he has no inkling. The honest idiocy of Cacurgus, it turns out, is a disguise, an aspect of his skill in intrigue and dissimulation. He is, in fact, the companion and counselor of Misogonus, protecting him from his father's wrath by tales that put the best construction of his worst behavior. On the other hand, he keeps the son posted on all his father's intentions and guides his countermoves. This reality behind appearances soon comes to the audience through the Vice's standard exposition, loud with his laughter, which in this instance, however, is shifted, ironically, upon his dissembled idiocy:

> Ha, Ha, Ha.
> You may perceive what I am, so much I doe laughe:
> A foole, yow knowe, can keepe no measure.
>
>   . . . .
>
> Yf yow knewe what delightes he taketh in my presence,
> Yow woulde laughe, I dare say now everyechoone.
> He talketh of me, I warrent yow, in my absence:
> Who but I to make him pastime who cham his none sonne.
> And proudly, I tell yow, to everie in commer
> He bragges what a naturall his lucke was to haue.
>
>   . . . .
>
> [And] when I am come, my properties he teles
> [How sim]ple how honest how faithfull and trewe.
>
>   . . . .
>
> Perswadinge him selfe that I tell him all
> What I can heare his servauntes to clatter
> [Of miso] gonus, his sonne, in kichin or haule.
> [A foole], he thinkes, can nether lye nor flatter.
> I tell him that I heare a verie good rumor;
> He is wilde, but what thoughe, he is not yet come to age.
>
>   . . . .
>
> And when I haue done, I goe showe my yonge master
> What he suspecteth, and bydde him beware;
> For he is a ruffin, a spendall and waster,
> He can doe nothinge but get stroute and stare.
>
>   [I.ii.13–44]

The homiletic candor of the last two lines saves us, however, from the easy misconception that he is simply on the side of the son against the father. Deceit is his constitutional activity and not likely to exhaust it-

THE HYBRID IMAGE IN FARCE

self upon a single victim. Although he is presented as the servant of his "yonge master" and his crony in dissipation, that is only the literalizing effort at work upon him, the fitful attempt to screw him into moral focus, against which his demonstrative amorality rebels. He dominates Misogonus rather than serves him, and he also deludes him. Having betrayed father to son, with no less pleasure he betrays son to father. He is the Vice, faithful to no one except the audience, and to nothing except his display of guile in respect to as many dupes as possible. When the situation offers him an opportunity for the most exquisite form of his destructive skill, he takes it, bending his energies upon a masterpiece of violent rupture between parent and child. While Philogonus laments what has already happened, Cacurgus promises more in an aside:

Nay softe, thouste haue yett sowe more thunder claps;
Ile make him defie the even face to face.

[II.iii.31–32]

He slips away from the tavern revels, consequently, while the orgy is at its height, with an announcement whose style and content are so familiar they need no comment:

Houle laughe now, my masters; and yow will, Ile make yow laughe:
Ile serve them, I trust, as coltish as they are.
I can anger them all and but tourne to a scofe.
Yest see a hurricampe straight way, Ile sett all at a Jar.
By promisse, as yow knowe, the old Jochum [Philogonus] I should certifye,
When his soone from burdinge home did retire;
Ile goe tell him now; the deed it selfe my wordes will verifye.
If I make yow no good sport, say Ime a lyer.

[II.iv.289–96]

Having thus directed the father to the scene of the son's dissipations, bringing them thereby to bitter words and an open break, he reverses himself and once more helps, or seems to help, son against father. When the rustics come forward with a tale of a second son spirited away at birth, he is stimulated to another piece of characteristic virtuosity, prefaced by the usual monologue of evolving intrigue:

There has bene blind tauke of another sonne, I dare say, this seven yeare;
But what saist thou to thy selfe, Cacurgus, hast thou no wile?
Ah ha, it shall go harde; but ere slepe weile haue somewhat here.

[III.ii.10–12]

THE HYBRID IMAGE IN FARCE 331

Disguising himself, therefore, as an Egyptian doctor, he imposes upon the country people's credulity by a show of occult knowledge, promising them supernatural punishment if they stand witness to the birth of another child. In this scene (III.iii) of fine bravura he advises Madge Mumblecrust to take for her toothache a "drame of Venus" together with "an ownce of poperye" and to add to both "an herbe cald envy that growes bith high ways," as well as other simples of like virtue; for in a play whose farce is incidental to its serious meaning he remains a moral satirist.

Finally, when in spite of his energetic guile the virtuous Eugonus is restored to his father and Misogonus is disinherited as prologue to his remorse and reformation, Cacurgus is turned out of service exactly as is the Vice Revenge in *Horestes,* regaling the audience with a long valedictory that is remarkably similar. He searches among them for a new employer, recites his talents in a formal proclamation, and goes off to seek his fortune elsewhere. Unlike Revenge, however, he is no longer transparent as a personification out of the abstract world, and the services he offers are a parody of actual domestic chores. The Vice, in his case, has been adapted to the human scene as an old servant and as a crony to Misogonus in his pleasures. But he is not so much adapted that his behavior has any moral consistency. If, superficially considered, he seems motivated by allegiance to his "yonge master," his crowning piece of mischief contradicts such a loyalty. His name, in fact, sums up his evil energy in all directions, for his aggressions, no longer disciplined by metaphor, have not yet become fully harnessed to a human, or moral, formula.

3

A few additional examples, briefly looked at, carry the performance of the Vice, specialized on its farcical side, deep within Elizabethan comedy. So exploited, his role degenerates, from both a moral and a dramatic standpoint, into outright comic bravura—into a running exhibition of his skill in deception and his resourcefulness in stratagem. He appears, under whatever literal name, as an artist in laughable intrigue, whose gratuitous knavery in a subordinate part of the play provides humorous relief to its serious story. The moral dissimulation at the heart of his serious role in the metaphorical drama congeals, in

332   THE HYBRID IMAGE IN FARCE

farce, into a grosser form of deceit: he becomes a master of physical disguise, imposing upon one victim after another, or upon the same one several times. The deception that once had a serious meaning survives mainly as a diverting skit, or a series of such skits, in that branch of his history which carries him into the secular drama on his lighter side. In this new environment farce takes what it can from his role and expands its unchanging formula into a repetitious series of comic frauds. We detect him in Elizabethan farce by this duplication of his single piece of business, by a performance whose method remains homiletic and demonstrative although it no longer has a homiletic content, and by a degree of harshness which often stretches the limits of comedy.

A play that illustrates unusually well this comic specialization of his role, because it also offers him, in the main division of its plot, in his more serious aspect, is one of the late moralities, *The Marriage between Wit and Wisdom,* which survives in a manuscript dated 1579. The title sufficiently reveals the educational theme of the moral plot. Young Wit, brought up diversely by his father Severity and his mother Indulgence, sets out to visit and woo Lady Wisdom. On the way he encounters Idleness the Vice, who leads him astray and deep into metaphorical trouble. Wit survives his dangers at the hands of Wantonness, Irksomeness, and Fancy, and in the end is united to the lady who personifies his object in life.

This part of the play qualifies it for a place within the central morality convention; but a subplot, built out of the adventures of the Vice, cultivates low comedy for its own sake. Idleness is put through a series of episodes, innocent of any moral aim, which exploit him at his crudest dramatic level—as a virtuoso in physical disguise, striving to escape the law after having cozened young Wit. He comes forward "araid like a phesitien" and entertains the audience with his impersonations until two soldiers, Snatch and Catch, come upon him, forcibly deprive him of the purse he has stolen from Wit, beat him, and leave him blindfolded. He next appears "like a rat-catcher" and encounters Search, the constable, who hires him to cry the proclamation for his own arrest. The Vice makes a comic garble out of the proclamation, and the constable cheats him out of his fee and sixpence besides.

THE HYBRID IMAGE IN FARCE 333

His next disguise turns him into a beggar, in which array he steals a pot of pottage from Mother Bee while her two servants, Doll and Hob, are amusing themselves in the barn. After "she beateth them vp and downe the stage" Inquisition brings in the Vice "with the potage pot about his neck" and takes him off to prison. Finally "Enter Idlenis like a preest" on his way to attend the wedding of Wit and Wisdom, having failed, in the end, to keep them apart. He assures the audience that he has not exhausted his shifts and "can turne into all Coullers like the com-million." A last minute recollection of his original, and serious, func-tion in the play provokes him to deliver a sermon against idleness, after which he goes off to "play the perueier Here in earth for the Deuell." The play is an example of the allegorical drama on its last legs, a hodgepodge of serious morality and broad comedy, with the play-wright mainly interested in the purely comic impersonations of the Vice; and these indicate the nature of his survival in Elizabethan farce.

One patent example of such survival is the role of Skink in *Look About You,* printed in 1600, a play whose chronicle setting is no more than a crust around an *olla podrida* of comic motifs.[12] The beginning and end attempt a serious reconstruction of the strife between Henry II and his sons, who rebel against their father because their mother, Eleanor of Aquitaine, has been imprisoned (according to the play's inaccurate version of history) for poisoning Fair Rosamond, Henry's concubine. The conclusion sees the reconciliation of the King and his children, and is full of patriotic sentiment against Gallic iniquity, with the last line a prayer upon the most fervent political theme of the Tudor age: "That England neuer know more Prince then one." Richard Coeur de Lion has a substantial role as a young prince, so does the wicked John, and a very sympathetic characterization is given to Richard's protégé, young Robert of Huntingdon, the Robin Hood to be.

What is historical in the play, however, is slight compared to what is farcical. Two thirds of it is given over to a bewildering succession of subtle shifts and disguisings, in which the prominent role belongs to Skink, shapeshifter extraordinary and, in fact, the Vice redesigned as a formal man. He is a comedian in his actions, but the overtones of seriousness are all about him. He has been Eleanor's instrument in the

THE HYBRID IMAGE IN FARCE

murder of Rosamond, and to the King he is a "murderous bloud-sucker." His comment upon himself is no less candid as he considers whether he ought to obey a summons to appear at court:

> but before I goe,
> Let mischiefe take aduise of villany . . .
> [ll. 47–48]

At court he is charged with murder but escapes, and the rest of his life in the play consists of one impersonation after another, accompanied by trickery that is of no use to his safety but, in fact, jeopardizes it. From having masqueraded as a hermit at Blackheath, cheating everyone who comes his way, he becomes successively a porter, the Duke of Gloster, Prince John, a drawer in a tavern, the hermit again, a falconer, the hermit a third time, before he finally lapses into mere Skink, abandoning his bravura demonstration of his "mother witt" and redeeming himself by becoming a soldier under the Duke of Gloster against the Moors in Spain. But he is not the only person in the play who dons the mantle and dimension of the Vice. Gloster himself, whose "braine flowes with fresh wit and pollicy," rivals Skink in transformations, putting off one disguise only to take on another: "Gloster wil be a proteus euery houre."

Before his identifiable character and unique method dissolve into the ocean of Elizabethan comedy, the degenerate Vice of secular farce has a moment of near brilliance. As Cocledemoy of Marston's *Dutch Courtesan* (1603–4) he is the life of the comic subplot of an essentially serious play, a knave of infinite resource in disguise and mischief who in the end defies moral definition.[13] In Cocledemoy the traditional performance and the features of the traditional dramatic image, although invested with the personality of a common type of London rogue, repeat themselves unmistakably. In the dramatis personae he is "a knavishly witty City Companion," a label which substitutes as well as possible for the original one no longer current. His wit and knavery are dedicated to a single end, the persecution of Mulligrub, a taverner in whom puritanism and sharp dealing make a greasy mixture. Before he is through with Mulligrub he has brought his tradesman's soul to despair and his neck to within an inch of the gallows. He begins to plague him by absconding with some of his best plate while a

THE HYBRID IMAGE IN FARCE

guest at his tavern, and continues with growing effrontery until the wretched victim is weary of his life. In the guise of a barber he trims him of fifteen pounds grubbed together to buy replacements for the stolen plate. As a French pedlar he overhears Mulligrub's transaction with a jeweler for some plate on credit, and as the jeweler's man he cozens Mulligrub's wife out of this purchase. He even returns to recover, by another trick, the "jole of salmon" he used as bait in the previous larceny. Mulligrub finally catches up with him and attempts to seize him, but seizes his cloak instead, whereupon Cocledemoy contrives to have the unhappy taverner stocked as a thief. To Mulligrub in the stocks "Re-enter Cocledemoy like a bellman," protests himself an old friend ("I knew your wife before she was married"), and offers his tearful sympathy: "Lord, I could weep, to see your good worship in this taking." Mulligrub gives the "honest bellman" his purse and entreats him to witness to his good character to the constable, which Cocledemoy does so effectively that the taverner is hauled off to jail for better safekeeping, his ears on his way out plagued by the laughter of the Vice:

wha, ha, ha! excellent, excellent! ha, my fine Cocledemoy, my vintner fists . . . to-morrow is the daye of judgment. Afore the Lord God, my knavery grows unperegall.

[IV.v.133–37] [14]

To Mulligrub about to be hanged comes Cocledemoy "like a sergeant" ("I am an honest man already"), invokes him to remember his sins and promises to look after his wife. The poor man makes a scaffold confession of what is deepest in his soul:

I do here make my confession: if I owe any man anything, I do heartily forgive him; if any man owe me anything, let him pay my wife.

[V.iii.95–97]

He even forgives Cocledemoy, hoping he will come from somewhere at this last moment and save him, whereupon Cocledemoy discovers himself and ends the "jest" just short of its extremity. As for the meaning of the whole enterprise, Cocledemoy makes his explanation to those who call him knave:

No knave, worshipful friend, no knave; for observe, honest Cocledemoy restores whatsoever he has got, to make you know that whatsoever he has

THE HYBRID IMAGE IN FARCE

done, has been only *euphoniae gratia*—for wit's sake . . . . all has been done for emphasis of wit, my fine boy, my worshipful friends.

[V.iii.137–42]

To someone who still insists he is "a flatt'ring knave" he admits it: "I am so; 'tis a good thriving trade"; and we are left to make our own choice between the knave and the witty fool.

He is richly drawn, as are the two Mulligrubs, and he seasons the comedy he offers with excellent satire, for he is a moralist who has read Montaigne. At the heart of his behavior, however, lies the traditional role and its characteristic dramaturgy, obscured, in the present instance, beneath the skin of a rogue called Cocledemoy. Farce converts the ancient aggression to its own mood and spares the aggressor the need for any further explanation beyond the wit he exhibits and the sport he provides, although even in farce the sport has about it a degree of harshness and suffering that suggests its darker possibilities. And Cocledemoy, in his ironic commentary upon himself, supplies an additional link between his performance in farce and the same performance in moral allegory or in tragedy. To the barber's apprentice whose tools he borrows he gives assurance that he will return them "As I am an honest man." With the condemned Mulligrub, who asks him whether he knows Cocledemoy, he enjoys the same joke: "Know him!—an honest man he is, and a comely; an upright dealer with his neighbors, and their wives speak good things of him." [15]

CHAPTER TEN

THE HYBRID IMAGE
IN SERIOUS DRAMA

*That was the old way, Gossip, when Iniquity
came in like Hokos Pokos, in a Iuglers ierkin,
with false skirts, like the Knaue of Clubs! but
now they are attir'd like men and women o'
the time, the Vices, male and female!*

BEN JONSON: THE STAPLE OF NEWS

I

If farce were the Vice's only destination he would scarcely be worth
the patience needed for the long journey he takes us. The greater goal is
his career in the serious drama—not always tragedy, for comedy is also
serious when it is not merely farce. To qualify for such a career he
undergoes a transformation relatively profound, for it is basically moral,
to render him worthy of his victims once his aggression is no longer
dignified by metaphor. In the hybrid plays they have become discrete
persons, subject to ruin and death through his machinations, and he has
become fitfully related to them in literal terms as servant, courtier, or
companion. As he moves thus into a context specifically human, he himself, we saw, becomes partially humanized while remaining in large part
obviously abstract. In its essential dynamic and method the role continues unchanged, but as it gradually loses its original anchorage in
metaphor it seeks, of necessity, another, and fumbles for it among the
impulses of human behavior. In the hybrid plays, however, his moral
adaptation to the human story is only slight, and could only be slight
because it is checked by the homiletic allegiance they still maintain. He
remains the incarnation of the abstract evil which the convention still
very much alive in them binds them to present, and his name remains
a pejorative abstraction even when it ceases to have a subjective mean-

THE HYBRID IMAGE IN SERIOUS DRAMA

ing but only describes his traditional role, as in the case of Ambidexter or Subtle Shift. The traditional performance grips the stage, but in the hybrid plays it is awkwardly suspended between the allegorical world it has lost and the literal one it tries to enter without quite being able to do so.

It is only when drama much more secular in its intention and method takes him over that he undergoes a thorough surface renovation toward human similitude, as we have already seen it in farce. As Jack Juggler, Diccon of Bedlam, Matthew Merrygreek, or Cocledemoy, he passes as native to any casual glance that is not on the lookout for what he really is, although to a second glance the role in each case must unclose its perplexity. He is much less obviously the Vice in farce because in the secular drama his adaptation to the human world is governed by an important change in method. He is no longer, as in the hybrid plays, merely literalized in some degree while remaining a manifest abstraction with a name like Ill Report, Politick Persuasion, or Common Conditions. In the secular drama he is *assimilated to someone else*. He becomes merged with some figure more normal to the play and already available to the dramatist out of the world of literal humanity. Since the Elizabethan playwright did not often create his plot out of the whole cloth, but adapted chronicle, biography, ready-made story, or pre-existing play to his own purpose, the role of the Vice is sheathed within the career and character of a person already formulated by history, legend, or art; or, when the author's originality is regnant, within some figure drawn by observation out of the English scene. Thus "the vyce," as Jack Juggler is still called, is integrated with an English version of the role belonging to Mercury in the *Amphitryon*. As Matthew Merrygreek the Vice shuttles in and out of an English version of the Roman stage parasite. He unites with the familiar figure of the roving Bedlam beggar to gain, as Diccon of Bedlam, a coloration that fits him into the human landscape of *Gammer Gurton's Needle*. His tenacious life, flowing out of allegory onto Marston's stage, invades the marrow of Cocledemoy, familiar rascal of the London stews and taverns. We can see how the traditional image, too established an institution to be abandoned, is redesigned to conform to a literal stage by surface conversion into a member of the human race.

THE HYBRID IMAGE IN SERIOUS DRAMA 339

When that conversion becomes so thorough, as eventually it does, that the role is transformed at its heart, we no longer recognize the Vice for the good reason that he no longer exists. That, however, is the end of his story. Before he reaches that point he survives by crossbreeding with humanity, and the hyphenated role shows its fission even in farce, although the nature of farce does not stimulate close character scrutiny. In the serious drama, especially in tragedy, where such scrutiny is unavoidable, this hyphenation is at the heart of the problem with which this study began.

In the serious drama he is assimilated not only to a literal figure, as in farce, but, what is more important in his transformation, to a serious moral nature. In tragedy the victims of the Vice suffer and die, just as they frequently do in the hybrid plays, and just as they suffer the even more serious tragedy of damnation in the moralities. But whereas metaphor sustained his tragic intrigues on the allegorical stage, in the literal drama they are sustained by fusion with the character and behavior of some person of serious stature, whose evil career has come to the attention of the dramatist out of literature or life. Such a villain and his history wrap the perennial role in the surface texture of human passion and appetite, beneath which it goes its ancient bravura way in the homiletic dimension and out of the organic compulsion with which we are familiar. Villainy thus dramatized becomes a demonstration, or, rather, as many demonstrations against as many dupes as the original story can be reorganized to supply. The motives of villainy, even when they are explicit, are robbed of vitality by the amoral temper of the performance and its homiletic showmanship. The Vice's exposition of his name, experience, and "property" survives, converted to villainy's exposition of its name, experience, and "property." And the Vice's unique intimacy with the audience survives, although progressively modified by an evolving sense of theatrical naturalism and by an equivalent withdrawal, therefore, from the homiletic method. The resulting performance, negotiable and enormously popular within the mixed dramatic tradition of its own time, when its hybrid nature was no trouble to an audience living on intimate terms with the larger hybrid of the transitional stage, defies any modern analysis that forsakes the history of the Tudor drama and resorts merely to psychology.

340　THE HYBRID IMAGE IN SERIOUS DRAMA

2

The play which ought, by chronological right, to stand first in this chapter, *The Jew of Malta,* is better deferred while we consider another that does not bemuse us by dramatic power or poetic brilliance. The author of *Edmond Ironside,* which has the alternate title *War Hath Made All Friends,* deserves his oblivion, for he is neither good enough for fame nor bad enough for notoriety. His play survives in a scribe's copy which "might have been written at any time within a generation or so before or after 1600," according to the modern editor, who also points out characteristics of the play indicating that its actual composition took place within the sixteenth century.[1] It offers itself as "A trew Chronicle History" and dramatizes the wars between Canute and Edmond as it found them in Holinshed. Almost all its roles are historical, and its episodes have historical integrity although their assimilation is sometimes fanciful. It exploits many of the stock techniques and motifs of the Elizabethan chronicle play: a plot based on an historical rivalry for the English throne, a spice of Senecan horror in addition to several stage battles, a dumb show and chorus, an element of romance and another of low comedy, a thrust against Catholicism, an English hero in Edmond, and a running thread of patriotic sentiment— all kneaded together by blank verse that has rhetorical dash even if little poetic power.

It also has in its leading role (despite its title) the figure of Edricus, who belongs half to Holinshed, half to homiletic allegory. He is a renegade Englishman on the side of Danish Canute, and in Holinshed he is described as "a man of great infamie for his craftie dissimulation, falshood and treason, vsed by him to the ouerthrow of the English estate."[2] In the play he is all these things, and by him Edmond, his benefactor, is deceived and betrayed more than once. His evil "character" is vehemently anatomized by morally outraged persons on both sides of the wars. To a Danish lord he is a

> Bace vild insinuatinge Sicophant
> Degenerat bastard falcely bred
> Foule mother killinge Viper traytor slave
> The scume of vices all the ill that may bee.
> 　　　　　　　　　　　[ll. 165–68]

THE HYBRID IMAGE IN SERIOUS DRAMA   341

Edmond, after one of several betrayals, denounces him as an "vngrate-full wretch, hellish incarnat divell . . . disloyall and vnfaithful Sico-phant." This is Edricus in his moral and historical dimension as the play derives him from Holinshed. He himself contributes to this focus by offering for his behavior fleeting explanations that have the bad validity of self-interest and ambition. He is willing and able to betray Canute also in order to keep on the winning side:

> And whilst Canutus here securely sleepes
> Hee [Edmond] wines with ease what wee with paine have gott
> Mas yf hee doe and fortune favour him
> I will soe woorke as Ile bee in his grace
> And keepe my liveinge and my self vnhurte.
>
> > [ll. 309–13]

In one or two places he points to kingship as the end he works for:

> The Crowne I levell at, I venter lyfe
> The Derest Iewell and of greatest price
> That anie mortall hath possession of.
>
> > [ll. 1145–47]

He is also, intermittently and vaguely, a revenger, shaped so by Elizabethan dramatic convention rather than by Holinshed; and at the end of the play, when Edmond and Canute unite in friendship, the last line is his: "By heaven Ile bee revengd on both of you." [3]

But this whole moral apparatus, although it must be taken at face value, is so much water in a sieve. It drains through the amoral artistry and homiletic showmanship of the Vice, now advanced to Villain, who demonstrates the craft of villainy from one end of the play to the other, at least half of his loquacity being naked communication with the audience:

> This Cottnes [sic] accordinge to my minde
> The kinge is angrie see hee faceth me.
>
> > [ll. 1305–306]

> See what dessemulacion bringes to passe
> Howe quicly I Cann make the kinge an asse.
>
> > [ll. 1427–28]

> See, See what witt and will can bringe aboute
> Canutus paies mee for my villa[n]ie
> And Edmund loves mee for my trecherye.
>
> > [ll. 1735–37]

342 THE HYBRID IMAGE IN SERIOUS DRAMA

The play is a succession of his stratagems, each more or less organized within the narrative logic of the story and in external conformity with the moral logic of evil behavior; but their narrative and moral reality is hopelessly compromised by the fusion of the historical Edricus with the traditional figure and stage image out of the morality drama. The intertwined elements of this conflation throw all his words and actions into double focus and complicate his mood into an inextricable mixture of passion and hilarity, mostly the latter. In fact, it is impossible to speak of "him" at all, although we must, just as it is impossible to formulate him in the language that describes human character, although we try to. He is dramatized in two contradictory dimensions, of which one is the pragmatic morality of the historic person, the other the naked homiletic exposition of the moral personification; and the Vice, in this case, has the dominant share in the ensemble. One scene (ll. 278–331) is nothing more than the long initial exposition of his *pedigree* by the Vice ("Enter Edricus solus"), defining himself by name, by moral quality, and by his characteristic behavior in the world —except that it is all translated into the literal terms of the historical situation. He begins with a pretense at secrecy, which is one sign of the gradual process, still slight in this play, by which the role of the Vice is bleached out of the secular drama over the years:

> What shall I thinke of him that means to begg
> And Canne thvs finely live vppon his witt
> I was as meane as anie bacely borne
> Fye saye not soe yt will discreditt thee
> Tut noe man heeres mee.
>
> . . . .
>
> Tis strange to see how I am favored
> Posses thy [my] duke dome and Canutus grace
> And am the Cheife of all his Counsellours
> When as my betters are exild the Courte
> Being discountenancd and out of grace
> They Cannot so desemble as I can
> Cloake, Cosen, Cogge and flatter with the kinge
> Crouch and seeme Courtious promise and protest
> Saye much doe naught in all thinges vse decept.
> [ll. 278–93]

THE HYBRID IMAGE IN SERIOUS DRAMA 343

This is a personification speaking in the homiletic pageantry of self-exposure, exactly duplicating the introductory declarations by any of the Seven Deadly Sins in *The Castle of Perseverance* two centuries before. The unbroken tradition is even more vivid in a later part of the same monologue when Edricus instructs the audience in his moral vita, vaunting his prowess and inviting their admiration:

> Hee that had hard my story from the eand
> How manie treasons I have practised
> How manie vild thinges I have brought to passe
> And what great wonders have bin Compassed
> By this deepe reachinge pate would thincke I wis
> I had bine bound apprentice to deceipt
> And from my bearth daye studied villanie.
>
> [ll. 300–306]

If he were only the naked personification, or even at some *pre-tragic* stage of development slightly beyond, like the Vice of *Common Conditions* or the Vice of *Clyomon and Clamydes,* the foregoing exposition of his villainy would be enough to explain his multiple deceptions. But the old image has now merged with the historical figure of Edricus, an English lord related to the literal persons and circumstantial events of serious story, and the hybrid has reached a point of naturalistic development that requires for its behavior a more advanced rationalization. His aggressions, therefore, invoke the anthropomorphic formula of his "hate," and for it even a moral explanation of sorts:

> For Edmonds father first did raise mee vppe
> And from a Plowmans sone promoted mee
> To be a duke for all my villanie
> And soe as often as I looke on him
> I must remember what hee did for mee
> And whence I did decend, and what I am
> Which thoughtes abace my state most abiecly
> Therefore I hate him, and desire his death
> And will procure his end in what I cann.
>
> [ll. 318–26]

Since, by hereditary prescription following the loss of the original disciplinary metaphor, his betrayals move indiscriminately in all directions, he is quite able to "hate" Canutus, his present patron, also.

344 THE HYBRID IMAGE IN SERIOUS DRAMA

"Hate," however, is no more than half the formula. The serial exhibition of deceit needs the two poles of reality and pretense, and the pretense, of course, is "love." We really do not need to derive the tradition within his words; they themselves reveal it:

> But for Canutus hee doth honor mee
> Because hee knowes not whence I did dissend
> Therefore of the Two I love Canutus best
> Yet I Can play an Ambodexters parte
> And sweare I love, yet hate him with my harte.
>
> [ll. 327–31]

On this stratified foundation the stratagems of Edricus arise to compose the main activity in the play, each an exemplification of the thesis the whole of the foregoing homily—for that is what it is—advances. Before and after each installment of his guile, moreover, he is the Vice outright, sharing his plot with the audience, preening himself on his wit and villainy, congratulating himself on his success—for these were the enormously popular rhetorical features of the role that helped keep it alive. To restore himself to Edmond's favor after betraying him outrageously, he writes a letter to him, whose devious art consists in its truth:

> *Truth needes noe cullors* though I meane to lye
> My simple writtinge shall deceave his eie
> I soe, O rare Conceyted peece of worke
> How cunningly thou canst convert thy shape
> Into an Angell when thou dost intend
> To flatter the plaine honest meaninge kinge.
>
> [ll. 1198–1204]

He also delivers it himself, disguised as his own servant. The letter contains the tears and "love" of the Vice:

> My love and zeale vnto your Maiestie.
>
> . . . .
>
> As sadly as the late espoused man
> Greeves to Departe from his new maried wife
> How manie sighes I fetched at my Departe
> How manie tymes I turned to Come againe
> How oft I plaind how often I did weepe
> Were too too longe to writte or you to reade.
>
> [ll. 1289–94]

THE HYBRID IMAGE IN SERIOUS DRAMA 345

As for the Vice's laughter, it is everywhere in his tone, as well as plainly in the text when he witnesses the "Crewell butchery" of two young and noble hostages whose noses and hands are cut off on stage:

> *Edricus.* Ha. Ha. Ha.
> *Canutus.* Whie laughest thou Edricus
> *Edricus.* I Cannot chuse to see the villaines rave.
> [ll. 730–32]

He has no loyalties, not even to himself, for he puts himself into danger to display his dexterity in getting out of it. Virtue is his natural enemy, and in this play of concrete incident and tragic scope the Psychomachia takes on its new coloring in words that are franker than Iago's because Edricus is nearer to the Vice. Yet the following monologue, in which he plans his last intrigue, must inevitably remind us of both Iago and the Vice:

> Oh gracious starrs inspire my nimble witt
> With some device, and as I ever have
> I will imploye yt to some villanie
> Soft, lett mee see, oh it is exelent
> Fountaine of witt, the springe of pollecye
> The flower of treason, and of villanie.
>
> . . . .
>
> Well Ile about it, meaninge noe man good
> But that my speech may sheed kinge Edmunds blood.
> [ll. 1841–59]

A few lines later he reminds us of both once more when he tells us why he wants to shed the blood of virtuous Edmond—it is the Psychomachia speaking:

> For I desire to Drinke kinge Edmundes blood
> Because hee ever sought to doe mee good.
> [ll. 1990–91]

Facing such an avowal, the modern reader, decently reared in the habits and preconceptions of the naturalistic drama, can only turn the page in the hope of finding elsewhere something more intelligible.

3

The Jew of Malta is a patriotic play, and we cannot fail to be reminded of the last lines of *King John* by the last speech of the island's governor to his Turkish prisoner:

> for come all the world
> To rescue thee, so will we guard vs now,
> As sooner shall they drinke the Ocean dry,
> Then conquer Malta, or endanger vs.
> [ll. 2405–408] [4]

It is also a Christian play, for patriotism in the sixteenth century still meant loyalty to a Christian commonwealth, and against the Turk it meant the defense of Christendom. Upon this twofold theme, which is everywhere woven into the story of Malta's heroic resistance, Marlowe draws the evil of Barabas in its largest outline. He is a bad citizen, or rather no citizen at all, for he insists on his rights as a stranger ("Are strangers with your tribute to be tax'd?") in the city where he lives and prospers. He is a bird of prey and passage, whose comment on Malta's great peril settles him into moral perspective within the large meaning of the play: "Why let 'em enter, let 'em take the Towne." [5] It does not redeem him that Marlowe's geographical flair, exploiting the romance of commerce, makes Barabas the Elizabethan drama's greatest cosmopolite. His talk and curses are polyglot, his ships and business associates are in every port, and all places owe him money:

> In Florence, Venice, Antwerpe, London, Ciuill,
> Frankeford, Lubecke, Mosco, and where not,
> Haue I debts owing; and in most of these
> Great summes of mony lying in the bancho;
> [ll. 1580–83]

But he is no more a citizen of the world than he is of Malta. His aggrandizing energy cuts him off spiritually from everyone, his egomania files him to a needle's point:

> How ere the world goe, I'le make sure for one.
>
> . . . .
>
> *Ego mihimet sum semper proximus.*
> [ll. 225–28]

THE HYBRID IMAGE IN SERIOUS DRAMA 347

> For so I liue, perish may all the world.
>
> [l. 2292]

His overweening sense of personal superiority does the same: he has no doubt that he is "born to better chance" and composed of "finer mould than common men."

His Jewishness defines his condemnation—to neglect this emphasis in the play is to be modern and romantic—but it condemns him much less for his faith than for his Jewish greed, pride, and insolence. Out of "the Blessings promis'd to the Iewes" he draws his right to benefits without a corresponding obligation, his right to exploit others because they are not Jews, his contempt for the state in which he thrives and for its citizens: "these swine-eating Christians, / Vnchosen Nation, neuer circumciz'd." [6] Marlowe's own time counts for much in these matters, and he is a great poet, not a Jew-baiter. He is also chilled by the shadow between the idea and the reality of Christianity, and the following words of Barabas belong no more to his own malice than to the severe insight of the poet:

> For I can see no fruits in all their faith,
> But malice, falshood, and excessiue pride,
> Which me thinkes fits not their profession.
> Happily some hapless man hath conscience,
> And for his conscience liues in beggery.
>
> [ll. 154–58]

The whole of this speech (ll. 141–77) is most useful, revealing what Marlowe finds worst in Barabas: his genius for amassing wealth is titanic because it is not disturbed by conflict with even the slightest spiritual impulse. By instinct as well as by practice he is total Mammon.

Early in the play, accordingly, Barabas is punished in some degree because he is a Jew, but mainly because of the kind of Jewish person he is—because of the way his character responds to a situation. By far the richest man in Malta, his only concern with Malta's need to pay the Turkish tribute is to escape the levy. His punishment, total confiscation, pivots on a thesis, just as does the punishment of Shylock, except that in Marlowe's play it pivots much more peremptorily. With the help of his daughter Abigail he recovers enough wealth to start anew, his heart filled with resentment and on fire for revenge. This

348 THE HYBRID IMAGE IN SERIOUS DRAMA

is the Barabas of the first act and part of the second—bad and brilliant on an heroic scale: cunning, resourceful, ruthless, self-righteous, and selfish. He is an evil character, but a character; a wicked man, but a man; morally vicious, but a moral figure. And if we wish, he is also a man mistreated: the victim of chicanery manipulated by prejudice. For so much of his role the homiletic stage offers no precedent, and Marlowe's genius is free.

For the rest of the play Barabas is something else, which nothing in the moral realm can explain—neither Machiavellianism, although the prologue puts him under the Florentine's auspices; nor the Devil, although he is frequently matched with the diabolic, and his Jewish nose is the same piece of facial furniture that adorns the Devil of the mysteries and moralities. He does not undergo a change in character, but something much more radical—a dramaturgic change, a change in theatrical method. From having been dramatized as a bad man he becomes the homiletic demonstration of serialized villainy, a demonstration, moreover, in which *he puts himself on show to the audience.* In other words, Marlowe resorts to the popular effectiveness of the older dramaturgy and Barabas becomes the Vice, although an occasional thread of his evil humanity weaves in and out of his changed dimension. From the middle of the second act his performance has only superficial connection with the premises of emotion and circumstance erected in the first part of the play. That they remain at all is concession to the fact that he is called Barabas, not Iniquity, in a play called *The Famous Tragedy of the Rich Iew of Malta.* But they have no real meaning any more and are, in fact, superfluous. The set exhibition of cunning villainy and the artistry of deceit against as many victims as possible is full of its own meaning and its own mood, both of which were self-explanatory to the audience of that time, and still are when we see them clearly.

The transformation does not come without warning. There is a portent of it in his dissembled passion with his fellow Jews (ll. 393–458) and another in his highly stylized dissimulation when Abigail pretends to become a nun (ll. 577–607). It is heralded in the slave market by his side remark to the audience, describing the double nature of the traditional role and its basic character as a demonstration:

THE HYBRID IMAGE IN SERIOUS DRAMA 349

Now will I shew my selfe to haue more of the Serpent
Then the Doue; that is, more knaue than foole.

[ll. 797–98]

And a moment later the convention about to take him over heralds
itself through his reply to the slave who protests himself "a very
youth":

A youth? I'le buy you, and marry you to Lady vanity, if you doe well.

[ll. 880–81] [7]

The actual catalyst is his meeting with the Turkish Ithamore. When
they come together as master and slave the transformation is complete in both of them, for Ithamore shares the role of the Vice with
Barabas and ekes out its characteristics, a development whose meaning
will get our attention later. The earliest of these characteristics is
rhetorical, the expository monologue of the Vice in which he proclaims his moral quality and its previous exercise in the world; and
Barabas falls into it exactly and lavishly, except that the moral injury
of the metaphorical aggression, as we saw it expressed in the allegorical plays, becomes in his case literal, inevitably:

> As for my selfe, I walke abroad a nights
> And kill sicke people groaning under walls:
> Sometimes I goe about and poyson wells;
> And now and then, to cherish Christian theeves,
> I am content to lose some of my crownes;
> That I may, walking in my Gallery,
> See 'em goe pinion'd along by my doore.
> Being young, I studied Physicke, and began
> To practise first vpon the Italian;
> There I enriched the Priests with burials.
>
> . . . .
>
> And after that was I an Engineere,
> And in the warres 'twixt France and Germanie,
> Vnder pretence of helping Charles the fifth,
> Slew friend and enemy with my stratagems.
> Then after that was I an Vsurer,
> And with extorting, cozening, forfeiting
>
> . . . .
>
> I fill'd the Iailes with Bankrouts in a yeare,
> And with young Orphans planted Hospitals,

THE HYBRID IMAGE IN SERIOUS DRAMA

And euery Moone made some or other mad,
And now and then one hang himselfe for griefe,
Pinning vpon his breast a long great Scrowle
How I with interest tormented him.

[ll. 939–63]

By the same process whereby it becomes literal, the original *significatio* of the moral personification also becomes external: the inward war of vice against the human soul emerges into the historical world and becomes the automatic aggression by Barabas against Christians everywhere, his *property* to use the old word, an index to his impending activity, and, of course, a rival principle of causation, nullifying the first part of the play. Shortly thereupon, speaking for Ithamore too, he announces his "villainy" and his "hate," and the allegorical circle of cause and consequence is complete, with everything that follows cast in the dimension of moral demonstration:

we are villaines both:
Both circumcized, we hate Christians both.

[ll. 979–80]

Remembering Abigail and the Turks he double-crosses, we need not take his "hate" and its object literally. His new career consists simply of one exhibition of villainy after another, and he makes no distinctions, for his impetus belongs to allegory and to theatrical convention, not to the natural world. He has neither friend nor foe, only victims, and he tells us so at the end:

And had I but escap'd this stratagem,
I would haue brought confusion on you all.

[ll. 2369–70]

The tricks of the Vice also belong to him—the weeping, for instance, which protests honesty and love when Mathias ripens into a subject for his art:

Oh, heauen forbid I should haue such a thought.
Pardon me though I weepe.

[ll. 1021–22]

Or again, when he manipulates one of his dupes onto the gallows: " 'Las, I could weepe at your calamity." The Vice's laughter is everywhere implicit in his voice and mood, and Edward Alleyn in the role

THE HYBRID IMAGE IN SERIOUS DRAMA 351

no doubt supplied it. For Ithamore, his alter ego, the text is explicit when he invites the audience to admire the stratagem by which his master has managed that the two friends, Mathias and Lodowick, should kill each other:

> Why, was there euer seene such villany.
> So neatly plotted, and so well perform'd?
> Both held in hand, and flatly both beguil'd?
>
> [ll. 1220–22]

Abigail enters at this moment and asks, "Why, how now Ithimore, why laugh'st thou so?" And he: "Oh, Mistresse, ha, ha, ha." As for Barabas, instead of pursuing him endlessly through the homiletic role with which the tragic figure of the play's beginning has been assimilated, we can find its history and its essence concentrated in the question he asks the audience when he undertakes to betray his benefactors, the Turks:

> why, is not this
> A kingly kinde of trade to purchase Townes
> By treachery, and sell 'em by deceit?
> Now tell me, worldlings, vnderneath the sunne,
> If greater falsehood euer has bin done.
>
> [ll. 2329–33]

The waning life of the allegorical stage revives intensely in such a speech: in its didactic and demonstrative principle, its ironic inversion of the homiletic point, its rallying impeachment of the audience, its celebration of deceit.

When we turn from this dimension of his performance to the nature of his stratagems, we find the Vice once more. In each of them what he demonstrates is his ability to deceive, and when he enters in the guise of a French Musician we recognize the Vice of secular farce. In spite of the effort the poet has made to organize them all within the moral logic of motive and intention, they clearly are parts of a theatrical formula to which such logic cannot adhere. They do not belong to the tragic plot, they invade it, and move by a momentum outside the premises set up in the first part of the play. The stratagem against Lodowick and Mathias literalizes the classic maneuver of the Vice throughout the homiletic drama:

THE HYBRID IMAGE IN SERIOUS DRAMA

So, now will I goe in to Lodowicke,
And like a cunning spirit feigne some lye,
Till I haue set 'em both at enmitie.

[ll. 1148–49]

What Diccon does in farce, Barabas does in tragedy, both actions having a single origin: the dissension stimulated by the Vice between the human hero of the moralities and his guardian personifications of virtue. Literalized by the secular stage and converted now to tragedy, it becomes the maneuver whereby Barabas turns the friendship of the two young men into rancor and their swords into each other's bosoms: "forc'd their hands diuide vnited hearts"; but it is still, as Ithamore applauds it, "braue sport." It is by the same sort of divisive artistry that he gets rid of the two friars:

Now I haue such a plot for both their liues,
As neuer Iew nor Christian knew the like.

[ll. 1626–27]

The emphasis is always on the artistry, not on the end; the serialized villainy flourishes as a demonstration, not as a means. From the second act to the end the structure of the play is linear and episodic, composed of successive variations on the single theme of his indefatigable guile, until he breathes out his "latest hate" (not "fate") in the boiling caldron.

Our habituation to naturalistic theater on the scenic stage leads us to read as soliloquies or asides speeches of Barabas that are outright communication with the audience from the platform of a homiletic stage. Our habituation to the mood of naturalistic tragedy is startled when T. S. Eliot classifies *The Jew of Malta* as "farce . . . farce of the old English humour." [8] The description is more cogent than the derivation. The play is racked by its seriocomic extremes because on the one hand, through the genius of its author, it presses toward the heights of Elizabethan tragedy; on the other, through its chief figure, it inherits the "tragical mirth" of the morality drama. In Barabas we see the Vice converting to tragedy as he moves through the gradual process of transition that eventually digests the allegorical role. Marlowe's poetic power did not emancipate him from the traditionary sway of his theater, but the intense fabric of human passion and motivation to

THE HYBRID IMAGE IN SERIOUS DRAMA 353

which he matched the Vice makes clear which is the recessive and which the dominant part of the hybrid he fashioned.

4

Although revenge is a prominent part of the business in both plays behind us, as indeed it is in serious drama everywhere and always, the more specialized form known as the Elizabethan Revenge Tragedy, with its absolute concentration on the theme and its distinctive language and apparatus, first enters this study as *The Tragedy of Hoffman or A Reuenge for a Father,* probably by Henry Chettle and probably composed in 1602. Its date and some of its characteristics suggest that Henslowe commissioned it as a play to rival *Hamlet* and to float on the latter's vogue.[9] The father who is being avenged does not indeed come on as a ghost, but he is even more an eye opener as a skeleton hung in chains, joined later by the skeleton of one of his son's victims. A virgin driven mad by the deaths of her father and sweetheart, her talk a medley of flowers and mortality, is surely Ophelia's sister. A burning crown as an instrument of death and other gruesome bric-a-brac, together with seven violent deaths on stage and numerous invocations to Rhamnusia, amply define the play's genre. Reading it, one is able better to appreciate the deep moral organization that Shakespeare could impose on this sort of melodrama. For all its melodramatic crudity, however, *Hoffman* has a certain tensile strength in its verse, in the energy and mordancy of its avenger, in the grotesquerie of Lucibella, and in its pervasive atmosphere of the gothic-romantic composed of wild seascapes, beetling cliffs, dank and menacing forests. It also has, especially in its suspensive last act, a strange resemblance to the modern detective story. In a later incarnation its author became Edgar Allan Poe.

The opening lines, spoken by Clois Hoffman, the avenger, sound like a postscript to *Hamlet:*

> Hence Clouds of melancholy
> Ile be no longer subject to your fittes.[10]

Thereupon, his father's bones to witness, he takes an oath of vengeance and asserts the justice of his cause: "Ill acts moue some, but myne's a cause of right." For the rest of the play he moves from one act of

354 THE HYBRID IMAGE IN SERIOUS DRAMA

revenge to another until he meets his own death under the iron crown that killed his father. His last words (a few verses are missing from the end of the play) are a lament that he allowed love to divert him and "slackt reuenge." In this opinion, however, he is too modest: he has been anything but slack, with five corpses to his credit and one near miss. His aim has been to kill all who judged his father to death, and all their heirs. It turns out, but only at the end, that four dukes are involved and five children—so that, in fact, his efforts are directed against almost everybody in the play. The fierce passion and lurid, sometimes brilliant, rhetoric of the Elizabethan stage revenger are plentifully his. In all these respects he is a choice specimen of the breed.

Entangled with this part of him, however, the archaic role of the Vice asserts itself throughout the play to create the double image with which we are familiar. His overweening and excessive vengeance makes him a villain; he is developed as such by the playwright and treated as such by others in the play; but this aspect of him is not important. What is important is that, in the homiletic dimension of the Vice, *he presents himself* as a villain, and that his behavior wanders out of its passionate premise and aim, into the characteristics and mood of the amoral stereotype with which personification endowed the popular stage. He and his instrument, Lorrique, share the Vice between them and strongly suggest, in this respect, Marlowe's Barabas and Ithamore. The imitation is almost confirmed by one of their stratagems and its victims. Two brothers, sons of the Duke of Saxony, are tricked into a situation whereby one kills the other, and their names are Mathias and Lodowick, duplicating exactly the names of the two friends who fall victim to Barabas in exactly the same way. Moreover, the bait in this device is Lodowick's sweetheart, Lucibella, who thus matches the use to which Barabas puts Abigail. As for the stratagem itself, it is once more the divisive aggression of the Vice against love and unity, and it is so emphasized beforehand by its deviser:

> Call in Mathias, if my plot proue good,
> Ile make one brother shed the others blood.
> [ll. 697–98]

and again afterward, as he stands over the deed and ironically defines its perpetrator:

THE HYBRID IMAGE IN SERIOUS DRAMA

> Then there is villany, practice, and villany
> Mathias hath bin wrong'd and drawne to kill
> His naturall brother, and with him to destroy
> The rarest peece of natures workmanship,
> No doubt by practize and base villany.
>
> [ll. 957–61]

He shows a slight advance toward naturalism, and in him we detect the gradual suppression of the inherited stereotype by the fact that he does not define himself in the formal rhetoric of homiletic allegory as the villain. But he does the same thing just as effectively by indirection and irony, as in the passage above or in the following one when he impresses Lorrique into his service:

> Were I perswaded that thou couldst shed teares,
> As doth the Egyptian serpents neere the Nile;
> If thou wouldst kisse and kill, imbrace and stabbe,
> Then thou shouldst liue, for my uindictiue braine
> Hath cast a glorious project of reuenge
> Euen as thou kneel'st, wilt thou turne villaine speake.
>
> [ll. 76–81]

And he is satisfied when Lorrique assures him that "villany is my onely patrimony." At both ends of the play he is the passionate avenger, a highly stylized murderer but a morally credible one: "Hoffman the son full of reuenge and hate." But in between he is mainly the Vice at work in the familiar style beneath his transformation; and Lorrique, the underling to whom the less dignified features of the Vice are transferred ("That fellow which is all compos'd of mirth"), never tires of defining his master, and himself at the same time, in his conversations with the audience:

> this is an excellent fellow
> A true villaine fitter for me then better company,
> This is Hannce Hoffmans sonne.
>
> [ll. 95–97]
>
> I laugh to see
> How I out-strip the Prince of villany.
>
> [ll. 2138–39]

Deceit and dissimulation are an art with which Hoffman is intensely preoccupied: "By slye deceit he acted euery wronge." For most of the play he wears the disguise of Otho, the first of his victims, and varies

356   THE HYBRID IMAGE IN SERIOUS DRAMA

from it only to take on another, "like a hermet." He is as fluent in compassionate weeping and scornful laughter as the Vice of old, and never
misses a chance to exercise this standard equipment of his guile. The
laughter comes early, like a signal to the audience that won't bear delay:

> Ha ha, I laugh to see how dastard feare
> Hastens the death doomd wretch to his distresse.
>
> [ll. 51–52]

His weeping is also prompt when he dissembles with young Otho a
moment before he kills him, so that the latter says: "I see thy true
hearts loue drope downe in teares." And the pretense of love and tears
sustains his successive stratagems throughout the play. He speeds his
fancy plot against the lives of the lovers Lodowick and Lucibella by
exciting Mathias with the falsehood that Lucibella has turned unfaithful
and fled with a "Grecian":

> My true seruant knowes
> How at the sight of such inconstancy
> My gentle heart was smitt with inward griefe
> And I sunk downe with sorrow.
>
> [ll. 744–47]

From the company assembled over the body of the slain Lodowick and
the apparently slain Lucibella he retires to nurse his grief:

> I pray you thinke me not in passion dull;
> I must withdraw, and weepe, my heart is full.
>
> [ll. 1017–18]

But this is what he withdraws to, five lines later, addressing Lorrique:

> Helpe me to sing a hymne vnto the fates
> Compos'd of laughing interiections.
>
> [ll. 1024–25]

And when the corpses of a duke and his son lie on the ground, both
of whom he has poisoned by employing Lorrique to the purpose "like
a French Doctor," he moves from tears to laughter so expeditiously
that we can trace him without skipping a verse:

> Goe on afore, ile stay awhile, and weepe
> My tributary teares paid on the ground
> Where my true ioy your Prince my vncle fell:
> Ile follow to driue from you all distresse

THE HYBRID IMAGE IN SERIOUS DRAMA 357

And comfort you, though I be comfortles.
Art not thou plumpt with laughter my Lorrique.
[ll. 1551–56]

Such tricks episodically repeated throughout the play do not establish the Vice in his composition, but they confirm it. What does establish the archaic stratum just beneath the surface is the whole tendency of his role to gambol from the purpose which defines him morally into successive homiletic demonstrations of villainy, attended by the temper and devices that for two centuries were part of such a performance. Like the other two figures reviewed so far in this chapter, he fluctuates between a naturalistic conception and an inveterate stage image which is not.

5

The play that follows can be treated briefly because, in the way we are concerned with it, it mainly repeats, with some dilution, the features of the three which have gone before. The title page of *Lust's Dominion, or The Lascivious Queen,* of which the earliest surviving edition is dated 1657, offers it as "Written by Cristofer Marloe, Gent." Modern scholarship is almost unanimous in rejecting this ascription, but there is equal agreement that the play is Elizabethan and an imitation of the Marlovian afflatus.[11] In addition to verbal resemblances to several of Marlowe's plays, it shows strong thematic affinities to one of them, *The Jew of Malta.* There is also distinct similarity in atmosphere and in details between it and Chettle's revenge tragedy of *Hoffman.* And its two main figures, Eleazar the Moor and the lascivious queen herself, clearly suggest the corresponding roles of Aaron and Tamora in *Titus Andronicus.* What is most obvious about all these relationships is their large dependence on one feature—the sensational role of the villain, whose lurid evil, enormous and bewildering energy in tragic intrigue, and utter immunity to moral or psychological formulation create a dramatic genre to which belong more plays than those already mentioned. The problems exist because in each case the homiletic dimension and stage image of the Vice has been draped with the mantle of tragedy, married to the serious motives of revenge or ambition, and inflated by the swelling verse of the tragic stage. Each of these figures is more or less grotesque because he is more or less hybrid—one part

358   THE HYBRID IMAGE IN SERIOUS DRAMA

of him drawn in naturalistic perspective as a criminal member of the human race, the other in the outright homiletic bravura of moral allegory. As the former, he is a villain advancing toward villainous ends through villainous means. As the latter, he is Villainy putting itself on display through exposition and tireless exemplification. From one moment to the next, and even from one word to the next, these two interwoven aspects of the single figure change him from an imitation of human life into an allegorical pageant, and back again. We may imagine that the popular Elizabethan audience liked him that way. Certainly their own tradition spared them criticism's modern headache.

The role of Eleazar the Moor in *Lust's Dominion* shows us this hybrid once more. The beginning of the play finds his savage nature fiercely committed to revenge, for, although maintained in the style of a nobleman, he is "Captive to a Spanish Tyrant" who has killed his royal father and deprived Eleazar of a kingdom. He is additionally committed by the "wrongs, dishonours, and . . . discontents" that come to him after the old king's death, when he is reviled for his adultery with the dead monarch's queen, degraded, and banished. His program, therefore, is "To cut down all that stand within my wrongs, /And my revenge." He is also passionately ambitious for the Spanish crown, as the dying monarch warns:

> Ambition wings his spirit, keep him down;
> What wil not men attempt to win a crown.
> [I:iii] [12]

He himself, after he actually becomes king, soars into a Tamburlainian celebration of royal power and glory:

> Kings indeed are deities.
> And who'd not (as the sun) in brightnesse shine?
> To be the greatest, is to be divine:
> Who among millions would not be the mightiest?
> To sit in God-like state, to have all eyes,
> Dazled with admiration, and all tongues
> Showting lowd Praiers, to rob every heart
> Of love, to have the strength of every arm.
> A Soveraigns name, why 'tis a Soveraign charm.
> [V.i]

This infusion of revenge and ambition into his passionate Moorish blood gives color, if we look on them alone, to his devious and endless

THE HYBRID IMAGE IN SERIOUS DRAMA   *359*

villainy, as he moves from one murderous stratagem to another with the express aim of making "all Spain a bonefire." We must notice, however, that, like all the other villains of this breed, he needs both motives together, and even they need stretching, to span the formula for this type of play, which demands that sooner or later he point his deceit and villainy against every important member of the cast: "By one, and one, I'le ship you all to hell."

But we are not allowed to focus on such motives alone, for he has a great deal more to say about himself in the monologues which regularly bracket each of his stratagems. The first words of the play are his, and they are almost a motto for the Vice through two centuries:

> On me, do's musick spend this sound on me
> That hate all unity?

The end of the second scene contrives to give him privacy for his first monologue, in which the revenger is hopelessly entangled with the Vice-*cum*-villain:

> now purple villany;
> Sit like a Roab imperiall on my back,
> That under thee I closelyer may contrive
> My vengeance.
>
> [I.ii]

When he considers the regions available to him in exile, his language and mood belong to a convention much older than the Elizabethan tragedy of revenge or ambition:

> Ther's Portugal a good air, & France a fine Country;
> Or Barbary rich, and has Moors; the Turke
> Pure Divell, and allowes enough to fat
> The sides of villany; good living there:
> I can live there, and there, and there,
> Troth 'tis, a villain can live any where.
>
> [I.iv]

And a later monologue combines with such sentiments the laughter that is their old accompaniment:

> Ha, ha, I thank thee provident creation,
> That seeing in moulding me thou did'st intend,
> I should prove villain, thanks to thee and nature
> That skilful workman; thanks for my face,
> Thanks that I have not wit [white?] to blush.
>
> [II.ii]

360 THE HYBRID IMAGE IN SERIOUS DRAMA

His hilarity, which rings throughout the play, becomes so frequent just before his end that his "jocund spleen" and "Crimson jollitie" compose an Elizabethan version of *Hubris*. In his last words, as he dies in his own snare, as well as in his speeches above, we hear the voice of Shakespeare's Aaron: "Devills com claim your right, and when I am confin'd within your kingdom then shall I out-act you all in perfect villany." What we actually hear in both, however, is the voice of the Vice, whose immunity, no longer to death, but to human sentiment about death, survives through this form of indifference, this defiance, this return to hell, this immortal pursuit by Villainy of its proper function. Eleazar could be as evil as possible, in crude imitation of Marlowe's heroic scale, without troubling us, if only he did not cease to be evil at all by forsaking a moral nature for the homiletic demonstration of Evil personified.

6

The period enclosing the four plays just examined, roughly the fifteen years from 1589 through 1603, when the popular drama is still only a stride away from a stage overtly homiletic, also encloses others in which the old convention merges with the new to produce villainy in double focus. A very brief inspection must serve for several plays in which his allegorical heritage governs the language of the villain more obviously than it does his behavior. In each of them the plot is no longer about him mainly, but has a scope which includes him only as a part, and an emphasis to which he is more or less incidental. His role, in consequence, is no longer an indefinite series of aggressions for the sake of display, patterned upon the exhibitive energy of the Vice. But his speeches, whatever pragmatic motives seem to sway him to evil, revert to that kind of absolute self-exposure which belongs only to homiletic allegory.

The role of Lorenzo in *The Spanish Tragedy* (1588–89), whatever other problem it offers, does not fall within our view; although his motivation seems slight, he is not radically complicated by the traits of the convention we are tracing. But the subplot of the same play, the business involving the Viceroy of Portugal and the two Portuguese noblemen, Alexandro and Villuppo, offers just such tight complication in a speech of three lines. Villuppo has falsely accused Alexandro of

THE HYBRID IMAGE IN SERIOUS DRAMA 361

treacherously slaying the Viceroy's son in the battle in which the latter was actually taken prisoner. Left alone on the stage for the purpose, Villuppo lets the audience know the why and wherefore of his lie:

> Thus haue I with an enuious forged tale
> Deceiued the king, betraid mine enemy,
> And hope for guerdon of my villany.
>
> [I.ii.93–95] [13]

Later on, when the truth is uncovered, Alexandro saved from death, and he himself doomed instead, Villuppo makes confession to the Viceroy:

> Rent with remembrance of so foule a deed,
> My guiltie soule submits me to thy doome,
> For, not for Alexandros iniuries,
> But for reward and hope to be preferd,
> Thus haue I shamelesly hazarded his life.
>
> [III.i.91–95]

Why he should want to deceive the Viceroy, why Alexandro is his enemy, or what reward he is after, are questions not worth the inquiry, for they have no answer. The whole episode is merely a sketch, its three main figures merely shadows; but even the shadow of a Villuppo is riven between his vague pragmatic aims, whatever they are, and villainy self-sufficient, self-defined, and stood up for exhibition by that most characteristic word of the morality drama: *thus*.

The same sort of contamination between villainy in naturalistic dimension and in homiletic pageant occurs from time to time in Marston's *Antonio's Revenge* (1599), the second part of his *Antonio and Mellida*. The gaudy wickedness of Piero belongs to the dramatic fashion that cultivated such paragons, and his gory bombast belongs to the same cause as well as to the self-indulgence of a playwright who is both John Marston and a young man. We can regard such excesses as a matter of style, even if we judge the style bad. Archaic convention, however, rather than contemporary style governs those moments—they are not many—when Piero ceases to be a villainous avenger and becomes instead a pageant of villainy—as in such questions as the following addressed to his tool, Strotzo, invoking his admiration:

> And didst thou ever see a Judas kisse,
> With a more covert touch of fleering hate?
>
> [I.i.] [14]

362 THE HYBRID IMAGE IN SERIOUS DRAMA

Canst thou not hony me with fluent speach,
And even adore my toplesse villany?

[I.i.]

A more substantial illustration of the same method occurs in *The Death of Robert Earl of Huntingdon* (1598) by Chettle and Munday, which follows a first part called *The Downfall of Robert Earl of Huntingdon*. The titular hero, Robin Hood, is celebrated throughout both plays as the mirror of knightly courtesy and Christian virtue, his story and behavior getting an emphasis which suggests a deliberate parallel with Christ. He disdains to seek revenge for his outlawry, lives chastely with Maid Marian in Sherwood, limits his band to acts of unimpeachable virtue, succors his enemies, and forgives them, as he lies dying, the death they inflict on him. His "virtuous mind" and "virtuous life" are thematic, and it is his virtue that costs him his life. His archenemy is Doncaster, a churchman, whose enmity gets a practical explanation at one point in the earlier play:

O, 'tis an unthrift, still the churchmen's foe;
An ill-end will betide him, that I know.
'Twas he that urged the king to 'sess the clergy,
When to the holy land he took his journey;
And he it is that rescued those two thieves,
Scarlet and Scathlock, that so many griefs
To churchmen did.

[*Downfall* III.ii] [15]

But in the second part he slips into a different perspective and will have nothing to do with so plausible a provocation. In this play his associate in malice against Robin is the Prior of York, and the two of them plot the hero's death by poison after their previous attempt upon him has failed. In a remarkable exchange at this point they query each other about their respective motives. "But tell, Prior," asks Doncaster, "Wherefore so deadly dost thou hate thy cousin?" The answer is forthright:

Shall I be plain? because, if he were dead,
I should be made the Earl of Huntington.

[*Death* I.ii]

In his turn the Prior asks the same question: "But tell me, Doncaster, why dost thou hate him?" Doncaster's reply, a long one, has the temper of farce and the absolute homiletic ingenuousness of moral allegory:

THE HYBRID IMAGE IN SERIOUS DRAMA   363

> By the mass, I cannot tell. O yes, now I ha't:
> I hate thy cousin Earl of Huntington
> Because so many love him as there do,
> And I myself am loved of so few.

In the rest of his reply, a bill of particulars, the Psychomachia takes over entirely:

> Nay, I have other reasons for my hate:
> He is a fool, and will be reconcil'd
> To any foe he hath: he is too mild,
> Too honest for this world, fitter for heaven.

—which reminds us somewhat of Richard of Gloucester's opinion of his brother Clarence—but Doncaster has more to say:

> He will not kill these greedy cormorants,
> Nor strip base peasants of the wealth they have!
> He does abuse a thief's name and an outlaw's,
> And is, indeed, no outlaw nor no thief:
> He is unworthy of such reverend names.

Next he develops his indictment of Robin Hood for chastity vis-à-vis Maid Marian, concluding:

> Another thing I hate him for again:
> He says his prayers, fasts eves, gives alms, does good:
> For these and such like crimes swears Doncaster
> To work the speedy death of Robin Hood.

Later, when both are doomed to death in spite of their victim's plea that they be forgiven, the Prior, a plausible villain, curses Doncaster exactly as the hero of moral allegory curses the Vice who has deceived, dominated, and damned him:

> High heavens, show mercy to my many ills!
> Never had this been done, but like a fiend
> Thou temptedst me with ceaseless devilish thoughts.
> Therefore I curse with bitterness of soul
> The hour wherein I saw thy baleful eyes.
> My eyes I curse for looking on those eyes!
> My ears I curse for hearkening to thy tongue!
> I curse thy tongue for tempting of mine ears!
> Each part I curse, that we call thine or mine;
> Thine for enticing mine, mine [for] following thine!
> <div align="right">[<i>Death</i> I.iii]</div>

364   THE HYBRID IMAGE IN SERIOUS DRAMA

But Doncaster is immune to curses, mocking them just as he mocks death itself; for his last words as he is led out to be hanged are a derisive "I thank you, sir" to his judge. What is more important, however, is the nature of his villainy as he himself proclaims it. It is his profession, his crime against Robin Hood being merely the latest product of a career devoted to nothing else. When he is accused of having ravished "Sir Eustace Stutville's chaste and beauteous child," he not only hastens to confirm the charge but delivers as well his whole moral pedigree in the style and with the zest that previously belonged to the Vice:

> I have a thousand more than she defil'd,
> And cut the squeaking throats of some of them—
> I grieve I did not hers.

His "thousand" might just as well be a million, for he inherits the universal range of his allegorical ancestor.

Another example comes to us out of *The First Part of Jeronimo* (1603?), which capitalized on the popularity of *The Spanish Tragedy* by offering, several years later, a dramatization of events preliminary to those in Kyd's play.[16] It opens with the King of Spain's appointment of an ambassador to claim from Portugal the tribute due and denied. Several candidates claim the post, among them Lorenzo, but it goes to Andrea, a gentleman full of virtue and honor. The preferment refused him makes Lorenzo a villain, just as it does Iago, and his first words seek out the audience:

> So, so Andrea must be sent imbassador?
> Lorenzo is not thought vpon: good,
> Ile wake the Court, or startle out some bloud.
> [I.i.70–72] [17]

An evil nature has its motive and its victim, and both are morally plausible—up to this point. But the end of the scene finds Lorenzo left alone for a long speech through which the homiletic method and the Psychomachia come flooding. It is outright homily, spoken by a villain inverted into a preacher, a technique which is normal only to a moral personification:

> Andreas gone embassador;
> Lorenzo is not drempt on in this age;
> Hard fate,

THE HYBRID IMAGE IN SERIOUS DRAMA 365

> When villaines sit not in the highest state.
> Ambitions plumes, that florisht in our court,
> Seuere authority has dasht with iustice;
> And pollicy and pride walke like two exiles,
> Giuing attendance, that were once attended,
> And we reiected that were once high honored.
>
> [I.i.97–105]

And in the remainder of this monologue the war of vice against virtue gets its literal reproduction, unenveloped by the art which in Shakespeare bemuses us with personality and poetry:

> I hate Andrea, cause he aimes at honor,
> When my purest thoughts work in a pitchy vale,
> Which are as different as heauen and Hell.
> One peeres for day, the other gappes for night.
>
> . . .
>
> Hee loues my sister; that shall cost his life;
> So she a husband, he shall lose a wife.
> O sweete, sweete pollicie, I hugg thee; good:
> Andreas Himens draught shall be in bloud.
>
> [I.i.106–24]

We need not go into Lorenzo's villainy, since he belongs with the foregoing examples, in which the dramatic pattern established by the Vice is prominent not in action but in the homiletic method on its verbal level. This emphasis is reversed, however, in another play, where the stage image out of the morality drama survives in a figure who has relatively little to say but a great deal to do. He is Roderick Duke of Orléans in *The Trial of Chivalry* (c. 1600), the popular ingredients of which are romantic love, knightly virtue, self-sacrificing friendship, and the patriotic comedy of "Caualiero Dicke Bowyer," who proves the English superiority over the French in both love and war. Warfare between the Kings of France and Navarre gives the plot its setting, and the opposed encampments of the two armies give the action its scene. Athwart this conflict, however, lies another—between love and war itself. The martial alignment is intersected by the love of Philip the Dauphin for Bellamira, daughter of Navarre, and by the same passion felt by Ferdinand, Navarre's son, for Katharina, daughter of the French King. All four are determined that war and politics must submit to love, and in an unusual scene the two young knights, together with

366 THE HYBRID IMAGE IN SERIOUS DRAMA

the Earl of Pembroke, flower of English chivalry, keep the opposing armies apart by force of their unaided valor.

This love which crosses the business of state is itself crossed by several complications. When Pembroke woos Katharina in behalf of Ferdinand, she finds him more attractive than his client. The latter, momentarily repulsed by her, turns violently against his friend, and the strong bond between the two men is severely tested. The other love affair also has its troubles, brought on by the passion, mixed with ambition, that the wicked Constable Bourbon feels for Bellamira. When she rejects him he smears her face with a poison that ruins her complexion. Philip nobly insists on marrying her, but she, no less nobly, runs away from him and from her family. In the end her face is restored by magic ointment, Pembroke and Ferdinand are restored to friendship, the latter restored to his Katharina, and peace restored between France and Navarre.

At the source of all the evil that frustrates love and peace is the aforesaid Roderick, whose scant and cryptic utterance, as he moves from one contrivance to another, covers the naked role of the Vice with only the barest shreds of rationalization. Like the Vice of the later hybrid plays, he offers vague and fleeting explanations that have to do with his advantage, but they are obviously the flimsiest accommodation to a set performance, disappearing with the words that utter them. He is the jeering enemy of every value the play upholds and of everyone it contains, and his indictment just before Philip kills him is compact rather than complete:

> Thou wert a party in all Burbons wrongs,
> Falsely term'd Ferdinand a Ravisher.
> Set discord 'twixt these kings,
> Practised my death.
>
> [V.ii] [18]

Discord is his achievement—the discord that destroys love and peace—and deceit his method, and his obituary so defines him:

> in him all hatred ends:
> The kings will now love peace, and soone be friends.
>
> [V.ii]

His obituary, however, since it belongs to the moral and dramatic dimension of the play, cannot define what he really is—the embodiment

THE HYBRID IMAGE IN SERIOUS DRAMA   367

of a stock aggression inorganic to the story, repeating itself with mechanical rigidity against one victim after another.

At the start of the play it is he who, for no discernible reason, urges war when a truce is in the offing. Later he actually creates war when out of a clear sky he announces to both sides that Navarre's Ferdinand has attempted to ravish France's Katharina, his purpose in this lie having no further substance than what can be found in the following, characteristic, monologue:

> Ha, ha! I laugh to see these kings at jarr.
> Now civill discord, like a raging floud
> Swelling above her banks, shall drowne this land
> Whilst Rodoricke on her ruines builds his hopes.
> The king of Fraunce, through my suggestion,
> Thinks Katherine his daughter ravished,
> Who onely, winged with love, is fled the Campe.
> Pembrooke and Ferdinand, in mutual strife,
> Slayne by eche other doth confirme my words
> And for revenge whets keene the two Kings swords.
>
> $\qquad$ [III.iii]

What his "hopes" are we shall never learn. They are only a forged passport, under an assumed name, to get the role into a play that is not a morality. Although for another stratagem his explanation is rather more specific, it has neither background nor continuity but lives and dies in a single speech. As Bourbon's friend he suggests to him the villainous revenge the other takes on Bellamira, and turns aside to inform the audience:

> Well howsoever I smooth it to the Duke
> My thoughts are bent on his destruction.
>
> $\qquad$ [I.i]

For this piece of deceit he offers his "reason" immediately after the deed:

> Zounds, he has don't: now, Rodorick, joy thy fill.
> Burbon is thine, the Dukedome is thine owne,
> For only he in the Inheritance
> Stood as an obstacle to let my clayme.
> This deed of his will take away his life:
> And then let me alone to enjoy his land.
>
> $\qquad$ [II.ii]

368   THE HYBRID IMAGE IN SERIOUS DRAMA

For this motive, as for any other, his role is rocky soil, however, and a later stratagem uproots it. He suddenly appears to Philip, who has cause enough against Bourbon, and entices him with an opportunity for revenge, offering to lead him into Bourbon's tent and to beguile Bourbon into the ambush; for which Philip promises him—

> if my complot take effect,
> Ile make thee Duke of Burbon.
>
> [V.i]

So far so good, but the next moment, when he leaves Philip within the tent, his aside must astonish anyone unfamiliar with his lineage: "Kill you the Duke (and after Ile kill thee)." And this, after Philip kills Bourbon, he tries most zealously to do to the man who has promised to make him the next Duke of Bourbon:

> *Rod.* Murder! murder! Burbon the Duke is slayne!
> *Phil.* Peace, Rodorick, I am Philip thy deare friend.
> *Rod.* Thou art a counterfet, I know thee not.
>
> [V.i.]

And so it goes, until he is surrounded and killed, defiant and unrepentant. It is impossible to read the play without being struck by the fact that from first to last his deceits and betrayals are so many beads on a string, and that they get their impetus from a dramatic formula to which motives, even when they do appear in his words, have no intrinsic relation. They are superfluous because beneath them his villainy is self-sufficient in the dimension of homiletic display. Because the talent that wrought him was meager he illustrates starkly the problem that stares at naturalistic criticism as a result of the confluence of an allegorical and a literal drama in the late years of the sixteenth century and the early years of the seventeenth. The stage image shaped and intrenched by metaphor in the moral plays persists in the secular drama, creating a succession of figures who participate in both worlds, creatures of a hybrid tradition from which the drama did not completely disengage itself in Shakespeare's day. When we turn to his plays we find that it is their tradition also.

7

We will follow our theme into Shakespeare with better understanding, however, if we resist the temptation to do so at once. An intervening

THE HYBRID IMAGE IN SERIOUS DRAMA 369

consideration, lacking which we lack perspective, concerns the gradual suppression of the image of the Vice by the sway of an alien dramatic environment. On a stage that has become literal, that steadily forsakes the techniques of its homiletic past as it increasingly commits itself to the naturalistic imitation of concrete events and human personality, the tenacious stereotype shaped by metaphor suffers slow but constant attrition. The human nature he dons, like the shirt of Nessus, consumes by degrees the personification underneath, and the rigid method of the Psychomachia crumbles against the circumstantial variety of dramatized history and legend. In this process of transfiguration, continuous through Shakespeare's career and beyond, the hybrid figures we have seen, as well as others we have not, are stages simply. Spaced over half a century, they form a spectrum of transition from the white light of abstraction to the moral colors of human passion and appetite. Our concern now is with the steady erosion of "the old Vice" in this hybrid by the naturalistic details that flow upon it, instinctively obedient to the current of the popular stage. For this purpose we return to the four figures examined earlier—Barabas, Edricus, Eleazar, and Clois Hoffman—in order to notice some of the gradations of change that make Hoffman in 1602 less obviously the Vice than Barabas in 1589–90. This partial conversion over thirteen or fourteen years tells us much about the several Shakespearian roles that partake of the old convention, and also of the difference between them—between Aaron the Moor, for instance, in 1592–93 and Iago in 1604.

The effect of tragedy is to sharpen the disparity we have been tracing through these chapters. Grief and hatred are serious emotions and require, by naturalistic standards, correlative seriousness in the behavior of persons possessed by them, especially when such persons inhabit the fatal scene of Elizabethan tragedy, which never "lacks deaths" and rarely inhibits the display of feeling. Passion offered to author and actor a verbal opportunity they grasped *con amore*, and often by both, as we know even without Hamlet's testimony, got torn to tatters. The set "speech of fire" through which suffering found its vent, known to the theatrical trade as "a passion," was constantly the playwright's effort and the audience's expectation. Old Hieronimo's lament for his son ("Oh eies! no eies but fountains fraught with tears") or Tamburlaine's for his Zenocrate ("Raving, impatient, desperate, and mad") illustrate,

370   THE HYBRID IMAGE IN SERIOUS DRAMA

at its beginning, a rhetorical mode that left its impress on almost every Elizabethan tragedy. Only when we come to some of the best of Shakespeare's silences does this convention give way to a greater subtlety for sorrow:

> What, man! Ne'er pull your hat upon your brows.
> Give sorrow words. The grief that does not speak
> Whispers the o'erfraught heart and bids it break.
>   [*Macbeth* IV.iii.208–10]

One part of the radical trouble afflicting the role of Barabas lies in the discord between the emotional gravity of the earlier figure—

> You partiall heauens, haue I deseru'd this plague?
> What will you thus oppose me, lucklesse Starres,
> To make me desperate in my pouerty?
> And knowing me impatient in distresse,
> Thinke me so mad as I will hang my selfe,
> That I may vanish ore the earth in ayre
> And leaue no memory that e're I was.
>   [ll. 494–500]

—and the absence of such sentiments in him during the last three acts (except for his dying curses). It is not the pleasure of revenge that breaks the mood of his role, for such a pleasure is serious and has its place in tragedy. What he loses is emotional caliber, replaced by a menial alacrity in word and action that is altogether comic. He is too busy with too many murderous contrivances to be distracted by an adequate sense of provocation for any of them. Lugging a pot of poisoned porridge, decked out as a French musician with a lute in his hand and a poisoned nosegay in his hat, bustling about his trapdoor with a carpenter's hammer, or welcoming Calymath to death with fleering dissimulation ("How the slaue jeeres at him"), he is disjoined absolutely from that kind of passional sentience that animates the original figure.

The foregoing, however, is only a naturalistic criticism and not particularly useful in the historical method of this study. More significant than the obvious disparity is the degree of assimilation. The earlier Vice, while equally pernicious, was much more frivolous, much less dignified. Not only has he been reclothed by tragedy in literal garments, he has also been relatively subdued by the tragic temper in

THE HYBRID IMAGE IN SERIOUS DRAMA 371

these plays. The horseplay and strident jesting are largely gone, along with the doggerel utterance now replaced by blank verse. Gone also are the more obvious verbal tricks and the more blatant obscenities. He has been stripped of his fustian patter and the gross physical humor of his gestures and brawls. The wide range of his coarse ebullience and a good deal of his raucous hilarity have been contracted by the pressure of his new seriousness. Even apart from his fusion with passion and provocation, even when he remains most obviously the Vice, the tone of his performance has acquired a notable increment of gravity compared to what formerly he was. And this assimilation is progressive over the span of time containing the four plays that now concern us. The disjunction of mood we find in Barabas is much less stark in Chettle's Hoffman, although that role has none of Marlowe's power, because there it is not so massively stratified. Not only are the elements of difference modulated in the later play, they also mingle in diffusion, almost every scene providing an emulsion of both the naturalistic avenger and the Vice. In fact the task of analysis and discrimination becomes increasingly difficult as it moves through time, confronting the slow dilution of the older image.

When measured against each other in respect to structure, again allowing for Marlowe's distinctive genius, these two plays chart the same direction of change. Structurally the first two acts of *The Jew of Malta* belong to the Elizabethan drama's naturalistic future, but they give way to its homiletic past. They give way, in other words, to a succession of episodes—to the serialized structure of repeated exemplification wherein against a parade of victims villainous deceit remains on display in a variety of forms. These episodes do not contribute to an organic plot because essentially they are an accumulation rather than a development. Marlowe, it is true, gives to each its provocative logic, sheathing it within the narrative meaning of literal story, for he is writing on that level also. Barabas poisons Abigail and the nuns because he can rely no longer on his daughter's silence; he tricks the two friars to death because he discovers they know too much; when Ithamore betrays and blackmails him he poisons Ithamore along with Bellamira and Pilia Borza; he betrays Malta to the Turks for reasons old and new; and he betrays the Turks in turn for the sake, as he says, of his profit and safety in Malta. But in these successive

372   *THE HYBRID IMAGE IN SERIOUS DRAMA*

events we detect the absence of genuine dramatic movement. Alongside the literal purpose within them, a rival purpose works in a different direction, and this part of the play forsakes the architectonic of action and character for the older homiletic method that enforces a moral point through repetitive display. By contrast *The Tragedy of Hoffman* achieves relative unity of action, marking a naturalistic advance toward essential dramatic action as we appraise it today. The successive stratagems of the Vice-avenger are all mounted on a single foundation, the comprehensive program of revenge that spans the plot. Unlike the scenic contrivance of Marlowe's play which makes its second part the obvious vehicle of the Vice, his movements in *Hoffman* obey, at least in essential outline, the pace and direction inherent in the revenge plot itself.

His partial transformation also modifies the homiletic principle in his role: he becomes less of a monologuist. His moral expositions, formerly confined to the ears of his audience, begin to recede into more naturalistic perspective by addressing themselves occasionally to some hearer on the stage. The moral vita with which Avarice once edified the playgoer becomes the pedigree of villainy Barabas recites to Ithamore. Edricus shares his stratagems with his servant Stitch. Between Clois Hoffman and his tool Lorrique there is the compact of candid villainy. Not only do these subalterns give homiletics a hearing inside the play, they also share the didactic burden in respect to the audience. Ithamore is an abridged edition of his master, the Vice in duodecimo, when he unrolls his own catalogue of iniquities or lectures the spectators on the latest stratagem achieved:

> Why, was there euer seene such villany.
> So neatly plotted, and so well perform'd?
> Both held in hand, and flatly both beguil'd?
>   [ll. 1220–22]

And so is Lorrique, who needs no prompting to evil ("Let me alone for plots and villany"), when he interprets the moral situation to the audience:

> Ile post vnto the Hermitage, and smile
> While silly fooles act treason through my guile.
>   [ll. 1321–22]

THE HYBRID IMAGE IN SERIOUS DRAMA 373

These tool villains, diminished copies of the same image stamped on their masters, represent a technical innovation of some consequence. Farce, which in the climate of tragedy slowly evaporates out of the Vice, does not actually depart from the play. It survives in the *sotteries* of such underlings, each a sliver of the old Vice, split off to free the major figure from impediments. They contribute to the development of the tragic process by supplying the absolute need for comic diversion in early Elizabethan tragedy while permitting the Vice, now a nobleman or merchant-prince, some accession of sobriety and decorum. They also contribute a new element of complication and flexibility to the old stratagems by doubling the conspiratorial manpower. In the end they die, as much the victim of the Vice's mechanical duplicity as any other dupe. The only reason Stitch does not reach his death is that *Edmond Ironside* does not reach its conclusion, only the first half surviving out of a two-part play. These secondary figures, Ithamore, Stitch, Lorrique, are almost identical offsets from a single formula of accommodation.

We can pursue this process of naturalistic accommodation a step further through a verbal detail. The word *policy,* as in every Elizabethan dramatization of "state villainy," is rife in the language of all four plays. Each is directly concerned with the behavior of "great ones" in the affairs of state, where *policy* has its most pertinent, though not exclusive, Elizabethan application. The word is older than the sixteenth century, but only from about 1550 onward does it become charged with pejorative meaning and expand into furious general use. In the dictionary of Elizabethan ideas it is an important trisyllabic, expressing as it does the acute contemporary awareness of the Renaissance by the Renaissance, especially of the political import in the great transvaluation of values then taking place. The Christian concept of society and government as earthly adumbrations of the Divine plan and as instruments of religious purpose felt just then the challenge of those secular absolutes that have since come to dominate the modern world. Derived from the same religious principle, the chivalric code of honorable overtness, whether killing an enemy or governing the state, confronted at the same time the rival doctrine of the new *natural* man, for whom the end justified any means in a world that was not God's

374   THE HYBRID IMAGE IN SERIOUS DRAMA

garden, however ruined, but nature's jungle. Although here and there
an Elizabethan radical, child of the future, could argue that *policy* is
inevitably the real mechanism of state beneath all pious professions, he
made the mistake, characteristic of the realist, of confusing standards
with practices. The age as a whole was making a more agonized transition from divine to secular sanctions, and we can glimpse the nature
of the issue in the following passage from the play of *Sir Thomas Wyatt*
(1602) which probes for their reconciliation:

> In actions roving from the bent of truth
> We have no precedent thus to persist
> But the bare name of worldly policy.
> If others have ground from justice and the law,
> As well divine as politic agreeing,
> They are for no cause to be disinherited.
>
> [p. 189] [19]

Policy, in other words, is the creature of this world's aims and goods,
the form that human energy takes when it is diverted from transcendental goals into competition for temporal objects: at its best it describes the foresight, indirection, and concealed intention of worldly
prudence; at its worst, devious and ruthless cunning unhampered by
moral scruple or religious conscience. Occasionally on the stage it was
a subject for comedy, as when Polonius, a decayed politician, is driven
by the habit of a lifetime to employ *policy* upon his son and "by in-
directions find directions out." But overwhelmingly, because of its intense association with Machiavelli, *policy* characterizes the behavior of
the villain who glories in the serpentine convolutions through which
he pursues power, wealth, or revenge.

In *The Jew of Malta,* it has been pointed out,[20] the word occurs
thirteen times, mainly in the utterance of Barabas as he moves through
his successive stratagems. It occurs at least as often in *Lust's Dominion,*
where Eleazar documents each of his conspirational successes by reference to his "reall policie," his "true pollicie," and his "pick-lock policie,
to whom all doors flye open." The voice of Edricus is practically never
without it as he pursues his "experiments of matchles pollicy." Hoffman is confident that nothing can "diuert my traine of pollicy." As
prominent as the word is in all these plays, however, its significance
need not be enlarged beyond the fact that the Vice has now climbed

THE HYBRID IMAGE IN SERIOUS DRAMA 375

into the society of "great men" and his performance has expanded to include the business of state. In both relationships the role has been stigmatized by a label, to which its essential character makes it acutely susceptible, that expresses the fashionable horror of Machiavellian *Realpolitik*. The older word, we recall, through which he vaunted his trickery was *gear*, for which *policy*, more applicable to the political theme which enters his evolving performance and more expressive of contemporary issues, is actually a later Elizabethan equivalent. When he survives in plays that are not political the word loses its iterated emphasis, and he is more likely to celebrate his *wit* than his *policy*.

Much the same point can be made about the renovation, whenever it occurs, of the old role by Machiavellianism in general. For all their distortion of his doctrine and their hysterical denigration of his character, the Elizabethans, standing as they did at the crossroads of two realities, probably grasped the import of the Florentine better than do we today, who have been carried four centuries out of sight of the great corner turned. That for us he is no longer of the Devil's party means chiefly that we have got rid of the Devil. For the sixteenth century, at least by inherited belief, the Devil was a vital and intelligible idea, the World his powerful ally, and worldlings the members of his party. By propounding the technique of worldly success without regard to any higher allegiance, Machiavelli elevated the most serious defect of human nature, from a Christian viewpoint, into a positive achievement. By defining power as the prize available to certain natural qualities he dissolved its divine auspices. By creating political science he abolished the religious principle in human society. The Elizabethans really understood him well enough, and indeed their traditional values within their transitional age taught them to apprehend the evil before they were actually aware of the man who later lent it his name. On their stage the Machiavellian villain, through his egoism, his ruthless energy unhampered by pious restraints, his deliberate disavowal of any law higher than his own appetite, his penetrating and cynical awareness of the animal impulses composing man's lower nature, enacts the thrust of the new *realism* against the traditional Christian sanctities applicable to the life of this world. Legitimacy, order, honor, loyalty, love, and the stable community of human creatures under God are the easy obstacles his purposes surmount because the pieties and simplicities of

376 THE HYBRID IMAGE IN SERIOUS DRAMA

honest men render them defenseless against his *policy*. It is a rare villain in the drama of that time who is not in some degree a Machiavel; for villainy in general, as the Elizabethans viewed and staged it, is rooted in an irreligious principle, to which the Florentine, from the same view, contributed not so much an origin as an affirmation, not so much a manifesto as a guidebook. The age was aware of Machiavellianism before it was aware of Machiavelli.

It was a normal consequence, therefore, that Machiavellian features should invade and qualify the four roles with which we are presently concerned, as well as others showing the same dramatic lineage. Barabas is certainly presented as the protégé of the Florentine, whose prologue begins the play and introduces its protagonist as one who "fauours me." Like prologues generally, this one spoken by "Macheuil" was probably written after the play itself and asks to be regarded as Marlowe's effective stroke of topical accommodation, his reformulation of the traditional stage image to match the climate of contemporary opinion and excitement.[21] The curious reader, it is true, will be struck by some discrepancy between the sentiments of master and disciple. Machiavel has only scorn for the pious legitimacy of hereditary rule:

> Many will talke of Title to a Crowne.
> What right had Caesar to the Empire?
> Might first made Kings, and Lawes were then most sure
> When like the Dracos they were writ in blood.
> [ll. 18–21]

But on the same theme Barabas expresses an opinion notably different:

> And Crownes come either by succession,
> Or vrg'd by force; and nothing violent,
> Oft haue I heard tell, can be permanent.
> [ll. 169–71]

And later in the play, after the Turks have made him governor of Malta, his reflections (ll. 2128–46) are remarkably un-Machiavellian as he rationalizes another act of treachery—this time against his Turkish benefactors—for deeper than the Florentine in his role is its prescriptive deceit, the only form of motion of which his dramatic life is capable. In the other three figures we can also discover the Machiavellian gloss, including a precise allusion in *Hoffman* and a very likely one in *Lust's Dominion*.[22] And it would not be wrong to apply the

THE HYBRID IMAGE IN SERIOUS DRAMA 377

same formula to all the Shakespearian figures participating in the same hybrid convention. Neither would it be very useful.

For the adjustment of the fissured role, on its moral side, to the conception of evil then sensationally current is only a topical detail of the naturalistic process at work upon it, and should no longer mislead us. To call such a figure a "Machiavellian villain," as a great deal of Elizabethan dramatic criticism is prone to do, explains almost nothing. Such a label hides the problem with a plaster. A villain is Machiavellian when he is morally organized to reach for some object by a method that obeys the precepts, or some lurid perversion of the precepts, of Machiavelli. But the side of Barabas and his brothers that troubles us is not morally organized at all; and if Machiavelli himself were dramatized the same way *he* would not be a Machiavellian villain for the simple reason that he would be cast in the homiletic dimension of a moral personification—one more version, in other words, of the Vice. The problem, to repeat, is not moral but dramaturgic, and in this fact Shakespeare's Richard of Gloucester instructs us. Where can we find another Elizabethan role that equals his in the right to be called Machiavellian? And he himself seems to arrogate that right at the close of a long monologue in *3 Henry VI* when, as climax to a series of comparisons (all the others classic) that proclaim his talent for deceit, he says:

> I can add colours to the chameleon,
> Change shapes with Proteus for advantages,
> And set the murtherous Machiavel to school.
> [III.ii.191–93]

Substantially the same speech appears elsewhere—in that variant text of the same play published in 1595 as *The True Tragedy of Richard Duke of York*. Whether *The True Tragedy* is a bad quarto of Shakespeare's play or an earlier version by another dramatist remains a subject for indefinite speculation, with the weight of evidence favoring the former view.[23] Whatever the relationship—the point is not material here—the corresponding lines to those above match Richard differently in *The True Tragedy:*

> I can adde colours to the Camelion,
> And for a need change shapes with Protheus,
> And set the aspiring Catalin to schoole.
> [p. 64] [24]

378 *THE HYBRID IMAGE IN SERIOUS DRAMA*

The sermon proper to these twin texts is that it is an indifferent matter in the role of Richard whether he outstrip "murtherous Machiavel" or "aspiring Catalin," the evil political allusion either way being sufficiently current and comprehensible. What does count is that in such a monologue the speaker should make either revelation about himself. The exact pointing of the evil announced is only a tittle beside the theatrical tradition that makes this kind of announcement possible in the first place.

Serving us this way, Richard also serves us another: he knits the whole investigation into a circle by bringing it back to Shakespeare.

CHAPTER ELEVEN

THE HYBRID IMAGE
IN SHAKESPEARE

I

A good critic helps us everywhere, and the remark of Longinus that the *Odyssey* belongs to the old age of Homer makes us more hospitable toward *Titus Andronicus* as the work of the young Shakespeare. It is a better play than *The Two Gentlemen of Verona,* but its theme and the popular mode to which it aspired solicited from the playwright a treatment that shocks us. Other such shocks—that the distinguished scholar Thomas Preston should have written *Cambises,* or Marlowe the last three acts of *The Jew of Malta,* for example—inure us to the popular Elizabethan stage and help us get over this one. *Titus* is an Elizabethan tragedy of violent revenge in the popular style, in imitation of Seneca and with borrowings from Ovid. It is not the only violent play that Shakespeare wrote, but it is the earliest of them, and it troubles us more than the others because its violence is so stark, because it lacks the rich moral organization and poetic subtlety by which the later Shakespeare of *Hamlet* and *Macbeth* sublimed melodrama and murder. The action in *Titus* lurches like a brazen engine in a field of blood. Most of its sounds—there are lovely exceptions—belong to the rhetoric of passion or oratory, and most of its gestures are sword thrusts. We should remember that here Shakespeare handles a Roman story for the first time, and, like all Elizabethans, he was very conscious of the special quality of the Roman *virtus.* He is aiming for the kind of character that fits the *Imperium* and the Forum—the high fashion of the antique Roman—and if his Romans in this play succeed chiefly in being *high,* they do much better in others which come later.

More pleasing perhaps than anything the Romans say and do is Aaron's affection for his child, and Aaron, although a Moor, is the one important figure unmistakably in the native dramatic tradition—

380   *THE HYBRID IMAGE IN SHAKESPEARE*

both halves of him. As Kittredge observes, after he outlines the classical derivation of the play, "The classical sources, however, give us no hint of Aaron." Neither, for reasons already stated, does Machiavelli, in spite of the inclination of Kittredge and of critics almost universally to wrap him up as a "Machiavellian villain." If "Aaron is Shakespeare's master-stroke in Titus," as Dover Wilson says,[1] the compliment finds its proper object in the effective combination between the young playwright's powers and the theatrical image which descended to him from the allegorical stage.

Aaron is not always the Vice, of course, for he is a hybrid. The other part of him is properly Aaron the Moor—in his first soliloquy, his vicious counsel to Chiron and Demetrius, his relations with Tamora and with his child, in much of the play in fact. But the older stage image weaves in and out of him, and we can see it best by placing him alongside his partner in evil, the villainous Tamora. Her deeds are no better than his, but she, although not profoundly drawn, is perfectly credible. She is a bad character whom revenge sets in motion; and she does not need to protest her villainy, she acts it. Her actions, moreover, are organic to the plot, not a stylized performance based on premises outside it. As Queen of the Goths she is the natural enemy of Rome who "will charm Rome's Saturnine / And see his shipwrack and his commonweal's." As a captive led in triumph she is the natural enemy of her captors, the Andronici. Her sharper cause against them, a consistent theme throughout, is their sacrifice of her son Alarbus; and when she turns Lavinia over to her remaining sons her words agree with her sentiments everywhere in the play:

> Remember, boys, I pour'd forth tears in vain
> To save your brother from the sacrifice;
> But fierce Andronicus would not relent.
> Therefore away with her, and use her as you will;
> The worse to her, the better lov'd of me.
>
>   [II.iii.163–67]

Her wickedness stays in clear moral focus because it belongs *exclusively* to her character and her motives, and she is not a dramatic problem. The only time she threatens to become one, it is none of her doing, but when Aaron, with his homiletic voice, describes her as

THE HYBRID IMAGE IN SHAKESPEARE 381

our Empress, with her sacred wit
To villany and vengeance consecrate . . .
[II.i.120–21]

But these words, of which the paired nouns in the second line expose
the hyphenated role, tell us about Aaron, and the dimension in which
he is intermittently cast, not about Tamora.

In Aaron the homiletic projection and bravura demonstration of the
old morality role, still relatively unsubdued by the crescent naturalism
to which it is united, create once more the familiar hybrid. The old
metaphor is gone, of course, but its traditional stage features remain
and combine with the historical or legendary Moor who, along with
the rest of the plot, may have come to Shakespeare out of some story
now lost [2]—combine with him to theatricalize him according to the
established dramatic formula that still counted for more with the
popular audience than the human validity of which it deprived him.
When Titus, by a benevolent deception ("Come hither, Aaron, I'll
deceive them both"), manages that his own hand, rather than that
of Marcus or Lucius, is cut off to redeem his condemned sons, Aaron
has his text for a sneering commentary that distills the essence of the
role whose history we follow—the bravura deceit that was once a moral
metaphor for the insinuation of evil into the human heart, but is now
superficially grafted to a new rationale in revenge and ambition:

[Aside] If that be call'd deceit, I will be honest
And never whilst I live deceive men so.
But I'll deceive you in another sort,
And that you'll say ere half an hour pass.
                    He cuts off Titus' hand.
[III.i.189–92]

A moment later his words shape themselves into a late version of the
Vice's verbal trick, breathe the Vice's laughter upon the grief of his
victims, and engage the audience with a directness to which the edito-
rialized direction does scant justice:

I go, Andronicus, and for thy hand
Look by-and-by to have thy sons with thee.
[Aside] Their heads, I mean. O, how this villany
Doth fat me with the very thoughts of it!

THE HYBRID IMAGE IN SHAKESPEARE

> Let fools do good, and fair men call for grace,
> Aaron will have his soul black like his face.
>
> [III.i.201–206]

We need not doubt his laughter in this scene, even though it is not explicit in the text, for later he refers to it expressly when he boasts to Lucius of his versatile iniquity ("Well, let my deeds be witness of my worth"):

> I play'd the cheater for thy father's hand,
> And when I had it, drew myself apart
> And almost broke my heart with extreme laughter.
> I pried me through the crevice of a wall
> When for his hand he had his two sons' heads,
> Beheld his tears, and laugh'd so heartily
> That both my eyes were rainy like to his.
>
> [V.i.111–17]

This is exactly the mood of the inherited role, just as the deed itself remains for Aaron exactly what it has always been for the Vice—sport:

> And when I told the Empress of this sport,
> She sounded almost at my pleasing tale
> And for my tidings gave me twenty kisses.
>
> [V.i.118–20]

The moral effect of his actions, no less than their style and mood, bears the impress of the same inheritance. In addition to mischief of every kind through which his deceit and cunning can illustrate themselves, enmity and internecine strife are his special object and the special mark of his achievement. The play has a large political theme, the unity of Rome, which is emphatic in the opening scene with its turmoil of rivalry between Saturninus and Bassianus for the vacant throne—rivalry which carries to the edge of civil war before it is put to rest by the patriotic efforts of Marcus and Titus. When the bloody events at the end vacate the throne once more and throw the populace into confusion and terror, Marcus invokes them in language expounding the most urgent of Elizabethan political tenets, the need for internal order and unity:

> You sad-fac'd men, people and sons of Rome,
> By uproar sever'd, as a flight of fowl
> Scatt'red by winds and high tempestuous gusts,
> O, let me teach you how to knit again

THE HYBRID IMAGE IN SHAKESPEARE 383

> This scattered corn into one mutual sheaf,
> These broken limbs again into one body;
> Lest Rome herself be bane unto herself,
> And she whom mighty kingdoms cursy to,
> Like a forlorn and desperate castaway,
> Do shameful execution on herself.
>
> [V.iii.67–76]

Creating and sustaining this unity, for the time it lasts, is the reconciliation in the first scene between the houses of Andronicus and Saturninus, sincere on the one side even if only pretended on the other. Having become the wife of Saturninus, Tamora announces that "this day all quarrels die," and her husband, the new emperor, follows suit by proclaiming "a love-day." The royal pair invite the Andronici to a double marriage celebration and become, in turn, their guests for the hunt of the day following.

Aaron's "excellent piece of villany" has its social meaning as an assault upon this harmony. He lays his snare for the sake of "their unrest / That have their alms out of the Empress' chest," and we shall see that one part of his vocational agenda consists in setting "deadly enmity between two friends." His contrivance incriminates the innocent sons of Titus in the murder of the Emperor's brother and is at the heart of a train of events inciting the Emperor to tyranny and the Andronici to rebellion and regicide. The deception by which he persuades Andronicus to cut off his own right hand is the straw that breaks the patience of Lucius and makes him leader of the Goths against Rome. In effect he pours the sweet milk of concord into hell, his achievement this way being standard for the role of the Vice in any morality with political or social implications, according to the bald formula expressed by Cloaked Collusion in *Magnificence*: "I sowe sedycyous sedes of Dyscorde and debates." [3]

In nothing, however, does his heritage reveal itself more clearly than in its liquidation of the conventional motives that naturalize him to the play as Aaron the Moor, follower and lover of evil Tamora as well as a criminal in his own right. Except for the moment he utters them they are everywhere annulled in his performance by its homiletic dimension and traditional impetus. The conventional ambition that appears in his adjuration to himself "To mount aloft with thy imperial mistress" and the conventional vengeance in his vague rhetoric to her

384   THE HYBRID IMAGE IN SHAKESPEARE

about "Blood and revenge . . . hammering in my head" not only
have neither coherence with his behavior nor even verbal endurance in
his utterance, they are sunk fathoms deep by the mood and method of
villainy for the sake of homiletic display. In the archaic stratum of his
performance his wickedness is neither acquisitive nor retaliatory; it is
demonstrative—a serial exhibition perpetuating the veteran stage image
of almost two centuries. His behavior has its absolute meaning in his
self-proclaimed villainy—that composite homiletic label which replaces,
of necessity, the exposition of his name and nature by the Vice of the
moralities. Shaped by the same homiletic perspective, his stratagems
exist, not as instruments of practical purpose, but as illustrations of a
talent in villainous deceit that, by his traditional intimacy with them, he
invites the audience to acknowledge:

> He that had wit would think that I had none
> To bury so much gold under a tree
> And never after to inherit it.
> Let him that thinks of me so abjectly
> Know that this gold must coin a stratagem,
> Which, cunningly effected, will beget
> A very excellent piece of villany.
>
> [II.iii.1–7]

Even more destructive of his moral status as a person with passions
and motives is his *moral pedigree* as he recites it in the fifth act. It is
overwhelming testimony to his lineage, being one more version of the
stylized rhetoric of exposure by which the Vice explains his aggressive
business in the play as just another example of his characteristic activity
always and everywhere. Barabas and Edricus, as we saw, translate into
literal villainies the precise method of this homiletic rhetoric, and in
Aaron we have it once more—the long speech of evil explication which
universalizes and immortalizes the Vice. No longer in naked intimacy
with the audience, he declaims it in response to the question of Lucius,
his captor: "Art thou not sorry for these heinous deeds?" after Aaron
has gleefully itemized his villainies throughout the play. But Aaron is
sorry only for his lack of industry:

> Ay, that I had not done a thousand more.
> Even now I curse the day (and yet I think
> Few come within the compass of my curse)
> Wherein I did not some notorious ill:

THE HYBRID IMAGE IN SHAKESPEARE

As kill a man, or else devise his death;
Ravish a maid, or plot the way to do it;
Accuse some innocent, and forswear myself;
Set deadly enmity between two friends;
Make poor men's cattle break their necks;
Set fire on barns and haystacks in the night
And bid the owners quench them with their tears.
Oft have I digg'd up dead men from their graves
And set them upright at their dear friends' door
Even when their sorrow almost was forgot,
And on their skins, as on the bark of trees,
Have with my knife carved in Roman letters
'Let not your sorrow die, though I am dead.
Tut, I have done a thousand dreadful things
As willingly as one would kill a fly;
And nothing grieves me heartily indeed
But that I cannot do ten thousand more.

[V.i.124–44]

In all these words we hear a personification speaking according to the formula of self-exposure once requisite for such a speaker on the abstract and didactic stage. The fifth, sixth, and seventh lines, let us notice, exactly document his activity in the play—against Bassianus, against Lavinia, and against the two sons of Titus; and the eighth decribes his divisive enterprise as we have already reviewed it. They also tell us all we need to know about the meaning of this activity and the source of its energy: it springs from what he everlastingly is and always does. The whole speech saturates his behavior with its allegorical explanation, and into this plenum motives such as revenge or ambition have no entry. They exist, of course, just as they exist for other figures we have examined, being part of the literal vesture without which the old role is no longer viable. But they have no real affinity with his mood and impetus, which imitate, not human life, but an entrenched theatrical image originating in metaphor.

Also, like the other members of his race who survive in the literal and serious drama, Aaron is homiletically fond of diabolic bravado: "If there were devils, would I were a devil." No less a sign of the unnaturalistic convention in his role is the bravery of his end. He confronts the ingenious torment awaiting him with a defiance that justifies nothing, extenuates nothing, repents nothing, but flaunts instead the

386 THE HYBRID IMAGE IN SHAKESPEARE

archaic allegiance of a performance whose meaning lies a world away from revenge or ambition. His last words transform, without concealing, the Vice's allegorical immunity to destruction and his inviolable commitment to his allegorical *property and kind*. In Aaron they become the Villain's unswerving addiction to villainy and his regret for nothing except the cessation of his enterprise on earth:

> I am no baby, I, that with base prayers
> I should repent the evils I have done.
> Ten thousand worse than ever yet I did
> Would I perform if I might have my will.
> If one good deed in all my life I did,
> I do repent it from my very soul.
>
> [V.iii.185–90]

A decade later, Iago, no longer able to say as much by way of valediction, says nothing.

2

By scholarship's best reckoning *Richard III* belongs to 1592–93, with good likelihood, therefore, that it is separated by not much more than a year from the composition of *Titus Andronicus*. Richard's opening lines—

> Now is the winter of our discontent
> Made glorious summer by this sun of York,
> And all the clouds that low'rd upon our house
> In the deep bosom of the ocean buried.

—except that they are better, duplicate the cadence and sentiment of the choric exposition with which Aaron begins his role:

> Now climbeth Tamora Olympus' top,
> Safe out of Fortune's shot, and sits aloft,
> Secure of thunder's crack or lightning flash,
> Advanc'd above pale envy's threat'ning reach.
>
> [II.i.1–4]

Furthermore, a locution that in the first part of *Henry VI*, unquestionably earlier than either of these plays, appears as

> She's beautiful, and therefore to be woo'd;
> She is a woman, and therefore to be won.
>
> [V.iii.78–79]

THE HYBRID IMAGE IN SHAKESPEARE 387

becomes for Aaron:

> She is a woman, therefore may be woo'd;
> She is a woman, therefore may be won;
> She is Lavinia, therefore must be lov'd.
> [II.i.82–84]

and is improved by Richard into

> Was ever woman in this humour woo'd?
> Was ever woman in this humour won?
> [I.ii.227–28]

Such links between the two plays are slight, but there is another of heavier metal. The features of the morality convention that survive in Aaron also survive, with but slightly diminished vitality, in Richard, and project him homiletically as another exponent of the art and achievement of villainy. This is not to say that he is less vital a creation than Aaron, for the reverse is true. Richard's is by all odds the greater role, and he dominates his play as Aaron, who is only a supporting member of a plot concerned with the suffering and revenge of Titus Andronicus, does not dominate his. We need, however, to discriminate the degree of homiletic starkness that survives in Richard from Shakespeare's brilliant exploitation of it. It is not only naturalism that makes great art possible, as we learn from a good deal of modern painting; and in this case the poet's crescent powers thrive on a waning image that is not naturalistic. By comparison with Aaron, Richard shows a slight but obvious dilution of the characteristics that come to him out of homiletic allegory, while at the same time enjoying them to much finer effect. What remains in him of the old role has wonderful *élan* and richness—Shakespeare's *élan* and richness—but it is also less radical in its nature and method.

The idea of Richard that the Elizabethans drew out of tradition and chronicle need not concern us except incidentally. He was morally organized by the history that Shakespeare knew as a very bad man of great energy and cunning, whose "execrable desire of sovereignty," as Sir Thomas More phrased it, led him from one outrage to another on his way to the throne, and also while sitting on it desperately. He was "malicious, wrathful, envious, and, from afore his birth, ever forward" —this last a reference to the legend that he was born feet first and

388   *THE HYBRID IMAGE IN SHAKESPEARE*

precociously equipped with teeth. His crimes, both personal and political, have their correlative aspect in his character as it is drawn by More and repeated with only trivial variation by Hall and Holinshed:

He was close and secret, a deep dissimulator, lowly of countenance, arrogant of heart, outwardly compinable [affable] where he inwardly hated, not letting to kiss whom he thought to kill; dispiteous and cruel, not for evil will always, but ofter for ambition, and either for the surety or increase of his estate.[4]

This moral portrait, along with the events it explains, is also available to us in Shakespeare's play, which amplifies or foreshortens the chronicles while remaining faithful to them, often literally. John Milton observed as much when he remarked that "throughout the whole Tragedie . . . the Poet us'd not much licence in departing from the truth of History." [5] But while the play does not do violence to the early historical estimate of Richard's character, it does do something which was not in Milton's province to observe. From time to time it has recourse to a dramatic method that has no relevance to either history or character, imitates neither, and, in fact, abrogates both.

Strictly speaking, then, to the extent that the play actually characterizes the historical Richard the role offers no problem that concerns us. Nor does one arise from the fact that Richard has continuous existence through three plays, the last two parts of *Henry VI* and *Richard III* itself. The *character* of Richard remains consistent with itself from first to last. His end fulfills his beginning, and the tyrant who dies at Bosworth is incipient in "Dicky your boy, that with his grumbling voice / Was wont to cheer his dad in mutinies." Already in *2 Henry VI* his valor makes him formidable, and so does his portentous mirth, chilling an enemy with its glint of death:

> *Young Clif.* And so to arms, victorious father,
>   To quell the rebels and their complices!
> *Rich.*   Fie! charity, for shame! Speak not in spite,
>   For you shall sup with Jesu Christ to-night.
> *Young Clif.* Foul stigmatic, that's more than thou canst tell.
> *Rich.*   If not in heaven, you'll surely sup in hell.
>   [V.i.211–16]

In both the earlier plays he thrusts through every obstacle of man and circumstance with that murderous alacrity and sovereignty of nature

THE HYBRID IMAGE IN SHAKESPEARE   389

which later send him crashing toward the throne, the only object that can finally sate his potency. From his first appearance his steel is distinguished from the softer metal of his kin and associates. His voice is peremptory and his betters heed it. His will is larger than theirs, and when his brother Edward and his uncle Montague demand their precedence over him in speaking to the Duke of York, they do not get it. It is he, not they, who sways the reluctant York, with casuistry and Marlovian glamour, to break his covenant and renew his effort for the throne:

> An oath is of no moment, being not took
> Before a true and lawful magistrate
> That hath authority over him that swears.
> Henry had none, but did usurp the place.
> Then, seeing 'twas he that made you to depose,
> Your oath, my lord, is vain and frivolous.
> Therefore, to arms! And, father, do but think
> How sweet a thing it is to wear a crown,
> Within whose circuit is Elysium
> And all that poets feign of bliss and joy.
> Why do we linger thus? I cannot rest
> Until the white rose that I wear be dy'd
> Even in the lukewarm blood of Henry's heart.
> [*3 Henry VI* I.ii.22–34]

He cannot rest—that is a main point about him, and his energy is fearful. While others talk before a battle he cries, "For God's sake, lords, give signal to the fight." In the short scene (*3 Henry VI* IV.v) in which he snatches Edward away from the custody of the Archbishop of York, his voice is a bell above the prattle of rescuers and rescued: "Brother, the time and case requireth haste" and "But wherefore stay we? 'Tis no time to talk" and "Come then, away. Let's ha' no more ado." When Queen Margaret, stricken by the loss of Barnet Field and the murder of her son before her eyes, asks for death, his dagger is upon her at once, only too prompt to render her that service—"Why should she live to fill the world with words?"—so that his brothers have to restrain him. Parried one way, his inspiration thrusts another in an instant, and he is off with no further explanation than a cry: "The Tower, the Tower!" The Tower holds old King Henry. Richard's brothers, left at Barnet, can talk while he is doing:

> *K. Edw.* Where's Richard gone?
> *Clar.*   To London, all in post; and, as I guess,

390   *THE HYBRID IMAGE IN SHAKESPEARE*

> To make a bloody supper in the Tower.
> *K. Edw.* He's sudden if a thing comes in his head.
>
> [*3 Henry VI* V.v.83–86]

The difference between him and Edward shows all the neat juxtaposition of a formal design. When a messenger brings them the news of their father's death, their reactions are matched opposites:

> *Edw.* O, speak no more, for I have heard too much!
> *Rich.* Say how he died, for I will hear it all.
>
> [*3 Henry VI* II.i.48–49]

The recital continues, therefore, and leaves Edward in tears, prostrate with despair, wishing to die: "Never, O never, shall I see more joy." Richard, in patterned contrast, is a furnace whose element is fire:

> I cannot weep, for all my body's moisture
> Scarce serves to quench my furnace-burning heart;
>
> . . . .
>
> To weep is to make less the depth of grief.
> Tears, then, for babes; blows and revenge for me!
>
> [II.i.79–86]

Edward is not weak, but he is unconcentrated, addicted to other things beside the throne—love, compassion, society, pleasure. Richard is addicted to nothing else. He serves up the crown to others, his father and his brother, like a chef who knows only one dish, until his own appetite gets the better of him. His single passion is made to turn upon a psychological point which also has contrasted reference to Edward. The elder brother is handsome, affable, gallant, his life mollified by the company of women and diverted by "stately triumphs, mirthful comic shows." But Richard, the foul stigmatic whose warped body and ugly face cut him off from all gentle commerce with humanity, concentrates his intense spirit upon the felicity of power and upon the golden round which is its badge. Since, unlike Edward, he cannot have love, a subtle form of power, he will have power in its most blatant form and most eminent degree. Since he cannot abolish the disabilities with which others taunt him throughout three plays, he will disable the taunters and triumph over the world of grace and beauty. It is exactly right that his first avowal of his regal aim, the long soliloquy beginning "Ay, Edward will use women honourably!" should be provoked by Edward's dalliance with Lady Grey:

THE HYBRID IMAGE IN SHAKESPEARE   391

> Well, say there is no kingdom then for Richard:
> What other pleasure can the world afford?
> I'll make my heaven in a lady's lap
> And deck my body in gay ornaments
> And witch sweet ladies with my words and looks.
> O miserable thought! and more unlikely
> Than to accomplish twenty golden crowns!
> Why, love forswore me in my mother's womb;
> And, for I should not deal in her soft laws,
> She did corrupt frail nature with some bribe
> To shrink mine arm up like a wither'd shrub;
> To make an envious mountain on my back,
> Where sits deformity to mock my body;
> To shape my legs of an unequal size;
> To disproportion me in every part,
> Like to a chaos, or an unlick'd bear-whelp,
> That carries no impression like the dam.
> And am I then a man to be belov'd?
> O monstrous fault to harbour such a thought!
> Then since this earth affords no joy to me
> But to command, to check, to o'erbear such
> As are of better person than myself,
> I'll make my heaven to dream upon the crown
> And, whiles I live, t'account this world but hell
> Until my misshap'd trunk that bears this head
> Be round impaled with a glorious crown.
>   [*3 Henry VI* III.ii.146–71]

The same general formula repeats itself twice in his later monologues, but with significant variations in detail to which we will
attend before long.

Much more could be said about the characterization Richard gets in
Henry VI, but perhaps the foregoing is enough to show that the same
man continues into the last part of Richard's trilogy. Whatever the
lapse of time between the completion of *3 Henry VI* and the writing of
Richard III—it cannot have been long—the shape of affairs in the later
play derives immediately from the earlier one and is closely knit up with
it. The speech of Edward which ends *Henry VI*—

> And now what rests but that we spend the time
> With stately triumphs, mirthful comic shows,
> Such as befits the pleasure of the court?
> Sound drums and trumpets! Farewell sour annoy!
> For here I hope begins our lasting joy.

—is exactly caught up by Richard in the first words of *Richard III:* his description of the "merry meetings" and "delightful measures," the gallantry and amorous sport, that have replaced "the winter of our discontent" with its war and rigor. His advance to the throne likewise proceeds in unbroken movement from his poised footfall at the end of *Henry VI,* where he announced, "Clarence, thy turn is next." For the turn of George of Clarence is indeed next in *Richard III,* in the first scene of which we see taking effect those prophecies respecting him and the letter "G" that Richard was just about to "buzz abroad" at the close of the earlier play. In every other way as well, including the whole complex of political circumstances, *Richard III* follows in tight sequence to the last part of *Henry VI.*

The moral portrait of Richard is no less continuous from one play to the other, if we disregard for the moment the intervention in both of the veteran dramatic image which is not, in fact, an aspect of his character, but rather the stock performance of our acquaintance, with its highly stylized homiletic bravura, that his character and stigmata invite. Disregarding this part of him, we discover that in his last play he is of a piece with what he has been before. He maintains his regal ambition, his enormous energy and sovereign force, his bonhomie and craft, to the end of his career. But after he reaches the throne events begin to harden against him. If he declines at intervals thereafter into a tyrant at bay, nervous and irascible, fearful, with good reason, of treachery, and on the night before Bosworth ghost-ridden and conscience-stricken—such or similar alterations in the heart are perfectly in keeping with Richard's mortal frailty.[6] They are, in fact, the common formula of intimation with which Shakespeare usually darkens the eve of disaster—as with the French before Agincourt, Macbeth before Dunsinane, Brutus before Philippi, and even Antony before Alexandria. If he confesses to the loss of "that alacrity of spirit" and "cheer of mind that I was wont to have," he acknowledges simply the turn in his life—he is fey; and Napoleon, dramatized by Shakespeare, might have made the same confession before Waterloo. And although he suffers the tyrant's destiny of having now everything to lose and nothing more to gain, Richard is Richard still in his last course. On the morning of battle he recovers completely from his trepidation of the night before and marshals his troops with his old dispatch and burly con-

THE HYBRID IMAGE IN SHAKESPEARE 393

fidence: "A thousand hearts are great within my bosom." The formula of his life and character remains clearly discernible even when he thrashes about, with animal fury, in the toils:

> I have set my life upon a cast
> And I will stand the hazard of the die.
> I think there be six Richmonds in the field;
> Five have I slain to-day instead of him.
> A horse! a horse! my kingdom for a horse.
> [V.iv.9–13]

What we see so far is something of the character of Richard as it maintains itself through all three plays in which he lives: the moral image of a formidable, if depraved, human nature, drawn from history and dramatized by the method of naturalistic art. What we have yet to see in combination with this image is another whose plastic stress transmutes the role, just as it does, in greater or less degree, all the others that have already come under review. For the playwright not only follows history, he *dramatizes* it for the theater; and he does so by the techniques native to his stage and unerring in their popular effect. The portrait of Richard in the chronicles, with its emphasis on his guile and depravity, invites and gets a dramatization in several notable scenes that reproduces once more the pungent *theatrical* image with which homiletic allegory endowed the popular stage. Shakespeare's rendition of Richard does not recast the historical figure, but from time to time it abrogates him entirely. It abrogates him because it applies to him the method of a performance designed originally for a timeless personification in a staged homily, not for a literal person in the moral dimension of human history.

Richard himself supplies the reference that documents this theatrical side of his lineage. Subjecting the young Prince Edward to the trick of verbal equivocation that identifies beyond peradventure the vested performance he imitates, he confirms the imitation by his comment immediately following and unmistakably directed to the audience:

> *Rich.* So wise so young, they say do never live long.
> *Prince.* What say you, uncle?
> *Rich.* I say, without characters fame lives long.
> [Aside] Thus, like the formal vice, Iniquity,
> I moralize two meanings in one word.
> [III.i.79–83]

394   THE HYBRID IMAGE IN SHAKESPEARE

To moralize two meanings in one word is, as we saw, a commonplace in the Vice's repertory of deceit, and Richard does not refer to any one version of the Vice. He refers rather to the composite role, for which *Iniquity,* a moral designation equally composite, became the common name after precise homiletic distinction between one Vice and another dissolved into the generalized figure who became a fixture of the stage. Thus one of the characters in Dekker's *Old Fortunatus,* evoking a recollection of the Vice, is addressed as "my little leane Iniquity." [7] Falstaff's affinity with the role is fortified by the description he gets as "that reverend vice, that grey iniquity." [8] It is the undiscriminated Vice of the moralities with the typical name of Iniquity who actually appears in Jonson's *The Devil Is an Ass,* before he is dismissed by the Devil as too old fashioned and ineffectual for the times:

> We must therefore ayme
> At extraordinary subtill ones now,
> When we doe send, to keep vs vp in credit,
> Not old Iniquities.
>
> [I.i.115–18]

And in the quotation from *The Staple of News* which begins the previous chapter the Vice is once more generalized as "Iniquity [who] came in like Hokos Pokos." [9]

It is not, therefore, the proper noun that carries the burden of Richard's meaning, but the adjective. In one of its common Elizabethan senses, "formal" means *conventional* or *regular,* and applies to anything which is unmistakable because it retains, to use Dr. Johnson's definition, "the proper and essential characteristic" of its informing nature, as in Cleopatra's advice to the messenger who brings her bad news:

> Thou shouldst come like a Fury crown'd with snakes,
> Not like a formal man.
>
> [*Antony and Cleopatra* II.v.39–40]

Richard uses the word to explain that, although he appears something different from the conventional and obvious Vice of the popular stage, he is imitating the method of that role. His words tell us even more. Directed as they are to the audience, their demonstrative force explicit in "thus," they proclaim also the homiletic demonstration and its nature. He is inviting the appreciation of the audience for his dexterity

THE HYBRID IMAGE IN SHAKESPEARE 395

in deceit, for his skill in that kind of exhibition which evolved out of the moral metaphor of the Vice. He has become for the nonce the artist, his ornate duplicity an end in itself. The historical figure who ruled England dissolves into the theatrical figure who ruled the English stage.

Although these two realities enclosed by the single name of Richard are as implicated with each other as the chequered features of a topographical map, we are able to mark the turn from one to the other. As his role rears itself out of the welter of historical incident in the last part of the *Henry VI* plays, it begins at the same time to shift from its previously recessed naturalism into a different perspective. The change is signaled at the end of the soliloquy already quoted in part, five sixths of which is a passionate debate inside the heart of the aspiring cripple who identifies his life's joy with the crown. Upon this passion intrudes, however, a very different note, for the long speech concludes with a piece of stylized rhetoric that is neither more nor less than another version of the *moral pedigree* of the Vice, although we notice a naturalistic modification. The catalogue of aggression which creates the background of allegorical meaning for the behavior of Barabas, Edricus, and Aaron, becomes in Richard's case potential rather than preterit—a catalogue of what *he can do*:

> Why, I can smile, and murther whiles I smile,
> And cry 'Content!' to that which grieves my heart,
> And wet my cheeks with artificial tears,
> And frame my face to all occasions.
> I'll drown more sailors than the mermaid shall;
> I'll slay more gazers than the basilisk;
> I'll play the orator as well as Nestor,
> Deceive more slily than Ulysses could,
> And, like a Sinon, take another Troy.
> I can add colours to the chameleon,
> Change shapes with Proteus for advantages,
> And set the murtherous Machiavel to school.
>   [III.ii.182–93] [10]

This is exposition in the homiletic dimension of the morality drama, as we have seen it before when the Vice comes forward to announce his moral identity and the nature of his timeless activity in the world; and we notice that all of Richard's self-comparisons converge upon a single

THE HYBRID IMAGE IN SHAKESPEARE

theme: his mastery of the art of aggression through deceit. In the last two scenes of *Henry VI* the dramatic method thus introduced begins to control the role. His monologue in the Tower, after he murders King Henry, moves unmistakably into the audience: *"See* how my sword weeps for the poor King's death!" and "Had I not reason, *think ye,* to make haste?" [11] In the very end of the play, Edward, now undisputed king and mellow with prosperity, sets up a target for the Vice to shoot at when he intones a hymn to the transcendent values of love and peace, invoking love from his brothers to his queen, his son, himself:

> Clarence and Gloucester, love my lovely queen,
> And kiss your princely nephew, brothers both.
>
> . . . .
>
> Now am I seated as my soul delights,
> Having my country's peace and brothers' loves.
> [V.vii.26–36]

The Vice is ready and rises to his cue. Richard in this scene becomes a creature of asides, an histrionic homilist who puts on a show of love and honesty and turns away with a grin to share his jest and register his art with the audience. The kiss of love and fealty he gives the young heir apparent, and his accompanying words, directed half one way and half another, are his last action in *Henry VI* and announces the bravura role to follow in the play that bears his name:

> And that I love the tree from whence thou sprang'st
> Witness the loving kiss I give the fruit.
> [Aside] To say the truth, so Judas kiss'd his master
> And cried 'All hail!' when as he meant all harm.

The traditional image thus initiated in the earlier play expands in *Richard III* in equal measure with the expansion of the figure to whom it is assimilated. By the end of *Henry VI* Richard has only begun to emerge from the press of men and events which diversifies that trilogy, although we become aware that already he has magnetized a change in dramatic perspective: the mural of national history in a succession of panels, its large population crowding through multiple phases of war and politics, by degrees surrenders foreground and focus to his looming portrait. In *Richard III* this portrait monopolizes the canvas, and its archaic features show a corresponding proliferation. They are enriched, moreover, by a consummate artistry such as the moralities never knew.

THE HYBRID IMAGE IN SHAKESPEARE 397

No "formal Vice" weeps more fluently than Richard, or uses that gaudy device to better effect upon his victims. None enjoys a happier intimacy with the audience, or titillates them more exquisitely in the ways prescribed by the old role's homiletic bravura. By none is the art of deceit so lavishly cultivated, so merrily held up for exhibition, or so richly organized around the paired antinomies of essential enmity and pretended love, essential turpitude and pretended virtue, essential villainy and pretended honesty. And in none of Richard's hybrid fellows in the secular drama does the ancient aggression show so plainly the twofold method that governed it originally; for the emphasis in his achievements, as often in his hyphenated role as he wears the mantle of Vicehood, is not on his progress toward the crown—that is the naturalistic Richard—but on his ability to create dissension in the place of unity and love, and on his cognate ability to seduce his victims from their virtuous allegiance and bend them to his will. In all these features of his role, but especially in the homiletic principle that binds them into demonstrative intimacy with the audience and supplies them with an impetus that has nothing to do with ambition, we recognize the archmetaphor that fathered them in the morality drama. The metaphor itself has been abolished by the literal play, but the dramaturgic personality of its chief exponent still flourishes in the role of Richard.

This hereditary pattern in his performance is so emphatic and stylized as to be unmistakable. Already humid with the weeping of its unhappy women, the play welters in the tears of Richard. Either as they are shed on stage or as they are reported they lubricate his fraud perpetually as he moves in episodic demonstration from one victim to another. In the first scene Clarence is on his way to the Tower, consigned there through Richard's plot and soon to die there at the hands of Richard's hired murderers. Richard fondly bids him good-by, promises to use every means to "enfranchise" him, and laments with double tongue "this deep disgrace in brotherhood." Clarence goes off to his doom solaced by Richard's love, and in the Tower he remains the dupe of the fraud even when his murderers try to undeceive him:

> 2 *Murd.* You are deceiv'd. Your brother Gloucester hates you.
> *Clar.*   O, no, he loves me and he holds me dear:
>
> · · · ·
>
> O, do not slander him, for he is kind.
>
> [I.iv.236–46]

398   THE HYBRID IMAGE IN SHAKESPEARE

Where does he get his strong faith in Richard's love and kindness? In large part it comes to him from his memory of Richard's affection and Richard's tears in the first scene. Although the drama has moved beyond "Let the Vice weep" as a stage direction, Clarence supplies its equivalent in the words with which he recalls, while pleading in the Tower for his life, Richard's behavior at their parting:

> Bid Gloucester think on this, and he will weep.
>
>   .   .   .   .
>
> . . . for he bewept by fortune,
> And hugg'd me in his arms, and swore with sobs
> That he would labour my delivery.
>
>   [I.iv.244–52]

Richard himself supplies the same direction for his behavior generally when he posts the audience on off-stage developments:

> Clarence, whom I indeed have cast in darkness,
> I do beweep to many simple gulls—
>
>   [I.iii.327–28]

One of these gulls is Hastings, who also believes that Richard loves him: "I thank his Grace, I know he loves me well." [12] With this belief he flatters himself to death, paying with his head for his simplicity. His simplicity indeed goes further and merits worse, for it provokes him to attempt the moral portrait of Richard:

> I think there's never a man in Christendom
> Can lesser hide his love or hate than he,
> For by his face straight shall you know his heart.
>
>   [III.iv.51–53]

His trunkless head, not long after, listens to even better irony from one who does not merely stumble into it, whose deliberate art in the ironic style is infinite:

> So dear I lov'd the man that I must weep.
> I took him for the plainest harmless creature
> That breath'd upon the earth a Christian;
>
>   .   .   .   .
>
> So smooth he daub'd his vice with show of virtue . . .
>
>   [III.v.24–29]

For Richard is tireless in lamenting the "world's deceit," and few of his victims lack his pious admonition on this subject.

THE HYBRID IMAGE IN SHAKESPEARE 399

His most memorable weeping and his most ardent protestations of love occur during his encounter with Lady Anne, and must wait for our notice of that episode. There remains, however, another confirmation of the lachrymose mask of love and honesty he wears whenever he is not grinning at the audience. The orphaned son of Clarence relates to the Duchess of York his version of how his father came to imprisonment and death. He has it from the unimpeachable lips of one who also gave him the tear of pity and the kiss of fatherly affection—

> for my good uncle Gloucester
> Told me the King, provok'd to it by the Queen,
> Devis'd impeachments to imprison him;
> And when my uncle told me so, he wept,
> And pitied me, and kindly kiss'd my cheek;
> Bade me rely on him as on my father,
> And he would love me dearly as a child.
>
> [II.ii.19–26]

The old Duchess, out of her bitter wisdom, knows better:

> Ah, that deceit should steal such gentle shape
> And with a virtuous visor hide deep vice!
> He is my son—ay, and therein my shame;
> Yet from my dugs he drew not this deceit.
>
> [II.ii.27–30]

She speaks even better than she herself knows. Her words, which her own meaning confines to a moral comment on the depraved nature of her son, belong to the unmistakable vocabulary of the moral play, and go straight to the heart of the formula that created the theatrical stereotype of the Vice. The side of Richard that inherits this formula is not on the stage to gain a crown but to offer another brilliant demonstration of "deep vice" masquerading under "a virtuous visor," beguiling a succession of victims—"simple gulls"—by the "gentle shape" of love and honesty. For love and honesty compose the substance of the fraud that his tears promote. Matched against them in the merry monologues through which he instructs the audience is the substance of the reality: his enmity and evil. The homiletic method of the old aggression, vice proclaiming its true nature and exhibiting its hostility to the soul's welfare, becomes, even when strained through a literal dramatic texture, a program only one step away from its cradle in allegory—Richard's program:

THE HYBRID IMAGE IN SHAKESPEARE

> I am determined to prove a villain
> And hate the idle pleasures of these days.
> [I.i.30–31]

On the role's permanent fulcrum of deceit ("I am subtle, false, and treacherous") his villainy and hate pivot neatly into the show of their opposites—the elaborate pretense of honesty and love, baited with his tears, by which he snares his dupes to their ruin. Even those who ought to know him better surrender their wisdom to the outrageous artistry of a performance that is guaranteed success over victims who are guaranteed fatuity by the Christian allegory from which it derives.

Equally derivative, and as richly arrayed in the homiletic panoply of the Psychomachia, is that side of his aggression that extends beyond victims to values, especially the paramount values of love and peace in human relationships. Clarence in the Tower recalls that

> our princely father York
> Bless'd his three sons with his victorious arm
> And charg'd us from his soul to love each other . . .
> [I.iv.240–42]

The fourth Edward's last energies are concentrated on the same fraternal bond and the peace it can insure, and while he is alive in *Richard III* he continues to seek what he sought at the end of *Henry VI,* when he invoked the love of his brothers for himself, his queen, and his son. His effort in *Richard III* is actually wider and more strenuous, for he strives to heal old rancors throughout the realm and to bind the peers of England into a "united league" of mutual amity.[13] The image of love and concord is thus erected in the play only to be shattered by its professed enemy. Richard wastes no time assuring the audience of his talent in this branch of villainy, of which both Edward and Clarence— no small irony—are his initial dupes. In his first monologue he announces the imminent success of his plot

> To set my brother Clarence and the King
> In deadly hate the one against the other.
> [I.i.34–35]

This compact job of alienation belongs, we remember, to the standard repertory of the Vice, and differs no whit in essence or method from what we have already seen in a score of plays. And it is a fascination to see history give way to dramaturgy in order that both victims may

THE HYBRID IMAGE IN SHAKESPEARE 401

qualify for their roles, becoming, in Richard's words, "Edward . . . true and just" (that is, innocent and gullible) and the other "Simple plain Clarence."

From this divisive achievement Richard moves ahead to another of wider scope. The third and fifth scenes of the play are given over to the dying monarch's attempt to draw his nobles together in friendship. To this end he summons Gloucester and Hastings to court in order "to make atonement" between them and the Queen's party, the latter being well disposed. The outcome matches Richard's aim, not Edward's. The lords of England, assembled for peace, are juggled into mortal enmity by one to whom they are all dupes indiscriminately. Under the exquisite sham of his slighted merit, his slandered innocence, his betrayed credulity—"I am too childish-foolish for this world"—he envenoms old wounds and inflicts new ones by every kind of insult and accusation. He provokes the quarrel and remains its whirling vortex, but he himself, let us note, is not quarreling essentially; rather he is demonstrating his ability to make others quarrel; and nowhere else is he more brilliantly the Vice. His wit stands apart to enjoy the effect of its own effrontery and to share his sport with the audience. At the end of this scene (the third) he is left alone with them for his choric and homiletic opportunity:

> I do the wrong, and first begin to brawl.
> The secret mischiefs that I set abroach
> I lay unto the grievous charge of others.
> Clarence, whom I indeed have cast in darkness,
> I do beweep to many simple gulls—
> Namely, to Derby, Hastings, Buckingham—
> And tell them 'tis the Queen and her allies
> That stir the King against the Duke my brother.
> Now they believe it, and withal whet me
> To be reveng'd on Rivers, Dorset, Grey.
> But then I sigh, and, with a piece of Scripture,
> Tell them that God bids us do good for evil;
> And thus I clothe my naked villany
> With odd old ends stol'n forth of holy writ,
> And seem a saint when most I play the devil.
>
> [I.iii.324–38]

We need only filter this speech, whose tenor Iago later borrows with improvements, through the more abstract style of the moralities to find

402   THE HYBRID IMAGE IN SHAKESPEARE

ourselves confronting the exact content and cadence of the Vice's monologue. The homiletic dimension and demonstrative logic of the old role were never more explicit. The central formula of deceit was never more comprehensive. The achievement in discord was never more triumphant. And the laughter, no longer raucous, remains unmistakable.

What he begins in the third scene he completes, the murder of Clarence intervening, in the fifth, where his "interior hatred" finally demolishes Edward's architecture of love. The treatment here is heavily thematic, even ritualistic, with "love" the sacramental word of every speech, almost every verse. Upon Rivers and Hastings the King urges the handclasp of love: "Dissemble not your hatred, swear your love." Rivers swears his "true heart's love" and Hastings his "perfect love." The same urging seeks out the Queen: "Wife, love Lord Hastings . . . do it unfeignedly," and she forswears "our former hatred." Hastings is invoked in a new direction: "Hastings, love Lord Marquess," and he and Dorset swear their "interchange of love." Edward turns to Buckingham, and the latter swears his "duteous love," inviting God to punish him "with hate in those where I expect most love. . . . When I am cold in love to you and yours." To the figure who just now enters Edward offers the happy news:

> Gloucester, we have done deeds of charity,
> Made peace of enmity, fair love of hate,
> Between these swelling wrong-incensed peers.
> [II.i.49–51]

On Richard's face love glows more brightly than on any other. He celebrates Edward's "blessed labour" and his own craving for "all good men's love," tenders peace and affection to everyone present, and screws the moment into excruciating irony with a hymn of thanksgiving:

> I do not know that Englishman alive
> With whom my soul is any jot at odds
> More than the infant that is born to-night.
> I thank my God for my humility.
> [II.i.69–72]

But now his jest grows ripe for harvest. The Queen prays Edward to admit to this agape one who, she recollects, is still outside it: Clarence

THE HYBRID IMAGE IN SHAKESPEARE 403

in the Tower. Whereupon Richard shatters concord and love with one blow, his victim now his instrument:

> Why, madam, have I off'red love for this,
> To be so flouted in this royal presence?
> Who knows not that the gentle duke is dead?
> [II.i.77–79]

It is one of the fine dramatic moments of the play, with Buckingham whispering, "Look I so pale, Lord Dorset, as the rest?" Dread and suspicion divorce his nobles in an instant while in the soul of the dying King bitterness marries despair. And into this breach Richard carves deeper with words that should remind us once more of Iago:

> This is the fruit of rashness! Mark'd you not
> How that the guilty kindred of the Queen
> Look'd pale when they did hear of Clarence' death?
> O, they did urge it still unto the King!
> [II.i.134–37] [14]

Although the ancient stereotype survives fitfully in him thereafter, notably in his exchanges with the young Edward (III.i) and in his solicitation to Queen Elizabeth for her daughter's hand (IV.iv), the foregoing scene is the last in which it is largely exploited. By the same token, that scene brings to a close a structural method whose archaic feature is plain even though encrusted within the play's organic fabric as history and as tragedy. With the exception of the fourth, concerned with the murder of Clarence in the Tower, these first five scenes belong to the episodic method by which the late moralities exhibited the Vice. In each of them Richard is on repetitive display as he demonstrates his talent upon King Edward, upon Clarence, upon Lady Anne, upon the nobility of England in general, as well as upon the values of love and concord. Having announced at the beginning that he is "determined to prove a villain," he proceeds to do so seriatim to the point where he is able to present the audience with his Q.E.D.—"And thus I clothe my naked villany," etc. These demonstrations are cumulative and, upon their own homiletic terms, self-sufficient. Through them we shall look in vain for anything in the temper of his performance that corresponds to a passion for sovereignty, or to any other motive that is morally intelligible. For as long as the archaic role grips him he is compelled by its homiletic principle to display himself as the type of

THE HYBRID IMAGE IN SHAKESPEARE

villainy, his regal ambitions lapsing into such obscurity that we remember them only by an effort. We saw how the crown shone to the grim-visaged cripple of *Henry VI* as the only prospect of joy available to him in this world since the joys of love were not. This theme is not forgotten, but by gradations it is reorganized and surrenders its original cogency. His dedication to royal power changes to a dedication that revives the homiletic transparency of a personification in the morality drama. He is on the way thither at the end of *3 Henry VI,* in the monologue that accompanies his murder of King Henry in the Tower:

> Then, since the heavens have shap'd my body so,
> Let hell make crook'd my mind to answer it.
> I have no brother, I am like no brother;
> And this word 'love,' which greybeards call divine,
> Be resident in men like one another,
> And not in me! I am myself alone.
>
> [V.vi.78–83]

In the speech he addresses to the audience at the beginning of *Richard III* he has fully arrived: the love he again abjures is now replaced by an alternative that has nothing to do with the crown:

> And therefore, since I cannot prove a lover
> To entertain these fair well-spoken days,
> I am determined to prove a villain
> And hate the idle pleasure of these days.

The jovial exhibitionist who from this point parades through his gallery of dupes in order to glorify his own villainy and his finesse in concealing it obeys a different law of motion inside a different dimension from that which governs the energy of ambition on the plane of the moral world.

Of these episodes the most memorable is Richard's florid manipulation of Lady Anne, so far neglected. She stimulates his most brilliant achievement in this kind because she is his most difficult undertaking, the immaculate intensity of her abhorrence for the murderer of her husband and her royal father-in-law corresponding to the more abstract enmity of virtue to vice that puts the Vice of the moralities on his mettle when faced with the equivalent situation. Shakespeare exploits this traditional crux to the uttermost by allowing Richard to intrude upon her at a moment the most hopelessly inauspicious for his enter-

THE HYBRID IMAGE IN SHAKESPEARE 405

prise, when she is following the corpse of murdered King Henry to its burial, her grief mingled with curses against the author of it. So contrived to extend his skill, the scene is Richard's masterpiece, its quality and method matched by only one other in Shakespeare—the great seduction scene in *Othello;* and both are amplifications of the typical beguilement effected by the Vice upon his victim in the pivotal scene of the moralities. At the end Anne has made the same moral reversal that marked the career of Mankind and all his descendants: she has thrown over her alliance with virtue and united herself to evil. And Richard at the end is left alone with the audience to share with them the homiletic jest and the familiar laughter, the latter diffused through all his words and explicit in the triumphant syllable of the last line:

> What? I that kill'd her husband and his father
> To take her in her heart's extremest hate,
> With curses in her mouth, tears in her eyes,
> The bleeding witness of my hatred by,
> Having God, her conscience, and these bars against me,
> And I no friends to back my suit withal
> But the plain devil and dissembling looks?
> And yet to win her—all the world to nothing?
> Ha!   [I.ii.230–38] [15]

Although dyed on its surface by the naturalistic colors of the historical play, the whole scene readily discloses its nuclear difference. Its grain is homiletic, not naturalistic, and we feel it as bravura because that is exactly what it is by hereditary principle—homiletic bravura in the dimension of display. Richard is putting on his happiest exhibition of villainous deceit in its most conventional masquerade, the pretense of love, in this instance romantic love: "I'll have her, but I will not keep her long." The ancient virtuosity is here wonderfully enhanced by the poet's finesse and power. Shakespeare's abundance crams the old image with dramatic wealth without defacing its familiar features. Anne succumbs, not because she is especially frail but because she is human, to a tempter who gets from Christian homiletics a prescriptive victory over her astonished heart; but the formula is now surcharged with great vitality and acuteness. Richard exerts upon her every artifice of moral and physical deceit, exploiting her human and feminine frailty with enormous effrontery and assurance, until he mesmerizes her out of her

406   THE HYBRID IMAGE IN SHAKESPEARE

passionate loathing and into a fascinated creature subdued to his will. She submits to an imperious skill that thrusts against her mood at its fiercest, engages it with flexible pressure while it struggles, and grasps it with careless, rough control when it melts. She is wooed out of her will by impassioned periods, impudent stichomythia, uninhibited flattery, outrageous sophistry, suicidal despair—by calculation so inspired and ironic it summons up the murder of the husband she mourns for testimony to the love of the murderer. Nothing, however, dissolves her more effectively than Richard's tears, for they rain on her incessantly:

> Thine eyes, sweet lady, have infected mine.
>
>   .   .   .   .
>
> Those eyes of thine from mine have drawn salt tears,
> Sham'd their aspects with store of childish drops—
>   [I.ii.149–54]

He who never wept before, not even for the piteous deaths of his father York and his brother Rutland, now offers her this humid proof of his desperate, honest love:

>   In that sad time
> My manly eyes did scorn a humble tear;
> And what these sorrows could not thence exhale,
> Thy beauty hath, and made them blind with weeping.
>   [I.ii.163–66]

On these buoyant waters he soon sails from the port of love into the port of conscience, and she, now won over, hears with pleasure that he will take Henry's burial off her hands and "wet his grave with my repentant tears." So prosperous is the old device that in his merry privacy with the audience he promises to continue it:

> But first I'll turn yon fellow in his grave,
> And then return lamenting to my love.
>   [I.ii.260–61]

His weeping and laughter do not by themselves establish the archaic source of Richard's performance, but they confirm it, alongside his other unmistakable tricks of language and behavior. The dominant trait in his descent appears in the unnaturalistic dimension of his role, in the repetitious and gratuitous deceit surviving out of the old Christian metaphor, in the homiletic method of the timeless personifica-

THE HYBRID IMAGE IN SHAKESPEARE 407

tion. It is the inspirational force of the method itself that gives birth to Richard's wooing of Lady Anne, for which there is no hint in the chronicles. That scene has its origin in theatrical convention, not in history, and its dramatic caliber sufficiently explains the playwright's recourse to the old dramaturgy. *His* caliber explains the great energy and brilliance we discover in this flashing version of the transformed Vice.

3

We learn something about the practical side of the Elizabethan dramaturgy when we discriminate between what Shakespeare borrowed and what he originated in the plot of *Much Ado about Nothing*. From the twenty-second tale in Bandello's *Novelle,* or from Belleforest's French translation of it in the *Histoires Tragiques,* he drew the story of Claudio and Hero, adding some details probably from the similar episode in *Orlando Furioso* (V.24–25). And no doubt he was also acquainted with another, abbreviated, version that Spenser, adapting from Ariosto, had worked into *The Faerie Queene* (II.iv.17–36). Despite some superficiality in the characterizations of hero and heroine, disturbing to readers who prefer the romantic passion writ large and deep in its votaries, this part of the play belongs to the serious literature of romantic love—in this case love almost destroyed by villainy but finally triumphant in matrimony. But the play intends to be a comedy, not simply in the technical sense of its happy ending, but a comedy full of laughter. What the Claudio-Hero plot suffers from is anemia, the playwright's inclination and energy flowing in another direction. If Claudio and Hero are ineloquent lovers, they really have no chance to be otherwise on a stage vibrant with the voices of Beatrice and Benedict.

Borrowing this much, Shakespeare originates the rest, and he does so by employing his powers upon the formula of contrast and relief inveterate in his art. The finished play, in fact, is an ingenious structure of patterned themes and moods. The serious romance of the derived story gets, with fine dramatic articulation, its gay counter-motif in the logomachy of Benedict and Beatrice, an outright dramaturgic tour de force. Their wit turns love's handsome garment the wrong way out and tugs at the underside's unhandsome seams and threads, until, of course, the same garment envelops their valiant but frail antiromanticism. And they also create a duplicating detail within the larger pattern of contrast, for they are deceived into love just as Claudio and Hero are deceived out of it. Again by way of contrast, this time not upon the theme of love but upon the mood of comedy, against the merry wit of Beatrice and Benedict the playwright matches the solemn witlessness of Dogberry and Verges. And in the name of the same formula he does something else whose intention escapes us unless we realize the deft distributive principle upon which the play is poised: he departs from the borrowed story to recreate the character, as well as the motive, of the villain, making him a melancholy, taciturn figure the sight of whose tart face, Beatrice says, gives her heartburn for an hour after. It should occur to us that Shakespeare's vivacious villains exist in tragedy and are, in fact, a form of comic variation within the serious movement of the tragic theme. In comedy, which needs a variation in reverse, his villains have solemn, even somber, natures. The distinction is moral as well as dramaturgic: when the good world is serious, its villainy is jovial; and the same proposition reverses itself for comedy. In the very gay and sociable world of *Much Ado* Shakespeare creates his effective contrasts, both dramaturgic and moral, through a gloomy, unsociable villain, the bastard Don John.

The fact that Don John is not only somber but wooden and trivial also, indicates that he suffers the same emaciation afflicting the romantic hero and heroine. The expansive wit of the merry pair squeezes the romantic story into a corner, and Don John is a part of that story. Wit, indeed, never gives itself any respite nor anything else in the play more than half a chance. When Beatrice surrenders, momentarily, her satiric humor to the moody seizure of love, she runs full tilt into the momentary verbal cleverness of Margaret, the waiting gentlewoman:

Beat. O, God help me! God help me! How long have you profess'd apprehension?
Marg. Ever since you left it. Doth not my wit become me rarely?
[III.iv.67–70]

And Benedict in the same mood gets the same treatment, not only from Margaret but from Claudio and Don Pedro as well. Such a dispensation allows only bare existence to both romance and villainy, and the latter is little more than a mechanism to trigger the plot. Its humiliating insignificance within the governing mood of the play is

THE HYBRID IMAGE IN SHAKESPEARE 409

sufficiently expressed through the last lines, which subject the villain to an indignity worse than any punishment: he is reduced to a tedious interruption in the merrymaking:

Mess. My lord, your brother John is ta'en in flight,
  And brought with armed men back to Messina.
Bene. Think not on him till to-morrow. I'll devise thee brave punishments
  for him. Strike up, pipers!

Dance. [Exeunt.]

Although meagerly sketched, Don John is a plausible villain most of the time, the homiletic link binding him to this study being a slight one. As John the bastard, his nature, in a general way, is defined through the stigma of the bar sinister. The effect upon character of the personal deprivation and social disesteem involved in illegitimacy was understood by the Elizabethans pretty much the same as we understand it today, except that they, without the doubtful benefit of our psychological terminology, spoke of such a man's "envy" and "discontent," whereas we now speak of his "aggressive impulses." [16] Thus disenfranchised, Don John nurses his malignant humor and his perpetual grievance against the ordered, legitimate, graceful society of the play, all its members falling within the circle of his displeasure: "Only to dispite them [Don Pedro, Claudio, Hero, Leonato] I will endeavor to do anything"; and "Let us to the great supper. Their cheer is the greater that I am subdued. Would the cook were o' my mind." General cause and effect are caught up together in the description applied to him by Benedict:

> The practice of it lives in John the bastard,
> Whose spirits toil in frame of villanies.
> [IV.i.189–90]

Actually in this respect he resembles Richard of Gloucester, whose own stigmata turn him against the "idle pleasures" of the handsome, courtly world, except that Don John, a shadow beside the hunchbacked Duke, is not carried through on the full tide of homiletic dramaturgy that works for Richard.

Within the large circle of his envious, canine disposition particular motives erect themselves. He has recently been in rebellion against the authority of his half-brother Don Pedro, has been "subdued," and is now, but only superficially, "reconciled" to the other's mastership and

THE HYBRID IMAGE IN SHAKESPEARE

his own "overthrow." Taken back into his brother's grace—such generosity itself a provocation to his nature—he is, nevertheless, under close supervision and on his good behavior ("I am trusted with a muzzle and enfranchis'd with a clog"). He cultivates his "discontent" and awaits his chance at retaliation:

John. If I had my mouth, I would bite; if I had my liberty, I would do my
liking. In the meantime let me be that I am, and seek not to alter me.
Con. Can you make no use of your discontent?
John. I make all use of it, for I use it only.

[I.iii.36–41]

Against "the most exquisite Claudio," as he calls him, his resentment finds even more specific ground in the fact that what he has lost the other has gained:

That young start-up hath all the glory of my overthrow. If I can cross him
any way, I bless myself every way.

[I.iii.68–71]

Although his invidious feeling is clear, his exact provocation is not, inviting alternative explanations: his "overthrow" may refer to a military engagement—even, perhaps, the very battle from which Don Pedro returns victorious at the play's beginning—in which Claudio has distinguished himself, winning both honor and affection from the Prince, as we know he has; or it may mean simply that, following his own disgrace and alienation, Don John finds himself replaced by Claudio in Don Pedro's affection and favor. Either way his prowling envy finds its exposed quarry in Claudio and Claudio's marriage; and his action against the lovers, since it is also an injury to Don Pedro, Claudio's friend and sponsor in his love-suit, finds all the provocation it needs:

Any bar, any cross, any impediment will be med'cinable to me. I am sick
in displeasure to him [Claudio], and whatsoever comes athwart his affection ranges evenly with mine. How canst thou cross this marriage?

[II.ii.4–8]

His intrigue thereafter follows the model supplied by the original story in Bandello or Belleforest, with the addition of some details that Shakespeare might have drawn from Ariosto.

But why does the playwright reject the motive for villainy supplied by his sources—the thwarted passion which turns the jealous rival to

THE HYBRID IMAGE IN SHAKESPEARE 411

intrigue in order to gain the heroine for himself? Such a question in isolation is probably the wrong way to deal with the role of Don John or, for that matter, with the Shakespearian method generally. It is likely to stimulate psychological subtleties that fly out of sight of an issue which, at its base at least, is technical. It is true that in Spenser's version of the same story the villain is described by his victim as follows:

> He either enuying my toward good [impending marriage],
> Or of himselfe to treason ill disposed . . .
> > [*The Faerie Queene* II.iv.22]

It seems, however, more suggestive, according to the viewpoint already advanced, that Shakespeare neither rejects nor imitates here, but moves in obedience to a dramaturgic principle much more positive and energetic—the principle, namely, of schematic contrast and balanced composition in the sense such words have for the fine arts. He recreates the role to make it serve a design apparent in all his love comedies, the design of the countertheme within the romantic world that each displays. It is, in fact, the theme of anti-love stitched in dark contrast, with more or less intensity, upon the bright fabric of love, the theme of sullen negation matched against a society of love and courtesy, of ebullience and generosity, of music and merriment. In *Twelfth Night* it takes form in the puritan rigor of Malvolio, whose name implies what his behavior confirms. The "melancholy Jaques" incorporates the same distinction in *As You Like It*. Shylock's mood and temperament (the melancholy Antonio's as well perhaps), even apart from his actions, stands in similar opposition to the amorous gaiety of Venice and Belmont. And in *Much Ado* the same antinomy fulfills itself exactly through the malignant humor of Don John. His role is denied the thwarted passion of love because the dramatist's primary organization of its characteristics within his broad dramaturgic design leaves no room for such a motive.

What then remains of Don John to make him a relevant subject for this volume? He has none of the alacrity which invests the role we are tracing with its conspicuous energy, nor the vivacity which gives it its characteristic humor, touching on farce. He is not a monologuist in communication with the audience, but addresses himself invariably to his henchmen, Conrade and Borachio, lacking in this respect the homiletic dimension with which we are familiar. And although his

THE HYBRID IMAGE IN SHAKESPEARE

intrigue is marked by the divisive purpose and deceptive method inherent in the activity of the Vice, it is, in fact, a straightforward adaptation by the playwright from his sources, unembellished by those dramaturgic features that expose the heritage of the allegorical drama. But that heritage does survive in the villain's language, especially in a single speech he addresses to his cronies. His words in this instance confuse his portrayal, slight as it is anyway, by a degree of moral clairvoyance in respect to himself that would not be possible in any naturalistic dramatization of villainy, no matter how wicked. He is speaking with reference to his brother Don Pedro:

I had rather be a canker in a hedge than a rose in his grace, and it better fits my blood to be disdain'd of all than to fashion a carriage to rob love from any. In this, though I cannot be said to be a flattering honest man, it must not be denied but I am a plain-dealing villain.

[I.iii.28–34]

Nor is he alone in this style. When, for the benefit of Conrade, Borachio describes his part in the deception perpetrated, he speaks with equal homiletic candor of "my villany."

As we have already seen in plays by Shakespeare's contemporaries, such sporadic instances of absolute self-exposure inherit the transparent style of homiletic allegory; and they do so, it seems most likely, whenever the intrigue they verbalize resembles the characteristic features of the morality plot. The seductive operation of deceit upon unsuspecting virtue and the divisive stratagem that shatters friendship, loyalty, love, or any other spiritual bond, attracts, in variable degrees of intensity, the homiletic language traditional in such an enterprise. Not only does the villainy of Don John, aggressive against both love and friendship, attract this style, but elsewhere in Shakespeare the same situation produces the same fitful dramaturgy, and thrusts the same confusion upon the modern canon of naturalistic verisimilitude. In all such cases, however, the homiletic heritage is slight, fleeting, and verbal, unproductive of the massive image interpenetrating the roles of Aaron, Richard, or Iago. In *Julius Caesar,* for instance, the intelligible movement of passion and politics leading to the assassination suddenly blurs and fades when Cassius' monologue screws a new and startling moral focus upon the action. Brutus has just left him, deeply moved by his vehement analysis of Caesar's ambition and Rome's danger:

THE HYBRID IMAGE IN SHAKESPEARE 413

Well, Brutus, thou art noble; yet I see
Thy honourable mettle may be wrought
From that it is dispos'd. Therefore it is meet
That noble minds keep ever with their likes;
For who so firm that cannot be seduc'd?
Caesar doth bear me hard; but he loves Brutus.
If I were Brutus now and he were Cassius,
He should not humour me.

[I.ii.312–19]

Although not so stark as Don John's words above, these of Cassius achieve the same effect: they dissolve the dramatic imitation of a limited human personality caught up in action and passion, replacing it by a detached and illimitable homiletic voice. At the same time, inseparable from this effect, they achieve another: in them the relationship of the two chief conspirators, as well as the conspiracy itself, is momentarily recast to fit the formula of the morality intrigue. Cassius' passionate exhortation of Brutus just before has now become, in Cassius' own words, an elaborate act of deception, he himself the villainous seducer, Brutus the noble innocent deceived, and the alienation of Brutus from Caesar the evil achievement. Although the plot is Roman, the dramaturgy, no less than the moral emphasis, is Elizabethan—a truism of which we sometimes need to be reminded. Not only is the play as a whole organized into the shape of an Elizabethan revenge tragedy, but in the particular episode before us it reverts to the veteran technique and intrigue of the allegorical drama.

The same technique, invited by the same kind of intrigue, penetrates the earlier part of Edmund's role in *King Lear*. His villainy enacts the type of moral evil increasingly prominent in plays after 1600—the insurrection of man's lower nature against the sanctities apprehended by his higher. Edmund's rebellion against the disqualifications of bastardy, his assertion of the "natural" qualifications inherent in strength, cunning, and appetite, his contempt for the ordered pieties of Christian society, and his actions in consequence, compose his portrait in accord with the deepest moral issues in the play as a whole. But these elements in his nature do not of themselves qualify him for attention here. It is the way he is fitfully dramatized that does: his gay alacrity in deception and dissimulation, the breach his stratagem achieves between father and son, and, beyond anything else, his absolute awareness of the moral

THE HYBRID IMAGE IN SHAKESPEARE

position. His own words, merry and cynical, promulgate his own villainy, although, in fact, this style in his performance is relatively subdued and confined to one scene—the second. To Edgar's exclamation, "Some villain hath done me wrong," his reply is deliberately ironic: "That's my fear." And he enjoys his joke again a few lines later: "Brother, I advise you to the best. Go arm'd. I am no honest man if there be any good meaning toward you." But the emphatic revelation of the dramaturgy at work upon him exists in the monologue with which he closes the scene:

> A credulous father! and a brother noble,
> Whose nature is so far from doing harms
> That he suspects none; on whose foolish honesty
> My practices ride easy! I see the business.
> Let me, if not by birth, have lands by wit;
> All with me's meet that I can fashion fit.

Here the other half of the homiletic equation, as he knows it and proclaims it, fulfills itself: on the one side his own villainy, on the other the susceptible credulity of one of his dupes and the equally susceptible nobility of the other. This formula, the evolved product of the Christian homiletic drama, returns us naturally to *Othello,* where its operation is neither incidental nor partial but envelops the play from first to last.

CHAPTER TWELVE

IAGO REVISITED

"O mistress, villany hath made mocks with love!"
EMILIA

I

Anyone reading in Giraldi Cinthio's *Hecatommithi* (1565) the story which supplied the plot of *Othello* must be struck by the revisions made by the playwright in dramatizing his source.[1] Apart from the measureless distance in quality between the great poetic drama and the arid, though competent, little tale of matrimonial tragedy out of which it originated, there remain specific and measurable differences in respect to persons and actions. These differences can be attributed either to Shakespeare's moral sentiment (including the reflective and "psychological" element in his work) or to his theatrical art, or even to a combination of both. What is useful, at least according to the method of this study, is the distinction, where it is possible, between the two; and even where it is not, it is still useful to consider theatrical purposes that seem to play a part in his alteration of the material on which he worked. Narration, whether fiction or history, transferred to the theater needs to be *dramatized,* which means a good deal more, of course, than simply turning it into dialogue and gesture. Those of us who do not write plays may assume that the technical difference between relating an action and imitating it on the stage is enormous. In this task of dramatization the initial recourse of the dramatist, however much he may modify them by his ingenuity or transcend them by his inspiration, is inevitably to the successful conventions of his stage.

Such a truism, paving the way back to Iago, is able to disgust any working playwright, but it is one of which the mere critic or scholar sometimes needs to be reminded. Otherwise he may unwisely substitute moral sentiment, of which he is likely to have a great deal, for

IAGO REVISITED

dramaturgic insight, of which he is likely to have less. Swinburne, who wrote unstageable plays, illustrates this danger. In his essay on *Othello* he observes that Iago's original in Cinthio's story had a three-year-old daughter whom Desdemona (Cinthio's spelling is Disdemona) at one moment fondled in her arms, giving the villain his chance to filch the handkerchief from her sash. The child, however, is missing from Shakespeare's play, and Swinburne finds the reason thus:

What can be the explanation of what a dunce who knows better than Shakespeare might call an oversight? There is but one: but it is all-sufficient. In Shakespeare's world as in nature's it is impossible that monsters should propagate: that Iago should beget, or that Goneril or Regan should bring forth. Their children are creatures unimaginable by man.[2]

From this kind of sentimental fallacy, however, the greater poet was free. He knew, with Job and the Preacher, that moral evil is not genetically sterile; and Aaron the Moor, whose villainy matches Iago's even if his dramatic portrait does not, treats with affection the infant borne him by Tamora. Shakespeare's reasons for deleting the ancient's daughter were not moral, they were dramaturgic. An incidental, arbitrary child, whose momentary appearance in the action is essentially meaningless, while tolerable in the relaxed method of the novel, is the kind of luxury the sterner economy of the dramatic plot cannot afford, and there are no such children in Shakespeare. But a second reason was by itself decisive: on the Elizabethan stage a child of three was an impossibility. Between the infant in arms or in the cradle, represented through a doll or shaped clout, and the lad of seven or eight, precociously voluble, the gap was technically unbridgeable, and is hardly less so on today's stage.

Moreover, by the very omission of the meaningless, impossible child, Shakespeare was able to dramatize another object very much to his purpose: he dramatized, upon its first appearance, the handkerchief. The technical achievement here is worth a moment's notice, since it helps us to understand what dramatization really means. The handkerchief first appears in response to Othello's abrupt, equivocal words: "I have a pain upon my forehead, here" (III.iii.284), flutters to the stage when he pushes his wife's hand away ("Your napkin is too little"), lies there for an intense moment before Emilia, left alone, picks it up, discourses upon it, and then allows Iago to take it from her. Left

IAGO REVISITED 417

alone in his turn, he dangles this trifle "light as air" and swiftly formulates its mission. Only careless criticism will object that here the
dramatist has carelessly substituted accident for the motivated incident
of his source. He is, in fact, revising with great skill and deliberation.
Getting rid of the literal act of theft, a physical trick worthy of farce
alone, not to speak of the child who would have encumbered it, he
reserves and emphasizes its essence, its element of deliberate contrivance: "I am glad I have found this napkin," says Emilia,

> My wayward husband hath a hundred times
> Woo'd me to steal it.
>
> [III.iii.292–93]

And a moment later, in her reply to his question, "What handkerchief?" the same thing appears: "That which so often you did bid
me steal." The whole episode, by its additions and subtractions, illustrates the theatrical art in obedience to theatrical necessity. Through
forty-four lines of the play the attention of the audience is fixed upon
the little square of cloth as it moves from hand to hand, its initial
triviality swelling into the portent of its ultimate operation. It has not
only been introduced, it has been staged, animated, transformed. Later
on, of course, it is dramatized another way—poetically, in Othello's
description of its history and magical powers. But something else behind Shakespeare's revision of the episode has equal dramatic value.
It concerns the character he gives Emilia and the use to which he puts
her. In Cinthio the villain's wife revealed the truth of the tragic events
some time after all the main actors were dead, and she was able to do
so because she had been aware of her husband's intentions at the time
they were unfolding, being his accomplice, in fact, through her silence.
In the play she is an ignorant instrument, but the revelation still belongs to her, and the lightning flash of the denouement is of her
kindling exactly because the handkerchief has passed through her
hands on its way to Iago:

> O thou dull Moor, that handkerchief thou speak'st of
> I found by fortune, and did give my husband;
> For often with a solemn earnestness
> (More than indeed belong'd to such a trifle)
> He begg'd of me to steal't.
>
> [V.ii.225–29]

IAGO REVISITED

Not only does Shakespeare unchild Iago, but for reasons not very different he unmarries Cassio. During one moment of his story Cinthio mentions that the lieutenant (Cassio) had a wife skillful with her needle, and that as she stood at her window copying the embroidery from Desdemona's handkerchief, the ensign (Iago) drew the Moor to view the object on which she was working. That is her whole history. Just as fleeting is Cinthio's reference to the courtesan the lieutenant visited the night he was waylaid and wounded. By any theatrical yardstick the two trivial women are one too many, and Shakespeare, abolishing the wife, gives her slight function in the plot to the courtesan, whose role he expands into significance. Perhaps it is not too much to suggest that his choice between the two illustrates the triumph of practical considerations over moral ones, since Cassio's "daily beauty" would have gained from a wife a degree of enhancement that the courtesan does not altogether supply. But the stage bristled with reasons pointing the other way, the least of them being that a married Cassio would have been less tractable a subject for Iago's intrigue. More important, however, was the blunt theatrical fact that with two respectable wives already inside a play dealing with matrimony a third would have had no dramatic virtue at all compared with the opportunity to stage a harlot. Such a statement will sound strange only if we ignore the radical technique of contrast governing the Shakespearian dramaturgy, or overlook the theatrical fashion in prostitutes (not to speak of bawds and pimps) during the early years of the seventeenth century, or neglect how much Iago's intrigue owes to the existence of Cassio's Bianca: "And to see how he prizes the foolish woman your wife! She gave it him, and he hath giv'n it his whore."

In a more general way the fine hand of the playwright reveals itself through the dramatic curtailment he imposes upon his material. Cinthio's method is historical and sprawls at its ease through time. His story begins in Venice with a sequential account of the valorous and worthy Moor, Desdemona's love for him and his for her, their marriage and happy life together, the Moor's military mission to Cyprus, and his wife's determination to accompany him there. After the murder of the heroine the narrative returns to Venice and lingers through a series of events that ultimately bring retributive justice upon those responsible for her death. Shakespeare's reconstruction at both ends of the story

IAGO REVISITED 419

exhibits the high art of his dramaturgy. His first act is not only a miracle of exposition, it is also, when measured against his source, a miracle of condensation. Character and situation, the ground of the past and the shadow of the future, spin like planets out of the cosmic whirl of an action concerned with the events of three quarters of an hour. And the final scene of the play merges climax and denouement into a continuous flare, lighting heroine, hero, and villain to their journey's end together. As for the action in between, the playwright's notable device of "double time" effects a similar transformation upon Cinthio's weeks or months of intrigue.

Stagecraft is also at work to rid the story of its original element of chance, and this intention is so clear it supplies its own comment on the handkerchief episode. In Cinthio the lieutenant's unsoldierly quarrel while on guard, provoking his dismissal, merely happened. Desdemona's intercession on his behalf was her own inspiration prompted by friendship. The Moor, because he returned home exactly at the moment the lieutenant was trying to return the handkerchief, heard him stealing away from Desdemona's vicinity and found thereby new food for his jealousy. In the play all these events are cut away from accident and grafted to design. Iago gets Cassio drunk and sends Roderigo to provoke the quarrel. Iago's prompting sends Cassio to Desdemona with an appeal for her intercession. Iago brings the Moor where he can see Cassio "soliciting his wife." Such revisions have two consequences at least: they deepen the organization of the intrigue and, therefore, of the play; they emphasize the villain by augmenting and ramifying his villainy.

But the way to the villain leads through his victims, and in their delineation it is Shakespeare's moral sentiment that asserts itself powerfully, especially in the transfiguration wrought upon Othello. Cinthio's Moor was valiant and affectionate enough, but otherwise a grim, prerogatived male, crude in his passion, in his sense of outraged masculine honor, and in his revenge. The revenge itself, instigated, contrived, and executed by the wicked ensign, was a ghastly business. Desdemona was beaten to death in her bedchamber by a stocking filled with sand wielded by him, whereupon both men pulled down upon her part of the ceiling to make the murder seem an accident. Hatred soon replaced friendship between the two murderers. Filled with the anguish of his loss, the Moor could not bear the sight of his ensign and deprived him of his office. The latter, returning to Venice, disclosed to the wounded lieutenant a version of events that put the blame entirely on the Moor, and the lieutenant accused him to the Signoria of Venice. He was subjected to torture but firmly denied his crime. Condemned first to prison and then to banishment, he was finally killed by Desdemona's kinsmen in the normal course of the Italian vendetta. In the delegated murder, in the attempt at concealment, and in the denial before the Venetian authorities, Cinthio's Moor is illuminated and Shakespeare's unrecognizable.

Cinthio does not press an enveloping moral upon his story beyond its obvious representation of a matrimonial tragedy brought about by egregious villainy and wild jealousy. But at one point he does insert the theme of miscegenation. Desdemona had married the Moor against the wishes of her relations, and when her suffering came upon her she offered her own riper experience as a warning to other Venetian women:

I know not what to say of the Moor; he used to treat me most affectionately; and I begin to fear that my example will teach young women never to marry against their parents' consent, and the Italians in particular, not to connect themselves with men from whom they are separated by nature, climate, education, and complexion.[3]

Shakespeare does not merely repeat this theme of miscegenation, he expands and elaborates it meticulously (an Othello "declin'd into the vale of years" is his invention)—but with the significant difference that it is no longer in the mouth or mind of Desdemona. Early in the play it is her father who repeatedly finds it incredible, unless witchcraft has corrupted her will, that she could abandon the refinements of her own delicate upbringing, not to speak of the habits, manners, morals of her own race and country, and run to "the sooty bosom" of a blackamoor, an alien, "an extravagant and wheeling stranger," a man many years her senior. Later in the play Iago presses the same point, with devastating effect, upon Othello, reminding him that

> She did deceive her father, marrying you;
> And when she seem'd to shake and fear your looks,
> She lov'd them most.
>
> [III.iii.206–208]

IAGO REVISITED

and that in her choice of him she displayed "a will most rank, / Foul disproportion, thoughts unnatural." In the final scene this whole aspect of the drama flashes through the electric outburst of Emilia: "She was too fond of her most filthy bargain."

It is, in fact, one of the play's dominant ideas, for the poet emphasizes it in order to transcend it. Through Desdemona and the Moor he dramatizes his own high sentiment on the spiritual possibilities in human love—that "marriage of true minds" of the sonnets which finds its precise echo in Desdemona's words. Their love is neither the fancy of the eye nor the lust of the blood but an essential attraction of soul overleaping the accidental barriers of race, place, habits, manners, years. Nor are these differences between them momentarily gilded over by the fragile moonlight of romantic ecstasy. It is important to the poet's purpose that Desdemona should see with open eyes the man she has married, that, while delighting in "his honours and his valiant parts," she should not overlook in him or in their union what all the world besides must stare and point at; and so she replies directly to the world upon the main issue:

> That I did love the Moor to live with him,
> My downright violence, and storm of fortunes,
> May trumpet to the world. My heart's subdu'd
> Even to the very quality of my lord.
> I saw Othello's visage in his mind . . .
>
> [I.iii.249–53] [4]

She knows what she is doing, and she knows it forever with that kind of firmness and clarity that astonishes her father, and us today as well. The regret with which Cinthio's heroine was shaken when gathering darkness signaled the tempest never occurs to Shakespeare's. "I would you had never seen him!" cries Emilia, whose inclinations, honest enough, are entrenched on the lower levels of reality. "So would not I," replies Desdemona, "My love doth so approve him."

The quality of the love she tenders the Moor is matched by the love she receives. It is no facile passion in him, aroused because his eye has encountered a beautiful, highbred Venetian girl. His years ("the young effects in me defunct"), the resources of his character, and the disciplined energy of his life are triple brass against "the light-winged toys of feather'd Cupid." Whenever he uses the word *love* one feels its slow arrival, its high and permanent residence:

IAGO REVISITED

> For know, Iago,
> But that I love the gentle Desdemona
> I would not my unhoused free condition
> Put into circumscription and confine
> For the sea's worth.
>
> [I.ii.24–28]

The feeling between them scales love's loftiest romance and expresses, more acutely than anywhere else in the English drama, the refinement of sexual love in the sentiment and literature of Renaissance Europe, the evolution of *l'amour courtois* to its richest spiritual possibilities. For the realization of such an effect the poet's means lie in the formidable disparity he places between them and in its resolution through the characters he gives them: in her the initial refinement and modesty, the admiration growing to love for character and achievement, the spirited rejection of convention and parental constraint, the depth and constancy of her feeling; in him the sheathed power and heroic largeness, the rich past instinct in every present word and act, the tenderness, the frankness, the noble ingenuousness. In a sense their union is a proposition and the play their battlefield, testing whether love so conceived and dedicated can long endure. But poetry is at work upon the proposition to transform it into sensation, and commentary at its best can only hint at the immediate experience the play gives us of gentle Desdemona and the noble Moor.

Romantic love, thus spiritualized and exalted, dominates the values that organize the moral meaning of the play. Somewhat less prominent, but emphatically dramatized nonetheless, is another form of love, for which our best, though inadequate, word is *friendship*. It creates through Cassio the image of unselfish devotion and links him to the romantic pair by his own feeling of adulation for them and by theirs of affection and esteem for him. In Cinthio he had no character at all, being merely the brave lieutenant "carrissimo al Moro," to whom Desdemona, to please her husband, showed kindness. In Shakespeare's hands he becomes a person: effusive, generous hearted, gallant and gay, subject to the easy ebullience and easy despondency of youth. Particularly he is Othello's friend and idolater, and in the subtle byplay of the poet's art their deepest feelings of affection shine through their words of greatest reproach: in the Moor's "How comes it, Michael, you are thus for-

IAGO REVISITED

got?" and in the lieutenant's "Dear General, I never gave you cause." Both forms of love, that between man and man as well as that between man and woman, express the upward nisus of the human spirit against which the play's evil is militant.

2

As for that evil itself, it is morally organized beyond almost anything else in the play. Cinthio's ensign ("di bellissima presenza, ma della più scelerata natura, che mai fosse uomo del mondo" [5]) was a depraved villain of the blackest stripe—lustful, revengeful, deceitful, cunning, and cowardly. But Shakespeare's figure is something else again—a man of principle, with a subtle coherence between what he believes in general and what he believes in particular. He entertains a comprehensive moral attitude toward the world, society, and the individual; and through that attitude appears the "new man," as he has been called, of the Renaissance, his contours sharp and grim against the orthodox values of the poet's age. To some extent he is a propaganda piece, with just enough exaggeration to send him crashing through the sensibilities of Shakespeare's contemporaries, but with not enough exaggeration to carry his meaning completely home to our own. Today our approval of some of his tenets is hampered only by our mystification that they should be the utterance of a villain: "If the balance of our lives had not one scale of reason to poise another of sensuality, the blood and baseness of our natures would conduct us to most prepost'rous conclusions" (I.iii.330–34). Where shall we find better doctrine? It was in respect to such a passage that an eminent Shakespearian once offered his students the opinion that Shakespeare's villains express some of the poet's most admirable sentiments. Alas, time devours things, among them the poet's meaning.

Provided we extend the significance of the label beyond Machiavelli, since it embraces concepts of which Tudor England was conscious without the Florentine's instruction, Iago is a Machiavel. Upon the traditional pieties, as they have already been summarized, and the system of belief behind them, his derisive assault is fundamental, extending to first principles. When Roderigo whimpers that he is ashamed to be so infatuated but "it is not in my virtue to amend it," the villain's response

IAGO REVISITED

becomes intelligible only when "virtue" is understood for what it almost certainly does mean: the divine grace flowing into the otherwise helpless nature of man, creating there the power toward good without which salvation is not possible. "Virtue? a fig!" replies Iago, " 'Tis in ourselves that we are thus or thus," demolishing in a phrase the theological foundation beneath the whole system of Christian ethics. He is *homo emancipatus a Deo,* seeing the world and human life as self-sufficient on their own terms, obedient only to natural law, uninhibited and uninspired by any participation in divinity. In addition to his animal nature, man possesses the equipment of will and reason with which to fulfill or regulate his natural appetites. He is the king of beasts, crowned by his superior faculties. And society, by the same token, is the arena of endless competition, more or less organized, between the appetites of one man and another, success attending him who knows "how to love himself" and how to manipulate the natures of other men. Nature is Iago's goddess as well as Edmund's, with the articles of the ancient's faith even more explicit and wider in their application.

Intellect and scorn, suppressing piety and reverence, compose the double-edged instrument with which he lops off life's idealisms. He has looked upon the world for four times seven years and has acutely seen what he has looked upon: the profane world, no more. His credo and conduct shape themselves accordingly. Loyalty in service is the dotage of "honest knaves" who deserve to be whipped for their folly. Candor in human dealings, whereby word and action faithfully mirror the sentiment of the heart, is as grossly inane as wearing the heart upon the sleeve "for daws to peck at." Rich idiots like Roderigo were made to be mulcted without scruple. Generous masters like Othello were made to be cheated. A truly good woman, assuming the doubtful existence of such a creature, is good for nothing except to exhaust herself upon child bearing and petty household accounts. As for love, it is simply physical appetite mediated by will and guided to fulfillment by libertine cunning. A sensible man of the world serves himself and does himself homage, takes his pleasure and profit wherever he finds them, plays to win by any trick, dissembles his intentions, and knows that only fools lament the loss of reputation as if it were a bodily wound. For he knows that the world belongs to the worldling, and that human

IAGO REVISITED

beings, whatever else they may profess, are in reality moved only by egotism, appetite, and personal advantage. A score of Machiavels on the Elizabethan stage know as much, except that they don't express themselves so effectively. Richard of Gloucester and the Bastard Edmund are past masters of this knowledge, and fragments of it also appear in a number of other Shakespearian characters, Falstaff for one and Antonio of *The Tempest* for another. The Bastard Faulconbridge is enrolled in the same school, but his sympathetic portrait allows him to wear his colors with a difference. Although his "mounting spirit" finds its proper traction in the courses of this world, he is careful, in his first monologue, to announce a pointed reservation:

> . . . though I will not practice to deceive,
> Yet, to avoid deceit, I mean to learn;
> For it shall strew the footsteps of my rising.
> [*King John* I.i.214–16]

The moral distinction in these words is explicit; what is not equally explicit, unless dramatic convention is allowed to assert its own relevant context of meaning, is the reference to the kind of role his is not going to be.

Labels, however, adhere only to surfaces and mock us with superficiality when we try to apply them to Shakespeare's depths. We detect the type with which he begins but lose it in the unique creation with which he ends. Applied to Iago, the Machiavellian label, while supplying some prefatory enlightenment, is too general to carry us very far into the moral meaning of his role. The high art that wrought him into the dense and exclusive design of his own play does not allow him to remain an undifferentiated specimen of villainous humanity according to the commonplace Elizabethan formula of the Machiavel. He is matched and specialized against a theme, and his evil refined into something rare through the ironic felicity of its polarization and the dramatic felicity of its operation within that theme. His cynical naturalism in respect to human motives and relationships is the first principle from which he moves, through a series of narrowing applications, until it creates his opinion of every other person in the play. It also creates something else: his opinion of his own situation. Unless we follow him closely through the descending gyres of his thought, we lose him and soon begin to wonder what he is talking about. Those of his words,

426 IAGO REVISITED

however, which apply to the way we are now concerned with him are invariably consistent with the way he is morally organized, and perspicuous in the terms of that organization. He is wonderfully opposed to the theme of the play as its anti-theme, and is, in fact, the most astonishing product of the Shakespearian technique of contrast.

If the play is about anything it is, as we have seen, about love. Its first words concern an elopement and its last the "heavy act" which has brought that elopement's history to its tragic end. Conceivably any sort of villain for any sort of villainous reason might have contrived the intrigue that produces the tragedy, and in Cinthio the motive was frustrated passion. But if one thing more than another can explain Shakespeare's departures from his sources, especially in matters of character and motive, it is his concern with dramaturgic patterns—in this case the pattern of opposites. Creating in Othello and Desdemona romantic love's most splendid votaries, he also creates in Iago its most derisive atheist. To the kind of love existing between hero and heroine, supplying the bright ideal of the play, the ancient is the dark countertype, the adversary. Although his naturalism is voluble upon a dozen topics, they are all ancillary to its main theme: nothing engrosses him so much as the subject of love or receives from him so mordant a negation. The marriage of true minds, or, for that matter, any level of love above sexual appetite, is exactly what he does not believe in. Nor does he believe that men and women exist in any relationship to each other apart from physical desire. He strikes his proper note in the first scene by the images of animal copulation with which he shocks Brabantio into attention,[6] and descants upon it thereafter through similar images and definitions that are, in fact, consistent deductions from a universal premise: Love, whose imagined mystery bemuses romantic fools like Roderigo, "is merely a lust of the blood and a permission of the will." Before he is through his nimble logic has roped everyone in the play, including himself, into his sexual syllogism. An Othello in love is merely "an erring barbarian" momentarily enticed but changeable in his appetites. A Desdemona in love is merely "a supersubtle Venetian" who married the Moor for lust and will leave him for youth "When she is sated with his body." Cassio is not handsome and young for nothing:

IAGO REVISITED

He hath a person and a smooth dispose
To be suspected—fram'd to make women false.
[I.iii.403–404]

Emilia, being a woman, is faithful to the promiscuous disposition of her sex:

> *Emil.* Do not you chide; I have a thing for you.
> *Iago.* A thing for me? It is a common thing—
> [III.iii.301–302]

He himself, being a man, obeys the disposition of his:

> Now I do love her too;
> Not out of absolute lust (though peradventure
> I stand accountant for as great a sin) . . .
> [II.i.300–302]

He thinks like a rigorous geometrician—from his basic proposition straight through to all its corollaries.

Being also a practical man of the world, from corollaries he moves to applications. Since the Moor is what he is and Emilia what she is, it follows that "I do suspect the lusty Moor hath leap'd into my seat." On the quay at Cyprus he stands spectator to an exchange of courtesies between Desdemona, who "must change for youth," and Cassio, who is "handsome, young, and hath all those requisites in him that folly and green minds look after," and soon imparts to Roderigo what it means: "Desdemona is directly in love with him." Social kissing between the sexes, though never quite free from equivocal suggestion, was permissible in Tudor England (to the astonishment of foreign visitors). Such a kiss between Cassio and Emilia in his presence suggests the interpretation natural to him: "For I fear Cassio with my nightcap too." His formulations are progressive, and parts of his second soliloquy (II.i.294–321) reach conclusions based on his observations during the reunion of the voyagers at Cyprus a few moments before. He is even obliged, with the air of a man of courage taking a calculated risk, to revise one of his previous estimates (for he has just seen and heard Othello's rapt greeting of Desdemona): "I dare think he'll prove to Desdemona / A most dear husband." In the same soliloquy he adverts to his discourse with his gull in order to save us from writing it off as sheer flimflam:

IAGO REVISITED

> That Cassio loves her, I do well believe it;
> That she loves him, 'tis apt and of great credit.

In other words, "I really do believe what I have just been saying to Roderigo." Something else will save us from the same skepticism—a part of his conversation with Cassio two scenes later:

Iago. Our general cast us thus early for the love of his Desdemona; who let us not therefore blame. He hath not yet made wanton the night with her, and she is sport for Jove.
Cas. She's a most exquisite lady.
Iago. And I'll warrant her full of game.
Cas. Indeed, she's a most fresh and delicate creature.
Iago. What an eye she has! Methinks it sounds a parley to provocation.
Cas. An inviting eye; and yet methinks right modest.
Iago. And when she speaks, is it not an alarum to love?
Cas. She is indeed perfection.
Iago. Well, happiness to their sheets!

[II.iii.14–29]

He does not get the confirmation for which he probes, but whether he changes his mind about Cassio too we shall never know. His separate suspicions bewilder us less and seem less absurd, at least to our theoretical consideration of him and them, when we see them for what they actually are—related local disturbances moving out from the broad weather front of his sexual doctrine. All of them together, by their mutual reinforcement, exhibit the disposition of his nature, and produce thereby an explanation for the existence of each individually, including the most prominent of them, his personal jealousy regarding his wife and Othello. We need also to reckon with the fact that on his own stage he was supported by a convention of which we are now largely bereft. It would take more than our fingers and toes to count the dramatized husbands round about him who jump to similar jealousies about their wives for no other reason than that they are women and, therefore, in Lear's sufficient phrase, "Down from the waist they are Centaurs"; or imagine a rival in every male who is not a certified eunuch.

To the extent that the foregoing interpretation is correct, his suspicions, which otherwise swirl like chaff in the wind, subside into an intelligible pattern. He has only two motives, one of them being his cynical Machiavellianism toward sex, which hovers over everyone in

IAGO REVISITED

the play and creates his personal provocation when it lights on his wife and "black Othello." The other requires only a word. We have no right to believe that he has a better claim than Cassio's to the lieutenancy, only that he craves it. And his craving is annexed to a credo of service which, at least in our own awareness of his moral qualifications, damns his claim. Besides, by every indication, he is intended as a coward, just as he was featured by Cinthio: "a very great coward, yet his carriage and conversation were so haughty and full of pretension, that you would have taken him for a Hector or an Achilles." [7] There is no reason to believe that the play changes this estimate. He is fluent with his dagger, but only in special circumstances: Cassio receives it anonymously in the dark, Roderigo already wounded and on his back, his wife when he is cornered ("Fie! your sword upon a woman?"); and he likes to stab and run. Finally, we can draw conviction on this point from the fact that to Cassio he is "the bold Iago" and to Lodovico "a very valiant fellow"; for, without exception, every moral attribute applied to him by anyone in the play is an ironic finger pointing to the truth of its opposite. As to his contempt for Cassio's "bookish theoric," it finds its precise equivalent in the feeling that today's master sergeant might entertain for the young second lieutenant just out of West Point. But unless the case is exceptional, we are able to assess the potential superiority of the trained, flexible, theoretical mind against the fossilized know-how of one who has merely slogged through a dozen years of practical experience. Iago's opinion notwithstanding, it tells us something of Cassio's qualifications that Othello should appoint him lieutenant before the beginning of the play and that the Signoria of Venice should appoint him governor of Cyprus before its end. But the question of Iago's justification or lack of it is ultimately meaningless beside the motive fact of his resentment, and his resentment, like his jealousy, belongs to his bad character. We neglect the intention within Shakespeare's irony unless we heed Emilia's inadvertent accuracy in respect to the nature and motives of her husband:

> I will be hang'd if some eternal villain,
> Some busy and insinuating rogue,
> Some cogging, cozening slave, to get some office,
> Have not devis'd this slander. I'll be hang'd else.
>
> . . . .

IAGO REVISITED

> The Moor's abus'd by some most villanous knave,
> Some base notorious knave, some scurvy fellow.
>
> . . . .
>
> Some such squire he was
> That turn'd your wit the seamy side without
> And made you to suspect me with the Moor.
>
> [IV.ii.130–47]

He has every reason for urging her to "Speak within door," for she has limned him to the life.

3

Such a portrait, or one reasonably like it, must be accepted because it exists, but it must also be rejected because it does not exist alone. Compromising it by addition and blurring it by invasion is his other life, his other set of features. They derive from nothing discoverable in Cinthio or in any naturalistic intention behind the playwright's revision of Cinthio, but have their source in the spectacular image of evil traditional on the popular stage. We need not expect, however, to find in Iago the massive dislocation visible in Richard ten years before, and even more obvious, because even earlier, in Barabas. The contrary elements of the conflation, no longer layered in broad distinction, are now relatively merged and granular, with the older image recessive and diminished. For one thing, the bravura image of multiple deceit, though ramifying upon as many victims as before, is no longer tandem and episodic, but deftly organized into a single complex intrigue within a comprehensive dramatic plot. For another, the amoral humor of the moral personification, having ceased to be explosive, has become pervasive—a mood and a tone penetrating Iago's role throughout. In the third place, the homiletic dimension of the role, its didactic voice and naked moral display, is relatively subdued and fragmentary, modified by indirection and mainly limited to sentences and half-sentences that twist in and out of his more relevant phraseology.[8] Finally, while the stark antinomy of the Psychomachia remains, supplying for his aggression an explanation that contradicts his motives, it has suffered attrition, and of the original formula only part survives: "I hate the Moor." To each of these aspects of the role we need to address ourselves briefly, allowing the long account already spun to piece out the explication proffered now.

IAGO REVISITED

One more comparison between Shakespeare and his source helps the matter forward. In Cinthio the wicked ensign's provocation was simple and compact, and so was his intention. Having fallen violently in love with Desdemona and found her oblivious to his furtive suit, he imagined she ignored him because she loved the lieutenant:

He then took it into his head, that this neglect arose from her being pre-engaged in favour of the lieutenant; and not only determined to get rid of him, but changed his affection for her into the most bitter hatred. He studied, besides, how he might prevent in future the Moor from living happily with Desdemona, should his passion not be gratified after he had murdered the lieutenant. Revolving in his mind a variety of methods, all impious and abominable, he at last determined to accuse her to the Moor of adultery with the lieutenant.[9]

The playwright's reformulation carries along with it a set of new conditions that point the direction he is taking. The aggression originally aimed at Desdemona and the lieutenant, with the Moor only an incidental victim, is in the play redirected full-front against Othello. The ensign's hatred for Desdemona has become Iago's hatred for Othello, and the principal target of his guile is now also the principal target of his enmity. In the second place, the theme of frustrated love has not disappeared; it has been pre-empted by a new figure, Shakespeare's one significant addition to the personae of the original story: Roderigo. Finally, the deception which originally operated exclusively on the Moor has in the play become diversified into a multiple exhibition of deceit exerted simultaneously upon Othello, Desdemona, Cassio, Roderigo, and even Emilia and Lodovico. These changes, like others already considered, are dramaturgic in the sense that they give dramatic body and color to a story redesigned for the stage; but by creating, at the same time, the opportunity for a series of images already familiar to us, they also reveal the *kind of dramaturgy* at work upon the play. It is with the last of them that we are immediately concerned.

Considered purely as an action, the intrigue is richly styled in several respects, all of them impressed upon it by its matrix in the homiletic convention. It remains plural even if it no longer remains serial, for, unlike Cinthio's ensign, who deceives only the Moor, Iago deceives everybody; and we have already seen that events occurring only by chance in the original story have been refashioned as direct products of his contrivance. By this expansion into multiplicity his plot receives its

IAGO REVISITED

homiletic conversion into an astonishing exhibit of guile and dissimulation. All the major characters are his dupes in addition to being his victims. In scene after scene he is immediately at work upon them, moulding their credulity or overcoming their incredulity, manipulating their innocence toward the abyss. And invariably each such episode is garnished by his monologue, inviting the audience to admire his virtuosity, to laugh at his gulls, and to understand the moral or tactical point within his latest imposture. Although all his actions are subdued to the dramatic plot, none of them marked by the pronounced quality of intercalated tour de force so conspicuous in Richard's wooing of Lady Anne, they achieve in their aggregate the same effect. He is not merely being put on display; like his ancestor the Vice he is putting himself on display, and what he displays has villainy for its subject and deceit for its method. Beneath the naturalistic refinements of character and situation lie the deep grooves of the old pattern, and in them he moves, carrying out a purpose that achieves its proper end through repetitive demonstration.

The pattern reveals itself another way, through the traditional faces of its masquerade. Having in the first scene, like a careful homilist, distributed his villainy into its two efficient aspects of dishonesty and hatred, he proceeds thereafter, in every possible way, to match against them the elaborate simulation of their opposites, and his dupes cooperate with him in weaving this design. The complex irony which identifies him to all of them as "honest Iago" allows him also, as criticism has abundantly noticed, a tireless gambol with this illusion, and he rarely forgoes the pleasure of invoking or protesting his honesty. Equally prominent, though less observed, is the pattern of his hate and "love." His iterated hatred of the Moor is matched by Othello's iterated conviction of his love, as if the victim embraced deception with as much zeal as deception embraced him:

> Honest Iago, that looks dead with grieving,
> Speak. Who began this? On thy love, I charge thee.
>
> [II.iii.177–78]

> I know, Iago,
> Thy honesty and love doth mince this matter,
> Making it light to Cassio.
>
> [II.iii.246–48]

IAGO REVISITED

> If thou dost love me,
> Show me thy thought.
>
> [III.iii.115–16]

> And, for I know thou'rt full of love and honesty
> And weigh'st thy words before thou giv'st them breath,
> Therefore these stops of thine fright me the more . . .
>
> [III.iii.118–20]

> I greet thy love,
> Not with vain thanks but with acceptance bounteous . . .
>
> [III.iii.469–70]

But while it is the artistic intention of the play that steeps his dupes in such unconscious irony, it is the homiletic intention within the role that creates his own deliberate use of it, and he lays it on with a trowel:

> And, good Lieutenant, I think you think I love you.
>
> [II.iii.315–16]

> I protest, in the sincerity of love and honest kindness.
>
> [II.iii.333–34]

> My lord, you know I love you.
>
> [III.iii.117]

> I am glad of it; for now I shall have reason
> To show the love and duty that I bear you
> With franker spirit.
>
> [III.iii.193–95]

> I humbly do beseech you of your pardon
> For too much loving you.
>
> [III.iii.212–13]

> I hope you will consider what is spoke
> Comes from my love.
>
> [III.iii.216–17]

> But sith I am enter'd in this cause so far,
> Prick'd to't by foolish honesty and love,
> I will go on.
>
> [III.iii.411–13]

Although his hate will be a subject for later discussion, in one respect it receives its explanation now. Its heavy iteration in the early scenes matches, in a balanced design, its heavy inversion into pretended love. It is through the emphatic statement and restatement of the reality that the stylized image of deceit achieves its effect in the illusion of him

434   *IAGO REVISITED*

entertained and endlessly expressed by Othello, and by everyone else in fact, as well as in his own avowals and protestations. His repetition of his hate, like his repetition of his dishonesty, is the amassed capital, as it were, that allows him to luxuriate in effusive declarations of love. The prominence of both motifs belongs to Shakespeare's artistry rather than to his originality: they are, as we have seen, typical parts of the convention in which he is working.

The mood of the role presents another side of the familiar image and pivots on the same axis of homiletic actuality and spectacular masquerade. The passion that should belong to the husband's and soldier's sense of injury is drowned, except for a single brief assertion, by the sardonic humor belonging by traditional right to the evil personification.[10] In all his intimate words to the audience his laughter lurks, modulated to scorn for honest fools or to self-satisfaction as he successfully pursues his sport and demonstrates his point:

> Thus do I ever make my fool my purse;
> For I mine own gain'd knowledge should profane
> If I would time expend with such a snipe
> But for my sport and profit.
>
> [I.iii.389–92]

It is no longer the coarse hilarity of the Vice of old, but if not loud it remains deep. And since his whole action in the play is absorbed into his intrigue, the laughter of the allegorical intriguer spreads throughout his role, gaining in extension what it loses in clamor, and suppressing the drastic *Stimmungsbruch* which cuts Barabas and Richard of Gloucester in two. At the end, in his comment on the wound he has just received, his gaiety even glints with the impervious immortality of his abstract forbears: "I bleed, sir, but not kill'd." Can we really be sure of his death? He and his more primitive brother Aaron are Shakespeare's only tragic villains still alive after the last word and the last scene. His intimate mood readily falls into focus when we stop peering for the character by way of the motives, but look instead at the *performance* by way of the tradition. In this tradition humor is not only the native mood of evil, it is also, along with the hate and the dishonesty, the indispensable predication for the massive operation of deceit.

For, while the essential face grins at the audience, its sober opposite, belonging to the man of love and probity, is the only countenance his victims see up to the denouement. At proper moments he is decently

IAGO REVISITED

jovial, but otherwise he is grave, he is solicitous, he is compassionate, he is loyal—a reluctant witness against a friend, a sympathetic counselor in time of trouble, an unhappy spectator of a woman's unhappiness, and especially a fervent ally of his injured master as he kneels and pledges "The execution of his wit, hands, heart / To wrong'd Othello's service." These are his feelings and his features. Surrounded by suffering, he himself becomes a man of sorrows, and tender sentiment melts the tough soldier, pouring out in tears or darkening his face with the shadow of tears—not once but many times if we allow the text its proper weight as a cue. When the drunken quarrel arouses Othello from his bed, he turns for explanation to the man on whose words he can rely, to "Honest Iago, that looks dead with grieving." Emilia, urging Desdemona to intercede for cashiered Cassio, assures her that "it grieves my husband / As if the cause were his." When the convulsed Moor seizes and bends him to the ground, demanding "the ocular proof," his protestation touches the lachrymose sublime:

> O grace! O heaven forgive me!
> Are you a man? Have you a soul or sense?—
> God b' wi' you! take mine office. O wretched fool,
> That liv'st to make thine honesty a vice!
> O monstrous world! Take note, take note, O world,
> To be direct and honest is not safe.
> I thank you for this profit; and from hence
> I'll love no friend, sith love breeds such offence.
> [III.iii.373–80]

In his reply to the bewildered Lodovico, who has turned to him for explanation after seeing Othello strike his wife, his words, restrained by loyalty, are less expressive than the anguish of his voice and hands:

> Alas, alas!
> It is not honesty in me to speak
> What I have seen and known. You shall observe him,
> And his own courses will denote him so
> That I may save my speech.
> [IV.ii.287–91]

When he tries to console Desdemona after the brothel scene, he himself is close to what he gently urges her against: "Do not weep, do not weep. Alas the day!" And when in the dark he bends over the man he has just stabbed, his tears drizzle by lantern light:

IAGO REVISITED

> Lend me a light. Know we this face or no?
> Alas, my friend and my dear countryman
> Roderigo? No. Yes, sure. O heaven! Roderigo.
> [V.i.88–90]

No Iago on the modern stage is likely to weep so much, or wring his hands so much, or carry out in other ways the original bravura of the role, our own taste scarcely being equal to so spiced a performance. We know we are not Elizabethans, and we may suspect we have not their palates. Richard of Gloucester is just as tearful; and the London citizen who saw the first *Othello* probably remembered the pleasure he had received fifteen years before from *The Jew of Malta*. The same man, allowing his memory to drift a little further back, could recall the evil merriment and pious grief, the simulated love and honesty, the multiple deceptions of "the formal Vice Iniquity." Today, without the benefit of his theatrical habituation, we pore with specialized eyes upon the surface of Iago's role, and try, whether as audience or as actor, to subdue its obscure depths to its intelligible mood and content. But these depths, it should now be obvious, assert their own mood and content.

And they also assert their own dramatic method, a point so often stressed in these pages that only its relevance to a good deal of Shakespearian criticism justifies this word of review. When William Hazlitt described Iago as "an amateur of tragedy in real life," when Bradley noted as "a curious point of technique" with Shakespeare that Iago's "soliloquies . . . read almost like explanations offered to the audience," and when other critics observe the "histrionic" or "artistic" element in the performance, they all respond to a phenomenon whose real nature, although they do not quite discern it, is by now sufficiently familiar to us. It is once more the homiletic dramaturgy of the moral play, where personified evil demonstrated its destructive operation and preached its own exposure, addressing itself as intimately to its audience as any minister to his congregation or pedagogue to his pupils, with the difference that the dramatized lesson was made trenchant by satire and by action. This method reached its culmination in the Vice and descended from him to the line of villains he fathered. All of them manipulate their victims into comic or tragic confusion in order to exhibit the name and nature of villainy. It is, as we have seen, a declining method, and

IAGO REVISITED

in Iago it is substantially diminished in its two principal features: the action loses as a demonstration what it gains as an organic plot, and the homily recedes before the enactment of the literal story. But although diminished it remains, exploited by the playwright at the height of his powers. That the action of the villain is still a moral demonstration is made clear by the language of demonstration: "Thus do I ever make my fool my purse . . ." and

> Thus credulous fools are caught,
> And many worthy and chaste dames even thus,
> All guiltless, meet reproach.
>
> [IV.i.46–48]

That the demonstration is addressed unequivocally to the audience is equally clear:

> And what's he then that says I play the villain,
> When this advice is free I give and honest,
> Probal to thinking, and indeed the course
> To win the Moor again?
>
> [II.iii.342–45]

And it is no less evident that his self-exposure is as absolute as it is inconceivable in any naturalistic estimate of wickedness, no matter how wicked:

> How am I then a villain
> To counsel Cassio to this parallel course,
> Directly to his good? Divinity of hell!
> When devils will the blackest sins put on,
> They do suggest at first with heavenly shows,
> As I do now.
>
> [II.iii.354–59]

A villain can act this way, but it is only Villainy in a Geneva gown that can talk this way; and the integrity of his sermon includes his victims as well as himself: they are grist for his mill, he says, because one is an "honest fool," another has "a free and open nature," and a third is a "worthy and chaste" dame. They qualify as his dupes, he says, because they are too honest to suspect him; but they also qualify in another sense: their virtue provokes him. His meaning on this last point, however, must wait until it is ripe for treatment under the rubric of his "hate."

438   *IAGO REVISITED*

4

Alongside such general observations on the role, several of its moments, briefly looked at, contribute their own testimony to its lineage. The seduction scene (III.iii), repeating, at greater length and with deeper subtlety, the method of Richard's wooing of Lady Anne, has the same source in the standard episode of spiritual manipulation by which the Vice of the moralities, resorting to all his tricks of sophistry and dissimulation, detaches his human dupe from allegiance to virtue and subjugates him to himself and to the sway of evil. Beneath the differences separating the literal story from allegory, the lines of force, the technique of the enterprise, and the nature of the achievement remain the same. Such a scene's acute theatrical effect lies, on the one hand, in its exhibit of perversion's cunning movement toward its goal, and, on the other, in its spectacular reversal, its peripeteia. In the allegorical plays the Vice begins his work when his destined victim is at the top of his virtue; Richard undertakes Lady Anne when she is at the top of her hatred; and Iago advances the first light tentacles of insinuation when Othello's love finds its most rapt expression:

> *Oth.* Excellent wretch! Perdition catch my soul
> But I do love thee! and when I love thee not,
> Chaos is come again.
> *Iago.* My noble lord—
>
> [III.iii.90–92]

The long dialogue that follows, interrupted by the brief interlude between Othello and Desdemona which introduces the handkerchief, almost defies analysis, so close is its texture, so artful its design. Only its own words afforded an adequate sense of what it is, and as well as anything in Shakespeare it exposes the distance between the conventions he uses and what he makes of them. Not the least remarkable thing about the web that is spun is that, in effect, it is spun unwillingly. The honest man talks by refusing to talk, insinuates his "thoughts" by resisting inquiry, inoculates his victim with jealousy's poison by warning him against it, and drives him to madness by reluctantly supplying the "proofs." It is all done because "I am bound" and "at your request" by a man constrained. And his achievement consists not only in perverting the mind of his dupe but in degrading and dominating him as

IAGO REVISITED

439

well—in reducing him from "my noble lord" to a creature he can interrupt and divert at will, to a thrall he can address with as little formality and as much contempt as he uses toward Roderigo: "Why, how now, General? No more of that!" And he is never more the Vice than in the ironic words with which he ends the scene: "I am your own for ever," for they mean, of course, "Now you belong to me."

A later scene (IV.i) intensifies this picture of degradation by arranging it into another imitation of its homiletic auspices. One of the most painful moments of the play occurs when Othello, racked to frenzy by his passion and by the sexual images his tormentor feeds to his imagination, gives way to a babble of disjointed words and sinks to the stage unconscious. Thereupon Iago contemptuously toes the prostrate body and delivers with down-pointed fingers his mocking sermon. It is an effective piece of theater, but more of a novelty to us than it was to its first audience. To them such an Image of Prostration, with Evil gloating over its stretched-out human victim, was traditional, going back at least to the time when the Malus Angelus of *The Castle of Perseverance* stood over the corpse of Humanum Genus and invited the spectators to acknowledge that the destination of the hero's soul had been ticketed by the depravity of his life:

> wyttnesse of al þat ben a-bowte,
> Syr Coueytyse, he had hym owte;
> þer for he schal, with-outyn dowte,
>   with me to hellë pytt.
>   [ll. 3031–34]

But the image reaches its more representative form in later plays. While the human hero of *Mankind* stretches in sleep on the ground, as sign of his spiritual decay, his seducer stands over him and elucidates the achievement:

> For-well, euerychon, for I haue don my game,
> For I haue brought Mankynde to myscheff & to schame.
>   [ll. 598–99]

Magnificence, in Skelton's play of that name, having been "beten downe and spoylyd from all his goodys and rayment," sprawls in similar prostration while several allegorical figures of ill omen, Adversity, Poverty, and Liberty, preach over him the causes and consequences of his fall.[11] In *The Four Elements* stupefied Humanity lies

440   *IAGO REVISITED*

asleep in a corner while Ignorance does the homiletic talking.[12] Confusion in *The Longer Thou Livest* does as much over the dying body of Moros.[13] In *Enough Is as Good as a Feast* the Vice points down to the stricken figure of Worldly Man and utters the relevant homily:

> This is the end alwaies wher I begin:
> For I am the root of all wickednes and sin.
> I neuer rest to teach and instruct men to euil:
> Til I bring them bothe body and soule to the Deuil.
> As we haue doon this worldly man heer as you see.
>
> [sig. G *recto*]

All the "wit" plays present the moral and intellectual decay of the hero through the same image of physical prostration while his personified foes use him as both text and pulpit.[14] Among the hybrid plays *Cambises* repeats this spectacle, with the depraved king stretched out *in extremis* and Ambidexter laughing and preaching over him.[15] Another example belongs to a play indebted to the morality convention only for the figure of the Vice, who brings with him, however, his traditional apparatus of deceit and homiletic mockery. In Heywood's *Play of Love,* the Vice (Neither Lover nor Beloved), involved in debate with The Lover Loved over the question whether there is more pleasure in love or out of it, promises the audience to make a fool of his opponent. He proceeds to do so by running in with the false announcement that the latter's sweetheart has just been burned to death. Thereupon the dupe faints with grief and lies prostrate while the Vice mocks him with words until he arouses him with blows.[16] This is the Vice of comedy, but the Image of Prostration attends him as part of his allegorical heritage. For the same reason it also attends Iago with all its homiletic trappings as he spurns his stricken prey and delivers the appropriate sermon:

> Work on,
> My medicine, work! Thus credulous fools are caught,
> And many worthy and chaste dames even thus,
> All guiltless, meet reproach.
>
> [IV.i.45–48]

Also, the first scene deserves a moment's notice in connection with one of the two figures with whom it begins. The only sizable role en-

IAGO REVISITED

tirely of Shakespeare's invention belongs to Roderigo, who derives from nothing more in Cinthio than his remark that the lieutenant waged his drunken quarrel on the court of guard "contra uno soldato." Apart from the same use to which Iago puts him in the play, Roderigo is scarcely significant in the tragic action, and his substantial portrait invites conjecture. It is at least part of the explanation that, to a considerable extent, he is what Shakespearian tragedy is never without, comic relief—a "silly gentleman" stricken into foolish love, maudlin in his unhappiness, and shrill in his petulance against the hand that masters him until its next touch resuscitates his mood and propels him on his next fool's errand. It is pure puppetry and the method is always the same: to each encounter with Iago he brings either despondency or rebellion, only to be twisted toward a new illusion and rewound like a toy. He is swindled, browbeaten, manipulated like wax, and allowed to feel the rough edge of contempt in the voice that rallies him. He is silly because he is weak, absurd because he is beyond his depth, and grotesque because he is dangled and jerked by the puppeteer. In the end, in the dark, he is granted sight of the truth by the gleam of the dagger entering his breast. But he serves a larger purpose. His comedy is only a variation within the principle governing the play as a whole in the way we are now concerned with it. Although he does not contribute very much to the tragic action, he contributes a great deal to Iago's traditional role. Not only does he render deceit more flexible by becoming its tool, he augments its achievement by becoming another one of its victims. He diversifies and multiplies its display and earns thereby his place in the story alongside all the other puppets: the hero, the heroine, the lieutenant, the wife. Both as the comic underling and as the tool destroyed he is created in obedience to the dramaturgic formula that previously created Ithamore for Barabas, Stitch for Edricus, Lorrique for Hoffman, and even Buckingham (without the comedy, for he is a nobleman) for Richard.

Like them also, Roderigo has another function which is only visible as a part of the process of historical change in the role to which his is subsidiary. He gives a hearing inside the play to its choric and homiletic voice, which otherwise would have to be directed, as in earlier plays, continually to the audience; and he aids, therefore, in its naturalistic transformation. His utility this way is especially clear in the first scene. What is sometimes called Iago's "credo," his exposition of his own behavior in contradistinction to that of "honest knaves" and his assertion of his talent in dissimulation ("I am not what I am"), is nothing else than another version of the prescriptive avowal by the evil personification of his *moral pedigree*—but now subdued in two respects: it refers to a literal situation and it is addressed no longer to the spectators but to a figure on the stage. The audience which a decade earlier had received Richard's lecture now simply overheard Iago's conversation. This difference in expository technique is significant, for the subject remains the same: the proclamation by the Vice-villain of his Villainy and of its attributes, his deceit and hatred. It is also true that Richard's announcement is more blatant because in it the *allegorical equation* is more compact. He leaves no doubt as to why and what he hates because he expresses it as part of a complete formula. On the same point Iago, though more emphatic, is less explicit because in his language the same formula is falling apart under the impact of the naturalistic elements invading his role. Certainly his first audience understood him well enough out of their habituation with the equation as a whole. Today we need to recover its pieces—they are all present in his words, though scattered—in order to understand him with equal clarity.

Why, then, does he hate the Moor? The question finds its answer where the whole Elizabethan drama of evil found its first principle: in the moral dualism of the Psychomachia. A quick backward glance helps us forward on this theme. The original allegory pitted personified vice against personified virtue on the field of battle, the most obvious metaphor for the eternal feud between them in the human soul. When the military image disappeared from the moralities, its substitute representation (in plays of the middle period mainly) for the strife between these natural enemies became a debate—sometimes dignified as in Medwall's *Nature* and Skelton's *Magnificence,* more often shrill billingsgate as in Rastell's *Four Elements,* Bale's *Three Laws,* and *King Darius.* Coexistence between vices and virtues being impossible, one side had to drive out the other from the soul of man, whether by original violence, later polemic, or the cunning intrigue of evil which soon became standard. Their enmity gets typical expression in the words of Envy in *Impatient Poverty:*

IAGO REVISITED

I hate conscience, peace loue and reste
Debate and stryfe that loue I beste
Accordyng to my properte.

[ll. 517-19]

Originally there was nothing for vice to "hate" in the generalized figure of mankind: he was a moral vacuum waiting to be filled by good or evil, and it was the job of the vices to capture, persuade, or deceive him while hating their proper adversaries, his guardian virtues. The later evolution of the morality drama brought about, however, a new alignment. All the virtues gradually melt away from the stage, and so do the subsidiary vices, while their leader swells into the portentous figure of the Vice. He, with unique theatrical éclat in the late moralities and in the hybrid plays, carries on the traditional program of moral evil, deceiving his victims into temporary jeopardy or permanent ruin. But in the hybrid plays the Psychomachia, by its adjustment to its new environment, indicates as well its future development in the secular drama. The Vice remains as militant as ever against virtues and values, but these are no longer externalized personifications, and the human hero no longer a moral cypher. Mankind has been replaced by men and women who carry their moral qualities inside them, and to the extent that such persons are good they become the virtuous side of the Psychomachia, attracting the enmity as well as the aggression of the allegorical foe. Although the formula of the Psychomachia is not always overt in the hybrid plays, exactly because they are hybrid and tran sitional, its new direction is clear and finds its new expression in the following words addressed to Politick Persuasion, the Vice of *Patient and Meek Grissill*:

The Scorpion forth will flinge, his poyson to anoye,
And passingers that passe him bye, with Vennome to distroye,
So thou whose mallice doth abound, thy stinge doste now prepare,
To vex and harme those wightes, whose liues most vertuous are.

[ll. 932-35]

And it is equally clear in his own words about the virtuous heroine:

Phie ont, it greeueth mee to the verie hart,
A Ladie honorable, naye a Whippe and a Cart.

[ll. 912-13]

IAGO REVISITED

All the hybrid plays, whether or not their language is explicit on the issue, inherit, along with the Vice, the moral structure of the Psychomachia, and present him arrayed, according to his allegorical "properte," against the virtues incorporated in such heroines as chaste Virginia, godly Susanna, patient and meek Grissill; or against the chivalric and romantic values inherent in the knights and ladies of the dramatized romances in which he appears. The old conflict, along with the enmity proper to it, has not changed, only shifted its ground, now that virtue is no longer distinguishable from its human possessor.

In the secular drama that follows, especially in tragedy, the villain who inherits the mantle of the Vice inherits as well this enmity. In his mouth it becomes the quintessential expression of the Psychomachia —the homiletic revelation of evil's hatred for its opposite. It is properly *allegorical* hatred, having neither psychological explanation nor appropriate emotional content, for it defines the elemental conflict within a moral antinomy, in the sense that Envy, as quoted above, hates Conscience, Peace, Love, and Rest "Accordyng to my properte." In the same sense the villain hates virtues and values, and the persons in whom they are embodied, because, as he says, he is a villain. His avowal to that effect simply repeats, in condensed version, the Vice's obligatory exposition of his name and nature; and it is also, as it was in the moral drama, a comprehensive statement of *allegorical* motivation. On this level of the role no other explanation is needed. Every human reason, good or bad, that can possibly be ascribed to Barabas for his villainy is made superfluous by what he says to Ithamore:

> we are villaines both:
> Both circumcized, we hate Christians both.
> [*The Jew of Malta,* ll. 979–80] [17]

"Christians," of course, is a virtue word, defining the composite enemy in this renewed declaration of the Holy War. In *Edmond Ironside,* Edricus is eager to describe himself as everybody's bane ("meaninge noe man good"), but he also has a more compact target in "the plaine honest meaninge kinge," whose goodness he emphasizes in every possible way in order to fit him to his role as victim. Because Edmond's father, he says, raised him from low estate "To be a duke for all my villanie" and because Edmond himself is to him the most generous of benefactors,

IAGO REVISITED

> Therefore I hate him, and desire his death
> And will procure his end in what I cann.
>
> [ll. 325–26] [18]

> For I desire to Drinke kinge Edmundes blood
> Because hee ever sought to doe mee good.
>
> [ll. 1990–91]

In *Lust's Dominion*, Eleazar's first words declare his membership in the same allegorical fraternity: "On me, do's musick spend this sound on me / That hate all unity" (I.i).[19] In *The Death of Robert Earl of Hungtingdon*, Robin Hood is Christlike in his virtues, provoking the villain Doncaster to shake against him the banner of the timeless feud:

> Another thing I hate him for again:
> He says his prayers, fasts eves, gives alms, does good:
> For these and such like crimes swears Doncaster
> To work the speedy death of Robin Hood.
>
> [I.ii] [20]

And in Lorenzo of *The First Part of Jeronimo* the Psychomachia is as explicit as possible for a figure no longer an overt personification:

> I hate Andrea, cause he aimes at honor,
> When my purest thoughts work in a pitchy vale,
> Which are as different as heauen and Hell.
>
> [I.i.106–108] [21]

Not only do such announcements expose the allegorical dynamic within this type of villainy, they also chart its consistent verbal formula pivoting on the word "hate"—a formula sufficiently bewildering to us today even when it is most explicit. On its own stage its expression was traditional and commonplace, even prescriptive, for the villain who drew all his energy, or part of it, from the allegorical heritage which characterizes, with varying intensity, many more Elizabethan plays than the few appearing in this study. But like every other feature of the same tradition it was a declining formula. Over time its elements lose their original cohesion, then crumble into decay and vanish. What remains longest is the pivotal expression of hate.

It is exactly in Shakespeare, because he used it so often, that the formula shows most clearly its stages of decline. In 1593 Richard of Gloucester utters it in its full dimension:

446

IAGO REVISITED

And therefore, since I cannot prove a lover
To entertain these fair well-spoken days,
I am determined to prove a villain
And hate the idle pleasures of these days.
[I.i.28–31]

These fair well-spoken days of peace, love, and courtesy, as well as the people in whose natures such qualities find expression, compose a system of values against which his villainy directs his hate and guile. Here the aggressive equation of the Psychomachia is complete. But it has begun to crumble a few years later (1593) when Shylock, in the most archaic moment of his role, invokes it, turning from Antonio to the audience to inform them that

I hate him for he is a Christian;
But more for that in low simplicity
He lends out money gratis . . .
[I.iii.43–45]

We are perhaps a little too comparative today in our religions and too comfortable in our economic Zion to receive from such an avowal the import it had for its own time. Its equivalent effect might come to a middle-class audience in some Midwest city if a caricatured villain of a commissar turned to the front seats in order to say of the hero, "I hate him because he believes in God, and even more because he believes in human liberty and free enterprise." In Shylock's words, at any rate, two thirds of the equation survives: the hate and its virtuous quarry are proclaimed; and if the villainy is not, an Elizabethan audience derived it very easily by extrapolation. But in Shylock even the hatred has become coy, and in the trial scene, where his reply to the Duke's appeal is not dictated by prudence, it retreats behind a doctrine of natural antipathies:

So can I give no reason, nor I will not,
More than a lodg'd hate and a certain loathing
I bear Antonio, that I follow thus
A losing suit against him.
[IV.i.59–62]

Three years later still it becomes even coyer. When Oliver of *As You Like It* comes to play his part in 1599 he employs his monologic opportunity to the following effect, his brother being the subject:

IAGO REVISITED

I hope I shall see an end of him; for my soul (yet I know not why) hates nothing more than he. Yet he's gentle; never school'd and yet learned; full of noble device; of all sorts enchantingly beloved, and indeed so much in the heart of the world, and especially of my own people, who best know him, that I am altogether misprised.

[I.i.170–77]

Although the hate remains explicit, its point has been blunted into an enigma; and although the solution is present, it is present only by indirection. But indirection gives way to revelation when old Adam warns Orlando against returning home:

> Know you not, master, to some kind of men
> Their graces serve them but as enemies?
> No more do yours. Your virtues, gentle master,
> Are sanctified and holy traitors to you.
>
> . . . .
>
> Come not within these doors! Within this roof
> The enemy of all your graces lives.

[II.iii.10–18]

We are watching, in short, the naturalistic disintegration less of the Psychomachia itself than of its homiletic war song. The hatred survives like a trunk stripped of its leaves, but the playgoer's recollection easily supplied the summer foliage, which, in reality, is not yet lost, merely scattered. It is chiefly as a result of this denuded tradition that the soliloquized profession of hate, no matter what the reason, marks the Elizabethan stage villain, while virtue marks his victim, in numerous plays not otherwise conspicuously indebted to the allegorical drama.

Othello, on the other hand, is very greatly indebted to it, almost as if the playwright, finding in his source a story of villainy highly susceptible to such a dramatization, deliberately undertook to give new brilliance to the old stage image. In Iago the image still retains its integrity as an action, but its verbal structure has crumbled, although all the fragments are still in sight. In his language all parts of the equation are copiously present, but in diffusion and modulated by indirection. In various places he reiterates his villainy, the virtue of his victims, and his hate; and occasionally he even puts two of the ingredients together, as in the following words, where his "howbeit" has the same deflected force as Oliver's second "yet":

IAGO REVISITED

> The Moor (howbeit I endure him not)
> Is of a constant, loving, noble nature . . .
>
> [II.i.297–98]

But the linked elements of the original formula, now interpenetrated by naturalism and yielding to the imperative of artistic change, have mainly fallen apart. The role has traveled through too much literal scenery to be able any longer to say, "My name is Iniquity and, according to my property, I hate Virtue"; or even to say less abstractly but with equal coherence, "I hate the Moor because he is a paragon of Christian and romantic virtue and I am a villain." Iago's hatred, in short, having become isolated from its allegorical predication, survives unattached, in spite of what he tells Roderigo about the lieutenancy in the first scene. It simply does not unite with the resentment he expresses then any more than it unites with the jealousy he expresses later, belonging to a realm where such causes have no status. On this point his words to his gull cannot compete in reliability with the testimony of his monologue. There it is starkly

> I hate the Moor;
> And it is thought abroad that 'twixt my sheets
> 'Has done my office.
>
> [I.iii.392–94]

What better motive for hatred than his suspicion that Othello has seduced his wife? and how tempting to read "for" instead of "and." But the "and" remains indestructible and wins a place in dramatic history, being the seam between the drama of allegory and the drama of nature, as well as between the kind of motivation proper to each. If he restates his hatred almost as much as he does his villainy, that is because both avowals are heavily stylized realities against his endless pretense of love and honesty:

> Though I do hate him as I do hell pains,
> Yet, for necessity of present life,
> I must show out a flag and sign of love,
> Which is indeed but sign.
>
> [I.i.155–58]

His deceit, to belabor an old theme, is theatrical bravura according to a traditional design, and designs in Shakespeare, when he is at the top of his powers, are massive as well as subtle, like the imagery and atmos-

IAGO REVISITED 449

phere in any of the great plays. As for his provocation against Cassio because

> He hath a daily beauty in his life
> That makes me ugly . . .
>
> [V.i.19–20]

that is the Psychomachia again, in language that naturalizes it slightly. The sense of the passage is future and its burden self-preservation: "If Cassio do remain" his virtues will, by contrast, show me up as evil and expose me for the villain I am. A certain tenderness about the time to come silts over what is, at bottom, as downright as Lorenzo's hatred of Andrea because "he aimes at honor,/ When my purest thoughts work in a pitchy vale . . ." For it is still the elemental strife between Good and Evil, the metaphor of the moral dualism sustained by the Christian imagination through the dozen centuries between Prudentius and Shakespeare, and it includes Desdemona as well.

5

A few words remain for the sake of a short supplement and an equally short generalization. Although this book ends with Shakespeare it would serve its subject badly if it left the impression that the convention with which it has been concerned also stops at the same point. It would be a strange convention indeed if it broke off so abruptly. Besides, nothing in the Tudor-Stuart drama really begins or ends with Shakespeare, except the contribution of his own genius, which was not eccentric, to an art which was profoundly traditional and moved through change with the biological pace of an organism moving through life. Iago's predecessors are not more numerous, though they are more obvious, than his successors, in whom the old dramatic image progressively fractures and fades. To point to a few of the villains who troop after him in the same hybrid convention becomes, therefore, a clarifying addition to its perspective, except that a book already too long allows them only the barest mention and confines them to figures who came to the stage while Shakespeare was still alive.

One such is the wicked Duke of Epire in *The Dumb Knight* (Pr. 1608) by Gervase Markham and Lewis Machin. Not only is the main plot of this play heavily indebted to *Othello,* but its villain, down to

450 *IAGO REVISITED*

his very language, is a palpable imitation of Iago, and shows the same fissure in his role. In Middleton's *The Phoenix* (Pr. 1607), a play which reveals its homiletic auspices through the fact that most of its roles are presented as types, the villain, transparently called Proditor, pursues his deadly feud against the very virtuous Prince Phoenix for no other reason than the compulsive one of the Psychomachia. Although the more opaque name of Horatio clothes the intriguer in John Day's *Law Tricks* (Pr. 1608), it is still in the bygone drama of abstraction that he finds at least part of his motivation and dramatic style. *The Faithful Friends,* which survived only in manuscript until it was published in 1812, may be by Beaumont and Fletcher and may be as early as 1605. In the role of Rufinus it presents another confusing product of the same mixed tradition. Finally, in Massinger's *The Duke of Milan,* written in 1616 or shortly after, a plot derived from the story of Herod and Mariamne (in Josephus) is given an Italian setting and twisted by the addition of the villain Francisco, derived from Iago, into an intrigue against love and marriage, derived from *Othello*. Only in the last act, after he has largely achieved his purpose, does Francisco produce a reason for the "revenge" he has been pursuing by devious tricks of policy and dissimulation since the beginning of the second. And this reason has every appearance of being the playwright's afterthought.[22] All these figures, as well as others that can be found in the drama surrounding Shakespeare by anyone who cares to look, are bewildering because they are, in part at least, traditional dramatic portraits of abstract evil out of the Psychomachia, moved by its original dynamic without, however, retaining with sufficient clarity its original language. Beneath the laminae of their exterior transformation the old image remains visible, but its relevant verbal formula has become disjointed, and they are rationalized by ambiguous explanations expressing revenge or ambition. Peeping through their monologues, however, the homiletic revelation still appears, though in dispersal, to explain that they themselves are villains and find their enmity in the virtue of their destined victims. Sometimes it even survives massively, as in the following words of the Duke of Epire in *The Dumb Knight,* respecting the hero Philocles:

> I am resolv'd, since virtue hath disdain'd
> To clothe me in her riches, henceforth to prove

IAGO REVISITED

A villain fatal, black and ominous.
Thy virtue is the ground of my dislike . .
[p. 134] [23]

For, by the same token that they inherit the malevolent side of the Psychomachia, their victims invariably inherit the other, and are presented, without exception, as persons of transcendent virtue. As for the action itself, it also retains its homiletic style by remaining, at bottom, a serial demonstration of villainous deceit (or "policy") at work against credulous innocence as well as against the spiritual ties of love and friendship. So much for the supplement.

As for the generalization, it brings the long theme back to Shakespeare. Now that scholarship has established the chronology of his plays with reasonable precision and assurance, we are able to view the whole evolution of his artistic career—and, to some extent, of his spirit— from a multitude of perspectives. As play follows play in time, the great organism unfolds its successive stages of maturity. Moving from phase to phase, vocabulary and idiom, verse and imagery, style and technique, moral sentiment and dramatic emphasis, and the sheer stride and turn of poetry and vision reveal the playwright's pilgrimage. In this regard we can neglect if we wish, once we have uncovered and based them, the premises of his age and stage, and concentrate our view on Shakespeare's private development. One phenomenon, as fundamental as it is elusive, exists, however, to complicate such a survey: the conventions of his stage are on a pilgrimage of their own—toward naturalism. The moving finger of the dramatist writes, as it were, on the moving surface of his dramaturgy. It is a truism that the Renaissance meant, among other things, the redirection of human energies toward the possibilities of mortal life on the plane of the natural world. And we are generally aware of the parallel redirection of Renaissance art when we speak of *quattrocento* painting and sculpture. But it is not yet a truism—in fact, it is scarcely a datum of our knowledge—that the dramatic art in which Shakespeare and his fellows worked was undergoing a similar revision of values and, consequently, of technique. The metaphoric dramaturgy that had preached the timeless crisis of the soul and enacted its impalpable world gave way, in his time, to the dramatic imitation of literal human life and historical event, marking the beginning of the great cycle of the naturalistic stage which reached its height perhaps in the plays of Ibsen's middle period and shows, in our own time, unmistakable symptoms of decay. To say that the drama imitates life or an action is to raise the question as to what we mean by either. It is probably more useful to say that technique imitates subject, and in the sixteenth century the English theater was in process of change from one great subject to another. Although by the time the drama reaches Shakespeare it ostensibly imitates natural forms, its dramaturgy still retains features, its stage properties, and its playwrights habits that belong to "the artifice of eternity."

Such survivals of the older subject and the older technique spread wide beyond the roles of villains merely, and invite further study as well as a new direction in critical method. Throughout its whole career Shakespearian criticism has been governed, and limited, by its heritage of naturalism, and limited further by a stubborn romantic mystique concerning the nature of art, especially the art of Shakespeare, for whom Swinburne's phrase still supplies the prevailing formula: "In Shakespeare's world as in nature's." The result has been that we are content not to understand, nor even to see, a perspective in his plays for which naturalism does not provide a focus. Elsewhere in literature, where critical canons have grown up in a less enchanted atmosphere, we learn more readily that great documents of the human spirit may be essentially composite or stratified when some traditional datum of sentiment, behavior, or technique gives way to changing convention, or is overlaid, without being consciously rejected, by the insight of individual genius—witness *The Iliad*, the *Alcestis* of Euripides, *Ecclesiastes, Job, Beowulf, Gargantua and Pantagruel*. Any of the other arts tell the same story and make much the same point. At bottom we are dealing with the everlasting fact of change, except that a great deal of the time it is gradual enough to be imperceptible, or it is confined within a single system of thought and values and, therefore, intelligible. When, however, its tempo accelerates to the degree that it becomes revolutionary, or if it creates one of those significant moments in the history of art or of institutions when one world of perception and sentiment gives way to another, the radical conflation that results can be understood only if we are, in the first place, open to the possibility of its existence, and, in the second, historically equipped to understand it. It is, of course, too easy to succumb to the fallacy of assuming that because

IAGO REVISITED

history explains something it explains everything. The historical method applied to Shakespeare can only throw light on what is common to him and other Elizabethans who were not Shakespeare—say Anthony Munday and Thomas Dekker. The quality of meaning and sensation distinguishing him from them is a matter of poetry, not of history. It is, however, a matter of history that the Elizabethan drama was preceded and deeply influenced by a popular dramatic convention that was not naturalistic, and this fact, according to the several hundred pages that have gone before, illuminates a good deal that has remained troublesome in Shakespeare, and equally troublesome in the plays of Munday and Dekker, if only we allowed those worthies to trouble us. Let the complete critic go on from there.

NOTES

I: IAGO

1. Achille Charles, duc de Broglie, "De l'Art Dramatique en France," *Revue Française*, XIII (1830). The article was inspired by the appearance of *Othello*, in the translation of Alfred de Vigny, upon the French stage. A more sensitive critic than Thomas Rymer, from whose "maggot" he was entirely free, Broglie was equally unbemused, as the following observation upon Iago reveals (p. 103):

Selon nous, le rôle a déplu parce qu'il n'est pas bon; parce qu'il est, non pas inconséquent (quoi de plus naturel à l'homme que l'inconséquence?) mais incohérent, parce que les parties dont il se compose ne tiennent pas ensemble, et qu'à son égard, on ne sait vraiment à quelle idée se prendre.

2. Harley Granville-Barker, *Othello* (*Prefaces to Shakespeare*, IV, London, 1945), p. 219.

3. The essence of this conception is contained in an article by C. F. Tucker Brooke, "The Romantic Iago," *Yale Review*, VII (1918), 349–59, wherein he describes "the tragedy of Iago" as "the tragedy of this honest, charming soldier," and pictures his "moral awakening" and his "weary detachment." But "Iago's tragedy" is also a prominent theme for A. C. Bradley, *Shakespearean Tragedy* (2d ed., London, 1905), pp. 218 and 222. More of the same appears in John W. Draper, "Honest Iago," *PMLA*, XLVI (1931), 724–37, and in Samuel A. Tannenbaum, "The Wronged Iago," *Shakespeare Association Bulletin*, XII (1937), 57–62. See also Henry J. Webb, "The Military Background in *Othello*," *Philological Quarterly*, XXX (1951), 40–52.

4. George Lyman Kittredge, ed., *The Complete Works of Shakespeare* (Boston, 1936), p. 1242. Unless otherwise noted, all Shakespearian citations are to this edition.

5. *Othello* V.i.11–22.

6. The line, of course, may be understood two ways: Iago either "fears" that his cuckoldry by Cassio has already occurred, or he regards it as imminent.

7. Bradley, *Shakespearean Tragedy*, p. 235.

8. George Woodberry, "Some Actors' Criticism of Othello, Iago, and Shylock," in *Studies in Letters and Life* (New York, 1891), pp. 171–73.

9. E. E. Stoll, *Shakespeare and Other Masters* (Cambridge, Mass., 1940), p. 232.

456   NOTES TO II: THE FAMILY OF IAGO

10. *Othello* I.i.6, I.i.155, I.iii.372–74, I.iii.392, II.i.297.

11. *Othello* II.iii.367–68.

12. T. S. Eliot, "Hamlet and His Problems," in *The Sacred Wood* (London, 1920), p. 92:

The only way of expressing emotion in the form of art is by finding an "objective correlative"; in other words, a set of objects, a situation, a chain of events which shall be the formula of that *particular* emotion; such that when the external facts, which must terminate in sensory experience, are given, the emotion is immediately evoked. . . . Hamlet (the man) is dominated by an emotion which is inexpressible, because it is in *excess* of the facts as they appear.

13. Bradley, *Shakespearean Tragedy,* pp. 223–26, *et passim.*

14. Theodore Spencer, *Shakespeare and the Nature of Man* (New York, 1942), p. 133.

15. *Othello* III.iii.300–305.

16. Bradley, *Shakespearean Tragedy,* pp. 234–35.

17. Levin L. Schücking, *Character Problems in Shakespeare's Plays* (London, 1922), p. 212.

18. E. E. Stoll, "Hamlet and Iago," in *Kittredge Anniversary Papers* (Boston, 1913), pp. 261–62.

19. A. J. A. Waldock, *Hamlet: A Study in Critical Method* (Cambridge, 1931), p. 98.

II: THE FAMILY OF IAGO

1. This characteristic of Iago's "soliloquies" has drawn frequent comment. Referring to them, and also to speeches by Aaron, Richard III, and Edmund, A. C. Bradley, *Shakespearean Tragedy* (London, 1905), p. 223, remarks: "It is a curious point of technique with him [Shakespeare] that the soliloquies of his villains sometimes read almost like explanations offered to the audience." See also Sir John Squire, *Shakespeare as a Dramatist* (London, 1935), pp. 210–12. The experience of the theater is even more conclusive, as in the observation of Margaret Carrington, who prepared John Barrymore for the role of Richard III, in respect to Richard's "soliloquy" at the end of the scene with Lady Anne (see Gene Fowler, *Good Night, Sweet Prince* [New York, 1944], p. 196): "To say the lines to himself lets the scene down. I suggested that Barrymore throw the speech right out into the auditorium. The effect was startling and at this point in the play he got a tremendous reaction from the audience by prolonged applause."

2. A. H. Thorndike, "The Relations of Hamlet to Contemporary Revenge Plays," *PMLA,* XVII (1902), 191–92.

3. Joseph Q. Adams, " 'Every Woman in Her Humour' and 'The Dumb Knight,' " *Modern Philology,* X (1913), 417.

NOTES TO III: THE PSYCHOMACHIA 457

4. Willard Farnham, *The Medieval Heritage of Elizabethan Tragedy* (Berkeley, 1936), p. 249.

5. A. H. Thorndike, "The Relation of 'As You Like It' to Robin Hood Plays," *Journal of English and Germanic Philology,* IV (1902), 69.

6. Richard G. Moulton, *Shakespeare as a Dramatic Artist* (Oxford, 1885), pp. 92–93.

7. *Much Ado,* ed. J. D. Wilson (Cambridge, 1923), introd. (by Sir Arthur Quiller-Couch), xviii.

8. *2 Henry VI* III.iii.30.

9. The artistic or histrionic bravura in these roles has been noted often, as in William Hazlitt's remarks about Iago ("an amateur of tragedy in real life") and Richard in his *Characters of Shakespeare's Plays.* See also Mark Van Doren, *Shakespeare* (New York, 1939), p. 35.

10. See, for instance, its use in *King John* II.i.46; *As You Like It* IV.i.201; *Hamlet* III.iii.8; *Antony and Cleopatra* V.ii.199. See also the *New English Dictionary* s.v. "Religion" (sect. 6a).

11. See, for example, Theodore Spencer, *Shakespeare and the Nature of Man* (New York, 1942); also E. M. W. Tillyard, *The Elizabethan World Picture* (London, 1943); John Danby, *Shakespeare's Doctrine of Nature* (London, 1949).

12. Bradley, *Shakespearean Tragedy,* p. 185.

13. G. Wilson Knight, *The Wheel of Fire* (Oxford, 1930), p. 107.

14. *Othello* I.i.19; the dash inserted by Kittredge and most modern editors between the third and fourth words of this sentence has neither Quarto nor Folio authority, and in this instance I have chosen to follow the original texts.

15. The most substantial work on this subject is by Eduard Eckhardt, *Die lustige Person im älteren englischen Drama* (Berlin, 1902). Shorter treatments occur in the following works: Charles M. Gayley, "An Historical View of the Beginnings of English Comedy," in *Representative English Comedies* (New York, 1903), Vol. I; Olive M. Busby, *Studies in the Development of the Fool in the Elizabethan Drama* (Oxford, 1923); Barbara Swain, *Fools and Folly during the Middle Ages and the Renaissance* (New York, 1932); A. P. Rossiter, *English Drama from Early Times to the Elizabethans* (London, 1950).

III: THE PSYCHOMACHIA

1. E. K. Chambers, *The Medieval Stage* (Oxford, 1903), II, 62–64 and 151–52.

2. See p. 108.

3. The documents for York are reproduced by Karl Young, "Records of the York Play of the *Pater Noster,*" *Speculum,* VII (1932), 540–46;

NOTES TO III: THE PSYCHOMACHIA

those for Lincoln and Beverley by Arthur F. Leach, "Some English Plays and Players," in *An English Miscellany* (Oxford, 1901), pp. 205–34. For a Creed play existing at York and performed every tenth year between c. 1440 and 1568, see E. K. Chambers, *English Literature at the Close of the Middle Ages* (Oxford, 1945), p. 33. Chambers suggests it was a group of saints plays rather than a morality.

4. For theories about this pageant, see Chambers, *The Medieval Stage,* II, p. 154; also Tempe E. Allison, "The Paternoster Play and the Origin of the Vices," *PMLA,* XXXIX (1924), 789–804. Chambers regards "Viciose" as "a typical representative of frail humanity"—the predecessor of Humanum Genus or Mankind in the early moralities. My alternative suggestion is that he was the leader of the Seven Deadly Sins, signifying vice in a composite sense, just as Vice is a separate figure, leader of the Deadly Sins in their battle against the assembled virtues, in Lydgate's *Assembly of the Gods* (c. 1420), ed. O. L. Triggs, Early English Text Society (London, 1896), ll. 596–620.

5. Young, "Records of the York Play of the *Pater Noster,*" p. 546.

6. See pp. 251–52.

7. R. Willis, *Mount Tabor: Or Private Exercises of a Penitent Sinner* (1639), pp. 110–14.

8. Throughout this study the words *historical* and *literal* will frequently appear as antonyms (for lack of better ones) to *allegorical*—not without the authority of the common medieval distinction, as it is expressed by Aquinas, *Summa Theologica,* I, 10, between "sensus historicus vel litteralis" and "sensus spiritualis, qui super litteralem fundatur et eum supponit." Dante makes the same distinction in his letter to Can Grande della Scala, *Epistolae,* ed. and trans. Paget Toynbee (Oxford, 1920), p. 199: "And although these mystical meanings are called by various names [moral, anagogical, and allegorical in the specific sense], they may one and all in general be termed allegorical, inasmuch as they are different (*diversi*) from the literal or historical."

9. The secularized version of the Parliament in Heaven in *Respublica* (1553); see p. 70.

10. The subject has been treated effectively by Theodore Spencer, *Death and Elizabethan Tragedy* (Cambridge, Mass., 1936), pp. 21–34; also by Eleanor P. Hammond, *English Verse between Chaucer and Surrey* (Durham, N.C., 1927), pp. 124–30.

11. John Skelton, *Poetical Works,* ed. Alexander Dyce (London, 1843), I, 18. The title of the poem in question makes its own contribution to the cadaverous literature of the late Middle Ages: "Skelton Laureat, Vppon a deedmans hed, that was sent to hym from an honorable jentyllwoman for a token."

12. *The Poems of William Dunbar,* ed. W. M. Mackenzie (Edinburgh, 1932).

NOTES TO III: THE PSYCHOMACHIA

13. François Villon, *Oeuvres Complètes,* ed. M. L. Moland (Paris, n.d.), p. 81.

14. The martial image, for instance, exists in *Piers Plowman,* ed. W. W. Skeat (Oxford, 1886), C-text, XXIII, 100–105:

> Deth cam dryuying after   and al to douste paschte
> Kynges and knyghtes   caysers and popes;
> Lered ne lewide   he lefte no man stande;
> That he hitte euene   sterede neuere after.
> Many a louely lady   and here lemmanes knyghtes
> Sounede and swelte   for sorwe of Dethes dyntes.

15. *The Castle of Perseverance,* ll. 2779 ff.

16. *Ludus Coventriae,* ed. K. S. Block, Early English Text Society (London, 1922), p. 176.

17. Other figures who perform the same function in late plays are Rumor in *Nice Wanton,* God's Judgment in *The Longer Thou Livest,* God's Plague in *Enough Is as Good as a Feast,* Severity in *Like Will to Like,* and the two figures of Justice and Reward in *Appius and Virginia.*

18. *King Lear* I.ii.145–47.

19. A characteristic version of the theme appears in *Middle English Reader,* ed. O. F. Emerson (New York, 1915), pp. 47–64. For a bibliographical statement, see J. E. Wells, *A Manual of the Writings in Middle English* (New Haven, 1916), pp. 411–13. See also Albert C. Baugh, *A Literary History of England* (New York, 1948), pp. 162–64.

20. *All for Money,* for which see pp. 233–35.

21. Robert Grosseteste, *Carmina Anglo-Normannica,* ed. Mathew Cooke, Caxton Society (London, 1852). Both versions are contained in this volume.

22. *Cursor Mundi,* ed. Richard Morris, Early English Text Society (London, 1874–92), ll. 9517–752.

23. Formerly attributed to Cardinal Bonaventura, the "seraphic doctor," the *Meditationes* is now generally regarded as the work of a lesser Bonaventura who was cardinal of Padua. The allegory of the Four Daughters appears in the English translation (before 1410) of the *Meditationes* by Nicholas Love, entitled *The Mirrour of the Blessed Lyf of Jesu Christ,* ed. Lawrence F. Powell, Roxburghe Club (Oxford, 1908), pp. 14–19.

24. *Gesta Romanorum,* ed. Sidney Herrtage, Early English Text Society (London, 1879), pp. 132–35.

25. *Piers Plowman,* ed. Skeat, B-text, XVIII, 110 ff.; C-text, XXI, 115 ff.

26. John Lydgate, *The Court of Sapience,* ed. Robert Spindler, *Beiträge zur englischen Philologie,* VI (1927), ll. 176 ff.

27. For an examination of these French plays as well as for a full study of the allegory, see Hope Traver, *The Four Daughters of God* (Philadelphia, 1907). A more recent study of the allegory, stressing its pictorial history, is by Samuel Chew, *The Virtues Reconciled; an Iconographic Study* (Toronto, 1947).

460 *NOTES TO III: THE PSYCHOMACHIA*

28. *Ludus Coventriae,* ed. Block, pp. 97–103.

29. *The Castle of Perseverance,* ll. 3130 ff. An additional English dramatization of the allegory, qualifying the limitation expressed in the text above, is indicated in the surviving MS. fragment called *Processus Satanae,* ed. W. W. Greg, Malone Society Collections (London, 1931), pp. 239–50. What survives is the actor's part for the role of God, Who argues for sinful mankind's redemption against Satan's negative plea; but the cues make it certain that the roles of Verity, Justice, Mercy, and Peace were included in the cast. The play is probably a good deal older than the MS., which seems to belong to 1570–80.

30. *Mankind,* ll. 832–35; *Hickscorner,* ll. 119–20.

31. *Respublica,* l. 1866.

32. *Everyman,* l. 442.

33. See also *Impatient Poverty,* ll. 1–7.

34. For Anaxagoras as well as for a general statement on the whole subject, see the *Encyclopedia of Religion and Ethics* s.v. "Dualism."

35. See Paul Elmer More, "Plato," in *Shelburne Essays,* sixth series (New York, 1909); also Simone Petrément, *Le Dualisme chez Platon, les Gnostiques et les Manichéens* (Paris, 1947).

36. *Faust,* trans. Bayard Taylor, I.ii. What is said above on moral dualism is, of course, short shrift for such a subject, and also perhaps an injustice to science, which latterly, through its best minds, progresses beyond its more youthful assumptions—both philosophical and moral. The biophysicist Lecomte du Noüy, for instance, expresses himself as follows in *Human Destiny* (New York, 1947), p. 108: "At a certain period of his metamorphosis, man became conscious of this fundamental dualism which is in reality the eternal theme of religions, philosophies, and arts. The awakening of this idea constitutes the most important event in all evolution."

37. Eusebius, *Ecclesiastical History,* ed. and trans. Kirsopp Lake, Loeb Classical Library (New York, 1926–32), I, 405–406.

38. *Ibid.,* I, 313.

39. *Ibid.,* II, 405.

40. Ephesians vi.11–17.

41. Galatians v.17.

42. *The City of God,* ed. Marcus Dods (New York, 1948), XIX.10.

43. Tertullian, *Writings,* trans. S. Thelwall *et al.,* Ante-Nicene Christian Library (Edinburgh, 1869–70), II, 34.

44. Cyprian, *Writings,* trans. R. E. Wallis, Ante-Nicene Christian Library (Edinburgh, 1868–69), I, 455.

45. Prudentius, *Writings,* ed. and trans. H. J. Thomson, Loeb Classical Library (Cambridge, Mass., 1949), I, 231 and 233.

46. *Ibid.*

47. *Ibid.,* I, 281.

48. *Ibid.,* I, 243.

NOTES TO III: THE PSYCHOMACHIA 461

49. *Ibid.,* introd. xiv–xvi.

50. C. S. Lewis, *The Allegory of Love* (Oxford, 1936), p. 68.

51. The proliferation of the Psychomachia in the art of the Middle Ages is richly examined and illustrated in the following books: Émile Mâle, *L'Art religieux de la fin du Moyen Age* (Paris, 1908); the same author's *L'Art religieux du XIIIe Siècle en France* (Paris, 1919); Louis Bréhier, *L'Art Chrétien* (Paris, 1928); Adolph Katzenellenbogen, *Allegories of the Virtues and Vices in Medieval Art* (London, 1939).

52. George Puttenham, *The Arte of English Poesie,* ed. Gladys Willcock and Alice Walker (Cambridge, 1936), p. 191.

53. Alanus de Insulis, *Anticlaudianus,* trans. W. H. Cornog (Philadelphia, 1935), pp. 145 ff.

54. Huon de Meri, *Li Tornoiemenz Antecrit,* ed. Georg Wimmer (Marburg, 1888).

55. John Lydgate, *Assembly of the Gods,* ed. O. L. Triggs, Early English Text Society (London, 1896).

56. Robert Grosseteste, *Carmina Anglo-Normannica,* pp. 16 ff.

57. *Piers Plowman,* ed. W. W. Skeat, B-text, XX, 213–15.

58. *Le Roman de la Rose,* ed. Ernest Langlois (Paris, 1914–24), ll. 15795–21860.

59. *The Faerie Queene* II.xi.

60. The following studies deal with figurative castles—religious, erotic, and anatomical—in medieval art and letters: Roberta D. Cornelius, *The Figurative Castle* (Bryn Mawr, 1930); Roger S. Loomis, "The Allegorical Siege in the Art of the Middle Ages," *American Journal of Archaeology,* 2nd Ser., XXIII (1919), 255–69; C. L. Powell, "Castle of the Body," *Studies in Philology,* XVI (1919), 197–205. See also G. R. Owst, *Literature and Pulpit in Medieval England* (Cambridge, 1933), pp. 77–85.

61. "Parabolae Sancto Bernardo vulgo ascriptae," ed. Migne, *Patrologia Latina,* CLXXXIII.

62. Owst, *Literature and Pulpit in Medieval England,* pp. 85–109; see also *Piers Plowman,* B-Text, V–VI.

63. Prudentius, *Psychomachia,* l. 550.

64. *The Castle of Perseverance,* ll. 2428 ff.

65. *Nature,* part II, ll. 471 ff.

66. For the literary and personal relationships among the figures of this "circle," see A. W. Reed, *Early Tudor Drama* (London, 1926), pp. 101–105, *et passim.* In his youth, undoubtedly while a member of Morton's household, Thomas More wrote and acted plays, according to the testimony of Bale's *Catalogue* and John Roper's *Life;* and the tradition gets strong support from the play of *Sir Thomas More.*

67. *Othello* II.iii.92–99. For the anatomy of Pride in its several aspects, see the following: "De Superbia" in the tale of Chaucer's Parson; Medwall's *Nature,* part II, ll. 1149–57; Phillip Stubbes, *Anatomie of Abuses,*

NOTES TO IV: THE MORALITY PLAY

part I, ed. F. J. Furnivall (London, 1877–79), pp. 26–49; description of the Palace of Pride in *The Faerie Queene* I.iv; *As You Like It* II.vii.70–82.

68. Cf. the speech of Pride, alias "Curiosity," in the Digby *Mary Magdalene*, ll. 491–506.

69. Compare, for instance, the scene between Falstaff and the Lord Chief Justice (*2 Henry IV* I.ii.62 ff.) with the encounter between the Vice Inclination and Sapience in *The Trial of Treasure* (Dodsley, III, pp. 276–79). For the banishment of Falstaff and his imprisonment in the Fleet, we have to reckon with the fact that exile, imprisonment, or hanging is the standard disposition of the vices (and the Vice) in moralities from about 1530 onward. See note 71 below and pp. 196–97.

70. The chief work on this subject, J. Dover Wilson, *The Fortunes of Falstaff* (New York, 1943), while it develops the influence of the moralities upon the structure and moral theme of the *Henry IV* plays, does not go deeply into the very precise correspondences between Falstaff and the morality vices, nor into the issues of interpretation which these correspondences create for the Falstaffian role.

71. It is very likely that such a battle also takes place in the lost portion of the morality *Good Order*, printed by William Rastell in 1533. The recently discovered fragment (131 lines) of the end of the play begins with the relation by Good Order to Old Christmas of just such a fray:

> Syr there hath ben here an vnthryfty company
> Here was hasarder / here was pariury
> And crakys and swerynge habomynably
> And as soone as I came they dyd me defye
> If I had not fledde I had ben slayne.

To which Old Christmas says:

> But this case to me is more fayne
> That these rebels be thus take
> Than a busshell of golde were gyuen for my sake.

The two "rebels" in question are Riot and Gluttony, and their fate is banishment out of England to "the new founde land."

72. John Lydgate, *Assembly of the Gods*, ll. 1831–32.

73. On this point, see Lewis, *The Allegory of Love*, p. 86.

IV: THE MORALITY PLAY

1. It is impossible to do more than mention in this place the long history of exegetical allegory, except to observe that at least from the time of Philo Judaeus (first century A.D.), whose Platonism relates him spiritually to the Christian tradition, the effort has been continual to liberate the literal sense of the Bible, especially of the Old Testament, into meanings more agreeable to the moral and spiritual vision of Christianity. Even earlier than the

NOTES TO IV: THE MORALITY PLAY 463

Christian era, the same impulse appeared in the Stoic commentators who allegorized the primitive gods of Homer in order to adjust them to a more sophisticated vision of deity. For at bottom the method of allegorical interpretation, wherever it is employed, is an act of piety—a way, as one student of the subject has expressed it, "of reading a new meaning into sacred tradition, and thus protecting it from the satire of its critics" (J. Geffcken in the *Encyclopedia of Religion and Ethics* s.v. "Allegory"). A similar piety, stimulated by the Fourth Eclogue, preserved Virgil for the Middle Ages by investing him with Christian dignity through quaint miracles of allegorical interpretation. See F. W. Farrar, *The History of Scriptural Interpretation* (London, 1886).

2. *Institutio Oratoria,* ed. and trans. H. E. Butler, Loeb Classical Library (New York, 1921–22), III, 326.

3. George Puttenham, *The Arte of English Poesie,* ed. Gladys Willcock and Alice Walker (Cambridge, 1936), p. 187.

4. See *Epistola X* in *Dantis Alagherii Epistolae,* ed. and trans. Paget Toynbee (Oxford, 1920). I do not regard the "selva oscura" or the animals of the first canto as metaphorical, but as the literal objects of a vision, and their meanings as symbolic.

5. *Grace Abounding and The Pilgrim's Progress,* ed. John Brown (Cambridge, 1907), p. 161.

6. It is perhaps necessary to add that such a discrimination has theoretical value chiefly, and would be misleading if it seemed to create absolute categories of separation. The allegorical imagination is scarcely so exclusive, and the metaphorical world of *The Faerie Queene,* for instance, is interpenetrated by symbolic figures and symbolic meanings.

7. The only other allegorical objects and properties that occur to me are the white, red, green, and black vestures of the Four Daughters of God in *Perseverance* (see the stage directions accompanying the diagram of the "platea"); the clothing of the principal figures in *Wisdom;* the vesture, signifying prosperity, with which Peace twice clothes Poverty in *Impatient Poverty* (ll. 218–20 and 1056); and the allegorical armor of St. Paul which appears in the following stage direction of *The Tide Tarrieth No Man* (ll. 1439 ff.): "Christianity must enter with a sword, with a title of pollicy, but on the other syde of the tytle, must be written gods word, also a Shield whereon must be written riches, but on the other syde of the Shield must be Fayth."

8. *Utopia,* trans. Ralph Robinson, Broadway Translations, p. 95.

9. E. N. S. Thompson, "The English Moral Plays," *Transactions of the Connecticut Academy of Arts and Sciences,* XIV (1908–10), 315. This essay (111 pages) is still the best examination and historical survey of the English moralities.

10. Prudentius, *Writings,* ed. and trans. H. J. Thomson, Loeb Classical Library (New York, 1949), ll. 709–14.

464 NOTES TO IV: THE MORALITY PLAY

11. *The Romaunt of the Rose,* in *The Complete Works of Geoffrey Chaucer,* ed. F. N. Robinson (Boston, 1933), ll. 6135-42.

12. *Piers Plowman,* B-text, V.

13. See pp. 60-61 and 100.

14. G. R. Owst, *Literature and Pulpit in Medieval England* (Cambridge, 1933), pp. 56-109 and 526-47.

15. John Wyclif, *English Works,* ed. F. D. Mathew, Early English Text Society (London, 1880), p. 429.

16. See also *Pride of Life,* ll. 187-90; *Wisdom Who Is Christ,* ll. 985-1000; *Mundus et Infans,* ll. 954-57.

17. The physical conditions of the morality stage are obscure, and over 150 years were probably anything but uniform. The outdoor "platea" and "sedes" of *Perseverance* are also indicated for *Pride of Life, Mary Magdalene* (Digby), *The Three Estates;* probably for *Everyman* and *Mundus et Infans;* and survive in *Thersites* (c. 1537). *Mankind* takes place within the precincts (courtyard?) of an inn. A number of moralities (*Four Elements, Impatient Poverty, All for Money*) in stage directions and dialogue refer to performance inside a "hall"; and *Nature,* in addition, was performed at the bidding of "my lord" (part I, l. 1438), at night (part I, l. 93), and used seats for stationary performers (first stage direction). But the almost universal word for the scene of the action is the "place," which may mean anything. It is, however, significant that almost without exception the "place" on which the moralities were performed was subject to encroachment by the spectators, and it was a standard function of the Vice to push back the audience with his invariable admonition of "Make room, sirs" (see the play of *Sir Thomas More,* IV.i.201–204), or words to the same effect. In *The Four Elements,* when the dancers are about to begin, Sensual Appetite urges the spectators to "make rome, syrs, and gyf them place" (p. 48). *Impatient Poverty* has this stage direction: "Here entreth the somner agayne, & pouerte foloweth him with a candell in his hande doyng penaunce about the place." Thereupon the summoner addresses the audience crowding the "place":

> Rowme syrs auoydaunce
> That thys man maye do hys pennaunce.
> [ll. 987 ff.]

Later plays begin to vary from the "place." A direction in *Appius and Virginia* advises: "Here let Virginius go about the scaffold" (l. 854); and the *Marriage between Wit and Wisdom* refers to "one cornor of the stage" (p. 29). For a summary of the staging of the moralities, see Chambers, *The Elizabethan Stage,* III, 21 ff.; also R. L. Ramsay, ed., *Magnificence,* introd. cxxviii ff.

18. The phrase originates with Charles M. Gayley, who discusses the subject in *Plays of Our Forefathers* (New York, 1907), pp. 334-38.

19. "An Apology for Poetry" in *Elizabethan Critical Essays,* ed. G. Greg-

NOTES TO V: EMERGENCE OF THE VICE 465

ory Smith (Oxford, 1904), I, 199. Together with other "grosse absurdities" on the English popular stage, Sidney observes "how all theyr Playes be neither right Tragedies, nor right Comedies; mingling Kings and Clownes, not because the matter so carrieth it, but thrust in Clownes by head and shoulders, to play a part in maiesticall matters, with neither decencie nor discretion: So as neither the admiration and commiseration, nor the right sportfulnes, is by their mungrell Tragy-comedie obtained." By way of distinction there is Sidney's reference to the genuinely "tragi-comicall" on p. 175 of the same essay.

20. *The Nature of the Four Elements,* p. 50. The prologue to *Virtuous and Godly Susanna* apologizes for the absence of songs in the play.

21. *Mankind,* ll. 655 ff.

22. *King John,* ll. 769–816.

23. *Wit and Science,* ll. 443 ff.

24. Tucker Brooke, *The Tudor Drama* (Boston, 1911), p. 65.

25. E. K. Chambers, *English Literature at the Close of the Middle Ages* (Oxford, 1946), p. 62.

26. *Mankind,* l. 879. Another appearance of Titivillus on the English stage is in *The Towneley Plays,* ed. George England, Early English Text Society (London, 1897), XXX, 206–367. For the doubtful meaning of his name and function, see L. W. Cushman, *The Devil and the Vice in the English Dramatic Literature before Shakespeare* (Halle, 1900), pp. 35–36; also G. R. Owst, *Literature and Pulpit in Medieval England,* pp. 512–14. That he is intended as an allegorical figure in *Mankind* is clear from the fact that he "syngnyfieth" something beyond himself. In a general way his homiletic significance is also clear: he is the antithesis of the virtue of strenuousness, both spiritual and physical, and corresponds to the vice of *Accidia.* His success in *Mankind* is signaled when his victim gives up his labors, his prayers, his church attendance, and goes to sleep.

V: EMERGENCE OF THE VICE

1. Left out of this account, for the reason that the play is not a morality, is the Devil who appears in a single scene of Thomas Ingelend's *The Disobedient Child* (1559–70). Probably adapted from a Latin dialogue, *Iuvenis, Pater, Uxor,* by Ravisius Textor (*Dialogi* 71), it has type roles: e.g., Rich Man, Rich Man's Son, Young Woman, Servingman, etc., but none of the personae or characteristics of the allegorical drama.

2. To put the same thing another way, the broad, unspecialized evil represented by the Devil is simply too gross a concept for the homiletic minutiae of the moralities. Their analytical method could have little use for a theological figure who comprehended all sins and whose characteristic announcement, like that of Satan in *The Disobedient Child* (see above, note 1), is that (Dodsley, II, 309):

NOTES TO V: EMERGENCE OF THE VICE

> Some I disquiet with covetousness:
> Some with wrath, pride and lechery;
> And some I do thrust into such distress,
> That he feeleth only pain and misery.
> Some I allure to have their delight
> Always in gluttony, envy and murder,
> And those things to practise with all their might,
> Either by land or else by water.

See also Belial's speech on the Seven Deadly Sins in *The Conversion of St. Paul,* in *The Digby Mysteries,* ed. F. J. Furnivall, Early English Text Society (London, 1896), ll. 487–95; and the address of Satan to the audience in the prologue of the First Passion Play of the *Ludus Coventriae,* ed. K. S. Block, Early English Text Society (London, 1922), pp. 225–29.

3. See L. W. Cushman, *The Devil and the Vice in the English Dramatic Literature before Shakespeare* (Halle, 1900), pp. 16 ff.

4. See *The Castle of Perseverance,* ll. 1–274, and *Mary Magdalene* (Digby), ll. 305–439.

5. Charles M. Gayley, ed., *Representative English Comedies* (New York, 1903–14), introd. li–lii.

6. See also *Nature,* part II, ll. 22–28.

7. *All for Money,* ll. 446–82.

8. Later on in the play (ll. 565–66) Ill Report explicitly defines his limited allegorical nature in a couplet addressed to the two Elders:

> But if you meane to haue my helpe, to fortefy your forte,
> All that I can doe is, to giue her an ill Reporte.

See also *The Conflict of Conscience,* ll. 838–40, and *The Tide Tarrieth No Man,* ll. 424–27.

9. No doubt the reader has already noticed that throughout these pages the capitalized word distinguishes the Vice proper from the numerous lower case vices in the moralities, out of whom he emerges.

10. The following plays, twenty in all, designate "the Vice" in their players' lists or stage directions, or both: *Weather, Love, Respublica, Jack Juggler, Mary Magdalene* (L. Wager), *Patient Grissill, Enough Is as Good as a Feast, Cambises, Appius and Virginia, King Darius, Horestes, Trial of Treasure, Like Will to Like, Virtuous Susanna, Sir Clyomon and Sir Clamydes, The Tide Tarrieth No Man, Common Conditions, All for Money, Marriage between Wit and Wisdom,* and *Tom Tyler.* To these must be added "Inclination the Vise" who appears in the morality performed within the play of *Sir Thomas More.*

11. From Rastell's original edition. Brandl's text, which I follow otherwise, reprints Waley's later edition (1584?) from a copy lacking the title page.

12. E. K. Chambers, *The Medieval Stage* (Oxford, 1903), I, 203–205.

13. R. L. Ramsay, ed., *Magnificence,* introd. xcv–cvi.

NOTES TO V: EMERGENCE OF THE VICE 467

14. For probable date of composition, see Honor McClusker, *John Bale, Dramatist and Antiquary* (Bryn Mawr, 1942), pp. 73–74. Bale himself mentions the play in the first of his several catalogues of English authors, the *Anglorum Heliades,* inscribed to John Leland and dated 1536. Dr. McClusker cites the evidence for supposing that the play "was composed as early as 1531, before Bale left the Cloister." See also *King John,* ed. Pafford and Greg, Malone Society Reprints (London, 1931), introd. xxii–xxiv.

15. See T. F. Henderson, *Scottish Vernacular Literature* (Edinburgh, 1910), p. 219.

16. This point, which seems so obvious, requires its present stress because it is frequently overlooked or disregarded, with a number of mistaken conjectures, in consequence, about the origin of the Vice. Cushman, for instance, although he affirms the allegorical origin of the Vice, states without justification in *The Devil and the Vice,* etc., p. 67, that

in the text itself of the plays in question, no reference whatever to the Vice as a character is to be found, except in the one passage, in the prologue to King Darius [Pr. 1565]. . . . The ordinary names of the Vice, as Hypocrisy, Folly, etc., are often referred to and played upon, why do we find no such reference to Vice?

17. *Wisdom Who Is Christ,* l. 769.

18. *Respublica,* ll. 1533–34.

19. Information on this point is provided by R. L. Ramsay in his edition of *Magnificence,* introd. cxxxi–cxxxiv. A division of the roles into the number of actors required to play them appears with fair consistency at the beginning or end of moralities printed after 1540. Thus *Three Laws* declares that its fourteen roles may be divided among "fyue personages." *Lusty Juventus, Impatient Poverty, Wealth and Health,* and *New Custom* all indicate four actors for roles ranging in number from seven to eleven.

20. Occasionally the Seven Deadly Sins are comprehended within a special-text Vice in moralities after 1500. That Folly, the single evil personification in *Mundus et Infans,* consolidates within himself all of the Deadly Sins is made clear by the following exchange between Manhood and Conscience (ll. 457–62):

> *Manh.* Folye? what thynge callest thou folye?
> *Consc.* Syr, it is Pryde, Wrathe, and Enuy,
> Slouthe, Couetous and Glotonye,—
> Lechery the seuente is:
> These seuen synnes I call folye.

See also *Everyman,* ll. 35 ff.; *Three Laws,* ll. 1098–1103; *The Life and Repentance of Mary Magdalene,* ll. 291–358; *All for Money,* ll. 432–38.

21. *The Plays and Poems of George Chapman,* ed. T. M. Parrott (New York, 1910–14).

22. *The Complete Works of Geoffrey Chaucer,* ed. F. N. Robinson (Boston, 1933), p. 285.

23. For a summary statement on this subject, see the *Encyclopedia of*

NOTES TO VI: MORAL METAPHOR

Religion and Ethics s.v. "Seven Deadly Sins." The formula of the *radix malorum* and its successive branches is pervasive in medieval homiletics beyond the possibility of comprehensive treatment here, and we must confine our attention to the authoritative voice of Gregory the Great, *Morals on the Book of Job* (Oxford, 1844–50), III, 489–90:

> For the tempting vices, which fight against us in invisible contest in behalf of the pride which reigns over them, some of them go first, like captains, others follow, after the manner of an army. For all faults do not occupy the heart with equal access. But while the greater and the few surprise a neglected mind, the smaller and the numberless pour themselves upon it in a whole body. For when pride, the queen of sins, has fully possessed a conquered heart, she surrenders it immediately to seven principal sins, as if to some of her generals, to lay it waste. . . . For pride is the root of all evil, of which it is said, as Scripture bears witness: *Pride is the beginning of all sin.* But seven principal vices, as its first progeny, spring doubtless from this poisonous root, namely, vain glory, envy, anger, melancholy, avarice, gluttony, lust . . . . they are, each of them, so closely connected with other, that they spring only the one from the other.

See also the *Ayenbite of Inwyt,* ed. Richard Morris, Early English Text Society (London, 1886), pp. 16 ff. The same theme became pictorial in the familiar *arbor mala* of medieval inconography, for which see Adolph Katzenellenbogen, *Allegories of the Virtues and Vices in Medieval Art* (London, 1939), pp. 63–68 and plates 64–67.

24. *Mankind,* l. 876; see also l. 297.

25. *Nature,* part I, l. 841.

26. *Three Laws,* l. 1854.

27. In *The Trial of Treasure,* Dodsley, III, 274–75, the Vice Inclination engages in a similar physical demonstration of his homiletic priority.

28. *Respublica,* l. 173.

29. See also sig. B4 *verso.*

30. Sig. C3 *recto.*

31. *Play of Love,* after l. 1293.

VI: MORAL METAPHOR AND DRAMATIC IMAGE

1. *Mundus et Infans,* l. 652.

2. The compact pattern of the twofold stratagem appears in the words with which the Devil, himself impotent, commissions the Vice against the hero of *Lusty Juventus,* Dodsley, II, 67:

> I would have thee go incontinent,
> And work some crafty feat or policy,
> To set Knowledge and him at controversy;
> And his company thyself greatly use,
> That God's Word he may clean abuse.

3. *Mundus et Infans,* l. 638.

NOTES TO VI: MORAL METAPHOR 469

4. *Respublica*, l. 507.

5. Gregory the Great, *Morals on the Book of Job* (Oxford, 1844–50), III, 491.

6. "The Bel-man of London" in *Non-Dramatic Works of Thomas Dekker*, ed. Alexander Grosart (London, 1885), III, 116.

7. *Morals on the Book of Job*, III, 544–46. See also, in the same source, I, 174–75; III, 18 and 455. Much earlier than Gregory, however, the same psychological principle of moral self-deception is developed by Plato in a notable passage of *The Republic*, where, for the sake of delineating the inner life of "The Democratic Man," he employs personification and gives us a Psychomachia as well. He is talking of the Democratic youth, son of the Oligarchic father:

One of the conflicting sets of desires in the soul of this youth will be reinforced from without by a group of kindred passions; and if the resistance of the oligarchical faction in him is strengthened by remonstrances and reproaches coming from his father, or his friends, the opposing parties will soon be battling within him. In some cases the democratic interest yields to the oligarchical: a sense of shame gains a footing in the young man's soul, and some appetites are crushed, others banished, until order is restored. . . . But then again, perhaps owing to the father's having no idea how to bring up his son, another brood of desires, akin to those which were banished, are secretly nursed up until they become numerous and strong. These draw the young man back into clandestine commerce with his old associates, and between them they breed a whole multitude. In the end, they seize the citadel of the young man's soul, finding it unguarded by the trusty sentinels which keep watch over the minds of men favoured by heaven. Knowledge, right principles, true thoughts, are not at their post; and the place lies open to the assault of false and presumptuous notions. . . . In the internal conflict they gain the day; modesty and self-control, dishonoured and insulted as the weaknesses of an unmanly fool, are thrust out into exile; and the whole crew of unprofitable desires take a hand in banishing moderation and frugality, which, as they will have it, are nothing but churlish meanness. So they take possession of the soul . . . bringing home Insolence, Anarchy, Waste, and Impudence, those resplendent divinities crowned with garlands, whose praises they sing under flattering names: *Insolence they call good breeding, Anarchy freedom, Waste magnificence, and Impudence a manly spirit.*

[my italics; trans. F. M. Cornford
(New York, 1945), pp. 284–85]

Nearly two thousand years later, in the very age of the moral plays and in their very language, Sir Thomas Wyatt makes the same point, explaining his voluntary rustication through the following description of court life:

> None of these poyntes would ever frame in me:
> My wit is nought—I cannot lerne the waye.
> And much the lesse of thinges that greater be,
> That asken helpe of colours of devise
> To joyne the mene with eche extremitie,

NOTES TO VI: MORAL METAPHOR

With the neryst vertue to cloke alwaye the vise:
  And as to pourpose like wise it shall fall,
  To presse the vertue that it may not rise;
As dronkenes good felloweshippe to call;
  The frendly ffoo with his dowble face
  Say he is gentill and courtois therewithall;
And say that Favell hath a goodly grace
  In eloquence; and crueltie to name
  Zele of justice and chaunge in tyme and place;
And he hath sufferth offence withoute blame
  Call him pitefull; and him true and playn
  That raileth rekles to every mans shame.
Say he is rude that cannot lye and fayn;
  The letcher a lover; and tirannye
  To be the right of a prynces reigne.
    [my italics; *Collected Poems of Sir Thomas
    Wyatt,* ed. Kenneth Muir (London, 1949),
    First Satire, ll. 56–75]

8. *Ludus Coventriae,* ed. K. S. Block, Early English Text Society (London, 1922), p. 228.

9. *Satire of the Three Estates,* version III, l. 722.

10. *Magnificence,* l. 710.

11. *Patient and Meek Grissill,* l. 917.

12. *Magnificence,* l. 698.

13. *Nature,* part II, after l. 81.

14. *The Tide Tarrieth No Man,* after l. 1751.

15. *Horestes,* l. 748.

16. Successively, *Magnificence,* after l. 2159; *The Trial of Treasure,* Dodsley, III, 287; *Impatient Poverty,* ll. 412–13; *Like Will to Like,* Dodsley, III, 309.

17. *Common Conditions,* ll. 896 and 1232.

18. This traditional association between the Vice and his "honesty" is affirmed by the whole of Ben Jonson's epigram (CXV) "On the Townes Honest Man," aimed perhaps at Inigo Jones. In order to conclude that "The townes honest Man's her errant'st Knaue," it describes him in terms that exactly particularize the stage behavior of the Vice, beginning as follows:

You wonder who this is! and why I name
Him not, aloud, that boasts so good a fame:
Naming so many, too! But this is one,
Suffers no name, but a description:
Being no vitious person, but the vice
About the towne; and known too, at that price.
A subtle thing, that doth affections win
By speaking well o' the company it's in.
    [Ben Jonson, *Works,* ed. Herford and
    Simpson, VIII (Oxford, 1947), 74–75]

NOTES TO VI: MORAL METAPHOR

19. *The Trial of Treasure*, Dodsley, III, 273.
20. *Impatient Poverty*, l. 517.
21. *Enough Is as Good as a Feast*, sig. D *recto*.
22. *Lusty Juventus*, Dodsley, II, 72.
23. The joke lingered on the stage, retaining its moral equivoque, as in the following lines between Bloodhound, a usurer, and his servant Sim, in *A Match at Midnight* (1633) by William Rowley (Dodsley, XIII, 57):

Sim. An old devil in a greasy satin doublet keep you company.
Blood. Ha, what's that?
Sim. I say, the satin doublet you will wear tomorrow will be the best in the company, sir.

24. *Wisdom Who Is Christ*, l. 494.
25. *Lusty Juventus*, Dodsley, II, 75.
26. See pp. 106 ff.
27. *Ludus Coventriae*, ed. Block, p. 124.
28. *Ibid.*
29. *Ibid.*, p. 125.
30. *Ibid.*, p. 132.
31. For other examples of this same coyness, see *Like Will to Like*, Dodsley, III, 337; *A Marriage between Wit and Wisdom*, pp. 16–17; *Patient and Meek Grissill*, ll. 99 ff.; *Virtuous and Godly Susanna*, ll. 504 ff.
32. *The Nature of the Four Elements*, p. 42.
33. *Love Feigned and Unfeigned*, l. 87.
34. *Mundus et Infans*, ll. 558–606; *John the Evangelist*, ll. 367–400. Exactly the same piece of expository rhetoric appears in the play of *Wily Beguiled* (S.R. 1606, but probably written before 1600), where Robin Goodfellow, a figure derived from the morality Vice, is urged by cudgels to "make a preachment of thy Pedigree, and how at first thou learnd'st this diuelish trade." He thereupon declaims his birth, his travels, his previous stratagems in the world, concluding:

> But the chiefe course of all my life,
> Is to set discord betwixt man and wife.
> [ed. W. W. Greg, Malone Society Reprints (London, 1912), ll. 2014–62]

35. *The Life and Repentance of Mary Magdalene*, l. 121.
36. *Ibid.*, l. 174.
37. *Mankind*, ll. 569 and 582.
38. *Ibid.*, l. 584.
39. *Three Laws*, l. 1787.
40. *King John*, l. 769.
41. *Lusty Juventus*, Dodsley, II, 68.
42. *Albion Knight*, l. 330.
43. *Like Will to Like*, Dodsley, III, 333.
44. *Virtuous and Godly Susanna*, l. 479.

NOTES TO VI: MORAL METAPHOR

45. *The Tide Tarrieth No Man*, l. 552.

46. See also ll. 1193 and 1665 of the same play.

47. See also ll. 610 and 1728 of the same play.

48. *Gammer Gurton's Needle*, in *Specimens of the Pre-Shakespearean Drama*, ed. J. M. Manly (Boston, 1897), II.iv.1.

49. *Three Laws*, ll. 1462–64.

50. *The Life and Repentance of Mary Magdalene*, l. 365.

51. *Enough Is as Good as a Feast*, sig. G recto.

52. *Like Will to Like*, Dodsley, II, 353.

53. *Martins Months Mind* (1589), in R. W. Chambers, *The Elizabethan Stage* (Oxford, 1923), III, 230.

54. *Magnificence*, l. 730.

55. Alois Brandl, *Quellen des weltlichen Dramas in England vor Shakespeare* (Strassburg, 1898), introd. xciv.

56. The corresponding lines in *Elckerlijk,* ed. Henri Logeman (Ghent, 1892), express the same idea but with the significant last clause omitted (ll. 422–24):

> Ghi hebt dat al v seluen ghedaen
> Dat me lief es te deser tijt,
> Ic moet daer om lachen.

57. *The Tide Tarrieth No Man*, after l. 1821.

58. *Nice Wanton*, after l. 415.

59. Thus Cushman, *The Devil and the Vice in the English Dramatic Literature* (Halle, 1900), p. 145, comes to the opinion, although his own analysis contradicts it, that "The Vice disappeared from the stage with the disappearance of the moralities." For similar viewpoints, see Gayley, *Representative English Comedies* (New York, 1903–14), introd. liv; Parrott and Ball, *A Short View of the Elizabethan Drama* (New York, 1943), p. 22. The same failure to realize the double significance of the Vice's role and the double nature of the morality plays is responsible for the statement of Sidney Thomas, *The Antic Hamlet and Richard III* (New York, 1943), p. 18, that the Vice "is, in almost every play in which he appears, predominantly a comic character." To Mr. Thomas's work the present study is otherwise much indebted. On the other hand, for opinions, conjecturally advanced, that anticipate the direction of my study, see Brandl, *Quellen,* introd. xciv; and Eduard Eckhardt, *Die lustige Person im älteren englischen Drama* (Berlin, 1902), p. 192.

60. Perhaps the earliest surviving reference, if we could trust it, to the role of the Vice occurs in an anecdote about a performance of a lost morality of Medwall's, *The Finding of Truth*, before Henry VIII in 1513. The story has its source in John Payne Collier, *The History of English Dramatic Poetry* (London, 1879), who claimed to have copied it from "a singular paper folded up" in a Chapter House roll of Revels Accounts still extant

NOTES TO VII: CHANGE AND DECLINE 473

in the Public Record Office. But the "singular paper" itself is untraceable and its existence at any time must be treated with caution in view of Collier's unhappy reputation. At any rate, his purported transcription goes as follows (I, 69):

Inglyshe and the oothers of the kynges pleyers . . . pleyed an Interluyt whiche was wryten by Mayster Medwall but yt was so long yt was not lyked: yt was the fyndyng of Troth who was carried away by ygnoraunce and ypocresy. The foolys part was the best, but the kyng departyed before the end to hys chambre.

If there is a chance that the quotation is valid, there can be little doubt that the "foolys part" refers to the role of the Vice, or that in his own time the Vice was commonly so regarded.

61. *Anatomie of Abuses,* part I, ed. F. J. Furnivall (London, 1877–79), p. 146.

62. *The Arte of English Poesie,* ed. Gladys Willcock and Alice Walker (Cambridge, 1936), p. 84.

63. Randle Cotgrave, *A Dictionarie of the French and English Tongues* (London, 1611) s.v. "mime."

64. *The Plays and Poems of George Chapman,* ed. T. M. Parrott (New York, 1910–14).

65. *The Works of Thomas Nashe,* ed. R. B. McKerrow (London, 1904–10).

66. *Anatomie of Abuses,* part I, p. 145.

67. *Like Will to Like,* Dodsley, III, 349.

68. *A Whip for an Ape: Or Martin Displaied* (1589) in *The Complete Works of John Lyly,* ed. R. W. Bond (Oxford, 1902), III, 417.

69. *The Conflict of Conscience,* marginal gloss following l. 390.

VII: CHANGE AND DECLINE IN THE MORALITY CONVENTION

1. For a detailed examination of the social criticism in these plays see Louis B. Wright, "Social Aspects of Some Belated Moralities," *Anglia,* LIV (1930), 107–48.

2. *Like Will to Like,* Dodsley, III, 340. On the whole subject of the theme of fortune in the moralities, see Willard Farnham, *The Medieval Heritage of Elizabethan Tragedy* (Berkeley, 1936), pp. 213–70, *et passim.*

3. *Nature,* part I, ll. 58 and 78.

4. The feminine virtues of *The Castle of Perseverance* do not alter this point. They are, of course, unimpeachable ladies, but they are the guardians of the hero in a maternal sense, and only incidentally feminine. Their relationship to him has about it nothing amatory or romantic.

5. G. W. Knight, "Lyly," *Review of English Studies,* XV (1939), 155–56.

474   *NOTES TO VIII: THE HYBRID PLAY*

6. *Playes Confuted in Fiue Actions* (1582), in *The English Drama and Stage,* ed. W. C. Hazlitt (London, 1869), p. 181.

7. See E. K. Chambers, *The Elizabethan Stage* (Oxford, 1923), III, 317; also p. 253 of the present text.

8. For a review of the Spira story and its connection with Woodes's play, see Celesta Wine, "Nathaniel Wood's [sic] *Conflict of Conscience,*" *PMLA,* L (1935), 661–78.

9. The comparison has both general and specific justification. Not only are the two plays related in theme and structure, but resemblances between them are so precise as strongly to suggest that Marlowe knew Woodes' play. Compare, for instance, ll. 1585–1619, 1671–1723, 2318–29 of *The Conflict* with ll. 1319 ff., 622–94, 1452–60, respectively, of *Doctor Faustus* in *The Works of Christopher Marlowe,* ed. Tucker Brooke (Oxford, 1929). Lily Bess Campbell, "Doctor Faustus: A Case of Conscience," *PMLA,* LXVII (1952), 219–39, examines the Spira story and compares the two plays, without, however, finding much in common between them. But she does not seem to take into sufficient account their very precise similarities. The relationship between Marlowe's plays and the English moral drama still needs its scholar.

10. See Celesta Wine, "Nathaniel Wood's [sic] *Conflict of Conscience,*" *PMLA,* L (1935), 661–78.

11. G. R. Owst, *Literature and Pulpit in Medieval England* (Cambridge, 1933), p. 535.

12. The same eschatological stress exists in the last two lines of *The Spanish Tragedy,* extending its theme of revenge into both worlds:

> For heere though death hath end their miserie,
> Ile there begin their endles tragedie.

13. *Inferno,* III, ll. 17–18.

14. See also *Mankind,* ll. 846–51; *The Castle of Perseverance,* ll. 3165–77; *Hickscorner,* ll. 116–20; *All for Money,* ll. 1455 ff. The warning is as common in the early moralities as it is in the later ones, and it is somewhat tendentious to offer it as a sign of a developing mood of tragedy in the moralities after 1500, as does Farnham, *The Medieval Heritage of Elizabethan Tragedy,* pp. 212 ff.

15. *Magnificence,* ll. 1896–1943.

VIII: THE HYBRID PLAY

1. Alfred Harbage, *Annals of English Drama, 975–1700* (Philadelphia, 1940).

2. E. K. Chambers, *The Elizabethan Stage* (Oxford, 1923), III, 177–78. The weight of the morality tradition in these decades has also been assessed by Willard Thorp, *The Triumph of Realism in Elizabethan Drama*

NOTES TO VIII: THE HYBRID PLAY 475

(Princeton, 1928). Using Chambers' abstract of the Stationers' Register, Thorp finds (p. 4) that out of seventy-nine plays published between 1557 and 1590, indicating "the kind of plays which the publishers . . . could obtain from their owners and thought capable of attracting trade," twenty-five were moralities and nine others had morality features; and he comes to the following conclusion (p. 5): "What it [the compilation of published plays] does show is the predominance of the morality form in English drama long after the classical impulse had transformed other native literary forms."

3. See the following "Documents of Criticism" as they are excerpted in *The Elizabethan Stage,* appendix C: Geoffrey Fenton, *A Forme of Christian Pollicie* (1574); Stephen Gosson, *Playes Confuted in Fiue Actions* (1582); Phillip Stubbes, *The Anatomie of Abuses* (1583); George Whetstone, *A Touchstone for the Time* (1584); *Martins Months Minde* (1589).

4. Stephen Gosson, *Playes Confuted in Fiue Actions,* as excerpted in *The Elizabethan Stage,* IV, 214.

5. *Ibid.,* pp. 216–18.

6. See W. W. Greg, ed., *The Interlude of Johan the Evangelist,* Malone Society Reprints (London, 1907), introd. According to the *Day-Book of John Dorne,* ed. F. Madan, Oxford Historical Society's *Collectanea,* Vol. I (Oxford, 1885), the Oxford bookseller John Dorne listed the sale of "1 saint jon euuangeliste en trelute" on November 8, 1520.

7. See W. H. Williams, " 'Irisdision' in the Interlude of Johan the Euangelyst," *Modern Language Review,* III (1908), 369–71.

8. In his introduction to his edition of *Godly Queen Hester (Materialien,* 1904), W. W. Greg points out the similarities respecting Wolsey that unite the play to Skelton's *Why Come Ye Not to Court* as well as to William Roy's *Read Me and Be Not Wroth.*

9. Compare the similar ending of Bale's *Three Laws,* which has the same theme and very much the same structure of debate between vices and virtues.

10. *The Life and Repentance of Mary Magdalene,* ll. 837–40.

11. For the relation of the play to Chaucer's Physician's Tale, see Willard Farnham, *The Medieval Heritage of Elizabethan Tragedy* (Berkeley, 1936), pp. 251–58; for the several versions of the Appius and Virginia story in English, see Otto Rumbaur, *Die Geschichte von Appius und Virginia in der englischen Litteratur* (Breslau, 1890).

12. Probably the same play as the *Orestes* performed at court in 1567–68; see Chambers, *The Elizabethan Stage,* III, 466, and IV, 84.

13. The dependence of *Horestes* upon Caxton's *Recuyell* has been analyzed by Friedrich Brie, "*Horestes* von John Pickeryng," *Englische Studien,* XLVI (1912), 66 ff., and by Farnham, *The Medieval Heritage of Elizabethan Tragedy,* pp. 259–60.

14. Farnham, *The Medieval Heritage of Elizabethan Tragedy,* pp. 263–

476 NOTES TO IX: THE HYBRID IMAGE

70, demonstrates that the immediate source of *Cambises* is Richard Taverner's *The Garden of Wysdom* (1539).

15. Ducange, *Glossarium Mediae et Infimae Latinitatis* s.v. "Ambidexter": "Judex, qui ab utraque parte dona accipit." Cowell's *Interpreter* (1607) offers: "Ambidexter is that jurour or embraceour that taketh of both parties for the giving of his verdict."

16. As it almost certainly is in this instance, the role of the foreign physician (French, Spanish, Italian, or Jewish) became a stock disguise on the stage, examples of which occur in the following plays: *Marriage between Wit and Wisdom, Misogonus, Rare Triumphs of Love and Fortune, 2 Return from Parnassus, Grim the Collier of Croydon, Hoffman* (Chettle), *Fair Maid of Bristow, Old Fortunatus* (Dekker), *Wonder of a Kingdom* (Dekker), *Duke of Milan* (Massinger), *Noble Soldier* (Samuel Rowley).

17. Some of these resemblances have been pointed out by Tucker Brooke in his edition of *Common Conditions* (see my bibliography). Worth noting, in addition, are the strong similarity between the two prologues and the "farewell" rhetoric of both plays (*Common Conditions*, ll. 468–77, 1873–79; *Sir Clyomon*, ll. 882–89). Compare also *Common Conditions*, l. 944 with *Sir Clyomon*, l. 345.

IX: THE HYBRID IMAGE IN FARCE

1. *The Cruel Debtor*, l. 176.

2. Among the multitude of Elizabethan asseverations on this issue the best known perhaps is Sidney's praise, in his *Apology*, of *Gorboduc* as "full of stately speeches and well sounding Phrases, clyming to the height of *Seneca* his stile, and as full of notable moralitie, which it doth most delightfully teach, and so obtayne the very end of Poesie." Chapman writes to the same effect in his letter of dedication for *The Revenge of Bussy d'Ambois*: "Material instruction, elegant and sententious excitation to virtue, and deflection from her contrary, being the soul, limbs, and limits of an autentical tragedy." Marston, fierce moralist though he is, even in the play in question, affirms the conventional canon by deliberate rebellion against it in the prologue to *The Dutch Courtesan*:

> And if our pen in this seems over-slight,
> We strive not to instruct, but to delight.

The age had no Aristotle to tell it that the drama, to the extent that it is art, is both instruction and delight because it is the kind of instruction that gives delight.

3. *The Complete Works of Geoffrey Chaucer*, ed. F. N. Robinson (Boston, 1933), p. 127.

4. See George Puttenham, *The Arte of English Poesie*, ed. Gladys Willcock and Alice Walker (Cambridge, 1936), pp. 152–53 ("Of the high,

NOTES TO X: THE HYBRID IMAGE

477

low, and meane subiect"). In our own time, of course, it is too easy to overlook the moral distinctions implicit in social division within an aristocratic structure of society.

5. For the date of the play, see Ewald Flügel, introd. to *Roister Doister,* in *Representative English Comedies,* ed. Charles M. Gayley (New York, 1903–14), I, 95–97.

6. *Roister Doister,* in *Specimens of the Pre-Shakespearean Drama,* ed. J. M. Manly (Boston, 1897).

7. *Roister Doister,* prologue, l. 24.

8. See Henry Bradley, introd. to *Gammer Gurton's Needle,* in *Representative English Comedies,* I, 197–202.

9. *Gammer Gurton's Needle,* in *Specimens of the Pre-Shakespearean Drama.*

10. Tucker Brooke, *The Tudor Drama* (Boston, 1911), p. 163.

11. For the authorship of *Misogonus* and its relation to the humanistic drama of the continent, see R. W. Bond, ed., *Early Plays from the Italian* (Oxford, 1911), introd. xci–cxvi and pp. 161–71. For the identification of Bariona as Laurence Johnson, author of a *Cometographia* in 1577, see G. L. Kittredge, "The 'Misogonus' and Laurence Johnson," *Journal of English and Germanic Philology,* III (1901), 335–41.

12. *Look About You,* ed. W. W. Greg, Malone Society Reprints (London, 1913).

13. How his role usurps dramatic prominence over the more serious main plot appears in the revival of the play for court performance in 1613 under the title of *Cockle de Moye.* See Chambers, *The Elizabethan Stage,* III, 431.

14. *The Dutch Courtesan,* in *The Works of John Marston,* ed. A. H. Bullen (London, 1887).

15. *The Dutch Courtesan* II.i.212 and V.iii.118–20.

X: THE HYBRID IMAGE IN SERIOUS DRAMA

1. Eleanore Boswell, ed., *Edmond Ironside,* Malone Society Reprints (Oxford, 1928), introd. vi–xii.

2. *Holinshed's Chronicles* (London, 1807), I, 728.

3. The play as it stands ends inconclusively, and very probably a second part, now lost, continued the chronicle on a more tragic note through the death of Edmond.

4. Christopher Marlowe, *Works,* ed. Tucker Brooke (Oxford, 1910).

5. L. 229; also ll. 191–92.

6. Ll. 768–69.

7. The allusion is to the "youth" and "wit" moralities with their consistent romantic metaphor for the errors, moral or intellectual, of inex-

NOTES TO X: THE HYBRID IMAGE

perienced adolescence. The morality performed as "The Mariage of Witt and Wisedome" within the play of *Sir Thomas More* (in *Shakespeare Apocrypha*, ed. Tucker Brooke, Oxford, 1908) has the following (IV.i. 215–18):

> *Enter Lady Vanitie singing, and beckning with her hand.*
> *Van.*   Come hether, come hether, come hether, come:
>   Such chere as I haue, thou shalt haue some.
> *Moore.* This is Lady Vanitie, Ile holde my life:
>   Beware, good Witt, you take not her to wife.

Although Lady Vanity does not actually appear as such in any of the surviving moralities, her name is probably composite for the numerous personified sirens who do, just as Iniquity became the undiscriminated name of reference to the Vice (see pp. 393–94), and allusions to her are common in the later drama: see *King Lear* II.ii.31–32; *Volpone* II.iii; *The Devil Is an Ass* I.i.

8. T. S. Eliot, *Selected Essays* (New York, 1932), p. 105.

9. See A. H. Thorndike, "The Relations of *Hamlet* to Contemporary Revenge Plays," *PMLA*, XVII (1902), 125–220.

10. Henry Chettle, *The Tragedy of Hoffman*, ed. Richard Ackermann (Bamberg, 1894).

11. See Tucker Brooke, "The Marlowe Canon," *PMLA*, XXXVII (1922), 406–12.

12. *Lust's Dominion*, ed. J. L. G. Brereton (Louvain, 1931).

13. Thomas Kyd, *The Spanish Tragedy*, in *Specimens of the Pre-Shakespearean Drama*, ed. J. M. Manly (Boston, 1897).

14. John Marston, *Works*, ed. J. O. Halliwell (London, 1856).

15. *The Downfall of Robert Earl of Huntingdon* and *The Death of Robert Earl of Huntingdon*, in Dodsley, *Old English Plays*, 4th ed. (London, 1874–76), Vol. VIII.

16. For the relation of *Jeronimo* to *The Spanish Tragedy*, see F. S. Boas, ed., *The Works of Thomas Kyd* (Oxford, 1901), introd. xxxix–xliv.

17. *The First Part of Jeronimo*, in *The Works of Thomas Kyd*, ed. Boas.

18. *The Trial of Chivalry*, in *A Collection of Old English Plays*, ed. A. H. Bullen (London, 1884), Vol. III.

19. John Webster, *Dramatic Works*, ed. W. C. Hazlitt (London, 1897), I, 18.

20. Harry Levin, *The Overreacher: A Study of Christopher Marlowe* (Cambridge, Mass., 1952), p. 61.

21. For the argument in favor of postdating the prologue, see Albrecht Wagner, ed. *The Jew of Malta* (Heilbronn, 1889), introd. iii–iv.

22. *The Tragedy of Hoffman*, ll. 476–79; *Lust's Dominion*, ll. 3678–85.

23. See Peter Alexander, *Shakespeare's Henry VI and Richard III* (Cambridge, 1929).

24. *The True Tragedy of Richard Duke of York*, in *Shakespeare's Li-*

NOTES TO XI: THE HYBRID IMAGE 479

brary, ed. J. P. Collier (London, 1875), Vol. VI. This variation between "Machiavel" and "Catalin" has been noted at least twice before, although to different effect: by Edward Meyer, *Machiavelli and the Elizabethan Drama* (Weimar, 1897), p. 59; and by Sidney Thomas, *The Antic Hamlet and Richard III* (New York, 1943), p. 12.

XI: THE HYBRID IMAGE IN SHAKESPEARE

1. *Titus Andronicus* (Cambridge Shakespeare, 1948), introd. lxiv.
2. Since this was written it has become fairly well established that the mid-eighteenth century chapbook called *The History of Titus Andronicus,* now in the Folger Shakespeare Library, accurately represents Shakespeare's source. But the role of Aaron, for reasons that compose the subject of the present study, is inevitably the dramatist's creation. On this point, see R. M. Sargent, "The Source of Titus Andronicus," *Studies in Philology,* XLVI (1949), 167–83: the Moor of the chapbook story "never emerges as an independent character; he remains, until his concluding confession, the instrument of the Queen." A recent editor of the play [J. C. Maxwell, ed. *Titus Andronicus* (Arden Shakespeare, 1953), introd. xxxvi–xxxvii] adds, "His [Aaron's] attitude toward his son, and his defiance at the end, are also peculiar to the play. . . . Perhaps the most interesting consequences of the assumption that we have in the chapbook what is substantially Shakespeare's source, are that it confirms the impression that Aaron is peculiarly Shakespearian, that it gives Shakespeare the typical concern . . . with civil order and the forces which threaten to overthrow it."
3. *Magnificence,* l. 737.
4. Sir Thomas More, *English Works,* ed. W. E. Campbell (London, 1931), I, 402.
5. John Milton, *Works,* ed. Frank A. Patterson (New York, 1931–38), V, 85.
6. Richard's words after he awakens from his dream (V.iii.178–200), though frequently misunderstood, are precisely in the tradition of the morality drama. They are a dialogue between himself and his half-personified Conscience. Cf. *Appius and Virginia,* ll. 501–508, for which see p. 271.
7. *Old Fortunatus* II.ii.
8. *1 Henry IV* II.iv.498.
9. See also *Club Law,* ed. G. C. Moore Smith (Cambridge, 1907), l. 1916; and Ben Jonson's Epigram (CXV) "On the Townes Honest Man," l. 27.
10. Richard's reference to "murtherous Machiavel" is dealt with on pp. 377–78.
11. *3 Henry VI* V.vi.63–72. The italics are mine.
12. *Richard III* III.iv.14.
13. *Richard III* II.i.1–6.

480   *NOTES TO XII: IAGO REVISITED*

14. Cf. *Othello* V.i.104–117.

15. The resemblance between Richard's wooing of Lady Anne and an episode in the morality *The Three Lords and Three Ladies of London* (1589) in which Lady Love is wooed by Dissimulation (Dodsley, VI, 420–21) has been noted by Sidney Thomas, *The Antic Hamlet and Richard III* (New York, 1943), pp. 28–30. To Dr. Thomas's work the present treatment of Richard is generally, sometimes specifically, indebted.

16. Cf. Bacon, "Of Envy": "Deformed persons, and eunuchs, and old men, and bastards are envious. For he that cannot possibly mend his own case will do what he can to impair another's; except these defects light upon a very brave and heroical nature, which thinketh to make his natural want part of his honour. . . . This envy, being in the Latin word invidia, goeth in the modern languages by the name of *discontentment*."

XII: IAGO REVISITED

1. The Italian original appeared as the seventh story of the third *deca* of *La Prima Parte de gli Hecatommithi di M. Giovanbattista Giraldi Cinthio* (appresso Lionard Torrentino), pp. 571–86. No Elizabethan translation is known. I have not been able to consult a French translation by Gabriel Chappuys of the *Hecatommithi* (Paris, 1584), and am content to rely on the estimate of H. B. Charlton, *Bulletin of the John Ryland's Library*, xxxi (January, 1948), 4: "It [the French translation of the Othello story] follows the original with a literal fidelity rare in such translations. Its closeness is such that it proffers not the slightest clue as to whether Shakespeare had the tale from the Italian or the French."

2. A. C. Swinburne, *Complete Works*, ed. Edmund Gosse and Thomas Wise (London, 1925–26), II, 245.

3. Translation by W. Parr in *Shakespeare's Library*, ed. W. C. Hazlitt (London, 1875), II, 300.

4. A hint for this quality of her love is supplied by the original story, where she loved him "tratta non da appetito donnesco, ma della virtù del Moro" (*Shakespeare's Library*, II, 285). But the sentiment is not only typical of Shakespeare, it is also profusely Elizabethan, as in the last stanza of Raleigh's *Walsinghame:*

> But love is a durable fire
>   In the mind ever burning;
> Never sick, never old, never dead,
>   From itself never turning.

5. *Shakespeare's Library*, II, 288.

6. *Othello* I.i.86–117. But he strikes the same note even earlier by his reference to Cassio as "A fellow almost damn'd in a fair wife" (l. 21), if we can accept what seems its most plausible meaning—that the hus-

NOTES TO XII: IAGO REVISITED

band of a pretty woman is damned in the sense that he is a predestined cuckold. To explain the meaning of the line does not, of course, explain its existence, since Cassio is unmarried, unless, as others have noted, it was Shakespeare's first intention, later revised, to retain the wife that Cassio's original has in Cinthio's story.

7. *Shakespeare's Library*, II, 288–89.

8. Except for his monologue at II.iii.342–68, where the homiletic revelation of villainy is massive and unimpeded.

9. *Shakespeare's Library*, II, 290.

10. The exception is at II.i.305–308, for which, see p. 17.

11. *Magnificence*, ll. 1875–2152.

12. *The Nature of the Four Elements*, pp. 41–43.

13. *The Longer Thou Livest*, ll. 1795 ff.

14. John Redford, *Wit and Science*, ll. 332 ff.; *The Marriage of Wit and Science*, Dodsley, II, 367–69; *A Marriage between Wit and Wisdom*, pp. 20–22.

15. *Cambises*, ll. 1173–86.

16. *Play of Love*, ll. 1293–1325.

17. Christopher Marlowe, *Works*, ed. Tucker Brooke (Oxford, 1910).

18. *Edmond Ironside*, ed. Eleanore Boswell, Malone Society Reprints (Oxford, 1928).

19. *Lust's Dominion*, ed. J. L. G. Brereton (Louvain, 1931).

20. *The Death of Robert Earl of Huntingdon*, Dodsley, VIII.

21. *The Works of Thomas Kyd*, ed. F. S. Boas (Oxford, 1901).

22. On this point see Maurice Valency, *The Tragedies of Herod and Mariamne* (New York, 1940), pp. 176–77.

23. *The Dumb Knight*, Dodsley, X.

BIBLIOGRAPHY OF
MORALITY PLAYS

Conjectural dates for the plays below are derived from E. K. Chambers, *The Medieval Stage* (1903), from *The Elizabethan Stage* (1923) by the same author, and from Alfred Harbage, *Annals of English Drama* (1940), except in a few instances where the evidence seems to warrant modification. The full title is quoted from the first extant edition, unless otherwise noted. The citation of modern editions is concentrated upon those after 1850, although a few before that date which seem especially useful are cited. Not cited are the short selections from several moralities that appear in A. W. Pollard, *English Miracle Plays, Moralities, and Interludes* (1890; 5th ed., revised, 1909). Also not cited are the photographic facsimiles of most of the plays below in J. S. Farmer, *Tudor Facsimile Texts* (1907–14; reissued in part as the *Old English Drama, Students' Facsimile Edition*). An asterisk denotes the edition used in the present work.

COLLECTIONS

Adams
: Joseph Quincy Adams. Chief Pre-Shakespearean Dramas. Boston, 1924.

Brandl
: Alois Brandl. Quellen des weltlichen Dramas in England vor Shakespeare. Strassburg, 1898.

Dodsley
: Robert Dodsley. A Select Collection of Old English Plays (4th ed., revised by W. C. Hazlitt). London, 1874–76. 15 volumes.

E.E.T.S.
: Early English Text Society. London. Publications 1864 to date.

Farmer
: John S. Farmer. Early English Dramatists. London, 1905–8.

Jahrbuch
: Jahrbuch der Deutschen Shakespeare-Gesellschaft. Berlin. Publications 1864 to date.

M.S.R.
: Malone Society Reprints, W. W. Greg, general editor. London. Publications 1907 to date.

Manly
: John M. Manly. Specimens of the Pre-Shakespearean Drama. Boston, 1897. 2 volumes.

Materialien
: Materialien zur Kunde des älteren englischen Dramas, W. Bang general editor. Louvain, 1902–14. Continued as, Materials for the Study of the Old English Drama, Henry de Vocht general editor, 1927 to date.

484 BIBLIOGRAPHY OF MORALITY PLAYS
INDIVIDUAL PLAYS

ALBION KNIGHT, 1537–65. [The surviving fragment, without title page, contains 408 lines.]
> J. P. Collier. Shakespeare Society Papers, I (1844).
> Farmer, 1906.
> * W. W. Greg. Malone Society Collections, I, 3 (1909).

ALL FOR MONEY, 1559–77. THOMAS LUPTON. A moral and Pitieful Comedie, Intituled, All for Money. Plainly representing the maners of men, and fashion of the world noweadayes. Compiled by T. Lupton. *Roger Warde and Richard Mundee, 1578.*
> J. O. Halliwell. Literature of the Sixteenth and Seventeenth Centuries Illustrated. London, 1851.
> *E. Vogel. Jahrbuch, XL (1904).

APPIUS AND VIRGINIA, 1559–67. R.B. A new Tragicall Comedie of Apius and Virginia, Wherein is liuely expressed a rare example of the vertue of Chastitie, by Virginias constancy, in wishing rather to be slaine at her owne Fathers handes, then to be deflowred of the wicked Iudge Apius. By R.B. *William How for Richard Jones, 1575.*
> Dodsley, IV.
> Farmer, 1908.
> *R. B. McKerrow. M.S.R., 1911.

CAMBISES, 1558–69. THOMAS PRESTON. A lamentable tragedy mixed ful of pleasant mirth, conteyning the life of Cambises king of Percia, from the beginning of his kingdome vnto his death, his one good deed of execution, after that many wicked deeds and tirannous murders, committed by and through him, and last of all, his odious death by Gods Iustice appointed. Doon in such order as foloweth. By Thomas Preston. *John Allde, n.d.*
> T. Hawkins. Origin of the English Drama, I. London, 1773.
> Dodsley, IV.
> *Manly, II.
> Adams.
> Baskerville, Heltzel, and Nethercot. Elizabethan and Stuart Plays. New York, 1934.

CASTLE OF PERSEVERANCE (MACRO MS.), 1400–1425.
> *F. J. Furnivall and A. W. Pollard. E.E.T.S., 1904.
> Adams (abbreviated text).

CLYOMON AND CLAMYDES, 1570–83. The Historie of the two valiant Knights, Syr Clyomon Knight of the Golden Sheeld, sonne to the King of Denmarke: And Clamydes the white Knight, sonne to the King of Suauia. As it hath been sundry times Acted by her Maiesties Players. *Thomas Creede, 1599.*

BIBLIOGRAPHY OF MORALITY PLAYS

A. Dyce. Works of George Peele, III. London, 1828–39.
A. H. Bullen. Works of George Peele, II. London, 1888.
*W. W. Greg. M.S.R., 1913.

COBBLER'S PROPHECY, 1580–94. ROBERT WILSON. The Coblers Prophesie. Written by Robert Wilson, Gent. *John Danter for Cuthbert Burby. 1594.*
W. Dibelius. Jahrbuch, XXXIII (1897).
*A. C. Wood. M.S.R., 1914.

COMMON CONDITIONS, 1576. An excellent and pleasant Comedie, termed after the name of the Vice, Common Condicions, drawne out of the most famous historie of Galiarbus Duke of Arabia, and of the good and eeuill successe of him and his two children, Sedmond his sun, and Clarisia his daughter: Set foorth with delectable mirth, and pleasant shewes. *William How for John Hunter, n.d.*
Brandl (fragmentary text).
Farmer, 1908 (fragmentary text).
*C. F. Tucker Brooke. Elizabethan Club Reprints. New Haven, 1915.

CONFLICT OF CONSCIENCE, 1575–81. NATHANIEL WOODES. [The early edition exists in two issues, the difference between them mainly in the title page, the prologue, and the speech of the *nuntius* which supplies the whole sixth act.] (*a*) An excellent new Commedie, Intituled: The Conflict of Conscience. Contayninge, The most lamentable Hystorie, of the desperation of Frauncis Spera, who forsooke the trueth of Gods Gospell, for feare of the losse of life and worldly goodes. Compiled, by Nathaniell Woodes. Minister, in Norwich. *Richard Bradocke, 1581.* [Spira's name is mentioned again in the prologue. At the end the *nuntius* brings in the "doleful newes" of the hero's tragic death by suicide.] (*b*) An excellent new Commedie, Intituled: The Conflict of Conscience. Contayninge, A most lamentable example, of the dolefull desperation of a miserable worldlinge, termed, by the name of Philologvs, who forsooke the trueth of Gods Gospel, for feare of the losse of lyfe, & worldly goods. Compiled, by Nathaniell Woodes. Minister, in Norwich. *Richard Bradocke, 1581.* [Also omits Spira's name from the prologue. At the end the *nuntius* proclaims the "ioyfull newes" of the hero's last minute conversion and peaceful death.]
J. P. Collier. Five Old Plays (Roxburghe Club). London, 1851 (combines title page of first issue with text of second).
Dodsley, VI (second issue).
*Herbert Davis and F. P. Wilson. M.S.R., 1952.

CRUEL DEBTOR, C. 1565. LEWIS WAGER OR W. WAGER. [Four leaves survive.]
F. J. Furnivall. New Shakespeare Society's Transactions, 1877–79 (reprints three leaves).
*W. W. Greg. Malone Society Collections, I, 4–5 (1911) and II, 2 (1923).

486   BIBLIOGRAPHY OF MORALITY PLAYS

ENOUGH IS AS GOOD AS A FEAST, 1560–69. W. WAGER. A Comedy or Enterlude intituled, Inough is as good as a feast, very fruteful, godly and ful of pleasant mirth. Compiled by W. Wager. *John Allde, n.d.*

    S. de Ricci. Huntington Facsimile Reprints. New York, 1920.

EVERYMAN, 1480–1500. Here begynneth a treatyse how the hye fader of heuen sendeth dethe to somon euery creature to come and gyue a counte of theyr lyues in this worlde, and is in maner of a morall playe. *John Skot, n.d.* [Skot's first edition, according to Greg, belongs to 1528–29. Parts of two earlier editions, both by Pynson, survive, but lack title pages.]

    T. Hawkins. Origin of the English Drama, I. London, 1773.
    Dodsley, I.
    H. Logeman. Ghent. 1892 (together with the Dutch *Elckerlijk*).
    A. W. Pollard. Fifteenth Century Prose and Verse. London, 1903.
    W. W. Greg. Materialien, IV (1904. First Skot ed.).
    Farmer, 1905.
    W. W. Greg. Materialien, XXIV (1909. Second Skot ed.).
    A. T. Quiller-Couch. Select English Classics. London, 1909.
    Ernest Rhys. Everyman's Library, 1909.
    W. W. Greg. Materialien, XXVIII (1910. Both Pynson fragments.).
    *Adams.
    (numerous modern editions besides)

FOUR ELEMENTS. *See* NATURE OF THE FOUR ELEMENTS.

FREE WILL, 1560–61. HENRY CHEKE. A certayne Tragedie wrytten fyrst in Italian, by F.N.B. entituled, Freewyl, and translated into Englishe, by Henry Cheeke. *John Tisdale, n.d.* [A translation of the *Tragedia del Libero Arbitrio* (1546) of Francesco Nigri de Bassano.]

    No modern edition.

GODLY QUEEN HESTER, 1525–29. A newe enterlude drawen oute of the holy scripture of godly queene Hester, verye necessary newly made and imprinted, this present yere. M.D.L.X.I. *William Pickering and Thomas Hacket.*

    J. P. Collier. Illustrations of Early English Popular Literature, I. London, 1863.
    A. B. Grosart. Miscellanies of The Fuller Worthies' Library, IV. London, 1873.
    *W. W. Greg. Materialien, V (1904).
    Farmer, 1906.

GOOD ORDER, 1500–1533. *William Rastell, 1533.* [The surviving fragment contains 131 lines of the end and Rastell's colophon.]

    G. L. Frost and R. Nash. Studies in Philology, XLI (1944), 483–91.

HICKSCORNER, 1513–16. Hycke scorner. *Wynken de Worde, n.d.*

    T. Hawkins. Origin of the English Drama, I. London, 1773.

BIBLIOGRAPHY OF MORALITY PLAYS 487

Dodsley, I.
*Manly, I.
Farmer, 1905.

HORESTES, 1567. JOHN PIKERING. A Newe Enterlude of Vice Conteyninge, the Historye of Horestes, with the cruell reuengment of his Fathers death, vpon his one naturtll Mother. By John Pikeryng. *William Griffith, 1567*.
J. P. Collier. Illustrations of Old English Literature, II. London, 1866.
*Brandl.

IMPATIENT POVERTY, 1547–58. A newe Interlude of Impacyente pouerte newlye Imprinted. M.C.L.X. *John King*.
Farmer, 1907.
*R. B. McKerrow. Materialien, XXXIII (1911).

JACK JUGGLER, 1553–58. A new Enterlued for Chyldren to playe named Iacke Iugeler, both wytte, very playsent and merye, Neuer before Imprented. *William Copland, n.d.*
J. Haslewood. Roxburghe Club. London, 1820.
F. J. Child. Four Old Plays. Cambridge, Mass., 1848.
A. B. Grosart. Miscellanies of The Fuller Worthies' Library, IV. London, 1873.
Dodsley, IV.
E. W. Ashbee. Dramatic Facsimiles. London? 1876.
Farmer, 1906.
W. H. Williams. Cambridge, 1914.
*E. L. Smart and W. W. Greg. M.S.R., 1933 (first ed.).
B. I. Evans and W. W. Greg, M.S.R., 1937 (third ed.).

JOHN THE EVANGELIST, 1520–57. Here begynneth the enterlude of Iohan the Euangelyst. *John Waley, n.d.*
*W. W. Greg. M.S.R., 1907.
Farmer, 1907.

KING DARIUS, 1559–65. A Pretie new Enterlude both pithie & pleasaunt of the Story of Kyng Daryus, Beinge taken out of the third and fourth Chapter of the thyrd booke of Esdras. *Thomas Colwell, n.d.*
J. O. Halliwell. London, 1860.
*Brandl.
Farmer, 1906.

KING JOHN (MS.), 1530–36. JOHN BALE.
J. P. Collier. Camden Society. London, 1838.
*Manly, I.
Farmer, 1907 (Dramatic Writings of John Bale).
W. Bang. Materialien, XXV (1909. Facsimile.).
J. H. P. Pafford and W. W. Greg. M.S.R., 1931.

488　BIBLIOGRAPHY OF MORALITY PLAYS

LIBERALITY AND PRODIGALITY, 1567–68. A Pleasant Comedie, Shewing the contention betweene Liberalitie and Prodigalitie. As it was playd before her Maiestie. *Simon Stafford for George Vincent, 1602.*

Dodsley, VIII.

*W. W. Greg. M.S.R., 1913.

LIFE AND REPENTANCE OF MARY MAGDALENE, C. 1550. LEWIS WAGER. A new Enterlude, neuer before this tyme imprinted, entreating of the Life and Repentaunce of Marie Magdalene: not only godlie, learned and fruitefull, but also well furnished with pleasaunt myrth and pastime, very delectable for those which shall heare or reade the same. Made by the learned clarke Lewis Wager. *John Charlwood, 1566.*

F. I. Carpenter. Chicago, 1902 and 1904.

LIKE WILL TO LIKE, 1562–68. ULPIAN FULWELL. An Enterlude Intituled Like wil to like quod the Deuel to the Colier, very godly and ful of pleasant mirth. Wherin is declared not onely what punishment followeth those that wil rather followe licentious liuing, then to esteeme & followe good councel: and what great benefits and commodities they receiue that apply them vnto vertuous liuing and good exercises. Made by Vlpian Fulwel. *John Allde, 1568.*

*Dodsley, III.

Farmer, 1906.

THE LONGER THOU LIVEST, THE MORE FOOL THOU ART, 1560–68. W. WAGER. A very mery and Pythie Commedie, called The longer thou liuest, the more foole thou art. A Myrrour very necessarie for youth, and specially for such as are like to come to dignitie and promotion: As it maye well appeare in the Matter folowynge. Newly compiled by W. Wager. *William Howe for Richard Jones, n.d.*

A. Brandl. Jahrbuch, XXXVI (1900).

LOVE, PLAY OF, 1530–33. JOHN HEYWOOD. A play of loue, A newe and a mery enterlude concernyng pleasure and payne in loue, made by Ihon Heywood. *William Rastell, 1534.*

*Brandl.

Farmer, 1905 (Dramatic Writings of John Heywood).

K. W. Cameron. Raleigh, N.C., 1944.

LOVE FEIGNED AND UNFEIGNED (MS. FRAG.), 1540–60.

A. Esdaile. Malone Society Collections, I, 1 (1908).

LUSTY JUVENTUS, 1547–53. R. WEVER. An Enterlude called lusty Iuuentus. Lyuely describing the frailtie of youth: of natur prone to vyce: by grace and good counsayll, traynable to vertue. *W. Copland, n.d.*

T. Hawkins. Origin of the English Drama, I. London, 1773.

*Dodsley, II.

Farmer, 1905.

BIBLIOGRAPHY OF MORALITY PLAYS 489

MAGNIFICENCE, 1513–16. JOHN SKELTON. Magnyfycence, A goodly interlude and a mery deuysed and made by mayster Skelton, poet laureate late deceasyd.

J. Littledale. Roxburghe Club. London, 1821.
A. Dyce. Poetical Works of John Skelton, I. London, 1843.
*R. L. Ramsay. E.E.T.S., 1908.
P. Henderson. Complete Poems of John Skelton. London, 1931.

MANKIND (MACRO MS.), 1461–85.
*Manly, I.
Brandl.
F. J. Furnivall and A. W. Pollard. E.E.T.S., 1904.
Farmer, 1907.
Adams.

MARRIAGE BETWEEN WIT AND WISDOM (MS.), c. 1579. FRANCIS MERBURY? The [Contract] of a Marige betweene wit and wisdome very frutefull and mixed full of pleasant mirth as well for The beholders as the Readers or hearers neuer before imprinted. *1579*.
*J. O. Halliwell. Shakespeare Society, XXXI (1846)
Farmer, 1908.

MARRIAGE OF WIT AND SCIENCE, 1568–70. A new and Pleasaunt enterlude intituled the mariage of Witte and Science. *Thomas Marsh, n.d.*
*Dodsley, II.
Farmer, 1908.

MARY MAGDALENE (DIGBY MS.), 1480–90.
T. Sharp. Ancient Mysteries from the Digby Manuscript (Abbotsford Club). Edinburgh, 1835.
*F. J. Furnivall. Digby Mysteries (New Shakespeare Society). London, 1882. Reprinted for E.E.T.S., 1896.
Adams (first part only).

MIND, WILL, AND UNDERSTANDING. *See* WISDOM WHO IS CHRIST.

MINDS, after 1575. Comoedia. A worke in ryme, contayning an Enterlude of Myndes, witnessing the Mans Fall from God and Christ. Set forth by H. N. and by him newly perused and amended. Translated out of Base-Almayns into English. [No date, imprint, or colophon. A translation from Low German of a work by Henrick Niklaes, founder of the sect of the Family of Love.]
No modern edition.

MISOGONUS (MS.), 1560–77. LAURENTIUS BARIONA? A mery and p[leasaunt comedie called ?] Misogonus. . . . Laurentius Bariona. Kettheringe. Die 20 Novembris, Anno 1577. [The prologue is followed by the signature "Thomas Rychardes."]

490   *BIBLIOGRAPHY OF MORALITY PLAYS*

*Brandl.
Farmer, 1906.
R. W. Bond. Early Plays from the Italian. Oxford, 1911.

MUNDUS ET INFANS, 1500–1520. Here begynneth a propre newe Interlude of the worlde and the chylde, otherwyse called /Mundus & Infans/ & it sheweth of the estate of Chyldehode and Manhode. *Wynkyn de Worde, 1522.*
    Roxburghe Club (editor unknown). London, 1817.
    Dodsley, I.
    *Manly, I.
    Farmer, 1905.

NATURE, 1490–1501. HENRY MEDWALL. A goodly interlude of Nature compylyd by mayster Henry Medwall chapleyn to the ryght reuerent father in god Iohan Morton somtyme Cardynall and arche byshop of Canterbury.
    *Brandl.
    Farmer, 1907.

NATURE OF THE FOUR ELEMENTS, 1517–18. JOHN RASTELL. A new interlude and a mery of the nature of the .iiij. elementes declarynge many proper poyntes of phylosophy naturall, and of dyuers straunge landys, and of dyuers straunge effectes & causis, whiche interlude yf the hole matter be playd wyl conteyne the space of an hour and a halfe, but yf ye lyst ye may leue out muche of the sad mater as messengers *p*te, and some of naturys parte and some of experyens *p*te & yet the matter wyl depend conuenyently, and than it wyll not be paste thre quarters of an hour of length. [The only surviving copy lacks all leaves between signatures C and E, and all leaves after E.]
    *J. O. Halliwell. Percy Society, XXII (1848).
    Dodsley, I.
    J. Fischer. Marburger Studien, V (1903).
    Farmer, 1905.

NEW CUSTOM, 1559–73. A new Enterlude No less wittie: then pleasant, entituled new Custome, deuised of late, and for diuerse causes nowe set forthe, neuer before this tyme Imprinted. *William How for Abraham Veale, 1573.*
    *Dodsley, III.
    Farmer, 1906.

NICE WANTON, 1547–53. A Preaty Interlude called, Nice wanton. *John King, 1560.*
    Dodsley, II.
    *Manly, I.
    Farmer, 1905.

BIBLIOGRAPHY OF MORALITY PLAYS 491

PATIENT AND MEEK GRISSILL, 1561–65. JOHN PHILLIP. The Commodye Of pacient and meeke Grissill, Whearin is declared, the good example, of her pacience towardes her husband: and lykewise, the due obedience of Children, toward their Parentes. Newly. Compiled by Iohn Phillip. *Thomas Colwell, n.d.*

W. W. Greg and R. B. McKerrow. M.S.R., 1909.

PLAY OF LOVE. *See* LOVE, PLAY OF.

PLAY OF THE WEATHER. *See* WEATHER, PLAY OF THE.

PRIDE OF LIFE (MS.), 1400–1425. [The surviving fragment of 502 lines lacks the final part of the play.]

J. Mills. Proceedings of Royal Society of Antiquaries of Ireland. Dublin, 1891.
Brandl.
*O. Waterhouse. E.E.T.S., 1909.

RESPUBLICA (MS.), 1553. A merye enterlude entitled Respublica, made in the yeare of our Lorde 1553, and the first yeare of the moost prosperous Reigne of our moste gracious Soverainge, Quene Marye the first.

J. P. Collier. Illustrations of Old English Literature, I. London, 1866.
Brandl.
*L. A. Magnus. E.E.T.S., 1905.
Farmer, 1907.
W. W. Greg. E.E.T.S., 1952.

SATIRE OF THE THREE ESTATES, 1535–40. SIR DAVID LINDSAY. Ane Satyre Of The Thrie Estaits, in commendation of vertew and vituperation of vyce. Maid be Sir Dauid Lindesay of the Mont, alias, Lyon King of Armes. *Robert Charteris, Edinburgh, 1602.* [The Bannatyne MS., 1568, contains several sections of the play, including what is not in the Charteris edition—the "Proclamatioun" introducing the performance at Cupar, Fifeshire, in 1552.]

G. Chalmers. Poetical Works of Sir David Lindsay. London, 1806.
F. Hall *et al.* Works of Sir David Lindsay (E.E.T.S.). London, 1865–71.
D. Laing. Poetical Works of Sir David Lindsay. Edinburgh, 1879.
*D. Hamer. Works of Sir David Lindsay (Scottish Text Society). Edinburgh, 1931–36.
J. Kinsley. London, 1954 (abridged).

SOMEBODY AND OTHERS, OR THE SPOILING OF LADY VERITY, c. 1550. [Two leaves survive. A translation of the French Protestant morality *La Verité Cachée.*]

S. R. Maitland. List of Early Printed Books at Lambeth. London, 1843.
*W. W. Greg. Malone Society Collections, II, 3 (1931).

SUMMONING OF EVERYMAN. *See* EVERYMAN.

BIBLIOGRAPHY OF MORALITY PLAYS

TEMPERANCE AND HUMILITY, C. 1530. [One leaf survives.]
W. W. Greg. Malone Society Collections, I, 3 (1910).

THREE LADIES OF LONDON, 1581. ROBERT WILSON? A right excellent and famous Comoedy called the three Ladies of London. Wherein is notablie declared and set foorth, how by the meanes of Lucar, Loue and Conscience is so corrupted, that the one is married to Dissimulation, the other fraught with all abhomination. A perfect patterne for all Estates to looke into, and a worke right worthie to be marked. Written by R.W. as it hath beene publiquely played. *Roger Warde, 1584.*
J. P. Collier. Five Old Plays (Roxburghe Club). London, 1851.
*Dodsley, VI.

THREE LAWS, 1530–36. JOHN BALE. A Comedy concernynge thre lawes, of nature Moses, & Christ, corrupted by the Sodomytes. Pharysees and Papystes. Compyled by Iohan Bale. Anno M.D. XXXVIII.
*A. Schroeer. Anglia, V (1882).
Farmer, 1907 (Dramatic Writings of John Bale).

THREE LORDS AND THREE LADIES OF LONDON, 1589. ROBERT WILSON? The pleasant and Stately Morall of the three Lordes and three Ladies of London. With the great Ioy and Pompe, Solempnized at their Mariages: Commically interlaced with much honest Mirth, for pleasure and recreation, among many Morall obseruations and other important matters of due Regard. by R.W. *R. Jones, 1590.*
J. P. Collier. Five Old Plays (Roxburghe Club). London, 1851.
*Dodsley, VI.

TIDE TARRIETH NO MAN, 1576. GEORGE WAPULL. The Tyde taryeth no Man. A Moste Pleasant and merry Commody, right pythie and full of delight. Compiled by George Wapull. *Hugh Jackson, 1576.*
J. P. Collier. Illustrations of Early English Popular Literature, II. London, 1864.
*E. Ruhl. Jahrbuch, XLIII (1907).

TOM TYLER AND HIS WIFE, 1550–80. Tom Tyler and His Wife. An Excellent Old Play, As It was Printed and Acted about a hundred Years ago. The Second Impression. 1661.
F. E. Schelling. PMLA, XV (1900), 253–89.
Farmer, 1906.
*G. C. Moore Smith and W. W. Greg. M.S.R., 1910.

TRIAL OF TREASURE, 1567. A new and mery Enterlude, called the Triall of Treasure, newly set foorth, and neuer before this tyme imprinted. *Thomas Purfoot, 1567.*
J. O. Halliwell. Percy Society, XXVIII (1850).

BIBLIOGRAPHY OF MORALITY PLAYS

493

*Dodsley, III.
Farmer, 1906.

VIRTUOUS AND GODLY SUSANNA, 1568–69. THOMAS GARTER. The Commody Of the moste vertuous and Godlye Susanna, neuer before this tyme Printed. Compiled by Thomas Garter. *Hugh Jackson, 1578*.
B. I. Evans and W. W. Greg. M.S.R., 1937.

WEALTH AND HEALTH, 1553–57. An enterlude of Welth, and Helth, very mery and full of Pastyme, newly at this tyme Imprinted.
*W. W. Greg and P. Simpson. M.S.R., 1907.
Farmer, 1907.
F. Holthausen. Festschrift der Universität Kiel, 1908 (rev. ed. 1922).

WEATHER, PLAY OF THE, 1530–33. JOHN HEYWOOD. The Play of the wether. A new and a very mery enterlude of all maner wethers made by Iohn Heywood. *William Rastell, 1533*.
*Brandl.
A. W. Pollard. [in] Representative English Comedies. New York, 1903–14.
Farmer, 1905 (Dramatic Writings of John Heywood).
Adams.

WISDOM WHO IS CHRIST—OR, MIND, WILL, AND UNDERSTANDING (MACRO MS.), 1461–85.
W. B. D. Turnbull. Abbotsford Club, 1837.
F. J. Furnivall. Digby Mysteries (New Shakespeare Society), 1882. Reprinted for E.E.T.S., 1896. [Only the first 754 lines of the play, as they survive in the Digby MS.]
*F. J. Furnivall and A. W. Pollard. E.E.T.S., 1904.

WIT AND SCIENCE (MS.), 1536–46. JOHN REDFORD. [The first part of the play is missing, but it ends with the colophon: "Thus endyth the Play of Wyt and Science, made by Master Jhon Redford."]
J. O. Halliwell. Shakespeare Society, 1848.
*Manly, I.
Farmer, 1907.
A. Brown and W. W. Greg. M.S.R., 1951.

WORLD AND THE CHILD. *See* MUNDUS ET INFANS.

YOUTH, 1513–29. Thēterlude of youth. *John Waley, n.d.*
J. O. Halliwell. Contributions to Early English Literature, 1849.
Dodsley, II.
*W. Bang and R. B. McKerrow. Materialien, XII (1905)
Farmer, 1906.

INDEX

Aaron the Moor (*Titus Andronicus*), 39, 43, 46, 58, 357, 360, 395, 412, 456, n. 1; and Iago, 35, 369, 416, 434; discrepancy between behavior and motives in, 35-36; artist-criminal, 43-44; hybrid, 379-86; and the Vice, 379-86; and Machiavellianism, 380; and Richard III, 386-87; Shakespeare's own creation, 479, n. 2

Adam (*As You Like It*), 447

Adams, Joseph Quincy, on Iago and the Duke of Epire, 34

Alanus de Insulis, 82, 106

Alarbus (*Titus Andronicus*), 380

Albany, Duke of (*King Lear*), 50

Albigenses, 75

Albion Knight, 181, 191, 209, 222

Alcestis (Euripides), 452

Allegorical, antonyms of, 458, n. 8

Allegorical castle, siege of, and the Psychomachia, 73

Allegorical journey, in Christian allegory, 101

Allegory, and the drama, 56, 60-63, 140, 252-53; 333; and Christianity, 58, 96; decay of, 59, 220-21; and history, 62-63, 90, 262-78; oldest form of, 69; themes of, 63-74; C. S. Lewis on, 81-82; Puttenham on, 82; definition of, 96; examples of, 97-98; and personification, 97-99; and symbolism, 98-99; method of, 99, 463, n. 1, 463, n. 6; literary and homiletic, 105-113; educational, 220; and the classics, 319; exegetical, 462, n. 1; *see also* Homiletic allegory, Morality plays, Psychomachia, the

Alleyn, Edward, in the role of Barabas, 350-51

All for Money (Lupton), 102, 112-13, 115, 131, 133-34, 182-83, 217, 233-35, 250, 306, 459, n. 20, 464, n. 17, 466, n. 10, 467, n. 20, 474, n. 14

Alphonsus, Emperor of Germany (at. to Chapman), 199

Amphitruo (Plautus), 316, 319, 338

Anatomy of Abuses (Stubbes), 199

Anaxagoras, dualism of, 74

Angelo (*Measure for Measure*), 37, 39, 41, 271

Annals of English Drama (Harbage), and number of morality plays, 251-52, 253

Anne, Lady (*Richard III*), 31, 46, 170, 399, 403, 404-7, 432, 438, 456, n. 1, 480, n. 15; and Mankind, 405

Antic Hamlet and Richard III, The (Thomas), 472, n. 59, 480, n. 15

Antichristus, 60

Anticlaudianus (Alanus de Insulis), 106; and the Psychomachia, 82

Antisthenes, 217

Antonio (*The Merchant of Venice*), 6, 411, 446

Antonio (*The Tempest*), a Machiavel, 425

Antonio's Revenge (Marston), hybrid image in, 361

Antony (*Antony and Cleopatra*), 392

Antony and Cleopatra, 394; and *Othello*, 51

Apology for Poetry, An (Sidney), 476, n. 2

Appius and Virginia, 115, 197, 213, 254, 269-72, 312, 314, 459, n. 17, 464, n. 17, 466, n. 10

Arbor mala, 143, 145, 468, n. 23

Ariosto, Ludovico, 407, 410

Aristotle, 216, 217

Art of English Poesie (Puttenham), 199

Assembly of the Gods (Lydgate), 92; and the Psychomachia, 82

496   INDEX

As You Like It, 26, 411, 446-47
Audience, the, and actors, 113, 119-20, 126, 394; and the Vice, 176-92, 339, 341, 464, n. 17; and monologues, 436, 437, 442, 456, n. 1
Augustine, St., 74; martial imagery of, 77

Bacon, Francis, on envy, 480, n. 16
Bale, John, 91, 93, 114, 117, 137, 139, 144, 169, 197, 209, 254, 263, 442, 467, n. 14, 475, n. 9
Bandello, Matteo, 407, 410
Barabas (*The Jew of Malta*), 34, 313, 354, 374, 384, 395, 434, 441, 444; and the Vice, 346-53, 369, 370-71, 372; and Machiavellianism, 376, 377; and Iago, 430
Bardolph (*1 Henry IV*), 87
Bariona, Laurentius, 327, 477, n. 11
Barrymore, John, as Richard III, 456, n. 1
Bassianus (*Titus Andronicus*), 382, 385
Beatrice (*Much Ado*), 407, 408
Beaufort, Cardinal (*2 Henry VI*), 41
Beaumont, Francis, 450
Belleforest, François de, 407, 410
Benedict (*Much Ado*), 407, 408, 409
Beowulf, 452
Bernard of Clairvaux, St., 69
Berowne (*Love's Labour's Lost*), 40
Beverley, *Paternoster* play at, 60-61, 108, 458, n. 3
Bianca (*Othello*), 56, 418
Biblical figures, and hybrid plays, 255-56, 259-61, 266, 269
Boccaccio, 312
Bonaventura, Cardinal, of Padua, 459, n. 23
Booth, Edwin, interpretation of Iago, 13
Borachio (*Much Ado*), 411
Bottom (*A Midsummer Night's Dream*), 219, 220
Brabantio (*Othello*), 55, 56, 426
Bradley, Andrew Cecil, 6, 28, 29, 204, 455, n. 3; on Iago, 12, 17, 24, 436; criticism of, 25-26; on *Othello*, 51, 54; on soliloquies of Shakespeare's villains, 456, n. 1
Brandl, Alois, on the Vice, 193, 472, n. 59
Broglie, Achille Charles, Duc de, on *Othello*, 3, 455, n. 1
Brooke, C. F. Tucker, on Iago, 4, 455, n. 3; on *Mankind*, 122; on Diccon the Bedlam and Iago, 327
Brutus (*Julius Caesar*), 392, 412, 413

Buckingham, Duke of (*Richard III*), 402, 403, 441
Bucolics (Virgil), 96
Bunyan, John, 83, 84, 99, 101, 105, 106, 231

Caesar, Julius (*Julius Caesar*), 412, 413
Cambises (Preston), 92, 115, 181-82, 186, 190, 224-25, 254, 284-91, 314, 379, 440, 466, n. 10
Cambridge, Earl of (*Henry V*), 26-27
Camus, Albert, 98
Canterbury Tales, The, homiletic allegory in, 107; on Seven Deadly Sins, 142
Canute, King, 340, 341
Carrington, Margaret, on John Barrymore as Richard III, 456, n. 1
Cassio (*Othello*), 5, 6, 8, 9, 10, 12, 13, 14, 15, 19, 20, 22, 29, 30, 31, 56, 245, 419, 422, 426, 427, 428, 429, 431, 435, 449, 480-81, n. 6; and his original in Cinthio's story, 418
Cassius (*Julius Caesar*), villainy of, 412-13
Castel of Love, The, 69
Castle of Perseverance, The, 61, 65, 66, 68, 70, 85, 86, 92, 94, 100, 101, 112, 119, 130-31, 138, 143, 162, 177, 207, 218, 242, 243, 343, 439, 463, n. 7, 473, n. 4, 474, n. 14
Catharine of Aragon, 258
Catholicism, and the morality plays, 222, 241, 245, 340
Cato the Elder, 217, 315
Caxton, William, 279
Chambers, E. K., 458, n. 3; on *Mankind,* 122; on number of morality plays, 252, 474, n. 2; on pageant of Viciose, 458, n. 4
Chapman, George, 141, 199; on tragedy, 476, n. 2
Charlton, H. B., on the French translation of the Othello story, 480, n. 1
Chasteau d'Amour (Grosseteste), 69; and the Psychomachia, 82
Chaucer, Geoffrey, 60, 107, 108, 109, 142, 143, 312, 316
Chettle, Henry, 34, 353, 357, 362
Chiron (*Titus Andronicus*), 380
Chivalry, and the morality plays, 218-26
Christianity, and the Psychomachia, 73-78; doctrine of Evil, 75; and history, 75-77; martial image in, 76-79; and allegory, 78, 96, 101

INDEX

497

Cicero, 217, 315

Cinthio (Giovanni Battista Giraldi), and source of *Othello*, 415-23, 426, 429, 430, 431, 441, 480, n. 1

Clarence, Duke of (*3 Henry VI* and *Richard III*), 392, 397-98, 399, 400, 401, 402, 403

Classic authors, and morality plays, 214-17

Claudio (*Much Ado*), 37, 407, 408, 409, 410

Claudius (*Hamlet*), 6, 37, 39, 203

Cleopatra (*Antony and Cleopatra*), 394

Clyomon and Clamydes, 128, 225-26, 254, 299-302, 308, 343, 466, n. 10

Cobbler's Prophecy, The (Wilson), 210, 235, 254

Cocledemoy (*Dutch Courtesan*), and the Vice, 334-36, 338

Coleridge, Samuel Taylor, 6; on Iago, 12, 24

Colin Clout's Come Home Again, 266

Collier, John Payne, on the Vice, 472-73, n. 60

Comedy, 59, 204, 205; and farce, 39; and the Vice, 57, 192-93; in morality plays, 113-23; homiletic purpose of, 116-23; range of, 117-20; and actors and audience, 119-20; distinguished from medieval comedy of evil, 121-22; and villains, 408

Comedy of evil, 121, 126

Comedy of Patient and Meek Grissill, see *Patient and Meek Grissill*

Comedy of the Most Virtuous and Godly Susanna, see *Virtuous and Godly Susanna*

Common Conditions, 164, 170, 191, 225-26, 254, 291-99, 313-14, 343, 466, n. 10

Conflict of Conscience, The (Woodes), 67, 115, 128, 131, 189, 202, 236-37, 238-39, 474, n. 8-9

Conrade (*Much Ado*), 410, 411

Contention between Liberality and Prodigality, The, 253

Corpus Christi, mystery cycle of, 61

Cotgrave, Randle, on the Vice, 199

Court of Sapience (Lydgate), 70

Cradle of Security, The, 61-62

Cromwell, Thomas, 137

Cruel Debtor, The (L. Wager or W. Wager), 162-63, 254, 308

Cursor Mundi, 69

Cushman, L. W., on the Vice, 467, n. 16, 472, n. 59

Cyprian, St., 76; and the martial image, 78

Danse Macabre, 64, 65

Dante, 50, 98, 99, 101, 105, 121, 240, 243; and personification, 97; distinction between historical and allegorical, 458, n. 8

Day, John, 450

Deadly Sins, *see* Seven Deadly Sins

Death, and the Middle Ages, 64-66; personification of, 65-67, 459, n. 14

Death of Robert Earl of Huntingdon, The (Chettle and Munday), 445; the hybrid image in, 362-64

Debate of Soul and Body, the, 211; morality theme, 63-64, 67-69, 71

Deceit, 126, 205, 298, 394, 395, 396, 412, 451; and the Vice, 155-76, 194, 198, 442; and Aaron the Moor, 384; and Richard III, 397, 402, 406; and Iago, 430, 432, 433, 434; in *Othello*, 431

Dekker, Thomas, 310, 394, 453; on the vices, 155

Demetrius (*Titus Andronicus*), 380

Desdemona (*Othello*), 9, 10, 12, 15, 17, 18, 19, 20, 22, 30, 32, 46, 51, 52, 418, 426, 427, 431, 435, 438, 449, 480, n. 4; and her original in Cinthio's story, 416-22, 431

Devil, the, 73, 76, 206, 348, 465, n. 1; and Iago, 52-53; Christian view of, 75, 78; and morality plays, 130-34, 465-66, n. 2; and the vices, 132-44

Devil and the Vice in the English Dramatic Literature, The (Cushman), 472, n. 59

Devil Is an Ass, The (Jonson), 199, 394

Diccon the Bedlam (*Gammer Gurton's Needle*), 338, 352; and the Vice, 191, 192, 193, 323-27; and Iago, 327

Dictionary of French and English Tongues (Cotgrave), 199

Diogenes, 217

Disobedient Child, The (Ingelend), 208, 465, n. 1, 465-66, n. 2

Divine Comedy, The (Dante), 105; and allegory, 97, 98, 99

Doctor Faustus (Marlowe), 131, 240; and *The Conflict of Conscience*, 236, 474, n. 9

Dogberry (*Much Ado*), 408

Doll Tearsheet (*Henry V*), 90

Doncaster (*The Death of Robert Earl of Huntingdon*), and the Vice, 362-64, 445

INDEX

Don John (*Much Ado*), 39, 43, 46, 58; and Iago, 35; discrepancy between behavior and motives in, 36-37; artist-criminal, 43-44; hybrid, 408-13; and Richard III, 409; and the Vice, 412-13

Don Pedro (*Much Ado*), 408, 409

Dorset, Marquess of (*Richard III*), 402, 403

Dualism, *see* Moral dualism

Duke of Milan, The (Massinger), 34; and *Othello*, 450

Dumb Knight, The (Markham and Machin), 34, 450-51; and *Othello*, 449-50

Dunbar, William, on death, 64

Duncan (*Macbeth*), 42

Dutch Courtesan, The (Marston), 334-36, 476, n. 2

Ecclesiastes, 452

Edgar (*King Lear*), 67, 323, 414

Edmond Ironside, 373, 444-45, 477, n. 3; hybrid image in, 340-45

Edmund (*King Lear*), 67, 424, 456, n. 1; villainy of, 413; a Machiavel, 425

Edricus (*Edmond Ironside*), 372, 374, 384, 395, 441; and the Vice, 340-45, 369; villainy of, 444-45

Education moralities, *see* Wit moralities

Edward IV, King (*3 Henry VI* and *Richard III*), 390, 396, 400, 401, 402

Edward, Prince of Wales (*Richard III*), 403

Edward, Earl of March (*3 Henry VI*), 389, 390, 396

Elckerlijk, and *Everyman*, 194, 472, n. 56

Eleazar the Moor (*Lust's Dominion*), 374, 445; and Iago, 34; and the Vice, 357-60, 369

Eliot, T. S., on Hamlet, 16, 456, n. 12; on *The Jew of Malta*, 352

Elizabeth, Queen, 59, 97, 253, 259

Elizabeth, Queen (*Richard III*), 403

Elizabethan drama, and soliloquies, 5; and adultery, 20-21; and naturalism, 33; beginnings of, 250; formative decades of, 254; and the Vice, 331-36; and tragedy, 369-70; and policy, 373-76; hybrid image in, 449-51; and the Psychomachia, 453

Elizabethan revenge tragedy, 353, 379

Emilia (*Othello*), 5, 10, 17, 19, 20-21, 30, 31, 52, 416, 421, 427, 429-30, 431, 435; and her original in Cinthio's story, 417

Enough Is as Good as a Feast (W. Wager), 114, 120, 131, 146-47, 162, 167, 171-75, 192, 207, 229, 249, 440, 459, n. 17, 466, n. 10

Envy, Bacon on, 480, n. 16

Epire, Duke of (*The Dumb Knight*), 450-51; and Iago, 34, 449-50

Ethics (Spinoza), 38

Eunuchus (Terence), 319-20

Eure, Sir William, 137

Euripides, 452

Eusebius, on Christian view of history, 75-76

Everyman, 63, 66, 67, 71, 72, 108-9, 193-94, 195, 207, 464, n. 17, 467, n. 20

Evil, and the family of Iago, 45-46; in Shakespeare's plays, 49-51; Christian doctrine of, 75; the Devil and, 130, 132; and personification of, 138, 140, 262, 436, 442; *see also* Psychomachia, the; Vice, the; Vices; Villains and villainy

Faerie Queen, The (Spenser), 151, 407, 463, n. 6; and the Psychomachia, 83; allegory in, 97

Faith, justification by, as theme of hybrid play, 262-63

Faithful Friends, The (Beaumont and Fletcher?), and the hybrid image, 450

Falstaff, Sir John (*Henry IV*), and the Psychomachia, 87-91; and the Vice, 203-4, 394, 462, n. 69; a Machiavel, 425

Family of Iago, the, 28-59: hybrid strain in, 33-37; discrepancy between behavior and motives in, 34-37; and Shakespeare's intelligible criminals, 37-43; artist-criminals, 43-47; and evil, 45-46; *see also* Hybrid image; Vice, the

Farce, 192, 411; and comedy and tragedy, 39; in morality plays, 116; hybrid image in, 304-36; and Latin comedy, 311, 315, 319; and serious drama, 314, 477, n. 4; and the Vice, 314-15, 337-39; and tragedy, 373

Farnham, Willard, on Iago and Politick Persuasion, 34

Faulconbridge, Philip (*King John*), a Machiavel, 425

Faust (Goethe), 74-75

Feste (*Twelfth Night*), 40

Finding of Truth, The (Medwall), 472, n. 60

First Part of Jeronimo, The, 445; hybrid image in, 364-65

INDEX

Fletcher, John, 450

Fletcher, Phineas, 83, 106

Formal, meaning of, 394

Fortunes of Falstaff, The (Wilson), 462, n. 70

Four Daughters, *see* Four Heavenly Sisters

Four Elements, The (Rastell), 86-89, 91, 114, 116, 117, 153, 158, 168, 183, 207, 208, 215, 439, 442, 464, n. 17

Four Heavenly Sisters, 69-70, 459, n. 23

Francisco (*The Duke of Milan*), and Iago, 34, 450

Friendship, and Iago, 4; and *Othello*, 422-23

Fulgens and Lucres (Medwall), 86, 257

Fulwell, Ulpian, 230, 253

Gammer Gurton's Needle (Stevenson), 328, 338; and the Vice, 191; hybrid image in, 322-27

Gargantua and Pantagruel, 452

Garter, Thomas, 266

Gascoigne, George, 208

Gayley, Charles M., on the Devil and the Vice, 132

Gear, and the Vice, 190-91, 326-27; and policy, 375

Geffcken, J., on allegorical method, 463, n. 1

Gentleness and Nobility, 257

Gertrude, Queen (*Hamlet*), 50

Gesta Romanorum, 69

Glass of Government (Gascoigne), 208

Gloucester, Earl of (*King Lear*), 49-50

Gloucester, Richard, Duke of, *see* Richard III

Gloucester, city of, morality play at, 60-61

Gnostics, 75

Godly Queen Hester, 254, 256-59, 475, n. 8

Goethe, 74-75

Goneril (*King Lear*), 37, 39, 40, 41, 416

Good and Evil, struggle between, dominant theme of morality plays, 73-75, 100, 304, 449. *See also* Psychomachia, the

Goodfellow, Robin (*Wily Beguiled*), and the Vice, 471, n. 34

Good Order (Rastell), 196, 462, n. 71

Gorboduc (Sackville and Norton), Sidney on, 476, n. 2

Gosson, Stephen, on romantic love in morality plays, 225, 308; attack on the Elizabethan stage, 252

Granville-Barker, Harley Granville, on

Iago, 3, 6

Gratiano (*Othello*), 56

Greban, Arnould, 70

Greg, W. W., on *Godly Queen Hester*, 475, n. 8

Gregory the Great, St., on vices, 155; on moral self-deception, 156, 469, n. 7; on Seven Deadly Sins, 468, n. 23

Grey, Lady (*3 Henry VI*), 390

Grim the Collier of Croydon, 131

Grindal, Archbishop, 61

Grosseteste, Robert, 69, 82

Guillaume de Guilleville, 83

Guillaume de Lorris, and the *Roman de la Rose*, 107

Hall, Edward, 388

Hamartigenia (Prudentius), and the Psychomachia, 79, 82

Hamlet (*Hamlet*), 21, 24, 40, 50, 51, 65, 203, 309; motives of, 6; T. S. Eliot on, 16, 456, n. 12; on the purpose of playing, 104-5

Hamlet (Shakespeare), 25, 70, 203, 353, 379; and *Othello*, 51

Hammurabi, Code of, 38

Harbage, Alfred, 251

Hastings, Lord (*Richard III*), 398, 401, 402

Hatred, 369; and Iago, 8, 13-16, 432-34, 437; and the family of Iago, 45-46; and the Vice, 165-67, 442; and the villains, 445, 447

"Haunted Palace, The" (Poe), 97

Hawes, Stephen, 218

Hazlitt, William, 6; on Iago, 436; on Iago and Richard III, 457, n. 9

Hecatommithi (Cinthio), 415, 480, n. 1

1 Henry IV, 203-4

2 Henry IV, 226, 462, n. 69, 462, n. 70; and the Psychomachia, 87-91; hybrid image in, 310-11

Henry V, 26-27

Henry VI, King (*3 Henry VI*), 389, 396, 404

1 Henry VI, 386

2 Henry VI, and Richard III, 388

3 Henry VI, 377; Richard III in, 388-96, 400, 404

Henry VIII, King, 216, 257, 472, n. 60

Henslowe, Philip, 253, 353

Hermione (*The Winter's Tale*), 6

Hero (*Much Ado*), 31, 37, 407, 408, 409

500   INDEX

Heywood, John, 136, 137, 147, 148, 188, 233, 235, 440
Hickscorner, 70, 157, 208, 474, n. 14
Histoires Tragiques (Belleforest), 407
Historical, used as antonym to allegorical, 458, n. 8
History, and allegory, 62-63, 90, 262-78; Christian view of, 75-77
History of English Dramatic Poetry, The (Collier), 472, n. 60
History of Horestes, The, see *Horestes*
Histriomastix (Marston), 131, 210, 310
Hoffman, Clois (*The Tragedy of Hoffman*), 441; and Iago, 34; and the Vice, 353-57, 369, 371, 372; and policy, 374
Holinshed, Raphael, 27, 340, 341, 388
Holy War (Bunyan), and the Psychomachia, 83
Homer, 379, 463, n. 1
Homiletic allegory, 81, 178, 204, 236, 267, 393, 412; and the Vice, 57, 151, 152, 153, 313; development of, 78; and the spiritual journey, 83-84; and morality plays, 176-78; decline of, 217, 225, 226, 238; and hybrid plays, 255, 277, 308-9, 312; tenaciousness of, 261; and Richard III, 387; and Iago, 430, 436-37, 439, 481, n. 8
Honesty, and Iago, 52, 54-55, 432-33, 434; and the Vice, 164-65, 470, n. 18; and Richard III, 397, 399
Honor and fame, as theme of morality plays, 213
Horatio (*Law Tricks*), a hybrid, 450
Horatius, **217**
Horestes (Pikering), 92, 163, 213, 223-24, 254, 279-84, 314, 331, 466, n. 10
Hugo of St. Victor, 69
Human Destiny (Lecomte du Noüy), 460, n. 36
Huon de Meri, 82
Hybrid image, and the family of Iago, 28-59; in farce, 304-36; in serious drama, 337-78; in Shakespearian drama, 379-414
Hybrid plays, 251-303; and the Vice, 189, 255, 278-303, 308, 311-15, 337-39, 443-44; and romantic love, 223-25; origin of, 227; and morality plays, 237-38; fusion of abstract and concrete in, 253, 262-78; characteristics of, 254-62; homiletic unity in, 255; and the Bible, 255-56, 259-61, 266, 269; stirrings of personality in, 278; defined, 305-6; and

personification, 308; and tragedy, 313, 339; and degradation of the hero, 440; and the Psychomachia, 443-44
Hybrids, principal, in Shakespeare: see Aaron the Moor, Don John, Iago, Richard III

Iachimo (*Cymbeline*), 37, 41
Iago (*Othello*), 192, 313, 345, 386, 401, 403, 412, 415; mystery of, 3-22; and the literal interpretation of his motives, 4-24; and hatred, 8, 13-16, 432-34, 437; and revenge, 9; and intrigue, 11, 12, 13, 430, 431-32, 434; monologues of, 11-12, 25, 31-32; jocularity of, 17-18, 434; and the Vice, 22-23, 29-32, 276-77, 432-49; and subjective interpretation of his motives, 24-27; family of, 28-59; two motive principles of, 29-32; and the hybrid strain, 33-37; and Clois Hoffman, 34; and Aaron the Moor, 35, 369, 434; and Don John, 35; and Richard III, 35, 430, 438, 442; artist-criminal, 43-44; moral significance of, 48; and the Devil, 52-53; and honesty, 52, 54-55, 432-33; and villainy, 53-54, 55-58, 429-30, 432, 437; and Diccon the Bedlam, 327; and his original in Cinthio's story, 416-19, 423, 429, 430, 431; and Machiavellianism, 423-25, 428; and love, 424, 426-29, 432-34, 480-81, n. 6; as anti-theme, 425; and deceit, 430, 432, 433, 434; and Barabas, 430; homiletic dimension of his role, 430, 436-37, 481, n. 8; and personification, 430; and the Psychomachia, 430, 442, 447-49; weeping of, 435-36; and Roderigo, 441-42; successors to, 449-52
Ibsen, Henrik, 452
Iliad, The, 452
Impatient Poverty, 104, 154, 162, 166, 169, 184, 186-87, 200, 207, 211-12, 244, 442-43, 463, n. 7, 464, n. 17, 467, n. 19
Inferno (Dante), 121, 240
Ingelend, Thomas, 465, n. 1
Interlude of Youth, 111
Intrigue, 140, 205, 412; and Iago, 11, 12, 13, 430, 434; and the Psychomachia, 58, 141; and the morality plays, 91, 92, 95; in *Othello*, 419, 431-32
Iuvenis, Pater, Uxor (Ravisius Textor), 465, n. 1

INDEX

Jack Juggler (*Jack Juggler*), and the Vice, 150, 316-18, 338

Jack Juggler, 94, 150, 315-18, 319, 466, n. 10

Jaques (*As You Like It*), 411

Jean de Meun, and the *Roman de la Rose*, 107

Jew of Malta, The (Marlowe), 25, 34, 340, 348, 357, 374, 376, 379, 436, 444; hybrid image in, 346-53; and *The Tragedy of Hoffman*, 371-72

Job, 416, 452

Johnson, Laurence, 477, n. 11

Johnson, Samuel, on meaning of formal, 394

John the Evangelist, 84, 158-59, 183, 254, 255-56

Jones, Inigo, 470, n. 18

Jonson, Ben, 199, 394, 470, n. 18; quoted, 337

Justification by faith, as theme of hybrid play, 262-63

Juvenal, 217

King Darius, 91, 93, 130, 158, 200, 254, 259-62, 267, 442, 466, n. 10

King John (Bale), 117-18, 144-45, 165-66, 190-91, 197-98, 200, 209, 254, 346

King Lear, 47, 50, 67, 257, 323, 413-14; and *Othello*, 51

Kittredge, George Lyman, 5, 28, 29, 457, n. 14; on Iago, 4, 14, 24; on Aaron the Moor, 380

Knack to Know a Knave, A, 131, 210, 310

Knight, G. Wilson, 6, 54; on *Othello*, 51, 54; on John Lyly, 223

Kyd, Thomas, 310, 364

Lactantius, 76

Lady. *For characters with this title, see under the proper name*

Lament for the Makaris (Dunbar), 64

Langland, William, 70, 108

La Peste (Camus), 98

Latin comedy, influence on hybrid farce, 311, 315, 319

Launce (*Two Gentlemen of Verona*), 202

Lavinia (*Titus Andronicus*), 31, 46, 380, 385

Law Tricks (Day), 450

Lear, King, 428

Lecomte du Noüy, Pierre, on moral dualism, 460, n. 36

Leonato (*Much Ado*), 409

Leontes (*The Winter's Tale*), 6

Lewis, C. S., on allegory, 80-81; on personification, 127

Liberality and Prodigality, 253

Life and Repentance of Mary Magdalene, The (L. Wager), 114, 129, 145, 154, 159-61, 185-86, 192, 209, 254, 262-66, 284, 309, 466, n. 10, 467, n. 20

Like Will to Like (Fulwell), 104, 114-15, 131, 165, 181, 183, 191, 192, 201, 212, 213, 230-31, 249, 253, 306, 459, n. 17, 466, n. 10, 473, n. 2

Lincoln, 108; *Paternoster* play at, 60, 458, n. 3

Lindsay, Sir David, 67, 137, 209, 228

Lingua, Or the Combat of the Tongue and the Five Senses (Tomkis), 253

Literal, used as antonym to allegorical, 458, n. 8

Li Tornoiemenz Antecrit (Huon de Meri), and the Psychomachia, 82

Livy, 269

Lodge, Thomas, 309

Lodovico (*Othello*), 56, 429, 431, 435

Longer Thou Livest, The (W. Wager), 114, 117, 140, 142, 159, 208, 229, 247-48, 307, 440, 459, n. 17

Longinus, 379

Look About You, 333-34

Looking Glass for London, A (Lodge and Greene), 210

Lord Chief Justice (*Henry V*), 90, 462, n. 69

Lorenzo (*The First Part of Jeronimo*), 445, 449

Lorenzo (*The Spanish Tragedy*), and Iago, 34

Love, and the Vice, 165-67; and Iago, 424, 432-34. *See also* Romantic love

Love, see *Play of Love*

Love Feigned and Unfeigned, 167, 183

Lucius (*Titus Andronicus*), 381, 382, 383, 384

Ludus Coventriae, 65-66, 67, 70, 156, 180-81

Lupton, Thomas, 112-13, 233

Lust's Dominion, 34, 357-60, 374, 376, 445

Lusty Juventus (R. Wever), 131, 153, 167, 170-71, 178, 187-88, 191, 200, 208, 209, 218, 467, n. 19, 468, n. 2

Lydgate, John, 70, 82, 83, 92

Lyly, John, and love as dramatic theme, 223

INDEX

Macbeth (*Macbeth*), 37, 39, 40, 41, 271, 392

Macbeth (Shakespeare), 370, 379; and *Othello*, 51

Macbeth, Lady, 21, 41, 42

McClusker, Honor, on Bale's *Three Laws*, 467, n. 14

Machiavelli, Niccolò, 380, 423; and policy, 374-76; and the hybrid image, 374-77

Machiavellianism, 348; and villainy, 374-78; and Iago, 428

Machin, Lewis, 34, 449

Macropedius, 246

Magnificence (Skelton), 67, 94, 102, 105, 112, 114, 136, 138, 153, 161, 162, 193, 207, 211, 215-17, 228, 232, 244, 383, 439, 442, 467, n. 19

Malvolio (*Twelfth Night*), 202, 411

Man, *see* Mankind

Manichaeism, and Good and Evil, 74

Manichees, 75

Mankind, and the morality plays: 92-94, 103-4, 126, 195, 207-8, 251, 304-7; a type figure, 100, 154; and the Devil, 133; limitation of, 227-28; division of, into specialized figures, 229-35, 237-38, 272; disappearance of, 250, 443; and the Psychomachia, 304, 305; and the Vice, 306-7

Mankind, 70, 73, 92, 109-10, 117, 122, 123-25, 144, 153, 189, 193, 207, 242, 439, 464, n. 17, 465, n. 26, 474, n. 14

Marcion the Gnostic, 79

Marcus (*Titus Andronicus*), 381, 382

Margaret (*Much Ado*), 408

Margaret, Queen (*3 Henry VI*), 389

Markham, Gervase, 34, 449

Marlowe, Christopher, 25, 34, 236, 346, 347, 354, 357, 360, 371, 376, 379, 474, n. 9

Marriage between Wit and Wisdom, The (Merbury?), 116, 191, 192, 208, 222, 332-33, 464, n. 17, 466, n. 10

Marriage of Wit and Science, The, 208, 221-22

Marston, John, 210, 334, 338, 361, 476, n. 2

Mary Magdalene (Digby ms.), 85-86, 92, 131, 218, 464, n. 17

Mary Magdalene (L. Wager), see *Life and Repentance of Mary Magdalene, The*

Massinger, Philip, 450

Master Builder, The (Ibsen), 98

Match at Midnight, A (Rowley), 471, n. 23

Maxwell, J. C., on Aaron the Moor, 479, n. 2

Measure for Measure (Shakespeare), 70

Meditationes Vitae Christi (Bonaventura), 69, 459, n. 23

Medwall, Henry, 73, 86, 87, 93, 102, 127, 162, 188, 214, 442, 472, n. 60

Merbury, Francis, 208

Mercadé, Eustache, 70

Merchant of Venice, The (Shakespeare), 40, 70, 157, 446

Mercy, and the morality plays, 240-43, 250; and Shakespeare, 241

Merrygreek, Matthew (*Roister Doister*), 319-22, 338

Metaphor, and personification, 99; and the morality plays, 100-1; tends to become opaque, 220-21; and the hybrid plays, 273

Microcosmus (Nabbes), 253

Middle Ages, 60, 78, 81, 82, 105, 121, 206, 257; concern with Death, 64-66

Middleton, Thomas, 450

Midsummer Night's Dream, A (Shakespeare), 206

Miles gloriosus, and the Vice, 311

Miles Gloriosus (Plautus), 319

Milton, John, on *Richard III,* 388

Miracle plays, 261; the Devil in, 130

Misogonus (Bariona), 191, 208, 327-31, 477, n. 11

Monologues, 271; and Elizabethan drama, 5; and Iago, 7-10, 11-12, 25; function of, in Shakespeare, 24-27; and Shakespeare's villains, 31-32, 456, n. 1; and Shakespeare's intelligible criminals, 41-42; as comic device in morality plays, 119-20; and the Vice, 189

Montague, Marquess of (*3 Henry VI*), 389

Montano (*Othello*), 56

Moral dualism, and the Psychomachia, 74-75, 77, 79, 442, 449, 460, n. 36

Moralia (St. Gregory the Great), 156

Morality plays, and the Vice, 56-59, 123-26, 151-76, 189, 306-8, 438; and the family of Iago, 58; survival of, 59; development of, 60-63, 108-9, 442-44; three groups of, 62; and the Psychomachia, 63, 72-73, 86-89, 91-95, 442; themes of, 63-74; homiletic pageantry in, 85-86; and Mankind, 92-94, 207-8, 227-35, 304-7; as allegories, 100; the basic metaphor of, 100-1; moral conflict and moral sequence in, 101-3; purpose

INDEX

of, 104; and homiletic and literary allegory, 105-13; homiletic technique in, 109-13; and the audience, 113; comedy in, 113-23; and farce, 116, 196-200; music as comic element in, 117; and dramatic monologues, 119-20; allegorical motivation in, 126-29; shift in emphasis of, 140-41, 206-11, 214-17; and the Devil, 130-34; number of actors in, 140, 467, n. 19; moral dissimulation in, 156-76; homiletic function of, 176-78; and names of personae, 180-82; tragedy and comedy in, 193-204; double nature of, 200-2; change and decline in, 206-50; and youth, 208; and the Reformation, 209; socio-political types, 209-11; and theme of fortune, 211-12, 473, n. 2; and increase of secular morality, 211-17; and theme of honor and fame, 213; new concept of virtue in, 213-16; and classic authors, 214-17; and chivalry and romantic love, 218-26; and Catholicism, 222; movement toward concrete and particular, 227-35, 305-6; decline of, 227, 237-38, 252-53, 271; and hybrid plays, 237-38; development of tragic resolution in, 238-50; and repentance-mercy formula, 240-44; and Protestantism, 245-46; and mercy, 250; three constitutional features of, 251; number of, 252, 474-75, n. 2; and tragedy, 313; physical conditions of stage, 464, n. 17

Moral metaphor, and dramatic image, 157-205

Morals on the Book of Job (Gregory the Great), 468, n. 23

More, Sir Thomas, 86, 108, 122, 461, n. 66; and the Psychomachia, 100; on Richard III, 387-88

Morgann, Maurice, 204; and Falstaff, 91

Morton, John, Cardinal, 86, 461, n. 66

Moulton, Richard, on Richard III, 36

Mucedorus, 310

Much Ado about Nothing (Shakespeare), 25, 35, 36; formula of contrast and relief in, 407-8

Munday, Anthony, 362, 453

Mundus et Infans, 92, 101, 104, 110-11, 113-14, 140, 153, 154, 167-68, 178-79, 183, 190, 207, 218, 244, 306, 464, n. 17, 467, n. 20

Music, as comic element in morality plays, 117

Mystère de la Passion (Greban), 70

Mystère de la Passion (Mercadé), 70

Mystery plays 95, 109, 180, 261; the Devil in, 130, 132, 133

Nabbes, Thomas, 253

Nashe, Thomas, 199, 253

Naturalism, and Elizabethan drama, 33; and Shakespearian drama, 451-52

Nature (Medwall), 73, 86-89, 93, 101, 102-3, 120, 127, 144, 153, 162, 184, 188, 207, 214-15, 240-41, 442, 464, n. 17

Nature of the Four Elements, The (Rastell), see *Four Elements, The*

New Custom, 93, 114, 127, 156-57, 201, 467, n. 19

Nice Wanton, 111, 197, 208, 229, 246-47, 459, n. 17

Novelle (Bandello), 407

"O Captain! My Captain!" (Whitman), allegory in, 97

Odyssey, 379

Old Fortunatus (Dekker), 310, 394

Oliver (*As You Like It*), 26, 446-47

"On the Townes Honest Man" (Jonson), quoted, 470, n. 18

Ophelia (*Hamlet*), 40, 353

Orlando (*As You Like It*), 447

Orlando Furioso (Ariosto), 407

Othello (*Othello*), 4, 5, 6, 8, 10, 13-16, 17, 18, 19, 20, 21, 22, 29, 30, 31, 46, 51, 52, 53, 416, 417, 424, 426, 427, 428, 429, 434, 435, 438, 439, 448; and his original in Cinthio's story, 418-22, 431

Othello (Shakespeare), 5, 6, 21, 30, 31, 33, 34, 35, 170, 192, 275, 405, 414, 436, 455, n. 1; difficulty of explaining, 3; evil in, 51, 54; in First Folio, 56; compared to its source by Cinthio, 415-22, 431; Swinburne on, 416; theme of miscegenation in, 420; and romantic love, 421-22; and friendship, 422-23; and intrigue, 431-32; and the Psychomachia, 447; plays derived from, 449-50

Ovid, 315, 379

Owst, Gerald R., 84; on allegorical pageantry, 108; on early morality plays, 239

Pageants, and allegory, 60-61; and morality plays, 108-9, 140, 141

Parables of Bernard (of Clairvaux), 83

Paradise Lost (Milton), 123

INDEX

Parasite, the, in Latin comedy, and the Vice, 311, 315, 320

Parliament in Heaven, morality theme, 63-64, 69-70, 71, 211; in medieval literature, 69-70

Pastime of Pleasure (Hawes), 218, 232

Paternoster plays, 63, 100, 108, 119; earliest moralities, 60-61, 457, n. 3

Pathomachia, Or the Battle of Affections (Tomkis), 253

Patient and Meek Grissill (Phillip), 34, 120, 161, 166-67, 191, 224, 254, 272-77, 443, 466, n. 10

Paul, St., 3; martial imagery of, 77

Peddler's Prophecy, The, 210

Pèlerinage de la Vie Humaine (Guillaume de Guilleville), 83

Periander, 217; quoted, 213

Perseverance, see Castle of Perseverance, The

Personification, 105, 134, 225-26, 369, 406-7; and the morality plays, 63, 126-27, 251, 254, 404; language of, and the Psychomachia, 77; and allegory, 78, 97-99; and Prudentius, 78-82; in Dante and Spenser, 97; and symbolism, 98-99; definition of, 99; and metaphor, 99; and the Vice, 197-98; of vices and virtues, 262, 264, 305, 442; and hybrid plays, 308; and Elizabethan drama, 310

Petrarch, 312

Phaedrus (Plato), 74

Phillip, John, 272

Philo Judaeus, 74, 462, n. 1

Phoenix, The (Middleton), 450

Piers Plowman (Langland), 70, 106, 121; and the Psychomachia, 82-83; homiletic allegory in, 107-8; personification of Death in, 459, n. 14

Pikering, John, 279, 280

Pilgrim's Progress, The (Bunyan), 83, 105; allegorical method of, 99

Plato, 217, 315; dualism of, 74; on moral self-deception, 469, n. 7

Plautus, 217, 316, 319

Play of Love (Heywood), 136, 137, 147-50, 188, 440, 466, n. 10

Play of the Weather (Heywood), 136, 137, 147-50, 235, 466, n. 10

Play of Wit and Science, The (Redford), 208

Plays Confuted in Five Actions (Gosson), 252

Pliny, 217

Plutarch, 315

Poe, Edgar Allan, 353; and allegory, 97

Policy, meaning of, in Elizabethan drama, 373-76

Polonius (*Hamlet*), and policy, 374

Pope, Alexander, quoted, 96

Preston, Thomas, 284, 379

Pride, and the Seven Deadly Sins, 142, 468, n. 23

Pride of Life, 61, 63, 66, 68, 71-72, 110, 114, 122, 127, 207, 214, 218, 228, 243, 257, 464, n. 17

Processus Satanae, 460, n. 29

Prodigal son play, 327

Promos and Cassandra (Whetstone), 308

Prosopopoeia, *see* Personification

Protestantism, and morality plays, 209, 245-46; and hybrid plays, 262-63

Prudentius, 85, 92, 106, 156, 304, 449; *Psychomachia* of, 78-82; on purpose of morality drama, 104

Pseudonyms, and the Vice, 158-61

Psychomachia, the, 56, 60-95, 100, 123, 132, 138, 155, 166, 167, 175, 253, 254, 260, 262, 267, 271, 278, 306, 345, 363, 369, 400, 444, 447, 450, 451, 469, n. 7; and the Vice, 58-59, 256; chief theme of morality plays, 72-73; and the spiritual journey, 83-84; as homiletic pageantry, 85-86; martial image in, 86-89, 91-95; and intrigue, 91, 125, 135, 141, 151; and the theater, 95; evolved form of, 126; metaphor of, 154; and morality plays, 251; and Mankind, 304, 305; and Iago, 430, 442, 447-49; and the hybrid plays, 443; decline of, 445-47

Psychomachia (Prudentius), 85, 156, 304; plot of, 79-82; quoted, 106-7

Purple Island, The (Fletcher), 106; and the Psychomachia, 83

Puttenham, George, on allegory, 82, 97; on the vices, 199

Pythagoras, 217

Queen (*Cymbeline*), 37, 41

Quiller-Couch, Sir Arthur, on Don John, 36-37

Quintilian, 78, 97; definition of allegory, 96

Radix malorum, the Vice as, 142, 145, 147, 149, 151, 152, 160, 266, 306; St. Gregory the Great on, 468, n. 23

Raleigh, Sir Walter, on love, 480, n. 4

INDEX

Ramsay, R. L., 136, 467, n. 19
Rastell, John, 86, 91, 116, 208, 215, 442
Rastell, William, 86, 136
Ravisius Textor, 465, n. 1
Read Me and Be Not Wroth (Roy), 475, n. 8
Rebelles (Macropedius), 246
Recuyell of the Historyes of Troye (Caxton), 279
Redford, John, 100, 118, 128, 208, 213, 219, 221
Reformation, the, and the morality plays, 47, 93, 131, 141, 209, 211, 222, 227, 234
Regan (*King Lear*), 40, 416
Religion, in Shakespeare, 48-50
Renaissance, 16, 43, 82, 83, 217, 266, 422, 423, 451; and the morality plays, 59, 62, 64, 67, 71, 86, 105, 206, 211; and the hybrid plays, 274, 314, 319; and policy, 373
Repentance, and the morality plays, 240-43
Republic, The (Plato), on moral self-deception, 469, n. 7
Respublica, 67, 70, 114, 139, 145-46, 158, 161, 188, 196, 209, 317, 466, n. 10
Revenge, and Iago, 9; significant theme in Elizabethan drama, 279, 283, 341, 353, 379
Revenge of Bussy d'Ambois, The (Chapman), 476, n. 2
Richard III (*2 and 3 Henry VI* and *Richard III*), 39, 43, 46, 58, 271, 412, 432, 434, 436, 441, 445-46, 479, n. 6, 480, n. 15; and Iago, 35, 430, 442; discrepancy between behavior and motives in, 36; and Shakespeare's intelligible criminals, 41; artist-criminal, 43-44; and the Vice, 170, 386-407; and Machiavellianism, 377-78, 425; and Aaron the Moor, 386-87; hybrid, 386-407; Sir Thomas More on, 387-88; character of consistent, 388-93; tears of, 397-99; and Lady Anne, 404-7, 438; and Don John, 409; John Barrymore as, 456, n. 1
Richard III (Shakespeare), 25, 35, 170, 404; hybrid image in, 386-407; Milton on, 388; and *3 Henry VI*, 388-93
Richardes, Thomas, 327
Rivers, Lord (*Richard III*), 402
Roderick, Duke of Orléans (*The Trial of Chivalry*), and the Vice, 365-68
Roderigo (*Othello*), 5, 9, 14, 15-16, 30, 419, 423, 424, 426, 427, 428, 429, 435-

36, 439, 448; an addition to original story, 431; function of, 441-42
Roister Doister (Udall), 323; hybrid image in, 318-22
Roman de la Rose (Guillaume de Lorris and Jean de Meun), 108; and the Psychomachia, 83; contrast between homiletic and literary temper in, 107
Romantic Iago, the, 4, 455, n. 3
Romantic love, 48; and the hybrid, 47; and the morality plays, 218-26; and *Othello*, 421-22; and Iago, 426-28
Romeo and Juliet (Shakespeare), 60
Rosalind (*As You Like It*), 40
Rowley, William, 471, n. 23
Roy, William, 475, n. 8
Rufinus (*The Faithful Friends*), 450
Rumour (*2 Henry IV*), and the Vice, 310-11
Rutland, Edmund, Earl of (*3 Henry VI*), 406
Rymer, Thomas, 455, n. 1

Sallust, 217
Satire, range of, in morality plays, 118
Satire of the Three Estates (Lindsay), see *Three Estates, The*
Saturninus (*Titus Andronicus*), 382, 383
Schelling, Felix E., quoted on plot of *Common Conditions*, 292
Schücking, Levin L., on motivation of Shakespeare's characters, 25
Sea, language of, in *Othello*, 52
Seneca, 115, 217, 310, 379, 476, n. 2
Seven Christian Virtues, 60, 108, 109, 140, 208, 214
Seven Deadly Sins, 60, 84, 85, 86, 108, 109, 121, 131, 140, 156, 208, 214, 306; and the Vice, 132, 135, 467, n. 20; in the *Canterbury Tales*, 142; St. Gregory the Great on, 468, n. 23
Shakespeare, William, 5, 6, 17, 34, 47, 353, 368, 392, 404, 410, 449; and Iago, 21, 24-27; and motivation, 27; and the hybrid image, 33, 449; humanity of, 39-40; moral vision of, 48-50; and morality plays, 61; theme of Sonnet CXLVI, 68-69; and the Psychomachia, 87-91, 309; and theme of mercy, 241; and *Titus Andronicus*, 379; and Richard III, 387; and *Much Ado about Nothing*, 407-9; and his source for *Othello*, 415-22, 431, 480, n. 1; and his villains, 423,

INDEX

Shakespeare, William (*Continued*) 434, 456, n. 1; evolution of his art, 451-53

Shakespeare's intelligible criminals, and family of Iago, 37-43

Shakespearian criticism, and Iago, 3-27, 436; and literal interpretation of Iago's motives, 4-24; and subjective interpretation of Iago's motives, 24-27; limitations of, 452

Shakespearian drama, evil in, 49-51; and reality, 157; and the Vice, 202-4; and personification, 310-11; hybrid image in, 379-414; villains in, 408; technique of contrast in, 418; Machiavels in, 425; decline of Psychomachia in, 445-47; and naturalism, 451-52

Shylock (*The Merchant of Venice*), 6, 17, 37, 40, 347, 411, 446

Sidney, Sir Philip, 309; contempt for "mungrell Tragy-comedie," 115, 464-65, n. 19; on *Gorboduc*, 476, n. 2

Sir Clyomon and Sir Clamydes, see *Clyomon and Clamydes*

Sir Thomas More, 464, n. 17, 466, n. 10

Sir Thomas Wyatt, 374

Skelton, John, 67, 94, 102, 105, 112, 136, 138, 207, 211, 216, 232, 439, 442, 458, n. 11, 475, n. 8

Skink (*Look About You*), and the Vice, 333-34

Socio-political moralities, themes of, 209-11

Socrates, 217, 315

Soliloquies, see Monologues

Soliman and Perseda, 310

Sonnet CXLVI (Shakespeare), theme of, 68-69

Spanish Tragedy, The (Kyd), 34, 310, 364, 474, n. 12; hybrid image in, 360-61

Speed (*Two Gentlemen of Verona*), 202

Spenser, Edmund, 83, 99, 101, 407; and personification, 97

Spinoza, Baruch, 38, 74

Spira, Francesco, and *The Conflict of Conscience*, 236-39, 474, n. 9

Spiritual journey, the, and the Psychomachia, 83-84

Staple of News, The (Jonson), 199, 394; quoted, 337

Stevenson, William, 322

Stoics, and allegorical interpretation, 463, n. 1

Stoll, Edgar E., 6; on Iago's hatred, 13-14; on Iago's monologues, 25

Summa Theologica (St. Thomas Aquinas), 38, 458, n. 8

Summer's Last Will and Testament (Nashe), 253; on the Vice, 199

Summons of Death, the, morality theme, 63-67, 71-72, 211

Swinburne, Algernon Charles, 6; on *Othello*, 416; on Shakespeare, 452

Symbol, definition of, 98

Symbolism, see Allegory

Tamora (*Titus Andronicus*), 310, 357, 383, 416; intelligible criminal, 380-81

Terence, 208, 217, 319, 320, 328

Tertullian, 76; and the martial image, 78

Themistocles, 217

Thersites, 464, n. 17

Thomas, Sidney, on the Vice, 472, n. 59; on Richard III, 480, n. 15

Thomas Aquinas, St., 38; distinction between historical and allegorical, 458, n. 8

Thompson, E. N. S., on morality plays, 103, 463, n. 9

Thorndike, A. H., on Iago and Clois Hoffman, 34; on Shakespeare's choice of subjects, 35

Thorp, Willard, and number of morality plays, 474-75, n. 2

Three Estates, The (Lindsay), 67, 137, 161, 196, 207, 209, 228, 229, 464, n. 17

Three Ladies of London, The (Wilson), 93, 164-65, 210, 213, 223, 235

Three Laws (Bale), 91, 93, 114, 137, 139, 144, 158, 163-64, 166, 169, 182, 190, 191-92, 200, 263, 442, 467, n. 14, 467, n. 19, 467, n. 20, 475, n. 9

Three Lords and Three Ladies of London, The (Wilson), 93, 210, 223, 235, 480, n. 15

Tide Tarrieth No Man, The (Wapull), 67, 114, 120, 158, 162, 190, 191, 197, 201, 213, 217, 231-32, 249-50, 306, 463, n. 7, 466, n. 10

Timaeus (Plato), 74

Time (*The Winter's Tale*), 310, 311

Timon of Athens (Shakespeare), 49

Titus Andronicus (*Titus Andronicus*), 381, 382, 387

Titus Andronicus (Shakespeare), 25, 35, 310, 357; hybrid image in, 379-86; source of, 381, 479, n. 2

Tomkis, Thomas, 253

Tom Tyler and His Wife, 254, 466, n. 10

INDEX

507

Tool villains, and the Vice, 372-73

Tragedy, 59, 204, 205, 305; and farce, 39; and the Vice, 57, 192-93; and the morality plays, 229, 238-50, 313; hybrid image in, 337-78; effect of, 369; and villains, 408

Tragedy of Hoffman, The (Chettle), 34, 376; hybrid image in, 353-57; and *The Jew of Malta*, 371-72

Tragical Comedy of Appius and Virginia, The, see *Appius and Virginia*

Tragical History of Doctor Faustus, The (Marlowe), see *Doctor Faustus*

Transitional plays, *see* Hybrid plays

Trial of Chivalry, The, hybrid image in, 365-68

Trial of Treasure, The, 67, 112, 113, 166, 169-70, 183, 185, 196, 207, 212, 217, 222-23, 229, 249, 307-8, 462, n. 69, 466, n. 10

Triumph of Realism in Elizabethan Drama, The (Thorp), and number of morality plays, 474-75, n. 2

True Tragedy of Richard Duke of York, The, 377-78

Twelfth Night (Shakespeare), 40, 202-3, 411

Two Gentlemen of Verona, The (Shakespeare), 202, 379

Udall, Nicholas, 318, 319, 320

Utopia (More), and the Psychomachia, 100, 122

Verges (*Much Ado*), 408

Vice, the, and Iago, 22-23, 29-32, 432-37, 438-49; and evolution as a hybrid, 33, 339; and morality plays, 56-59, 63, 306-8, 443; emergence of, 57, 130-50, 151-52, 467, n. 16; survival of, 59, 265-66; and the Psychomachia, 95, 256; homiletic exposition of, 111, 158, 178-84; allegorical motivation of, 127-29; and the Devil, 132-44; homiletic purpose of, 134, 151, 152, 153, 178-84; and the vices, 135, 141-47, 443, 466, n. 9; as *radix malorum,* 142-50, 160, 266; dramatic image of, 151-76; twofold stratagem of, 152-54, 468, n. 2; and moral dissimulation, 155-76; and deceit, 155-76, 194, 198, 442; and pseudonyms, 158-61; and physical disguise, 160-61; tears and laughter of, 161-64, 291; and honesty, 164-65, 298, 470, n. 18; and hatred, 165-67, 198, 442; and love, 165-67; and homiletic metaphor, 175; and the audience, 176-92, 339, 341, 464, n. 17; as moralizer, 184-88; and monologues, 189; double nature of, 193-205; and farce, 196-200, 314-15, 331-36, 337-39; and personification, 197-98; and death, 198; and cursing, 200-2; and villains and villainy, 201-2, 298, 303, 339, 341, 357-60, 372-73, 436-37, 442, 444-46; Shakespearian drama and his double nature, 202-4; and hybrid plays, 238, 255, 262-78, 278-303, 308, 311-15, 337-39, 443-44; hanging of, 270-71; ceases to be metaphorical, 279; and Mankind, 306-7; and his name, 313; and comic specialization, 332-33; and tragedy, 337-78; and Edricus, 340-45; and Barabas, 346-53; and Eleazar the Moor, 357-60; erosion of, in the hybrid image, 369-78; and Machiavellianism, 374-78; and Aaron the Moor, 379-86; and Richard III, 386-407; and Don John, 412

Vices, 304, 305; homiletic expositions of, 111-13; contest for leadership among, 118; and comedy, 121; in morality plays, 121, 123, 126, 140-42, 207, 208, 210, 218, 231, 251; and the audience, 126; and the Devil, 132-44; and the Vice, 135, 141-47, 443, 466, n. 9; homiletic function of, 178; in hybrid plays, 265; personifications of, fade, 278

Viciose, pageant of, at Beverley, 60-61, 458, n. 4

Vigny, Alfred Victor, Comte de, 455, n. 1

Villains and villainy, and Richard III, 36, 387, 397, 400, 404, 405; and Don John, 36-37; and Iago, 53-54, 55-58, 432, 437; and the Vice, 201-2, 205, 298, 303, 339, 341, 357-60, 436-37, 442, 444-46; and the hybrid image, 360-61; and Machiavellianism, 374-78; and Shakespeare, 408, 423, 434, 456, n. 1; and *Othello,* 419

Villon, François, Prayer of Villon's Mother to the Virgin, 65

Virgil, 96; allegorical interpretation of, 463, n. 1

Virtue, new concept of, in morality plays, 213-16; personifications of, 262, 278

Virtue plays, 262, 268, 269

Virtues, 304, 305; in allegorical pageantry, 108, 109; in morality plays, 123, 126,

508   *INDEX*

Virtues (*Continued*)
208, 251, 271; homiletic function of,
178
Virtuous and Godly Susanna (Garter), 116,
131, 134, 164, 191, 196, 224, 254, 266-
69, 314, 466, n. 10
Vision Concerning Piers Plowman, The
(Langland), see *Piers Plowman*

Wager, Lewis, 114, 129, 145, 154, 159,
185, 209, 262, 263, 264, 284; on acting,
308-9
Wager, W., 247
Waldock, A. J. A., on motives, 25
Walsinghame (Raleigh), 480, n. 4
Wapull, George, 231
Warning for Fair Women, A, 310
Wealth and Health, 181, 209-10, 229, 230,
308, 467, n. 19
Weather (Heywood), see *Play of the
Weather*
Whetstone, George, quoted, 308
Whitman, Walt, allegory in, 97
Why Come Ye Not to Court (Skelton),
475, n. 8
Widow's Tears, The (Chapman), 141
Willis, R., and description of a morality
play, 61-62
Wilson, J. Dover, on Aaron the Moor, 380;
and Falstaff, 462, n. 70
Wilson, Robert, 93, 210, 223
Wily Beguiled, 471, n. 34

Winter's Tale, The (Shakespeare), 6, 310
Wisdom, 93, 130, 133, 138, 170, 241, 463,
n. 7
Wit and Science (Redford), 100, 118, 128,
213, 219-20, 221
Wit and Wisdom (Merbury?), see *Marriage between Wit and Wisdom, The*
Wit moralities, 101, 292, 440, 477-78, n. 7;
examples of, 208, 218-22
Wolsey, Thomas, Cardinal, 256, 257-58,
475, n. 8
Women, frailties of, prominent satirical
theme, 118
Woodberry, George, on Edwin Booth's interpretation of Iago, 13
Woodes, Nathaniel, 236-37, 238, 239,
474, n. 9
Wyatt, Sir Thomas, on moral self-deception, 469-70, n. 7
Wyclif, John, 60; on York *Paternoster*
play, 108

York, city of, *Paternoster* play at, 60, 61,
108, 457-58, n. 3
York, Duchess of (*Richard III*), 399
York, Richard Plantagenet, Duke of (*3
Henry VI*), 389, 406
Youth, 149, 158-59, 208
Youth moralities, 477-78, n. 7; examples
of, 208, 246, 247

Zoroastrianism, and Good and Evil, 74